MW00910157

Other McGraw-Hill Books of Interest

Informix

Client/Server Application Development

Paul R. Allen

Joseph J. Bambara

Richard J. Bambara

McGraw-Hill

New York San Francisco Washington, D.C. Auckland Bogotá
Caracas Lisbon London Madrid Mexico City Milan
Montreal New Delhi San Juan Singapore
Sydney Tokyo Toronto

Library of Congress Cataloging-in-Publication Data

Allen, Paul R.
    Informix : client/server application development / Paul R. Allen,
  Joseph J. Bambara, Richard J. Bambara.
       p.   cm.
    Includes index.
    ISBN 0-07-913056-9 (pbk.)
    1. Client/server computing. 2. Application software—Development.
  I. Bambara, Joesph J.   II. Bambara, Richard J.   III. Title.
  QA76.9.C55A52 1997
  005.75'85—dc21   96-47947
                                          CIP

McGraw-Hill

A Division of The McGraw-Hill Companies

Copyright © 1997 by The McGraw-Hill Companies, Inc. All rights reserved. Printed in
the United States of America. Except as permitted under the United States Copyright
Act of 1976, no part of this publication may be reproduced or distributed in any form or
by any means, or stored in a data base or retrieval system, without the prior written
permission of the publisher.

1 2 3 4 5 6 7 8 9 0   DOC/DOC 9 0 2 1 0 9 8 7

P/N 005996-9
PART OF
ISBN 0-07-913056-9

The sponsoring editor for this book was Jennifer Holt DiGiovanna, the editing supervi-
sor was Lori Flaherty, and the production supervisor was Donald Schmidt. It was set in
Century Schoolbook by Jana Fisher through the services of Barry E. Brown
(Broker—Editing, Design and Production).

Printed and bound by R. R. Donnelley & Sons Company.

 This book was printed on recycled, acid-free paper containing a minimum of
50% recycled de-inked fiber.

McGraw-Hill books are available at special quantity discounts to use as premiums and
sales promotions, or for use in corporate training programs. For more information,
please write to the Director of Special Sales, McGraw-Hill, 11 West 19th Street, New
York, NY 10011. Or contact your local bookstore.

LIMITS OF LIABILITY AND DISCLAIMER OF WARRANTY
The author and publisher have exercised care in preparing this book and the programs contained herein. They make no representation, however, that the programs
are error-free or suitable for every application to which the reader may attempt to apply them. The author and publisher make no warranty of any kind, expressed or implied, including the warranties of merchantability or fitness for any particular
purpose, with regards to these programs or the documentation or theory contained in
this book, all of which are provided "as is." The author and publisher shall not be liable
for damages in connection with, or arising out of the furnishing, performance, or use
of these programs or the associated descriptions or discussions.
    Readers should test any program on their own systems and compare results with
those presented in this book. They should then construct their own test programs to
verify that they fully understand the requisite calling conventions and data formats
for each of the programs. Then they should test the specific application thoroughly.

To Martha, Francesca, and Freddie
Paul R. Allen

To Roseanne, Vanessa, and Michael
Joseph J. Bambara

To Maria, Ricky, and Michelle
Richard J. Bambara

Contents

Chapter 20. Standards and Guidelines   541

Preface

In recent years the information technology industry has undergone a renaissance of development. Large firms are downsizing, rightsizing, or smartsizing from being mainframe host-based to using multiplatform applications that incorporate networks of cooperative processing. Smaller firms are outgrowing their stand-alone PC applications and migrating them to local area networks (LANs) that include file and database servers. There are a tremendous number of new development efforts underway in the computing industry. Thankfully, there is also a common denominator to facilitate this wealth of new development. There are a number of relational database management systems, like Informix, and each provides some showcased feature. They are all good, but none to date provides as comprehensive an environment as Informix. It is a tool that provides cross-platform, full-function RDBMS, soon to be ORDBMS, features, coupled with the ability to easily connect from a wide variety of GUI front ends. For this reason, it is the choice of many development efforts that have emerged from this downsizing, rightsizing, and upsizing process.

The book is intended to 1) introduce you to the best approach to learning Informix, 2) educate those new to client/server world about the concepts and theories behind this paradigm, and 3) present an understanding of the graphical user interface, object oriented programming (OOP) techniques, and relational database access, including data definition, data manipulation, and stored procedure language. The book will also help experienced developers migrate their skills from large mainframe environments or stand-alone PC environments to the client/server paradigm. The book encourages experienced developers to leverage their old skills with new skills in order to develop applications that involve multiple tiers of platform architecture, weaving these components together to deliver applications in tune with current presentation possibilities.

Paul R. Allen
Joseph J. Bambara
Richard J. Bambara

Acknowledgments

As always, first and foremost, I must give praise and thanks to my wife, Martha, for tolerating me while writing another book. Martha, I could not have done any of this without your patience and understanding, you are still the one!

Very special thanks to my co-authors, Joseph J. Bambara and Richard J. Bambara, for their continuous encouragement, strength, and perseverance to "chip away" during this endeavor. Special thanks to Dawn Mattina and Dawn Goodchild for keying and revising a sizable portion of the text. I wish to thank Jay Ranade for giving us this opportunity and I would like to thank everybody else at McGraw-Hill, especially Barry Brown and Kellie Hagan, for their patience and hard work in producing the book.

I would like to thank my friends and colleagues at the New York Stock Exchange, Securities Industry Automation Corporation (SIAC), Merrill Lynch, Chemical Bank, Bain Securities, Wilco, MK Electric for giving me the opportunities to learn and work in such dynamic and challenging environments. Specifically I would like to thank Angela Posillico, Tom McNally, Dan Carlucci, John Ginelli, John Strampfer, Jim McAna, Dave Pavero, Ed Keenan, Don Trojan, Paul Potwardski, Sheila Saye, Gerardo Raimato, John Cantrell, Martin Lehrman, Everett Young, Marty Eisen, Holly Bowers, Christine Reagan, Christine Colbert, Bob Friedman, Roy Staines, Terry Wing, Bob Elliott, and Jon Loom. Special thanks to John Pezzullo of ICS Consulting Group.

I would like to acknowledge and thank Informix Software, Inc., for making such great products and for all of your assistance in writing this book. Very special thanks to George Anderson at Enterprise Engineering for his friendship, advice and support during our many endeavors.

Special thanks to Johnny Bauer and Rene Madsen at United Consultants for encouraging us to travel, consult and lecture around the world, many times over. Also thanks to Potter Palmer, Peter Koletzke and Dennis Green for giving me the opportunity to lecture at Columbia University of New York.

I would also like to thank Sandra and Goran Jovicic, Paul Baneky, Rodney Erb, Joe Licata, Kailash Chanrai, Lawrence Byron-Sinclair, Sahba St. Clair,

Tom and Lisa Jardine, Steve Adamson, and Ian Stokes for their friendship, heart-to-heart advice, direction and support.

It is also my pleasure to thank Carmen, Luz-Mery, Hernan, Rodrigo, Julie Goodchild and Jaime, Edwin, Juan-Carlos, Andy, Carolina, and Jerry for welcoming me into their families and for always being there when I need them. I would like to give special thanks to Maureen Allen and Brian Holmes who, back in England, take care of what I hold most dear.

As always, I would like to thank my parents, Carole and Terence, my sisters, Lorisa and Hayley, and the rest of my family for their never-ending love, optimism and support.

Finally, to my niece Francesca and my nephew Freddie, I hope and pray that you believe in the beauty of your own dreams.

Paul R. Allen
New York, New York

I would like to thank Jay Ranade for presenting the opportunity to write this book. I would also like thank Barry Brown and Kellie Hagan and all of the folks at McGraw-Hill for their hard work and dedication in producing the book. I would like to thank my friends and colleagues from Duane Reade (Steve Clark, Dane, Reggie Smith, Yuri Fridman and Fabian), Merrill Lynch (John Strampfer, Bob Dieckmann et al.), General Foods (Jerry Feldman), Philip Morris, Viacom (Minna Silventoinen), First Boston, Goldman Sachs (George Smith), AIG (Chris Caracappa), Bank of New York (James Stormont), and Gilder, Gagnon and Howe (Tom Borgason). Thanks to Paul Baneky and Joe Licata and all of the cooperative folks at Informix for providing encouragement. Special thanks to Johnny Bauer and Rene Madsen at United Consultants for providing us with opportunities to present our materials in Europe and Scandinavia. Special thanks to Dawn Mattina for helping with the page edits.

I also wish to especially thank Professors Lawrence Wein and Brian Comerford for facilitating key career opportunities which helped me develop the skills required to write the book. Thanks to Brian Holmes and Carole (Paul's mom) for taking care of us in London.

Thanks to all the hockey people and players (Neubs , Rock, Brian et al.) at the Port Washington Skating Academy for providing an environment in which I could get up a good sweat and relieve any latent stress built up during the seven months it took to complete the text. A very special thanks to Chanel's Steve Koyfman (one of NY's best CIOs) for providing opportunities and for being a great friend and person. Thanks to George Anderson, Helen Chin and Herb Karlitz for their friendship and encouragement. A very special thanks to my co-author Paul R. Allen for his friendship, consistent hard work, energy, excellent team play and for being a great partner no matter what we try.

Thanks to my dad Joseph, my mom Millie, my brothers Vincent and Richard, my sister Patricia, my father in law Joseph and the rest of my family who are always there when I need them.

Foremost, I thank my wife Roseanne and my children Vanessa and Michael who are and have always been patient, loving, helpful and encouraging no matter what new career challenge I attempt to pursue. Roseanne, thanks for simultaneously reviewing and keying a good deal of the text while preparing the world's best food. I could not have done it without you.

Joseph J. Bambara
Greenvale, New York

I would like to thank Jay Ranade for first presenting the opportunity to write this book. I also want to thank Barry Brown and Kellie Hagan and all of the folks at McGraw-Hill for their hard work and dedication in producing the book. I would like to thank my friends and colleagues from First Boston (Bob Rogan, who has always been an unflappable team player, Makhan Lalli, friend and colleague, Frank Fanzilli, for his excellent advice and all the members of the IS staff) who I have worked with throughout the years of my career.

A very special thank you to my co-author and brother Joe for giving me the opportunity to work with him on this project as well as for all of the guidance which he has provided to me throughout my career in the computer field. My brother has always been a true mentor and dear friend throughout my life. I would also like to thank Paul R. Allen for sharing this opportunity with me as well, for his friendship, consistent hard work, energy, excellent team play and encouragement.

Thanks to my dad Joseph, my mom Millie, my brothers Vincent and Joseph, my sister Patricia, my father-in-law Armando, my mother-in-law Celia and the rest of my family who are always there when I need them. I love you all.

Foremost, I thank my wife Maria and my children Ricky and Michelle who are and have always been patient, loving, and helpful encouraging me no matter what new career-enhancing project I pursue. Maria, thanks for all of your assistance in the typing and review of the chapters , as well as keeping up with your regular duties of raising our two children. This could not have been possible without your help, thank you.

Richard J. Bambara
Manalapan, New Jersey

Introduction

This introduction contains a roadmap for navigating the book.

Part I is comprised of Chapters 1 through 6. It will introduce the reader to Informix. Chapter 1, *Informix: the Company and the Products*, describes the history of the company and its flagship products that database administrators and development managers are choosing. It also contains almost everything you need to know about development using the complete Informix database product line. This information will assist new development efforts when planning the software and hardware procurement stages.

Chapter 2, *The Informix Environment*, defines the comprehensive database environment. In an introductory fashion, object-oriented development techniques are reviewed, the Informix components and tools used to develop the Informix objects are identified, and the steps required to build an Informix-based application are described.

Chapter 3, *Designing an Application*, is an overview of client/server process modeling and data modeling techniques. Data design and modeling tools like Erwin are showcased. These topics are also covered in an iterative fashion throughout the book.

In Chapter 4, *Setting Up the Development Environment*, you will learn how to set up your sandbox environment. This chapter will help you plan the environment, including standards, guidelines, and good practices. Also discussed is the proper planning required to use Informix and the "how tos" of sketching out the application flow in order to produce consistent, stable, reliable application delivery.

Chapter 5, *Managing the Database*, will teach you how to create and maintain database objects using a GUI administration tool. In this instance, Power-Builder is used to illustrate what a comprehensive administration tool can provide. Illustra and Informix NT, which were not generally available at the time of this writing, will provide a similar look and feel.

Chapter 6, *Developing the Application*, provides a detailed overview of how to develop an application and outlines the prerequisites for the development environment. The importance of database design and the need to virtually complete the database design before full-scale development begins is emphasized. The chapter also describes how to choose a window menu interface architecture, and introduces the "how" and "when" of building basic application components (GUI windows, data access, and basic batch processing).

Part II, Development, is comprised of Chapters 7 through 15, and will expand and extend the concepts introduced in Part I, especially those presented in Chapter 6.

Chapter 7, *Defining an Application*, provides an overview of client/server and object-oriented computing, including its architecture, strategies, and theories. The phases of a development effort, which include many that will be familiar to an experienced developer, are presented. The book, however, goes further and includes the additional steps required in most client/server application development efforts.

We will also draw distinctions between mainframe development and client/server development by examining the traditional techniques and contrasting them with contemporary variations on the same themes. Chapter 8, *Administration Utilities*, discusses some of the command-line utilities provided by Informix OnLine. Chapter 9, *Creating the User Interface*, covers the components of a database application that uses the Windows graphical user interface. It provides an overview of the various types of document interfaces and subcomponents common in many of today's Windows products.

Chapter 10, *Building the Data Definition Language (DDL)*, and Chapter 11, *Building the Data Manipulation Language (DML)*, introduce and expand on the development and use of the relational database constructs (DML, DDL, and SPL) and components (tables, columns, indexes, etc.). Once you have mastered the database creation basics, the text continues with the essence of the database transaction: connecting to the SQL database. Database manipulation and definition language are presented with a developer's perspective. You'll go behind the scenes to discover how the actual database update takes place and how to control the cost of database access. Moreover, you will learn how to construct and manipulate SQL to provide specialized features such as ad-hoc database query tools for performing dynamic business functions. Chapter 12, *Building C Programs with ESQL*, reviews the use of embedded SQL within the confines of a C language program. The construction (design, coding, compiling, and testing) of C programs using the Informix ESQL preprocessor is discussed in detail.

Chapter 13, *Debugging Your Code*, presents the philosophy of debugging. Additional validation and performance benchmarking techniques are also discussed.

Chapter 14, *Tuning Your Environment*, provides an overview of the performance and tuning of an Informix database application. It covers the server resources that affect performance: CPU, memory, and disk. The chapter also covers the tuning of Parallel Database Query (PDQ) parameters and the issues surrounding the network configuration.

Chapter 15, *Building Common Database Procedures*, introduces Informix-stored procedures and implementation techniques. At some point during Informix development, you begin to realize that you repeat (over and over again) a particular database access. With a little work you can write this functionality so it is extendible and, above all, reusable by other developers and other applications. The stored procedure functionality might range from a simple singleton select to a complex multiple table update for an application. Hopefully, the chapters in Part II will provide some ideas necessary to catalyze and show you this development direction.

Part III, Deployment, is comprised of Chapters 16 through 19. Chapter 16, *Preparing the Operational Database*, discusses the tools that allow you to install and maintain Informix products on a UNIX platform. In addition, it shows you how to configure the files required to initiate Informix OnLine and create a test database. Chapter 17, *Distributing the Application*, examines the issues surrounding the packaging, deployment, and distribution of an application. Chapter 18, *Related Tools and Publications*, covers the myriad of third-party tools you can use to develop an application with Informix. Chapter 19, *Getting Familiar with the Development O/S*, introduces developers to the UNIX platform. The VI editor is covered, as well as basic UNIX utilities that allow users to manipulate data on the UNIX platform. Chapter 20, *Standards and Guidelines*, provides an example of areas that should be standardized, especially when implementing large-scale, enterprise-wide solutions. Chapters 15, 16, and 17 describe features and options typically deployed in larger-scale development.

Note that you can and probably should read Chapters 18, 19, and 20 early on in reading or using the book. Their content is referenced in many places throughout the book. We encourage you to jump to them when interest dictates. We attempted to follow the development life cycle in a stepwise fashion, especially in Chapters 7 through 17.

This book will not only provide an introductory treatment of Informix development, but it will also be useful later on as you reach each milestone in the development life cycle as a checklist to ensure that you have considered your options. No book can satisfy all needs, but this guide was written by three developers who have been implementing computer-based solutions for a period fast approaching 60 years. In any event, we hope you enjoy reading the book and that it improves your Informix development capabilities.

1

Informix: The Company and the Products

This chapter introduces the company that brings you the product Informix. It starts by reviewing the history of the Informix company, then introduces the product line. The chapter concludes by explaining the various ways you can obtain help with using Informix products.

1.1 The History of Informix

1.1.1 The past

The company, which started out with the name Relational Database Systems, Inc., was begun by Roger Sippl, now CEO of Visigenic Software Inc., and Laura King. Table 1.1 lists the company highlights.

Summary financial results

The results of Informix Corporation's fourth quarter and full year, ending December 31, 1995, are listed in Table 1.2.

Figure 1.1   The Informix logo.

TABLE 1.1

Date	Highlight
1980	Established as Relational Database Systems, Inc.
1981	First product released was C-ISAM, with the initial name Marathon
1982	Release of the pre-SQL product suite: Informer query language, Perform form manager, Ace report writer
1983	Inform[er] plus the desire to associate it with UNIX operating system led to the new name: Informix
1984	Release of SQL-based products, first being Informix-SQL and Informix-ESQL/C and the companion C-ISAM
1986	Release of Informix-4GL
1986	Informix-Turbo was introduced in 1986, with the former database product being renamed to Informix-SE
1988	The company changed its name to Informix Software, Inc.
1988	Informix-4GL/RDS and Informix-4GL/ID, the p-code versions of Informix-4GL were introduced
1988	Released WingZ on the Macintosh, a graphical spreadsheet
1990	Informix-Turbo replaced by Informix-OnLine
1993	Informix-OnLine Dynamic Server released
1994	Informix-NewEra, the GUI object-oriented langauge released
1995	Informix-NewEra, new version released
1996	Informix merges with Illustra

TABLE 1.2

Results	Q495	Q494	Percent change
Revenue	$217,070,000	$150,068,000	+4.5%
Operating income	$57,825,000	$37,342,000	+55%
Pretax income	$59,743,000	$37,243,000	+60%
Net income	$38,834,000	$23,836,000	+63%
Net income per share	$0.28	$0.18	+56%

Results	1995	1994	Percent change
Revenue	$708,985,000	$468,697,000	+51%
Operating income	$159,253,000	$102,561,000	+55%
Pretax income	$166,140,000	$103,430,000	+61%
Net income	$105,333,000	$66,196,000	+59%
Net income per share	$0.76	$0.49	+55%

Mergers and acquisitions

1995 was a very active year for Informix in its effort to consolidate and extend its domestic and international presence. During this time, Informix acquired the following companies:

- The database division of ASCII Corporation
- Daou Technology
- Stanford Technology Group
- Illustra Information Technologies

In January 1995, Informix acquired 90% (now 100%) of the database division of ASCII Corp. of Japan, now called Informix ASCII, K.K. This division is the primary distributor of Informix software in Japan. Also in early 1995, Informix acquired Daou Technology, its primary distributor in Korea.

In October 1995, Informix acquired Stanford Technology Group Inc. (STG). STG sells multidimensional data access and relational online analytical processing (OLAP) technology, called MetaCube. The is a leading technology in the data warehousing market because it is an OLAP/relational solution, as opposed to most of the competition's proprietary approaches. The relational approach combines powerful, flexible query capabilities with a scalable multi-tier architecture, while leveraging the benefits of a parallel server.

In late December 1995, Informix announced its intention to acquire Illustra Information Technologies in a stock deal reportedly worth around $386 million, positioning Informix as the dominant player in the object-relational database management system (ORDBMS) market. The growth of the Internet and multimedia applications has brought about the need for complex data types, ones that traditional RDBMSs cannot handle.

Other announcements

At the worldwide user conference in San Jose, California in July 1995, Informix announced:

- Informix-OnLine Extended Parallel Server (XPS), which extends dynamic scalable architecture to clustered SMP and MPP environments.
- Informix-NewEra v2.0, including new features for rapid application development, application partitioning, and character-based deployment.
- Informix database servers available in the Netscape Internet family of turnkey software solutions.

Informix has been shipping with SAP's R/3 application programs for more than two years now and averaged a new account per day over the first 18 months. Informix on Hewlett-Packard hardware announced a sub-1.6-second

SD benchmark (1,110) for SAP's leading R/3 sales and distribution module. This benchmark demonstrated the high-end scalability of Informix OnLine Dynamic Server. This performance positions Informix as the database of choice for large customers for their R/3 implementations.

Informix announced that it has optimized Informix OnLine Dynamic Server for 64-bit UNIX-based computer systems, available in mid-September for Digital's AlphaServer. The database server features very large memory capabilities, which will provide customers with significant performance increases for their very large database (VLDB), business-critical applications such as OLTP, decision support, and data warehousing.

Early testing of Informix OnLine Dynamic Server optimized for 64-bit architectures has revealed significant performance increases over 32-bit environments. Informix OnLine Dynamic Server with 64-bit enhancements allows customers to run their VLDB applications—traditionally available only in a mainframe environment—in the cost-effective symmetrical multiprocessing environment.

The release of OnLine Dynamic Server v7.2 has taken a step toward reaffirming Informix's lead position for companies that want to create data warehouses. For example, TransAmerica Commercial Finance Corp., in Chicago is reported to be using a 52-gigabyte data warehouse based on Informix OnLine Dynamic Server. OnLine Dynamic Server 7.2 has added text and video storage and search capabilities through an optional add-on called Extensible Framework. The framework allows users to add support for additional data types through an API for linking third-party text, workflow, and imaging products to the OnLine Dynamic Server database. It also enables Informix-only replication and is currently working with third-party vendors (Platinum and Praxis) to provide replication tools for linking other databases.

Other features are support for 64-bit parallel processing and object data types (ANSI SQL 3.0 specification).

1.1.2 The present

Financially, the company appears to be in great shape, despite the fact that their earnings have declined compared to the prior year. These lower earnings reflect the effect of the acquisition of Illustra. Informix's announced results for the first quarter ending March 31, 1996 are shown in Table 1.3.

TABLE 1.3

Results	Q1 96	Q1 95	% Change
Revenue	$204,021,000	$148,037,000	+38%
Operating income	$23,302,000	$26,326,000	–12%
Pretax income	$25,224,000	$27,978,000	–10%
Net income	$15,891,000	$17,646,000	–10%
Net income per share	$0.10	$0.12	–17%

ILLUSTRA

Figure 1.2   The Illustra logo.

During the first quarter of 1996, Informix announced a record setting TPC-C benchmark on Digital Equipment Corporation's 64-bit AlphaServer 8400 5/350 system. Informix OnLine Dynamic Server 7.2 delivered 13,646 tpmC at an outstanding price/performance level of $277/tpmC. This result significantly exceeds those of Informix's major competitors.

Informix generally has great technology. However, the company's biggest weakness is getting the word out that they have such good architecture.

1.1.3 The future

Informix's goal is to obtain the number-one spot outright (from Oracle). The company has already made market headway against the former number-two vendor, Sybase Inc. With the acquisition of Illustra and the plans for Universal Server, Informix is very well positioned in the fully extensible relational database management system market. The following sections provide some more details surrounding the merger and the upcoming products.

Illustra merger

In February, 1996, Informix completed the acquisition of Illustra Information Technologies, Inc., and Illustra became a wholly-owned subsidiary of Informix Software, Inc. Approximately 12.9 million shares of Informix common stock were issued to acquire all outstanding shares of Illustra. The acquisition was accounted for as a tax-free pooling of interest.

The acquisition enabled Informix to integrate Illustra's dynamic content management system into its core parallel database technology, Dynamic Scalable Architecture (DSA). This technology integration should give Informix a significant market advantage over competing database vendors in providing a powerful database engine to support the next wave of object relational database applications, such as Web applications, which require high performance and scalability coupled with dynamic content management capabilities.

Both companies realize that the Web is driving a large and rapidly growing new market for information management. This new market, which is driving a shift from static and fixed data types to dynamic data with rich content, requires users to interact with three-dimensional graphics, video, audio, HTML, spatial data, and other complex data. To effectively manage this new content, users are demanding a sophisticated database engine that combines the robust, scalable, enterprise solutions offered by relational databases with the flexible, extensible, content management capabilities pioneered by Illustra. The integration of Informix and Illustra products will offer users the ideal solution. With this merger, no other database vendor is better positioned in the Web market and the overall information management market today.

Before the merger, Illustra Information Technologies, Inc., founded in 1992, was the leading worldwide supplier of content management systems and tools for applications in multimedia and entertainment, digital media publishing, and financial services. The company's Illustra Server allowed users to store, manage, and analyze complex multimedia data such as audio, video, and images in a single database, along with traditional characters and numbers.

---

24 Hours in Cyberspace

On February 8, 1996, more than 100 photojournalists covered the globe to document how online technology is changing people's lives. Their focus was on the human stories behind online technology: the ways in which the digital revolution has changed how people all over the world interact, learn, and conduct business. Illustra technology enabled the staff to publish a new Web site every 30 minutes over a 24-hour period. Illustra was very proud to have been selected as the sole database system to manage all content associated with 24 Hours in Cyberspace. Illustra was chosen because of its ability to manage all types of user-defined data.

Universal Server

The merged company will create Informix: Universal Server, an extensible, relational database management system. Universal Server will combine the best features of two proven, leading database technologies: Informix's core parallel database technology, Dynamic Scalable Architecture (DSA), and the unique extensible architecture from Illustra, which includes existing DataBlade modules. The combination of extensibility and high-performance scalability will help position Informix as an industry leader for several years.

Traditional RDBMS systems can work only with simple data types. However, the business environment now requires the ability to intelligently manage all sorts of data assets, including complex financial instruments, time series, spatial, 2-D, 3-D, video, sound, and other types of rich data.

Figure 1.3   24 hours in Cyberspace.

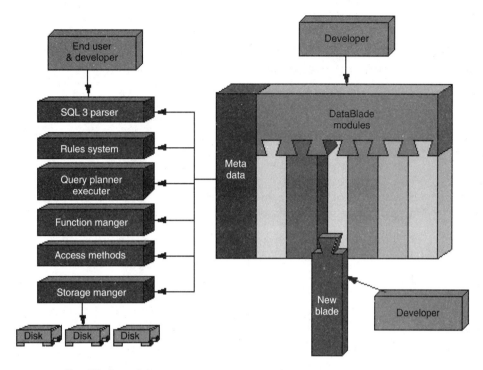

Figure 1.4 DataBlade modules.

The Illustra, now Informix, technology was designed to support rich, multimedia content natively, via DataBlades (see Figure 1.4). Developers will be able to extend the Universal Server to accommodate these new data types. This flexibility will allow users to quickly react to change by either inventing new data types or purchasing them from a third party. In a short space of time, many third-party developers will create data types for specific, or vertical, markets such as data warehousing, telecommunications, financial services, Internet and Intranet applications, multimedia asset management, and sciences.

To help this market develop, Informix announced the DataBlade Developers Program, an early access program intended for experienced C and SQL programmers. The program supplies a developers kit, which consists of documentation, sample code, and support software to assist developers in understanding Illustra DataBlade modules and in producing DataBlade modules of their own. The sample code is a collection of example DataBlade modules that demonstrate what is required for DataBlade module development. The existing DataBlade modules were developed by Illustra and a number of solution provider partners. Existing DataBlade modules include:

Text. Basic text search

PLS. Advanced text search

2D, 3D Spatial. Manipulation and retrieval of spatial data

Drawing. Storage and manipulation of graphics

Time series. Time-sequenced analysis and manipulation

S-Plus. Statistical and graphical data analysis

Image. Management, manipulation, and retrieval

Video. Management, manipulation, and retrieval

Web. Interface to Web browsers and Web pages

Sybase, Oracle. Gateways to these database servers

The Illustra architecture, which will be integrated into the Universal Server, is comprised of two components: a core engine and a series of DataBlade modules. Illustra's core engine provides:

- The ability to create new data types and new functions.
- A SQL parser that understands new data types and functions.
- An optimizer that understands the costs of running user-defined functions against rich data.
- Extensible indexing schemes.

DataBlades, as described earlier, are collections of data structures and the functions that manipulate them, and optionally new access methods. In object-oriented terms, DataBlades are class libraries for the server.

The Informix-Illustra merger changed the entire competitive landscape of the database industry. The Universal Server will couple infinite extensibility made possible by unique DataBlade technology with high-performance scalability. The Universal Server will enable customers to shift from a world of simple data types to a new world of rich, user-defined content that can be extended as business needs change.

Universal Server roll-out plans

The initial version of Universal Server has been rolled out in three phases over the course of 1996, as follows:

Phase 1. Customers can link Informix's DSA technology with Illustra databases through a new gateway product. Using the Informix gateway, customers will be able to build Illustra applications that transparently integrate complex data stored in the Illustra Server with traditional data stored on Informix. This is available now.

Phase 2. A DataBlade module developer's toolkit, which provides the guidelines for building data structures, functions, and access that will run against both Illustra and the Universal Server. This is also currently available.

Phase 3. The full-blown Universal Server, which will blend "industrial-strength" relational database technology with "snap-in" DataBlade modules. This should be available by the end of 1996.

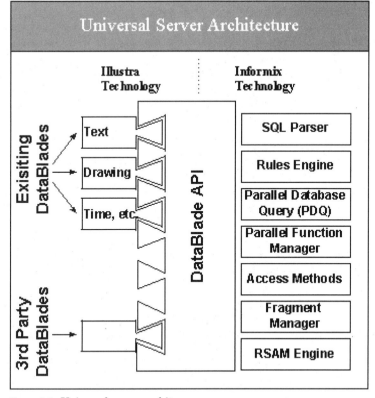

Figure 1.5   Universal server architecure.

Migration plans

Current and prospective customers of both Informix and Illustra can start development immediately, because their applications and DataBlade extensions will be supported by Universal Server. Informix-based applications will run on the Universal Server without recompilation or changes. Illustra-based applications can be easily migrated to Universal Server. Existing and new Illustra customers who buy Illustra database licenses with support will be able to upgrade to the Universal Server at no additional charge.

1.2 The Informix Product Line

The Informix product line-up can be broken up into the following areas:

- Database servers
- Connectivity
- Application development tools
- End-user information access tools
- Online analytical processing tools

1.2.1 Database servers

Informix has several database engines that are either capable of understanding SQL (structured query language) commands or provide routines that allow for the creation and use of databases.

Dynamic Scalable Architecture (DSA) is the company's database architecture that allows developers to take advantage of the processing power of parallel computing. DSA is the technology used in the following scalable server products:

- Informix-OnLine Extended Parallel Server
- Informix-OnLine Dynamic Server
- Informix-OnLine Workgroup Server

These server products scale to service the enterprise, workgroup, and departmental applications, as well as large-scale transaction processing (OLTP) and data warehousing (DW) applications. The server line is designed so it can run on a variety of clustered processing (SMP) and massively parallel processing (MPP) platforms.

Informix-OnLine Extended Parallel Server (XPS) extends the architecture to loosely coupled or shared-nothing computing architectures, including clusters of symmetric multiprocessors (SMP) and massively parallel processors (MPP). XPS supports large database environments for OLTP, data warehousing, imaging, document management, and workflow database applications.

Informix-OnLine Dynamic Server is a database server available for UNIX and Windows NT platforms that provides support for large distributed databases, stored procedures, triggers, and referential integrity. It features high availability, the ability to back up while the database is available for query, and imaging. It also supports enhanced data types to cope with binary data, while providing fast response times under heavy transaction volumes. Optical enhancement adds the mass storage capabilities of optical disk subsystems for storing binary large objects (BLOBs). Informix-OnLine has higher administration requirements than SE, and typically runs on "raw" as opposed to "cooked" file systems. The Secure option is designed to meet stringent international government and commercial security requirements.

Informix-OnLine Workgroup Server is available for the Windows NT platform and is designed for the workgroup or departmental environment. It is easy to install, use, and administer (see Figures 1.6 and 1.7). It incorporates multimedia datatypes, provides high system availability, and is scalable to accommodate growth.

Informix-SE is an easy-to-use database server that provides good performance and data consistency with low administration requirements. It is best suited for small to medium databases and runs on "cooked" as opposed to raw file systems.

C-ISAM is a library of C routines and functions that allows you to create and access indexed sequential files (a.k.a. ISAM, or Indexed Sequential Access

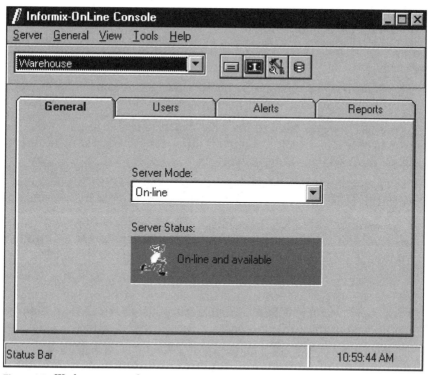

Figure 1.6 Workgroup console.

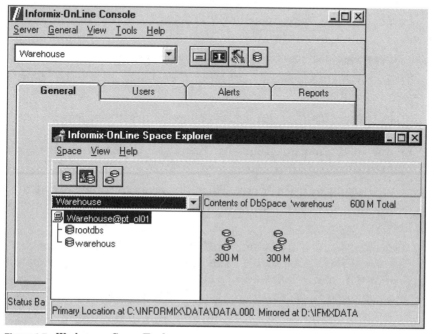

Figure 1.7 Workgroup Space Explorer.

Method). This product was Informix's first commercial offering and continues to be offered as a low-cost solution to database management.

1.2.2 Connectivity

The following are software products that let you connect various client applications and database server machines to provide database access:

Informix-Enterprise Gateway. Provides both SQL and remote procedure call access to over 60 relational and nonrelational data sources on different hardware platforms and operating systems.

Informix-Gateway with DRDATM. Integrates IBM DB2TM relational databases with Informix applications without the need for IBM host-resident software.

Informix-DCE/NET. A DCE-based connectivity product to allow transparent access to Informix and other relational databases via ODBC, while taking advantage of DCE features such as security and naming services.

Informix-CLI. A Call Level Interface that enables application developers to dynamically access Informix database servers. Based on Microsoft's Open Database Connectivity (ODBC) architecture, it provides a standard means of connecting to Informix databases.

I-STAR. The networking software you need on a database server machine. It provides distributed database capabilities that include multisite joins and updates with a transparent two-phase commit/rollback recovery feature.

I-NET. The software you need on a client machine in order to talk to an Informix database server machine.

1.2.3 Application development tools (programming languages)

These products let developers build a user interface to the data held in Informix databases.

Informix-4GL. This is Informix's older, character-based programming language. It supports two platforms: Informix-4GL/GX is for X-Motif environments, and Informix-4GL for Windows is for the Microsoft Windows environment.

Informix-ESQL for C and COBOL. This allows you to embed SQL statements that access Informix databases directly into the source code of C and COBOL languages.

Informix-NewEra. This is Informix's newer development language and is already a version 2.0 product. The code is similar to and compatible with Informix-4GL source, but also has object-oriented programming (OOP) features and enhanced GUI support for the Microsoft Windows and UNIX X-Motif environments.

1.2.4 End-user access tools

These tools are intended to enable end users to be able to construct applications that maintain data in a database without having to know some of the underlying complexities of locking, triggers, and stored procedures.

Informix-NewEra ViewPoint is a graphical SQL database access tool that provides end users with the ability to develop fill-in forms, reports, and queries in a quick and intuitive way. The tool is designed to simplify end-user access to data while retaining control over security and integrity within the systems or database administration groups.

1.2.5 Online Analytical Processing (OLAP) tools

The MetaCube product family is a collection of decision-support software that was acquired when Informix purchased STG (see section 1.1.1). The product range is designed specifically for developing and managing data warehouse applications. It consists of the following modules:

Informix-MetaCube. An engine providing the online analytical processing (OLAP) backbone for data warehouse applications.

Informix-MetaCube for Excel. Allows Excel users to perform multidimensional analysis of very large data warehouses directly from spreadsheets.

Informix-MetaCube Explorer. An ad-hoc software for end-user access.

Informix-MetaCube Warehouse Manager. A graphical tool for administering meta data that describes your data warehouse in a logical, easy-to-understand manner.

Informix-MetaCube Agents. Facility allowing users to perform queries and administrative tasks in either foreground (exclusive) or background mode.

Getting Help with Informix Products

If you need assistance when using Informix, in addition to this book and the manuals that came with Informix, the following sources of information are available:

- The Internet: World Wide Web (WWW), Usenet newsgroups, and FTP sites
- CompuServe
- InformixLink bulletin board service
- Sales and marketing
- Customer support
- Education/training and consulting services
- Informix Certified Professional Program
- Annual user meeting
- Local user groups

1.3.1 On the Internet

There is an ever-increasing list of users requiring access to information via a combination of World Wide Web (WWW) pages, Usenet newsgroups, and file transfer protocol (FTP) sites, so Informix now provides the following sources of support and information:

World Wide Web (WWW)
Informix provides information on the company and its product line on the following Web sites:

```
http://www.informix.com
http://www.illustra.com
```

Usenet newsgroups
To join the Usenet newsgroup, you need to subscribe to:

```
comp.databases.informix
```

The newsgroup provides a forum to post questions and allows other subscribers to respond either directly to your e-mail account or, more usefully, back to the newsgroup.

File transfer protocol (FTP)
For file transfer, use the following FTP address:
```
ftp.informix.com
```

1.3.2 Help from Informix Corporation

The following is a list of facilities and services that Informix provides to assist Informix developers:

1.3.2.1 InformixLink bulletin board service
The InformixLink BBS enables you to download fixes, sample code and technical write-ups. You can also upload files for review by the technical support team. To use the bulletin board service, call 1.800.331.1763 to subscribe. The InformixLink BBS is available 24 hours a day.

1.3.2.2 Sales and marketing
To inquire about a product or speak to a sales or marketing representative, call +1.800.331.1763 or +1.415.926.6300.

1.3.2.3 Customer support
Informix provides the following services for customer support:

Informix Assurance. The minimum level required to maintain your Informix technology and environment.

Informix OpenLine. All the benefits of Assurance level, plus quick-response telephone support, case escalation, extended support hours, and more.

Regency Support. Top-of-the-line service and support, with direct access to an account manager.

TechInfo Center. A special 24-hour support section of the WWW InformixLink service, providing the latest information, such as alerts, porting reports, defect reports, publications, product release information, and events. The system also allows you to register products and submit cases to the Technical Support department.

1.3.2.4 Education, training, and consulting services

Informix Corporation provides many training classes and courses. The classes are either given by Informix Corporation or held at approved Informix Corporation education centers. There are courses available for the following paths:

- Application Design and Development Tools
- Database Server and Connectivity
- Computer-Based Training and Video
- On-Site Customized Training

For details on training class schedules, approved education centers, and computer-based training, call 800-331-1763 or send a fax to 913-599-8767.

Application Design and Development Tools

The specific courses available are:

- Relational Database Design
- Structured Query Language
- Forms and Reports Using Informix-SQL (1996)
- Developing Applications Using Informix-NewEra ViewPoint Pro
- Building Forms and Reports Using Informix-NewEra ViewPoint
- Developing Applications Using Informix-NewEra I
- Developing Applications Using Informix-NewEra II
- Developing Applications Using Informix-4GL
- Advanced Informix-4GL Development
- Developing Applications Using Informix-ESQL/C
- Developing Applications Using Informix-ESQL/COBOL
- Developing Applications Using Informix-Ada/SAME

Database Server and Connectivity

The specific courses available are:

- Informix-SE System Administration
- Informix-OnLine 5.0 Database Administration

- Informix-OnLine 5.0 System Administration
- Informix-OnLine 5.0 Internal Architecture and Advanced Administration
- Upgrading to Informix-OnLine Dynamic Server
- Managing and Optimizing Informix-OnLine Dynamic Server Databases
- Informix-OnLine Dynamic Server System Administration
- Archiving Informix-OnLine Dynamic Server
- Informix-OnLine Dynamic Server Performance Tuning
- Using Stored Procedures and Triggers
- Informix-OnLine/Secure Administration and Management
- Distributed Transaction Processing with Informix-TP/XA and Informix-TP/ToolKit

Computer-Based Training and Video
The CBT courses available are:

- Understanding Relational Databases
- Using Informix-SQL
- Advanced Informix-SQL
- Developing Applications Using Informix-4GL Self-Paced Training
- Introduction to Object-Oriented Technology
- Object-Oriented Analysis and Design

The video courses available are:

- Relational Database Design Workshop
- Fundamentals of ANSI SQL
- The UNIX System for Users
- UNIX System Administration I
- UNIX System Administration II
- Windows 3.1
- ANSI C Language for Programmers
- TCP/IP Concepts
- OSF/Motif Part I: An Introduction to OSF/Motif
- OSF/Motif Part II: Programming OSF/Motif

On-site Customized Training
Informix instructors will come to your company to teach these training courses. In addition, Informix can also tailor a course to your exact requirements.

Professional services

Informix has a group of consultants and managers that can work with you to tailor the ideal and most effective level of support for any situation or requirement. Their expertise includes the following areas: planning, conversion, migration, system design, leadership, team augmentation, development, production, and training.

For further details on professional services, call 800-331-1763 or contact you local Informix supplier.

1.3.2.5 Informix Certified Professional Program

The Informix Certified Professional Program consists of a series of examinations, based on job experience and training courses, designed for system professionals to validate and enhance their proficiency with Informix technology.

Informix is currently certifying individuals in the areas of Database Administrator (DBA), Systems Administrator (SA), and Support Engineer (SE) for Informix-OnLine Dynamic Server. The program will soon be expanded to include Developer (D) and Support Engineer (SE) for Informix-NewEra. Once enrolled and successfully completed, you get:

- Access to TechInfo Center, the 24-hour support section of the WWW InformixLink.

- Toll-free technical support with a valid customer support contract.

- Access to the ICP BBS.

- Use of the ICP logo (see Figure 1.7) and a certificate of achievement.

To enroll or obtain more information on certification, call 800-977-3926 (800-977-EXAM) in North America. For all other locations call the Sales and Marketing number listed in section 1.3.2.2.

Figure 1.8 The Informix Certified Professional logo.

1.3.2.6 Annual User Conference & Exhibition

The Informix Worldwide User Conference & Exhibition takes place at a location in the U.S. In 1996 it was held at the Navy Pier Convention Center in Chicago, Illinois. These conferences provide an environment for discussion, demonstration, and training sessions for the Informix product line and, in addition, the exhibition of third-party add-on products. They also provide a relaxed forum for people to swap the invaluable "war-story" experiences gained by actually using and implementing the product features.

1.3.2.7 Local user groups

There are countless user groups being run around the world. They provide developers and users of products in the local communities with a forum for exchanging information. They also allow the Informix Corporation partners to demonstrate and sell their wares. For a list of user groups in your area, call the Sales and Marketing number listed in section 1.3.2.2.

2

The Informix Environment

Informix is a tool that provides an integrated development environment packaged into a software suite. We will mention all the components in this chapter, but the book will concentrate on Informix RDBMS, which is viewed as the number-two or -three database management system in the client/server arena. As discussed earlier, Informix can run on most existing client/server platforms (for example, UNIX and NT). The environment has also expanded. Many third-party vendors have added Informix interfaces to their products (for example, PowerBuilder). Others have development tools and function libraries that can be installed as instant development standards (for example, ERwin). This combination makes Informix one of the most comprehensive environments available for today's client/server development. This chapter will present definitions and terminology that will be expanded upon later. If you are familiar with these ideas, quickly browse through this material and move on to the next chapter.

2.1 Definition

Informix is a relational database management system. Using Informix, you can develop powerful applications that are executable on a multitude of platforms, e.g., Microsoft NT and UNIX. If you are new to Informix, read through this chapter and then spend the two hours it takes to work with the demonstration database. The name will be "demo" followed by the release number, for example demo7 for release 7 of Informix. This will guide you through the process of building a Informix database. It is not exciting, but it is a good first step in the iterative learning process that will lead most experienced developers to become Informix-productive in the short term.

2.1.1 Database servers

What is OnLine? What is SE? OnLine is a database server. A database server is a software package that manages access to one or more databases for one or more client applications. It is the principal component of a database-management system. Early access methods included IBM's ISAM and VSAM, which provided random access of file records identified by key fields in the record. This was faster than sequentially accessing the whole file, and has evolved to provide a standard language for the access: SQL. Informix supports and embraces this access language.

Specifically, OnLine is a database server in a relational database-management system (RDBMS). In a relational database, data is organized in tables that consist of rows and columns. If OnLine is like a Mercedes 450, then the SE or standard edition is the Mercedes 190. SE is a function and feature subset of OnLine. Where significant, we will point out the differences from a development point of view. For the purposes of this chapter, however, we will refer to both OnLine and SE as "OnLine."

The OnLine database server offers the following features:

- Client/server architecture
- Scalability
- High performance
- Fault tolerance and high availability (SE is less recoverable—more on this later)
- Multimedia support
- Distributed data queries
- Database server security

2.1.2 Client/server architecture

OnLine is a server for client applications. More specifically, OnLine is a database server that processes requests for data from client applications. It accesses the requested information from its databases, if possible, and sends back the results. Accessing the database includes activities such as coordinating concurrent requests from multiple clients, performing read and write operations to the databases, and enforcing physical and logical consistency on the data.

The client is an application program (e.g., the PowerBuilder GUI front end) that a user runs to request information from the database. Client applications use Structured Query Language (SQL) to send requests for data to OnLine. Client programs include the DB-Access utility and programs that you write using Informix-ESQL/C, Informix-NewEra, or a host of third-party tools like PowerBuilder and Visual Basic.

Client processes are independent of OnLine processes. Database users run client applications as the need arises to access information. The OnLine administrator starts the OnLine processes by executing the oninit utility. OnLine processes are presumed to execute continuously during the period that users access the databases.

A client application communicates with OnLine through the connection facilities that OnLine provides. For example, client/server communications with PowerBuilder are carried out using I-NET, the Informix network access tool. I-NET handles the conversation using logonid, protocol, dbserver names, and service information provided by the client at database connect time. See Figure 2.1 for a look at how the pieces fit in an enterprise client/server solution using Informix and PowerBuilder to connect to "legacy" mainframe data. At the source-code level, a client connects to OnLine through a SQL statement. Beyond that, the client's use of OnLine connection facilities is transparent to the application. Library functions that are automatically included when a client program is compiled enable the client to connect to OnLine.

The OnLine administrator specifies the types of connections that OnLine supports in a connectivity information file called sqlhosts. The sqlhosts file contains the names of each of the database servers (called the dbservernames) and any aliases to which the clients on a host computer can connect. For each dbservername and each alias, you specify the protocol that a client must use to connect to that database server. When the client connects to OnLine through a SQL statement, the client transparently accesses this information and makes the connection using the specified protocol.

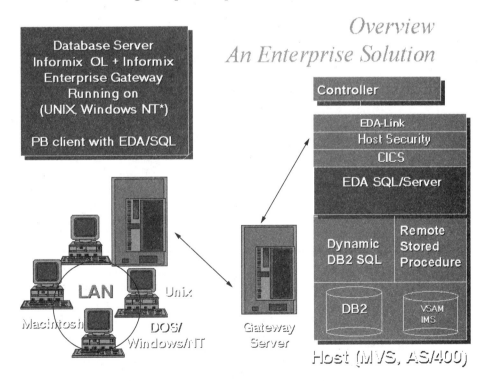

Figure 2.1 An enterprise solution.

2.1.3 Scalability

The OnLine Dynamic Scalable Architecture (DSA) enables you to add both processes and shared memory while OnLine is in online mode. The SE version does not provide this capability. OnLine is designed to handle high volume and dynamic activity; for that reason it provides more functionality and the settings to facilitate tuning.

2.1.4 Potential for high performance

One of the problems with client/server database solutions is performance. Early attempts to displace legacy systems with client/servers have failed because they could not provide the required performance users grew to expect. OnLine provides the potential to achieve high performance through the mechanisms outlined in the following sections.

2.1.4.1 Raw disk management

OnLine can use both UNIX file-system disk space and raw disk space. When using raw disk space, however, OnLine performs its own disk management using raw devices. By storing tables on one or more raw devices instead of in a standard operating system file system, OnLine can manage the physical performance advantages. OnLine is not restricted by operating system limits on the number of tables that can be accessed concurrently. OnLine optimizes table access by guaranteeing that rows are stored contiguously.

OnLine also eliminates operating system I/O overhead by performing direct data transfer between disk and shared memory. If these issues are not a primary concern, you can also configure OnLine to use regular operating system files to store data.

2.1.4.2 Dynamic shared-memory management

All applications that use a single instance of an OnLine database server share data in the memory space of the database server. After one application reads data from a table, other applications can access whatever data is already in the memory cache. Disk access and the corresponding degradation in performance is sometimes avoided. This intelligent caching is a step towards the ultimate goal of never having a page fault, i.e., the data you need is in memory and no disk access is required.

OnLine shared memory contains both data from the database and control information. Because the data needed by various applications is located in a single, shared portion of memory, all control information needed to manage access to that data can be located in the same place. OnLine adds memory dynamically as it needs it and you, as the administrator, can also add segments to shared memory if necessary.

2.1.4.3 Dynamic thread allocation and parallelization

OnLine supports multiple client applications using a relatively few number of processes, called virtual processors. A virtual processor is a multithreaded process that can serve multiple clients and, where necessary, run multiple threads to work in parallel for a single query. In this way, OnLine provides a flexible architecture that is well-suited for both online transaction processing (OLTP) and decision-support applications. In other words, the process footprint is a small one. Each user does not require a large amount of memory and therefore many users can be in a partial state of execution at the same time without choking the machine.

OnLine can allocate multiple threads to work in parallel on a single query. This feature is known as the parallel database query (PDQ) feature. OnLine allows a table to be fragmented over multiple disks according to a distribution scheme. This feature is known as fragmentation. The PDQ feature is most effective when you use it with the fragmentation feature. The reason for this is that a large table scan can be broken up into parts and execute in parallel, increasing the speed of execution by a multiple of the number of fragments. For example, five fragment table scans can be done almost five times as quickly.

2.1.5 Online fault tolerance and high availability

Another shortcoming of early client/server systems was reliability. Informix OnLine uses various logging-and-recovery mechanisms to protect data integrity and consistency in the event of an operating system or media failure.

2.1.5.1 Archives and backups of transaction records

OnLine allows you to archive the data it manages and also store (back up) changes to the database server and data since the archive was last performed. The changes are stored in logical log files, so you have a database backup and all the incremental updates performed since the update. OnLine allows you to create the archive tapes and the logical log backup tapes while users are accessing OnLine. You can also use online archiving to create incremental archives. Incremental archiving enables you to back up only the data that has changed since the last archive, which reduces the amount of time required for archiving.

After a media failure, if critical data was not damaged (and OnLine remains in online mode), you can restore only the data that was on the failed media, leaving other data available during the restore.

2.1.5.2 Fast recovery

When OnLine starts up, it checks if the physical log is empty, which implies that OnLine shut down in a controlled fashion. If the physical log is not empty, OnLine automatically performs an operation called fast recovery. Unfortunately, SE does not include this feature, so you must devise your own recovery when starting up after a failure. Online fast recovery automatically restores OnLine databases to a state of physical and logical consistency after a system failure that might leave one or more transactions uncommitted. During fast recovery, OnLine uses its logical and physical logs to perform the following operations:

- Restore the databases to their state at the last checkpoint.

- Roll forward all committed transactions since the last checkpoint.

- Roll back any uncommitted transactions.

OnLine spawns multiple threads to work in parallel during fast recovery.

2.1.5.3 Mirroring

When you use disk mirroring, OnLine writes data to two locations. Mirroring eliminates data losses due to media (hardware) crashes. If mirrored data becomes unavailable for any reason, the mirror of the data is accessed immediately and transparently to users.

2.1.5.4 Data replication

If your organization requires a very high degree of availability, you can replicate OnLine (not SE) and its databases, running simultaneously, on a second computer. Sybase has a similar feature called the Replication Server. Replicating OnLine and its databases provides you with a backup system in the event of a catastrophic failure; if one site experiences a disaster, applications can be directed immediately to use the second database server in the pair.

Running data replication also allows you to balance read-only applications (for example, decision support) across both database servers in the data replication pair. Replication is not a trivial pursuit. It requires careful planning and additional resources to bring an integrated replication scenario to fruition.

2.1.5.5 Multimedia support

OnLine supports two blob (binary large object) data types—TEXT and BYTE—that place no practical limit on the size of the stored data item. OnLine stores this blob data either with other database data or in specially designated portions of the disk called blobspaces.

2.1.6 Distributed data queries

OnLine allows users to query and update more than one database across multiple OnLine database servers within a single transaction. The OnLine database servers can reside within a single host computer or on the same network. OnLine supports both TCP/IP and IPX/SPX networks. A two-phase commit protocol ensures that transactions are uniformly committed or rolled back across the multiple database servers.

You can use Informix-Gateway with DRDA to make distributed queries that involve both Informix- and DRDA-compliant databases. This is of particular importance if you require data from a "heritage" system using DB2 or native MVS files stored with the VSAM access method. You can also use OnLine in a heterogeneous environment that conforms to X/Open.

2.1.7 Database server security

The databases and tables managed by OnLine enforce access based on a set of database and table privileges, which are managed through the use of GRANT and REVOKE SQL statements. In addition to this type of security, OnLine allows you to audit database events on a database server-wide basis. Auditing, described in the Informix OnLine Dynamic Server Trusted Facility Manual, enables you to track which users performed which actions to which objects at what time. You can use this information to monitor database activity for suspicious use and thereby deter ill-intended users. You can also use it as post-facto evidence of database server abuse.

2.1.8 Who uses and maintains Informix Online?

Relational database management systems are complex software systems that include database engines and database data. They need care and feeding to provide good service. OnLine administrators understand that OnLine combines fault-tolerant, OLTP performance with multimedia capabilities and a dynamic architecture to take advantage of available hardware resources, but not all users of OnLine understand it that way. The question "What is OnLine?" means different things to different users. The following types of individuals who interact with OnLine all have a different perspective:

2.1.8.1 End users
End users almost unknowingly access, insert, update, and manage information in databases using a structured query language (SQL), often embedded in a client application. The client application could be implemented with a GUI front-end tool such as PowerBuilder or Informix New Era. These end users of OnLine might be completely unaware that they are using OnLine. To them, OnLine is a nameless aspect of the system being used. As long as the data is delivered in a timely and reliable fashion, they will be happy.

2.1.8.2 Application developers
For the developers of a client application, OnLine is a database server that offers a number of possibilities for data management, multimedia, isolation levels, and so on. OnLine can integrate information objects such as scanned and digitized images, voice, graphs, facsimiles, and word-processing documents into a SQL-based relational database. The concept of relational databases managed by Informix database servers is explained in the remainder of the book. This book is primarily targeted to the development group.

2.1.8.3 Database administrators
The database administrator (DBA) of a database is primarily responsible for managing access control for the database. The DBA uses SQL statements to grant and revoke privileges to ensure that the correct individuals can perform the actions they need to, and that untrained or unscrupulous users are kept from performing potentially damaging or inappropriate resource-intensive activities.

2.1.8.4 Online administrators
Unlike the DBA, an OnLine administrator is responsible for maintenance, administration, and operation of the entire OnLine database server, which might entail managing many individual databases. This individual works with On-

Line as a set of software and operating system files that require care and feeding commensurate to the use and stress created by the application.

2.1.8.5 Operations and database support

OnLine operators are responsible for carrying out routine tasks associated with OnLine administration, such as backing up and restoring databases. The same person might fill the roles of both the administrator and the operator.

2.2 The Development Tools

You build the components of your application using the Informix development software, which provides an assortment of tools for building and testing objects, e.g., database, tables, and indices.

For completeness, we will mention the Informix application development tools. As mentioned earlier, the book will primarily address the Informix database. The development tools include but are not limited to the following: The Informix-4GL product family, comprised of Informix-4GL Rapid Development System, Informix-4GL Interactive Debugger, and Informix-4GL Compiler. Together, they make up a comprehensive fourth-generation application development and production environment that provides power and flexibility without the need for third-generation languages like C or COBOL.

Third-party products that can access Informix exist as well and, in our experience, the Informix database is commonly used with tools like Erwin (database modeling) and PowerBuilder (graphical front-end development tool). Informix is touted as a self-contained application development environment that:

- Provides rapid development and interactive debugging capabilities.

- Offers high performance in the production environment.

- Integrates all the functionality you could possibly need for building even the most complex applications.

- Doesn't require the use of a third-generation language, although we commonly see PowerBuilder used instead of NewEra (Informix GUI tool).

- Allows you to easily maintain your applications for years to come.

- Is based on industry-standard SQL and is easily portable.

The Informix-4GL product family gives you tools to create database applications—in three packages with one interface. Used together, Informix-4GL Rapid development System and Informix-4GL Interactive Debugger provide an environment for developing applications, while Informix-4GL Compiler provides high-performance application execution in the production environment. For building menus, forms, screens, or reports, Informix-4GL performs all development functions and allows for integration between them. More sophisticated applications will, however, require external development packages such as PowerBuilder.

2.2.1 Application development environment

For creating customized applications, Informix-4GL has pop-up windows, color, built-in help, nonprocedural report specifications, complete procedural flow control, and other facilities. You can also create your own ring menus and use flexible scrolling arrays—all of which increase productivity during development and production.

Informix-4GL's combination of procedural and nonprocedural statements gives you development alternatives for using 4GL without third-generation languages such as C or COBOL. Procedural statements give developers flexibility, while nonprocedural statements such as OPEN WINDOW, MENU SELECT, DISPLAY, FORM, and INPUT save developers from writing hundreds of lines of detailed code. Less code also means less time spent maintaining your applications. Informix-4GL is concise and English-like, making it easy for programmers to get up to speed quickly when it's time to view, edit, and update existing applications.

Like all Informix application development tools, the Informix-4GL product family is built on the industry standard, SQL. SQL speeds database access and manipulation, and allows easy integration with applications built using any Informix SQL-based tool. These include Informix-SQL and Informix-ESQL/C (embedded SQL for C that allows SQL commands to be used in applications created with the C programming language).

2.2.2 Informix-4GL Rapid Development System

Informix-4GL Rapid Development System, the interpreted version of Informix-4GL, increases developer productivity by decreasing compilation time. Informix-4GL Rapid Development System is optimized to reduce compile time. Code written with the Informix-4GL Rapid Development System is compiled into pseudocode (p-code), read into memory, and executed by a p-code runner.

Informix-4GL Interactive Debugger

Informix-4GL Interactive Debugger enables you to "single step" a running program to perform debugging operations in a friendly, easy-to-use environment. Programmers are able to:

- Control the execution of running programs.
- View and change contents of variables.
- Analyze program execution step-by-step.

The Informix-4GL Interactive Debugger is also a powerful tool for maintaining Informix-4GL programs because it reduces the time required for developers to understand an existing application, and allows them to locate bugs quickly and easily.

Informix-4GL Compiler

Once you've completed development and are ready to move into the production environment, you'll want the fastest possible performance. Informix-4GL Compiler maximizes application performance by taking the Informix-4GL source code and compiling it into standard C code, which is then compiled into machine code. By compiling the source code into machine code, Informix-4GL Compiler allows users to take full advantage of the speed of the computer.

Features and functions

Informix-4GL allows applications created in Informix-4GL to be flexible and have more functionality with statements such as: ALTER TABLE, CONSTRUCT, CREATE TABLE, INPUT, INPUT ARRAY, MENU, OPEN FORM, OPEN WINDOW, OPTIONS, SELECT, and WHENEVER.

For example, the CONSTRUCT statement now allows 4GL programmers to control the manner in which users use screens to create queries. CONSTRUCT also allows developers to monitor the queries that users are building.

The OPEN FORM statement allows developers to specify character variables for each filename display in a window. This eliminates the need to write separate OPEN FORM statements for every form in an application.

Another example of enhanced syntax, the MENU statement, includes a BEFORE MENU clause, a HIDE OPTION statement, and a SHOW OPTION statement. These new options allow you to name menu options that begin with the same letter or letters, and to place menus anywhere on the screen.

You also have greater flexibility to specify character variables for menu names, option names, and option description.

4GL Application Programming Interface (API)

Many 4GL programs are able to call C functions, but C programs have not been able to call 4GL functions. Informix-4GL frees you from this restriction. The API allows you to call 4GL functions directly from a C program.

Interrupting 4GL queries

Informix-4GL allows applications that give you the choice of either allowing or disallowing aborting queries, depending on your specific requirements.

Online error messages

Informix-4GL makes it easier to access error information. First, an electronic version of error information, including error numbers, descriptive text, and corrective actions, is delivered in both ASCII and Postscript format. This allows you to print out a personal version of the error information. Second, a new utility called finderr displays the error text and corrective action, so you no longer need to have a manual handy to decipher error numbers.

Portability

Informix-4GL runs on over 450 hardware machines from 85 manufacturers—and it's portable to any of these platforms with no application recoding. Informix SQL is a leading database application development system featuring the speed, power, and security required by both large and small database applications. To retain a competitive edge, successful companies rely on powerful database applications to manage vital corporate information. An increasing number of these companies rely on Informix SQL.

Informix SQL gives you some of the tools you need, right out of the box. It features a suite of five application development tools: a forms package, a report writer, an interactive SQL editor, a menu builder, and an interactive schema editor. Each of these products is integrated, allowing you to develop complete database applications with a single software package. These tools are helpful, but we prefer more robust tools such as PowerBuilder and Delphi because they are friendlier and more commonly known application development database front ends.

2.2.3 Development tools (Perform and Ace)

With Informix SQL, you can access five built-in tools that share a common interface and easy-to-use menu options. With Perform, the custom screen generator, users can build and compile data-entry screens with little prior experience.

Perform's programming features allow developers to design and compile forms using columns from several database tables, multiple-field data displays, and multiscreen forms to create an interactive relationship between tables. Perform also ensures the integrity of your information using a variety of data validation checks, thus preventing incorrect data entry. PowerBuilder's Data Window is a similar component, which has been patented.

Ace, the relational report writer that is included with Informix SQL, allows you to control and format the information returned from a SQL query. Custom reports that include data from multiple tables can be easily developed with little programming.

Application developers can use some of Ace's sophisticated features, including prompting for input at runtime, passing parameters, and high-level language controls like IF-THEN ELSE statements and FOR and WHILE loops. Helpful formatting features include automatic page headers, trailers, and adjustable page layouts.

The interactive SQL editor allows experienced SQL users to write any SQL statement to be processed by the database engine. This is a particular advantage to developers who want to prototype SQL transactions using the standard Informix-SQL interface, before embedding the code into an ESQL or Informix-4GL application for complete customization.

The complete menu builder lets you create custom vertical menus without any programming. This helpful tool integrates the pieces of the application, including tying together forms, reports, SQL statements, and other menus.

Rather than using SQL syntax to create database schemas, the menu-driven interactive schema editor assists you in defining and modifying database design, table structures, and indexes.

2.2.4 Informix SQL and portability

Informix SQL is portable between a complete array of hardware and software environments. It is available on over 450 hardware environments from 85 different manufacturers, which saves you time and money. Complete database applications can be developed in Informix SQL and later transferred across a variety of major operating environments, including UNIX, XENIX, DOS, and OS/2. As mentioned, with Informix-SQL you can access two powerful Informix database engines. Informix-OnLine is designed for intensive online transaction processing environments, and Informix-SE is ideal for low-maintenance environments where ease of use is essential. Other Informix products are completely compatible with Informix SQL at the database level.

Productivity, flexibility, portability, and standards are what programmers can achieve by using Informix-ESQL for C or COBOL. Developers can continue to use these familiar third-generation languages (3GL) for developing applications, and also gain the advantage of using SQL to access data from those applications. Developers do not have to build their own database functions, thus saving development time and effort.

Informix-Embedded SQL (ESQL) allows developers to access highly efficient SQL database capabilities, including high-level data definition and manipulation commands and SQL query optimization facilities. In addition, Informix ESQL conforms to the ANSI SQL standard, so developers don't have to learn different data access methods when accessing data from Informix database servers as well as other database servers such as IBM's DB2 and DB2/400. Embedding SQL syntax into 3GL programs means developers use less code for accessing data from a SQL-based relational database management system (RDBMS). Data manipulation routines are quick and simple when developers use the short, English-like statements of SQL. Developers can create and alter databases and tables, and retrieve and modify data. All it takes are a few short SQL statements.

Commands

With SQL, efficiency also means power. With short SQL statements like CREATE DATABASE or CREATE TABLE, developers eliminate the need to develop the many lines of conventional 3GL code needed to set up a database and its associated objects. Single commands like SELECT, INSERT DELETE, and UPDATE let developers query, add, remove, and change data. Developers simply place EXEC SQL at the beginning of the first line of SQL code that needs to be embedded and processed. The preprocessors for Informix ESQL search the program for the SQL statements and convert the SQL to "C" movement and CALL statements—thereby encapsulating them within the appropriate Informix function calls. Informix ESQL will then invoke the 3GL compiler, which compiles the program and links the Informix libraries into the final executable application. In addition, the Informix preprocessors allow just the pure 3GL code or only the object modules to be built.

English-Like statements

As you will see in more detail later, the WHERE clause of a SQL UPDATE, SE-
LECT, or DELETE statement determines the rows that will be processed. The
WHERE clause might contain conditions on individual fields, multiple fields,
join conditions, and subqueries. The example, later in the chapter, shows a
simple subquery condition combined with a single field condition.

Standard compliance

Informix SQL statements are ANIS SQL-92 entry-level compliant. This means
developers can build applications that are portable to other environments or
work with different database servers without any code changes. Developers
can build applications that work with both Informix database servers and
other servers such as IBM's DB2 and DB2/400 using TCP/IP or IPX/SPX protocols. Of course, developers can still take advantage of Informix-specific SQL.
Informix recently added new commands (extensions) for added power and flexibility. In addition, Informix ESQL supports X/Open commands such as GET
DIAGNOSTICS and ALLOCATE DESCRIPTOR to provide improved portability of application code.

Connection management

Application developers can build applications that connect to multiple database
servers simultaneously using the advanced ANSI-standard CONNECT, SET
CONNECTION, and DISCONNECT statements. With these statements, applications can work with multiple databases using different/dynamic user IDs and
passwords. For instance, with Informix ESQL, transactions can be held from
one database server while switching to another database server for separate execution. The following is sample code from an Informix-ESQL/C application:

```
EXEC SQL BEGIN DECLARE SECTION;
double percent raise:
EXEC SQL END DECLARE SECTION;D
EXEC SQL CONNECT TO @bigserver1 USER thebigguy USING PASSWD;
EXEC SQL DATABASE consultdb;
if (SQL ERROR) return (SQL ERROR);
EXEC SQL UPDATE consultbucks
  SET rate =rate*(1.0+:percent raise)
 WHERE (year(contract date)<1996) AND
     EXISTS (SELECT keyguy FROM offices
            WHERE keyguy IN ("Paul","Joe","Rich");
if (SQL ERROR) return (SQL ERROR); return (SUCCESS);
EXEC SQL DISCONNECT CURRENT
```

2.2.5 Informix ESQL and the client/server architecture

Once the application is developed, Informix ESQL automatically links the Informix communication libraries into the application. The application is "network ready" and can work in a client/server environment without any
additional products. With the latest release, new syntax has been added, al-

lowing programmers to adjust client/server communication buffer sizes for more efficient performance.

2.3 Building an Application

This section outlines the basic steps you follow when building an Informix application. After completing step 1, you can work in any order. That is, you can define the objects used in your application in any order, as you need them. To develop an application you might:

1. Create the database. The database is the hub of the application. It includes the description and content of all information and data stored to facilitate the operation of the business.

2. Create the application object. This is the entry point into the application. The application object names the application, specifies which libraries to use to save the objects, and specifies the application-level scripts.

3. Create windows. You must place control in the window and build scripts that specify the processing that will occur when events are triggered.

4. Create data access objects. Use these objects to retrieve data from the database, format and validate data, analyze data through graphs and crosstabs, create reports, and update the database.

5. Create menus. Menus in your windows can include a menu bar, drop-down menus, and cascading menus. You can also create pop-up menus in an application. You define the menu items and write scripts that execute when the items are selected.

6. Create user objects. If you want to be able to reuse components that are placed in windows, define them as user objects and save them in a library. Later, when you build a window, you can simply place the user object instead of having to redefine the components.

7. Create functions and structures. To support your scripts, you probably want to define functions to perform processing unique to your application and structures to hold related pieces of data.

8. Test and debug your application. You can run your application anytime. If you discover problems, you can debug your application by setting breakpoints, stepping through your code statement by statement, and looking at variable values during execution.

Prepare a release candidate executable when your application is complete. Then you have a dress rehearsal system test involving the user. If all goes well and the user signs off, you can then prepare a final executable version to distribute to your users.

This is the whole Informix environment in a brief overview fashion. We will concentrate on the database environment as well as the process of developing database applications in greater detail in the following chapters.

3

Designing an Application

Designing computer applications is one of those things where some things change and some remain the same. The tools and methodologies have changed (become more refined and more plentiful), but the problem or opportunity—depending on your viewpoint—is that we still need smart but not necessarily clever business systems to provide accurate and timely information.

3.1 Model the Target Business Process

Whether you are trying to understand and modify an existing computer-based business system or create an entirely new one, the biggest obstacle to successful engineering is an inability to analyze and communicate about the myriad of interacting activities that comprise the business process. Conversational languages, such as English, are too ambiguous to be effective, while formal languages remain unintelligible to most functional (business) experts. What is needed are techniques that structures conversational language in such a way as to eliminate ambiguity and facilitate effective communication and understanding.

To put the current state of business software modeling technology in context, at this point in 1996 there is good news and bad news. The good news is that database modeling has come a long way in the last two years. There are a variety of good tools emerging, and the competition moves the techniques along everyday. The bad news is that process modeling has not progressed as well. There is a reason for this. Process modeling is more difficult. Database modeling tools cater to the current RDBMS standard, SQL.

There is still only the beginning of process models because there is no standard process language. 3GLs and 4GLs are being used in a myriad of combinations. COBOL, C, and Pascal are mixed with PowerBuilder and Visual Basic development in the same shop and sometimes on the same project. There is hope, however; many vendors are working to create process models that generate target code for many popular process program languages. Fortunately, this book is about Informix so we will concentrate on database modeling. But be aware that a good database design is not just a nice relational model but also one that supports the business processes with data manipulation SQL that provides for "fast access" coupled with integrity.

3.1.1 Why create a model?

Modeling can be an effective technique for understanding and communicating, and has been used for centuries. In a process model, extraneous detail is eliminated, thus reducing the apparent complexity of the system under study. The remaining detail is structured so as to eliminate ambiguity and highlight important information. Graphics (pictures, lines, arrows, graphic standards) can provide much of the structure, which is why most people think of process models as pictorial representations. However, well-written definitions of the objects appearing in the model, as well as supporting text, are also crucial to the model serving its role as a communications tool.

In engineering disciplines, it is expected that a model will be constructed before an actual working system is built. In the automotive industry, scale models of cars are constructed for the purpose of extensive testing. In most if not all cases, modeling the target business process is an essential first step in developing any database application. It is an essential roadmap that will establish the destination. Determining the exact functionality of your target destination is essential. It must be captured and represented in as much detail as possible. Figure 3.1 is a graphical representation of a mainframe AS400 database connected to multiple AIX servers with Informix SE databases. A picture can make the objective clear. As the Cheshire cat in *Alice in Wonderland* says: "If you don't know where you are going, any road will get you there."

Once a model is developed and available for the developers, the product can then be refined at the logical level. This ensures a successful software product. Architects create blueprints before they actually construct a house. The blueprints are a logical representation of the physical building. There are many advantages to refining the design at the logical level, before the first brick is set.

There are tools available to facilitate the construction of the model. Unfortunately, no tool to date can tell you what you want to do. You must determine this yourself. Once you have begun to formulate your requirements, tools can be helpful. Currently available tools such as VISIO can be used to create graphical representations of almost anything (see Figure 3.2). These graphical depiction of the process can be augmented with text. Another tool, Integration Framework/2000 (see Figures 3.3 and 3.4), can be used to capture information about each life-cycle step in a system integration. They can also be linked with OLE to other tools, e.g., Word, Excel, and Powerpoint. You can also use a tool such as BPWIN to capture graphics and text. You still need to do the modeling with the business experts. These tools help with presentation and control.

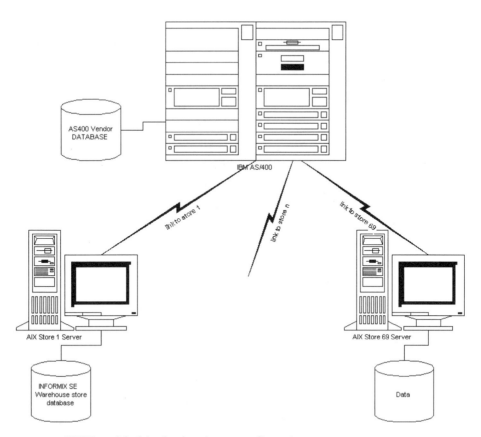

Figure 3.1 VISIO model of the database/server configuration.

Process modeling allows you to look at a system of interest in depth, so you can analyze, understand, and—perhaps most importantly—communicate to others the subtle nuances of your organization. There are many reasons that might motivate a process modeling project. One of the by-products is documentation of a multiple-step business process. One of the rules of thumb of business is that the longer a document is, the less it will be read. Give busy people a one- or two-page document with a VISIO or Powerpoint diagram, and there is a pretty good chance they will look it over in a reasonable amount of time. Give those same people a 30-page, single-spaced document, and there is a very good chance that it will sit on their desks for months unread.

Process modeling is a valuable technique to gain consensus on what is being done and quickly proposing alternative new approaches. It costs much less to develop a model than it does to develop a new information system or reorganize a department, only to find out that the new approach has merely created a new set of problems and inefficiencies.

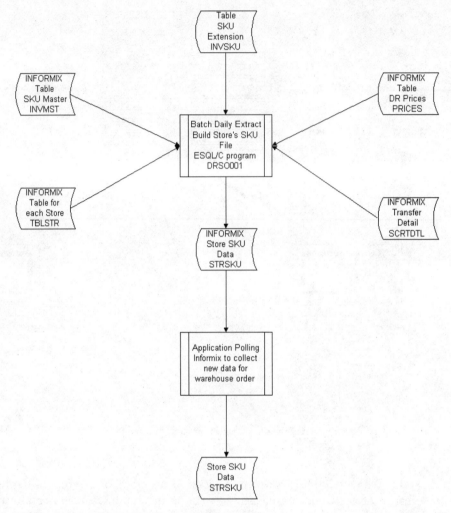

Figure 3.2 System flow for collecting Warehouse orders.

3.2 Develop an Entity Relationship

Once you have a basic model of the business process functionality, you then capture information about the data requirements to support the functionality. Before CASE tools became available, this was a tedious process, and even CASE was sometimes too large to handle. Thankfully the tools have evolved and now there are a host of viable alternatives.

3.2.1 Entity relationship basics

The design process for the application database is unique to each development environment. We will discuss it in general terms and then show how CASE

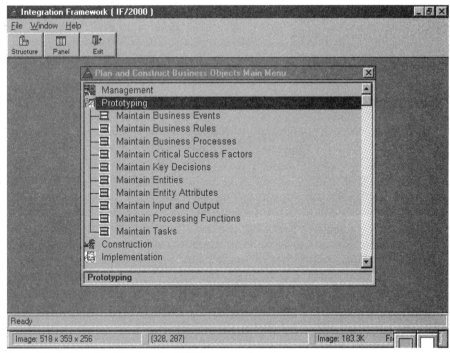

Figure 3.3 Integration Framework / 2000.

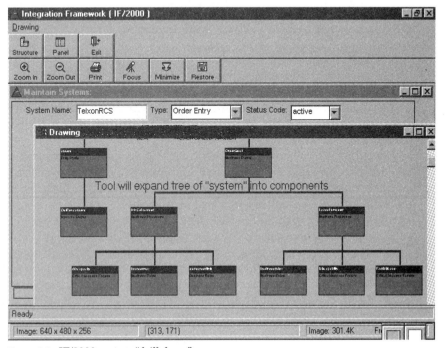

Figure 3.4 IF/2000 system "drill down".

tools can facilitate the process. The specifics of the process might vary from shop to shop. In any event, this is a crucial item and the degree to which it is completed before full-scale development will facilitate the process greatly.

3.2.1.1 Determine the application entities

An entity is a person, place, object, event, or activity of interest to the functionality you are creating, i.e., any noun that can represent information of interest to the organization. In the logical database design, you try to build an entity/relationship model by identifying the entities and their attributes as well as the relationships between the different entities. The database logical design starts as soon as you meet the users. Listen for entities in interviews with the user. If you are developing a database to track the schedules at one television station, the entities might include series and episodes. The attributes of an entity are the things that describe and define it. For example, a series has a descriptive name, so the name is an attribute of the series. The date it was originally produced might also be an attribute. Make sure to listen for relationships in the user interviews.

What is a relationship? If an entity cannot exist without a parent, it is dependent, i.e., it "belongs to" another entity. This is a relationship. Important subsets of an entity with special attributes are subentities. For example, a TV series might be of the "special" type, with attributes that pertain only to that type of series. There might also be a "special" subentity. So a special would be part of a series, i.e., it could be merged with the series and have the same primary key. A dependent entity, e.g., an episode, belongs to a series and has a primary key that contains the parent key and an additional key to identify the dependent.

3.2.1.2 Refine each entity and attribute

After you have collected the business entities and attributes from interviews with the user, check the project standards for naming conventions. See Chapter 19 for an example. Also, if applicable, use firmwide abbreviations to ensure consistent naming. Next, attempt to capture a description and validation criteria for each entity and attribute.

Does the project have a data dictionary? If so, enter the description and validation criteria here. Also check the dictionary to determine if the attribute or entity already exists. PowerBuilder has its own catalog tables, the extended attributes, which can house descriptions and validation rules. These attributes can be populated with CASE tools like ERwin or LBMS.

Determine the primary key for each entity, which uniquely identifies entity instances (rows). The primary key of a dependent entity includes parent key and descriptive column. For example, the primary key for the episode entity is the series_code and episode_cde concatenated. Document past or future states in description, i.e., add last_update_timestamp. The primary key will promote database integrity as you will be inhibiting table row duplicity and the creation of database orphans, i.e., rows in a dependent table with no parent.

3.2.1.3 Determine relationships

Here again, listen for relationships in interviews with the user. Document the roles of entities in recursive relationships. A series might be a part of another series. Determine the cardinality of the relationship, which will facilitate the choice of keys or indices to access the entity. For example, how many episodes are in a series? Does the identifying key to the relationship have many different values?

Decide on a formal name by checking the standards for naming keys. Don't confuse relationships with entities or attributes. Attributes that designate entities are relationships. If the primary key of an entity consists of other primary keys, it might be a relationship. For example, the TV episode entity would have a primary key consisting of the TV series identifier and the episode identifier. The TV series identifier is the primary key of the series entity.

3.2.2 CASE tools "lite"

So how do you create an entity relationship diagram? ERwin and S-Designor are generally considered to be the best choices for serious developers when it comes to CASE tools. They are similar and both perform the really important functions. For the purposes of this book, we will use ERwin to illustrate the capabilities of these "new wave" CASE tools.

ERwin's stated focus is on quickly creating high-quality, robust physical databases. ERwin is sold as a database design tool. ERwin does not create processing modeling diagrams, just entity relationship diagrams (known as ER diagrams—thus the name ERwin). ERwin's specialization is on the physical side. At press time, ERwin 2.5 had been released with support for Informix 7 among other database management systems. When you finish modeling the database you can have ERwin build the data definition language. This is essentially what has been missing from upper CASE tools. Using ADW or LBMS, we have found that, after spending a couple of years designing something, we still didn't know that much more about good relational database design . . . which is crucial for client/server success.

Tools like ERwin and S-Designor show you the physical definition right from the start, not hiding it like upper CASE tools do. To build a good database model for physical implementation using Informix, you have to think like a relational database.

3.2.3 Benefits of "lite" CASE

We can break the benefits into two categories. The first one you will notice is increased productivity. This is true for those projects that already have an existing database, and also for those of us lucky enough to work on new projects with a blank slate for a data model.

You will see the second benefit after you create your database. The quality and robustness of the physically generated SQL DDL (data definition language) is unsurpassed by even the largest and most expensive CASE tools on the market. An interesting point to note is the lifespan of ERwin's usefulness on a project. We have found that when tools like ERwin are chosen they are used throughout the entire project, without exception. Where upper CASE tools are used (LBMS, ADW, etc.), the tool is usually abandoned somewhere during the initial development phase. We've never seen a project that adopted an upper CASE tool in the middle of development. However, on many occasions, we've seen projects that weren't using any form of CASE tool easily pick up ERwin in midstream and keep with it to the end.

3.2.4 Data modeling using ERwin

ERwin uses a traditional methodology called IDEF1X. Not unlike other tools, with ERwin you start creating an ER diagram by placing entities (tables) on your diagram and adding relationships between them. Figure 3.5 shows the ERwin environment, which allows you to do this.

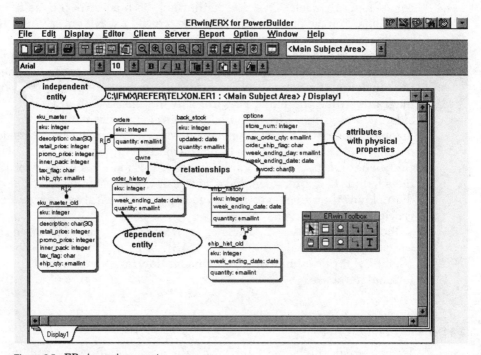

Figure 3.5 ERwin environment.

3.2.5 Reverse engineering

Sometimes the data you will use is contained in a legacy data or existing "heritage" data model. Both ERwin and S-Designor include the capability to reverse-engineer from any of the supported databases. Reverse engineering is the process of examining the previously existing table structure and getting your ERwin data model up to date with what's going on in the real database. In previous versions of ERwin, reverse engineering required you to have the original SQL DDL that was used to create your tables. However, you might find yourself with a DDL that is out of date or even, in the worst case, with no DDL. ERwin solves this problem by providing a "database server suck" in a SERVER/CONNECT/SYNC ERWIN option (see Figure 3.5).

If you prefer, you can still use the traditional approach in the latest version. You are basically using the ERwin OPEN command to read in SQL and create a model. Here are the steps:

1. Start ERwin, usually as an icon (ERWIN16.EXE or ERWIN32.EXE, depending on operating system).

2. From the File menu, select OPEN.

3. Change the File type to SQL, and specify the SQL file that you want to reverse engineer from.

4. Specify the DBMS type that the SQL syntax is written for.

In the Reverse Engineer window, you now have several options. You can specify which components of SQL you want to capture. You must reverse-engineer tables for obvious reasons, but you can capture foreign keys and indexes as well. You also have the ability to set case conversion options. Lastly, for the inquisitive, you can display the parse of the SQL as it is happening. When all options are set, press the Reverse Engineer button. Now would be a good time to calculate how much time you are saving by letting ERwin do the reverse engineering as opposed to doing it yourself! Unfortunately, you might not even have time—it's pretty fast. It even runs in the background, so you can press Alt–Tab and go do something else.

There is a much better method of reverse engineering in ERwin 2.5. With this capability, ERwin will actually connect to your DBMS and read directly from the system catalogs. This is not a one-time process, but an ongoing synchronization. Basically, you connect to the Informix database you want to re-engineer. Then you choose SYNC ERWIN with INFORMIX. The ERwin tool will read the Informix system catalog and build the model based on the tables, columns, indices, etc., found in the system catalog (see Figures 3.5, 3.6, and 3.7). If a developer makes a change directly on the database, you can easily pick it up the next time you synchronize. This capability can only strengthen the product's project longevity.

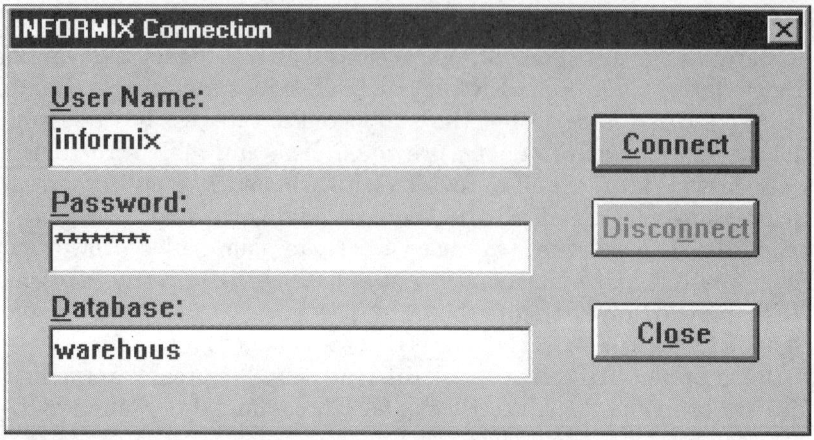

INFORMIX Connection   ☒

User Name:
informix   **Connect**

Password:
********   **Disconnect**

Database:
warehous   **Close**

Figure 3.6 Connecting to Informix.

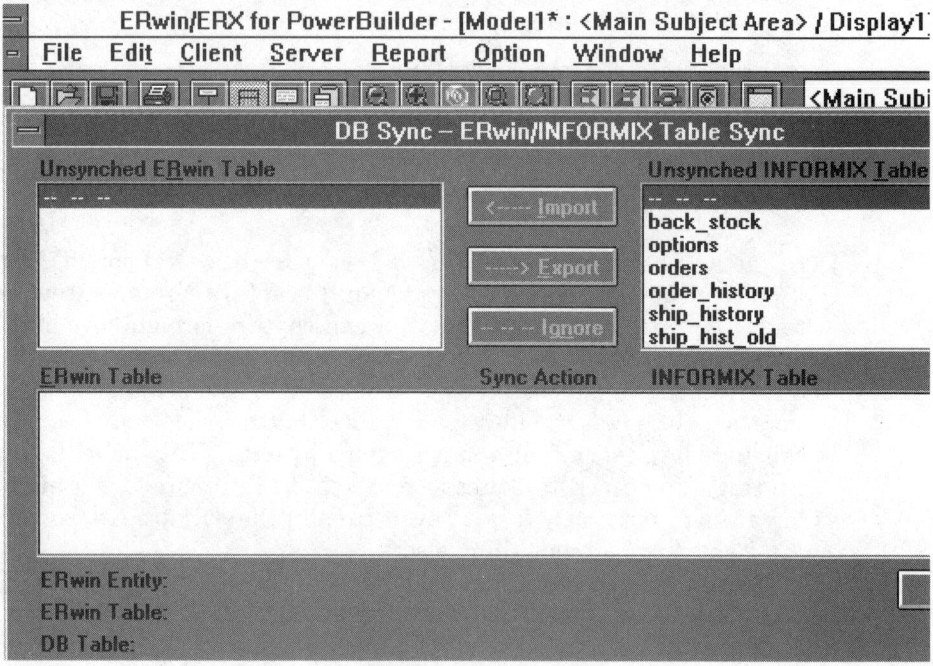

ERwin/ERX for PowerBuilder - [Model1* : <Main Subject Area> / Display1]

File   Edit   Client   Server   Report   Option   Window   Help

<Main Subj

DB Sync – ERwin/INFORMIX Table Sync

Unsynched ERwin Table   **Unsynched INFORMIX Table**
-- -- --   -- -- --
                  <---- Import   back_stock
                                                options
                  ----> Export   orders
                                                order_history
                  -- -- Ignore   ship_history
                                                ship_hist_old

ERwin Table   **Sync Action**   **INFORMIX Table**

ERwin Entity:
ERwin Table:
DB Table:

Figure 3.7 Synchronizing ERwin with Informix.

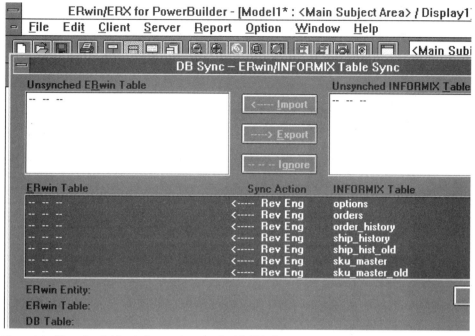

Figure 3.8 Choosing tables to be synchronized with ERwin.

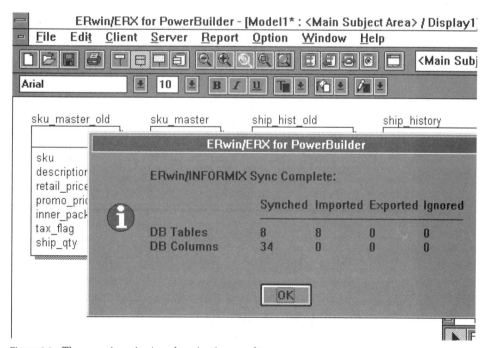

Figure 3.9 The reengineering/synchronization result.

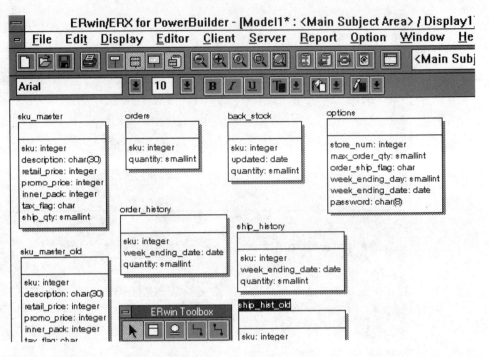

Figure 3.10   Design sans primary keys.

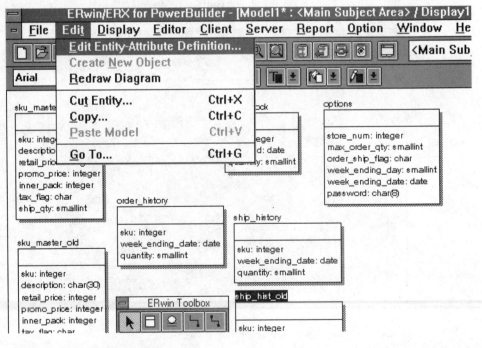

Figure 3.11   Editing the entity/attribute.

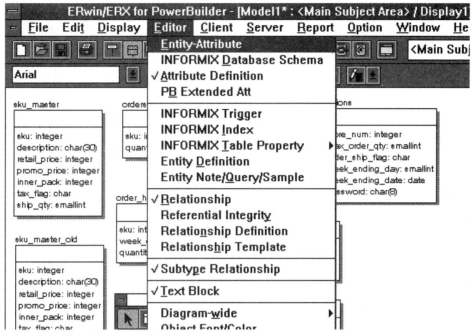

Figure 3.12 Choosing among editors.

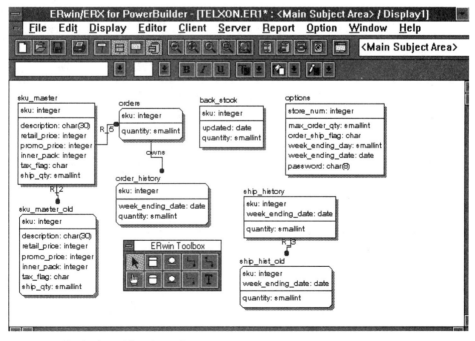

Figure 3.13 Designing with primary keys.

3.2.6 Entity modeling

Whether or not you are starting from scratch or working with an existing database, there are two types of entities, independent and dependent, as shown in Figure 3.5. You can uniquely identify independent entities without depending on relationships to other entities. Conversely, you cannot uniquely identify dependent entities without depending on relationships to other entities. Both types are available within the ERwin environment, shown in Figure 3.5. The sharp-cornered entities are independent. The entities with rounded corners are dependent. To add an entity to your diagram, select the appropriate icon from the toolbox and click anywhere on your diagram. ERwin will give your entity a default name. To change the name, use the right mouse button and click on the entity to bring up the list of available editors for that entity. Then Invoke the Entity Attribute Editor.

The Entity Attribute Editor, shown in Figure 3.14, allows you to enter not only the entity name, but the attributes (fields, columns) for the entity. When you enter attributes, you need to decide whether an attribute forms part of the primary key or not, and enter it into the appropriate window. Keep in mind that what you have entered so far are only logical names for attributes and entity. These names can have spaces in them. The logical names will be used to generate default physical names. It might be wise to limit your logical names according to the specifications of your particular database. That way you might never need to adjust your physical names.

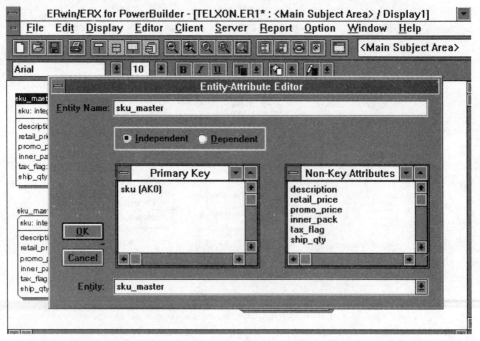

Figure 3.14 The Entity-Attribute editor.

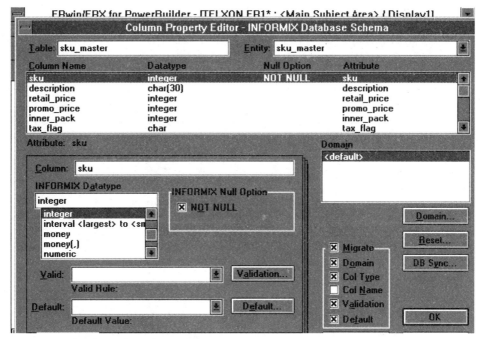

Figure 3.15 The Physical Attribute editor.

The Physical Editor, shown in Figure 3.15, allows you to enter the data type and other physical properties of the particular attribute (table column) within each entity.

3.2.7 Relationship modeling

One of the nicest features of ERwin is its foreign key migration capability. It's a feature you really need to understand before you start adding relationships between entities. In the IDEF1X terminology, there are two types of relationships between entities, identifying and nonidentifying. You use identifying relationships when a child entity is identified through its association with the parent entity. In other words, The foreign key column of the child table is also part of the primary key.

Nonidentifying relationships indicate that the child entity is not identified by its relationship to the parent entity. Identifying relationships and nonidentifying relationships are represented by solid and dashed lines, respectively.

Relationships in ERwin are generally referred to as foreign keys on the physical level. In fact, the way foreign keys are graphically displayed in the Power-Builder Database Painter is often mistaken for an ER diagram. Normally, when you create foreign keys you first define the parent table (with a primary key) and the child table (with some columns in common). Then you add a foreign key on the child table's related columns, and make it point to the primary key of the parent table. You'll always get an error if the number of columns in the foreign key is not the same number of columns in the primary key of the parent table (or if the data types don't match). This is where foreign key migration comes into place.

To create a relationship in ERwin, select the appropriate icon (identifying/nonidentifying) from the ERwin toolbox, click on the parent table, and then click on the child table. ERwin will automatically migrate the primary key attributes of the parent table into the child table. PowerBuilder will also migrate the physical name and data types of those columns. If you draw an identifying relationship (solid line), the primary key attributes of the parent table will migrate into the primary key section of the child entity. Conversely, nonidentifying relationships will migrate the primary key columns of the parent table into the non-key area of the child entity.

Take a look at Figures 3.10 and 3.13, which are before-and-after looks at adding a nonidentifying relationship. You'll notice that ERwin automatically added the SKU number field in the Order table. The relationship was a nonidentifying one, so the customer number was automatically inserted in the nonprimary key of the Order table.

The best part about this foreign key migration is that it is dynamic. If you change the data type of a primary key column in a parent table, the change is reflected in all child tables. If you add columns to the primary key of a parent table, they are migrated down to the child tables.

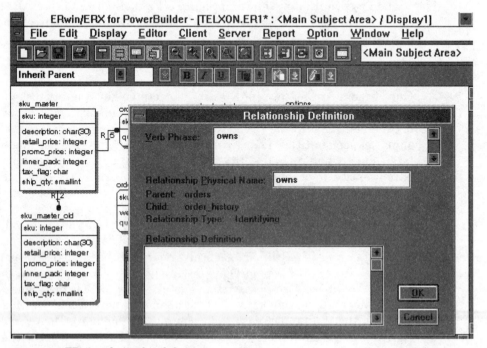

Figure 3.16 ERwin relationship definition.

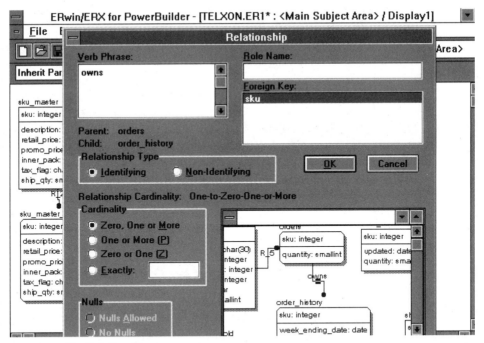

Figure 3.17 The Relationship menu.

3.2.8 Referential integrity

After a relationship has been added between tables, ERwin lets you control the referential integrity between them. To access this feature, you need to right-click on the relationship line to bring up the relationship's menu, and select Referential Integrity (see Figure 3.17).

Once in the Referential Integrity Editor, ERwin will display the parent and child table names, as well as the name of the relationship. The first thing you can do is change the verb phrase and physical name of the relationship. This will be used for the name of the foreign key.

ERwin allows you to control the behavior for an insert, delete, or update on either the parent or the child. Your options for any given action are Restrict, Cascade, Set Null, Set Default, and None.

Restrict. This option will cause the database to return an error if the action will violate referential integrity. For example, on a Parent Delete Restrict setting, if an attempt is made to delete a customer who has orders, the deletion will fail.

Cascade. This option will cause the database to trickle any changes between the related entities. A Parent Delete Cascade setting would attempt to delete a customer with orders and also to delete the associated orders. A Parent Update Cascade setting would result in any attempt to change a customer number (the primary key of the Customer table) also changing the customer number for all orders that belong to that customer.

Set Null. The Set Null option will cause the database to null-out the foreign key columns in the child table during a deletion or an update. For example, a Parent Delete Set Null option would result in Order records having a null customer number for any orders that once belonged to a deleted customer.

Set Default. This is very similar to Set Null, but instead of setting the foreign key columns to null, it resets them to their original default values.

Not all the options are available for each action. For example, a Child Update Set Null setting doesn't make much sense if you think about it for a minute. Also, not all the options are available for foreign key declaration syntax in your particular DBMS. In fact, most of the options are not supported by the popular DBMSes. However, ERwin provides physical support for all of its options through the use of triggers. If your DBMS supports triggers, you can take advantage of most, if not all, of the options.

ERwin accomplishes this through a set of trigger templates. These templates are created with a large and feature-filled set of macros. You can customize and even create your own triggers, but the macro language is poorly documented. This same macro language has now been extended in version 2.5 to support stored procedures and ad-hoc scripts. You can create your own stored procedure templates and apply them to tables or to the schema as a whole. This can be powerful for creating standard select, insert, update, and delete stored procedures to use in your DataWindows.

3.2.9 Supported databases

One of ERwin's big strengths is its support for various databases. Figure 3.18 shows the Target Server dialog with all the supported databases. ERwin doesn't make a big deal out of it, but you can change databases on the fly. ERwin maintains a data-type map between databases, so the process of porting from one database to another is only a few clicks.

It might also be noteworthy to mention that ERwin/ERX 2.5 supports physical storage parameters for most DBMSs, including Informix 7.

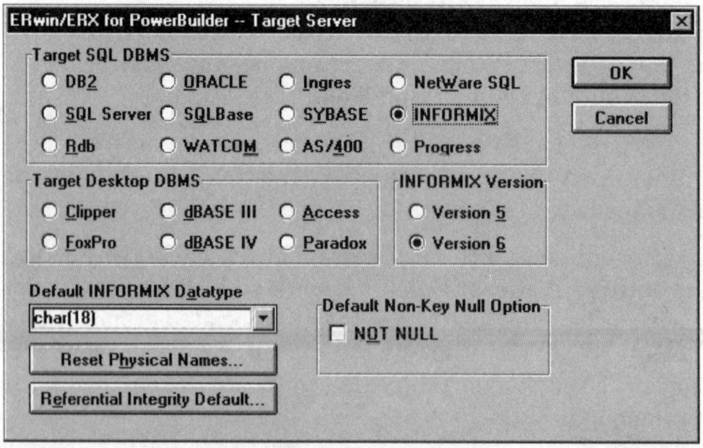

Figure 3.18 Supported databases.

Setting Up the Development Environment

This chapter is divided into two sections. The first covers the general areas and issues that need to be addressed when developing a client/server application. The second covers the specifics of setting up the development workstation environment. (This is a multistep process that covers library management and development preferences.) You must establish a working framework that is flexible enough so it can mature, reposition itself, and adapt to change.

4.1 Planning and Setup

The plan outlined in this section assumes that the following list of hardware and software resources either are or are soon to be put in place:

- One or more database servers (e.g., Sequent, IBM/RS6000, Sun, or IBM-compatible PC running Windows/NT or OS/2).

- Database management software (e.g., Informix, Oracle, SYBASE, or DB/2).

- Network file servers with the necessary connections (e.g., routers, bridges, and gateways) and software (e.g., Netware) installed.

- Client machines for all developers (e.g., workstations with file space and memory).

- A plan for source management (e.g., ObjectCycle, PVCS, MKS, or SourceSafe).

4.1.1 Development team

Client/server projects, like most projects, require that you combine a range of skills in order to complete the development of an application successfully. The skill sets you'll typically need for most client/server development project are listed in Table 4.1.

TABLE 4.1

Skill area	Involves
Project management	Ability to make decisions within a short period of elapsed time, scheduling of team tasks, coordination in and between projects
End-user representation	Understanding what users want the application to do and how they want to interact with it
System architecture	Designing the application to meet its requirements and to fit well in the computing environment where it is intended to operate
Database administration	Development and management of test and production databases
Network administration	Configuration and monitoring of server computers and the networks that connect client computers to them
Standards control	Establishment and enforcement of conventions and standards for such things as user-interface design, coding style, documentation, and error processing
Object management	Administration of the application components that developers create (with particular attention to facilitating the reuse of these components in multiple applications)
Application development	Creation and maintenance of application components (which includes painting them and coding logic for them), proficiency with SQL, and familiarity with the client computer's operating system and any other programs to be accessed from the application
Documentation	Writing comments, documents, or online help about the application for reference by developers or end users
Multimedia artistry	Creation of pictures, sounds, or other multimedia elements to be used in the user interface of the application
Quality assurance	Testing and debugging the application

Dividing the work

For a large project, the application development can typically be broken down into subsystems, with three to four developers per subsystem. It is still important to coordinate the overall project and keep the channels of communication open at all times, particularly when changes in one of the subsystems affect any of the others. It's a good idea for changes to be published through memos or e-mail in advance, so anyone who is affected will be aware and can subsequently make the necessary adjustments when appropriate.

Code review and walkthrough

It's a good idea to institute an ongoing code review and walkthrough session during the development of an application. This can be especially helpful on large projects that have several developers with varying PowerBuilder proficiency. For example, when a particular window or large section of functionality is coded, the code review meeting can be scheduled. At the review meeting, preferably in a conference room, the developer brings multiple copies of all the scripts and the original design specification for the particular window or section of functionality. If possible, a quick demonstration of the code is given while the group refers to the original design specification to note any differences in functionality. If the group comes across any differences, a decision must be made as to whether to change the specification or to change the code. If the functionality of the code is wrong, then it must be changed and a meeting rescheduled. If there are no or very minor differences, then the group can proceed to look at each piece of the code in detail. There are several purposes to this scrutiny:

- To check that the code will work as per the specification.
- To examine any new techniques and transfer the knowledge to the whole group.
- To make sure that the code is in line with the accepted conventions.

For this kind of code review to work requires that the team check their egos at the door so they don't take the criticism personally. The idea is to improve the quality of the product that is being developed. Once the code has passed through this kind of review, it is no longer the responsibility of the original coder; it is now owned by the review team. In the event of a problem arising later on, this change in responsibility will help prevent either the "not invented here" or the "Oh, it was Richie who developed that window" kind of responses.

Developer tools

It's also important to make sure that the developers have adequate hardware (e.g., a high-end PC with print capabilities), the appropriate software to produce documentation (e.g., Word, Excel, Powerpoint), access to database administration tools (e.g., Desktop DBA, DB-Access, DB-Load), and case-tools for modeling (e.g., S-Designor, ERWin, LBMS). In addition to the documentation provided with these tools, very often developers need to access the wealth of information available electronically through services like the Internet, bulletin board systems, CompuServe, America Online, and Prodigy. These services provide many newsgroups, forums, and libraries that can be scanned for possible solutions to issues that arise during development.

4.1.2 Sample planning chart

The sample planing chart shown in Table 4.2 shows columns for task and subtask descriptions, including any prerequisites and comments. To use this in your environment, could add columns for human resources, scheduled completion dates, a status, or anything else pertinent to your environment.

4.1.3 Standards, guidelines, and good practices

To start the task, you must develop a framework for and subsequently add to and modify some standards, guidelines, and practices/procedures. One of biggest mistakes is trying to come up with the ultimate standards guide before publishing it. This needs to be put in place early in order to help with produc-

TABLE 4.2

Task	Subtask
Establish system envirnonment for	Acquire copies of development tool
	Acquire local or LAN disk space for development tool
	Setup LAN directory structure (source, documentation, class)
	Setup backup and recovery procedures
	Establish source control procedures
	Provide copies of development tool and DB documentation to prepare basic startup document for new developer
Install development tool	
Local:	Run setup for each developer, including DB connections
Network:	Run setup, installing to network location
	Set up network development tool Icons for each developer
	Add network development tool's location to PATH
Install database connection layers	Determine any addressing (e.g., IP)
	Install transport layer (e.g., Named pipes, TCP/IP)
	Install database connection (e.g., SQL*NET, DBLIB, Open)
	Modify WIN.INI and other configuration files
	Test the database links
Configure development tool	Install any third-party class libraries
	Allocate library for reusable ojects and classes
	Establish and publish standards and naming conventions
	Establish guidelines document
	Establish development libraries

tivity, especially with developers who are getting up to speed with products like PowerBuilder, Visual Basic, or Delphi. After all, not everyone can always remember the best technique for a given situation. The payback for this up-front administration normally comes much sooner than you might expect. The thought process will naturally slow the project down to begin with, but surging ahead with what first comes to mind can come back to haunt you later on! Consider the following questions:

- What can be leveraged from the organization's current standards?

- What existing resources can be leveraged?

- How can I implement version control?

- Are there any source code and database naming conventions?

- What standard user and technical documentation is required?

- What are the database resources and requirements?

4.1.4 Network file server access

If you arc in or plan to be in a network environment, take some time to plan the directory structures and user groups that will access these directories on the shared file server. You might want to separate the project into coders, testers, and integrators and grant access rights accordingly. You can start off with a fairly simple directory structure such as the one shown in Figure 4.1.

You might also want to establish a review committee that is responsible for and meets periodically to discuss any modifications to the directory structure.

4.1.5 Database server access

You can use roles (such as DBO and DBA) to govern access to the data tables. You should create the tables and views, etc., using the DBO login, and develop any application code using a regular developer database login. This will ensure that the correct prefix for any database table is included in a fully qualified reference for that table. It will also prevent any problems in determining table identity during the runtime execution of the application. There will be several databases to consider:

- Development (default)
- System or integration test
- Quality assurance
- User acceptance
- Production

Directory Architecture

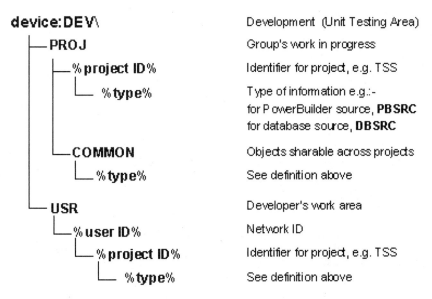

device:DEV	Development (Unit Testing Area)
PROJ	Group's work in progress
%project ID%	Identifier for project, e.g. TSS
%type%	Type of information e.g.:- for PowerBuilder source, **PBSRC** for database source, **DBSRC**
COMMON	Objects sharable across projects
%type%	See definition above
USR	Developer's work area
%user ID%	Network ID
%project ID%	Identifier for project, e.g. TSS
%type%	See definition above

Figure 4.1 Sample directory structure.

4.1.6 Backup and recovery procedures

The client/server environment is not immune to hardware failure and accidents, so design backup and recovery procedures for both the file server (development tool objects) and the data server (database objects and data).

Once the procedures are in place, make a point of testing them on a regular basis, i.e., once a month or more frequently, so you can determine if the recovery procedures actually work and continue to work on an ongoing basis. Catching problems before they become nightmares is the goal here. Remember to store the backups off-site, so if the building goes up in flames you can still operate in an emergency replacement installation.

4.2 Development Preferences

There are several more development considerations, such as the developer workstation configurations, the steps necessary to migrate objects through the development life cycle, the check-in and check-out procedures, establishing and maintaining object class libraries, the placement of the development tools, and the testing strategies.

4.2.1 Developer workstations

The developer workstations are a crucial factor in the development process. If the machines are not configured correctly or inefficiently, then the possibility of delay increases. Here are some of the issues surrounding developer workstations:

4.2.1.1 Workstation configuration

With the geometric advances in the speed and capacity of computers, workstations have become obsolete almost overnight, but your basic hardware and software setup should be as follows:

- High-end Pentium or Pentium Pro processor
- 32MB of memory, depending on the operating system (more is always better)
- 2GB hard disk drive
- CD-ROM drive for installation and later access to CD-based material
- 3.5-inch high-density disk drive, necessary for floppy disk installation only
- Network card (if necessary)
- Microsoft Windows 95 or Windows NT Workstation 4.0
- Most recent video driver for your monitor

Table 4.3 lists some configuration ideas for the DOS/Windows 3.1 environment. There was not much evidence when this book was being written, but we hope that the new PowerBuilder platforms like NT and other operating systems that support true multitasking will avoid many of the memory problems associated with the PowerBuilder DOS/Windows interface.

TABLE 4.3

Resource	Performance point	Comments
Memory	Use extended memory.	Windows does not use expanded memory.
Memory	Load drivers in high memory.	This frees up base memory, that which is below the 1 MB mark. With DOS 6.0 you have better control over where applications go. MemMaker and other memory managers can also provide help.
Memory	Use disk caching.	Use disk caching, and give as much memory as possible to the buffer.
Memory	Stay away from wallpapers or anything that is form over substance.	Using a wallpaper as a background can eat up a lot of memory. If you find it necessary to have a background, use a color pattern rather than a wallpaper.
The CONFIG.SYS and AUTO EXEC.bat	Understand what each item in your CONFIG.SYS and AUTOEXEC.BAT means, and remove unnecessary items.	You should understand the configuration of your machine in order to control it. Read the DOS and Windows configuration manuals.
Swap files	Use a permanent swap file.	Windows knows exactly where the swap file is and how big it is.
	Do not put a swap file or TEMP directory on the network.	You will be in constant contention with other network users.
Hard Drive	Defragment your hard drive on a regular basis.	Use DEFRAG or another tool.
	Performance will be affected by the hard drive speed and the drive's interleaf setting.	Both Windows and the server are hard drive intensive.
Display	Use the lowest-resolution display that will meet your needs.	The higher the resolution or the monitor, the slower the application will run.
WIN.INI and SYSTEM.INI	Understand what each item in your WIN.INI and SYSTEM.INI means.	There are WRITE files for both of these files. The Windows Resource Kit provides documentation. Note that the 386 enhanced section can greatly affect performance.

4.2.1.2 Application initialization/registration

For each application you develop, it's a good idea to create an application initialization file (.INI) that contains a profile of the user preferences used during the application execution. When you build your application, it should have its own INI file that contains the database transaction connection parameters, with the exception of password, for the application database. Here is a sample contents for a PowerBuilder application initialization file:

```
[Database]
DBMS= IN5
```

```
ServerName=tribecao11
Database=
UserID=allenp

[Toolbar]
toolbarvisible=yes
toolbaralignment=top
toolbartext=no
```

It addition to the connection information, this is a good place to store user profile information so you can refer to it at execution time. For example, this information can provide certain user interface preferences, such as toolbar configuration.

Most Windows application initialization files (those with the extension .INI) are placed in one of two locations: the WINDOWS directory (most often) or the directory of the application (less often). If you do not specify a path for the initialization file, most application development tool functions will look for an INI file in the following locations:

- The current directory

- The directory where Windows is installed, or where WIN.COM is executed

- The SYSTEM subdirectory for Windows, or where GDI.EXE is installed

- The working application directory, if not the current directory

- Sequentially through each directory listed in the path

4.2.2 Administration of libraries

The migration of objects between libraries should be tightly controlled either by a version control system or a set of well-defined procedures that allow an administrator to determine which objects in the development libraries have changed and need to be promoted into the next set of libraries. These libraries or files include the following type of objects:

- User interfaces, e.g., windows, menus, etc.

- Problem domain items, e.g., nonvisual functions, C programs, stored procedures, and triggers

- Operating system objects, e.g., UNIX shell scripts and NT batch files

- Database data manipulation and definition languages (DML and DDL)

- Check in/out procedures

In multideveloper environments, where teams with many members are involved in the coding and testing of objects and libraries, version control is an important consideration. There are several third-party version control systems available with interfaces to many different development tools.

To provide the team with greater security throughout the development life cycle, version control systems provide check-out and check-in functionality for the source code. We suggest you take advantage of these capabilities.

Check-out and check-in functionality also includes other features designed for the protection of the development environment. Objects that have been checked out cannot be checked in when an application using that object is currently being executed. Although this feature helps to maintain the integrity of the development library, it can be frustrating trying to find out who is running the executable and asking him or her to stop the application so you can check in your work. In addition, we recommend that you set up separate and discrete library environments for the unit test (DEV), system test or quality assurance (SYS or QA), and user acceptance test (UAT)—as well as an actual copy of what will ultimately be migrated to production (PRD).

An example of the initial setup might be:

1. The LAN administrator sets up the following directories on the network:

   N:. This would be distinct for each developer.

   P:\SYS. This would be common to all developers.

   P:\UAT. This would be common to all developers.

   P:\PRD. This would be common to all developers.

   Note: The logical mapping of N:\ would physically map to:

   ServerName/VolumeName:DEV\UserID\AppDir, e.g.,
   SIAC1/VOL1:DEV\ALLENP\FOCUS

   and the logical mapping of P:\ could physically map to:

   ServerName/VolumeName:DEV\PROJ, e.g., SIAC1/VOL1:DEV\PROJ

2. Designate two members of the team with the role of library managers (librarians). Only the librarians have write privileges to the UAT and PROD libraries. They are responsible for moving the system-tested (quality-assured) objects from the SYS directory to the UAT directory, ready for user acceptance testing. When this is satisfactorily completed, the objects are moved from UAT directory to the PRD directory, ready for production. The PRD libraries ultimately contain the final versions of the libraries that will be moved out to the production environments.

3. The librarians create the new libraries on PRD, UAT, and SYS.

4. The developers create their own work in progress libraries and files on N:\, and set up their library search paths. The following PowerBuilder example assumes that there are eight production libraries in the project, when in reality there could be many more:

```
N:\MYWIP.PBL
P:\SYS\SYSWIP.PBL
P:\UAT\UATWIP.PBL
```

```
P:\PRD\WHAPP.PBL
P:\PRD\WHMAIN.PBL
P:\PRD\WHLIB1.PBL
P:\PRD\WHLIB2.PBL
P:\PRD\WHCLS.PBL
P:\PRD\SYS.PBL
P:\PRD\UTLWIN.PBL
P:\PRD\UTLFUNC.PBL
```

If the object already exists, an example of the development procedures might be:

1. The developer requests a librarian to copy the object from the relevant PRD library to SYSWIP.PBL.
2. The developer then checks the object out from SYSWIP.PBL to N:\MY-WIP.PBL, makes the necessary changes, and then tests them.
3. After successful testing, the developer checks the object back into SYSWIP.PBL.
4. The system test/quality assurance team then runs the regression test(s) for the areas affected by the change (or, better still, use an automated testing tool that runs regression tests for the complete application overnight).

If the object is new, the development procedures might be:

1. The developer creates the object in N:\MYWIP.PBL and then tests it.
2. After successful testing, the developer moves the new object to SYSWIP.PBL.
3. The system test/quality assurance team then develops an appropriate test or tests for the new object (possibly in conjunction with the developer), and runs the test(s) for at the new object. (The test team might also want to run regression tests for the complete application overnight.)

Once the object is considered of a high enough standard (i.e., it works as expected), the test team notifies a librarian that the object (or a series of objects) are ready to be moved from the SYS library to the UAT library, ready for testing in accordance with the test plan developed by the user community. The testing will probably take place using an executable, in order to simulate the production environment. Upon successful testing in this environment, the object (or series of objects) is ready for the PRD library. The librarian can then determine which production library the object(s) must be moved to prior to building the executable (and dynamic libraries).

It is important to note that most development tools are not version control systems. The success of these techniques relies, in great part, on the cooperation of the development team as a whole.

TABLE 4.4

Library name	Contains
whapp.pbl	Application and project objects only
whmain.pbl	Application MDI frame library
whlib1.pbl	Application object library
whlib2.pbl	Application object library (repeat if necessary)
whcls.pbl	Application library descendants (an isolation layer)
pfcys.pbl (*)	Application library (system management)
pfcnvo.pbl (*)	Application library (nonvisual)
pfcwin.pbl (*)	Application library (user interface)

(*) indicates that the library is a foundation class library

When you begin the development of a new application, you need to think about the libraries that make up the application. You might not have this information at the very beginning, however, particularly if this is your first application. Table 4.4 shows an example using PowerBuilder.

4.2.3 Using class libraries

Developers new to client/server systems should consider using any of the sample application code and foundation class libraries (if any) that are supplied with the development product. Or you might consider purchasing one of the many available third-party class libraries. Then, after some experimentation and education, you can add features to the library or build your own from scratch.

4.2.4 Development tool location

When it comes to installing development software, there are a couple of questions about the environment you need to answer. The answers determine how you will proceed with the installation:

- Is this a stand-alone or network installation?
- If it's a network installation, should the development environment be installed on each developer workstation or on the network file server?

If this is a stand-alone installation or if the development environment is to be loaded on each developer workstation, then install the product from either CD-ROM or diskettes.

4.2.5 The daily "build and test"

It is rumored that, at the end of the working day at Microsoft, a complete recompile or rebuild of all the products takes place. Once they are rebuilt, they are tested using standard product regression tests. Project leaders are notified of any problems or issues that occur during the build or regression tests. Consequently, it is easier to determine which piece of code is causing a problem simply because less code can be changed in a 24-hour period. If you wait a month between builds, you might be left scratching your head trying to sift through the list of modules that have changed, particularly on a project involving a large development team.

You might want to consider doing this for your application development environment, perhaps on a less aggressive basis—maybe once a week. This technique also requires that you have the test scripts built and available for the parts of the product as they are being implemented. It will probably also require that you invest in one of the many automated test tools that have become an absolute necessity for overnight regression testing on a large scale.

5

Managing the Database

The hub of the typical application, especially one developed in PowerBuilder, is the database. This chapter describes how you can design, administer, and manage the database from within PowerBuilder, as well as other tools that can facilitate database design and maintenance.

We choose to use PowerBuilder because the DB-Access tool that comes with Informix is character-based and cryptic. Informix on NT comes with a GUI database administration tool, but it was not generally available at the time we wrote this book. Also, PowerBuilder is graphic and illustrates the points of this chapter well, and you can use it to perform some if not most database management functionality. For example, small applications using Informix SE as the DBMS can be managed with PowerBuilder exclusively. While larger deployments where the DBMS is Informix O/L might be better managed by a central database group using a database administration tool, PowerBuilder still provides some useful database functions, especially for the developer who does not have access to all available DBA tools.

5.1 Overview

Before we move on to the technical material, let's look briefly at the administrative issues. Most organizations have several database administrators who design, implement, and manage data on one or more DBMSs. The responsibilities of the database administrator include design and construction of database objects, performance monitoring, tuning, and data security.

5.1.1 Data administration

In the 1980s, a new organizational role emerged within information services, commonly known as data administration. Despite the similarity of names, this activity is quite different from database administration. The data administrator does not focus on a specific database and DBMS. The emphasis is on early life-cycle phases (analysis) and a global view of data. Responsibilities include naming standards, data models that cut across organizational boundaries, and long-range planning.

Nowadays, most large organizations have a data administration function, perhaps under a different job title. We address functions of both data administration (analysis) and database administration (design, construction, and maintenance). As you saw earlier in the book, under the discussion of the development life cycle, all these activities are related and covered by the term *database design*.

Both data and database administrators rely on a dictionary to document their designs and models. A dictionary stores data about your data-table specifications, columns, indexes, even specifications for application software and hardware. The early difficulties with data dictionaries involved problems in translating the dictionary meta-data into usable development objects, e.g., a data definition language. Because the dictionary database is one level above the humble operational database, it is sometimes called a meta-database. Some CASE tools bridge the translation gap. PowerBuilder has its own system tables, which are a form of dictionary database. They can be populated with CASE-like vendor tools such as ERwin and LBMS. These catalog tables augment the RDBMS system catalog tables to provide data that can describe rules for editing, validating, and displaying database table and column information.

5.1.2 Dictionaries and system catalog tables

There are many alternate terms for a dictionary. Vendors of CASE (computer-aided software engineering) tools (e.g., ADW and LBMS) often refer to the internal CASE dictionary as an encyclopedia or repository, and the two terms are basically synonymous. Relational DBMS have an internal catalog that contains limited but crucial data about user tables, columns, indexes, and security. Although these terms differ in some respects, they all maintain meta-data (data about your data). If you are using a tool such as ERwin or LBMS, you can use the logical model to create the DDL to define the database.

For the purposes of this discussion we will assume that you have a dictionary of some kind. This is your database; it stores all information about your emerging design.

Dictionaries can either be online or offline to development and production systems. A dictionary that is actively referenced during data entry is dynamic. One that is offline and used strictly for documentation is passive. An active dictionary is online to development, but not production systems, e.g., the Brownstone data dictionary for DB2/MVS. The direction of the technology is moving towards active dictionaries.

Dictionary technology is currently in a state of flux, with a number of official and de-facto standards emerging. LBMS and ADW are two of the more popular CASE tool dictionaries in use today, LBMS on the Windows/NT side and ADW on the OS2 platform. In any CASE, it is the usual start point for large system development.

Now what do you do with this data dictionary meta-data? In basic relational design, you convert data dictionary entities, relationships, and attributes to physical database tables foreign keys and columns. The goal is simply to move from the language of analysis suitable for client interviews to the language of relational database demanded by the computer. If the tools and methods used do not produce this result, it will severely affect the development. Ensure that proper target Informix translation is possible before proceeding with a particular data dictionary tool. Otherwise, all the analysis work will amount to a lost effort and a waste of time and resources.

5.1.3 Physical database objects

Once you start to get physical, the application's database consists of the following components:

Tables and columns. These are the basic building blocks of a good database. They should be grouped by usage and named in a standard way. They start off as entities and attributes in the logical model, where they are arranged to satisfy the business processes. A large application usually begins with a CASE tool that develops the entity relationship diagram whose entities and attributes are converted to physical tables and columns. Converting to the physical requires that you understand the target, Informix. ERwin, a third-party tool, can convert a logical model into any one of 15 physical DBMSs including, but not limited, to Informix, SyBase, Oracle, DB2, and Watcom.

Indexes. These, as the name implies, provide a way to search and sometimes control the data rows within a table. One or more columns can be grouped together to form an index. Most tables should have a unique index that serves not only as a search mechanism but also as a control to avoid duplication. For example, a table containing employee information should use a unique index to ensure that information about a particular employee is not entered twice. An index can also be clustered to maintain the physical placement of inserted rows in a specified order. For example, at a television station an acquired television series will include one or more episodes. A clustered unique index for the episode table might be series_code and episode_code concatenated together. This would make sure all of a series' episodes on database pages were stored in close proximity, which would speed up any access involving all the episodes within a series.

Keys (primary and foreign). Keys are indexes that provide for database integrity. For example, a network television station showing "Leave It to Beaver" reruns might have a series table. The series table would have a primary key, series_code. The primary key is typically a unique table row identifier. It also establishes the first part of the key in any dependent table, e.g., episodes belong to and dependent on a series. The episode table would have a foreign key, series_code, to connect the episode to the series and also to ensure that a series cannot be deleted if any episodes belonging to the series exist. Design tools such as ERwin can be used to define the logical database model and also create the physical components, including the referential definitions required to enforce database integrity.

Views. The name view describes its object's function: to provide a particular view of base tables. Views are vertical tables made up of columns from one or more tables, usually joined by the same key or keys they share in common. Views facilitate access to the data. They can provide security as well, e.g., you can restrict the selection of employee column data such as salary. Views containing columns from more than one table are typically not updateable; check the target DBMS for specifics.

Of particular importance are the data types supported by each DBMS. The database design and physical manifestation must consider which data types are available in the target DBMS. For example, date and time data types vary widely from DBMS to DBMS.

5.2 Database Administration Tools

Database administrators have been waiting for comprehensive database administration and maintenance software for a long time. The advent of menu- and GUI-based software has provided some help. For large organizations it might not be suitable, but for small developers it is more than adequate and fairly easy to use. In the Database painter, you can:

- Create, alter, and drop tables.
- Drop views.
- Create and drop indexes.
- Create, alter, and drop primary and foreign keys.
- Define and modify extended attributes for columns.

From the Database painter, you can also open three related painters:

- The Data Manipulation painter, where you retrieve and manipulate data from the database.
- The View painter, where you create views.
- The Database Administration painter, where you control access to the database and execute SQL directly.

You can also do some other fairly useful things, like:

- Create database profiles to quickly connect to any of the databases you might be using or supporting in development and production.
- Add EDIT styles, and display formats and validation maintenance, i.e., the extended attributes mentioned in other parts of the book. See the

OBJECTS menu item. These features are often overlooked, but can increase development productivity significantly, especially when using data windows. More on this later.

5.2.1 Invoking the database administration tools

To open the Database painter:

1. Click the Database icon in the PowerBar or double-click the Database icon in the PowerPanel. The Select Tables window will be displayed (see Figure 5.1).

2. You can select tables to work on now or click Cancel to go to the painter workspace. You can open tables later from the workspace.

Like the other PowerBuilder painters, the Database painter contains a menu bar, a customizable PainterBar, and a workspace (see Figure 5.2). To work with database components, you open them in the workspace.

Tables are expanded, so they show the table's columns, keys, and indexes. You can move objects around the workspace by dragging them with the mouse. For example, to move a table, press the left mouse button on the title bar for the table and drag the table. You can also select and modify objects in the work-space by pointing and clicking them with the mouse, as described throughout this chapter. Select the table for which you want to display or alter the information, then press Enter. Scroll in the painter workspace. If you open more tables and views than can be displayed in the Database painter workspace at one time, you can scroll up or down to view all the tables and views.

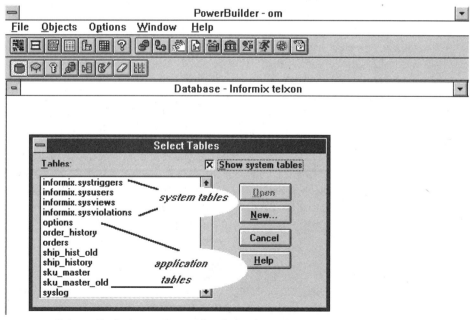

Figure 5.1 Painter displaying preference database.

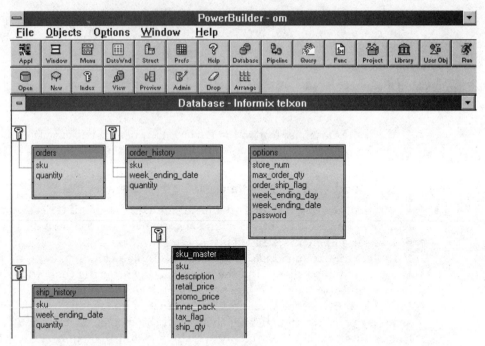

Figure 5.2   Selected tables of the preference database.

First-time users should build a test table with each possible data type in the target DBMS. Experiment with the DBMS before beginning serious development. As you work with your database, you will probably generate SQL/DDL statements. You might want to save a copy of the SQL statements generated by PowerBuilder. They might be helpful if you have to migrate or rebuild a database object. For example, as you define a new table in the Create Table window in the Database painter, PowerBuilder is building a SQL CREATE TABLE statement internally. When you click the Create button, PowerBuilder sends the SQL statement to the DBMS to create the table. Similarly, when you add an index, PowerBuilder is building a CREATE INDEX statement.

You can record all SQL statements generated in a painter session in a log file. This allows you to have a record of your work and also makes it easy to duplicate the work if you need to create the same or similar tables in another database. In addition, each time you create or modify a database component such as a table, you can generate just the SQL to a log file. You can then submit the statement to the database at a later date.

To start logging your work in a text file:

1. Open the Database painter.
2. Select Start/Stop Log from the Options menu.

PowerBuilder will open a log file and display the Activity Log icon at the bottom of the screen. From this point on, all of your work will be saved in a temporary file. To save the log to a permanent text file:

1. Select Save Log As from the Options menu. The Save the Log window will be displayed.

2. Name the file and click OK. The default file extension is .SQL, but you can change that if you want.

PowerBuilder will save the log as a text file with the specified name. You can later open a saved log file and submit it to your DBMS in the Database Administration painter. Using the log might be helpful if you have been developing in one DBMS, e.g., Informix NT, and migrating to a new platform, e.g., Informix on a UNIX machine. You could use the log to create a new DDL or perhaps as input to a reengineering tool like ERwin, which will accept DDLs from one DBMS, build a model, and then convert it to another DBMS syntactically.

To clear the log, select Clear Log from the Options menu. PowerBuilder will delete all statements in the log, but leave the log open. To stop the log, select Start/Stop Log from the Options menu or close the Activity Log window. PowerBuilder will close the log, and your work will no longer be logged. However, the log file still exists. You can open it again and continue logging from where you left off.

5.2.2 The database connection

Always be mindful that when you open the Database or DataWindow painters, PowerBuilder connects you to the preference DBMS, i.e., the database you used last (the information is recorded in the PB.INI file). Be careful, because you are not necessarily connected to the database used in your default application. You can change to a different DBMS and/or to a different database anytime. See the end of this chapter for Informix connection specifics.

There are two ways to change your database connection: by being prompted for the connection parameters and by defining and using database profiles. To change the database connection through prompts:

1. Open the Database painter or DataWindow painter.

2. Select Connect from the File menu. A cascading menu will be displayed.

3. Select Prompt for existing profiles from the menu. You will be prompted to specify the DBMS.

4. Select the DBMS. The installed DBMS interfaces are listed in the DBMS drop-down listbox.

5. PowerBuilder will display additional windows asking you to specify connection parameters. Specify all the appropriate parameters.

For complete information about the connection parameters required by your DBMS, see the end of this chapter or the PowerBuilder interface manual for your DBMS. Once you have answered all the prompts, you will be connected to the database and can work with its tables.

If you are working with multiple DBMSs or databases, the easiest way to move between them is by defining and using database profiles, which are

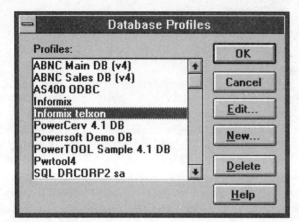

Figure 5.3 Connecting to a database using an existing profile.

named sets of parameters that specify a particular database connection. They are saved in your PB.INI file. To define a database profile:

1. Open the Database or DataWindow painter.

2. Select Connect from the File menu. A cascading menu will be displayed.

3. Select Setup from the Database Profiles window display (see Figure 5.3). It lists the existing profiles and allows you to edit or delete them, or to define a new one.

4. Click New to create a new profile. The Database Profile Setup window will be displayed (see Figure 5.4).

5. Specify a name for the profile. The name you enter here will be displayed on the File/Connect menu in the Database and DataWindow painters.

6. Specify the DBMS. The installed DBMS interfaces are listed in the DBMS drop-down listbox.

7. Click OK. PowerBuilder will display additional windows asking you to specify necessary connection parameters.

8. Specify all the appropriate parameters. Once you have answered all the prompts, you'll return to the Database Profiles window, with the new profile listed. Note if PowerBuilder tries to make the connection to verify the profile. This sometimes causes response delays, especially with a new and untried connection.

9. To connect to the database, select the appropriate profile and click OK.

To connect to a database using a database profile:

1. Open the Database or DataWindow painter.

2. Select Connect from the File menu. A cascading menu will be displayed, listing the defined profiles.

3. Select the appropriate profile. PowerBuilder will connect you to the specified database and return you to the painter workspace. You can also customize your PowerBar with an icon to perform database connects from anywhere in PowerBuilder.

5.3 Building a Physical Database

In PowerBuilder, you work within an existing database. With one exception— a Watcom local database—creating and deleting databases are administrative tasks not performed directly in PowerBuilder. For information about creating and deleting databases, see your Informix documentation.

5.3.1 Creating and deleting a database

To create an Informix SQL database you should review the later chapters regarding the following issues:

- Size the database.
- Choose a standard name.
- Specify the name and path of the database you are creating.
- Contact your DBA.

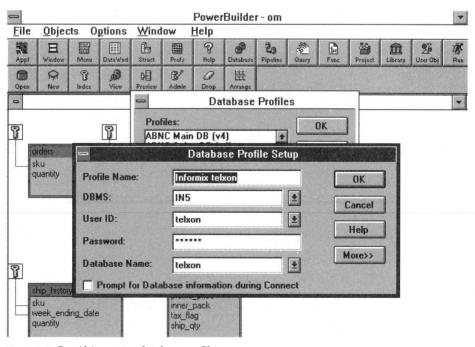

Figure 5.4   Specifying a new database profile.

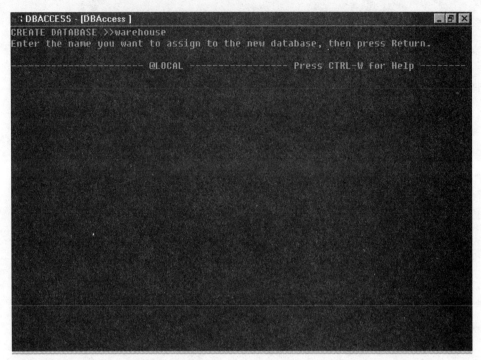

Figure 5.5 Creating a new database.

When you use the basic DB-Access tool, Informix:

- Creates a database with the specified name in the specified directory. If a database with the same name exists, you will be asked whether you want to replace it.
- Prompts you regarding the location of the LOG file.
- Prompts you regarding whether the database will be ANSI-compliant. ANSI requires that a LOG file be set up.
- Allows you to return to PowerBuilder after the CREATE to use it as a GUI administration tool.

When you open the Database painter, the Select Tables window lists all the tables and views in the current database (including tables and views that were not created using PowerBuilder). You can create a new table or open existing tables. If you set the TableDir variable in the [Database] section of PB.INI to 0, Power-Builder will not display the table list when you open the Database painter.

5.3.2 Opening tables

To open a database table:

1. If the Select Tables window is not displayed, open it by clicking the Open icon in the PainterBar or by selecting Tables from the Objects menu. To display system tables, select the Show system tables checkbox.

2. Select the tables to open by doing one of the following:

- Clicking the name of each table you want to open in the list displayed in the Select Tables window, then clicking Open to open the selected tables.

- Double-clicking the name of each table you want to open. Each table will be opened immediately.

- Clicking Cancel to close the Select Tables window.

The selected tables will be displayed in the Database painter workspace (see Figure 5.6). By default, PowerBuilder shows only user-created tables in the Select Tables window. There are many techniques for limiting what to access and see. There are typically parameters in the DBPARM section of the database profile as specified in the PB.INI or application .INI file.

If you select Show System Tables in the window, PowerBuilder will also show system tables. There are two kinds of system tables:

System tables provided by your DBMS See your DBMS documentation for details on this. These tables usually contain the object particulars for each DBMS. For example, in Informix the catalog table known as SYSTABLES contains a row for each database table.

PowerBuilder system tables These tables also contain the object particulars for each PowerBuilder-defined or PowerBuilder-interface-generated object in the

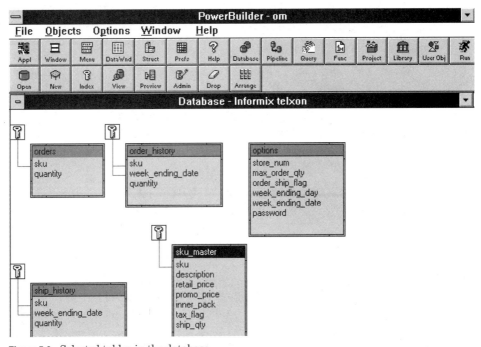

Figure 5.6 Selected tables in the database.

particular DBMS. For example, project.pbcattbl contains a row for each database table known to PowerBuilder.

You can also use DBMS system tables to develop DBMS-specific system applications. For example, you could set up an application to provide statistical reports on your DBMS space capacity, performance, or anything of interest for the system maintenance.

PowerBuilder extended attribute tables store information you provide when you create or modify a table (such as the text to use for labels and headings for the columns, validation rules, display formats, and edit styles) in system tables in your database. As mentioned, these system tables are a kind of database dictionary. The five PowerBuilder system tables are listed in Table 5.1. You can open these tables in the Database painter just like other tables.

When you open a table, PowerBuilder shows only the name of the table in a window-like representation. You can expand the representation to show the rest of the information.

To show information about the table, click the up arrow in the upper right corner of the table's title bar. PowerBuilder will expand the display to illustrate the table columns in a list format.

5.3.3 Creating a table and its columns

Analyzing the data: the entity/attribute relationship

Your organization might have used the entity relationship approach to data analysis. Entity relationship has two major advantages. First, it is very close to natural language. An entity is like a noun, a relationship is like a verb, and an attribute is like a prepositional phrase. This makes it easy to convert information gleaned in an interview with the user into a data model. Second, most CASE tools have adopted this approach. Learning entity relationship is good preparation for CASE. An entity is a person, place, object, concept, activity, or event of interest to your organization. You can determine entities within an application by listening for important nouns during interviews with the users.

An entity type is a set of objects. TV Series and Episode are examples of different entity types. An entity instance is an element of the set. Leave It to Beaver, the series, and Beaver Flunks Math, the episode, are examples of entity types.

TABLE 5.1

PB extended attribute table name	Content
pbcatcol	Stores information about columns
pbcatedt	Stores information about edits
pbcatfmt	Stores information about formats
pbcattbl	Stores information about tables
pbcatvld	Stores information about validation

Entity types usually become tables in relational design and entity instances usually become rows. However, entities and tables are not identical. You can split an entity into several tables for better performance, or you can merge several entities in one table. Occasionally, entities are listed merely for documentation and disappear in relational design.

Designing tables

The formal definition of a table, according to the relational godfathers (Codd and Date), is that it consists of two parts: a heading and a body. The heading is the specification for the table, and does not change in time. The body, or contents of the table, is a time-varying set of rows. Each row is a set of column-value pairs.

This definition has three important consequences. First and most significantly, a table is defined as a set of rows, and each row is defined as a set of column-value pairs. Since elements of a set are not ordered, the rows and columns of a table have no logical order. It is impossible to refer to the "fourth row" or "second column" of a table in SQL, for example. Of course, rows and columns are ordered internally on storage media, but this physical order is always invisible to the user in a relational DBMS. This is called physical data independence.

Second, sets should not contain duplicate elements. Consequently, tables should not contain duplicate rows or column names—in theory. In practice, most systems allow unstructured tables with duplicate rows, but this is not particularly useful. After all, it is impossible to distinguish duplicate rows. You would not be able to delete the "first" duplicate and retain the "second" because rows have no logical order. In practice as well as in theory, tables should have unique primary keys and therefore no duplicate rows.

Third, the table definition implies that each row-and-column cell contains exactly one value, not several. This point is fundamental to database design. It means that plural attributes are harder to implement than singular attributes. Sometimes a column is denormalized into a repeating value, i.e., an array for performance purposes. Natural arrays are the best because they do not change over time. For example, there will always be seven days in a week and twelve months in a year. A table with seven columns each representing a day of the week might reduce the physical I/O by 84%, i.e., you get all the data in one access instead of seven. Moreover, it might also reduce the required physical storage.

Another concept of the relational data structure is the null value. Null is a special symbol that means either unknown or inapplicable. These two meanings are different; a null social security number for an employee means unknown, presumable, but a null commission for a sales person means inapplicable. Regardless of meaning, null is always represented as the same symbol: NULL. This symbol is the same regardless of data type; NULL is used for integers and characters alike. With null values, a new arithmetic and logic is necessary. What is the value of the expression 10 + null? In SQL the answer is null, or unknown. What about 10 > null? Again, the answer is null. In fact, any arithmetic or comparative expression involving null evaluates to null.

Creating the table within PowerBuilder

Although in a large environment table definition will be done by central DBA group, we will review the process using PowerBuilder. This exercise will also give developers new to SQL a sense of how database objects are created and maintained.

You can create tables from within PowerBuilder. Before proceeding, you should know what you are going to define and whatever standards are applicable. To create a table in the current database:

1. Click the New icon in the PainterBar and the Create Table window will be displayed (see Figure 5.7).

2. Enter the following required information the table once and once for each column:

   - The name of the table you are creating. Check the naming standards.

   - The name of each column in the table. Check the naming standards as well as the project recommendations regarding data types. Note: if the database will be migrated to another DBMS, use common data types.

   - The data type and other required information for each column (such as column length, number of decimal places, and whether null values are allowed). All data types supported by the current DBMS are displayed in the Type drop-down listbox. Specifying No in the Null drop-down listbox means nulls are not allowed; users must supply a value. Index fields are usually specified as not nullable.

Optionally, you can specify the following information now or later when you modify the table:

- Fonts used to display the headings and data for the table when it is used in a DataWindow object (Font button in the Table group).

- Comments about the table (Comment button in the Table group).

- Keys used to control and access the table (Primary and Foreign Key buttons in the Table group), although keys can be modified later. You should spend the time to analyze the database relationships and define them before any serious development begins. This will provide you with the basic referential integrity. Again, in a large environment the primary and foreign keys will probably be defined by the central DBA group, who will choose between the DBMS declarative referential integrity or using database triggers to the same effect.

- Extended attributes for columns, which specify how data for the columns is displayed and validated and specifics the text that is used to label the columns in DataWindow objects.

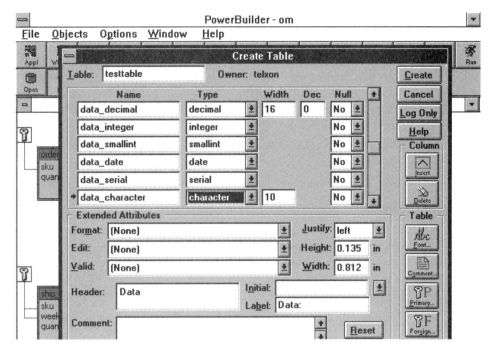

Figure 5.7 Creating a new table.

Notes about the extended attributes

Extended attributes are an often overlooked feature of PowerBuilder. This is something that the development team should embrace. The central DBA group can help, but here is where the developer can define the format, editing, and validation rules for each column in each table in the database. You can click the Object menu item to define edit styles, display formats, and validation rules. Once defined, you can use the extended attribute drop-down listboxes to associate them with database columns. Doing this early in the development will greatly facilitate data window creation. Erwin and LBMS can predefine the tables and their extended attributes.

After the definition is completed, save your work by doing one of the following:

Clicking the Create button. PowerBuilder will submit the CREATE TABLE statement it generated to the DBMS. The table will be created in the DBMS.

Clicking the Log Only button. The CREATE TABLE statement will be written only to the log file, not submitted to the DBMS. You can submit the statement later if you choose.

You will be returned to the Database painter workspace.

Altering a table within PowerBuilder

Once a table has been created, you can do the following:

- Append columns to the table. Appended columns must allow null values.
- In some DBMSs, you can also increase the number of characters allowed for data in an existing character column and allow null values. However, you cannot prohibit null values in a column that had been defined to allow null values.
- Add or modify all PowerBuilder-specific information about the table and its columns.

To alter a table:

1. Open the table in the Database painter.
2. Double-click the name of the table as represented in the workspace. The Alter Table window will be displayed (see Figure 5.8). Make your changes and do one of the following:
   - Click the Alter button. PowerBuilder will submit the ALTER TABLE statement it generated to the DBMS. The table will be altered in the DBMS.
   - Click the Log Only button. The ALTER TABLE statement will be written only to the log file, not submitted to the DBMS. You can submit the statement later.

You will be returned to the Database painter workspace.

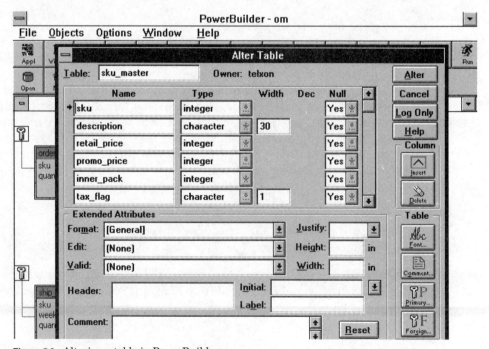

Figure 5.8   Altering a table in PowerBuilder.

TABLE 5.2

Extended attribute	Meaning
Comment (Comment:)	Describes the column. Whenever the table is opened in the database painter, you can see the comment to understand the purpose of the column.
Heading and label (Header:, Label:)	Text that is used in DataWindow objects to identify columns.
Alignment and size (Justify:, Height:, Width:)	How data is aligned and how much space to allocate to the data in a DataWindow object.
Display format (Format:)	How the data is formatted in a DataWindow object.
Edit style (Edit:)	How the column is presented to the user in a DataWindow object. For example, you can display column values as radio buttons or in a drop-down listbox
Validation rule (Valid:)	Criteria that a value must pass in order to be accepted in a DataWindow object
Initial value (Initial:)	Specifies the initial value for the column (choices include: fill with spaces, set to zero, set to today, and set to null)

Specifying the extended attributes

The extended attributes act as default, or standard, for all development. Time spent on the extended attributes for each database item (column) is well spent and can significantly enhance developer productivity. When you create or alter a table, you can choose the fonts used to display information from the table in a DataWindow object in your application. If you don't specify fonts for a table, PowerBuilder will use the font information specified in the application object. As mentioned earlier, in addition to providing the information required to create a table, you can specify extended attributes for each column in the table. An extended attribute is PowerBuilder-specific information that enhances the definition of the column. The extended attributes PowerBuilder provides for a column are listed in Table 5.2.

Extended attributes are stored in the repository (in the PowerBuilder system tables in the database). PowerBuilder uses the information to display and validate data in the Data Manipulation painter, in the DataWindow painter, and during execution. When you create a view, the extended attributes defined for the table columns used in the view are used by default.

You can create extended attributes in the Database painter's Object menu item under edit style, display format, and validation maintenance. An example of edit style extended attribute specification is depicted in Figure 5.9.

Creating indexes

Data in tables has both a relational and a physical order. The relational order of values is the usual arithmetic sequence for numbers, or dictionary sequence for character data. The physical order of rows in a table is the combination of the sequence of pages on the disk drive, and the sequence of rows within each

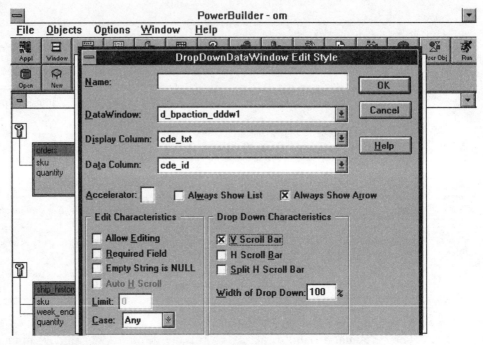

Figure 5.9 Specifying an edit style (extended attribute).

page. Of course, disk drives are not serial devices; pages are spread across tracks and around sectors.

A table is clustered on a column when the physical order of rows matches the relational order of values in the column. For example, series is clustered on series_cde. In some database systems, clustering can be imperfect; a table is considered clustered even when some rows are on the wrong page. Some databases maintain a cluster ratio or the percent of rows that are clustered.

An index on a column is a list of column values, with pointers to the location of the row containing each value. A composite index is defined over several columns. A clustering index, sometimes called a primary index, is defined on a clustering column, i.e., a column ideally with a uniform distribution of values with which to group rows together for common/fast access. A nonclustering index, sometimes called a secondary index, is not defined on a clustering column. A dense index contains one entry for each row of the table. A nondense index contains one entry for each page of the table with the low and high index values. Nondense indexes are possible only on clustered columns. Nondense indexes have a great advantage over dense indexes because they have far fewer entries and therefore occupy fewer pages. As a result, they are more efficient. In Informix, for example, clustering indexes are nondense. In some other database systems, rows might be out of sequence, so a clustering index must be dense.

How does this structure handle insertions and updates? Informix places a new row on the correct page based on its clustering column. If this page is full it splits in two to create free space, and a new entry is inserted at the bottom level of the index. If this index page is full it splits in two to create more space, and a new entry is necessary in the bottom level of the index. If this index page is full it splits to create more space, and another entry is necessary at the next higher level of the index. In the worst case, these splits propagate all the way through the top of the index, and a new level is created. Because the new level is created at the top of the index, all branches of the index tree are always the same length.

This kind of index is often called a B tree; the B stands for *balanced*. In theory, the system could reverse the process when rows are deleted, merging pages and reducing the index. However, this is not supported by Informix and other vendors, since deletions are less frequent than insertions.

Occasionally a table will not have a clustering index. In this case, new rows are always inserted at the end of the table. When a row is deleted, the empty slot is not reused until the table is physically reorganized. Since there is no clustering index, rows remain in order of the initial load or insertion. Because no meaningful order is maintained, this structure has limited utility. It is useful for tables of five pages or less; after all, if a table is small, the system can scan it quickly without an index. It is also useful for archival or temporary tables.

A table can have only one clustering index, but any number of nonclustering indexes. Nonclustering indexes are necessarily dense. When and how can nonclustering indexes accelerate queries? A crucial factor is the percentage of rows selected by a query, variously known as hit ratio, filter factor, or selectivity. When the hit ratio is high, nonclustering indexes are useless.

For example, suppose you set up a nonclustering index on the holiday column within the TV Episode table. The holiday column contains a code that lets you know which episodes have a holiday theme, e.g., Halloween. Suppose you select all episodes not associated with a holiday. The hit ratio will be quite high; most or all pages will contain qualifying rows because most days are not holidays. It is faster to ignore the index and scan the entire table. In contrast, if you select all episodes associated with the holiday of Halloween, the hit ratio will be low. Less than 5% of episodes qualify. A nonclustering index on Holiday will quickly locate the few pages of interest.

In the Database painter workspace, you can create as many single- or multivalued indexes for a database table as you need, and you can drop indexes that are no longer needed. As we mentioned earlier, indexes can facilitate integrity rules and they are also added for performance. An index and a table work like a book's index. Rather than scanning the entire table's data to find a particular piece of information, the DBMS looks for the value in the index and follows a page pointer directly to its location. Well-designed indexes can save I/O and processing time because the DBMS SQL optimizer uses the indexes to quickly access the database rows. The choices developers make in designing indexes determine how well the database will perform. Note: you can update a table in a DataWindow object only if it has a unique index or primary key.

To create an index using the PowerBuilder database painter:

1. Select the table that you want to create an index for.

2. Click the Index icon in the PainterBar or select Index from the New cascading menu on the table's pop-up menu. The Create Index window will be displayed (see Figure 5.10).

3. Enter a name for the index, and check the naming conventions.

4. Select whether or not to allow duplicate values for the index.

5. Specify any other information required for your database (in Informix, for example, specify whether the index is clustered, and the order of columns within the index).

6. Click the names of the columns that make up the index. The selected column names will be displayed in the Index On box.

7. Save your work by doing one of the following:

   ▪ Click the OK button. PowerBuilder will submit the CREATE INDEX statement it generated to the DBMS. The index will be created in the DBMS.

   ▪ Click the Log Only button. The CREATE INDEX statement will be written only to the log file, not submitted to the DBMS. You can later submit the statement if you choose.

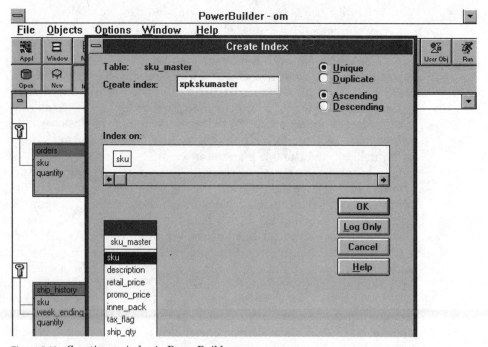

Figure 5.10 Creating an index in PowerBuilder.

After this is done, return to the Database painter workspace. The new index is shown as a key connected to each column in the index.

5.3.5 Creating primary and foreign keys

There are several kinds of keys in relational theory, but only two are of practical importance: primary and foreign keys. The primary key of an entity identifies and distinguishes instances. The primary key must always be unique, i.e., two instances should never have the same value. It must also be known and available at all times. social_security_number might make a bad primary key of an Employee table, for example, because it might be unavailable for foreign employees. Not always but most of the time, the primary key and the clustering index are one and the same in content.

To make it simple, primary keys must always be unique and known. If possible, they should also have four additional characteristics. First, they should be stable. A changing primary key leads to confusion and errors. Second, they should not contain descriptive information like color or size. If the color changes, the primary key will be unstable. Third, short and simple alphanumeric codes or integers are best because they are easy to input and are unambiguous. Finally, users should be familiar with the primary key so they can enter it in database queries.

Names can change and are prone to data-entry errors, so they usually make bad primary keys. If you cannot find a good primary key, develop an artificial one, either a random integer or a short alphanumeric code. To discover the primary key of an entity, ask the user how the entity is identified. If you cannot determine a primary key, reconsider the entity. Perhaps it represents data and not a thing, is not important to your organization, or is poorly defined.

A key is not the same as an index. Keys are logical; they identify rows. Indexes are physical; they locate rows. Identifying a murder suspect is not the same as locating the suspect. A foreign key is a column (or group of columns) that matches the primary key of some table. For example, series_cde in the Episode table is a foreign key to the Series table. Most joins compare a foreign key to its matching primary key. This is the case in the example join. This is called a primary/foreign key join. Because primary and foreign keys are frequently compared, they must be comparable; in other words, they must be defined over the same data type.

So far we have discussed two rules for relational databases: primary keys must be unique and non-null. The rule that primary keys must be non-null is sometimes called entity integrity. Another rule, called referential integrity, governs foreign keys. Referential integrity requires that a foreign key must either be null or match some value of its primary key. It makes sense to allow a null foreign key.

Referential integrity (RI) is easy to state and important for error-free database management. It is hard to enforce, however, unless you are using a tool for generating triggers, e.g., and ERwin or DBMS can enforce them with a declarative style of RI. Foreign key rules specify how to preserve referential integrity when foreign keys are inserted or updated, and then primary keys are updated or deleted. Now we will examine alternative foreign key rules, but first the deletion of a primary key value.

There are four main options for primary key deletion. When the database administrator specifies the restrict option, the primary key value should not be deleted as long as there are any matching foreign key values. The data entry user must first change or delete all matching foreign keys. The second option is cascade. When a primary key is deleted, all rows containing matching foreign keys are also automatically deleted. This is dangerous. Deletes automatically trigger deletes, which in turn trigger other deletes. If you specify this rule often, you might find that a single deletion will cause an entire database to disappear. The third and fourth options are nullify and set default. These automatically set all matching foreign keys to null or default when a primary key value is deleted. A fifth option is to simply allow violations of referential integrity, but this is not usually recommended. The fifth option will invariably lead to disaster when the orphans and broken links between database entities causes errors in the application components. Even application-enforced integrity is better than nothing. Rely on your DBA staff if you have a large database with lots of lineage, i.e., many relationships.

Similar options apply when a primary key is updated. For example, cascade automatically propagates the new primary key value to all matching foreign keys. Updates to primary keys are strongly discouraged, however, since primary keys should be stable. For this reason, the options for primary key updates are not as important as deletes. Similar options also apply when a foreign key is inserted or updated. The restrict option is usually specified, which says that new foreign key values should not be entered unless a matching primary key value already exists.

If your DBMS supports primary and foreign keys, you can work with the keys in PowerBuilder. When you open a table with keys, PowerBuilder gets the information from the DBMS and displays it in the painter workspace. If your DBMS supports them, you should use primary and foreign keys to enforce the referential integrity of your database. If you use keys, you can rely on the DBMS to make sure that only valid values are entered for certain columns instead of having to write code to enforce valid values. Say you have two tables, Series and Episode. The Episode table contains the column series_code, which holds the name of the series. You want to make sure that only valid series are entered in this column, that is, the only valid values for series_code in the episode table are values for series_code in the Series table. To enforce this kind of relationship, you define a foreign key for series_code that points to the series table. With this key in place, the DBMS disallows any value for series_code that does not match a series in the series table.

In the Database painter you can do the following:

- Look at existing primary and foreign keys.
- Open all tables that depend on a particular primary key.
- Open the table containing the primary key used by a particular foreign key.

- Create keys.
- Alter keys.
- Drop keys.

For the most part, you will work with keys the same way for each DBMS that supports keys, but there are some DBMS-specific issues. For complete information about using keys with your DBMS, see your DBMS documentation. When you open and expand a table containing primary and/or foreign keys, PowerBuilder displays the keys in the workspace. The keys are shown as icons with lines connected to the table. When working with tables containing keys, you can easily open related tables.

To open the table that a particular foreign key references:

1. Open and expand the table containing the foreign key.
2. Click the right mouse button on the icon representing the foreign key.
3. Select Open Referenced Table from the pop-up menu. PowerBuilder will open and expand the table referenced by the foreign key.

To open all tables referencing a particular primary key:

1. Open and expand the table containing the primary key.
2. Click the right mouse button on the icon representing the primary key.
3. Select Open Dependent Table(s) from the pop-up menu. PowerBuilder will open and expand all tables in the database containing foreign keys that reference the selected primary key.

Defining primary keys using PowerBuilder

If your DBMS supports primary keys, you can define them in PowerBuilder. To define a primary key:

1. Display the Create Table window for a table you are now creating, or the Alter Table window for an existing table.
2. Click the Primary Key button in the Table group. The Primary Key Definition window will be displayed (see Figure 5.11). Some of the information in the window is DBMS-specific.
3. Select each of the columns comprising the primary key in the Table Columns box. PowerBuilder will display the selected columns in the Key Columns box.
4. If you want, you can reorder the columns in the key by dragging them with the mouse.
5. Specify any information required by your DBMS (such as a name for the primary key). For DBMS-specific information, see your DBMS documentation.
6. Click OK. You will return to either the Create Table or Alter Table window.
7. Save your work by clicking either the Create or Alter buttons.

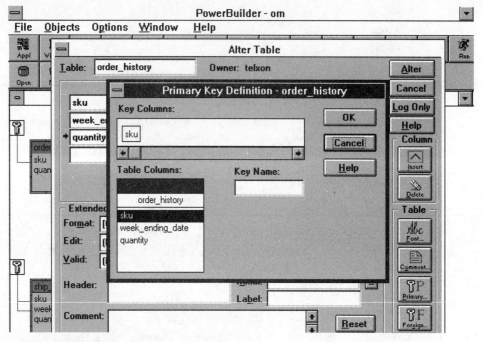

Figure 5.11 Defining a primary key.

PowerBuilder will submit the CREATE TABLE or ALTER TABLE statement to the DBMS. Some DBMSs automatically create a unique index when you define a primary key, so you can immediately begin to add data to the table. Others require that you separately create a unique index to support the primary key before populating the table with data. To see what your DBMS does, see your DBMS documentation.

Defining foreign keys using PowerBuilder

If your DBMS supports foreign keys, you can define them in PowerBuilder. To define a foreign key:

1. Display the Create Table window for a table you are now creating, or the Alter Table window for an existing table.

2. Click the Foreign Key button in the Table group. The Foreign Key Selection window will be displayed, listing all foreign keys defined for the current table.

3. Click New to define a new foreign key. The Foreign Key Definition window will be displayed. Some of the information in the window is DBMS-specific.

4. Name the foreign key in the Foreign Key Name box. Check the naming standards.

5. Select the columns for the foreign key in the Select Columns listbox. The selected columns will be displayed in the Foreign Key Columns box. You can reorder the columns by dragging them with the mouse.

6. In the Primary Key Table listbox, select the table containing the primary key referenced by the foreign key you are defining. PowerBuilder will display the selected table's primary key in the Primary Key Columns box.

7. Specify any information required by your DBMS (such as a delete rule). For DBMS-specific information, see your DBMS documentation.

8. Click OK. You will return to the Foreign Key Selection window.

9. Click Done. You will return to the Create Table or Alter Table window.

10. Save your work by clicking either the Create or Alter buttons. Power-Builder will submit the CREATE TABLE or ALTER TABLE statement to the DBMS.

General note about databases, keys, and indexes

It is probably easier in most cases to use a tool like ERwin or LBMS to build a complex database with many entities and relationships. The interaction can be planned analyzed and designed. These tools also have comprehensive schema generation to provide database triggers and DDL. We have mentioned index and key creation for completeness, but warn against its casual use. Relationships and their update ramifications must be clearly thought out before definition.

5.3.6 Creating database views

A base table is stored on disk. So far in this chapter we have discussed only base tables. A view table is not stored. It is really just a query; the rows of the view are derived by executing the query. When you construct a view with the CREATE VIEW statement, the definition is recorded in the catalog. When you run a query against the view, the system merges your query with this definition and executes the merged query. As you can see, views do not significantly affect performance; they are used primarily for convenience.

Views are quite useful. Sensitive information like salaries can be stored in a base table but excluded from a view. By giving users access to the view but not the base table, you secure the salary data. Views are also used like macros, as a way of packaging complete queries in the guise of a table. You can use views to present data in a format requested by the user without affecting your database design.

Unfortunately, views have one major limitation. Select statements work well against views, but inserts updates and deletes might not. Suppose a view contains all the table columns except the primary key. Insertions to this view might create a null primary key, and will be rejected. If you have specified NOT NULL, updates and deletions might be ambiguous because the primary key is not available to positively identify rows.

You can define and manipulate views in PowerBuilder. Typically you use views for the following reasons:

- To give names to frequently executed SELECT statements.
- To limit access to data in a table. For example, you can create a view of all the columns in the Employee table except Salary. Users of the view can see and update all information except the employee's salary.
- To combine information from multiple tables for easy access.

A view is a set of columns that can be chosen from one or more tables. Views are typically not updateable, but they can provide a simple way to access natural database table joins or secure sensitive database data. In PowerBuilder, you can create single- or multiple-table views and use a view to create a new view. You open and manipulate existing views in the Database painter, and you define views in the View painter.

5.3.7 Exporting database objects

You can export the syntax for a table or view to the log. This feature is useful when you want to create a backup copy of the table or view before you alter it, or when you want to create the same object in another DBMS. To export to another DBMS, you must have the PowerBuilder interface for that DBMS. To export the syntax of an existing table or view to a log:

1. Select the table or view in the painter workspace.
2. Select Export Table/View Syntax To Log from the Objects menu. If you selected a table, the DBMS window will be displayed.
3. Select the DBMS where you want to export the syntax.
4. Click OK (see Figure 5.12).

PowerBuilder will export the syntax to the log. The syntax is in the format required by the DBMS you selected in the DBMS window. Note that the PowerBuilder catalog table rows that describe the object being exported will also be generated and added to the log. They can be quite extensive because they generate all the SQL inserts you are required to populate.

5.3.8 Manipulating data

Now we turn to the second part of the relational model, the operators used to manipulate tables. Codd defined eight operators in his 1970 paper, called restrict, project, join union, difference, intersect, product, and divide. Of these eight, only five are necessary. Join, difference, and divide can be derived from the other five. Additional operators can also be defined, such as outer join. Thus, the original eight operators are a useful but somewhat arbitrary collection.

The operators act on tables just as arithmetic operators act on numbers. When an operator is applied to one or two tables, the result is another table. Consequently, there is an algebra of tables, just as there is an algebra of arithmetic. Codd called this relational algebra. In this section, we will examine the three most important operators—restrict, project, and join and show you how they are implemented in SQL.

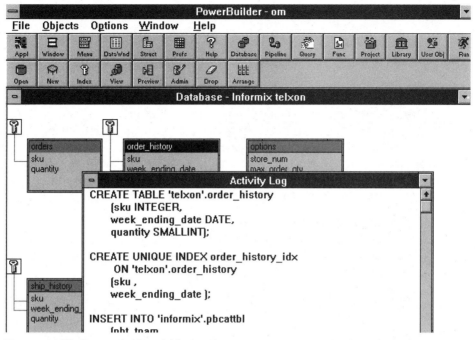

Figure 5.12   The log created by a table export.

Let's begin with restrict. Restrict eliminates rows from a single table. In the example query, we have selected comedy shows. The query result conforms to the definition of a table, although it does not physically exist. In SQL, the result of every query is another table; this principle is known as closure.

```
SELECT SERIES_CDE, SERIES_NAME
FROM SERIES
WHERE GENRE_CDE = "COMEDY"
```

The project operator eliminates columns from a single table. In the example, only series_cde and series_name were selected.

Most SQL queries combine restrict and project. The operator that best characterizes relational database management is join. Join combines two tables by comparing one column from each. The comparison here uses the equal sign, =, and is called an equijoin. Joins involving > or < are possible but less common. An equijoin results in a table with two identical columns. To conform the definition of a table, one of these columns must either be eliminated with a project or renamed. An equijoin that eliminates the duplicate column is called a natural join. The example on this page is a natural join, with additional columns eliminated for clarity.

```
SELECT episode.series_cde, pgmtrk.track_datetime,
episode.episode_cde,
episode.episode_name,
episode.eps_desc_txt,episode.eps_quest_star_txt
```

```
FROM pgmtrk, episode
WHERE ( episode.episode_cde = pgmtrk.episode_cde )
  and ( episode.series_cde = pgmtrk.series_cde )
  and  (pgmtrk.track_datetime between
        '1994-02-01 00:00' AND '1996-0401 23:59:00')
ORDER BY  episode.series_cde ASC,  pgmtrk.
          track_datetime ASC;
```

As you work on the database, you will often want to look at existing data or create some data for testing purposes. Also, you will want to test display formats, validation rules, and edit styles on real data. PowerBuilder provides the Objects menu and particularly the Data Manipulation painter for such purposes (see Figure 5.7). In this painter, you can retrieve and manipulate database information. You can also save the contents of the database in a variety of formats (for example, Excel, dBASE, or Lotus 1-2-3).

Opening the Data Manipulation painter

To open the Data Manipulation painter, select the table or view whose data you want to manipulate from the list of tables (see Figure 5.13). Then do one of the following:

- Click the Preview icon in the PainterBar. This will display the data in a grid format.
- Select Data Manipulation from the Objects menu and choose the format option from the cascading menu to display:

Grid. This uses a rigid spreadsheet format.

Tabular. This uses rows and columns, i.e., multiple rows per page, that you can arrange as you like.

Freeform. This resembles a freeform data entry form, i.e., you can place selected columns anywhere and you have one row per page displayed.

After you choose a form, the Data Manipulation painter will open and retrieve all rows (see Figure 5.14). As the rows are being retrieved, the Retrieve icon changes to a Cancel icon. You can click the Cancel icon to stop the retrieval. This is a good idea if you get back more rows than you could possibly review. The Data Manipulation painter is actually a DataWindow. The format style you have chosen corresponds to a type of DataWindow object, i.e., grid, tabular, or freeform.

To retrieve rows from the database, click the Retrieve icon in the PainterBar or select Retrieve from the Rows menu. PowerBuilder will retrieve all the rows in the current table or view. As the rows are being retrieved, the icon changes to Cancel. You can click it to stop the retrieval.

You can add, modify, or delete rows. When you are finished manipulating the data, you can apply the changes to the database. If you are using a view, you cannot update data in a view where it is comprised of columns from more than one table.

To modify existing data. Tab to the field and enter a new value. The Data Manipulation painter uses validation rules, display formats, and edit styles that

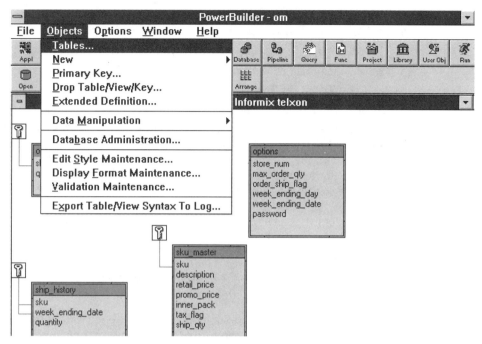

Figure 5.13 Object painter with data manipulation.

Sku	D	Retail Price	Promo Price	Inner Pack	Tax Flag	Ship Qty
10007 CREST TO(		259	0	24	T	
10010 CREST T/P REG 8.2 OZ		299	279	24	T	
10017 COLGATE TP REG 8.2Z BN		279	0	24	T	
10022 COLGATE TP GEL 8.2Z BN		279	0	24	T	
10024 AIM REG STR TP 6 OZ		129	0	24	T	
10034 AQUA FRESH TP REG 6.4 OZ		199	0	24	T	
10042 SENSODYNE TP REG 4 OZ		399	0	36	T	
10047 TOPOL TOOTH POLISH 2.7Z		329	0	12	T	
10050 PEARL DROP SPEARMNT 3 OZ		379	0	12	T	
10056 POLIDENT TABS 40'S		299	0	12	T	
10062 ORAL B AMOSAN POWDER 40'9		999	0	12	N	
10065 ACT FLOURIDE RIN CIN 18OZ		399	0	12	T	
10068 FLUORIGURD DENT RINSE 16 (		349	0	12	T	
10074 SUPER POLI-GRIP 1.4OZ		299	0	12	T	

Figure 5.14 Data manipulation grid form.

you have defined for the table in the Database painter. To save the changes to the database, you must apply them, as described later.

To add a row. Click the Insert Row icon and PowerBuilder will create an empty row. Enter data for a row. To save the changes to the database, you must apply them, as described later.

To delete a row. Click the Delete Row icon and PowerBuilder will remove the row from the display. To save the changes to the database, you must apply them, as described in the next paragraph.

To apply changes to the database, click the Update Database icon. Power-Builder will update the table with all the changes you have made. You can define and use sort criteria and filters for the rows. The sort criteria and filters you define in the Data Manipulation painter are for testing only and are not saved with the table or passed to the DataWindow painter.

To sort the rows. Select Sort from the Rows menu. The Specify Sort Columns window will be displayed. Select the columns you want to sort the rows by and specify whether you want to sort in ascending or descending order. The order in which you select the columns determines the precedence of the sort. Click OK.

To filter the rows. You can limit which rows are displayed by defining a filter. Select Filter from the Rows menu and the Specify Filter window will be displayed. Enter a Boolean expression that PowerBuilder will test against each row. If the expression evaluates to TRUE, the row will be displayed. You can paste PowerScript functions, columns, and operators in the expression. Click OK and PowerBuilder will filter the data. Only rows meeting the filter criteria will be displayed.

About filtered rows and database updates

When you update the database using PowerBuilder-generated SQL, filtered rows are ignored. They are not deleted when you update the database, and the value of any filtered rows that has changed since they were retrieved is not updated in the database.

You can display information about the data you have retrieved. To display the row information, select Described from the Rows menu and the Describe Rows window will be displayed. The Describe Rows window shows the number of rows that have been

- deleted in the painter but not yet deleted from the database
- displayed in Preview
- filtered
- modified in the painter but not yet modified in the database

All row counts are zero until you retrieve the data from the database or add a new row. The count changes when you modify the displayed data or test filter criteria (see Figure 5.15).

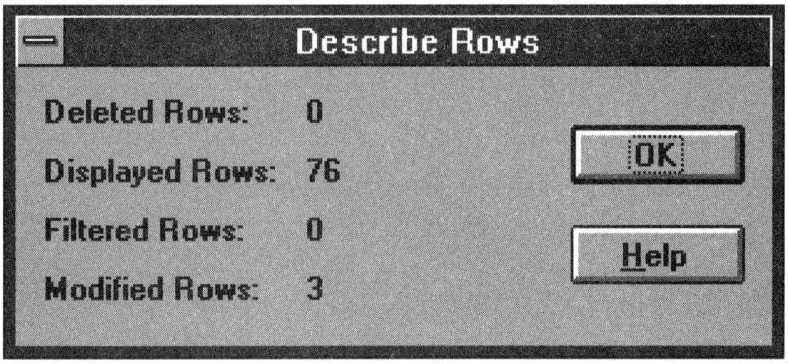

Figure 5.15 Describing rows.

Importing data

You can import data from an external source and display it in the Data Manipulation painter, then save the imported data in the database. To import data:

1. Select Import from the Rows menu and the Select Import File window will be displayed.

2. Specify the file from which you want to import the data. The types of files that you can import into the painter are shown in the List Files of Type drop-down listbox.

3. Click OK.

PowerBuilder will read the data from the file into the painter. You can then click the Update Database icon in the PainterBar to add the new rows to the database. You can save the displayed data in an external file. You can also invoke the SaveAs function programmatically by using a script and the DataWindow SaveAs function. This is a powerful way to save database data to another form, e.g., an Excel spreadsheet (see Figure 5.17). To save the data in an external file:

1. Select Save Rows As from the File menu. The Save Rows As window will be displayed.

2. Choose a format for the file (see Figure 5.16) and name the file.

3. If you want the column headings saved in the file, select the Include Headers box.

4. Click OK.

PowerBuilder will save all displayed rows in the file and all columns in the displayed rows. Filtered rows are not saved. You can use the Database Administration painter to control access to the database and to create SQL for immediate execution.

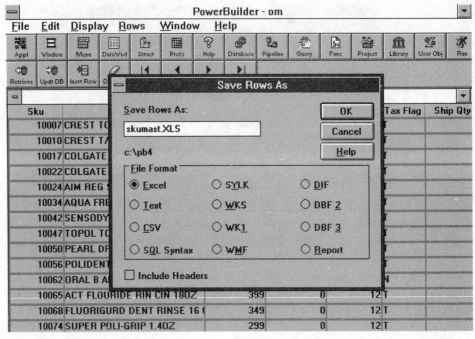

Figure 5.16 SaveAs function.

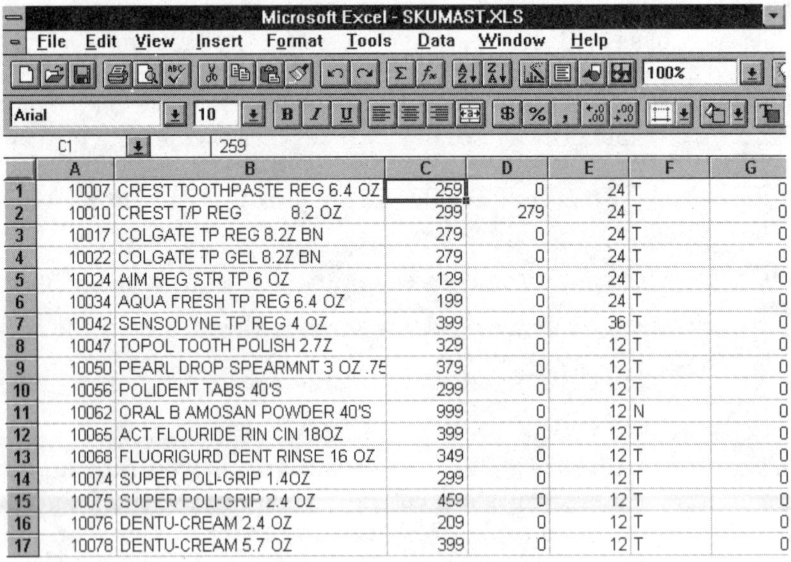

Figure 5.17 Rows SaveAs Excel spreadsheet.

Opening the Database Administration painter

To open the Database Administration painter, click the Database Administration icon or select Database Administration from the Objects menu in the Database painter (see Figure 5.18). The Database Administration painter, which is very much like the PowerScript painter, will be displayed. But instead of building scripts in it, you will build SQL statements to submit to the DBMS. The Database Administration painter provides the same editing capabilities as the PowerScript painter. It provides a series of windows you can use to control access to the database. The windows are tailored to your DBMS. For information about PowerBuilder support for security options in your DBMS, see the PowerBuilder interface manual for your DBMS. You can also use the Database Administration painter to build SQL statements and execute them immediately. The painter's workspace acts as a notepad in which you can enter SQL statements.

You can enter a SQL statement in three ways:

- Pasting the statement.
- Keying the statements into the painter workspace.
- Opening a text file containing the SQL.

You can paste SELECT, INSERT, UPDATE, and DELETE statements to the workspace (see Figure 5.18). To paste a SQL statement to the workspace:

1. Click the Paste SQL icon in the PainterBar or select Paste SQL from the Edit menu. The types of SQL statements you can paint will be displayed in a window.
2. Double-click the appropriate icon to select the statement type. The Select Table window will be displayed.
3. Select the tables you will reference in the SQL statement.
4. Go to the Select, Insert, Update, or Delete painter, depending on the type of SQL statement you are painting.
5. Follow the procedure described in Table 5.3 for the statement you are painting. In each case, you can select Show SQL Syntax from the painter's Options menu to see the SQL as you dynamically build it.

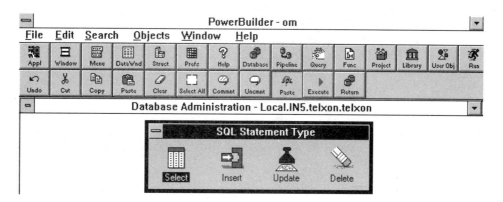

Figure 5.18 Pasting SQL.

TABLE 5.3

Type of statement	Actions taken to gain desired result
SELECT	Define the statement exactly as in the Select painter when building a view. You choose the columns to select. If you want, you can define computed columns, specify sorting and joining criteria, and WHERE, GROUP BY, and HAVING criteria.
INSERT	Type the values to insert into each column. You can insert as many rows as you want.
UPDATE	First, specify the new values for the columns in the Update Column Values window. Then specify the WHERE criteria to indicate which rows to update.

When you have completed painting the SQL statement (see Figure 5.19), click the Return icon in the PainterBar in the Select, Insert, Update, or Delete painter. You will return to the Database Administration painter with the SQL statement pasted into the workspace (see Figure 5.20). If you want, you can simply type one or more SQL statements directly in the workspace. You can enter any statement supported by your DBMS. This includes statements you can paint as well as statements you cannot paint (for example, a database-stored procedure or CREATE TRIGGER).

You can read a SQL statement that has been saved in a text file into the Database Administration painter. To read a SQL statement from a file:

1. Select Paste From the Edit menu. The DOS File Open window will be displayed.
2. Select the file containing the SQL statement.
3. Click OK. PowerBuilder inserts the SQL statement at the current insertion point.

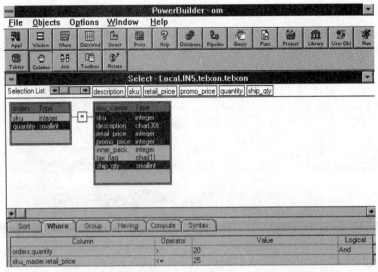

Figure 5.19 Developing a SELECT statement using pasted SQL.

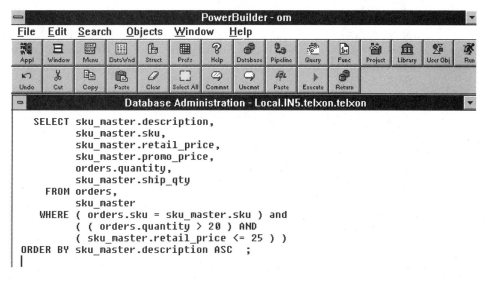

Figure 5.20   Returning to the Data Administration painter with SQL.

Sometimes there is more than one way to code SQL statements to obtain the desired results. When this is the case, you can use Explain SQL on the Objects menu to help you select the most efficient method. Explain SQL displays information about the path that PowerBuilder will use to execute the statements in the SQL Statement Execution Plan window. This is most useful when you are retrieving or updating data in an indexed column or using multiple tables. The information displayed in the SQL Statement Execution Plan window depends on your DBMS. For more information about the SQL execution plan, see your DBMS documentation. When you have the SQL statement you want in the workspace, you can submit it to the DBMS. If the SQL retrieves data, the data will appear in a window identical to a grid in the Data Manipulation painter. If there is a database error, you will see a message box describing the problem.

5.4 Connecting to Other DBMSs

A LAN-based client server application can use a growing number of DBMS platforms as a back end to the PowerBuilder. A PowerBuilder database interface is a native (direct) connection to a database or DBMS. If your site uses one or more of these databases and if you have the required database server and client software installed, you can access the data by installing the corresponding Powersoft database interface that comes with PowerBuilder or InfoMaker.

For example, you can access an Informix database by installing the Powersoft Informix interface. A Powersoft database interface does not go through ODBC to access a database, i.e., you go native. Therefore, you do not complete the ODBC Configuration dialog box to define the data source. Instead, you create a database profile in which you specify connection parameters for accessing the database.

Many Powersoft database interfaces are supported in PowerBuilder Enterprise. Check the availability of each interface at application deployment time to ensure that the DBMS and PowerBuilder are at the same release level. Otherwise, you might have to stay at one release of a database or avoid new features until the two components are at the same release level set.

This list includes the following databases interfaces for PowerBuilder release 4 at the date of this book's publication:

- ALLBASE/SQL
- Oracle 7 (OR7 interface)
- IBM DRDA-DRDA
- SQL Server
- Informix 4 (IN4 interface)
- SQLBase
- Informix 5, 6, and 7 (IN5 interface)
- Sybase Net-Gateway Interface for DB2
- Micro Decisionware Database Gateway (MDI) Interface for DB2
- Sybase SQL Server System 10
- Oracle 6 (OR6 interface)
- XDB

5.4.1 Connecting Powerbuilder to Informix

Powersoft currently supports the following versions of Informix database products:

- Informix SE 5.0
- Informix SE 6.0
- Informix SE 7.0
- Informix OL 5.0
- Informix OL 6.0
- Informix OL 7.0

Software and hardware requirements

For Informix drivers, the software required on the client is Informix-Net PC. Informix-Net PC supports different TCP/IP drivers. For UNIX drivers, the following is supported:

- .PC-NFS from Sun Microsystem, Inc., version 4.0
- .PC.TCP from FTP Software, Inc., version 2.2

- .Pathway Access from Wollongong Group, Inc., version 2.0
- .StarGroup (not actually TCP/IP protocol) from AT&T, version 3.1

Novell's NetWare using IPX/SPX protocol instead of TCP/IP is also supported. InformixDIR is the directory where Informix Software is located. The path should read: InformixDIR\BIN.

Here again the setup involves the typical prerequisites and first-time use implications. Purchase and install the PowerBuilder Interface for Informix (PBINF040.DLL) from Powersoft. Install the Informix database according to the vendor's instructions. Set the database variables in Prefaces to the appropriate values for Informix.

Connecting to Informix

Except for the specification of the database, the connect essentially takes place outside of PowerBuilder and Windows. The connection occurs when you load I-Net.

For Informix connections via PowerBuilder 5, use PBINF050.DLL as opposed to PBINFM40.DLL or PBIN5040.DLL. PBIN5050.DLL resides in the Power-Builder directory. If connecting Informix through TCP/IP, the Informix.INI file must have a [INet_Connection] section. See the following example:

```
[INET_CONNECTION]
User=telxon
Host=196.200.1.32
Service=sqlexec
Protocol=tcp-ip
Passwd=EP 12 10 2120 53 52 90 90 90 90 90 90 90 90 90116101108
```

Remember, setting the client's I-Net does not guarantee the ability to connect. The attributes set in the client's I-Net simply identify the preferences in the client's net layer that is used to communicate to the host. If the client has Informix-SQL, there is an executable named ISQL.EXE or PISQL.EXE that you can use to access the database from DOS. This is a quick way to determine your ability to connect. If you can access the database from DOS, you can probably use PowerBuilder to connect to the database. If the client does not have Informix-SQL, use the command PING *hostname* to PING the host; this will test access to the host.

Informix database preference variables

To connect to Informix, set the database variables in Preferences to the values shown in Table 5.4.

These variables are used only for Informix Online databases that were created with transaction support executes. SQLReturnData will cause the serial number of the row to be stored after an INSERT statement executes. If an error occurs during a connection, a message box will display the error message. After you click OK, a window will be displayed so you can change the database variable set in Preferences. PowerBuilder then uses the new values to connect to the database.

TABLE 5.4

Preference variable	Set to
Vendor	INFORMIX
DBMS	IN5
Database	The name of the desired database
Lock values	Values:
	DIRTY READ
	COMMITTED READ
	CURSOR STABILITY
	REPEATABLE READ

Informix database environment variables

The DbDate environment variable specifies the following formats for date values:

- The order of the month, day, and year in a date.
- Whether the year should be printed with two digits (Y2) or four digits (Y4).
- The separator between the month, day, and year.

The default value for DbDate is MDY4/, where M represents the month, D represents the day, Y4 represents a four-digit year, and the slash (/) is a separator, for example, 12/25/1994.

Other acceptable characters for the separator are a hyphen (-), a period (.), or a zero (0). (Use the zero to indicate no separator.) The maximum length is five characters.

This user-entered data is stored without validation in the [ENVIRON-MENT] section of the INFORMIX.INI file in the Windows directory when Save is selected. To specify the following statement:

```
INET_DBPATH, INET_PROTOCOL, INET_SERVICE parameter
```

in a database profile, type the following in the DBParm box in the Database Profile Setup dialog box:

```
INET_DBPATH = '/home/informix'
```

To specify the statement in a PowerBuilder application script, type the following:

```
SQLCA.dbParm = "INET_DBPATH = '/home/informix'"
```

You can specify values for INET_DBPATH, INET_PROTOCOL, and INET_SERVICE in the same DBParm statement. This statement specifies that the directory /INFORMIX contains Informix databases, and that you want to connect using the SE5 service and the TCP/IP network protocol. Enter the statement on a single line.

```
INET_DBPATH = '/informix',
INET_SERVICE = 'se5',
INET_PROTOCOL = 'tcp-ip'
```

Informix connection to PowerBuilder: server-side troubleshooting

- Is the Informix server version 5 or higher? Informix 4 is not supported.

- Is the sqlexecdd daemon running on the Informix server? It goes in the UNIX etc/rc. Make sure to SET and EXPORT the INFORMIXDIR.

- Was sqlexecd started correctly, i.e., started by root with INFORMIXDIR and SQLEXEC environment variables set? Was the service name used when sqlexecd was started?

- Is the database running, walking, or crawling?

- Do the service names, port numbers, and ip addresses match? (Check /etc/services to verify. Check /etc/hosts if you are not running NIS to verify that machine ip addresses match.)

- If the service name is not sqlexec, does $INFORMIXDIR/etc/hosts exist and is the format correct? If the service name is not sqlexec, is SQLSERVICE set on the client side?

Informix connection to PowerBuilder: client-side troubleshooting

- Can you connect via INFORMIX-SQL (I-SQL)?

- Is INFORMIXDIR set? INFORMIXDIR is the directory where Informix software is located. The path should be INFORMIXDIR/BIN.

- Is LDLLSQLW.DLL in the path?

- For multiple DLL versions, remove all LDLLSQLW.DLL versions from $path except for the I-Net PC 5.01 DLL.

- Has PowerBuilder PBIN5050 DLL been properly installed? There was a problem with PB4 PBINFM40.DLL. It had to be manually PB-unzipped. It is no longer required.

- Are you using a supported TCP/IP or IPX vendor?

- Are the host and username/password valid?

- Is the machine turned on?

6

Developing the Application

Developing an application is one of those catch phrases that can mean of host of different things. For the purposes of this book, we will focus on the tasks (as well as the relative sequence in which the tasks are undertaken) that comprise the average application development life cycle. Each of these steps will probably be taken during the course of development, and some will need to be done more than once. In fact, sometimes a whole group of steps will be iteratively performed. This is not unique to developing with a relational DBMS such as Informix. It is common in most development efforts, but effective planning and hard work can keep these reiterations to a minimum. This will save time and money, and perhaps maintain the integrity of the objects that are developed. In any event, this chapter will, at first read, provide a quick overview; later it can be a basic checklist of the steps involved in Informix application development.

6.1 Prerequisites

Before you begin the actual construction portion of the development life cycle, you need to make sure that certain prerequisite tasks are either complete or in an advanced state of existence. The project team should have a development approach and accompanying plan, with skilled players to carry it to fruition. They will also need a logical database model and physical manifestation, as well as adequate workstation resources. These are the components of successful development.

6.1.1 Logistic prerequisites

The developers must decide on the separation of application components. The lead developers on a larger project, let's say more than 30 developers, will incorporate an application design based upon either a two-tier (2T) or three-tier

(3T) approach. Exactly what a tier is and when it begins and ends can be a somewhat nebulous concept. In any event, the developers must decide how to break out the functional requirements into logistic tiers that promote a consistent, reusable, and maintainable application system that performs to the users' satisfaction. They must consider how this can be accomplished. There are many aspects of development to consider, aspects that will dictate the type of developers you will staff the effort with, i.e., which skills are required to implement the architecture.

Next, what exactly is a 2T or 3T approach? In fact, it is largely in the eye of the beholder. The classic 2T approach implemented ad infinitum using a CICS/COBOL/MVS client with a DB2/MVS server residing on the same host platform MVS includes:

Tier 1/server. Database server: stores and requests data.

Tier 2/client. Application objects: receives and presents data.
The majority of the application is on the client end, including the database access language (SQL). Another approach is to put the data access (e.g., stored procedures) and database on the server and use the client as a presentation tool only. The best implementations are flexible and include the proper mix of client SQL with presentation windows and the use of stored procedures for performance problematic functions. This approach must be made on a case-by-case basis.

To complicate matters further, three-tier (3T) development explicitly breaks everything in the application into a separate layer. The architecture includes the following tiers:

Tier 1/presentation logic. Developers build Informix windows and menus to provide application presentation and navigation.

Tier 2/business rules. Separate developers build all the business rules and processes, perhaps using nonvisual objects.

Tier 3/database management. DBA develops database design and access modules, e.g., stored procedures.

The 3T approach requires three separate teams of developers and a better coordination of effort. It will also separate the types of Informix objects developed, as well as which external items will have to interface with a GUI presentation tool. For example, the GUI presentation tool objects might call external .DLLs for business logic or message switching.

Depending on the requirements of the application, either approach can be useful. The vast majority of client-server systems we have seen and worked on require an interface into a legacy system, e.g., a mainframe-based application. A 2T approach is useful when the legacy system has a large amount of business rules and database access integrated together, e.g., mainframe COBOL/CICS programs with embedded SQL to access DB2. Breaking the application into separate components is usually not feasible, so development usually consists of extending or enhancing the current system to include a GUI presentation to client.

For example, this breakout could cause the following connections: a Power-Builder client workstation to access a UNIX-based Informix database server and return the data down the chain to the client for presentation. So a 2T architecture consists of business rules and database access integrated together.

A 3T approach is useful when the requirements for the application consist of migrating processing requirements from a legacy system onto the client or a middle-layer server. This breakout could cause the following connections: a Power-Builder client1 workstation of a UNIX Informix server1/client2 to issue a remote procedure call (RPC) to an Informix gateway server2/client3 to access a mainframe CICS transaction to select from a mainframe DB2 database server3, then return the data down the chain to the client for ultimate presentation. The legacy system is being viewed mainly as a database server, with the business rules aspects of the application being moved onto an intermediate server, and presentation on the end-user client machine. The business rules have been placed on the client machine, resulting in a physical 2T system with a 3T architecture, with security and performance concerns mandated by an intermediate server to effect load balancing between database and file servers. This results in freeing up a lot of expensive mainframe time (database server) and a much more efficient system.

Three-tiered development is much more complex and expensive. It requires faster network communication to support the increase in messaging between the three tiers. Extensive planning, design, and coordination is also required. 3T systems we have worked on have been well over budget and behind schedule. This is not only due to a lack of appropriate planning, but also undereducated and miscast management and developers. Neither approach is better than the other; each should be taken on its own merit and used where appropriate.

6.1.2 Physical prerequisites

Before you begin physically constructing the application components, certain prerequisite physical items must be in place for use by the development team. Besides an adequate workstation and the appropriate server(s), accessible project libraries (GUI presentation tool should also be available and appropriate permissions in place. You should have access to Informix with current maintenance and third-party or in-house class library software ready for use from each workstation. Developers should be aware of the guidelines and naming standards the project team has agreed to use to develop the database and application. These suggestions might seem a bit pedantic, but they will save precious time later in the process. They will also reduce the usual start-of-project confusion. Developers will not hesitate because they know that the objects (i.e., database tables) are named properly, and they will follow suggested guidelines (e.g., unique index for each table).

6.2 Designing the Database

The design process for the application database is unique to each development environment. We will discuss it in general terms. The specifics of the process

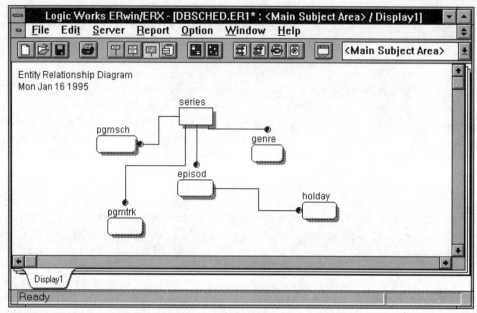

Figure 6.1   Database logical design.

might vary from shop to shop. In any event, this is a crucial item and the degree to which it is completed before full scale development will affect the process greatly.

6.2.1 Determining the application entities

An entity is a person, place, object, event, or activity of interest to the functionality you are creating, i.e., any noun that can represent information of interest to the organization. In the logical database design, you try to build an entity/relationship model by identifying the entities and their attributes, as well as the relationships between the different entities. The logical database design starts as soon as you meet the users. Listen for entities in interviews with the user.

If you are developing a database to track the schedules at one television station, the entities might include series and episodes. See Figure 6.1 for the logical database design of an ERwin-based logical entity model. The attributes of an entity describe and define it. For example, a series has a descriptive name, which is an attribute of the series. The date it was originally produced might also be an attribute.

Listen for the relationships in user interviews. What is a relationship? If an entity cannot exist without a parent, then it is dependent, i.e., it "belongs to" another entity. This is a relationship. Important subsets of an entity with special attributes are subentities. For example, a TV series might be a "special" with attributes that pertain only to a "special" series, so there would be a "special" subentity. Special is, therefore, a part of a series, i.e., it could be merged with the series and have the same primary key. A dependent entity, e.g., an episode, belongs to a series and has a primary key that contains the parent key and an additional key to identify the dependent.

6.2.2 Refining each entity and attribute

After you have collected business entities and attributes from interviews with the user, check the project standards for naming conventions. Also, if applicable use firmwide abbreviations to ensure consistent naming. Next, attempt to capture a description and validation criteria for each entity and attribute. Does the project have a data dictionary? If so, enter the description and validation criteria here. Also, check the dictionary to determine if the attribute or entity already exists. Informix has its own catalog tables, i.e., extended attributes, which can house descriptions and validation rules. These attributes can be populated with CASE tools like ERwin or S-Designor. Both of these vendor tools have interfaces to Informix that can be used to populate the extended attributes of the GUI tool of choice, e.g., PowerBuilder.

Determine the primary key for each entity. The primary key of an entity uniquely identifies entity instances (rows). The primary key of a dependent entity includes parent key and descriptive column. For example, the primary key for the episode entity is series_code and episode_cde concatenated. Document past or future states in the description, i.e., add last_update_timestamp. The primary key will promote database integrity as you will inhibit table row duplicity and the creation of database orphans, i.e., rows in a dependent table with no parent.

6.2.3 Determining relationships

Here again, listen for relationships in interviews with the user. Document the roles of entities in recursive relationships. A series may be a part of another series. Determine the cardinality of the relationship. This will facilitate the choice of keys or indices to access the entity. For example, how many episodes are in a series. Does the identifying key to the relationship have many different values. Decide on a formal name by checking the standards for naming keys. Don't confuse relationships with entities or attributes. Attributes which designate entities are relationships. If the primary key of an entity consists of other primary keys, it may be a relationship. For example, the TV episode entity would have a primary key consisting of the TV series identifier and the episode identifier. The TV series identifier is the primary key of the series entity.

6.2.4 Creating tables and columns

Typically, using the completed logical design, independent entities become independent tables. Similarly, dependent entities become dependent tables. Refer back to Figure 6.2 for an example of the physical design of the logical model depicted in Figure 6.1. Before getting physical, i.e., defining the database in

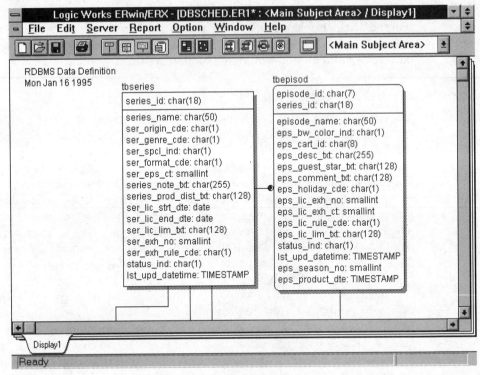

Figure 6.2   Database physical design.

the development DBMS, the designers should verify that tables are in Third Normal Form (3NF), i.e., every nonkey column depends on the key, the whole key, and nothing but the key. Designers should attempt to retain normalized subtables unless the cost of application-required table joins is unacceptable, or merging with a super table creates few inapplicable nulls. Consider merging tables linked by one-to-one relationships. This merger works best if minimum cardinality is also one-to-one and stable. Denormalize for performance as a last resort. You should exhaust physical solutions first, denormalize selectively, and apply updates directly to 3NF tables.

The attributes of each entity usually become table columns. These table columns should have well-thought-out data types, e.g. ones that do not use a decimal for a number that is always an integer. These table columns should be specified as NOT NULL for required attributes and relationships. You can cause the DBMS to enforce unique attributes/columns by defining them as an index. Attributes of relationships then go with a foreign key. Implement vectors column-wise unless physical size, user access, or number of tables forces row-wise design. Where possible, avoid alternating, encoded, or overlapping columns.

6.2.5 Creating keys

Besides the primary key and index, secondary keys and indexes might be required. In a many-to-one relationship, place the foreign key in the "many" side of the table. In a one-to-one relationship, place the foreign key in the table with fewer rows. The many-to-many relationship becomes an associative or junction table. Consider an artificial primary key such as a random number when there are many incoming foreign keys and the natural key is null—not unique, unstable, complex, or meaningful.

6.2.6 Completing the database's physical design

Now you have tables and columns and a cluster index, but you are not done yet. To really know if your design will perform, you must list, examine, and explain crucial queries and transactions. Crucial queries are ones that are high volume and frequently executed, where a quick response is required. They are a point of reference for physical design.

Create and use clustered indexes for most if not all tables (usually on primary key), for reference and access. Occasionally some other column is more important for access, and will get the clustered index. Small or temporary tables might have no clustered index. Create nonclustered indexes (consider foreign key columns) for other columns that are used to search or order the data. Review crucial queries after you have assigned a clustered index, and determine which of them cannot use the clustered indexes for access. For these queries, consider nonclustered indexes on column(s) specified in a WHERE clause, particularly join columns. Create a nonclustered index only when the hit ratio is low. Create at most three or four indexes per table (unless they're read-only). The rest is DBMS-dependent. The DBAs usually determine partitions, locking, granularity, and device assignments. Have whoever is responsible complete the physical design and notify the developers at each significant milestone.

6.2.7 How do you know how big the database will be?

It is a good practice to know how much volume your database is expected to have for the first years of production. This will help in the physical design of the database and SQL access. To this end, it is wise to build a spreadsheet to estimate and finalize storage requirements. The steps in this process are as follows:

1. Build a spreadsheet to estimate and finalize storage requirements:
   - Estimate the number of tables.
   - Estimate the length of each row.
   - Estimate the number of rows for each table (including a year's worth of growth).
   - Procure additional storage if needed.

2. Build a spreadsheet to estimate and finalize access requirements:

- Estimate the number of users.
- Determine user transaction types (EIS, DSS, or OLTP).
- Calculate the cost and frequency of each access.

6.2.8 Setting up the development database environment

It is also good practice to set up your development database to have the first year of production data loaded in a simulated fashion. This will help to certify the physical design of the database and SQL access as well. The steps in this process are as follows:

1. Create development database, tables, indexes, and user permissions.

- Use ERwin to generate the database schema.
- Use DB-Access/PB Data Admin/Desktop DBA to administer and maintain database objects.

2. Build batch and online procedures to populate/access the database.

- Use flat file extracts to load the initial testbed of data.
- Develop batch procedures for periodic mass updates (C with SQL).
- Develop OLTP using stored procedures, SQL, and data windows.
- Develop techniques for EIS and DSS database summary tables, and build ad-hoc query tools (dynamic data windows).
- DBMS-explain all SQL, which can be performance-problematic.
- Refine the database's physical design (add secondary indexes to facilitate access and improve performance, and repartition/relocate physical components).

6.3 Defining the Application

After establishing the development environment, the first step is to create the application object. Defining the application includes not only the setup and definition of the application object, but also the rules of interaction between developers. The developers must buy in to the sharing objects they will jointly develop. They should "check in" and "check out" development objects, and use basic teamwork to maximize project productivity.

6.3.1 The application object

This object constitutes the entry point into the application. This is similar to a transaction ID in CICS. The application object names the application and specifies which libraries, i.e., GUI presentation tools, will be used to save the objects and run the application. The library list also includes class libraries, which are used to inherit base objects. Finally, it specifies the application-level scripts. This application OPEN event script usually includes a function to initialize application variables, test the database connection, and launch or OPEN the application window frame (in an MDI application). Other events in the application object include things like IDLE, SYSTEM ERROR, and CLOSE. Application GUI presentation tools are manipulated and default preferences are set for the application development workstation using the respective painter.

6.3.2 The application standards

At this point you and your developer colleagues should be familiar with certain application defaults. The standard font and size can be set in the application object, e.g., MS sans serif 8. The number and names of Informix libraries (GUI presentation tool) should be determined. You can set up libraries and store objects based on application functionality or by object type. Defining an application object is usually done once for an application, but the application object can be copied onto each developer's workstation so the developer can include his or her own GUI presentation tool in the library list (usually first). This is a good technique for setting up a development environment where object sharing is accomplished (library list 2-N contains project-wide GUI presentation tools) and developers can test new objects (library list item 1 contains individual developer GUI presentation tools). More on this later.

6.4 Creating a Batch Interface

Even a predominantly OLTP system will require some form of batch interface. By batch interface, I mean jobs or processes consisting of a command language (e.g., UNIX shell script) that executes a sequential series of utilities and application programs (C/ESQL) to access and manipulate the application database. For example, you might have a gateway data transfer from a mainframe (e.g., IBM MVS or AS/400) that contains reference data. The flat ASCII reference data, when received, is then loaded into an Informix table for use by the OLTP. The LOAD might be followed by a script call to Informix to execute a stored procedure to update other tables based on the downloaded data. For example, an ASCII price file is downloaded from IBM DB2 and used to update the Informix price table. The new prices are then used by an Informix-stored procedure to update client positions in an Informix portfolio table.

Maybe you need a job that is started at a certain point in time to poll Informix tables containing orders. The following example uses the UNIX cron facility to start a job at a specific time and day of the week. The UNIX crontab is a somewhat cryptic mechanism, but it works for basic batch processing. The script located at /Warehous/ordering/bin/pollchain is executed daily using crontab.

Each crontab entry consists of a line with six fields separated by spaces and # tabs that contain, respectively:

```
# 1) The minute          (0 through 59)
# 2) The hour            (0 through 23)
```

```
# 3) The day of the Month     (1 through 31 ; * is everyday)
# 4) The Month of the year    (1 through 12 ; * of everymonth)
# 5) The day of the week (0 through 6 for Sunday - Saturday)
# 6) The UNIX shell command
# pollchain runs every day of the year at 11:30 pm
30 23 * * * su warehous /Warehous/ordering/bin/pollchain
# n.b. most machines are cycled weekly
# Reboot the Machine every Sunday Morning @ 3:00am.
00 3 * * 0 /etc/shutdown -r +2
```

6.4.1 Initially loading the data

Every table has to start somewhere when it comes to the content. If you have an existing system, you might have a conversion where the old system's data is downloaded and used to seed/populate the new system tables. Informix provides a variety of utilities and options to LOAD flat ASCII data into an Informix table. The choice between utilities is based on speed and flexibility. The utilities and their options are discussed in Chapters 11 and 16.

6.4.2 Creating base-class stored procedures

When the database is designed and you hopefully know the set of accesses required by the functionality, then you can begin to build procedures to access the Informix database. A powerful option available with Informix is the stored procedure. Using stored procedures, you can group SQL statements and a control-of-flow stored procedure language (SPL) in one object to improve the performance of Informix. Stored procedures are collections of SQL statements and SPL. They are stored in the database and the SQL is parsed and optimized. An execution plan is prepared and cached when a procedure is run, so subsequent execution is very fast. The SQL is reoptimized at execution only if necessary. Stored procedures can:

- Receive parameters passed by the calling object (e.g., PowerBuilder GUI front end).
- Call other procedures.
- Return a status value to a calling procedure or GUI front end to indicate success or failure, and the reason for failure.
- Return values of parameters to a calling procedure or GUI front end.
- Be executed on remote Informix, i.e., remote procedure calls (RPC).

The ability to write stored procedures greatly enhances the power, efficiency, and flexibility of SQL. Compiled procedures dramatically improve the performance of SQL statements and batches. In addition, stored procedures on other Informix servers can be executed if your server and the remote server are both set up to allow remote logins. You can write triggers on your local Informix that execute procedures on a remote server whenever certain events, such as deletions, updates, or inserts, take place locally. Stored procedures differ from ordinary SQL statements and from batches of SQL statements in that they are precompiled.

6.4.3 Batch C programs with embedded SQL

Sometimes a table does not require an entire LOAD because only a small percentage of the table needs to be modified, for example, Informix C/ESQL, which cause an interface to code embedded SQL (including stored procedures) in a C program. A small transaction file can be read, and selective updating can be applied using a SELECT/UPDATE combination. The choice between using C with ESQL and Informix utilities is again based upon speed and flexibility. ESQL and C are discussed in Chapter 12.

6.4.4 Batch utilities for database tuning and repair

Sometimes a table becomes fragmented and unorganized, degrading your performance. You need to know about this as soon as possible. Sometimes a table gets corrupted, which you need to amend as soon as possible. Informix provides a host of utilities to reorganize and repair disorganized and damaged tables. These utilities are discussed in a later chapter.

6.4.5 Batch utilities for backup and recovery

Every serious database application should include a scenario for backup and recovery in case of a system failure (hardware or software that destroys the database). These scenarios range from simple, for a SE-based database on one machine, to extremely involved, where multiple OL databases are arranged in a replicated string across many sites. Informix provides various solutions that can support each particular environment.

6.5 Creating a Window/Menu Interface

After you have developed the basic presentation/navigation of the application and received user approval, you can build the windows and menus that present the data. You should also develop the menu(s) that allow users to move from window to window and perform application tasks. On-Line Transaction Processing applications (OLTP) should provide easy-to-understand, user-approved, data-entry characteristics as well as a quick, understandable response to each user action. Note that user-approved application presentation and navigation should be done at or near the beginning of the development cycle. Make sure users have seen and used a prototype or example of how the basic system components will look and feel. Make sure they sign off on the design for that application version.

6.5.1 Choosing an interface style

In the early days of client/server development, OLTP systems resembled either old dBASE systems or mainframe CICS implementations, i.e., single-document applications with only one document or sheet open at a time. As the use of software like Word and Excel increased in popularity, their look and feel became the de-facto standard. A growing number of users are familiar and accustomed to using Word-like application interfaces. These applications are based on the so-called "multiple document interface" (MDI). The MDI consists of a window frame to house the main menu and one or more window sheets that present the application data to users for update and inquiry. The MDI provides the ability to open more than one window sheet at a time, i.e., work on different parts of an application at the same time. It also provides a consistent and common interface to all the operating system features. For example, a Save menu item on an application's main menu that is created once will be used by all the application components, and each user can access the full range of data manipulation features.

6.5.2 Setting up the class library for an interface style

In simple terms, a class library is a collection of Informix objects (windows, menus, and user objects) that have generic functionality the developer can use by inheriting the class object. For example, you inherit a class object menu that includes item FILE and subitem PRINT, which triggers an event script to print the current window. Inheriting this class object provides all windows that use this menu with a consistent print interface. Moreover, the interface is coded only once. Each time you inherit it you save time and money. Eventually, the class library will pay for itself.

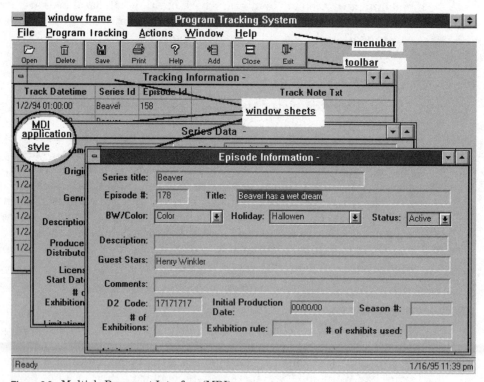

Figure 6.3   Multiple Document Interface (MDI).

Assuming you will use the MDI interface, the organization will have either purchased a class library including a MDI implementation kit, or developed its own class library. This will obviate having to redo the application-launching objects (window frame and base menu) that aggressive developers will create if the class objects are not determined and available early on. Once the base frame, menu, and sheets are created, the developers need only inherit the sheet and they can create windows, place controls in the window, and build scripts that specify the processing that will occur when events are triggered.

6.6 Building Windows

Windows are the main interface between the user and Informix applications. Windows can display information, request information from a user, and respond to mouse or keyboard actions.

There are six types of windows. Where class libraries are used, the developer will typically inherit a main type window. The MDI frame with MicroHelp type window is usually built once. The other four are typically used to provide information for a Main type window. For example, Informix uses a child window type when you add a drop-down data window to provide only valid choices for a field on a main window. Most of the windows you develop in a MDI application will be type main. Each window object has:

A style. This is determined by the attributes, which are things that describe an object—in this case a window. The attributes of a window include but are not limited to: whether or not it is enabled, its height, the menu name (if one is associated with the window), the window title, and (for MDI frames and sheets) toolbar attributes.

Events. These can trigger script execution. The basic window events include OPEN and CLOSE as well as user events, which are defined to perform special processing in a MDI application. For example, the base menu might have the item SAVE, which has a script to trigger the event ue_filesave. It will have been defined to contain a user-defined event called ue_filesave. The script associated with this event will be executed.

Functions. These are part of the definition of the window; they are used in scripts to change the style or behavior of the window, or to obtain information about the window. The window might contain a function, wf_update, which contains a script that performs update processing particular to the current window sheet.

Structures. These are part of the definition of the window and are used in scripts to define groups of window-pertinent variables.

6.6.1 Determining the type of window

The type of window you use to implement a particular feature of the application is an important decision when trying to make your application consistent with other Windows applications. Table 6.1 lists some general considerations.

TABLE 6.1

Window type	Window type properties
Main	• Is a stand-alone window, i.e., has no dependencies • Has a title bar (is there a project standard for setting the title?) • Is independent of other windows (main sheet windows encapsulate functionality), e.g., w_series_sheet maintains series and w_episode_sheet maintains episodes. • Is sometimes called a parent or overlapped window • Can be minimized or maximized • Can have its own menu (is there a standard class library menu?)
Child	• Is always subordinate to its parent window, e.g., drop down Data Access windows • Is never the active window • Can exist only within the parent window • Can have a title bar • Is automatically closed when its parent window is closed • Is clipped when you move it beyond the parent window • Is clipped when you move it beyond the parent window • Moves with the parent window because its position is always relative to the parent window • Has no menu
Popup	• Has a parent window • Can have a title bar or menu • Can display inside or outside the parent window • Can never disappear behind its parent window • Can be minimized; when minimized, it is displayed as an icon at the bottom of the screen • A pop-up window minimizes with its parent
Response	• Obtains information from and provides information to the user, e.g., the row you are trying to add already exists! Continue? Yes or No • Remains the active window until the user responds by clicking a control • Is application-modal, i.e., a fixed path and menu items are disabled. The user must respond before any other action can be taken. • When the response window is open, the user cannot go to other windows in the application from which the response window was opened. • The window cannot be minimized, but can be moved.

Multiple Document Interface windows

You use a main window as the frame and sheets for a MDI application. This is probably the most common window type you will create. The main window suits the open application because you can add user events (ue) common to applications, e.g., ue_filesave and ue_fileopen, and include the specific processing in a script behind the event. You can then use the same common main_menu for all the main sheet windows, saving all the expense of a menu. For example, the menu item Save will trigger the event ue_filesave in the current window. Whatever script is embedded in that event will be executed. The script can be different for each window; the basic function, i.e., Save, is the same.

Child windows are useful when an application needs to display a variable number of subordinate entities, tables, or data views. If an application's style calls for heavy usage of response windows, try to find an open solution using a menu or toolbar item if possible. The downside to response windows is that the approach makes the applications modal or less open, i.e., the user must go down a predefined path to perform a task. There are few options for change. When deciding how to use response windows, look at other Windows applications for some precedents before you commit to an approach. Both child and pop-up windows can have an explicit parent window. If a parent window is not named when the child or pop-up window is opened, the last active main window will become the parent window.

The base or frame window of a MDI application

Every Windows application needs a base or frame window. This is usually the first window you see either when you invoke the application or after you have supplied log-on information (In Word, for example, a frame window containing a menu, toolbar(s), and a blank open sheet). The base window should be a main type window since it is at the highest level in your application hierarchy. It is not subordinate to any other window in the application. This window usually remains on the screen throughout the application session. The MDI frame in a MDI application is a prime example of a base window. It is usually the first window that appears that has a menu on it in a combination interface application.

Sheet windows of a MDI application

As mentioned earlier, sheets are defined as main windows. After the base frame is defined, you will build as many sheets as are necessary to perform the application functionality, for example, one sheet per table for basic maintenance plus others for special functions. Each sheet acts like a main window and follows most of the rules of child windows.

A sheet is always subordinate to its parent window, the MDI frame. A sheet is activated at the same time as the MDI frame. This is one exception to the child window rules. A sheet can exist only within the MDI frame. Sheets always have title bars, which can be dynamically populated. Sheets are closed automatically when the MDI frame is closed. Sheets move only within the MDI frame because their position is always relative to the MDI frame. They occupy the workspace, remaining after the menu and toolbar real estate is established. You can minimize sheets. When minimized, they display as an icon inside the MDI frame. Sheets can have menus, but developers should keep the number of menus to a minimum. Find the common denominator of menu functionality in your application. Sheets can be activated when the user clicks anywhere within the sheet boundary; the menu associated with the sheet will also become active.

The rest of the windows in the MDI

Child windows are subordinate to the sheets (for example, the Table windows used in the Database painter). This nesting can continue, but MDI does not provide for the nesting of sheets within sheets. Pop-up windows are generally not used in MDI applications because they replace the need for pop-up windows. Response windows, although modal, are used as Yield or Stop signs to draw the user's attention.

While response windows aren't frequently invoked directly from the MDI frame, they can be used to open or print application entities, or some similar actions. For example, a response window can be used with a Data Access window control to search for existing database rows and return the key values to the main window sheet for subsequent retrieval and update. The About box is a response window as well.

Response windows are usually used within the context of a sheet, to further refine the definition of an application entity or to specify options for an action. Response windows can also be invoked from other response windows. This is useful when a generic entity interface needs to be invoked, or space limitations on the surface of a response window dictate that additional information needs to be gathered elsewhere. Response windows should never nested more than one level down.

6.6.2 Adding controls to a window

After choosing the window type, you'll want to add one or more controls to enhance the functionality. In the MDI style, the number of controls should be kept to a minimum. The menu and toolbar should be used to carry out application tasks. The most common control will probably be the Data window control, which can provide a good deal of functionality. It can be used to receive, edit, validate, display, print, and maintain data. Most of the window controls can be built within a data window. The data window can but does not need to be associated with a database table. For determining an option or value, you can use the external-source Data Access windows. More on this later. Table 6.2 is a brief summary of controls.

The Data Access window control should be the most commonly used control. You can use it with a menu to trigger event processing on the window sheet and the Data Access window object currently associated with the control. To build a window, use the Window painter, described in detail later.

6.7 Creating Menus

Menus in your windows can include a menubar, drop-down menus, and cascading menus. You can also create pop-up menus in an application. You define the menu items and write scripts that execute when the items are selected. These scripts launch the particular application component. In the MDI application style, menubars are usually accompanied by toolbars. Toolbar buttons map directly to menu items. Clicking a menu toolbar button is the same as clicking on its corresponding menu item (or pressing the accelerator key for that item).

TABLE 6.2

Control	Executes a script	Determined option or value	Notes
CheckBox	No	Yes	Try to use the menu in-
button	Yes	No	stead; common on response windows
Data access, i.e., a control that accesses the database to select, insert, update, or delete base or system meta data	Yes	Yes	Should be the most common control; you can use it as a better alternative to almost all the other controls. The data access control includes its own control styles, e.g., drop-down list box.
DropDownListBox	Yes, but only on the editable and show list	Yes	
Edit Mask	No	No	Display and enter format-ted data
Graph	Yes	No	
GrouGUI presentation toolbox	No	No	Used to group available se-lections
HScrollBar and VscrollBar	No	No	
ListBox	Yes	Yes	
MultiLineEdit	No	No	Used to enter data; try an external Data Access win-dow instead
Picture	Yes	Yes	Cosmetic as well; expen-sive and large
RadioButton	No	Yes	
SingleLineEdit	No	No	Used to enter data; try an external (nondatabase) Data Access window in-stead
SpinBox	No	Yes	
StaticText	No	No	Used to display text infor-mation
User Object	Yes	Yes	

6.7.1 Designing menu interaction

Develop your menus carefully. Poorly designed menus can cause latent prob-lems detected only when the application is used heavily, e.g., the first month of production. Menus are expensive (they are one of the larger objects in an Informix library) and their misuse can seriously degrade application performance. Poor planning with menus can also cause problems that manifest themselves as inconsistent responses to user actions. These errors are hard to detect, reproduce, and correct.

The menubar/toolbar combination is the backbone of a MDI application. It provides a common user interface to all the application components. If you are using a class library, you will probably build menus by inheriting a class object menu and adding your custom items to the existing list of common items, e.g., File, Window, and Help. Improperly handled menus can make the trivial seem complex. Be aware of the way Informix sets the current menu and toolbar, and follow some basic rules and guidelines for working with menus.

6.7.2 Optimizing menu usage

The MDI frame should always have a menu. If the currently active sheet does not have a menu, then the menu and toolbar (if any) associated with the last active sheet will remain in place and operative while that previous sheet remains open. So to avoid unpredictable results, all sheets should have a menu.

Another nuance of Informix menu/toolbar workings is the toolbar. If the currently active sheet has a menu but no toolbar, and the previously active (and still open) sheet has both a menu and a toolbar, then the menu that's displayed will be the menu associated with the currently active sheet, but the menu toolbar that's displayed will be the toolbar for the previously active sheet. This will totally confuse users and must be avoided.

Here again, if you are using toolbars (a virtual "gimme" in the MDI application) then all sheets should have a menu toolbar. Disabling a menu item will disable its toolbar button as well, but it will not change the appearance of the button. If you want it to appear gray, you must do this programmatically. Hiding a submenu item will not cause its toolbar button to disappear or be disabled. If you want the button to disappear or be disabled, you must do this programmatically as well. To build a menu, use the Menu painter. More on this later.

6.8 Creating Data Access Objects

You can create Data Access objects to retrieve data from the database, format and validate data, analyze data through graphs and crosstabs, create reports, and update the database. A Data Access object is a window object that allows the user to display and manipulate database information using SQL statements in scripts or stored procedures developed for the particular function. You build a Data Access object in the Data Access painter and save it in a library that is available to the application.

To build serious Data Access objects (known as data windows in Power-Builder), i.e., those used for data entry and mission-critical applications, the database design should be in the 90% complete zone.

6.8.1 Building Data Access objects with completed database entities

A good database design will make data access creation easy. This is because good design provides consistent column names, data types that are not overly exotic, unique indexes that provide uniform data distribution, and primary/foreign keys that create relationships promoting integrity and facilitating "full statement" information joins. When the database is completed, you will probably know all the accesses required to provide the desired functionality.

Now is a good time to create the Informix-stored procedures to speed up and simplify your processing. These are the database qualities that allow developers to easily build a usable Data Access object (e.g., DataWindow). If your database has these qualities, then you are ready to proceed. If not, stop here, get out your database design book, and read it again carefully. Set up meetings with the database administrators. Take the time to get it right. The lack of a good database design signifies either a lack of business knowledge or database administration talent—or both. The database design is the most crucial component. The presentation can be easily changed and modified; the database cannot. A poor database design can cause integrity as well as performance problems.

At some point, the database design becomes workable, and all developers are granted permissions and are ready to build Data Access objects. To use a Data Access object in a window, place a Data Access control in the window of the Window painter and then associate a Data Access object with the control in the Window painter or in a script. During execution, Informix will create an instance of the Data Access object. Every Data Access control has:

A style. These are determined by its attributes.

Events. These can trigger the execution of scripts.

Functions. These are part of the definition of the Data Access control. They are used in scripts to change the style or behavior of the Data Access control, or to obtain information about the Data Access control.

You might want to customize the data windows and allow for dynamic changes in the base data window SQL. Informix provides some functions that can help.

PowerBuilder data windows are designed to be intelligent database controls. See Figure 6.4, the Data Window painter for an example of a data-entry data access. You can include other objects in a data access for cosmetic purposes. Data access also allow you to display columns of data in the form of Edit, CheckBox, RadioButton, DropDownListBox, or DropDownData access control. The DropDown data window is a powerful edit style and can be used to create firmwide edit capability for code or subject area data.

6.8.2 Uses of a Data Access object

The primary strengths of Data Access objects are as follows:

Data display. You do not have to code variables to contain column values and data formatting, translate data varies to display values, or map column values to nontextual display forms (pictures and OLE).

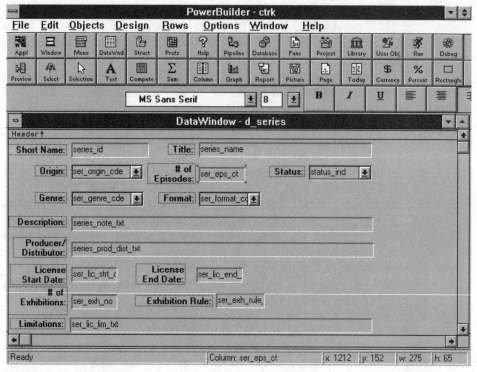

Figure 6.4 Data Access painter.

Data entry layout. To define a window with normal controls for data entry, the programmer would need to manage many separate controls collectively.

Scrolling. Data access deals with all the scrolling page formatting issues without any programmer code.

Reporting. Data access objects also provide extensive reporting capabilities. Calculated columns, formatting, and grouping can all be managed by Data Access objects without any coding.

Data validation. Data can be validated by Data Access objects. This is important for database validity and consistency, especially if you have used the DB painter to create edit styles and validation rules.

Automatic SQL. It is not necessary to code the appropriate SQL statements to access data from the database.

Performance. Data entry often requires many different slots for the user to enter or display data. It would require many other controls if you were to implement such an interface without using the Data Access control. When a Data Access control displays information, it doesn't use a collection of individual Windows controls; it paints the information on the screen as needed. By detecting when the user clicks the mouse, the Data Access control knows where to activate a particular column. The more complicated a Data Access control is, the greater the performance benefits achieved. A Data Access control with 40 objects on its surface requires nearly the same resources as a Data Access control with ten objects, or only one object on its surface. This is because the Data Access control is actually managed internally by Informix, not the Windows environment. The Data Access control also provides many other performance advantages. It requires fewer resources. Since Windows paints each control separately and Data Access is only one control, the speed of painting is significantly increased because Informix handles it all at once. Because the Data Window control manages many form-oriented tasks internally, you write less code to perform validation and cursor control. Windows considers Data Access to be a single control and, therefore, it uses fewer resources compared to multiple-standard controls.

Updates. One of the most difficult database programming problems is identifying what needs to be updated based on what the user selected and modified. How do you select the appropriate required syntax? The Data Window object does this for you. The PowerScript UPDATE statement builds the correct SQL based on the data window (DW) settings.

6.8.3 Using Data Access or standard controls

Some situations call for a Data Access control and some call for other controls; some situations can use either a Data Access or other control. In general, most windows require both Data Access controls and standard controls. Data Access controls improve performance and reduce programming effort for data access, presentation of data, and data entry. A large percentage of controls within an application will probably be Data Access. Anytime you need to access the database (DB), you should use a Data Access control (DAW). The external DAW with no DB access is also useful as a data-entry display object.

Some situations straddle the line between using a Data Access control and a standard control. An example of this is a database logon window. There is no database information to display, none that originates from a table by use of a Select statement. There is no formatting, reporting, or update requirements. On the other hand, there is data entry, where the user is required to enter several pieces of related information onto a window and then the information is collectively processed. This means that you should consider an external Data Access control. Either way does the job, but the code to accomplish the task will be slightly different depending on the technique you choose. To build data windows, use the Data Access window painter.

6.9 Adding Scripts

Scripts determine the actions that are initiated when an event takes place. For example, when a user runs an Informix application, the system opens the application and executes a script in the application for the Open event. The application Open event might open an application frame window and test the database connection to see if it is active before the user begins processing. The PowerScript Application Open might look like this:

```
OPEN (w_appl_frame_window)
CONNECT using SQLCA ;
IF SQLCA.SQLCODE 0 THEN f_db_error(SQLCA)
```

6.10 Validating Your Code

You can run your application anytime during development. If you discover problems, you can debug your application by setting breakpoints, stepping through your code statement by statement, and looking at variable and structure values during execution.

6.10.1 When to use the debugger

When you compile a script, the compiler detects obvious errors (such as incompatible data types or a misspelled function name), and the script will not compile until you fix these errors. In addition to compiler errors, you might have errors (such as dividing by zero) that will stop execution of the application, or logical errors that might not stop the script from running but produce incorrect results. A debugger helps you find these errors. Debug allows you to suspend the application at selected points in a script (stops) and review the contents of variables used in the application.

6.10.2 Selecting the scripts to breakpoint

In Debug mode, you select the script you want to debug, insert stops in the script, and then run or single-step through the script. When Informix encounters a stop, it suspends execution of the application and displays the Debug window. See Figure 6.5 for an example of the Debugger and a suspended script. In the Debug window, you can:

- Display the objects and user-defined functions in the application, the current values of the objects, the instance variables, and the attributes of the objects.
- Display the current values of the global, shared, and local variables.
- Edit stops, i.e., add or modify the existing stops.
- Select another script to debug.
- Modify variable values.
- Select the variables you want to watch during the Debug session.
- Continue executing the application to the next stop, or step to the next executable statement.

Using PowerBuilder, the stops remain in the scripts until you remove them or exit the application. When you close Debug, you suspend the Debug session. If

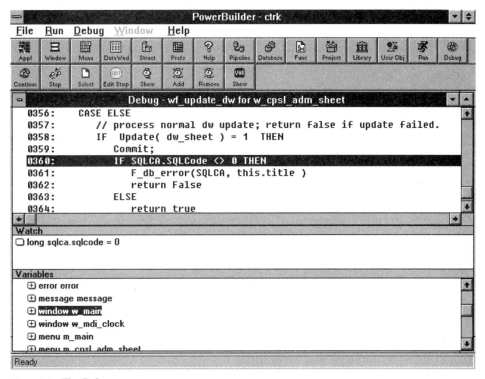

Figure 6.5 The Debugger.

you run Debug again during the same session, Debug will resume processing at the point at which you closed Debug. The Debug settings are saved for you in your .INI file so you can continue an existing Debug trail the next time you are ready.

6.11 Refining Your Code

At some point in the application development, key developers will see that certain patterns are repeated frequently within the application. This might mean that certain application functions are repeated, certain database accesses are repeated, or certain user tendencies are emerging. The developers must respond and refine those parts of the application so they perform in an optimal fashion. This point in the development cycle will make or break an application's acceptance and use. Things to consider are how you can accomplish:

- Code reusability and reducing development time.
- Code modularity.
- Reduced maintenance costs.
- Improved consistency (visual look and feel, nonvisual standards).
- Improved performance.

You will accomplish these objectives by carrying out the following tasks:

- Optimizing Informix.
- Removing redundant classes.
- Minimizing levels of menus and toolbar inheritance.
- Minimizing the use of large bitmaps.
- Minimizing or isolating array processing outside of window open processing.
- Minimizing the loading of list- and drop-down listboxes in the open event (use Data Access controls or drop-down Data Access controls instead).
- Putting inherited GUI presentation tools first in the library search path (in reverse order).
- Placing the directory that contains the Informix runtime DLLs first in the network search path.
- Optimizing libraries, for example, if you use Novell, resetting the Sharable attribute after optimizing a library.

6.12 Creating Functions and Structures

To support the refinement effort for your scripts, you probably want to define functions to perform processing unique to your application and structures to hold related pieces of data. If you want to be able to reuse components placed in windows, define them as user objects and save them in a library. Later, when you build a window, you can simply place the user object instead of having to redefine the components.

6.13 Creating an Executable

When your application is complete, you will prepare an executable version to distribute to your users. Before you deliver your application to users, however, you need to prepare a standard .EXE file in the Application painter. The .EXE file contains:

- A bootstrap routine
- The application icon (optional)
- The compiled version of each object in the application

6.13.1 Preparing to create the executable

To create an .EXE file, you must perform a series of steps that we will mention not for the procedure's sake but because each of these items must be fashioned properly long before this point in the development cycle. When you open the Application painter from the PowerPanel or the PowerBar, there is an icon/menu item that you select to create the executable file. The Create Executable window will display the name of the current application with the file extension .EXE. It will also display the name of the current directory, a list of available directories, and the libraries in the search path for the current application. Make sure you have considered the placement of the executable library components.

6.13.2 Creating the deployable application executable

Use the GUI tool to create the executable, store it in the specified directory, and close the Create Executable window. Consider its size. How many libraries must be packaged? If the application is large, can it be broken up into smaller deliverables? Is the security in place? Has the production database been defined with the proper sizing and partitioning? Is it available for use? Are the user identifiers in place with the proper permissions? Do the users have connectivity? Has the user acceptance team been put in place? Are the database support people ready? These are the types of issues you must be address before deploying an Informix production application. We will expand upon each of these issues and options throughout the remainder of this book. This iterative style will hopefully minimize the amount of time and effort required to understand how to develop applications in the client/server world.

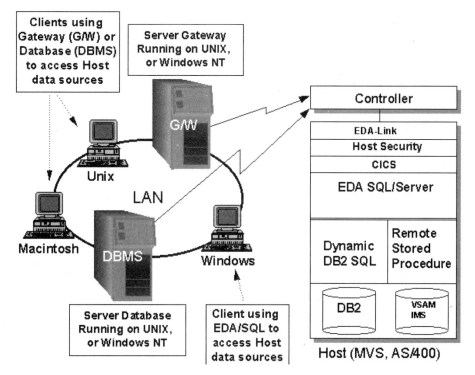

Figure 6.6 The enterprise solution using Informix.

Chapter

7

Defining an Application

This chapter focuses on designing and defining an object-oriented client/server application for Informix. What do we mean by that? When defining an application, the lead developer typically starts by attempting to determine the application's technical architecture, that is to say, the definition of all the interacting software and hardware components that combine to make up the application or system. This is true for reengineering an existing computer system or developing a brand-new system.

The task often begins at a very high level and, through various iterations of refinement, results in a very detailed architecture document that can be updated during the life of a project if, as is often the case, requirements change. At its most simplistic or high level, you can divide the application into a couple of pieces: the online portion and the batch portion. (Even if your online application is required to be "available 24 hours a day, 7 days a week, 365 days a year," you will still have to factor in time for tasks such as cleanup processing or hardware/software upgrade processing during the year.)

This chapter is divided into three sections. The first is an introduction to the concepts surrounding client/server and object-oriented development, and how they can affect the development of an application. The second section examines the most popular approaches to the system development life cycle and shows how these phases can be implemented during a project. The third section expands on the partitioning strategies, introduced in the first section, that exist for an application.

7.1 Client/Server and Object-Oriented Systems

In the past six years the terms "client/server" and "object-oriented" have become very popular in the information systems industry, if not overused. Unfortunately for some, you must be very familiar with the terms and be able to use them to implement an application in order to be able to find a programming job these days. The good news is that once you look behind the covers, the processes involved are neither complicated nor particularly new and innovative. However, these paradigms will be around for some time, so if you haven't had time to learn about it, now is the perfect opportunity.

7.1.1 The basics

As with any new technology, the first thing you have to concentrate on is the terminology. By becoming familiar with the jargon, you will at least be able to converse with your peers in order to obtain some assistance. So let's start there. Once we get the definitions out of the way, we can move on to the architecture, life cycle, and partitioning strategies commonly available.

7.1.1.1 Client/server terminology

Client. The client (see Figure 7.1) is a consumer of services. It is the process that begins a conversation by issuing a request to be serviced by another process, known as the server process.

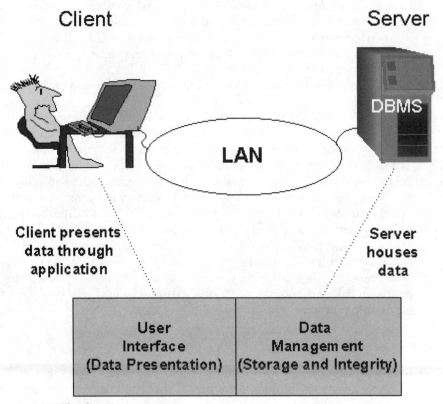

Figure 7.1   The client/server system.

Server. The server (see Figure 7.1) is a provider of service. It is a process that waits for requests. When it receives a request, it carries out a service and returns a response (or result) to the calling client. A server process is capable of handling requests from several client processes and is responsible for the management of responses. This relationship can be likened to a customer (client) placing an order (request for service) to a waiter or waitress (server) in a restaurant.

The client/server model provides the developer with an opportunity to partition the application and distribute it in several distinct processes. The client/server paradigm has given corporate developers the ability to downsize, rightsize, or smartsize large mainframe host-based applications to relatively inexpensive hardware and software. It has also provided the platform in which to upsize stand-alone PC applications that have outgrown their single-processor constraints and become inadequate for sharing data across the enterprise.

7.1.1.2 Object-oriented terminology

Object-oriented languages have been promoted as a technology that has the ability to deliver high-quality products to market more quickly, with lower on-going maintenance cost. Object technology, through the use of modeling, provides the link between the real world and computer technology.

Object-oriented analysis

This is taking a set of user requirements and reducing them to business objects. A business object is made up of its data, or what it knows, and its methods, or what it can do.

Object-oriented design

This means taking a set of business objects, designing them for an object-oriented programming language, and possibly implementing the business objects in conjunction with a user interface and database objects.

Object-oriented programming

This takes an object-oriented design, which includes the user interface and business and database objects, and implements them in the chosen object-oriented programming language. Object-oriented programming languages achieve this by providing developers with the following object-oriented features, which are also useful in controlling software complexity:

- Abstraction
- Encapsulation
- Polymorphism
- Inheritance

Abstraction. Object-oriented languages release developers from the restriction of fixed data types. Using these new languages, developers can create new data types, known as abstract data types or classes. Abstraction is the ability to consider and extract the essential characteristics required and packaging them into a convenient and compact data type. Another advantage to object technology is that it treats these new user-defined data types as though they were part of the language that originally came out of the box!

Encapsulation. Encapsulation is closely associated with modularity, or information hiding, which allows ongoing modifications to be made to the internals of an object—provided these changes do not affect the public interface. This reduces complexity and prevents internal changes from causing errors in other objects.

Polymorphism. Polymorphism, meaning "many forms," allows the developer to define the same name operation in different objects of an inheritance tree. The name is the same, but often the operation is implemented in a different way. For example, you can define a print function for a wide range of objects. Each object has its own definition of how the print function is implemented. One object responsible for printing trade confirmations might print several copies of the trade confirmation, one at the trader's desk and another in a back-office operations room for follow-up processing. A second object, responsible for printing sales commissions, might print only at the sales trader's desk. Polymorphism can increase the complexity of an object-oriented development project, but with careful planning and continual review it can be a valuable time-saver.

Inheritance. Inheritance allows programmers to define classes by reusing, or inheriting, previously defined classes as the basis for new objects. There are two approaches to classifying inheritance: single versus multiple inheritance and specification versus implementation inheritance. Single inheritance allows a subclass to have only a single parent class. Existing OO programming languages and methodologies permit extending the parent's definition, including redefining some or all of the properties of the parent class. With redefinition capabilities, it is possible to introduce an inheritance conflict, that is, a property of a subclass with the same name as a property of an ancestor class (a class one or more levels "higher" in the inheritance tree/lattice). Multiple inheritance occurs when a subclass inherits from several parent classes. This multiplies the inheritance conflicts, because it is now possible to have conflicts between two (or more) of the parent classes of the subclass. Inheritance conflicts increase the difficulty of understanding an inheritance structure and individual object in the structure. Many development tools do not support the multiple inheritance feature, and some industry pundits even go so far as to say that the lack of this feature is not usually an issue.

"Dealing with the lack of multiple inheritance is really an implementation issue, but early restructuring of a model is often the easiest way to work around its absence."

— James Rumbaugh, et al. (Object-Oriented Modeling and Design, Prentice Hall, 1991)

When using inheritance, there is a risk of increasing the complexity of a system instead of decreasing it.

Don't let anybody tell you that client/server and object-oriented development are the "silver bullet" solutions to application development because there aren't any! In fact, the transition to C/S and OOP might take some time before you begin seeing any payback. It might take several years in order to train the staff needed to reengineer or migrate (basically rewrite) legacy mainframe applications to the client/server and OOP platforms. You will find the first application to be the hardest, just like anything else that is new, but stick to it and you will find that by using these techniques you can get:

Scalability. Moving to a more modular architecture enables you to add hardware power to match demand without rewriting software.

Usability. Since client/server and graphical user interface (GUI) go practically hand-in-hand these days, applications have become more usable. GUI is an excellent environment to handle sophisticated user interfaces (Windows, Mac, Motif), as opposed to the character-based terminals attached to mainframe hosts.

7.1.2 Architecture

Client/server applications can be designed and implemented using one or more levels, or tiers. The tiers are typically, but not always, synonymous with the number of processors involved. These architectures are commonly known as:

- Single-tier
- Two-tier
- N-tier

Single-tier

In a single-tier architecture (see Figure 7.2), both the client and the server processes are running on the same machine's processor. For example, when you purchase PowerBuilder it comes with a stand-alone user-user version of the SQL Anywhere database. When you run the client example, it connects to the server database. The performance of a single-tier production application is linked not only to the design of the application, but to the speed of the processor and workstation hardware. They are subject to decreased performance because the processor is being shared by the client and server processes. Some commercial software uses this architecture, such as Microsoft's OLE implementation. When you embed an Excel spreadsheet in a Word document, Excel becomes a server to the Word client.

This type of client/server implementation is suited to small-scale or "startup" environments. The application can be implemented on a single processor and, when the need arises, upgraded to a distributed environment. It is also good for prototyping an application, but bear in mind that it will not provide a means to validate the performance or integrity of a scaled-up application.

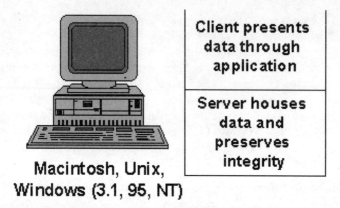

**Macintosh, Unix,
Windows (3.1, 95, NT)**

Figure 7.2   A single-tier client/server system.

Two-tier

In a two-tier architecture solution (see Figure 7.3), the concept of a network is introduced. Both the client workstation and server are connected by a network (e.g., TCP/IP or IPX/SPX). The client process running on the client workstation issues its requests via the network to the server process running on a server.

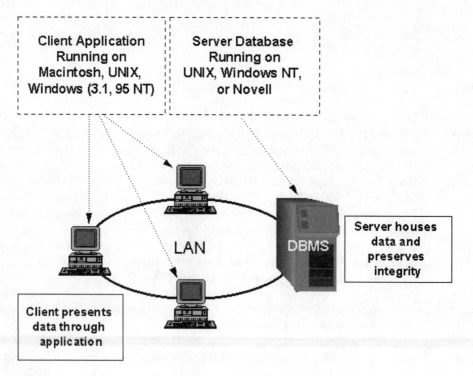

Figure 7.3   A two-tier client/server system.

Until fairly recently, two-tier architecture was the more common choice for client/server development, simply because it was the only straightforward way available. Typically, the client workstation handles presentation of information while the server provides the container for and access to the data. The actual logic, or business rules, are handled either exclusively by the client or the server, or by a mixture of both, i.e., declared constraints such as unique indexes, or procedural code such as stored procedures and triggers. This technique is well suited to the "departmental," or small- to medium-size environment, but might not be sufficient for large-scale, enterprise-wide solutions to data processing.

N-tier

An N-tier architectural solution (see Figure 7.4) is similar to the two-tier solution, in that they are both implemented across a network with the client process running on a client workstation issuing a request to server process running on a server. However, how the service is carried out is where N-tier comes in.

The server that receives the request can in turn become a client to another server process. For example, a client process sends a specific request, which is handled by a process completely within the server. The same client process could also send a different request to the server, in which the server becomes a

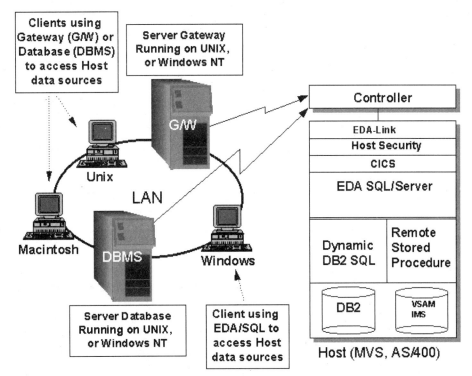

Figure 7.4 An N-tier client/server system.

client process and sends a request to another server process on the network. This second server process responds with data to the first server process, which in turn passes the data back to the original client process.

There are many possible implementations of this type of architecture. In the example, the first client process could be a PowerBuilder application running on an IBM-compatible PC workstation, the first server process an Informix gateway running on a Windows NT machine, the gateway process sending a message to the second server process, which executes on an IBM mainframe retrieving information from a DB/2 database. An N-tier architecture is better suited for enterprise-wide data contained on a (third-tier) host that needs to be accessed by local work groups, which also store data on their (second-tier) server. The client does not need to know the intricacies of where the data is stored, just the name of the procedures to interact with the servers that contain the data. The advantages of an N-tier architecture are that it:

- Helps to overcome performance limitation of two-tier client/server:
- By making use of remote CPU power (ultra-fast number crunchers).
- By providing access to specialized resources (e.g., host data).
- Improves access to heterogeneous data sources.
- Helps to eliminates database server bottlenecks.
- Allows you to scale an application without upgrading client workstations.

The distribution of data determines the architecture you will need for your project(s). Whatever approach you take, the chosen development tool must be capable of being implemented. Now let's see how the strategy affects the choice of tools, architecture, and development approach for client/server environments.

7.1.2.1 Application partitioning

Client/server implementations can range from slapping a graphical user interface onto an existing application to completely engineering or reengineering a distributed database application. The client/server strategy is the distribution of the process layers (see Figure 7.5) in an application, the process layers being presentation, business rules, and data access.

The strategies are defined in terms of distributing the layers for presentation, business rules, and data access logic across the client and the server. The presentation layer is responsible for all that is involved with the processing of the user interface, including formatting the information for display. The business rules layer is responsible for implementing the rules defined for the data. The data access layer handles all processing related to retrieving and maintaining data. Client/server tools, like PowerBuilder, implement a layered architecture to provide maximum flexibility in distribution decisions. This section illustrates some of the more popular client/server strategies, indicating which situations prompt for the use of the strategy.

Application Processing Layers

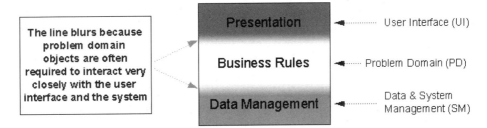

The line blurs because problem domain objects are often required to interact very closely with the user interface and the system

Presentation — User Interface (UI)

Business Rules — Problem Domain (PD)

Data Management — Data & System Management (SM)

Figure 7.5 Application presentation layers.

Distributed presentation strategy (DP)

The distributed presentation (see Figure 7.6) is the simplest form of client/server implementation. The presentation layer is present on the client and the server, typically a character-based host mainframe application. This approach provides a quick way to get the much in-demand GUI front end on an existing application that is too costly to rewrite or might take too long to reengineer at this point in time.

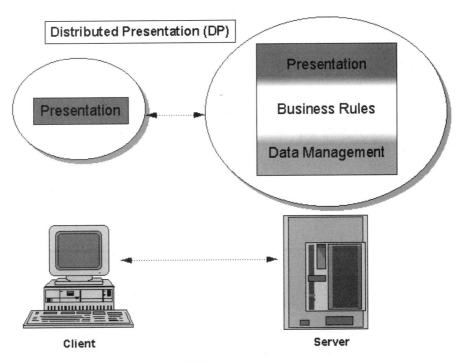

Distributed Presentation (DP)

Presentation

Presentation

Business Rules

Data Management

Client

Server

Figure 7.6 Distributed presentation (DP).

Using this strategy, the majority of processing takes place on the server, including a large percentage of the presentation component. The remainder of the presentation component runs on the client, typically using a graphical user interface (GUI). The client will probably need some additional logic that is aware of the navigation of the existing legacy host application. This is sometimes referred to as "screen scraping" because the host-based screen information is scraped off and translated into the GUI running on the client. This implementation is suited for integrating multiple, existing applications on a workstation or front-end mainframe applications with PC products, such as Microsoft Excel.

Remote presentation strategy (RP)

The remote presentation strategy (see Figure 7.7) places all the presentation logic on the client, but leaves the business rules and data access processing on the server. These are also known as "skinny" applications because they do not take up much space or require substantial processing on the client machine.

This strategy is most often applied where there is a mix of client workstations, e.g., Windows, Mac, and Motif. Because of the similarities among the GUI components, products support a single-source presentation component running on all platforms. The business logic and data access layers remain on the server. This type of implementation is suitable for data-centric or simple transaction processes with no database validation on the client or low-powered client workstations.

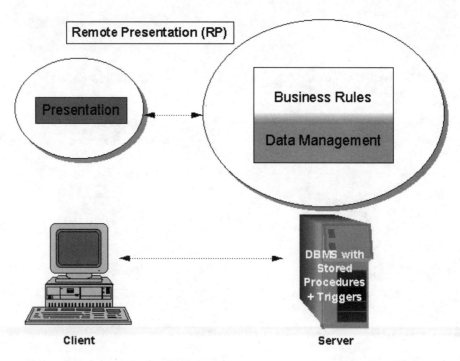

Figure 7.7   Remote presentation (RP).

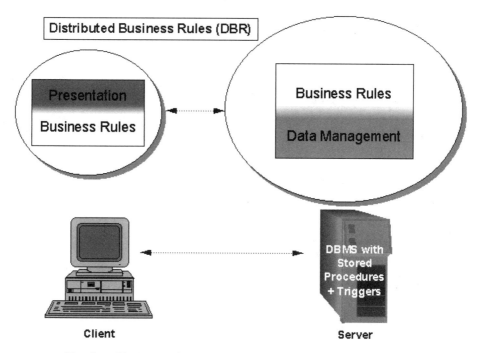

Figure 7.8 Distributed business rules (DBR).

Distributed business rules strategy
The distributed business rules strategy, see Figure 7.8, can be complicated by the need to synchronize the business rules processes running on both client and server. The data remains server based. This type of implementation is suitable for a mix of data and presentation level processing, complex processing demands or downsizing an existing mainframe application.

Remote data management strategy
The remote data management strategy (see Figure 7.9) has the entire application running on the client, but the data remains on the server. It is a common model for two-tier client/server applications, driven largely by the capabilities of common tools. Depending on the DBMS in use, there might be some business rules running on the server as triggers and stored procedures. This type of implementation is suitable for powerful workstations or presentation-oriented processing.

Distributed database strategy
In the distributed database model (see Figure 7.10), the data is stored on several servers and might be split across the client and the server. The distribution model used and the complexity of the transactions will determine how complex the distributed database implementation will be. This type of implementation is suitable for naturally segmented usage and storage of data or simple, single-location, single-table updates.

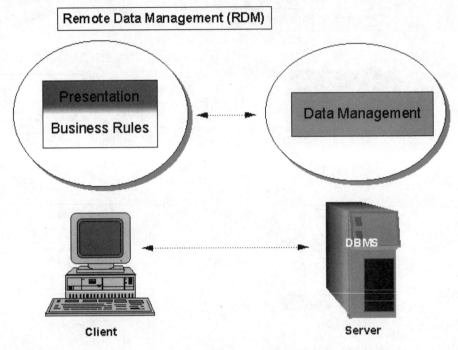

Figure 7.9 Remote data management (RDM).

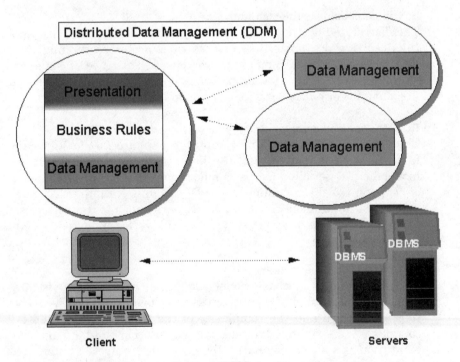

Figure 7.10 Distributed data management (DBM).

7.1.3 Recent demand

The client/server and object-oriented technology that has been made available in the last six years is largely responsible for the recent attraction and demand from corporations, small businesses, and individuals. We are now going to review the technology highlights that are the major reasons for the success of client/server computing today.

The graphical user interface (GUI)

A graphical user interface is an essential part of most client/server systems. The user interface is the external view of the system as it is presented to the user of the system. The appeal of the user interface is constrained by the presentation system (e.g., MS-Windows and OSF Motif), the development tool (e.g., Delphi, PowerBuilder, and Visual Basic), and the visual painting skills of the developer. However, the development tool might not exploit the presentation system to its fullest. Similarly, an inexperienced designer will not get the best from the tool. A good GUI is easy to learn, satisfying to use, effective for the task, and consistent in appearance and interaction, with the same look and feel as other popular GUIs, e.g., Word and Excel. Other design features should prevent the user from making errors, put the user in control, and above all be intuitive. Ugly GUIs make a product much harder to sell and less pleasurable to use. Additional considerations for GUI design are that they:

- Accommodate unskilled or infrequent users.
- Give immediate feedback.
- Permit reversible actions.
- Display descriptive and helpful messages.
- Allow the use of symbols and visual metaphors (icons and toolbars).
- Are aesthetic.
- Are in proportion.
- Have different typefaces.
- Use different colors.

For further reading on graphical user interface design, see the *Microsoft Application Design Guide* and *CUA91 Guide To User Interface Design*.

Distributed intelligent database

Data often has both localized and global use; distributed databases provide the opportunity to service both needs. Distributed database technology provides the ability for a single logical database to reside across a network on several computers. By putting data closer to where it is used, you will reduce network traffic and improve throughput. The biggest issue is processing transaction updates. There are currently two methods for distributed update:

Two-phase commit. This is an approach where the distributed computers all coordinate to either accept or reject the updates together. The overhead of ensuring that all databases are updated simultaneously usually has an adverse effect on the performance.

Replication. This is an approach where the computer that initially accepts the transaction takes responsibility to replicate it on the other databases. There is a lag before all databases are consistent, and a storage overhead. However, performance is considered better using this approach.

Most of today's database management systems use some form of procedural intelligence in the database, in the form of triggers or stored procedures. This processing logic is separate and distinct from the programs that invoke it. A trigger is a piece of processing logic that is not explicitly called by a program; it is initiated by an action, such as an insert, update, or delete on a table within the database. They are typically used to enforce referential integrity so you cannot delete a customer who has outstanding orders. A stored procedure is a function written in SQL that is explicitly called by a program in order to retrieve and/or maintain information in the database.

Networks

When several computers are involved in processing, the network is an essential component providing the means to link them together. In a client/server architecture, a local area network often connects a workstation to file or data services running on local servers. The architecture might also include a wide area network linking together local area networks.

End-user tools

End-user computing allows users to access data on the server by means of tools like Forest & Trees or Microsoft's Excel (via MS query and ODBC), providing reporting against server data.

7.1.4 Improved communication

The process of object-oriented analysis and design focuses on things that users interact with in the real world. Products, customers, and orders are common business examples. If you use items with which users are familiar to actually construct an application, communication not only improves greatly, but the software you build should correctly represent what the users want.

7.1.4.1 Design stability

Systems are traditionally based on data and processes, which typically are separate but interrelated elements. However, business processes and data change over time, which affects the underlying software. If you build software based on an architecture that depends on something that changes often, then the whole architecture must be reworked whenever the processes or data changes.

Over time, customers order products from businesses. This relationship among customer, order, and product is relatively stable and will probably remain that way. If you build software based on these components, you will end up with systems that are more stable over time. As a result, you should be able to build more robust systems.

7.1.4.2 Flexibility

Applications built out of well-designed objects tend to be more flexible than traditional systems. An object that is self-contained and serves a single, well-defined purpose can be modified internally with minimal impact on the entire system. It can also be readily removed from a system and replaced with another object that provides similar functionality.

New objects can also be added to a system more easily because they have a distinct method for connecting to other objects in the system. As a result, you can extend the application with much less effort than with traditional systems.

7.1.4.3 Reuse

Reuse is one of the primary benefits of the object-oriented approach. To reuse objects, they must be designed and built based on a fairly strict set of principles, such as abstraction and encapsulation.

In the older, more procedural language developments, code modules were constructed, tested, saved in libraries, and then documented for use by other developers. This provided some reuse, but these "copybooks" were typically very specific and could seldom be used across the enterprise. Object-oriented analysis and design has changed the way corporations capture their business and data requirements. Business rules and data are now being considered assets of companies, and systems that are being developed to support these assets are constructed with a view to being reusable across the enterprise. So the ease and extent that reuse plays a part in an OO environment is significantly enhanced.

7.1.4.4 Client/server integration

Objects interact with each other as clients and servers, sending and receiving messages to and from each other. This is the primary reason that object-oriented techniques are used extensively for client-server system development.

One of the benefits of a client/server architecture is that it allows different systems to interoperate. Applications built using objects can be designed to be highly compatible, or to interoperate with each other, much like client/server systems do now.

7.1.5 How to succeed

In order to be successful in client/server development, you have to pay attention to the following areas: consistency, stability, quality, and usability.

Consistency

The single greatest factor that contributes to user satisfaction is consistency. A consistent, weak interface design is preferable to an excellent but inconsistent one. Users expect that the same types of actions will occur in the same way each time they encounter them. The challenge is not only to provide one consistent system, but rather to provide a consistent work environment. That means consistency across systems and the other tools the user accesses.

Consistency is provided for in the planning stage and by means of a new approach to user interface design. The planning stage provides a cross application view of client/server development, and the design approach (i.e., visualize, abstract, and detail) ensures consistency within an application by maximizing reuse and inheritance.

Stability

Client/server technology is still relatively immature. This, combined with possible wide distribution, creates a fragile environment. The distribution also adds complexity in providing support and analyzing breakdowns. Therefore, it becomes the responsibility of the designer to build stability into the system.

Designing applications for a perfect world where businesses always work as expected and the technology always performs as promised is easy, but unreal. Creating stable applications means anticipating problems and expecting the unexpected. Throughout the methodology, you must address integrity checking, risk analysis, and stability design. In analysis, you collect business rules and also examine the resilience of the business model to future change. In design, you implement the integrity rules (sometimes twice to cater for end-user access and front-end checks) and introduce design integrity constraints such as referential integrity checks. In stability design, you must specifically examine and correct for weaknesses of client/server implementations.

Quality

Quality is an essential attribute for all applications, but it takes on a special meaning in a client/server implementation. This is primarily due to the complexities involved in distributing and upgrading the applications. Changing a mainframe application is relatively simple. New code can be installed on the mainframe overnight and everyone has access to it in the morning. Perhaps there is a need to reorganize the database and that can be done over the weekend. Translate that into a distributed client/server environment, however, and the increase in complexity is dramatic. The code must find itself to 400 workstations at 20 sites nationwide; each site has a piece of the distributed database. These demands require that you minimize the number of software releases and that each release is of high quality. You achieve quality by applying a robust methodology and testing the quality at each point in the process.

Usability

In spite of the emphasis placed on cost savings by product vendors, the lead time to realize the benefit for most organizations is lengthy. Due to a combination of learning costs, the need to migrate from existing hosts, and the cost of installing new hardware and software, it can be up to three years before promised savings materialize. Short-term benefits are realized from the enhanced usability of the applications. A client/server application can improve user productivity and enjoyment by providing the user with:

- A graphical user interface (GUI), which provides for easier manipulation and access to information.
- Integration of information and processing with familiar desktop tools (e.g., MS Word for Windows or MS Excel).
- Easier access to data resident locally to the user.
- Consistency in the user interface across applications and tools.
- Access to and analysis of data through end-user tools and executive information systems.

Unfortunately, these benefits do not come automatically. A client/server tool does not guarantee good GUI design, and an intelligent DBMS does not in itself imply data that the user can access. Usability must be a focus for the development team and of the development method.

If you roll out an application without paying special attention to these characteristics, you might find that what should have been a success quickly becomes an embarrassment.

Other considerations

There have been distributed systems before the emergence of the client/server architecture. Digital Equipment Corp., built its reputation on real-time and distributed applications. IBM's midrange System 38 and AS 400 were regularly used to implement distributed systems. In these previous generations of commercial applications, distribution usually indicated that separate processes were being executed on different processors. In other words, the application was distributed. In a client/server architecture, it is a single business process itself that is distributed. A single process can now run on different machines. This brings some new design challenges and issues.

Objects and events

In the client/server methodology, you examine objects and events in both analysis and design. There are two primary reasons for this:

- Object and event analysis permits you to model real-world concepts in your analysis. This in turn allows you to base the user interface on real-world concepts. Most experts in the field agree that this is the best basis for a graphical user interface.
- Leading client/server development tools support class hierarchies and inheritance in design. Using an object and event approach maximizes the use of those tools.

Business rules

You use business rules as an analysis technique in the client/server methodology. This replaces the older and more traditional action diagram or structured

English representation of business logic. Business rules have the advantage of being not only a more modular representation of business facts, but also simpler for business people to review and refine.

The modularity of business rules provides a distinct advantage in a client/server methodology. You have the flexibility to decide at the design stage where you will implement the rule (i.e., on the client, on the server, or on both). The classification of rules also guides you in deciding where the rules should be implemented.

Application suitability

Client/server is a wonderful technology. However, in spite of its power and capabilities, it is not a panacea. Some application characteristics suggest a client/server solution, and some are risky to implement with client/server technology. In other words, some applications play to client/server strengths while others are at risk from its weaknesses. It is certainly worth acknowledging those strengths and weaknesses. The strengths are:

- Graphical presentation of data.
- Integration of application and end-user tools.
- Access to shared data.
- Download/export for local analysis.
- Single-record updates.

And the weaknesses are:

- Complex or long-running update transactions.
- Distributed transaction update.
- Very large database support on servers.

The following application types are ranked by increasing risk in a client/server environment. The lower numbered applications are more suitable for client/server development with today's technology.

1. Information retrieval
2. Information analysis
3. Image and graphic presentation
4. Simple (single-table) transaction update
5. Multimedia presentation
6. Multiple-table update transactions
7. Long transaction updates
8. Distributed database updates

Client/server is here to stay for the long run.

7.2 Managing the Development

The primary goal of any software development team is to produce high-quality products that fit the business requirements. Client/server systems that use object-oriented analysis, design, and programming techniques have the potential to improve the quality and functionality of software. However, adopting and succeeding with this development approach requires investing in education and practice to become really effective. So why make the investment? Simply because everybody else is, so why be left behind? Another question you might be asking yourself is: "Are object-oriented client/server systems any different from others?" The obvious answer is yes. The differences usually relate to either the management of the project, with items such as human resources, software development life cycle, version, and quality control or the object-oriented technology itself, with its abstraction, classes, reuse, and messaging.

We've mentioned the possible improvements in quality and functionality, but what about the other factor, time? Well, if everything works out, the payback will usually not be apparent until the third or fourth application is developed. By this time you will have had plenty of practice at developing the right kind of generic and specific objects that can be reused, with no change, by the new application.

Be aware, however, that although these techniques might reduce costs to the enterprise over the long term, the fruits will probably be harvested by a different department from the one that originally cultivated them. While the organization as a whole benefits, the gains might need to be accounted for with an alternative business model.

7.2.1 Software development goals

Object-oriented development techniques are not visible to users. Users care only that the application completes the business functions, and this is typically confirmed through certain external qualities. Object-oriented techniques can help you provide the following characteristics in an application:

Correct. The application should perform its task exactly as defined by the user. An integrated process of object-oriented analysis, design, and programming can help ensure correctness.

Robust. The application must be able to function under resource constraint or abnormal conditions. An object-oriented architecture can provide a foundation to help applications operate under such constraints or unusual conditions.

Extendible. The application should be easy to modify due to changes in the user's requirements. An application built from modular pieces is easier to modify.

Reusable. The modular pieces of an application often contain elements that are common across the enterprise, and as such should be reusable in other applications.

Compatible. You should be able to easily combine well-designed and well-constructed software with others products in order to solve similar business problems. Application components that are designed and constructed with simple interface methods will be more compatible with other applications.

7.2.2 Project management

Project management relies on information being collected in order to determine the amount of progress within the project. Some specific OO issues that must be taken into account are the appropriate team structure, managing the library organization, the phases of the life-cycle model being used, the overall goal of quality, moving from a project to a product culture in software engineering, and the need to measure the project for future reference.

7.2.3 Team structure

An important consideration in the development of a product is the composition of the team that is involved with the design and construction. The goal is always to have a project team with a good balance of disciplines and skills in analysis, interviewing, writing, construction, and testing. As mentioned in Chapter 4, the team needs to be comprised of personnel in the following skill areas:

- Project management
- End-user representation
- System architecture and design
- Database administration
- Network administration
- Standards control
- Object management
- Application development
- Documentation
- Multimedia artistry
- Quality assurance

These skills are rare in a single individual, so teams of people that specialize in the different disciplines are typically put together in the hope that they will forge into a cohesive unit. This takes a great deal of effort from all concerned and requires regular monitoring by project management, with realistic goal setting and follow-up.

Another important factor is the location of and facilities for the development team. It will be detrimental to the project if the team members are not in close proximity to each other. It is important to provide satisfactory working facilities, such as access to a conference room with an adequate amount of whiteboard space. Conference rooms are good for "just in time" education, presentation of development ideas, and code reviews.

For the prototyping and construction elements of the team, one approach might be to split the development team into groups that are responsible for specific areas of vertical functionality, such as maintenance and reporting subsystems. This setup still requires communication and the close cooperation between subsystem teams during the full extent of the life cycle.

7.2.4 Object management

The management of objects, or classes, is intrinsically linked with software reuse. A project consists of teams of developers responsible for creating and integrating the horizontal (generic) and vertical (specific) classes. Some object-oriented languages have matured to the point that the language or tool vendor supplies a foundation class library that provides many of the horizontal classes required by developers. This provides an excellent jump-start and framework for an application developer.

As a project progresses, these objects are published for other teams and team members to use. This can create a few problems unless good procedures are in place to control versions and ensure quality. As time passes, with the enterprise-wide adoption of object-oriented languages, developers will find that many of the classes required for a specific application will already exist in libraries prior to the commencement of the specific project. This reuse of pre-coded classes will improve developer productivity and application reliability, while reducing the amount of resources consumed by the duplicate or near-duplicate code that already exists, scattered across older applications that support the business lines of the enterprise.

As you can see, the management of class libraries needs to be addressed at the enterprise level instead of at the business line—or worse still, the individual application level. This requires an organization's commitment to an integrated set of libraries.

7.2.5 System development life cycle (SDLC)

The system development life cycle is the name of the major steps involved in transforming a set of user requirements into an object-oriented application.

One of the ways to deliver a quality product is to follow a procedure (or methodology) that has proven to be successful at producing a quality product. There are many methodologies available that lead you through the life cycle of planning and executing application development, but the essence of them all can be summarized into the following list of tasks or phases to be carried out:

- Planning
- Analysis
- Design
- Construction
- Testing

- Implementation
- Maintenance

Now each methodology that exists today might have a different name for any one or all of these tasks, but they typically occur. Methodologies are a documented path that details what to do, how to do it, and what should be delivered at each point. There is no ultimate methodology and there probably never will be, but the actual experience of implementing a methodology and then continuously refining and improving it with feedback will result in the best methodology—one that's configured to suit your needs and the way you work.

What follows is an overview of each of these phases or tasks. Then we will examine how these tasks were carried out using both a traditional technique and a more contemporary technique.

7.2.5.1 Planning
This phase of the project is where you should determine the scope and objectives, and draft the plan for the overall project. This plan is subject to change, which is to be expected, especially if the development group is new to client/server or unfamiliar with the business area.

Understand the existing system
The existing business process does not necessarily have to involve computers. It could be a collection of very detailed manual operations that are carried out by individuals of various skill levels. The reason that more advanced technology is brought in is because it is widely accepted as a means to make a business more efficient, provide better service, and therefore become more profitable. However, in order to suggest a new system to replace the old, you need to know and document as much as possible about the business and its existing system(s).

Determine requirements
The task of determining requirements, or information gathering, is typically achieved when the systems people meet with or interview the business clients to discuss what they want in a new system. The meeting interview will generally flow from the description of what currently happens to what they would like to see happen with a new system, and address why they think it will make their jobs easier. It is best to clarify unfamiliar terminology or familiar words used in an unfamiliar way when first used. It might be a little difficult to begin with, especially when you have people without any knowledge of the business process. However, it will help if everybody starts to use the same words to describe the processes involved.

Just as in purchasing a product from a retail store or hiring an employee or consultant, you can reduce the process of acquiring a shrink-wrapped, custom-built, or somewhere-in-between system to the following basic areas:

Functionality. Can the product do what I require it to do? How close does the product's capabilities match the requirements?

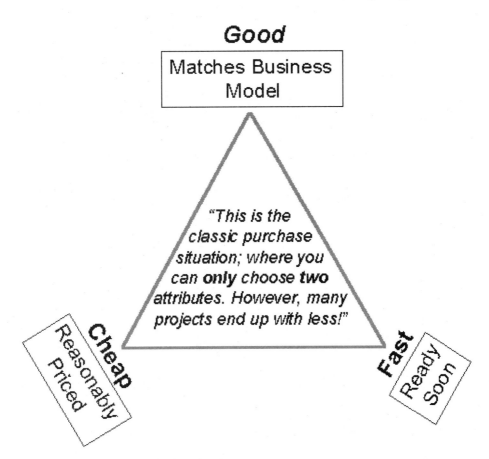

Figure 7.11 The classic purchasing triangle.

Availability. Can I get the product soon?

Cost. Can I get the product inexpensively?

It is also valid to apply the general rule that it is very difficult to get a product that will satisfy *all* the requirements (see Figure 7.11).

Technical architecture analysis

During the planning stages, you evaluate the current platform and plan for the future technical environments. To facilitate the planning and scheduling of development, it is a good idea to gather some information to quantify the project. You can gather this information during the life of the project, but it's normally started during the business analysis phase. In order to assist in technical evaluations, you will need to develop pilot or proof-of-concept applications.

The following is a list of areas that should be discussed and reviewed when developing a client/server application:

- Evaluations for hardware, software, and networks.
- Strategies for location, migration, operation, and support.

Each of these issues must be addressed for both the development and the production environments. We will now discuss each point in more detail.

Hardware evaluation

For hardware you will need to establish the configurations, size and type of processor, size and type of memory, and size and type of storage space for the following items or multiples thereof:

- Workstation
- File server
- Local database server
- Enterprise database server

If any of the hardware is not currently available, you need to plan to acquire it. To help determine what type and size of hardware, you should ask questions like:

- How big will the database be in the short, medium, and long term?
- What are the data requirements?
- How big is each table (rows × columns, including column width)?
- How much file server space is required for items such as the development tools and the user and technical documentation?

Software evaluation

The tools and libraries that the organization decides to purchase or build should be supported by the underlying technical architecture and development life cycle. Object-oriented tools often do not fit well into organizations structured for traditional system development. There are few object-oriented tools and libraries for mainframes. Structured methods and processes do not adapt well to the use of object-oriented tools.

Once again, if any of the software is not currently available, you need to acquire it. The software list might also includes standard office productivity tools for word processing, spreadsheets, presentations, electronic mail, and scheduling meetings. You will also need to consider other supporting products such as version control, entity-relationship modeling, and database query tools. In terms of the GUI development side, here are some specific areas for consideration:

- What GUI platform (Windows, Mac, UNIX) should you use? During development, where will development tools and source libraries reside: on each developer's workstation or in a directory on the shared file server?
- In the production environment, where will executables reside: on each client workstation or in a directory on the shared file server?
- How many developers, testers, administrators, support people (database server, file server), and end-user clients will be involved?

- What are the printing and reporting requirements? This covers simple screen print to possibly large outputs. How can you design a system so your users don't need that mountain of paper anymore? If they do need a large amount of output on a daily/weekly basis, can you print it elsewhere and deliver it, so you don't tie up the local laser printer?

- You can extend the life of your product if you provide the means to export data for additional analysis with a tool like Microsoft Excel or Lotus 1-2-3. You might also want to specifically restrict this kind of process due to the sensitivity of the data.

- Discuss and establish standards to satisfy the security issues for connecting the application to the database: using standard SQL statements, using views and stored procedures to facilitate all (or possibly update) access, using cursors to populate window control and variables, and using embedded SQL.

- Plan the development library setup with respect to the number and purpose of libraries, procedures for checking out entries under version control, and the backup and restore procedures (Note: many people forget to test the recovery procedure until it's too late!)

- Establish development standards, guidelines for naming conventions, screen sizes, fonts, colors, and technical documentation.

- Consider the following application design issues: using and maintaining the database meta-data catalog via third-party tools, using a multiple document interface (MDI) as a standard environment for all applications, and using object-oriented programming (inheritance, encapsulation, and polymorphism).

- Consider creating common functions or objects, providing runtime context-sensitive help, application/menu/window-level security, a common login screen, and simple but familiar error handling and problem reporting in the event that something goes wrong in the production environment.

Network infrastructure

The network plays an essential part in the success of a client/server project. The product might perform perfectly under laboratory conditions, but work less than satisfactorily when it is rolled out. If you have any network engineers within reach, involve them from the start of the project to help with the prediction and resolution of network traffic bottlenecks. A common resolution to this is to make sure all the application is stored on each client machine. That way the network isn't being flooded with requests to load application code (executables, dynamic libraries, etc.) onto a client processor. It might pay to create a model of the application or consult with the many books that provide formulas for determining load on networks.

Location strategy

If the project involves the implementation of a distributed system, you will need to consider the other locations and where necessary, involve support staff in those to manage remote database and file servers, including backup and disaster recovery procedures for each site. You will also find it necessary to buy or construct a "watchdog" application that can alert support staff in the event of an impeding or actual failure of a component of the client/server implementation.

Migration and transition strategy

As will all software products, for the users to maximize their use of the new system, you should consider establishing some form of training prior to the production date. This education will help to smooth out the process of production and allow you to re-acquaint the users with the proper procedures in the event of any real or perceived failure of the system.

If you are reengineering an existing system, consider if you can and how you will migrate/replicate all the data that exists to the new system. This might involve writing and testing conversion programs and routines, downloading or transferring the data via other media, and uploading it to the new database. You should completely perform this exercise on several occasions in order to iron out any problems and get a feel for how long the process will take when the production date comes around. Prior to the production date, you might plan to have a subset of the production users execute a planned test-drive of the new system, possibly in conjunction with the prior system, to ensure that the system is performing as expected. This user acceptance period will give you the opportunity to optimize the end-user workstation configurations as well as test the application and runtime environment software distribution techniques.

Operation strategy

Any day-to-day operations required to make the system flow smoothly, including backups and scheduling the submission of jobs, should be documented in an operations guide.

Support strategy

In the event of a failure in any part of the system, format a standard message with as much diagnostic material as possible to uniquely identify where the error occurred and for what reason. For severe errors, consider some kind of paging utility to notify key support personnel.

Before anything does go wrong, however, consider building in some kind of capture utility that allows you to gather information, such as transaction usage or frequency. Reviewing this information might provide insight into improving the process the next time around.

7.2.5.2 Analysis

The task of analysis is really structuring and organizing the information gathered by meetings or interviews with the business clients. Again, there are many tools and techniques designed to do this: flow charts, information flow diagrams, entity-relationship models, etc. For more information on tools, see Chapter 18.

7.2.5.3 Design

The design task is taking the results of the analysis of the requirements, and turning it into a detailed description of the new system. What are the platforms, the architecture, and the construction tools? How will it look and feel? What are the subsystems, the inputs, the processes, and the outputs?

7.2.5.4 Construction

The construction task is taking the detailed design specification and implementing it. At various points throughout building the application, some questions or issues will arise that might prompt a small amount of redesign, but this is not uncommon and is usually due to a misinterpretation of the requirements during the design phase. Any large-scale redesign at this point will be a major setback to the schedule for the project, and will obviously affect any subsequent planning dates and ultimately the roll-out date.

7.2.5.5 Testing

The testing phase is responsible for ensuring that the product that's built performs the way the detailed design documentation specifies. There are various testing levels that are typically carried out by specific personnel during the development life cycle. Each testing level must be successful before the next level is attempted.

The very lowest level is unit or component testing, where the programmer who writes the code tests the code according to detailed specifications. The next level is system or integration testing, where a project leader or systems analyst tests all the components to see that they interact correctly when combined as a system. The next level is quality assurance testing, where a series of tests that worked on the previous version of the product are run against the new version.

If any test fails, then the product will not progress forward through the testing phases. The problem is investigated and fixed, and the tests are repeated until the results are successful. This quality assurance testing phase has more recently been addressed by the use of automated test tools. The more advanced test tools allow you to create or record small test cases that can be grouped together to test a large piece of functionality. These test cases can then be run automatically, often overnight, revealing any unexpected results (i.e., potential errors) from the product. Once the product has its QA stamp, the next level is user acceptance testing, where the users get to exercise the product in a pre-production mode and hopefully give an approval for the product to be placed into production.

See Chapter 13 for more information on tracking down existing and preventing future bugs.

Testing can also be broken down into two types: integrity and performance. Integrity testing breaks down into availability (Does the application provide access to the production data as required?) and consistency (Does the application process the transaction entirely, taking the database from one known state to another known state?) Integrity is also about the products resiliency (Does the application detect errors, report them, and recover correctly, or is it able to prevent problems from occurring?) Performance is typically the measurement of response times (Is the system designed and implemented to avoid bottlenecks, e.g., on the LAN or file server?) This type of testing usually involves the simulation of multiple users requesting the maximum amount of data to be transferred, or the simulation of low or inadequate resources, such as constraints on workstation memory and disk, or network bandwidth.

7.2.5.6 Implementation

The implementation phase is the roll-out of the production version of the system to the client community. This involves tasks like backing up the existing system (data and programs), data conversion, producing user documentation, user training, software distribution (push, pull, e-mail, sneaker-net), and setting up the infrastructure for supporting the new system. See Chapter 17 for more information on deploying an application to the client environment.

7.2.5.7 Maintenance

The maintenance phase is a post-production phase for all new implemented systems. Maintenance can be considered a project of its own, depending on how much change is required, and it determines how many of the previous tasks should be repeated to implement a revision of the system.

7.2.6 Implementing the project plan

The methodology that an organization chooses for application development should complement its choice of technical architecture. A methodology is a series of steps specified for constructing a system. Structured methods were primarily designed to build applications for implementation in a host-terminal architecture, which were usually written in common business-oriented language, or COBOL.

Structured methods have had difficulty in adapting to the client/server architecture. By contrast, object-oriented methods generally result in applications that are well-suited for deployment on an underlying client/server architecture. Object-oriented system development and maintenance incorporate many of the same elements involved in the traditional system development process. Analysis, design, building, testing, and implementation are steps the two processes have in common. Object-oriented components must pass through additional stages to become generalized and included in application libraries and frameworks.

Many stages of the system development cycle can be conducted concurrently and/or repeatedly due to the nature and characteristics of objects. This iterative, or spiral, process differs significantly from a traditional "waterfall" development process.

Now let's review what a methodology is going to do for you if you follow it: "For the project to be a success, one must firmly establish the business requirements. By performing business analysis one will document the data and process requirements. Detailed design will document how the data and process requirements are to be met. Construction will attempt to meet the requirements. Testing will ensure that construction does meet the requirements." — Anon

The system development life cycle is a way of categorizing development processes within the information technology architecture. There are two primary types of life-cycle models to describe the information system development process: waterfall and iterative. The waterfall model is widely recognized and extensively used in older system development. The iterative model is the newer approach and manifests itself with slight variations in every development area.

7.2.6.1 Traditional application development

Traditional application development (see Figure 7.12) is quite simply the execution of the project tasks, as described at the beginning of this chapter, in an almost serial fashion. In other words, before you start design you have to complete (or almost complete) the analysis, and you have to have a detailed design specification before you start construction. At the end of the process you deliver the complete system.

This all seems fairly logical, right? Well, a number of issues arise when you build a system in this fashion. Systems, especially large ones, are invariably delivered late, with budget overruns. By the time the system is implemented, the user needs have expanded or changed. In other words, what you give them now they needed last year!

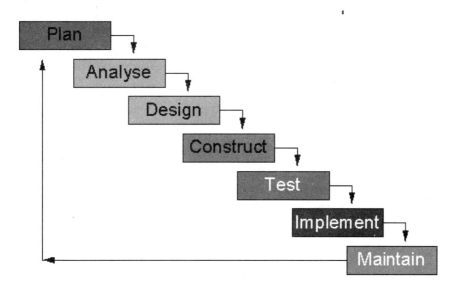

Figure 7.12 Traditional "waterfall" development life cycle.

The waterfall process breaks the development cycle into a series of sequential steps:

1. The system plan is developed.
2. Once management signs off on the plan, system analysts work with users to develop requirement specifications.
3. Once the specs are complete and management signs off on them, the system design is constructed.
4. Once the design is approved, the system is built.
5. The system is tested.
6. The system is delivered to the user.

Note that the user participates in this process both at the beginning and the end. Also, each step must be completed and approved before work can begin on the next stage.

With development life cycles structured around this approach, it is difficult, if not impossible, for developers to work back "up the waterfall." The nature of this process is such that if requirements change or the plan must be altered, it is hard to make adjustments. The waterfall approach is usually effective for systems that are well understood and not subject to changing business conditions, such as practical business systems. Tactical systems usually provide back-office support and automate existing business processes to make them more efficient. Such processes generally change little over time and few, if any, alterations are anticipated in the future.

For example, accounting processes (such as the general ledger, fixed-asset accounting, and tracking) are suitable for the waterfall approach. The only changes to these systems are usually in accounting practices and regulations. These changes typically have a long gestation period while the industry reviews and comments on proposed modification before mandating them.

7.2.6.2 Contemporary application development

Contemporary development life cycle uses rapid application development (RAD) and prototyping (see Figure 7.13), which are techniques that allow a group of users and developers to get together and interact during the gathering and implementation of the application objectives or requirements. This helps to ensure that everyone understands what must be delivered. The presentations or discussions might range from stepping through a simple sequence of screens and reports to an SQL query involving user- or industry-supplied equations and calculations. There are times when rapid application development (RAD), joint application development (JAD) sessions, and prototyping can fill in the gaps left in the business analysis phase. You will find that it is very effective if you begin prototyping before completing the analysis to enable the user/client to better visualize the processes. It is important to note that RAD and JAD sessions and prototyping do not necessarily replace the need for traditional business analysis.

Contemporary RAD/JAD Technique

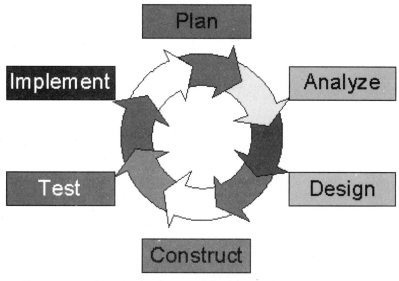

Figure 7.13 Contemporary iterative development life cycle.

In iterative development, you specify the objectives for a system and then build and deliver a series of partial but increasingly complete implementations. You can start with a shell type of application or prototype and, with each successive implementation, add functionality. With this style of development, it is possible to build, integrate, and demonstrate the sections of the application in a short space of time, keeping everybody involved interested and providing valuable input. This early and regular integration will reduce the likelihood of encountering major problems near the end of the project. Each iteration allows you to incorporate the latest feedback and refinements from the JAD session. This regular interaction becomes part and parcel of the acceptance process, with the eventual users of the application getting comfortable and accepting the interface, functionality, and performance during its development. The feedback becomes a part of the quality assurance process. The comments also provide feedback on the usability of the product that is being developed jointly. During each subsequent JAD session the prototype features are refined to a point where, piece by piece, the design is accepted. Discussing and incorporating feedback during these sessions is likely to improve the overall success of the project. Because this is the most effective way to agree on what the system should look like in production, more and more corporations have turned to this form of development.

Using contemporary development tools, like PowerBuilder, with RAD techniques will allow the development team to quickly turn the prototype into production-standard code. During these phases, it makes sense to keep any documentation up to date to prevent any creeping scope. It's also important to continue JAD sessions throughout the construction and make an effort to record any metrics during the process. This can help to improve the process in review meetings after the project is implemented and before you embark on the next project.

In any case, the methodology should demand and produce a clear set of deliverables. It is also crucial that reuse be factored in and supported by the chosen methodology. Many methodologies just pay "lip service" to reuse. Others discuss the creation of objects *for* reuse and not *with* reuse (or vice versa). A good methodology will support both:

For reuse. Which is the creation of new library classes for use in the future?

With reuse. Which are the techniques to locate and reuse existing library classes and capitalize on your investment in object technology so far?

7.3 Application Partitioning

In essence, this is a template for designing software applications. It separates all the objects into three groups, or partitions: the problem domain partition, the user interface partition, and the system management partition.

This separation promotes modularity and reusability. It specifies that each object performs a particular type of task: user interface, problem domain, or system management. As a result, problem domain objects can be reused throughout numerous related applications, each of which might have completely different user interface requirements. The same is true for interface objects that can be reused across domains, and system management objects that can be reused independent of an interface or domain.

A common practice that has evolved over the past five years is partitioning an application into three distinct segments: the user interface, the business rule objects, and the data and system management objects. This architecture provides the basis for modular and extendible object-oriented applications. Table 7.1 shows these layers and a few of the alternate names for them. This evolution of application partitioning resembles that of cell division in the natural world (see Figure 7.14).

What follows in the remainder of the chapter is a detailed definition of these layers and the questions you should ask yourself during the planning and de-

TABLE 7.1

Layer	Alternate name
Presentation	User interface or UI
Business rules	Problem domain or PD
Data/system access	Data and system management, or DASM

Application Partitioning Evolution:
"The Splitting Of The Process Cell"

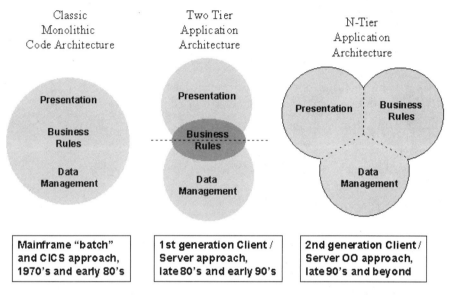

Figure 7.14 Application partitioning evolution.

sign stages in order to create a satisfactory application. However, this practice can often be summarized into the following:

1. Use any existing code directly (reuse) or as a model for new code (reengineer).

2. Consider purchasing third-party code or libraries, even if all you do is examine the code for educational reasons.

3. Construct the remaining objects or classes.

4. Document the layers, classes, and objects that you create, use, and/or modify.

5. Finally, provide easy-to-access documentation for the development team (e.g., Windows help files, HTML-formatted files for a Web browser, or a documentation database in Lotus Notes).

Once the layers have been defined and documented, they should be formally presented to the whole development team, including any management, for educational purposes, to provide a feeling of technical direction, and to obtain feedback from the team. General questions you can pose to help determine an object's value:

- What is the machine scope of the object (local machine, remote machine, both)?

- What is the object supposed to do (initially restricted functionality, expanding as the project continues)?

- How will it work with other objects (properties, events, attributes, functions, data, methods, etc.)?

- What platforms will be supported (16- or 32-bit issues, Windows NT, Windows 95, Windows 3.x, UNIX, Mac)?

- What level of performance is required? (memory/other resource usage and technique, i.e., cache and refresh or reread every request)?

- How will it be maintained in the future (distribution, documentation, or revision)?

Build a table (see Table 7.2) showing the object's design.

7.3.1 Partitioning the online portion

The online portion of an application, or system, is usually the only part a user talks or knows about, if you're lucky. The application will usually break down into one of the following types: online transaction processing (OLTP) or some form of decision support system (DSS). DSS might by the name of either executive information system (EIS) or management information system (MIS). The difference between these types is that OLTP systems capture information from the user for storing in a database, and DSS systems extract information from the database, analyze it, and report it to the user (see Table 7.3).

Some systems are a combination of both types, but if you try to create a database that is used for capturing many transactions as well as providing extensive query capability, you'll get very poor performance.

TABLE 7.2

Type	Visual	Nonvisual
Public method	of_ShowRate	of_GetRate
Private method		of_InitRates
Protected method		
Public property		

TABLE 7.3

Type	Flow of online information	Example
OLTP	More data IN than OUT	Transactions capture, or data population
DSS	More data OUT than IN	Analysis, reporting, what if?

7.3.2 User interface (UI)

The user interface portion contains all the objects that directly interact with the end user of the application. These include objects such as windows, menus, and toolbars. The user interface objects must not contain any other partition's logic, but delegate the processing by sending a message to the appropriate service in the other partition.

7.3.3 Problem domain (PD)

The problem domain contains all the classes and objects that provide specific business-related functionality, also known as business rules or business logic. Many companies have passed through the information realization age, which is the recognition of just how valuable the information that is stored in databases is, into the age of wondering how to keep control over, and keep benefiting from, this increasing amount of information.

Business rules are here, with a positive force for our applications, because:

- End users can easily relate to them.

- Data, process, and object-oriented developers can easily relate to them.

- They focus energy on maintaining data quality.

You can measure your organization's acceptance of business rules as valid components of an information system by comparing your situation to each of the following stages:

Stage 1. The organization has no awareness or recognition of business rules as such. The company is aware of only two components of application: data and process. At best, you might hear that the process component does something to process the data.

Stage 2. Some developers appreciate the business rule component, which is more stable than the process component and less stable than the data component—for example, DBAs implementing stored procedures and triggers to protect data by enforcing business rules or logic.

Stage 3. The business rules exist primarily for businesspeople and secondarily for programmers and database designers, but are independent of any programming language or modeling technique.

Stage 4. The business rules move up from the departmental level and are considered and discussed at the company-wide or enterprise level.

Stage 5. The business rules are considered a business asset, where they are used to shape organizational behavior, instigate change, serve customers, and compete creatively. This level of business rules is the responsibility of companies leaders and visionaries, and can be used to create and reward productivity and prevent ineffective behavior.

Most problem domain objects relate to real-world objects, such as an order, client, or manufactured component. They are implemented without any visual component, so they can work independently of the presentation layer.

7.3.4 Data and system management (DASM)

The data and system management portion contains the objects used to handle database or system-related services or tasks, such as printing, file access, and security. If one of the system management classes needs to display information to the user or obtain information related to the problem domain, it should message the appropriate class or object in the presentation partition via the problem domain partition.

You can measure your organization's acceptance of data as a valid component of an information system by comparing your situation to each of the following stages:

Stage 1. There is no awareness of data as an asset. A system is considered to be just a process or procedural. The systems process something, which just happens to be data.

Stage 2. The company formally recognizes two components: the data component as well as the process component. System developers see physical data structures as separate from the procedures, or programs, that access and manipulate them.

Stage 3. The company is conscious that the business semantics of the data are important, and recognizes a need to present and capture data in the same way across various projects.

Stage 4. The company moves its focus from a departmental approach to data awareness to a company-wide or enterprise level.

Stage 5. Data is considered a business asset, where it must be shared and leveraged throughout the enterprise. The quality and availability of the data becomes a enterprise business issue rather than a centralized IS responsibility.

7.3.5 Partitioning the batch portion

Although the batch portion of a system is less complex, it still requires some attention with respect to the partitions. Consider the following areas of the batch system:

Batch interface (BI)
- Scheduling packages (CRON, NT, 95)
- Program parameters (including input files)

Batch problem domain (BPD)

- Standard business processing modules
- Common file layouts

Batch system management (BSM)

- File/system I/O modules
- Database processing modules

Using client/server and object-oriented technology requires some understanding of the technical details, but it also requires an appreciation of the way these technologies affect the whole organization. Reuse and library management has perhaps the greatest affect on the corporate culture, which will most likely result in a flexible, reliable, high-quality software with reduced ongoing maintenance costs.

Administration Utilities

In this chapter we will discuss some of the utilities provided by Informix On-Line. These utilities will allow you to perform routine administrative duties, which are a necessary function of day-to-day operations. The functions they perform include startup, shutdown, backup, restore, monitoring, error recovery, and performance.

8.1 Oncheck: Check, Repair, or Display

By using the various options provided by the oncheck utility, you can examine specified disk structures for inconsistencies, repair index structures that contain inconsistencies, and display information about the disk structures that are part of your database. By using oncheck, you can find background information on the various disk structures managed by Informix OnLine.

8.1.1 Check and repair options

When it comes to repairs, oncheck can be used only to repair indexes. Should oncheck detect any inconsistencies in another type of structure, it will issue a message notifying you of the inconsistency, but oncheck will not resolve the problem. In addition, oncheck will repair only attached indexes—those indexes created without a distribution scheme. The oncheck utility will not repair detached indexes; these indexes are created with a distribution scheme for the index keys and a set of dbspaces that contain the fragments. When oncheck detects an inconsistency in a detached or fragmented index, it displays a message similar to the following:

```
Please Drop and Recreate Index index_name for table_name
```

TABLE 8.1

Object	Check	Repair	Display
Blobspace blobs			–pB
Chunks and extents	–ce		–pe
Data rows, no blobs	–cd		–pd
Data rows, blob pages	–cD		–pD
Index (key values)	–ci	–ci –y –pk –y	–pk
Index (keys plus row IDs)	–cI	–cI –y –pK –y	–pK
Index (leaf key values)		–pl –y	–pl
Index (leaf keys plus rowids)		–pL –y	–pL
Pages (by table of fragment)			–pp
Pages (by chunk)			–pP
Root reserved pages	–cr		–pr
Space usage (by table or fragment)			–pt
Space usage (by table, with indexes)			–pT
System catalog tables	–cc		

Any user can execute oncheck by using the check options, but only users with the ID of "informix" or "root" can display database data or perform index repairs.

8.1.2 Oncheck option descriptions

The options used in the execution of oncheck fall into three categories: display, check, and repair. Table 8.1 lists the options that can be used with the oncheck utility.

The various display options, which start with –p, function in the same manner as the check options, which start with –c, but the display options provide additional information about the data being checked as the oncheck utility executes. In general, the –c options check for consistency and will display a message on your screen only if an error or inconsistency is found.

8.1.3 Locks and oncheck

The oncheck utility places a shared lock on tables when it checks indexes. It also places a shared lock on system catalog tables when they are checked. It places an exclusive lock on a table when it repairs an index.

When oncheck checks the consistency of an index, it locks the associated table in shared mode. However, if you indicate that oncheck is to repair an index with the –y option, oncheck will place an exclusive lock on the associated table.

8.1.4 Execution options

You can execute the oncheck utility with the options described in the following sections.

8.1.4.1 Checking system catalog tables with the –cc option

The –cc option checks each of the system catalog tables for the specified database. If the database is omitted, all system catalog tables for all databases will be checked. Before you execute oncheck, execute the SQL statement UPDATE STATISTICS to ensure that an accurate check occurs.

To check a table, oncheck compares each system catalog table to its corresponding entry in the tblspace. The –pc option performs the same checks and also displays the system catalog information as it checks it, including extent use for each table.

```
% oncheck -cc
% oncheck -cc warehous
```

8.1.4.2 Checking pages with the –cd and –cD options

The –cd option reads all nonblob pages from the tblspace for the specified database, table, or fragment and checks each page for consistency. Entries in the bitmap page are checked against the pages to verify mapping. It is important to note that oncheck will not repair bitmap pages if they have errors; it will only notify you of the problem in this case.

If the database contains fragmented tables and you do not specify a fragment, all fragments in the table will be checked. If a table is not specified, all tables in the database are checked. (The –pd option displays a hexadecimal dump of specified pages, but does not check for consistency.)

The –cD option performs the same checks as –cd, but includes dbspace blob pages if any exist. To monitor blobspace blobpages, refer to oncheck –pB, later in this chapter.

```
% oncheck -cD warehous:catalog
```

In oncheck finds an inconsistency, a message similar to the following will be displayed:

```
BAD PAGE 20001c:pg_addr 20001c != bp-. bf_pagenum 200045
```

If no inconsistencies are found, oncheck will display a header, similar to the following example, for each table it checks:

```
TBLSPACE data check for warehous:order_history
```

The oncheck utility will display a header similar to the following example for fragmented tables, one per fragment:

```
TBLSPACE data check for warehous:informix.tabl
Table fragment in DBspace dbl
```

If you specify a single fragment, oncheck will display a single header for that fragment. The oncheck utility locks each table as its indexes are checked for both the –cd and –cD options.

8.1.4.3 Checking the chunk-free list with the –ce option

The -ce option checks each chunk-free list and corresponding free space, and each tblspace extent. The oncheck process verifies that the extents on disk correspond to the current control information describing them. The –pe option performs the same checks and also displays the chunk and tblspace extent information as it checks it.

```
% oncheck -ce
```

8.1.4.4 Checking index-node links with the –ci and –cI options

The –ci option checks the ordering of key values and the consistency of horizontal and vertical node links for all indexes associated with the specified table. If an index is not specified, all indexes will be checked. If a table is not specified, all tables in the database will be checked.

If inconsistencies are detected, you'll be prompted for confirmation to repair the problem index. If you specify the –y (yes) option, indexes will automatically be repaired. If you specify the –n (no) option, the problem will be reported but not repaired. No prompting occurs. If oncheck does not find inconsistencies, the only message displayed will be the following:

```
validating indexes
```

The message will be followed by the names of the indexes that oncheck is checking. Be aware that index rebuilding can be time-consuming if you use oncheck. Processing is usually faster if you use the DROP INDEX and CREATE INDEX SQL statements to drop the index and re-create it.

The –cI option performs the same checks as –ci, but also checks that the key value tied to a row ID in an index is the same as the key value in the row. The same –ci repair options are available with –cI. The following example checks all indexes on the order_history table:

```
% oncheck -cI -n warehous:order_history
```

The following example checks the index sku on the order_history table:

```
% oncheck -cI -n warehous:order_history#sku
```

The oncheck utility locks each table as its indexes are checked for both the -ci and –cI options.

8.1.4.5 Checking reserved pages with the –cr option

The –cr option checks each of the root dbspace reserved pages, as follows:

- It validates the contents of the $INFORMIXDIR/etc./$ONCONFIG file with the PAGE_CONFIG reserved page.

- It ensures that all chunks can be opened, that chunks do not overlap, and that the chunk sizes are correct.

- It checks all logical-log and physical-log pages for consistency.

If you have changed the value of a configuration parameter and have not yet reinitialized shared memory, oncheck –cr will detect the inconsistency and return an error message. The –pr option performs the same checks and also displays the reserved-page information as it checks the reserved pages.

```
% oncheck -cr
```

If oncheck –cr does not display any error messages after you execute it, you can assume that all three items in the preceding bulleted list were checked successfully.

8.1.4.6 Indicating no repair with the –n option
The –n option is used with the index repair options (–ci, –cI, –pk, –pK, –pK, –pl, and –pL) to indicate that no repair should be performed, even if errors are detected.

8.1.4.7 Displaying blobspace statistics with the –pB option
The –pB option displays statistics that describe the average fullness of blobspace blobpages in a specified table. These statistics provide a measure of storage efficiency for individual blobs in a database or table. If a table or fragment is not specified, statistics will be displayed for the entire database.

```
% oncheck -pB photo_base:photos
```

8.1.4.8 Displaying system catalog information with the –pc option
The –pc option performs the same checks as the –cc option. In addition, –pc displays the system catalog information as it checks it, including extent use for each table.

```
% oncheck -pc
```

Displaying rows in hexadecimal format with the –pd and –pD options
The –pd option takes a database, a table, a fragment, and a specific row ID or tblspace number and logical page number as input. In every case, –pd prints page header information and displays the specified rows for the database object (database, table, fragment, row ID, or page number) you specify in hexadecimal and ASCII format. No checks for consistency are performed.

- If you specify a row ID (expressed as a hexadecimal value), the row ID will map to a particular page and all rows from that page will be printed.

- If you specify a logical page number (expressed as a decimal), all the rows of the tblspace number with the logical page number will be printed.

- If you specify a fragment, all the rows in the fragment will be printed, with their row IDs, forward pointers, and page type.

- If you specify a table, all the rows in the table will be printed, with their row IDs, forward pointers, and page type.

- If you specify a database, all the rows in all the tables in the database will be printed. Blob descriptors stored in the data row will be printed, but the actual blob data won't.

The –pD option prints the same information as –pd. In addition, –pD prints blob values that are stored in the tblspace or blob-header information for blobs stored in a blobspace blobpage.

```
% oncheck -pd warehous:order_history,frgmnt1
% oncheck -pd warehous:order_history
% oncheck -pD warehous:order_history 0x101
```

8.1.4.10 Displaying chunk and extent information with the –pe option
The –pe option performs the same checks as the –ce option. In addition, –pe displays the chunk and tblspace extent information as it checks it.

```
% oncheck -pe
```

8.1.4.11 Displaying index information with the –pk, –pK, –pl, and –pL options
For each of the following execution options, you can also perform repairs by executing with them with the –y option. The –pk option performs the same checks as the –ci option. In addition, –pk displays the key values for all indexes on the specified table as it checks them.

The –pK option performs the same checks as the –cI option. The –pK option displays the key values and row IDs as it checks them. The –pl option performs the same checks as the –ci option and displays the key values, but only leaf-node index pages are checked. The root and branch-node pages are ignored. The pL option performs the same checks as the –cI option and displays the key values and row IDs, but only for leaf-node index pages. The root and branch-node pages are ignored.

```
% oncheck -pk -n warehous,order_history
```

The following example displays information on all indexes on the order_history table:

```
% oncheck -pl -n warehous:order_history
```

The following example displays information about the index sku, which was created on the order_history table:

```
% oncheck -pl -n warehous:order_history#sku
```

8.1.4.12 Displaying contents of a logical page with the –pp and –pP options

The –pp option requires either of the following values for input:

- A table name and a row ID. If the table you want to check is fragmented, you must also supply the name of the dbspace in which the fragment is located.

- A tblspace number and logical page number.

Use the –pp option to dump the contents of the logical page number contained in the row ID. The page contents appear in ASCII format. The display also includes the number of slot-table entries on the page.

To obtain the row ID of a specific data row, use oncheck –PD. The –pP option provides the same information as the -pp option, but requires a chunk number and logical page number as input.

```
% oncheck -pp warehous:order_history,frag_dbspcel 0x211
% oncheck -pp warehous:back_stock 0x211
% oncheck -pP 0x100000a 25
% oncheck -pP 3 15
```

8.1.4.13 Displaying reserved-page information with the –pr option

The –pr option performs the same checks as the –cr option. In addition, –pr displays the reserved-page information as it checks the reserved pages. Reserved pages are the first 12 pages of the initial chunk of the root dbspace. The contents of each reserved page provides OnLine with specific control and tracking information.

```
% oncheck -pr
```

If you have changed the value of a configuration parameter and not yet reinitialized shared memory, oncheck –cr will detect the inconsistency, print both values, and display an error message.

Displaying tblspace information for a particular table or fragment with the –pt and –pT options

The –pt option prints a tblspace report for a given table or fragment whose name and database you specify when you execute oncheck at the command line. The report contains general allocation information including the maximum row size, number of keys, number of extents and their sizes, pages allocated and used per extent, current serial value, and date the table was created. The Extents fields lists the physical address for the tablspace (tblspace) entry for the table, and the address of the first page of the first extent. If a table is not specified, this information will be displayed for all tables in the database.

The –pT option prints the same information as the –pt option. In addition, –pT displays index-specific information and page-allocation information by page type (for dbspaces).

Output for both –pt and –pT contains listings for the number of pages used. The value shown in the output for this field is never decremented because the disk space allocated to a tblspace as part of an extent remains dedicated to that extent, even after you free the space by deleting rows. For an accurate count of the number of pages currently used, refer to the detailed information on tblspace use (organized by page type) that the –pT option provides.

```
% oncheck -pT warehous:order_history
```

8.1.4.14 Suppressing checking and validation messages with the –q option
The –q option suppresses all checking and validation messages. Only error messages are displayed if the –q option is invoked.

```
% oncheck -cc -q
```

8.1.4.15 Repairing indexes when needed with the –y option
Use the –y option with the index-repair options (–ci, –cI, –pk, –pK, –pl, and –pL) to indicate that oncheck should repair any index where errors are detected.

```
% oncheck -cI -y warehous:order_history
```

8.2 Oninit: Initializing Online

Executing oninit from the command line initializes OnLine shared memory and brings OnLine online.

Before you initialize OnLine, consider setting the INFORMIXSERVER environment variable to the dbservername you chose when you set the configuration parameter DBSERVERNAME. Strictly speaking, INFORMIXSERVER is not required for initialization. However, if INFORMIXSERVER is not set, OnLine will not build the sysmaster tables. In addition, INFORMIXSERVER is required when using the ON-Monitor and DB-Access utilities.

If you use specific options when executing oninit, you can also initialize disk space. You must be logged in as "root" or "informix" to execute oninit.

8.2.1 Initializing shared memory only

OnLine should be in offline mode when you initialize shared memory. You can make it offline by using the onmode utility, described later in this chapter.

8.2.1.1 Initializing shared memory with no options
If you execute oninit without options, OnLine will be left in online mode after shared memory is initialized. For example, the following commands take OnLine offline and then reinitialize shared memory:

```
% onmode -ky
% oninit
```

8.2.1.2 Initializing shared memory with the –p option
The –p option directs oninit not to search for (and delete) temporary tables. If you use this option, OnLine will return to online mode more rapidly, but the space used by temporary tables left on disk is not reclaimed.

8.2.1.3 Initializing shared memory with the –s option
The –s option initializes shared memory and leaves OnLine in quiescent mode. The following commands take OnLine offline, then reinitialize shared memory and leave OnLine in quiescent mode:

```
% onmode -ky
% oninit -s
```

8.2.2 Initializing disk space and shared memory

When using the –i option of oninit, you should be especially careful. This option will initialize your disk space, and destroy all data currently managed by your OnLine database server. OnLine must be offline when you initialize disk space.

8.2.2.1 Initializing disk space and shared memory with the –i option
If you use only the –i option, OnLine will initialize disk space and shared memory. The –i option leaves OnLine in online mode after initializing the disk space.

8.2.2.2 Initializing disk space and shared memory with the –s option
If you use the –i and –s options, OnLine will be left in quiescent mode after disk initialization.

8.3 Onload: Creating a Database or Table

The onload utility creates a database or table in a specified dbspace and loads it with data from an input tape or disk file created by the onunload utility. The onunload utility is discussed later in this chapter. During the loading process, you can move blobs stored in one blobspace to another blobspace.

8.3.1 Onload parameters

You can execute the onload utility in the following format:

```
onload [source parameters] [create options] database [:owner.table]
```

When you execute onload without specifying any source parameter options, onload uses the device specified as TAPEDEV in your ONCONFIG file. The block size and tape size are the values specified as TAPEBLK and TAPESIZE, respectively.

When you execute onload without specifying any creation options, onload stores the database or table in the root dbspace.

8.3.2 Source parameter options

The –l option tells onload to retrieve the values for tape device, block size, and tape size from the configuration parameters LTAPEDEV, LTAPEBLK, and LTAPESIZE, respectively.

To override LTAPEDEV, LTAPEBLK, or LTAPESIZE, you can specify the –l option, and optionally –b, –s, or –t. The value(s) you specify will override the value(s) contained in the configuration file, for example:

```
onload -l -b blocksize -s tapesize -t input_source
```

where the values for blocksize, tapesize, and input_source must conform to the descriptions in Table 8.2.

8.3.3 Creating option parameters

As an extension to the onload parameters, you can also supply create options, which direct the onload utility to store the output into a specific dbspace or re-name a table index, for example:

```
onload -l -d dbspace
```

TABLE 8.2

Parameter Options	Function	Restrictions	Syntax
blocksize	Specifies in kilobytes the block size of the tape device. This option overrides the default value in TAPEBLK or LTAPEBLK.	Must specify the block size of the tape device.	Unsigned integer
tapesize	Specifies in kilobytes the amount of data that OnLine can store on the tape. This option overrides the default value in TAPE SIZE or LTAPESIEZE.	Must specify the amount of data that OnLine can store on the tape.	Unsigned integer
input_source	Specifies the fully qualified pathname of the file on disk or of the tape device where the input tape is mounted. This option overrides the tape device specified by TAPEDEV or LTAPEDEV.	Must be a legal pathname.	This parameter is site-specific and you should refer to your system documentation.

TABLE 8.3

Parameter options	Function	Restrictions	Syntax
dbspace	Specifies the dbspace where the database or table will be stored.	The dspace must exist.	The dbspace name
oldindex newindex	Directs onload to rename the table index when it stores the index on disk. Use the –i option to rename indexes during the load to avoid conflict with existing index names.	You must specify a table name in the command line.	Identifier segment

or

```
onload -l -i oldindex newindex
```

where dbspace and oldindex newindex take on the values as described in Table 8.3. When you execute onload without specifying any create options, the onload utility stores the database or table in the root dbspace.

8.3.4 Restrictions that affect the usage of onload and onunload

The original database and target database must be from the same release level of OnLine. You cannot use onunload/onload to move data from one release level to another.

The tape that onload reads contains binary data stored in disk-page-sized units. For this reason, the computer receiving the data and the computer that creates the tape must share the same OnLine page size. The two computers must also have the same byte alignment on structures and unions.

The onunload utility can unload data more quickly than either dbexport or the UNLOAD command because it copies data in binary and in page-sized units. However, this places the following restrictions on its use:

- You must load the data on the onunload tape into a database or table managed by OnLine.
- When you unload a complete database, you cannot modify the ownership of database objects (such as tables, indexes, and views) until you have completely reloaded the database.
- You must load the tape written by onunload onto a computer with the same page size and representation of numeric data as the original computer.
- Onunload does not preserve the access privileges defined on the original tables.
- Onunload does not preserve the synonyms defined on the original tables.

The onload utility performs faster than the dbimport, dbload, or LOAD options. In exchange for this higher performance, the following five restrictions exist:

- Onload will create only a new database or table; you must drop or rename an existing database or table of the same name before you can run onload. (Onload will prompt you to rename blobspaces during execution, if necessary.)

- Onload locks the database or table exclusively during the load.

- When you load a complete database, the user executing onload becomes the owner of the database.

- Onload creates a database without logging; you must initiate logging after onload has completed loading the database.

- When you use onload to load a table into a logged database, you must turn off logging for the database during the operation.

8.3.5 Logging when using onload

The onload utility performs all its loading within a transaction. This allows the changes to be rolled back if an error occurs.

When you use onload to create tables from an onunload input tape, onload can only load information into a database without logging. Thus, before you load a table into an existing, logged database, end logging for the database. You also might want to consider loading during off-peak hours. Otherwise, you might fill the logical-log files or consume excessive shared-memory resources. After you load the table, create a level-0 archive before you resume database logging.

When you use onload to create databases from an onunload input tape, the databases that result are not ANSI-compliant and do not use transaction logging. You can make the database ANSI-compliant or add logging after you load the database. To make your database ANSI-compliant, you must use different commands for your database, which is dependent on whether or not you are using transaction logging.

If you have a database called warehous, which is currently using transaction logging, execute the following command:

```
% ontape -A warehous
```

If you have a database called warehous, which does not use transaction logging, execute the following command:

```
% ontape -s -A warehous
```

In addition to making the database ANSI-compliant, this command will also create an archive. When you are prompted, you must specify a level-0 archive.

8.3.6 Relocating blobspace blobs

If you load a table that contains blobs stored in a blobspace, onload will ask you if you want to move the blobs to another blobspace. If you respond "yes," onload will display the blobspace name where the blobs were stored when the tape was created. It will then ask you to enter the name of the blobspace where you want the blobs stored. If you enter a valid blobspace name, onload will move all blob columns in the table to the new blobspace. Otherwise, you will be prompted again for a valid blobspace name.

8.3.6.1 Ownership and privileges

When you load a new database, the user who runs onload becomes the owner. Ownership within the database (tables, views, and indexes) remains the same as when the database was unloaded to tape with onunload.

To load a table, you must have resource privilege on the database. When onload loads a new table, the user who runs onload becomes the owner unless you specify an owner in the table name. (To perform this function, a DBA privilege for the database is required.)

The onunload utility does not preserve synonyms or access privileges. To obtain a listing of defined synonyms or access privileges, use the dbschema utility.

8.3.6.2 Exclusive locks

During the load operation, onload places an exclusive lock on the new database or table. Loading proceeds as a single transaction, and onload drops the new database or table if an error or system failure occurs.

8.4 Onlog: Displaying Logical-Log Contents

The onlog utility displays the contents of an OnLine logical-log file, either on disk or on a backup tape created by ontape. The onlog output is most useful in debugging situations, when you want to track a specific transaction or see what changes have been made to a specific tblspace. Any user can run onlog. If OnLine is in offline mode when you execute onlog, only the files on disk will be read. If OnLine is in quiescent or online mode, onlog will also read the logical-log records stored in the logical-log buffers in shared memory after it has read all records on disk.

When reading a log file with status U (unreleased) from disk while in online mode, OnLine denies all access to the logical-log files, effectively stopping database activity for all sessions. If at all possible, you should wait to read the contents of the logical-log files after the files are backed up, and then read the files from tape.

8.4.1 Onlog syntax

The output produced by the onlog utility is controlled by two parameter sets called filters. These filters fall into two different classes: read and display. If you want to use onlog's output as input to a report writer, you can use the –q option to suppress the initial header and the one-line header that appears every 18 records by default.

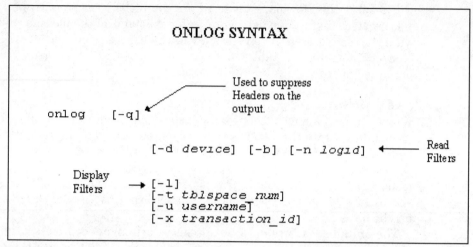

Figure 8.1

8.4.1.1 Read filters
The onlog read filters allow you to read the following portions of the logical log as it searches for records to include in the output display:

- Records stored on disk.
- Records stored on tapes created by ontape.
- Records from the specified logical-log file.

By default, onlog displays the logical-log record header, which describes the transaction number and the record type. The record type identifies the type of operation performed. In addition to the header, you can use the read filters to direct onlog to display the following information:

- Copies of blobpages from blobspaces (copied from the logical-log backup tape only, not available from disk).
- Logical-log record header and data (including copies of blobs stored in a dbspace).

8.4.1.2 Display filters
You can display every logical-log record header or you can limit the output based on the following criteria:

- Records associated with a specific table.
- Records initiated by a specific user.
- Records associated with a specific transaction.

8.4.1.3 Error detection

If onlog detects an error in the log file, such as an unrecognizable log type, it will display the entire log page in hexadecimal format and terminate.

8.4.2 Log-record read filters

The read filters use the following parameters to control input to the onlog utility.

8.4.2.1 Displaying blobpage logical-log records with the –b option

The –b option directs onlog to display logical-log records associated with blobspace blobpages. OnLine stores these records on the logical-log backup tape as part of blobspace logging.

8.4.2.2 Specifying the pathname of your tape device with the –d option

The –d option names the pathname of the tape device where the logical-log backup tape whose contents you want to display are mounted. If you do not use the –d option, onlog will read the logical-log files stored on disk, starting with the logical-log file with the lowest log ID.

8.4.2.3 Displaying logical-log records from a single log file with the –n option

The –n option directs onlog to read only the logical-log records contained in the log file you specify using log ID. If you do not use the –n option, onlog will read all logical-log files available (either on disk or on tape created by ontape).

The onlog utility uses the pathnames stored in the root dbspace reserved pages to locate the logical-log files.

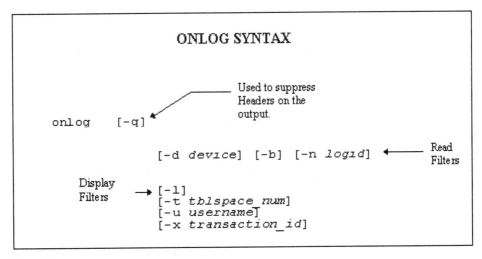

Figure 8.2

TABLE 8.4

Parameter options	Function	Restrictions	Syntax
device	Specifies the pathname tape device where the logical-log backup tape created by ontape is mounted.	The device you name must be the same as the pathname of the device assigned to the configuration parameter LTAPEDEV.	Pathname must be the fully qualified device pathname.
logid	Specifies the identifier assigned by OnLine to each logical-log file.	Value must be an unsigned integer between 3 and the value assigned to the configuration parameter LOGMAX.	Unsigned integer

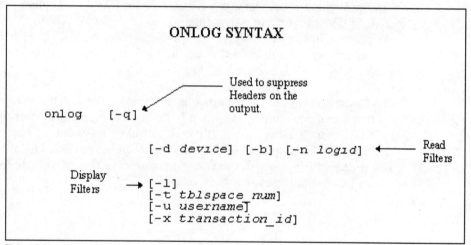

Figure 8.3

8.4.3 Log-record display filters

For clarity, Figure 8.3 shows the diagram of onlog's syntax. Table 8.5 outlines the function of each parameter and the restrictions for usage.

If no options are specified, onlog will display a short listing of all the records in the log. You can combine options with any other options to produce more selective filters. For example, if you use both the –u and –x options, only activities initiated by the specified user during the specified transaction will be displayed. If you use both the –u and –t options, only the activities initiated by the specified user and associated with the specified tblspace will be displayed.

8.4.3.1 Displaying the long listing of logical-log records with the –l option

The –l option directs onlog to display the long listing of the logical-log records. The long listing of a log record includes a rather difficult-to-understand hexadecimal and ASCII dump of the entire log record. This form of the display is not intended for the casual user.

TABLE 8.5

Parameter options	Function	Restrictions	Syntax
tblspace_num	Specifies the tblspace number of a table whose records you want to display. To determine the tblspace number of a particular tblspace, query the systables system catalog table.	Numbers greater than 0 must be contained in the partnum column of the systables system catalog table. Can be specified as either an integer or hexa-decimal value. (If you do not use an 0x prefix, the value is interpreted as an integer.)	Unsigned integer
transaction_id	Specifies the transaction ID of a particular trans-action.	An integer between 0 and TRANSACTIONS −1, inclusive.	Unsigned integer
username	Specifies the login name of the user whose records you want to display.	Must be an existing login name.	User name must conform to operating-system-specific rules for login name.

8.4.3.2 Determining a transaction ID with the –x option

The –x option directs onlog to display only records associated with the transaction you specify. You should need to use the –x option only in the unlikely case that an error is generated during a roll forward. When this occurs, OnLine sends a message to the message log that includes the transaction ID of the offending transaction. You can use this transaction ID with the –x option of onlog to further investigate the cause of the error.

8.5 Onparams: Modifying Log-Configuration Parameters

You can use the onparams utility to perform three basic functions. Depending upon which execution options you select, it will perform one of the following operations:

- Add a logical-log file.
- Drop a logical-log file.
- Change the size or location of the physical log.

Note that OnLine must be in quiescent mode, and you must be logged in as "root" or "informix" to execute onparams.

8.5.1 Automatic response

The –y option causes OnLine to automatically respond "yes" to all prompts. Any onparams command will fail if an OnLine archive is in progress. If no options are specified, onparams will return a usage statement.

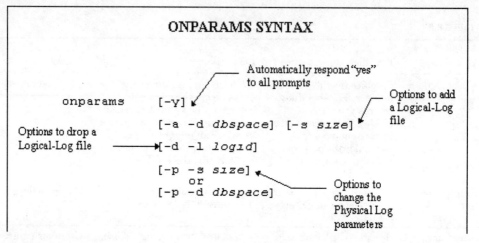

Figure 8.4

TABLE 8.6

Parameter options	Function	Restrictions	Syntax
dbspace	Names the dbspace where the logical-log file will reside.	The space allocated for a logical-log file must be contiguous. OnLine does not allow you to add a log file to a dbspace without adequate contiguous space. You cannot add a log file during an archive (quiescent or online).	Identifier segment
size	Indicates the size of the new logical-log file, in kilobytes.	Value must be greater than or equal to the minimum of 200 kilobytes. If you do not specify a size with the -s option, the size of the log file is taken from the value of the LOGSIZE parameter in the ONCONFIG file when OnLine disk space was initialized.	Unsigned integer

8.5.2 Adding a logical-log file

To add a logical-log file, execute onparams using the following format:

```
onparams -a -d dbspace [-s size]
```

Where the values of dbspace and size are supplied as described in Table 8.6.

The −a option adds a logical-log file in the dbspace specified in the metavariable dbspace. The newly added log file or files retain a status of A and do not become available until you create a level-0 archive. If you use ON_Archive as your backup tool, you only need to create a level-0 archive of the root dbspace for the log file to become available.

The −d followed by dbspace is required when adding a new logical-log file. Optionally you can use −s, followed by the size in kilobytes, to make the new logical-log file a specific size.

Using the –a option of onparams to add a logical-log file is one of the steps in the procedure for moving logical-log files to another dbspace.

8.5.3 Dropping a logical-log file

To drop a logical-log file, execute onparams with the following format:

```
onparams -d -l logid
```

Where the value of logid is supplied as described in Table 8.7.

The –d option of onparams allows you to drop a logical-log file. You specify which logical-log file you want to drop by using –l followed by a log ID. (You can obtain the log ID of a logical log from the number field of onstat –l.) After your configuration reflects the desired number of log files, create a level-0 archive. If you use ON-Archive as your backup tool, you need to create only a level-0 archive of the root dbspace.

The onparams command to drop a logical-log file is one of the steps in the procedure for moving logical-log files to another dbspace.

8.5.4 Changing physical-log size or location

To change the size or location of a physical-log file, execute onparams with the following format:

```
onparams -p -d dbspace (to change the physical location)
onparams -p -s size (to change the physical size)
```

Where the values of dbspace and size are supplied as described in Table 8.8.

Use the –p option to change the location or size of the physical log. Note: If you move the log to a dbspace without adequate contiguous space, or increase the log size beyond the available contiguous space, a fatal shared-memory error will occur when you attempt to reinitialize shared memory with the new value.

TABLE 8.7

Parameter options	Function	Restrictions	Syntax
logid	Names the logical-log file to be dropped.	Value must be an unsigned integer greater than or equal to 0. OnLine requires a minimum of three logical-log files at all times. You cannot drop a log file if OnLine is configured for three logical-log files. OnLine must be in quiescent mode before you drop a logical log. You drop log files one at a time. You can drop only a log file that has a status of free (F) or newly added (A). Use onstat -1 to view the status of your logical logs.	Unsigned integer

TABLE 8.8

Parameter options	Function	Restrictions	Syntax
dbspace	Names the dbspace where the physical log will reside.	The space allocated for the physical log must be contiguous.	Identifier segment
size	Indicates the size of the physical log in kilobytes.	Value must be greater than or equal to the minimum of 200 kilobytes.	Unsigned integer

To change the size of the physical log, use the −s option followed by a size in kilobytes. To change the location of the physical log, use the −d option followed by a dbspace that is the new location for the physical log.

Changes to the physical log do not take effect until you reinitialize shared memory. To immediately reinitialize shared memory, execute the command with the −y option.

Note: Create a level-0 archive immediately after you reinitialize shared memory. This archive is crucial for proper OnLine recovery. If you use ON-Archive as your backup tool, you need to create only a level-0 archive of the root dbspace.

If you move the log to a dbspace without adequate contiguous space, a fatal shared-memory error will occur when you attempt to reinitialize shared memory with the new value.

8.6 Onspaces: Modifying Blobspaces or Dbspaces

The onspaces utility allows you to perform the following functions:

- Create a blobspace, dbspace, or temporary dbspace.
- Drop a blobspace or dbspace.
- Add a chunk.
- Drop an empty chunk.
- Start mirroring.
- End mirroring.
- Change chunk status.
- Set the DATASKIP parameter.

To perform these functions, you must be logged in as "root" or "informix."

8.6.1 Onspaces syntax

In addition to the parameters in Figure 8.5, you can use the −y option, which instructs OnLine to respond "yes" to all prompts.

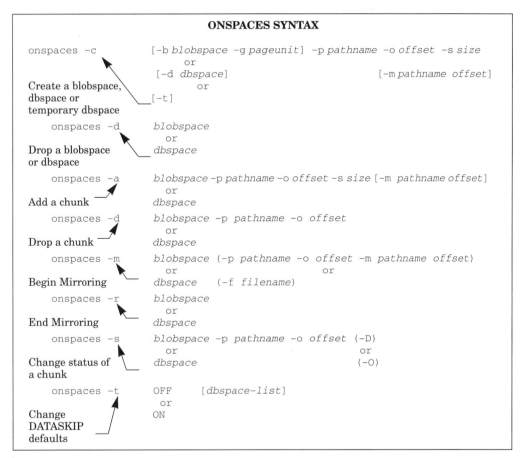

ONSPACES SYNTAX

```
onspaces -c        [-b blobspace -g pageunit] -p pathname -o offset -s size
                                     or
                   [-d dbspace]                              [-m pathname offset]
Create a blobspace,                  or
dbspace or         [-t]
temporary dbspace

   onspaces -d     blobspace
                        or
Drop a blobspace   dbspace
or dbspace

   onspaces -a     blobspace -p pathname -o offset -s size [-m pathname offset]
                        or
Add a chunk        dbspace

   onspaces -d     blobspace -p pathname -o offset
                        or
Drop a chunk       dbspace

   onspaces -m     blobspace (-p pathname -o offset -m pathname offset)
                        or                           or
Begin Mirroring    dbspace    (-f filename)

   onspaces -r     blobspace
                        or
End Mirroring      dbspace

   onspaces -s     blobspace -p pathname -o offset (-D)
                        or                         or
Change status of   dbspace                         (-O)
a chunk

   onspaces -t     OFF      [dbspace-list]
                        or
Change             ON
DATASKIP
defaults
```

Figure 8.5

8.6.2 Creating a blobspace, dbspace, or temporary dbspace

To create a blobspace, dbspace, or temporary dbspace, execute onspaces using the following format:

```
onspaces -c [-b blobspace -g pageunit] -p pathname -o offset -s size
```

or:

```
[-d dbspace] [-p pathname -o offset -s size] or [-m pathname offset]
```

or:

```
[-t]
```

The –c option creates a nontemporary dbspace or blobspace.

8.6.2.1 Creating a temporary dbspace with the –t option

The –t option creates a temporary dbspace. Temporary dbspaces are reserved for the exclusive use of temporary tables. It is important to note that OnLine

TABLE 8.9

Parameter options	Function	Restrictions	Syntax
blobspace	Names the blobspace to be created.	Before creating a blobspace, you must first allocate a raw or cooked disk space. Verify that the number of dbspaces and blobspaces does not exceed the value you set for DBSPACES in your configuration parameters.	Identifier segment
dbspace	Names the dbspace to be created.	Verify that the number of dbspaces and blobspaces does not exceed the value you set for DBSPACES in your configuration parameters. Check with your system administrator to ensure that you are not using track zero on a particular disk. Use the fully qualified pathname. The device and slice or partition if *raw*, and the UFS filesystem name if cooked.	Identifier segment
offset	After the –d option, *offset* indicates, in kilobytes, the offset into the disk partition or into the device to reach the initial chunk of the new blobspace or dbspace. In case *offset* follows the –m option, it specifies the offset to reach the mirror chunk of the newly created dbspace or blobspace.	Value must be greater than 0. The offset has two purposes. It prevents OnLine from overwriting the UNIX partition information (especially important if you are using partition 0 on a disk). Another use of the offset is to allow you to define multiple chunks on a partition, disk device, or cooked file.	Unsigned integer
page_unit	Specifies the blobspace blobpage size in terms of page_unit, the number of disk pages per blobpage.	Value must be greater than zero. To determine the OnLine page size, you can use the oncheck utility with the –pr option to view the contents of PAGE_ZERO.	Unsigned integer
pathname	Indicates the disk partition or device of the initial chunk of the new blobspace or dbspace.	The chunk must be an existing raw device or cooked file. When specifying a pathname, you can use either a full pathname or a relative pathname. However, if you use a relative pathname, it must be relative to the directory that was the current directory when you initialized OnLine.	Pathname must be the fully qualified pathname (UFS filesystem) or device name (raw partition).
size	Indicates, in kilobytes, the size of the initial chunk of the new blobspace or dbspace.	Value must be greater than 0. Size must not exceed 2 gigabytes.	Unsigned integer

TABLE 8.10

Parameter options	Function	Restrictions	Syntax
blobspace	Names the blobspace to be dropped.	The paragraphs following this table describe the restrictions.	Identifier segment
dbspace	Names the dbspace to be dropped	The paragraphs following this table describe the restrictions.	Identifier segment

will never drop a temporary dbspace unless you explicitly ask that it be done. The reason these dbspaces are called temporary is because OnLine does not preserve the contents of the dbspace when it is shut down abnormally. When you initialize OnLine, all temporary dbspaces are reinitialized.

When you create a temporary dbspace using onspaces, OnLine will not use it until you perform the following steps:

1. Add the name of the temporary dbspace to your list of temporary dbspaces in the DBSPACETEMP configuration parameter or the DBSPACETEMP environment variable, or both.

2. Reinitialize OnLine.

8.6.2.2 Specifying a mirror chunk with the –m option
Use the –m option to specify an optional pathname and offset to the chunk that will mirror the initial chunk of the new blobspace or dbspace.

8.6.3 Dropping a blobspace or dbspace

To drop a blobspace or dbspace, execute onspaces using the following format:

```
onspaces -d (blobspace or dbspace) -p pathname -o offset
```

The –d option indicates that either a blobspace or a dbspace is to be dropped. Before you drop a dbspace, you must first drop all databases and tables that you previously created in the dbspace. Before dropping a blobspace, all tables that include a TEXT or BYTE column referencing the blobspace must be dropped. Execute oncheck –pe to verify that no table currently stores data in the blobspace or dbspace.

When you drop a blobspace, OnLine must be in quiescent mode. Note: Do not specify a pathname when you are dropping a dbspace or blobspace.

8.6.4 Adding a chunk

This action is performed when you need to increase the amount of disk space allocated to a dbspace or blobspace. To add a chunk, execute onspaces with the following format:

```
onspaces -a (blobspace or dbspace) -p pathname -o offset -s size [-m pathname
offset]
```

The –a option indicates that a chunk is to be added. Use the –m option to specify an optional pathname and offset to the chunk that will mirror the new chunk.

TABLE 8.11

Parameter options	Function	Restrictions	Syntax
blobspace	Names the blobspace to which you are adding a chunk.	Verify that you will not exceed the maximum amount of chunks for your configuration, the CHUNKS parameter in your ONCONFIG file. If the blobspace or dbspace is mirrored, you must also add a mirror chunk.	Identifier segment
dbspace	Names the dbspace to which you are adding a chunk.	Verify that you will not exceed the maximum amount of chunks for your configuration, the CHUNKS parameter in your ONCONFIG file. If the blobspace or dbspace is mirrored, you must also add a mirror chunk.	Identifier segment
offset	After the –a option, *offset* indicates, in kilobytes, the offset into the disk partition or into the device to reach the initial chunk of the new blobspace or dbspace. In case *offset* follows the –m option, it specifies the offset to reach the mirror chunk of the newly created dbspace or blobspace.	Value must be greater than 0. The offset has two purposes. It prevents OnLine from overwriting the UNIX partition information (especially important if you are using partition 0 on a disk). Another use of the offset is to allow you to define multiple chunks on a partition, disk device, or cooked file.	Unsigned integer
pathname	Indicates the disk partition or device of the initial chunk of the blobspace or dbspace you are adding.	The chunk must be an existing raw device or cooked file. When specifying a pathname, you can use either a full pathname or a relative pathname. However, if you use a relative pathname, it must be relative to the directory that was the current directory when you initialized OnLine.	Pathname must be the fully qualified pathname (UFS filesystem) or device name (raw partition).
size	Indicates, in kilobytes, the size of the initial chunk of the new blobspace or dbspace.	Value must be greater than 0. Size must not exceed 2 gigabytes.	Unsigned integer

TABLE 8.12

Parameter options	Function	Restrictions	Syntax
blobspace	Names the blobspace from which the chunk will be dropped.	OnLine must be in quiescent mode. All pages other than the overhead pages must be freed. The initial chunk of a blobspace cannot be dropped.	Identifier segment
dbspace	Names the dbspace from which the chunk will be dropped.	All pages other than the overhead pages must be freed. The initial chunk of a dbspace cannot be dropped. To determine the initial chunk of a dbspace use onstat –d and look at the fchunk column.	Identifier segment
pathname	Indicates the disk partition or device of the initial chunk of the blobspace or dbspace you are dropping.	The chunk must be an existing raw device or cooked file. When specifying a pathname, you can use either a full pathname or a relative pathname. However, if you use a relative pathname, it must be relative to the directory that was the current directory when you initialized OnLine.	Pathname must be the fully qualified pathname (UFS filesystem) or device name (raw partition).
offset	Indicates, in kilobytes, the offset into the disk partition or into the device to reach the initial chunk of the blobspace or dbspace you are dropping.	Value must be greater than 0. The offset has two purposes. It prevents OnLine from overwriting the UNIX partition information (especially important if you are using partition 0 on a disk). Another use of the offset is to allow you to define multiple chunks on a partition, disk device, or cooked file.	Unsigned integer

8.6.5 Dropping a chunk

Before you can begin this process, you must ensure that all pages other than the overhead pages are freed. If any pages are allocated, onspaces will return the following error message:

```
Chunk is not empty.
```

You can execute the oncheck utility with the –pe option to determine which On-Line entity is still using space within the chunk. To drop a chunk, execute onspaces with the following format:

```
onspaces -d (blobspace or dbspace) -p pathname -o offset
```

Use the –d option to drop a chunk. Note: You must specify a pathname to indicate to OnLine that you are dropping a chunk.

8.6.6 Beginning mirroring

To begin mirroring, you must create a mirror chunk for each primary chunk in a dbspace or blobspace. To perform this, you must specify a disk space that you

TABLE 8.13

Parameter options	Function	Restrictions	Syntax
blobspace	Names the blobspace that you want to mirror.	You are required to mirror an entire blobspace. OnLine does not permit you to select individual chunks within a blobspace. When you select a space to mirror, you must create mirror chunks for each chunk within the space.	Identifier segment
dbspace	Names the dbspace you want to mirror.	You are required to mirror an entire blobspace. OnLine does not permit you to select individual chunks within a blobspace. When you select a space to mirror, you must create mirror chunks for each chunk within the space.	Identifier segment
filename	Allows you to indicate to onspaces that chunk-location information is located in a file named *filename*.	The file must be an existing UNIX cooked file.	Pathname must be the fully qualified pathname (UFS filesystem) only.
offset	The first time *offset* occurs in the syntax diagram, it indicates, in kilobytes, the offset into the disk partition or into the device to reach the initial chunk of the newly mirrored blobspace of dbspace. The second time *offset* appears in the syntax diagram, it indicates the offset to reach the mirror chunk of the newly mirrored dbspace or blobspace.	Value must be greater than 0. The offset has two purposes. It prevents OnLine from overwriting the UNIX partition information (especially important if you are using partition 0 on a disk). Another use of the offset is to allow you to define multiple chunks on a partition, disk device, or cooked file.	Unsigned integer

TABLE 8.13   (Continued)

Parameter options	Function	Restrictions	Syntax
pathname	The first time *pathname* occurs in the syntax diagram, it indicates the disk partition or device of the initial chunk of the blobspace or dbspace you wish to mirror. The second time *pathname* occurs in the syntax diagram, it indicates the disk partition or device of the initial chunk of the blobspace or dbspace that performs the mirroring.	The chunk must be an existing raw device or cooked file. When specifying a pathname, you can use either a full pathname or a relative pathname. However, if you use a relative pathname, it must be relative to the directory that was the current directory when you initialized OnLine.	Pathname must be the fully qualified pathname (UFS filesystem) or device name (raw partition).

have already allocated. If your primary space is raw, then you should also make your mirror a raw device; alternately, if your primary space is a standard UNIX file system, then your mirror should also be a standard UNIX file system. To begin mirroring, execute onspaces using the following format:

```
onspaces -m (blobspace or dbspace) (-p pathname (-o offset or -f filename) -m
pathname offset)
```

Use the –m option to add mirroring for an existing dbspace or blobspace.

You can create a file that contains the chunk location information. Then, when you execute onspaces, use the –f option to indicate to OnLine that this information is contained in a file whose name you specify in the filename variable.

If the dbspace you are mirroring contains multiple chunks, you must specify a mirror chunk for each of the primary chunks in the dbspace you want to mirror. To mirror a dbspace that has multiple chunks, use the following syntax:

```
$ onspaces -m my_dbspace\
-p /dev/db_data1 -o 0 -m /dev/dbmirror_data1 0\
-p /dev/db_data2 -o 0 3000 -m /dev/dbmirror_data2 3000
```

where /dev/db_data1 and /dev/db_data2 are two chunks in my_dbspace.

8.6.7 Ending mirroring

When you end mirroring for a dbspace, OnLine will make the mirror chunks available immediately. You can reassign these chunks to another dbspace or blobspace. To perform this function, you must be user "root" or "informix." To end mirroring, execute onspaces using the following format:

```
onspaces -r (blobspace or dbspace)
```

TABLE 8.14

Parameter options	Function	Restrictions	Syntax
blobspace	Names the blobspace for which you want to end mirroring.	You cannot end mirroring if any of the primary chunks are down.	Identifier segment
dbspace	Names the dbspace for which you want to end mirroring.	You cannot end mirroring if any of the primary chunks are down.	Identifier segment

TABLE 8.15

Parameter options	Function	Restrictions	Syntax
blobspace	Names the blobspace whose status you want to change.	A chunk can be taken down or restored only if it is part of a mirrored pair. Optionally, you can take down a primary chunk or its mirror chunk, as long as the other chunk from the pair remains online.	Identifier segment
dbspace	Names the dbspace whose status you want to change.	A chunk can be taken down or restored only if it is part of a mirrored pair. Optionally, you can take down a primary chunk or its mirror chunk, as long as the other chunk from the pair remains online.	Identifier segment
offset	Indicates, in kilobytes, the offset into the disk partition or into the device to reach the chunk.	Value must be greater than 0. The offset has two purposes. It prevents OnLine from overwriting the UNIX partition information (especially important if you are using partition 0 on a disk). Another use of the offset is to allow you to define multiple chunks on a partition, disk device, or cooked file.	Unsigned integer
pathname	Indicates the disk partition or device of the chunk. The chunk can be a raw device or a cooked file in a standard UNIX file system.	When specifying a pathname, you can use either a full pathname or a relative pathname. However, if you use a relative pathname, it must be relative to the directory that was the current directory when you initialized OnLine.	Pathname must be the fully qualified pathname (UFS filesystem) or device name (raw partition).

Use the –r option to indicate to OnLine that mirroring should be ended for an existing dbspace or blobspace.

8.6.8 Changing the status of a mirrored chunk

To change the status of a mirrored chunk, execute onspaces with the following format:

```
onspaces -s (blobspace or dbspace) -p pathname -o offset ((-D) or (O))
```

TABLE 8.16

Parameter options	Function	Restrictions	Syntax
dbspace-list	Specifies the name of one or more dbspaces for which DATASKIP will be turned ON or OFF.	The configuration parameter can be set to OFF, ON, or ALL. If it is set to OFF, then OnLine will not skip any fragments. If a fragment is unavailable, then the query will return an error. ALL indicates that any unavailable fragment is skipped. ON followed by a specific dbspace(s) will skip any fragments located within the dbspace(s).	Identifier segment

Use the –s option to indicate to onspaces that you want to change the status of a chunk. Use the –D option to take the chunk down. Use the –O option to restore the chunk and bring it online. You can change the status of a chunk only in a mirrored pair.

8.6.9 Specifying the DATASKIP parameter

To control whether or not an unavailable fragment is skipped, the OnLine administrator can execute onspaces using the DATASKIP parameter. To use the DATASKIP option of onspaces, execute onspaces using the following format:

```
onspaces -f (OFF or ON) [dbspace-list]
```

The –f option allows you to indicate to OnLine that you want to change the DATASKIP default for specified dbspaces. The onspaces utility allows you to specify DATASKIP on a dbspace level or across all dbspaces.

If you use OFF (or ON) without a dbspace list, then DATASKIP will be turned OFF (or ON) for all fragments. If OFF (or ON) is used with a dbspace list, then only the specified fragments will be set with DATASKIP OFF (or ON). All changes in the system-wide DATASKIP status are recorded in the OnLine message log.

8.7 Ontape: Logging, Archives, and Restore

The ontape utility allows you to perform several different tasks:

- Archive data managed by an OnLine database server.
- Change the database-logging status.
- Backup the logical-log files.
- Start continuous logical-log file backups.

- Restore data from an archive tape.
- Use data replication.

To perform these functions, you must be logged in as user "root" or "informix."

8.7.1 Ontape syntax

8.7.2 Backing up the logical-log files

OnLine automatically switches to a new logical-log file when the current log file fills. The full logical-log file displays a status of unreleased, U. When you back it up, the status changes from U to B. You should attempt to back up each log file as soon as it becomes full. To backup all logical-log files, execute ontape with the following format:

```
ontape -a
```

When executing ontape with the −a option, perform this function in the foreground. Do not execute the command using the UNIX operator &, since this will place your job in the background and you will not receive any responses.

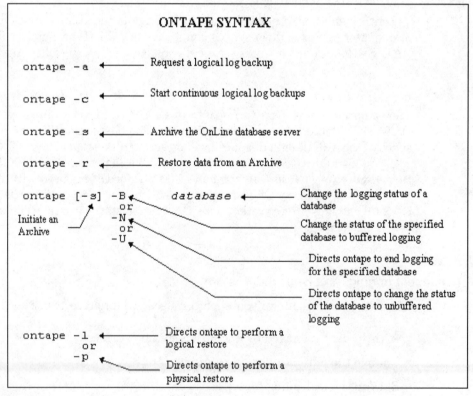

Figure 8.6

The ontape process initiates an interactive dialogue, which will prompt you for additional tapes if required.

8.7.3 Starting continuous logical-log backups

When you initiate the continuous backup option, OnLine automatically backs up each logical-log file as it becomes full. By using this option, you are protected from losing no more than a partial log file. To continuously back up logical-log files, execute ontape using the following format:

```
ontape -c
```

To end the continuous backup, you must cause an interrupt at the terminal that is dedicated to the backup. If you use the interrupt key while a backup is in progress, ontape will complete the backup before terminating. Once you have interrupted the continuous backup, you must continue performing the backups explicitly. See the previous section, 8.7.2.

When executing ontape with the –c option, perform this function in the foreground and do not execute the command using the UNIX operator &. The ontape process initiates an interactive dialogue that will prompt you for additional tapes if required.

8.7.4 Archiving the OnLine database server

An archive might require more than one tape. Once a tape is full, OnLine rewinds it and prompts the operator with the tape number for labeling. Next, OnLine prompts the operator for an additional tape, if needed. You can create an archive when OnLine is in online or quiescent mode. Each time you create a level-0 backup, you should also back up the configuration file as it exists at the beginning of the archive. If you are required to perform a restore from tape, you will need this information. To create an archive of the database server, execute ontape with the following format:

```
ontape -s
```

When you are prompted for a label, provide some meaningful data, such as the archive level, date, time, and the tape number. For example:

```
Level 0: Monday Jan 01,1996 23:00 Tape # 2 of xx
```

When executing ontape with the –s option, perform this function in the foreground and do not execute the command with the UNIX operator &. The ontape process initiates an interactive dialogue that will prompt you for additional tapes if required.

The tape device that is used is the one you specified for the TAPEDEV parameter of your ONCONFIG file.

Note: If you attempt to create an archive and the total available space in your logical files is less than half of a single log file, OnLine will not create the archive. Back up the logical files and then request an archive again. Also note that, while you are performing an archive, you cannot add a logical-log file or mirroring.

8.7.5 Restoring data from an archive

Three types of situations could occur in an OnLine environment that would require you, as an OnLine administrator, to perform a data restore:

- You want to replace one or more disks.
- Your disk experiences a media failure.
- Your OnLine data experiences extreme corruption.

A data restore re-creates the OnLine system that was in effect at the time of your most recent archive, plus any changes that have been backed up to a logical log tape. To perform a restore from an archive tape, execute ontape using the following format:

```
ontape -r
```

8.7.5.1 All data is restored, with no selectivity of tables

You cannot restore a selected table or database. Since you perform a data restore from the complete set of archive and logical log backup tapes, OnLine restores the complete contents of those tapes, which includes all OnLine databases.

8.7.5.2 Data restore procedure

This section outlines the main steps that are part of the data restore procedure. If you press the Interrupt key at any time during the restore, you must repeat the entire procedure.

1. Gather all archive and logical-log backup tapes needed for the restore.
2. Verify that your current shared-memory parameters are set to the maximum value assigned since the last archive (any level).
3. Verify that your current device (and mirroring) configuration matches the configuration that was in effect at the time of the last archive (any level).
4. Verify that all raw devices in use since the last archive are available.
5. Take OnLine to offline mode.
6. Execute ontape –r, and mount the first level-0 archive tape on TAPEDEV. The ontape process will read reserved page information from the tape and verify that the current configuration and the tape are compatible.
7. Back up any logical-log files remaining on the disk, if prompted by ontape, and mount the tape on LTAPEDEV. The ontape process will read each page of data from the archive tape(s) and write the page to the address contained in the header. After the last archive tape is restored, the oninit daemon

process clears the physical log to prevent fast recovery activity. The oninit process initializes shared memory, and the ontape process prompts for the logical logs to be rolled forward.

8. Mount the correct tape (as prompted) on LTAPEDEV. The oninit process will roll forward the logical logs, prompting for more tapes as required. After the roll forward is complete, OnLine remains in quiescent mode and oninit returns control to the administrator.

8.7.6 Changing database logging

By using the ontape utility, you can make one of the following changes to your database:

- Add logging to a database.
- End logging for a database.
- Change logging from buffered to unbuffered.
- Change logging from unbuffered to buffered.

To modify your database's logging status, execute ontape with the following format:

```
ontape [-s] (-B or -N or -U) database
```

To add logging to your database, you can execute one of the following commands:

```
ontape -s -B database (buffered logging)
ontape -s -U database (unbuffered logging)
```

To end logging for your database, execute the following command:

```
ontape -s -N database (turn off logging)
```

In addition, you can use the same commands to add logging, to modify the type of logging that is performed. For instance, if you are currently using unbuffered logging and want to begin using buffered logging, then perform the following command:

```
ontape -s -B database
```

The opposite is true, as well. If you are using buffered logging and want to use unbuffered logging, then do the following:

```
ontape -s -U database
```

8.7.7 Preparing for data replication

The design and setup of a data replication server is beyond the scope of this chapter. Other required tasks include tailoring various systems files, such as sqlhosts, and the UNIX files /etc/hosts and /etc/services. In addition, you must review most of the steps that were required for your initial setup. This section discusses using ontape as part of that process. The syntax to execute ontape for data replication is as follows:

```
ontape -p
```

Execute ontape using the –p option when preparing for data replication, because it performs a physical restore only. If you used ontape with –r, you would be performing both a physical and a logical restore.

8.7.7.1 Performing a logical restore using the –l option
The –l option directs ontape to perform a logical restore on all the dbspaces that were physically restored on the OnLine database server in a data-replication pair. It rolls forward logical-log records from the last checkpoint up to the last available logical-log record on disk.

8.7.7.2 Performing a physical restore using the –p option
The –p option directs ontape to perform a physical restore of an OnLine database server. It is expressly for replicating data prior to initiating the data-replication feature. The –p and –l options are used for initially replicating data in a pair of database servers using data replication.

8.7.7.3 Things to consider
If more than one tape is needed during data replication, ontape will prompt for each additional tape. Do not run ontape in background mode using the UNIX & operator because you might be required to provide input from the terminal or window.

8.7.7.4 Exit codes
The ontape utility has two exit codes:

0. Indicates a normal exit from ontape.

1. Indicates an exceptional condition.

```
                    ONUNLOAD SYNTAX

onunload -l                 database
         [-b blocksize]              [:table]
             and or                     or
         [-s tapesize]               [:owner.table]
             and or
         [-t source]
```

Figure 8.7

TABLE 8.17

Parameter options	Function	Restrictions	Syntax
database	Specifies the name of a database.	The database name cannot include a database server name (*database@dbserver*).	Identifier segment
owner	Specifies the owner of the table.	The owner name must not include illegal characters.	Refer to your operating-system documentation.
table	Specifies the name of the table.	The table must not exist.	Table name segment

8.8 Onunload: Transferring Binary Data in Page Units

The onunload utility writes a database or table into a file on tape or disk. The program unloads the data in binary form in disk-page units, making it more efficient than dbexport.

8.8.1 Onunload syntax

You can execute the onunload utility in various formats. Table 8.17 describes the various parameters used in the execution of onunload.

If you do not specify any destination parameter options, onunload will use the device specified by TAPEDEV. The block size and tape size are the values specified as TAPEBLK and TAPESIZE, respectively.

8.8.2 Specifying destination parameters

The destination parameters include the device for input, the blocksize, and the tapesize. Table 8.18 describes values that are acceptable.

The –l option directs onunload to use the values for tape device, block size, and tape size from LTAPEDEV, LTAPEBLK, and LTAPESIZE, respectively.

8.8.3 Restrictions that affect onunload

You must read the file created by onunload using the onload utility of the same release level of OnLine. You cannot use onunload/onload to move data from one release level to another. For example, you cannot use onunload and onload to move a database from OnLine version 5.0 to OnLine version 6.0.

The computers where the original database resides (where you use onunload) and where the target database will reside (where you use onload) must have the same page size, use the same representation of numeric data, and have the same byte alignment for structures and unions. If the page sizes are different, onload will fail. If the alignment or numeric data types on the two computers are different (for example, with the most significant bytes 1st instead of first, or different float- type representations), the contents of the data page could be misinterpreted.

TABLE 8.18

Parameter options	Function	Restrictions	Syntax
blocksize	Specifies in kilobytes the block size of the tape device. This option overrides the default value in TAPEBLK or LTAPPEBLK.	Must specify the block size of the tape device.	Integer
tapesize	Specifies in kilobytes the amount of data that can be stored on the tape. This option overrides the default value in TAPESIZE or LTAPESIZE.	Must specify the amount of data that OnLine can store on the tape.	Integer
source	Specifies the pathname of the file on disk or of the tape device where the input tape is mounted. This option overrides the tape device specifies by TAPEDEV or LTAPEDEV.	Must be a legal pathname.	Must be the fully qualified pathname to the file or the full pathname for the tape device, such as /dev/rst0.

The tape or disk file produced by onunload contains binary data stored in disk-page-size units.

8.8.4 Unloading a database or table

To unload a database, you must have DBA privileges for the database. To unload a table, you must be the owner of the table or have DBA privileges for the database in which the table resides. (Users "informix" and "root" cannot use onunload unless they also have DBA privileges.)

8.8.4.1 Unloading a database

If you unload a database, all the tables in the database, including the system catalog tables, will be unloaded. All the triggers, stored procedures, defaults, constraints, and synonyms for all the tables in the database will also be unloaded.

Unloading a table

If you unload a table, onunload will unload the table data and information from the following system catalog tables:

- systables
- syscolumns
- sysindexes
- sysblobs

This means that onunload does not unload information about constraints, triggers, or default values associated with a table. In addition, access privileges defined for the table and synonyms or views associated with the table are not unloaded.

8.8.5 Logging mode

The onunload utility does not preserve the logging mode of a database. After you load the database with onload, you can make a database ANSI-compliant or add logging, as described earlier in this chapter under the sections on the onload utility.

8.8.6 Locking during the unload operation

During the unload operation, the new database or table is locked exclusively. An error will be returned if an exclusive lock cannot be obtained.

8.9 Onmode: Mode and Shared-Memory Changes

The various execution options that accompany onmode determine which of the following operations is performed:

- Changing the OnLine operating mode.
- Forcing a checkpoint.
- Changing residency of OnLine resident shared memory.
- Switching the logical-log file.
- Killing an OnLine database server session.
- Killing an OnLine transaction.
- Setting data-replication types.
- Adding a shared-memory segment to the virtual shared-memory portion.
- Adding or removing virtual processors.
- Changing data to version 5.0 or version 6.0.
- Regenerating the .infos file.
- Setting decision-support parameters.
- Freeing unused memory segments.

You must be user "root" or "informix" to execute onmode.

8.9.1 Onmode syntax

Figures 8.8A and 8.8B outline the different execution options that can be used with the onmode utility. If you use the –y option, OnLine will automatically respond "yes" to all prompts. The following sections provide more detail, describing the execution options displayed in the figures.

8.9.2 Switching OnLine to offline mode using the –k option

The –k option takes OnLine to offline mode and removes OnLine shared memory. You might want to use this option to reinitialize shared memory. A prompt will ask for confirmation. Another prompt will ask for confirmation to kill user threads before OnLine comes offline.

8.9.3 Switching OnLine from quiescent to online mode using the –m option

The –m option of onmode takes OnLine from quiescent to online mode.

8.9.4 Shutting down OnLine gracefully with the –s option

The –s option performs a graceful shutdown of OnLine. Users already using OnLine are permitted to finish before OnLine switches to quiescent mode, but no new connections are permitted. When all processing is completed, –s takes OnLine to quiescent mode. The –s option leaves shared memory intact. A

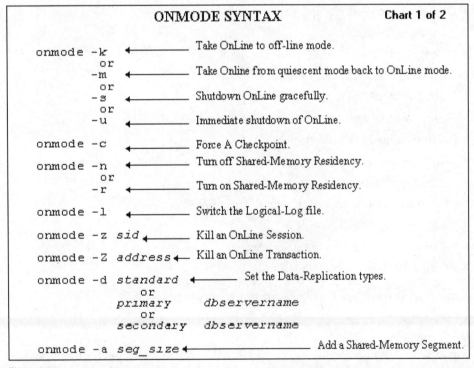

ONMODE SYNTAX   Chart 1 of 2

onmode -k ◄──────────── Take OnLine to off-line mode.
      or
      -m ◄──────────── Take Online from quiescent mode back to OnLine mode.
      or
      -s ◄──────────── Shutdown OnLine gracefully.
      or
      -u ◄──────────── Immediate shutdown of OnLine.

onmode -c ◄──────────── Force A Checkpoint.

onmode -n ◄──────────── Turn off Shared-Memory Residency.
      or
      -r ◄──────────── Turn on Shared-Memory Residency.

onmode -l ◄──────────── Switch the Logical-Log file.

onmode -z sid ◄──────── Kill an OnLine Session.

onmode -Z address ◄──── Kill an OnLine Transaction.

onmode -d standard ◄─────── Set the Data-Replication types.
      or
      primary   dbservername
      or
      secondary dbservername

onmode -a seg_size ◄──────────── Add a Shared-Memory Segment.

Figure 8.8a

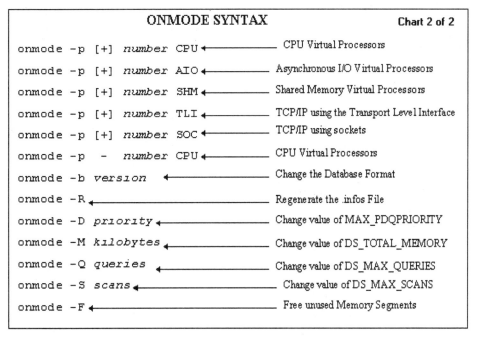

ONMODE SYNTAX   Chart 2 of 2

```
onmode -p [+]  number  CPU ◄──────────  CPU Virtual Processors

onmode -p [+]  number  AIO ◄──────────  Asynchronous I/O Virtual Processors

onmode -p [+]  number  SHM ◄──────────  Shared Memory Virtual Processors

onmode -p [+]  number  TLI ◄──────────  TCP/IP using the Transport Level Interface

onmode -p [+]  number  SOC ◄──────────  TCP/IP using sockets

onmode -p  -   number  CPU ◄──────────  CPU Virtual Processors

onmode -b  version     ◄──────────────  Change the Database Format

onmode -R ◄────────────────────────────  Regenerate the .infos File

onmode -D priority ◄───────────────────  Change value of MAX_PDQPRIORITY

onmode -M kilobytes ◄──────────────────  Change value of DS_TOTAL_MEMORY

onmode -Q queries ◄────────────────────  Change value of DS_MAX_QUERIES

onmode -S scans ◄──────────────────────  Change value of DS_MAX_SCANS

onmode -F ◄────────────────────────────  Free unused Memory Segments
```

Figure 8.8b

prompt asks for confirmation. If you want to eliminate this prompt, execute on-mode using both the –y and the –s options.

8.9.5 Shutting OnLine down immediately with the –u option

The –u option brings OnLine to quiescent mode without waiting for users to finish their sessions. Their current transactions are rolled back and their sessions are terminated. A prompt asks for confirmation. Another prompt asks for confirmation to kill user threads before OnLine comes to quiescent mode.

8.9.6 Forcing a checkpoint

The –c option causes OnLine to force a checkpoint if the most recent checkpoint record in the logical log prevented the logical-log file from being freed (status U-B-L).

8.9.7 Changing shared memory residency

To change the forced residency setting in the ONCONFIG configuration file, use onmode –r to turn on residency immediately or onmode –n to turn off residency immediately. You can turn residency on or off while OnLine is in online mode. You must be user "root" or "informix" to perform this function. Note: This change is not permanent; to make it permanent, you must modify the RESIDENT parameter within your ONCONFIG file.

8.9.8 Ending forced residency with the –n option

This option immediately ends forced residency of the resident portion of OnLine shared memory. This command does not affect the value of RESIDENT, the forced residency parameter in the ONCONFIG file.

8.9.9 Beginning forced residency with the –r option

This option immediately begins forced residency of the resident portion of OnLine shared memory. This command does not affect the value of RESIDENT, the forced-memory parameter in the ONCONFG file.

8.9.10 Killing an OnLine session

The –z option kills the session you specify in sid. To use the –z option, first obtain the session identification (sessid) onstat –u, then execute onmode –z, substituting the session identification number for sid.

When you kill a session using onmode –z, OnLine attempts to kill that session and, if successful, frees any resources held by the session. If OnLine cannot free the resources, it will not kill the session.

If the session does not exit the section or release the latch, user "informix" or "root" can take OnLine offline by executing onmode with the –k option to close all sessions.

8.9.11 Killing an OnLine transaction

The onmode –Z command is not valid until the amount of time specified by the ONCONFIG parameter TXTIMEOUT has been exceeded. The format of this command is as follows:

```
onmode -Z address
```

TABLE 8.19

Parameter options	Function	Restrictions	Syntax
sid	Identifies the session number you want to kill.	A value greater than 0 must be the session identification number of a currently running session.	Unsigned integer

TABLE 8.20

Parameter options	Function	Restrictions	Syntax
address	Kills a distributed transaction associated with the shared-memory address *address*. The address is available from onstat -x output.	Must be the address of an ongoing distributed transaction that has exceeded the amount of time specified by TXTIMEOUT.	Address must conform to the operating-system-specific rules for addressing shared memory.

The –Z option should rarely be used, and then only by an administrator of an OnLine database server involved with another OnLine database server in distributed transactions.

Note: If applications are performing distributed transactions, killing one of the distributed transactions can leave your client/server database system in an inconsistent state. Avoid this if possible.

8.9.12 Setting data-replication types

You can use the –d primary and –d secondary options only when OnLine is in quiescent mode. You can use the –d standard option when OnLine is in quiescent, online, or read-only mode.

The dbservername of the other database server in the data-replication pair and the type of a database server (standard, primary, or secondary) is preserved across reinitializations of shared memory.

–d standard. This option drops the connection between database servers in a data-replication pair (if one exists) and sets the database server type of the current database server to standard. This option does not change the mode or type of the other database server in the pair.

–d primary dbservername. This option sets the database server type to primary and attempts to connect with the database server specified by dbservername. If the connection is successful, data replication will be turned on (the primary database server goes into online mode, and the secondary database server goes into read-only mode). If the connection is not successful, the database server will switch to online mode, but data replication will not be turned on.

–d secondary dbservername. This option sets the database server type to secondary and attempts to connect with the database server specified by dbservername. If the connection is successful, data replication will be turned on (the primary database server goes into online mode, and the secondary database server switches to read-only mode). If the connection is unsuccessful, the database server will switch to read-only mode, but data replication will not be turned on.

TABLE 8.21

Parameter options	Function	Restrictions	Syntax
dbservername	Identifies the database server name of the primary or secondary databaser server.	The *dbservername* argument must correspond to the DBSERVERNAME parameter in the ONCONFIG file of the intended secondary database server. It should *not* correspond to one of the servers specified by the DBSERVERALIASES parameter.	Default value is equal to the hostname, 18 characters or less. First character must be a lower-case letter. Cannot contain any upper-case characters, spaces, tabs, new-line, or comment characters.

8.9.13 Adding a shared-memory segment

The –a option of onmode allows you to add a shared-memory segment of the size you choose. Ordinarily, you do not need to add segments to the virtual portion of shared memory because OnLine automatically adds segments as they are needed. You can execute onmode using the following format to add a shared-memory segment:

```
onmode -a seg_size
```

Note: As segments are added, it is possible for OnLine to reach the operating system limit for the maximum number of segments before it acquires the memory it needs. This typically occurs when SHMADD is set to a small value, and causes OnLine to exhaust the number of available segments before it can acquire the memory it needs to perform some operation.

By manually adding a segment that is larger than the segment specified by SHMADD, you can avoid exhausting the operating system limit for segments while meeting the need OnLine has for additional memory.

TABLE 8.22

Parameter options	Function	Restrictions	Syntax
seg_size	Allows you to specify the size, in kilobytes, of the new virtual shared-memory segment.	Value must be a positive integer. Must not exceed the operating-system limit on the number of shared-memory segments.	Unsigned integer

8.9.14 Adding or removing virtual processors

The –p option enables you to add or remove virtual processors. You can use the –p option only when OnLine is in online mode, and you can add to only one class of virtual processors at a time. To add or remove virtual processors, execute onmode using the following formats:

```
onmode -p [+] number CPU
onmode -p [+] number AIO
onmode -p [+] number SHM
onmode -p [+] number TLI
onmode -p [+] number SOC
onmode -p - number CPU
```

8.9.15 Changing the database format

The –b option changes the format of your databases. When you begin using a new version of OnLine that uses disk space initialized and managed by an older version of OnLine, several modifications can make the format of the database incompatible with the older version of OnLine. Use the –b option to revert to the older format. To change the format of your database, execute onmode using the following format:

```
onmode -b version
```

TABLE 8.23

Parameter options	Function	Restrictions	Syntax
number	Specifies the number of virtual processors to add or drop.	Minimum is 1. If dropping, maximum cannot be greater than the actual number of processors of the specified type. If adding, the maximum is less than 64K; however, that *number* cannot be greater than the number of physical processors.	Unsigned integer

TABLE 8.24

Parameter options	Function	Restrictions	Syntax
version	Specifies the version number.	Version number must be 5.0 or 6.0.	Unsigned integer

Before you use the –b option, notify users that you are going to bring OnLine offline. The –b option includes an implicit –ku. Before the reversion starts, all other users are removed; after the reversion is complete, OnLine is offline.

8.9.15.1 Reverting to version 5.0

Before you use the –b option, you must free any resources that you allocated beyond 5.0 limits. Observe the following limits:

- The number of logical logs must be less than 61.
- The number of dbspaces must be greater than 38.
- The number of chunks must be less than 58.

In versions of OnLine prior to 6.0, the maximum number of chunks is dependent on the length of the chunk pathnames, but cannot exceed 58. During the reversion, the changes that take place can include the following, depending on which version of OnLine you are reverting from:

- Verify that no NLS databases exist.
- Verify that data replication is off.
- Remove the second slot in an archive-reserved page for data replication.
- Drop the sysmaster database.
- Rewrite the leaf pages of all indexes.
- Free the reserved-page extensions.
- Remove the data-replication slot from the archive-reserved page.
- Rewrite all partnums on disk (systables, database tablespace, tablespace pages, blob freemap pages) in their old formats.
- Rewrite dbspace page in the old format.
- Write a 5.0 format checkpoint record to a clean logical-log file.

Reformatting does not make the data space identical to its earlier format. Some of the changes made during conversion from an earlier version to version 7.1 do not make the space incompatible with earlier versions, and these changes are not modified by the –b option.

8.9.15.2 Reverting to version 6.0

Before you use the –b option, you must free any resources that you allocated beyond 6.0 limits. Observe the following limits:

- The number of page-cleaner threads must be less than 33.
- The number of LRU queues must be less than 32.

You set the maximum number of page-cleaner threads with the CLEANER configuration parameter and the maximum number of LRU queues with the

LRUS configuration parameter. During the reversion, the following changes take place:

- Verify that none of the existing tables or indexes are fragmented.
- Drop the sysmaster database.

Before you run onmode –b with the 6.0 option, also run $INFORMIXDIR/etc/smi_unld under the following conditions:

- Configure OnLine for secure auditing.
- Use ON-Archive to preserve the associated catalog information.

Executing $INFORMIXDIR/etc/smi_unld preserves any data in the sysmaster database permanent tables. After you run onmode –b, OnLine informs you of the smi_load script, which you can use to import your data for the permanent tables back into the sysmaster database once you initialize version 6.0 of On-Line.

8.9.15.3 Using tbcheck or oncheck or after you revert

After you use onmode –b to revert to version 5.0 or 6.0, you might want to run the version 5.0 utility tbcheck or the 6.0 utility oncheck. When you do, OnLine displays the following message:

```
OLD pn_nbytes != NEW pn_nbytes
```

This message does not require any action on your part. It merely indicates that the 7.1 version of the OnLine database server has accessed your database.

8.9.16 Recreating the .infos file

OnLine uses information from the $INFORMIXDIR/etc/.infos.dbservername file when it accesses utilities. This file is created and managed by OnLine, and you should never need to do anything to this file. However, if the .infos.db-servername file is accidentally deleted, you must either re-create the file or reinitialize shared memory.

Before you use the –R option, you must set the $INFORMIXSERVER environment variable to match the DBSERVERNAME parameter from the ON-CONFIG file. Do not use the –R option with $INFORMIXSERVER set to one of the DBSERVERALIAS names. To re-create the .infos file, execute onmode using the following format:

```
onmode -R
```

8.9.17 Modifying decision-support parameters

You can use onmode to modify the performance of your parallel database queries by executing it with the following format:

```
onmode -D priority
onmode -M kilobytes
onmode -Q queries
onmode -S scans
```

These options allow you to modify the OnLine configuration parameters while OnLine is online. The new values affect only the current instance of OnLine, and are not recorded in the ONCONFIG file. If you reinitialize shared memory, the values of these parameters will revert back to the values in the ONCON-FIG file. The following ONCONFIG parameters are overridden for the current instance of OnLine:

onmode –D priority. Modifies the value of MAX_PDQPRIORITY.

onmode –M kilobytes. Modifies the value of DS_TOTAL_MEMORY.

onmode –Q queries. Modifies the value of DS_MAX_QUERIES.

onmode –S scans. Modifies the value of DS_MAX_SCANS.

8.9.18 Free unused memory segments

When you execute onmode –F, the OnLine memory manager examines each memory pool for unused memory. When the memory manager locates unused memory, it is immediately freed. After checking each memory pool, the memory manager begins checking memory segments and frees any that OnLine no longer needs. To free unused memory segments, execute onmode with the following format:

```
onmode -F
```

Run onmode –F on a regular basis using the UNIX cron facility or some other scheduling facility (if one is installed on your system). In addition, consider running onmode with the –F option after you direct OnLine to perform some

TABLE 8.25

Parameter options	Function	Restrictions	Syntax
kilobytes	Specifies the maximum amount of memory available for parallel queries, in kilobytes.	Minimum of 128 × DS_MAX-QUERIES, Maximum of 1024 × 1024	Unsigned integer
priority	Specifies the maximum.	Must be an integer between 0 and 100, or OFF, LOW or HIGH	Unsigned integer
queries	Specifies the maximum number of concurrent parallel queries.	Minimum of 1, Maximum of USERTHREADS	Unsigned integer
scans	Specifies the maximum number of concurrent queries.	Minimum of 10, Maximum of 1024 × 1024	Unsigned integer

function that creates additional memory segments such as large index builds, sorts, or backups.

Executing onmode with the –F option causes a significant degradation of performance for any users who are active when you execute the utility. Although brief (one to two seconds), degradation for single-user systems can reach 100%. Systems with multiple CPU VPs will experience proportionately less degradation.

To confirm that onmode has freed unused memory, check your message log. If the memory manager frees one or more segments, it will display a message indicating how many segments and bytes of memory were freed.

9

Creating the User Interface

The user interface, or presentation, is what will really sell your application during its initial use. If the application is awkward or difficult to handle, the user will avoid using it. It might end up in the software graveyard, despite the fact that functionally it was a wonderful application. The user interface is affected not just by the interaction of menus, toolbars, and windows, but also by the multimedia aspects of today's personal computers, such as sound and motion. It is these aspects and an easy navigation between the various elements that makes the user interface one of the most important aspects of any application.

> The recent emergence of the Internet, the World Wide Web, and the myriad of Web browsers (specifically Netscape Navigator and Microsoft Explorer) is changing the landscape of client/server application development. Some pundits are lauding this technology as the great equalizer because of its scalable cost of entry and potential. There is still an air of uncertainty about the security of the Internet, but many companies are hard at work trying to address this issue. Improvements in communications hardware and software will also be required. So far, this development platform had remained the domain of hopeful individuals pressing for the technology to be adopted into corporations.
>
> One thing that does appear to be happening is that client/server systems and internet/intranet systems will converge (see Figure 9.1). Many companies need to provide access to the latest information, but static Web pages will not suffice. Similarly, many companies would like to provide customers, or their field sales people, with access to information stored within in-house client/server systems, but remote connections are too complicated and cumbersome to establish. Companies are tackling these issues from one or both ends. That is, client/server applications are being

enabled for internet/intranet access and Web applications are being connected to databases. Pretty soon these lines will more than likely become blurred.

Some early online transaction processing (OLTP) applications circa 1972 were run on IBM's CICS—a transaction processing program environment. It became the most popular mainframe OLTP development environment. As graphics-capable front-end environments have become more popular, character-based system development using CICS has been limited. Character-based systems have data-entry and presentation limitations; you are limited to a small set of keyboard-based controls and can display only in characters. The GUI enables you to dictate actions like saving and printing by pointing the mouse arrow and clicking on symbols, icons, or data as well as the basic keyboard interface. The older OLTP equivalent was the program function key (PF key), whose meanings also had to be standardized to promote ease of use and end-user acceptance.

The typical GUI window is navigable by way of a menubar/toolbar running along the top of the window. The bar contains items like File, Edit, Windows, and Help. By choosing (clicking on a menu item or its toolbar counterpart—a picture or symbol), the application responds in kind, e.g., opens a new window. Within an enterprise, developing standards of presentation and user appeal for this new GUI interaction is important. You can also look at other popular GUI applications, e.g., Word and Excel. They will give you some idea about the look and feel of the GUI, and they both conform to a standard. They are both developed in the multiple-document interface style (MDI).

The limitations of a character-based transaction system like CICS have fostered the need to develop new applications using graphical user interface (GUI) front-end tools like PowerBuilder. CICS did teach us some important lessons about large-scale OLTP development. OLTP applications should have a

Client/Server-Internet Convergence

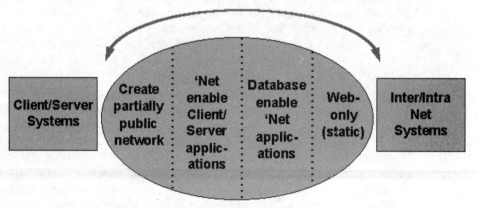

Figure 9.1 Client/server and Internet convergence.

consistent look and feel across an enterprise. The windows, menus, and controls should look and function consistently. The obvious prerequisite to accomplishing consistency would be that OLTP development should be standardized within an organization. Developing firm-wide standards and guidelines for OLTP and building firm-wide libraries containing shareable class objects, functions, and database interfaces is both practical and cost-effective, and promotes consistency. An organization does not evolve to that level after one project, but strategy and appropriate initiatives can be deployed early enough to facilitate the transition.

To the extent that it is possible, an organization should try to create a client/server and internet/intranet developer support group consisting of the firm's best application developers. Included in this group should be individuals who are knowledgeable in the firm's existing systems and are able to create procedures to facilitate development-tool setup and database connectivity. Network and connectivity knowledge will help to develop firm-wide procedures for software and data distribution. Probably the most important function and the most difficult to install on a firm-wide basis is a set of libraries containing visual and nonvisual class objects that can be used by all developers to create the necessary parts of an application.

9.1 User Interface: The Focal Point

The reason that graphical user interfaces (GUIs) have been a success is because the attention is focused on the user and the user's task in hand. The user interface is an essential part of most client/server systems. The appeal of a user interface is typically constrained by three things: the presentation system (e.g., MS-Windows, OS/2 PM, or OSF Motif), the development tool used (e.g., Delphi, PowerBuilder, or Visual Basic), and the visual painting skills of the developer. However, the development tool might not exploit the presentation system to its fullest. Similarly, an inexperienced designer will not get the best from a tool.

A good user interface is something that is easy to learn, satisfying to use, effective for the task, and consistent in appearance and interaction, with the same look and feel as the popular user interfaces, e.g., Word and Excel. Other interface features should help prevent the user from making errors, put the user in control, and above all be intuitive. An ugly user interface will make a product much harder to sell and less pleasurable to use. Other considerations for a user interface design are that it must:

- Accommodate unskilled or infrequent users.
- Give immediate feedback.
- Permit reversible actions.
- Display descriptive and helpful messages.
- Use good symbols and visual metaphors (icons and toolbars).
- Be aesthetically pleasing.

- Be in proportion.
- Use different typefaces.
- Use color carefully.

For further reading on graphical user interface design, see *The Windows Interface Guidelines for Software Design* and the *CUA91 Guide To User Interface Design*.

9.1.1 Give control to the user

An important principle of contemporary application design is that the users must always feel as if they are in control of the computer, rather than the opposite. The users must play an active, instead of reactive, role; even if the situation is extensively automated, the application should still be implemented in a way that allows the users to maintain overall control. There is nothing more frustrating than an hourglass that provides no clue to how much longer a task will take and no means of canceling the process. Users will typically tolerate only a few seconds of an unresponsive interface. In this case, it is better to show the progress of the task (see Figure 9.2).

Another suggestion for a GUI application is that it should accommodate the widely varying skills and individual preferences of the end users. Microsoft Windows provides users with the ability to change system default properties, such as colors, screen size, and fonts. A well-constructed application should take these settings into account and adjust appropriately.

9.1.2 Be consistent

Consistency allows users to transfer existing knowledge to new applications, learn new tasks quickly, and focus on the results—because they don't need to spend time trying to remember how to interact with specific parts of a system. Consistency provides a sense of stability, because it makes the interface familiar and therefore more predictable. See Figure 9.3, which shows the now familiar File, Window Help menu structure.

Consistency should play a part of all aspects of the interface, including names of commands, visual presentation of information, and operational behavior. To design consistency into software, you must consider several aspects:

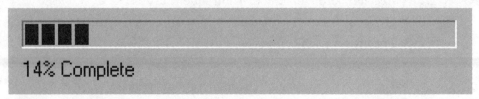

14% Complete

Figure 9.2 Showing progress for a lengthy task.

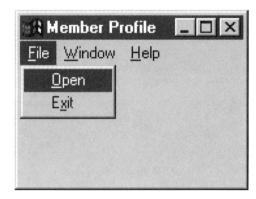

Figure 9.3 Using existing standards.

Application consistency. Present common operations using a consistent set of commands and interfaces. For example, you want to avoid a print command that immediately carries out the operation in one situation but presents a dialog box that requires user input in another.

Operating system consistency. Be consistent with the interaction and interface conventions provided by Windows. The application will then benefit from the users' ability to apply already learned skills.

Metaphor consistency. If a particular behavior is more characteristic of a different object than its metaphor implies, user might have difficulty learning to associate the behavior with the object. For example, the wastebasket icon conveys an element of recoverability for objects thrown into it.

9.1.3 Be direct

Design your software so users can manipulate data directly. Users should immediately see the results of acting upon the objects on the screen. The information that is displayed coupled with the choice of new possible actions should help guide users through the application.

A visual metaphor will help support user recognition rather than recollection. Many users will recognize functionality represented by an icon more easily than they can recall a command-line syntax equivalent (see Figure 9.4).

9.1.4 Give immediate feedback

Always provide feedback for user actions as close to the point of the users' interaction as possible. Visual and audible cues can confirm that the application is responding to user input and also to communicate details that characterize the action. When the application is processing a particularly lengthy task, it is a good practice to provide information regarding the progress of the process and, if possible, the ability to cancel the task. For example, feedback for a simple task might be mouse pointer changes or a status bar message, whereas feedback for a complex process might display a dialog indicating the task's progression (see Figure 9.2, shown earlier).

Junk.txt

Figure 9.4 Metaphors in action.

Recycle Bin

9.1.5 Be forgiving

People often explore and learn about new things by trial and error. A good user interface displays appropriate sets of choices and warns about potential situations where previous versions of data will be overwritten, or become unrecoverable.

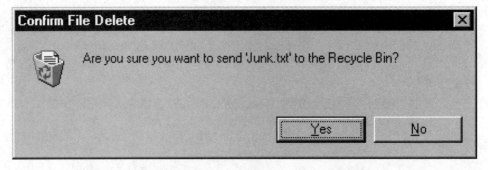

Windows itself has two warning stages
before any possible data loss...

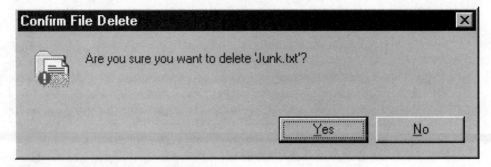

Figure 9.5 Generating a warning before data loss.

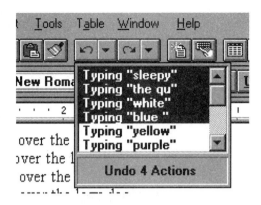

Figure 9.6 Sample of Word's undo capability.

However, the best intentions of any user can still result in mistakes. How many times have you pressed the No button when you really needed to press Yes? For this reason, you should consider building a form of undo capability into your application (see Figure 9.6). This will probably involve some log file that preserves the prior version of the data concerned, so if the users so choose, they can scroll back to a prior copy of the data.

In summary, a well thought-out user interface design can help users avoid making mistakes and, when they do, allow them to easily recover from them.

9.1.6 Keep it simple

Visual controls should communicate helpful impressions of and important cues to the required interaction of objects. Every visual control competes for the user's attention, so it pays to keep an interface as simple, easy to learn, and easy to use as possible. This is not to be confused with simplistic, because the user interface must provide access to all functionality provided by an application. It is the balance between simplicity and functionality that leads to very pleasing application. An example of simplification would be to use concise descriptions for commands and messages.

9.2 The Interface Components

The interface components can be broken down into the following areas or types:

- Windows
- Menus
- Toolbars
- Controls

9.2.1 Windows

A window is the main conversation medium between an application and a user. It is used to display information to the user and can accept information from a

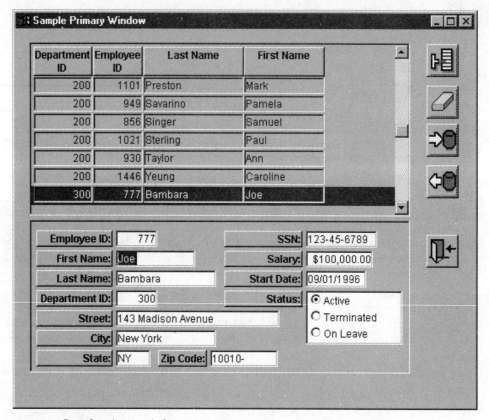

Figure 9.7 Sample primary window.

user via the keyboard and the mouse. Windows provide access to a wide variety of information and are typically classified into two main types: primary and secondary.

A primary window is a main window used to view and edit a specific amount of data, e.g., customer information. It consists of a title or caption that usually identifies the type and key information of what is being displayed in the window (see Figure 9.7).

Secondary windows can be used to supplement the primary window information. Some common examples are a property sheet, an open dialog, and a message box. They differ from primary windows in various ways. When the primary window is closed, the secondary windows are automatically closed. Secondary windows do not have maximize and minimize buttons, they do not appear on the taskbar/tasklist, and they do not have any individual icon associated with them. They are typically not resizable, although they will sometimes contain a button (typically containing > or the word More) that will expand, or unfold, the window—revealing more options and settings.

Another property that affects how secondary windows work is whether they are modeless or modal. A modal window requires that the user complete the interaction with the secondary window before being allowed to interact with the primary window, so modal windows are often called response windows. A modeless secondary window, on the other hand, will allow the user to continue to interact with the primary window independently of the secondary window. These modeless windows are often called child or pop-up windows.

9.2.1.1 Manipulating the window

Users can perform the following basic actions on a window:

- Activate and deactivate
- Open and close
- Move and resize

Activate and deactivate

Users can activate a window by either switching to it or clicking anywhere within its border. At any one time, only a single primary window can be considered active and ready for user input. When one window becomes active, therefore, all others naturally become deactivated.

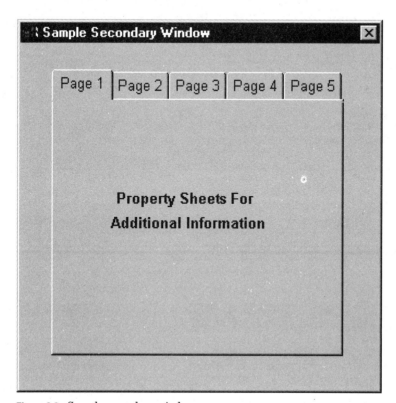

Figure 9.8   Sample secondary window.

Open and close

When users open a primary window, its name and icon are entered onto the taskbar/tasklist and it becomes the active window. A common feature of a well-designed interface is that a window is opened in the same place and in the same size as it was when it was previously closed. This is typically done by saving the coordinates in either an initialization file or the Windows registration database for the current user.

Move and resize

You can move a window either dragging its title bar with a mouse or by using the Move command on the window's control menu. Most primary windows will be defined as resizable. Users can resize a window using several different techniques. They can drag the border that is displayed around the edge of a window or they can use the sizing grip displayed at the bottom right-hand side of the window. You can also quickly expand or shrink an application by using a window's maximize, minimize, and restore buttons (see Figure 9.9.)

The maximize button increases the size of the window to the size of the full screen. This is often used to allow more information to be displayed in the window without requiring scroll bars, so you might find it necessary to resize the controls within a window accordingly. In the case of primary windows, the minimize button reduces the window to an entry in the taskbar. In MDI child windows, the minimize button reduces the window to a similar sized entry within the MDI frame window.

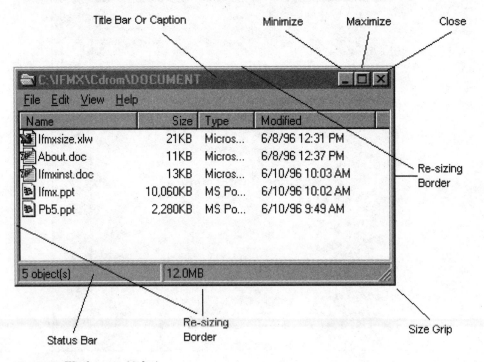

Figure 9.9 Window manipulation.

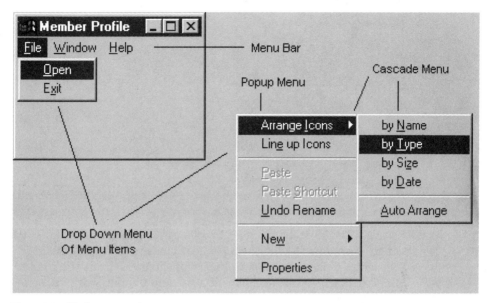

Figure 9.10   Various menu types.

9.2.2 Menus

Menus provide the user with an easy way to issue commands and select options in an application. There are four types of menus (see Figure 9.10):

Menu bar. A horizontal grouping of functional areas (e.g., File).

Drop-down menu. A vertical group of specific commands or functions (e.g., Exit or Close).

Cascading menu. A submenu to a drop-down menu.

Pop-up menu. Another kind of menu that has no fixed screen location and is typically invoked with the alternate mouse button. Mature application development environment should use a standard menu that has been set up as a base class object to be inherited. It should contain all the standard menu items, such as File, Window, and Help, and should also contain filler slots for application-specific processing. For more examples of standard menu and toolbar combinations, take a closer look at either Microsoft Word or Excel.

Menus are extensively featured in a multiple-document interface (MDI) application, with a menu for the frame window and a specific menu for each child window or sheet. For more information regarding MDI, see *Document interfaces* under section 9.2.4 later in this chapter.

9.2.3 Toolbars

To make your application easy to use, you might want to add a toolbar with icons that users can click as a shortcut for choosing an item from a menu (see

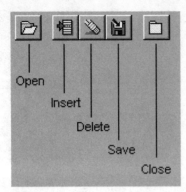

Figure 9.11 Sample toolbar and associated text.

Figure 9.11). Most development tools provide an easy way for you to add a tool-bar to a window. Toolbars are typically associated with menu items, so when you define a menu item, simply specify that you want the item to also display in the toolbar with a specific picture. The toolbar works the same way as in other Windows products. Your users can select items from the toolbar, choose to display or not display text in the toolbar, move the toolbar around the frame, make the toolbar float, and so on. All without writing a line of code.

Often you want to provide a toolbar for users of a MDI application. Toolbars can be defined for the most common menu items, such as open window and save rows, or it can execute commands, such as run the current report, delete the selected records, and exit the window. A toolbar without text has become more popular now that Windows provides balloon (tooltip) help for the cur-rently focused toolbar item.

9.2.4 Window controls

A window is the vehicle for showing information to a user and collecting data from a user, via the keyboard or mouse clicks. It does this with objects, known as controls, that are painted onto the surface of the window. A window must have these controls in order to be of any use. An example of all the controls that can be placed onto a window is shown in Figure 9.12.

DataWindows

DataWindows are the best way, in PowerBuilder, to display any information to capture information from the user (see Figure 9.13). In fact, almost every vi-sual control for a Window can be inserted into a DataWindow control. In PowerBuilder, the DataWindow has its own dedicated engine in the runtime environment and is processed considerably faster than any of the other win-dow controls. This is because it does not matter how many controls exist within a DataWindow; Microsoft Windows needs to deal with only one control. If this were implemented with non-DataWindow controls inside a window, Microsoft Windows would need to manage each control, consequently using more of the valuable graphics device interface (GDI) resources.

Although the DataWindow control is the most powerful control in Power-Builder, you might find that you still need to use some of the other controls, especially if you are not using PowerBuilder!

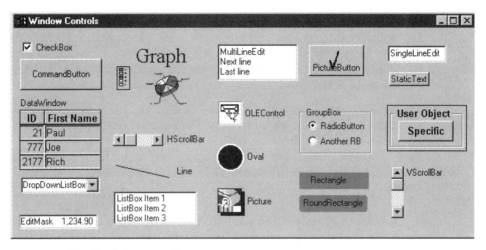

Figure 9.12   Sample window controls.

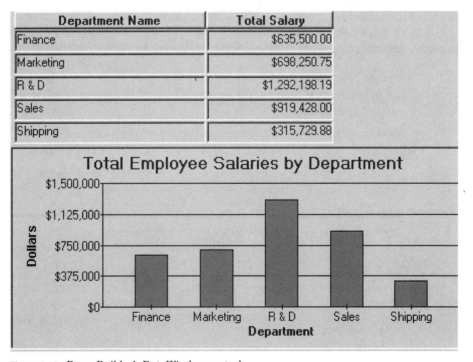

Figure 9.13   PowerBuilder's DataWindow control.

Button controls

Button controls allow a user to begin actions, via command and picture buttons, or change properties, via check boxes and radio buttons.

Check box. Check boxes are square boxes that display one of two states: checked or unchecked (blank). These states typically represent options such as yes or no, or on or off. However, a check box can also represent a third state (gray). For example, a window containing medical information for a patient might have a check box to indicate whether the patient has been immunized for Cholera. In certain situations the information might not be known, so the third state of the check box can represent the unknown state.

Command and picture button. Command buttons are typically used to initiate or confirm an action, e.g., Cancel or OK. When clicked, they visually simulate a pushed-down look during the time the mouse button is held down. Because of the amount of window real estate that a command button uses, it makes sense to avoid using them in most windows except response windows, which cannot make use of the menu. For common functionality, such as saving the current sheet's data or closing the current sheet, you should implement the logic via the menu or its associated toolbar. A picture button is a command button with, you guessed it, a picture on it. You can associate two pictures with a picture button, one for the enabled state, when the user can press the control, and another for the disabled state, when the user cannot press down the control.

Radio button. A radio button is a round object that indicates a selection: on or off. When the option is on, the button has a dark center. When the option is off, the center is blank. Radio buttons are often contained in a group box, so the user can select only one button from the group.

Text field controls

Text fields are the basic window controls that allow the application to display or accept a text value.

Simple text box. This is also known as a single-line edit and multiline edit. A simple text box is a control where the user can enter one or more lines of data.

Rich text box. A rich text box is similar to a simple text box, but it allows the developer to apply a specific mask or picture for the values that are entered during execution.

Spin box. A spin box is also similar to a simple text box, but it allows the developer to apply a specific spin-style mask to allow values to be specified when the spin arrows are pressed during execution.

Static text box. A static text box is useful for labeling or describing the contents of other window controls placed on a window surface.

List box controls

List boxes allow an application to display a list of choices to or accept a list of choices from the user. The list box can contain text as well as graphic information.

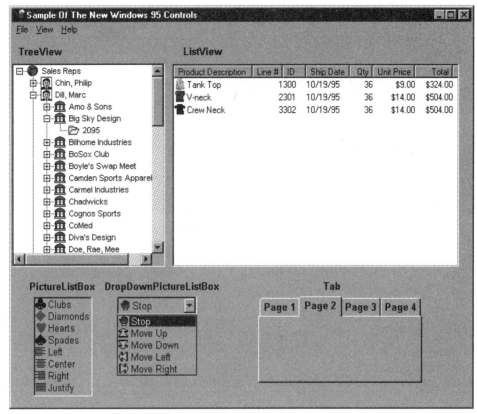

Figure 9.14 Sample of the new Windows 95 controls.

List box. A list box can display a list of data items. These items can be either specified at design time or added via development tool functions.

Drop-down list box. A drop-down list box is similar to a simple edit box. However, when a user clicks on the down arrow, a list of data items is displayed. These items can be either specified at design time or added via development tool functions.

Picture list box. The picture list box is the same as the list box, but it also allows the application to display a graphic picture along with each text item.

Drop-down picture list box. A drop-down picture list box is the same as a drop-down list box, but also allows the application to display a graphic picture along with each text item.

List view. The list view is an extension to the picture list box that allows the list to be displayed in four different views: icon, small icon, list, and report.

Tree view. The tree view is an extension to the picture list box that allows the list to be displayed in an indented fashion according to a logical hierarchical relationship.

Other controls

Some of the other popular controls that make up the windows environment are:

Group box. A group box is used to visually group controls that are closely related, typically radio buttons. For example, you might have three radio buttons inside a group box to indicate that the user can select only one radio button at a time.

Scroll bar. The scroll bar (horizontal and vertical) control can provide relative information that pertains to a combination of controls displayed in a window.

Simple graphic. Simple graphic controls, e.g., a line, oval, rectangle, or picture, are drawing or bitmap objects that can make a window more interesting and visually appealing.

OLE control. An OLE control contains a linked or embedded object, such as a spreadsheet or word-processed document, that was created by an OLE 2.0-compliant application. Users can activate the object and edit it in the application in which it was originally created.

Document interfaces

Before you get into the mechanics of building an application, you must decide on a framework for the entire application. Decisions about the style of application, what the base application processing will consist of, the organization, and the presentation to the users should be resolved to a good degree before proceeding. One of the first questions you should ask yourself is whether the application will follow either the single-document interface (SDI) or multiple-document interface (MDI) convention.

Single-document interface. In some situations, all an application requires is a single primary window and some additional secondary windows. This kind of application, commonly known as a single-document interface (SDI), allows the user to easily switch between main windows with the taskbar. This window model is also called "docucentric" or "data-centered" because of the one-to-one relationship between the window and the type of document or data being viewed or maintained.

Multiple-document interface. In some cases, the application is required to provide a uniform housing for windows that present different, but related, views of data. For this kind of situation, a multiple-document interface (MDI) is more often the choice for window model implementation. Within a MDI application, users can open multiple main windows (also known as sheet) within a single window, commonly known as a frame window. The users navigate between the open sheets by clicking on the sheet with a single click of the mouse button or by selecting the desired sheet from a list of open sheets that appear below a menu option (usually labeled Window). The MDI frame window has three parts: the frame itself, the client area, and sheets opened within the client area. The frame is the perimeter or shell that typically contains a menu; a toolbar; minimize, maximize, and close buttons; and microhelp. It acts as a main window that helps users to navigate through the application components, and it provides the capability of having multiple application components (window sheets) in a partial state of execution. The sheets represent application components and are manipulated using the menu associated with them. The menu of the active sheet is displayed in the frame's menu bar. It is a good idea, if practical for the application, to have one menu (attached to the frame) for the entire application and to have each window enable/disable pertinent menu items. This will promote consistency and help performance. You can also have a menu (inherited from a base menu and extended) for custom sheets within the application.

Other interface models. To date, it has been pro forma to develop large-scale client/server applications using the MDI window model. Although MDI provides a useful technique for managing a set of related windows, it is not the only way of handling tasks. Microsoft has also provided some examples for alternatives to the MDI style that present a single window design while preserving some of the MDI window management benefits. They are Workspace, which is almost the same as MDI, Workbook, which is similar to the tab interface provided within an Excel workbook, and Project, which is similar to the SDI variant provided in the Visual Basic and Visual C++ development environments.

9.3 Other Interface Features

There are other features Windows provides that can either help a user navigate an application or provide various forms of assistance.

9.3.1 Accelerator keys

You can define accelerator keys for your controls to allow users to change the focus to the control by pressing Alt and an accelerator key. How you do it depends on whether the type of control has displayed text associated with it. Be aware that these accelerators will work only if they do not clash with the accelerators attached to the menu. If you use the same accelerator key, the menu option will be performed, not the window control.

9.3.2 Equipping your application with help

Windows provides various ways to provide the user with assistance. They are:

- Context-sensitive help
- Reference help
- Status-bar help
- Task-oriented help
- Tooltips
- Wizards

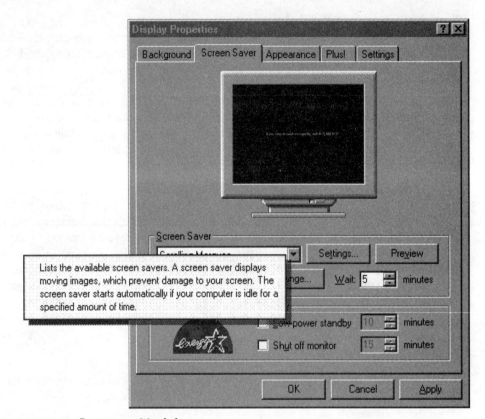

Figure 9.15   Context-sensitive help.

However, not all development tools can make use of or display each type. Check with your development tool documentation for details.

9.3.2.1 Context-sensitive help
The most common form of context sensitive help is implemented by a pop-up window that provides assistance for the particular object on a window or the window itself (see Figure 9.15).

9.3.2.2 Reference help
Reference help is more commonly known as online documentation, where the application features are described in a combination of text and graphics (see Figure 9.16).

9.3.2.3 Status-bar help
You can also use the status bar to provide context-sensitive help in an application (see Figure 9.17). Because of its size, location, and temporary nature, it should not be the primary form of user assistance.

9.3.2.4 Task-oriented help

Task-oriented help is useful for describing the steps necessary to complete a task successfully (see Figure 9.18).

9.3.2.5 Tooltip help

Tooltip help is another form of context-sensitive help specifically for toolbar icons (see Figure 9.19). Users can conserve their valuable visual real estate by turning off the display of toolbar text and relying on the help provided by tooltips.

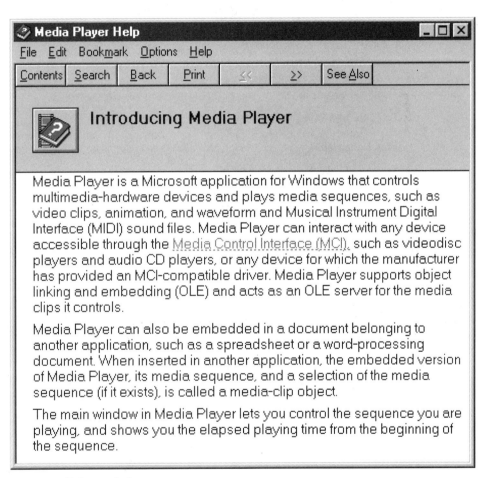

Figure 9.16 Reference help.

Edit the seleced object with the appropriate painter

Figure 9.17 Status bar help.

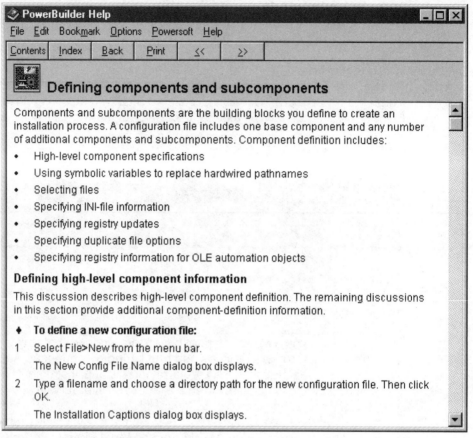

Figure 9.18 Task-oriented help.

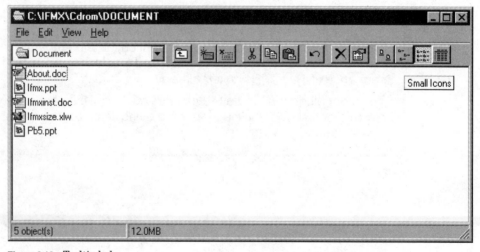

Figure 9.19 Tooltip help.

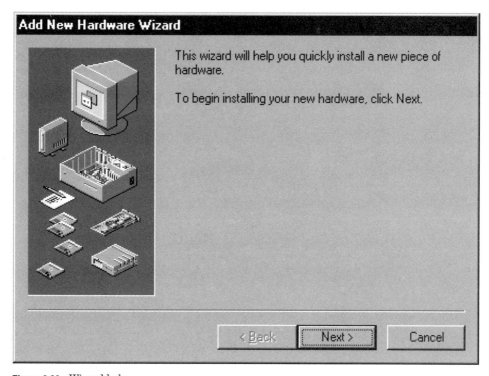

Figure 9.20   Wizard help.

9.3.2.6 Wizard help

Wizards are a very useful form of help that assists users in completing a complex or new task by stepping them through the process (see Figure 9.20). This is especially useful for tasks that users might find difficult to learn.

Chapter

10

Building the Data Definition Language (DDL)

The hub of the typical application is the database. The database contains the entities, attributes, and relationships required to satisfy the application data objective. The relational database consists of the tables/views, columns, indexes, etc.

10.1 Overview

Once you start to get physical (see Figure 10.1)—converting the logical model to a physical Informix database—the application's database will consist of the following components:

Tables and columns. These are the basic building blocks of a good database. They should be grouped by usage and named in a standard way. They start off as entities and attributes in the logical model where they are arranged to satisfy the business processes. A large application will usually begin with a CASE tool, which develops the entity relationship diagram. The entities and attributes in this diagram are then converted to physical tables and columns. Converting to the physical requires that you understand the target database management system—in this case, Informix. ERwin, a third-party tool, can convert a logical model into any one of 15 physical DBMSs, including Sybase, Oracle, DB2, Watcom/SQLAnywhere, and of course Informix (including release 7). A similar tool, S-Designor, can perform the same database design functions, and also includes some process design and construction. There are a host of other vendors who provide tools with similar functionality.

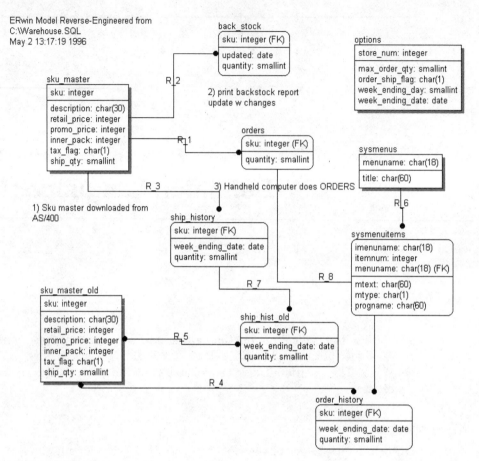

ERwin Model Reverse-Engineered from
C:\Warehouse.SQL
May 2 13:17:19 1996

Figure 10.1 ERwin physical model.

Indexes. Indexes, as the name implies, provide a way to search and sometimes control the data rows within a table. One or more columns can be grouped together to form an index. Most tables should have a unique index that can serve not only as a search mechanism but also a control to avoid duplication. For example, a table containing employee information should use a unique index to ensure that information about a particular employee is not entered twice. An index can also be clustered to maintain the physical placement of inserted rows in a specified order. For example, at a television station an acquired television series would include one or more episodes. A clustered unique index for the episode table might be series_code and episode_code concatenated together. This would group all of a series' episodes on database pages stored in close proximity, which would speed up access involving all the episodes within a series.

Keys (primary and foreign). Keys are that which provide for database integrity. For example, the series table would have a primary key of series_code. The primary key is typically a unique table row identifier. It also establishes the first part of the key in any dependent table, e.g., episodes belong to and dependent on a series. The episode table would have a foreign key of series_code to connect the episode to the series and also to ensure that a series cannot be deleted if any episodes belonging to the series exist. Design tools such as ERwin can be used to define the database logical model and also create the physical components, including the referential definitions required to enforce database integrity.

Views. The name view describes its object's function: to provide a particular view of base tables. Views are vertical tables made up of columns from one or more tables, usually joined by same key or keys they share in common. Views facilitate access to the data. They can also provide security, e.g., you can restrict the selection of employee column data such as salary. Views containing columns from more than one table are typically not updatable; check the target DBMS for specifics.

10.2 Creating a Database

Creating a new database usually happens at two distinct points in project's life cycle. The first is just before development and the second is at the point where production is imminent. The first development database is done without full knowledge of the application, i.e., it is still being constructed, hence it is not optimally configured. The second database that is built (production) will hopefully be based on how the database is to be deployed and will include all the Informix features available for optimizing data access. To create a database, the syntax is different depending upon whether you are using the Standard Edition (SE) or OnLine (OL). The differences and how these choices affect database performance are explained in the following sections.

SE syntax
```
create database database_name
[with log in database_device [MODE ANSI]
```

OL syntax
```
create database database_name
[in dbspace.]
[with [buffered] ulog] ![with log mode ANSI]
```

Example to create the warehouse database
```
create database warehouse with log in
'/Strorddb/warehouse.log' mode ANSI;
```

Keywords and options
The name of the new database is database_name. This name must conform to the rules for identifiers. It can be as simple as dbname.

- It can also be dbname@dbservername or '//dbservername/dbname/' for OL.

- It can be dbname or '//dbservername/pathname/dbname' or 'pathname/dbname@dbservername' for SE.

The keyword indicating that you want to specify a location and (optionally) a size for the database is in dbspace (see Figures 10.2 and 10.3). The specification of the logical name of the device that will be used to store the database logs is with log in.

10.2.1 Preparing to create a database

Before creating a database, the database administrator must decide:

- The logging mode.
- ANSI-standard compliance.
- The location of the database.

These choices have the following ramifications on a database:

The database administrator must decide on the logging mode of the database. Databases that perform transaction processing that are not created with logging cannot be recovered to their current state if a severe failure occurs. The SE Informix engine does not forward recover after a system failure.

The developer must recover the database using the backup and then code routines to access the log. The database administrator must decide if the database will be ANSI-complaint. ANSI databases must conform to certain rules laid out by the ANSI standards committee. For example, programs accessing ANSI databases cannot use the BEGIN WORK statement; the program is always in a transaction and the COMMITWORK statement will implicitly start a new transaction once the current transaction has been committed.

The database administrator must decide the dbspace location of the database. This decision is usually made in conjunction with the Informix-OnLine Dynamic Server system administrator, who creates and manages dbspaces within the OnLine system. Some more examples of creating a database for OL are as follows:

```
CREATE DATABASE warehous CREATE DATABASE warehous in DBSPACE 1 with log
CREATE DATABASE warehous IN DBSPACE 1 WITH BUFFERED LOG
CREATE DATABASE warehous IN DBSPACE 1 WITH LOG MODE ANSI
```

As mentioned, you create a database with the CREATE DATABASE statement. This statement creates the system catalog tables necessary to store information about the tables in the database. More on this later. The previous examples show different ways to create a database with the Informix-OnLine Dynamic Server.

```
CREATE DATABASE warehous
```

This statement will create a database in the default location, which is the root dbspace. It is not recommended to create databases in the root dbspace. The database is created without logging.

```
CREATE DATABASE warehous IN dbspace1 WITH LOG
```

This example will create a database in the dbspace called dbspace1, with unbuffered logging.

```
CREATE DATABASE warehous IN DBSPACE1 WITH BUFFERED LOG
```

This example will create a database in the dbspace called dbspace1, with buffered logging.

```
CREATE DATABASE warehous IN DBSPACE1 WITH LOG MODE ANSI
```

This example will create an ANSI database in the dbspace called dbspace1. An ANSI database uses unbuffered logging.

10.2.2 The system catalog

The system catalog is a set of tables that describe the structure of the database (see Figures 10.4 and 10.5). It is automatically generated when you create a database. Each time a SQL statement is processed, the database server accesses the system catalog for many purposes, including determining system privileges and verifying table and column names. The system catalog tables do not appear with other tables when the TABLES option of DB-Access is used. You can, however, select data from these tables using a standard SELECT statement.

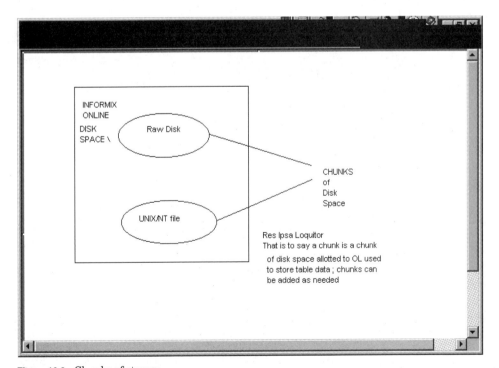

Figure 10.2   Chunks of storage.

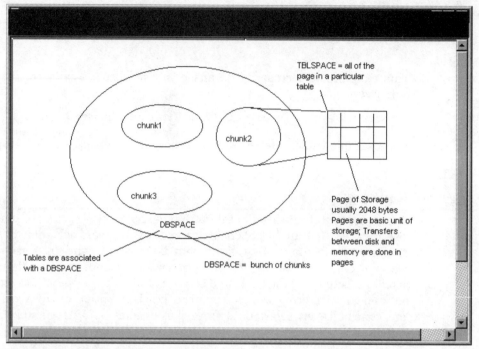

Figure 10.3   DBSPACE = collection of chunks.

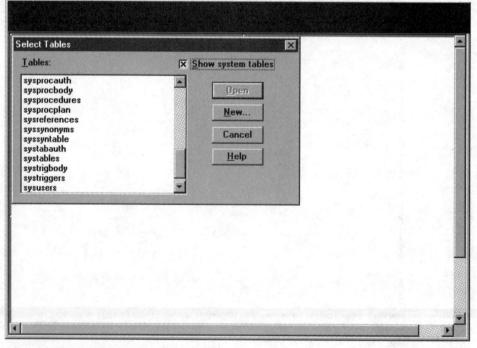

Figure 10.4   Partial list of system catalog.

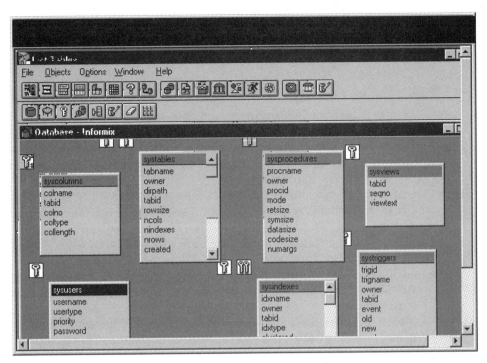

Figure 10.5   PowerBuilder database painter, Informix system catalog.

10.2.3 Databases and dbspaces

Using OnLine (OL), you can specify that a database be created in a specific db-space. This means, for nonfragmented tables and indexes, that all the space used by that database, including all system catalogs, the data, and corresponding indexes, will be located in the chunk or chunks assigned to that dbspace. A chunk is a unit of space assigned to OL. It might be a raw disk space or a UNIX file. Disk management in OL is performed by the raw sequential access method (RSAM). It is suited for database management and superior to the UNIX file system. Separating databases into different dbspaces has several advantages:

- A database cannot grow beyond the space available in the dbspace. By limiting the size and number of chunks assigned to a dbspace, you also limit the size of the database.

- You can assign databases to different devices by assigning them to separate dbspaces that have chunks on different devices. Should one of the devices suffer a failure, you will lose access to only the database stored in the dbspace on that device. Other databases will be unaffected.

If you do not specify the dbspace in which to create the database, the database will, by default, be created in the root dbspace. It is recommended not to create databases in the root dbspace, and to create other dbspaces for holding database data. For details on the creation and management of dbspaces in the Informix-OnLine Dynamic Server, refer to the Informix-OnLine Dynamic Server system administration manuals.

10.3 Creating Tables

Your organization might have used the entity-relationship approach to data analysis. This type of approach has two major advantages. First, it is very close to natural language. An entity is like a noun, a relationship is like a verb, and an attribute is like a prepositional phrase. This makes it easy to convert information gleaned in an interview with the user into a data model. Second, most CASE tools have adopted this approach, so learning it is good preparation for CASE. An entity is a person, place, object, concept, activity, or event of interest to your organization. You can determine entities within an application by listening for important nouns during interviews with the users.

An entity type is a set of objects. TV Series and Episode are each different entity types. An entity instance is an element of the set. "LEAVE IT TO BEAVER" the series and "Beaver flunks math" the episode are instances of our entity types.

Entity types usually become tables in relational design, and entity instances usually become rows. However, entities and tables are not identical. You might split an entity into several tables for better performance, or merge several entities in one table. Occasionally entities are listed merely for documentation, and disappear in relational design.

10.3.1 Designing tables

The formal definition of a table, according to the relational godfathers (Codd and Date), is that it consists of two parts: a heading and a body. The heading is the specification for the table, and does not change in time. The body, or contents of the table, is a time-varying set of rows. Each row is a set of column-value pairs.

This definition has three important consequences. First and most significantly, a table is defined as a set of rows, and each row is defined as a set of column-value pairs. Since elements of a set are not ordered, the rows and columns of a table have no logical order. It is impossible to refer to the "fourth row" or "second column" of a table in SQL, for example. Of course, rows and columns are ordered internally on storage media, but this physical order is always invisible to the user in a relational DBMS. This is called physical data independence.

Second, sets should not contain duplicate elements. Consequently, tables should not contain duplicate rows or column names—in theory. In practice, most systems allow unstructured tables with duplicate rows, but this is not particularly useful. After all, it is impossible to distinguish duplicate rows. You would not be able to delete the "first" duplicate and retain the "second" because rows have no logical order. In practice as well as in theory, tables should have unique primary keys and therefore no duplicate rows.

Third, the table definition implies that each row-and-column cell contains exactly one value, not several. This point is fundamental to database design. It means that plural attributes are harder to implement than singular attributes. Sometimes a column is denormalized into a repeating value, i.e., an array for performance purposes. Natural arrays are the best because they do not change over time. For example, there will always be seven days in a week and twelve months in a year. A table with seven columns each representing a day of the week might reduce the physical I/O by 84%, i.e., you get all the data in one access instead of seven. Moreover, it might also reduce the required physical storage.

Another concept of the relational data structure is the null value. Null is a special symbol that means either unknown or inapplicable. These two meanings are different; a null social security number for an employee means unknown, presumable, but a null commission for a sales person means inapplicable. Regardless of meaning, null is always represented as the same symbol: NULL. This symbol is the same regardless of data type; NULL is used for integers and characters alike. With null values, a new arithmetic and logic is necessary. What is the value of the expression 10 + null? In SQL the answer is null, or unknown. What about 10 > null? Again, the answer is null. In fact, any arithmetic or comparative expression involving null evaluates to null.

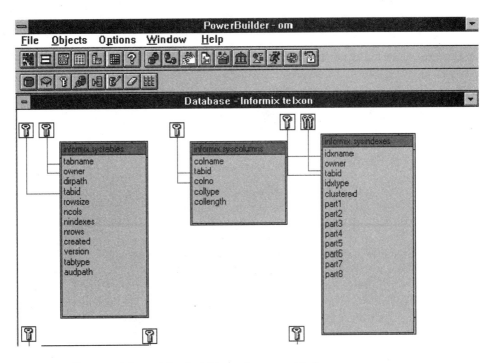

Figure 10.6 System catalog entries for tables, columns, and indexes.

10.3.2 The syntax for create table

The syntax for create table in Informix is not unlike any other DBMS. The statement creates new tables and optional integrity constraints within the specified database. The syntax, which will appear confusing, follows. See the examples within the section to get a more typical flavor for table definition.

General syntax

```
create table [database.[owner].]table_name
  (column_name datatype
    [default {constant_expression | user | null}]
    {[{SERIAL | null | not null}]
    | [[constraint constraint_name]
    | references [[database.]owner.]ref_table
        [(ref_column)]
    | check (search_condition)}]}...
    | [constraint constraint_name]
      {{unique | primary key}
       (column_name [{, column_name}...])
    | foreign key (column_name [{, column_name}...])
      references [[database.]owner.]ref_table
      [(ref_column [{, ref_column}...])]
    | check (search_condition)}
      [{, {next_column | next_constraint}}...])
```

For example:

```
— drop an existing table
drop table order_history;
— create next version of the table
create table order_history
    (
      sku integer,
      week_ending_date date,
      quantity smallint
    );
— create an index table

create unique index order_history_idx on order_history (sku,
week_ending_date);
```

Keywords and options

The name of the new table is `table_name`. It must be unique within the database and to the owner. If you have set quoted_identifier on, you can use a delimited identifier for the table. Otherwise, it must conform to the rules for identifiers.

You can create a temporary table either by preceding the table name in a create table statement by preceding the table name with `temp table`. Such tables can be accessed only by the current Informix session. They exist until they are explicitly dropped by their owner, or until Informix reboots. You can create a table in a different database, as long as you are listed in the sysuser's table and have create table permission for that database.

column_name. The name of the column in the table. It must be unique in the table.

datatype. The data type of the column. System or user-defined data types are acceptable. Certain data types expect a length, n, in parentheses: datatype(n). Others expect a precision, p, and scale, s: datatype(p,s). See section 10.3.6 for more information.

default. Specifies a default value for a column. If you have declared a default and the user does not provide a value for this column when inserting data, Informix will insert this value. The default can be either a constant expression to insert the name of the user who is performing the insert, or null to insert the null value. Defaults declared for columns with the SERIAL property have no effect on column values.

constant_expression. A constant expression to use as a default value for the column. It cannot include the name of any columns or other database objects, but you can include built-in functions that do not reference database objects. This default value must be compatible with the data type of the column.

SERIAL. Indicates that the column has the SERIAL property. Each table in a database can have one SERIAL column with a type of integer. SERIAL columns are not updatable and do not allow nulls. SERIAL columns are used to store sequential numbers, such as invoice numbers or employee numbers, that are generated automatically by Informix. The value of the SERIAL column uniquely identifies each row in a table.

null : not null. Specifies that Informix assigns a null value if a user does not provide a value during an insertion and no default exists (for null), or that a user must provide a non-null value if no default exists for not null. If you do not specify null or not null, Informix will use not null by default.

constraint. Introduces the name of an integrity constraint. This keyword and constraint_name are optional.

constraint_name. The name of the constraint. It must conform to the rules for identifiers and be unique in the database. If you do not specify the name for a referential or check constraint, Informix will generate a name using the following two options:

unique.

Constrains the values in the indicated column or columns so that no two rows can have the same non-null value. This constraint creates a unique index that can be dropped only if the constraint is dropped, using ALTER TABLE.

primary key.

Constrains the values in the indicated column or columns so no two rows can have the same value, and so the value cannot be NULL. This constraint creates a unique index that can be dropped only if the constraint is dropped, using ALTER TABLE.

Here is another example:

```
CREATE TABLE ORDERS (
order_num INTEGER NOT NULL,
```

```
customer_nme CHAR (32),      Columns and their data types
order_charge_amt FLOAT,      Columns and their data types
order_dte DATE)
IN dbspace1          Location of the table
EXTENT SIZE 64 Size in pages of the initial extent in kbytes
NEXT SIZE 32   Size in pages of the second and nth extent in kbytes
LOCK MODE Lock level
```

The CREATE TABLE statement has the following by-products:

- Inserts the table and column information into the systable's and syscolumn's system catalog tables.
- Sets aside contiguous space for the table in the dbspace. The amount of contiguous space set aside depends on the size requested in the EXTENT SIZE clause.
- Sets the lock level of the table.

The previous example CREATE TABLE statement creates a table named orders, with three columns. The table is located in the dbspace dbspace1, and 64K is allocated for the first extent. Every extent after that is allocated 32K. When locks are applied to data in the table, they are applied at the row level.

10.3.3 Creating a temporary table

Sometimes you need a temporary work space to mix and match result sets from other SQL operations. To solve this problem, you can explicitly create a temporary table that is similar to a permanent table except it is valid only for the duration of the program and is not logged. If you close the current database, the

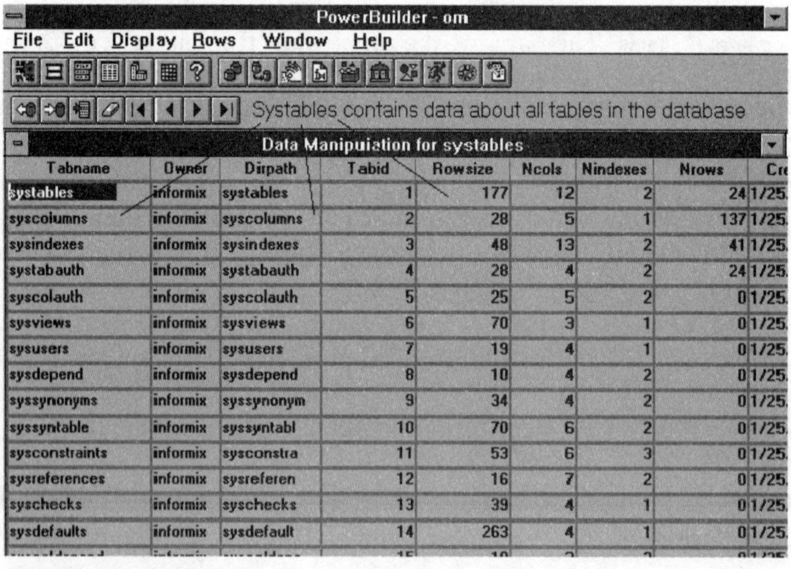

Tabname	Owner	Dirpath	Tabid	Rowsize	Ncols	Nindexes	Nrows	Cr
systables	informix	systables	1	177	12	2	24	1/25.
syscolumns	informix	syscolumns	2	28	5	1	137	1/25.
sysindexes	informix	sysindexes	3	48	13	2	41	1/25.
systabauth	informix	systabauth	4	28	4	2	24	1/25.
syscolauth	informix	syscolauth	5	25	5	2	0	1/25.
sysviews	informix	sysviews	6	70	3	1	0	1/25.
sysusers	informix	sysusers	7	19	4	1	0	1/25.
sysdepend	informix	sysdepend	8	10	4	2	0	1/25.
syssynonyms	informix	syssynonym	9	34	4	2	0	1/25.
syssyntable	informix	syssyntabl	10	70	6	2	0	1/25.
sysconstraints	informix	sysconstra	11	53	6	3	0	1/25.
sysreferences	informix	sysreferen	12	16	7	2	0	1/25.
syschecks	informix	syschecks	13	39	4	1	0	1/25.
sysdefaults	informix	sysdefault	14	263	4	1	0	1/25.

Figure 10.7 Systables after development tables have been created.

temporary table will no longer be valid. Temporary tables should be created in a dbspace that is specifically designated for temporary tables within the On-Line system. The dbspace is created with no logging regardless of the logging mode of the database. The designation of a dbspace for temporary objects is performed at the time the dbspace is created. The DBSPACETEMP environment variable can be set to one or more of the specifically designated dbspaces. If the DBSPACETEMP environment variable is not set, OnLine will use the value of the DBSPACETEMP OnLine configuration parameter.

There are no entries for the temporary table in the systable's or syscolumn's system catalog tables. You can create indexes on temporary tables, and you can drop temporary tables when you are finished by using the DROP TABLE statement:

```
DROP TABLE temp order;
```

10.3.4 Table extents

When you create or build a table, disk space for a table is allocated in units called extents. This concept dates back to the early 1960s when IBM OS2 (as in mainframe 360) data sets were allocated with a primary and 15 secondary extents. Informix calls the primary and secondary extents EXTENT and NEXT. An extent is an amount of contiguous space on disk; the amount is specified for each table when the table is created. Each table has two extent sizes associated with it:

EXTENT SIZE. The size of the first extent allocated for the table. This first extent is allocated when the table is created.

NEXT SIZE. The size of each subsequent extent added to the table.
When an extent is added, it is empty at first, except for one or more bitmap pages. When the first allocated extent has no more space (i.e., all pages are filled) another extent is allocated for the table, when this extent is filled another extent is allocated, and so on.

What is a tablespace/tblspace?

In a fashion similar to IBM's DB2, all Informix extents allocated for a given table are logically grouped together, and are referred to as a table space (tbl-space). While the space within an extent is guaranteed to be contiguous, the space represented by the tblspace might not be contiguous because extents can be spread across a device as availability permits.

Extent size

The minimum size that an extent can be is four pages. There is no maximum size in practical terms. Typically, it will be in the range of two gigabytes, depending upon the operating system. The extent size must be an even multiple of the page size for the system. It is important to calculate extent requirements for your tables. A spreadsheet with built-in calculations would be a helpful tool for this purpose.

Extent growth

There are special situations that can alter the next size of subsequent extents from the size specified at the time the table is created. Extent concatenation occurs when an extent for a table is allocated and physically contiguous with an existing extent for the same table. The existing extent is simply made larger. This effect is most often seen when performing batch table loads in a sequential fashion, i.e., one at a time. Generally, each new allocated extent is contiguous with the previous extent. A large table loaded onto a relatively empty disk space could end up occupying a single large extent. The size of the first extent and subsequent extents is specified when the table is created. It is possible to alter the extent size using the ALTER TABLE command. You can increase or decrease the extent size for any subsequent extents, but it will not alter the size of the extents currently allocated for the table.

If the amount of contiguous free space in a dbspace is less than the size of the current extent allocation, the amount of available space will be allocated to the extent even though it is less than the desired amount. The minimum available space will be used for an extent.

10.3.5 Table lock modes

The Informix locking strategy for tables is comprehensive, especially when compared to other RDBMSs like Sybase (see Figure 10.8).

Page locking will lock an entire page of data, effectively locking all data on that page. Index locks are also at page level. Page is the default level. This is curious since Informix always touts their row-level locking as being superior to the page-level locking in databases like Sybase. The bottom line is that row-level locking can solve a bad design, but it comes at a price. Well-chosen indexes with proper use of clustering can make page-level locking a good choice. Row-level locking locks only the row needed. Index locks are placed only on the key values.

Locks are used to prevent one user from accessing data that is being used by someone else. Page-level locking locks an entire page; row-level locking locks a single row at a time. The level OnLine uses depends on the locking mode of the table. The owner of the table sets the locking mode when the table is created or altered.

Page-level locking

Page-level locking provides the most efficient method for locking several rows of data. Because you lock every row on the page whether you are using it or not, however, other users cannot access that data. Page-level locking decreases concurrency, or the availability of the data to other users. Since a page lock actually locks more than one row with only one resource, it is useful if you are processing rows in the same order as they occur physically on disk. For example, if you are processing a table in its physical order, page-level locking allows you to update many rows with a fewer number of locks.

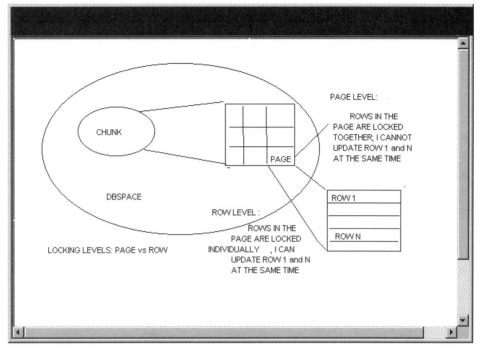

PAGE LEVEL:

ROWS IN THE
PAGE ARE LOCKED
TOGETHER; I CANNOT
UPDATE ROW 1 and N
AT THE SAME TIME

CHUNK

PAGE

DBSPACE

ROW 1

ROW LEVEL :

ROW N

LOCKING LEVELS: PAGE vs ROW

ROWS IN THE
PAGE ARE LOCKED
INDIVIDUALLY   , I CAN
UPDATE ROW 1 and N
AT THE SAME TIME

Figure 10.8   Page vs. row locking.

Row-level locking

One of Informix's premier features is row-level locking. Row-level locking increases concurrency because only one row is locked. OnLine uses row-level locking on the system catalog tables to provide the highest level of concurrency. When the number of locked rows is high, however, not only do you risk exhausting the number of available locks, but the overhead of lock management can become significant.

10.3.6 Data types

Defining data types amounts to specifying the type of information, size, and storage format of columns, stored procedure parameters, and local variables (see Figure 10.9). Informix provides a number of system data types, and allows you to build user-defined data types based on these types. For simplicity's sake, system data types are printed in lowercase characters, although Informix allows you to enter them in either upper- or lowercase. Most Informix-supplied data types are not reserved words, and can be used to name other objects.

Exact numeric data types: integers. Informix provides two data types to store integers (whole numbers): smallint and integer. These are exact numeric types; they preserve their accuracy during arithmetic operations. Choose between the

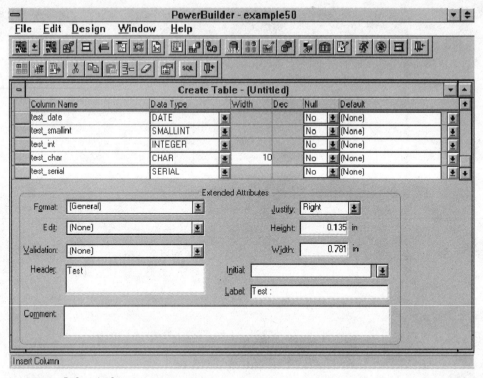

Figure 10.9 Informix data types.

integer types based on the expected size of the numbers to be stored. Internal storage size varies by type between two and four bytes.

Exact numeric data types: decimal numbers. Informix provides numeric types for numbers that include decimal points. Data stored in decimal columns is packed to conserve disk space, and preserves its accuracy to the least significant digit after arithmetic operations. The decimal types accept two optional parameters, precision and scale, enclosed within parentheses and separated by a comma:

```
decimal [(precision [, scale])]
```

Informix treats each combination of precision and scale as a distinct data type. The precision and scale determine the range of values that can be stored in a decimal or numeric column. Precision specifies the maximum number of decimal digits that can be stored in the column. It includes all digits, to the right and left of the decimal point. You can specify a precision of 1 to 16 digits, or use the default precision of 16 digits. Scale specifies the maximum number of digits that can be stored to the right of the decimal point. Note that the scale must be less than or equal to the precision. You can specify a scale of 0 to 16 digits, or use the default scale of 0 digits. Exact numeric types with a scale of 0 are displayed without a decimal point. If you enter a value that exceeds either the precision or scale for the column, Informix will return an error message. The storage size for a numeric or decimal column depends on its precision. The minimum storage requirement is two bytes for a 1- or 2-digit column. Storage size increases by one byte for each additional two digits of precision, up to a maximum of nine bytes.

Informix provides approximate numeric types for numeric data that can tolerate rounding during arithmetic operations. The approximate numeric types are especially suited to data that covers a wide range of values.

The real and double precision types are built on types supplied by the operating system. The range and storage precision for all three types is machine-dependent. You enter approximate numeric data as a mantissa followed by an optional exponent. The mantissa is a signed or unsigned number, with or without a decimal point. The column's binary precision determines the maximum number of binary digits allowed in the mantissa. The exponent, which begins with the character e or E, must be a whole number. The value represented by the entry is the following product:

```
mantissa * 10exponent
```

For example, 2.4E3 represents the value 2.4 times 103, or 2,400.

Numeric data types
So to reiterate and summarize, there are five numeric data types: INTEGER, SMALLINT, FLOAT, SMALLFLOAT, and DECIMAL.

INTEGER. Whole numbers –2, 147, 483, 647 to +2, 147, 483, 647

SMALLINT. Whole number –32, 767 to +32, 767

FLOAT. Binary floating-point numbers, double precision

DECIMAL. Precision and scale designation up to 32 significant digits
INTEGER values hold numbers from –2, 147, 483, 647 to +2 147, 483, and 647. SMALLINT values hold numbers from –32, 767 to +32, and 767. An INTEGER uses four bytes and a SMALLINT uses two bytes of disk space. The two-byte savings is probably not significant in small tables, but it can make a substantial difference in large tables. You can always convert a SMALLINT to an INTEGER without loss of data.

FLOAT AND SMALLFLOAT values store binary floating-point numbers. The precision for these data types is as follows:

FLOAT. Double-precision, 16 significant digits (corresponds to the C double data type)

SMALLFLOAT. Single precision, up to 8 significant digits (corresponds to the C float data type)
The number of significant digits can vary from machine to machine. FLOAT can store twice as many digits as SMALLFLOAT data types. FLOAT columns

do not necessarily store larger numbers; they store numbers with greater precision. A FLOAT uses eight bytes and a SMALLFLOAT uses four bytes of disk space.

DECIMAL and MONEY values store numbers with the number of digits specified by the user. You can specify up to 32 siginficant digits. The range of numbers that you can store is:

```
10 × 10 –128 to 10 × 10 128
```

However, only 32 digits are significant. DECIMAL numbers can be formatted with a given precision and scale. Precision is the total number of digits. Scale is the number of digits to the right of the decimal point. A DECIMAL column with a definition (5,2) would store a five-digit number with three digits before the decimal point and two digits after the decimal point. However, specifying precision and scale is optional.

No Precision. DECIMAL is treated as DECIMAL (16), a floating-point decimal with a precision of 16.

No Scale. DECIMAL is treated as a floating-point decimal.
You can calculate the number of bytes it takes to store a DECIMAL value by taking the precision of a DECIMAL column, dividing it by two, and adding one. (If the precision is odd, add one to it, then divide by two.) For example, a DECIMAL value with a precision of 16 would take nine bytes to store:

```
Precision/2+1= 16/2+1+9
```

How do you choose between FLOAT and DECIMAL? The advantages of using the DECIMAL data type over the FLOAT data type are that DECIMAL allows greater precision (32) over FLOAT (7 or 14) and the ability to round a number. It requires some amount of processing to convert, however. The available precision of FLOAT might differ from machine to machine, which could be significant when transferring data across a network. FLOAT is less CPU-intensive when it comes to conversion and processing.

Character data types
The character data types store strings consisting of letters, numbers, and symbols. Use the fixed-length type, char(n), and the variable-length type, varchar(n), for single-byte character sets such as English. Possibly consider using the text type for strings longer than 255 characters. Character literals are treated as variable-length types. You can use the like keyword to search character strings for particular characters, and the built-in string functions to manipulate their contents. Strings consisting of numbers can be converted to exact and approximate numeric types with the convert function, then used for arithmetic. Use n to specify the length in characters for the fixed-length types, char(n). Entries shorter than the assigned length are blank-padded; entries longer than the assigned length are truncated without warning. Fixed-length columns that allow nulls are internally converted to variable-length columns.

Use n to specify the maximum length in characters for the variable-length types varchar(n) and nvarchar(n). Data in variable-length columns is stripped of trailing blanks; the storage size is the actual length of the data entered. Data in variable-length variables and parameters retains all trailing blanks, but is not padded to the full defined length. Fixed-length columns tend to take more storage space than variable-length columns, but are accessed somewhat faster. CHAR columns (character) store any combination of letters, numbers, and symbols. Tabs and spaces can be included. No other nonprintable characters are allowed. The maximum length of a CHAR column is 32,767 bytes. CHAR columns are of fixed length. If a character column is defined with a width of 400 bytes, data for that column will take up that amount of space on disk, even if the data is less than 400 bytes.

VARCHAR columns store variable-length character data. They are not available in the SE version of Informix. The primary benefit of using the VARCHAR data type is that, when used correctly, it can increase the number of rows per page of storage on disk. VARCHAR is most effectively used when the majority of rows need only a small amount of space and some rows require significantly more. For example, a comments column might not be used in 80% of the rows in a table. However, when it is populated, VARCHAR can increase performance on sequential reads of tables and reduce disk-storage waste when compared to the same data stored in CHAR data-type fields. VARCHAR columns can store between 0 and 255 bytes of character data. When specifying a VARCHAR data type, make sure to include a maximum length in the syntax of the column definition.

The max-size parameter sets the upper limit on the length of the characters allowed within the data item, and the min-size parameter sets a minimum amount of disk space that is always reserved for data within the data item. When a row is written, OnLine sets aside either the number of bytes needed to store the data or the number of bytes specified in min-size for the column, whichever is greater. If the column later grows to a size greater than the space available in the row, the row might have to be moved to another place on a page, or part of the row might have to be moved to another page. You can see why it is important to specify an accurate average min-size when the table is created. Besides the actual contents of the VARCHAR column, a one-byte length indicator is stored at the beginning of the column. The bottom line in choosing between VAR and VARCHAR is as follows:

CHAR. Use this if the content of the column is predictable (fixed), e.g., a street address or area code. CHAR and INTEGER are common to all RDBMSs and will probably be the most frequent type of data used.

VARCHAR. Use this if the majority of the rows use a small amount of space, and the maximum size of the column is the exception. Use it when you must save space, e.g., there is a large number of table rows.

Character strings must be enclosed in single or double quotes. If you have set quoted_identifier on, use single quotes for character strings or Informix will treat them as identifiers.

Strings that include a double quotation symbol should be surrounded by single quotes. Strings that include the single quotation character should be surrounded by double quotes.

10.3.7 Other data types

Relational database systems introduced special data types in inconsistent ways before RDBMS. Informix includes special data types for generating sequential numbers, and storing dates, times, and large objects.

SERIAL data type

SERIAL columns contain unique numbers that are assigned by the system to each row of the table. They are stored as INTEGERS. When a new row is entered, the serial column is assigned the next number in the sequence. The default starting number is one, and the highest serial number that can be assigned is over 2.1 billion. Sybase also uses a similar data type known as IDENTITY, but it uses DECIMAL to store the values.

When you need a unique row identifier with sequencing, consider SERIAL. Serial columns make good primary keys (see Figure 10.10) because of their small size and inherent uniqueness. Only one SERIAL column can be specified in a table. If the starting number is 100, the first row to be entered will be assigned the serial value 100.

When a row or rows are deleted, the data is removed but the SERIAL values continue to increase. That is, when a new row is added, it is assigned the next number in the sequence. SERIAL numbers cannot be reused without special programming.

You can use SERIAL data types to store identification numbers such as customer numbers and order numbers. A SERIAL data type uses four bytes.

DATE, DATETIME, and INTERVAL

An example of the way special data types were used inconsistently before RDBMS is storing a date as a six-character field (MMDDYY), an eight-character field (MMDDYYYY), a decimal number, or an integer. This created a need for special programs and functions to calculate and compare dates. Relational databases including Informix provide a consistent way of storing, calculating, and comparing dates. Informix includes the following special data types for storing dates and times:

DATE. Used to store calendar dates

DATETIME. Used to specify a particular point in time, for example:

```
DATETIME (1996-5-15 12:00) YEAR TO MINUTE
DATETIME (16 12:23) YEAR TO MINUTE
DATETIME (31.234) SECOND TO FRACTION
```

INTERVAL. Used to specify a span of time, for example:

```
INTERVAL (5-3) YEAR TO MONTH (5 YEARS, 3 MONTHS)
INTERVAL (11:15) HOUR TO MINUTE
```

A DATE column is specified in programs, forms, and SQL in the default format mm/dd/yyyy, where mm is the month (1 to 12), dd is the day of the month (1 to 3l), and yyyy is the year (0111 to 9999). You can change the default format with the environment variable DBDATE. The DATE data type if the number of days since December 31, 1899. January 1, 1900 is day one.

DATETIME is an advance over the DATE data type in that the granularity to which a point in time is measured is selectable; that is, data items that store points of time with granularities from a year to a fraction of a second can be defined. The value ranges for each DATETIME field are:

YEAR. (A.D.) 1 to 9999

MONTH. 1 to 12

DAY. 1 to 28, 29, 30, or 31

HOUR. 0 (midnight) to 23

MINUTE. 0 to 59

SECOND. 0 to 59

FRACTION(n). Where n is 1–5 significant digits (default of 3)

INTERVAL is used to store values that represent a span of time. An INTERVAL data item can express spans of time as great as 9,999 years and 11 months, or as small as a fraction of a second.

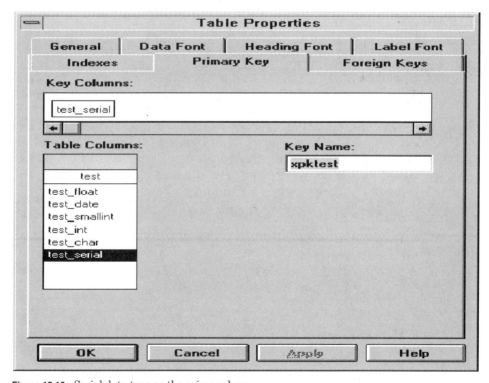

Figure 10.10   Serial data type as the primary key.

INTERVAL data types cannot contain both months and days. This is because the number of days in a month varies with the month; May has 31 days, while September has 30. The number of days in a month might also vary with the year; the number of days in February changes from 28 to 29 every four years, with special exceptions for particular centuries.

Because of these necessary peculiarities in calendars, ANSI divides the INTERVAL type into two classes: year-month intervals and day-time intervals. Year-month interval classes are:

- YEARs
- MONTHs

Day-time interval classes are:

- DAYs
- HOURs
- MINUTEs
- SECONDs
- FRACTIONs of a second

Binary large objects

Binary large objects (BLOBs) are streams of bytes of arbitrary value and length. A BLOB might be a digitized image or sound, a relocatable object module, or a legal contract. For this reason they are becoming more and more popular. The Informix merger with Illustra will no doubt create new uses for BLOBs. A BLOB can be any arbitrary collection of bytes for any purpose. Anything that you can store in a file system of a computer can be stored in a BLOB.

OnLine allows BLOBs to be stored as columns within a database. The theoretical limit to their size is over 2.1 billion bytes; this size is based on the highest value that can be held in a four-byte signed integer. Internal to the BLOB, 56 bytes of space are reserved in the row for general BLOB information. The BLOB itself is stored in pages separate from the rest of the row. There are two types of BLOB data types: BYTE and TEXT.

BYTE. Large amounts of unstructured data with unpredictable contents

TEXT. Large amounts of data containing ASCII values Control–I, Control–J, and Control–1
A data object of type TEXT is restricted to a combination of printable ASCII text (and a few specific control characters) such as:

- Word processing files
- Manual chapters
- Engineering specifications
- Program source-code files

Control-I, Control-J, and Control-1 characters are allowed in a TEXT data type. The BYTE data type can store any type of binary data, such as:

- Spreadsheets
- Program modules
- Digitized images; for example, photographs and drawings
- Voice patterns

The BYTE data type is an undifferentiated byte stream. OnLine knows only the length of the BLOB and storage location on the disk. Other programs can be called to display the BLOB information.

10.3.8 Determining column types

You must determine the contents of a column. What is the smallest/largest value for numeric columns? What is the size of character columns? You need to determine how data will be accessed. Will arithmetic operations be performed? Will character columns be involved in filters?

Database administrator should analyze the potential column contents and the way a column will be accessed before deciding the data type of every column. Determine the contents of a column. This step is important in deciding whether a column should be SMALLINT, DECIMAL or INTEGER, etc. For character columns, administrators must choose between VARCHAR, CHAR, and TEXT. The maximum size of a character column might disqualify the use of VARCHAR (which has a maximum size of 255). If the administrator determines that a column is usually empty except for a small percentage of rows, then VARCHAR might be the best choice.

Determine how data will be accessed. For example, if a zip code is not involved in arithmetic operations, perhaps it should be created as a character column. Another example of a difficult choice is a comments column. Should a comments column be VARCHAR, CHAR, or TEXT? If queries do not involve the character column in a filter and the comments column is vary large, perhaps it should be a TEXT column so it can be stored apart from the row itself.

10.3.9 Determining how big the database will be

1. Build a spreadsheet to estimate and finalize storage requirements (see Figure 10.11).
   - Estimate the number of tables.
   - Estimate the length of each row.
   - Estimate the number of rows for each table (including a year's worth of growth).
   - Procure additional storage.

2. Build a spreadsheet to estimate and finalize access requirements.

- Estimate the number of users.
- Determine user transaction types (EIS, DSS, OLTP).

10.4 Creating Indexes and Keys

Data in tables has both a relational and a physical order. The relational order of values is the usual arithmetic sequence for numbers, or the dictionary sequence for character data. The physical order of rows in a table is the combination of the sequence of pages on the disk drive and the sequence of rows within each page. Of course, disk drives are not serial devices; pages are spread across tracks and around sectors.

A table is clustered on a column when the physical order of rows matches the relational order of values in the column. For example, SERIES is clustered on SERIES_CDE. In some database systems clustering can be imperfect; a table is considered clustered even when some rows are on the wrong page. MVS/DB2 maintains a cluster ratio, or the percent of rows that are clustered. An index on a column is a list of column values, with pointers to the location of the row containing each value. A composite index is defined over several columns.

A clustering index, sometimes called a primary index, is defined on a clustering column, i.e., a column ideally with a uniform distribution of values with which to group rows together for common/fast access. A nonclustering index, sometimes called a secondary index, is not defined on a clustering column.

Table	Table Description	Number of Rows	Bytes /Row	Growth /Year	Num Pages	Data Size MBytes	Index Bytes	Index Filfactor	Index Pages	Index MBytes	Total MBytes
TBSSCUST	Stampsheet Customer	5,000,000	290	90%	1,583,333	3,092	10	10%	12,998	266	3,359
TBCTCUST	Catalog Customer	350,000	260	90%	95,000	195	10	10%	780	16	211
TBSSTRAN	Stampsheet Transactions	7,000,000	100	90%	738,889	1,513	18	10%	9,342	191	1,705
TBSSITEM	Stampsheet Items	40,000,000	45	90%	2,000,000	4,096	27	10%	34,921	715	4,811
TBCTTRAN	Catalog Transactions	700,000	50	90%	38,000	78	18	10%	480	10	88
TBSSITEM	Orders for Stampsheet Items	10,000,000	45	90%	500,000	1,024	27	10%	8,730	179	1,203
TBCTITEM	Orders for Catalog Items	2,000,000	45	90%	100,000	205	27	10%	1,746	36	241
TBORDXRF	Order Cross Reference	3,500,000	13	90%	66,500	136	13	10%	653	13	150
TBDEMOG	Demographic	30,000	638	90%	19,000	39	9	10%	145	3	42
TOTALS:					5,140,722	10,378			69,795	1,429	11,807

Figure 10.11   Sizing a database with the spreadsheet approach.

A dense index contains one entry for each row of the table. A nondense index contains one entry for each page of the table with the low and high index values. Nondense indexes are possible only on clustered columns. Nondense indexes have a great advantage over dense indexes because they have far fewer entries, and therefore occupy fewer pages. As a result, they are more efficient.

How does this structure handle insertions and updates? Informix places a new row on the correct page based on its clustering column. If this page is full, it will split in two to create free space, and a new entry will be inserted at the bottom level of the index. If this index page is full, it will split in two to create more space, and a new entry will be necessary at the bottom level of the index. If this index page is full, it will split to create more space, with another entry at the next higher level of the index.

In the worst case, these splits will propagate all the way through the top of the index, and a new level will be created. Because the new level is created at the top of the index, all branches of the index tree are always the same length. Consequently, this kind of index is often called a B-tree, the B for balanced. In theory, the system could reverse the process when rows are deleted, merging pages and reducing the index. However, this is not supported by Informix and other vendors, since deletions are less frequent than insertions.

Occasionally a table will not have a clustering index. In this case, new rows are always inserted at the end of the table. When a row is deleted, the empty slot is not reused until the table is physically reorganized. Since there is no clustering index, the rows remain in order of their initial load or insertion. Because no meaningful order is maintained, this structure has limited utility. It is useful for tables of five pages or less; after all, if a table is small, the system can scan it quickly without an index. It is also useful for archival or temporary tables.

A table can have only one clustering index, but any number of nonclustering indexes. Nonclustering indexes are necessarily dense. When and how can nonclustering indexes accelerate queries? A crucial factor is the percentage of rows selected by a query, variously known as hit ratio, filter factor, or selectivity. When the hit ratio is high, nonclustering indexes are useless. For example, suppose you set up a nonclustering index on the holiday column within the TV Episode table. The holiday column contains a code that lets you know which episodes have a holiday theme, e.g., Halloween. Suppose you select all episodes not associated with a holiday, i.e., a normal day. The hit ratio will be quite high; most or all pages contain qualifying rows because most days are not holidays. It would be faster to ignore the index and scan the entire table. In contrast, if you select all episodes associated with the holiday of Halloween, the hit ratio will be low. Less than five percent of episodes qualify. A nonclustering index on HOLIDAY will quickly locate the few pages of interest.

10.4.1 The CREATE INDEX statement

Use the CREATE INDEX statement to create a unique or duplicate index, and optionally to cluster the physical table in the order of the index.

Syntax

```
create [unique| distinct] [cluster] index index_name
on [[database.]owner.]table_name (column_name [ASC|DESC] [,
    column_name]...)
[{fillfactor percent}]    (OL only)
[in dbspace] | [fragment by expression in dbspace remainder
in dbspace2]   (OL only)
```

For example:

```
create table ship_history
( sku integer,
week_ending_date date,
quantity smallint );
```

sku will be the unique and clustered index for the shipment history table
create unique cluster index ship_history_idx on ship_history (sku);

Keywords and options

unique. Prohibits duplicate index (also called key) values. The system checks for duplicate key values when the index is created (if data already exists), and checks each time data is added with an insert or update. If there is a duplicate key value or if more than one row contains a null value, the command will be aborted and an error message giving the duplicate will be printed. Update or insert commands that generate duplicate key values are canceled. Composite indexes (indexes in which the key value is composed of more than one column) can also be unique. The default is nonunique.

cluster. Means that the physical order of rows on this database device is the same as the indexed order of the rows. The bottom or leaf level of the clustered index contains the actual data pages. A clustered index almost always retrieves data faster than a nonclustered index. Only one clustered index is permitted per table. A clustered index is often created on the table's primary key (the column or columns that uniquely identify the row). If clustered is not specified, nonclustered is assumed.

nonclustered. Means that there is a level of indirection between the index structure and the data itself.

index_name. The name of the index. Index names must be unique within a table, but need not be unique within a database.

table_name. The name of the table in which the indexed column or columns are located.

column_name. The column or columns to which the index applies. Composite indexes are based on the combined values of up to 16 columns. The sum of the maximum lengths of all the columns used in a composite index cannot exceed 256 bytes. List the columns to be included in the composite index (in sort-priority order) inside the parentheses after table_name.

fillfactor. Specifies how full Informix will make each page when it creates a new index on existing data. The fillfactor percentage is relevant only at the time the index is created. As the data changes, the pages are not maintained at any particular level of fullness. The default for fillfactor is 90; this is used when you do not include with fillfactor in the CREATE INDEX statement. When specifying a fillfactor percentage, legal values are between 1 and 100. If the fillfactor is set to 100, Informix will create both clustered and nonclustered indexes with each page 100% full. A fillfactor of 100 makes sense just for read-only tables (tables to which no additional data will ever be added). Fillfactor values smaller than 100 (except 0, which is a special case) cause Informix to create new indexes with pages that are not completely full. A fillfactor of 10 might be a reasonable choice if you are creating an index on a table that will eventually hold a great deal more data, but small fillfactor values cause each index (or index and data) to consume more storage space.

IN dbspace. Specifies that the index is to be created on the named dbspace. Before this option can be used, you must initialize the dbspace and add it to the database. See your system administrator for a list of the dbspace names available in your database.

10.4.2 Choosing index candidates and options

You use an index to find a row quickly, similar to the way you use an index in a book. Indexes are organized in a binary tree of pages containing encoded data. In other words, the binary tree (B+ tree) is a set of nodes that contain keys and pointers arranged in a hierarchy. The B+ tree is organized into levels. Level 0 contains a pointer, or address, to the actual data. The other levels contain pointers to nodes on different levels that contain keys less than or equal to the key in the higher level.

When you access a row through an index, you read the B+ tree starting at the root node, and follow the nodes down to level 0, which contains the pointer to the data. It is important to keep key size to a minimum for two reasons:

- One page in memory holds more key values, potentially reducing the number of read operations to look up several rows.

- A smaller key size might cause less B+ tree levels to be used. This is very important from a performance standpoint. An index with a four-level tree will require one more read per row than an index with a three-level tree. If 100,000 rows are read in an hour, this means there will be 100,000 less reads to get the same data.

In OnLine, the size of a node is the size of one page, typically 2K (2048 bytes).

Binary tree splits

The binary tree responds to growth in a set way. When a node gets full, it must be split into two nodes (see Figure 10.12). B+ trees grow toward the root. Attempting to add a key into a full node forces a split into two nodes and promotes the middle key value into a node at a higher level. If the key value that causes the split is greater than the other keys in the node, it will be put into a

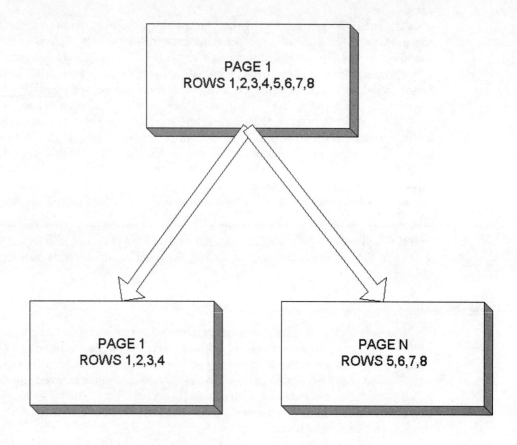

B-TREE SPLIT
It's like the Amoeba's you
learned about in grammar
school

Figure 10.12 B-tree split.

node by itself during the split. The promotion of a key to the next higher level can also cause a split in the higher-level node. If the full node at this higher level is the root, it will also split. When the root splits, the tree grows by one level and a new root node is created. Using this method, it is impossible for a B+ tree to be unbalanced (having different levels in different parts of the tree).

Unique and duplicate indexes

There are four characteristics associated with indexes: unique, duplicate, composite, and cluster. An index must be either unique or duplicate. In addition, it can be composite and it can be clustered. A unique index allows no more than one occurrence of a value in the indexed column. Therefore, a unique index prohibits users from entering duplicate data into the indexed column. For column(s) serving as a table's primary key, a unique index ensures the uniqueness of every row. As a general rule, a unique index should be chosen for each table. The choice of a unique key for a table should be carefully considered. A duplicate index allows identical values in different rows of an indexed column.

Composite index

An index on two or more columns is a composite index. The principal functions of a composite index are to:

- Facilitate multiple column joins, e.g., orders by sku and date.
- Increase the uniqueness of indexed values, e.g., order number and sequence number for items within an order.

Composite indexes can be very helpful in improving the performance on a query. OnLine allows up to 16 columns in a composite index, with a maximum key size of 255 bytes.

Cluster indexes

Information stored in a database is extracted from the hard disk in blocks (sections of disk space). Through clustering, you can cause the physical placement of data on the disk to be in an indexed order. This can increase the efficiency of data retrievals when the retrievals are in a similar order as the index. In the previous example, if a cluster index is put on 1name, the data row would be ordered physically by 1name. A SELECT statement retrieving many rows in the customer table in order by 1name will therefore be more efficient, especially if the table is large.

The cluster index physically alters the placement of data stored on the disk. Only one cluster index can exist per table. Cluster indexes are not updated when rows are added to the table or data is updated. Therefore, cluster indexes are most effectively used on often-queried static tables, and are less effective on dynamic tables.

Although the index is not altered when data is added to or updated in a table, you can recluster a cluster index with the following statement:

```
ALTER INDEX index name TO CLUSTER
```

To maintain the effectiveness of a cluster index, it is a good idea to update the cluster index used on a nonstatic table frequently.

When the ALTER INDEX TO CLUSTER statement is executed, Informix will make a copy of the entire table on disk in index order before dropping the old index. Therefore, you must have sufficient space available in the dbspace to hold a copy of the table. The following examples show different ways to create an index:

```
create unique cluster index x1_sku_master on sku_master (sku);
create unique index x1_back_stock on back_stock (sku);
```

The index fill factor is the percentage of each index page that will be filled during the index build. It is available only with Informix OL. This percentage can be set with the CREATE INDEX statement. If it is not specified with CREATE INDEX, the default will become the value specified in the OnLine configuration parameter FILLFACTOR. If the fill factor is not specified in either location, the default fill factor will be 90 percent.

If you do not anticipate many new inserts into the table after the index is built, you can set the FILLFACTOR higher when you create the index. If you are expecting a large number of inserts into the table, you can leave the FILLFACTOR at the default value or set it lower. If the FILLFACTOR is set too low, you risk a decrease in the cache rate and an unnecessary increase in the amount of disk space needed for the index. The fill factor is not kept during the life of the index. It is applied only once as the index is built. Note that the DBSCHEMA utility will not list the fill factor if it is specified in an index.

Altering and dropping an index

You can change an index to cluster on the key with the ALTER INDEX statement, as in the first example in the previous section. If, over time, your table becomes unclustered, you might need to recluster it. To recluster, you can run the ALTER INDEX statement. For example:

```
alter index ix cust to cluster;
```

To drop an index, use the DROP INDEX statement. To drop an index, you must know the index name. You can determine the index name using the TABLE option in DB-Access, or by using the DBSCHEMA utility.

Fast indexing allows you to sort index keys first, before they are inserted into a new index created with the CREATE INDEX statement. This feature reduces the amount of binary tree manipulation and disk access needed to retrieve the node that the key belongs in (the node pages will most likely already be in memory).

The temporary space is taken from disk in the following order for the Informix-OnLine Dynamic Server:

- If PSORT DBTEMP is enabled for parallel sorting on machines with multiprocessors, the temporary disk space will be taken from the directory specified with the PSORT DBTEMP environment variable.

- If the DBSPACETEMP environment variable or configuration parameter is set, temporary disk space will be taken from the dbspace it specifies.

- If neither variable is set, temporary disk space will be taken from the /TMP directory.

You can calculate the amount of space needed for sorting with the following algorithm: (the size of keys in bytes plus four bytes for handling) multiplied by the number of rows in the table.

10.4.3 Benefits of indexing

There are several performance benefits associated with indexing database tables. Performance improves when indexes are applied to the following:

- Columns that are used to join two tables.
- Columns applied as filters to a query.
- Columns in an ORDER BY or GROUP BY.

In these cases, using the index to find the desired rows greatly reduces the time needed. Without an index, you must access tables sequentially, reading each row until the WHERE condition is satisfied. An index can reduce that I/O considerably. You can use an index on a column or columns to retrieve data in a sorted order. When performing an indexed read (reading the table via an index), returned rows are automatically in sorted order. This prevents the database server from having to sort the output data. You can create an index on a column with the UNIQUE keyword, so only one row in the table can have a column with that value. You still need to perform any uniqueness checking through the application program and return the appropriate response, but you are assured that the table contains no duplication.

Also, when all columns listed in the SELECT clause are part of the same index, OnLine does not read the data rows, as all the data is already available via the index. This can greatly reduce the amount of I/O needed to process such a query.

10.4.4 Costs of indexing

The first cost associated with an index is one of disk space. An index contains a copy of every unique data value in the indexed column(s), plus a four-byte pointer for every row in the table and a one-byte delete flag. This can add many blocks or pages to the space requirements of the table. It is not unusual to have as much disk space dedicated to index data as to row data.

The second cost is one of time while the table is modified. Before inserting, updating, or deleting a row, you must first look up the index key in the B+ tree. Assume an average of two I/Os to locate an index entry. Some index nodes are in shared memory, though other indexes that need modification might have to be read from disk. Under these assumptions, index maintenance adds time to different kinds of modifications as follows:

- When a row is deleted from a table, the related entries are deleted from all indexes. Null values are entered in the row in the data file.
- When a row is inserted, the related entries are inserted in all indexes. The node for the inserted row's entry is found and rewritten for each index.
- When a row is updated, the related entries are looked up in each index that applies to a column that was altered. The index entry is rewritten to eliminate the old entry, then the new column value is located in the same index and a new entry made.
- Many insert and delete operations can also cause a major restructuring of the index (as they are implemented using B+trees), requiring more I/O activity.

Some basic guidelines for choosing an index candidate are as follows:

- Look for index columns involved in joins.
- Look for index columns that are used as selective filters and have a large range of values (> 25).
- Look for index columns frequently used for ordering or sorting (e.g., popular reports).
- Avoid highly duplicate indexes.
- Limit the number of indexes to those that give you the most bang for the buck, i.e., do *not* index everything.

There should be an index on at least one column named in any join expression. If there is no index, the database server will either build a temporary index before the join and perform a sort merge join or nested loop join, or sequentially scan the table and perform a hash join.

When there is an index on both columns in a join expression, the optimizer has more options when it constructs the query plan. As a general rule in OLTP environments, you should place an index on any foreign key column, and on any other column that is frequently used in a join expression. If, however, only one of the tables in a join is chosen to be indexed, give preference to the table with unique values for the key corresponding to the join column(s). A unique index is preferable to a duplicate index for implementing joins. As a general rule, in DDS environments where large amounts of data is read and sequential table scans are performed, indexes might not play an optimal role in implementing joins since hash joins are the preferred method.

If a column is often used to filter the rows of a large table, consider placing an index on it. The optimizer can use the index to pick out the desired rows, avoiding a sequential scan of the entire table. An example is a table containing a large mailing list. If you find that a zip-code column is often used to filter out a subset of rows, consider putting an index on it even though it is not used in joins.

This strategy will yield a net savings of time only when the selectivity of the column is high, that is, only when there are not a lot of duplicate values in that column. Nonsequential access through an index takes more disk I/O operations to retrieve many rows than sequential access, so if a filter expression causes a large percentage of the table to be returned, the database server might as well read the table sequentially.

Generally, indexing a filter column will save time when:

- The column is used in filter expressions in many queries or in queries of a large table.
- There are relatively few duplicate values.

When a large quantity of rows has to be ordered or grouped, the database server has to put the rows in order. The database server will sort the selected rows via a sort package before returning them to the front-end application. If, however, there is an index on the ordering column(s), the optimizer will sometimes plan to read the rows in sorted order through the index, avoiding the final sort. Whether or not the index is used depends on the complexity of the query.

Since the keys in an index are in sorted sequence, the index really represents the result of sorting the table. By placing an index on the ordering column(s), you can eliminate many sorts during queries.

When duplicate keys are permitted in an index, the entries that have any single value are grouped in a list. When the selectivity of the column is high these lists are short, but when there are only a few unique values the lists become quite long. For example, in an index on a column whose only two values are male and female, all the index entries are contained in just two lists of duplicates. Such an index is not very useful.

When an entry has to be deleted from a list of duplicates, the server has to read the whole list and rewrite some part of it. When adding an entry, the database server puts the new row at the end of the list. Neither operation is a problem until the number of duplicate values becomes very high. The server is forced to perform many I/O operations to read all the entries in order to find the end of the list. When it deletes an entry, it typically has to update and rewrite half of the entries in the list.

When such an index is used for querying, performance can also degrade, because the rows addressed by a key value might be spread out over the disk. Imagine an index addressing rows whose location alternates from one part of the disk to the other. As the database server tries to access each row via the index, it must perform one I/O for every row read. It would probably be better off reading the table sequentially and applying the filter to each row in turn.

If it is important to index a highly duplicate column, consider forming a composite key with another column that has few duplicate values.

Because of the extra reads that must occur when indexes are updated, some degradation will occur when there are many indexes on a table that is being updated frequently. An extremely volatile table should probably not be heavily indexed unless you feel that the amount of querying outweighs the overhead of maintaining the index file. Indexes can be dropped and recreated. During periods of heavy querying (for example, for reports), you can improve performance by creating an index on the appropriate column. Creating indexes for a large table, however, can be a time-consuming process. Also, while the index is being created, the table is exclusively locked, preventing other users from accessing it.

Because an index can require a substantial amount of disk space to maintain, it is best to keep the size of the index small relative to the row size. This is because of the way key values are stored in the index: the larger the key value, the fewer keys will fit in a node of the B+ tree. More nodes require more I/O operations to access the indexed rows.

When the rows are short or the key values are long, it might be more efficient to just read the table sequentially. There is, of course, a certain break-even point between the size of a key and the efficiency of using that index, though this varies according to the number of rows in the table.

An exception to this is key-only selects. If all columns selected in the query are in the index, the table data will not be read, thus increasing the efficiency of using such an index.

Composite indexes are created on more than one column. They facilitate joining tables on multiple columns, and can increase the uniqueness of indexed values.

When you create a composite index to help improve query performance, some of the component columns can also take advantage of this index. A composite index on three columns, say a, b, and c, can be used for queries on the two columns a and b or just on column a. You would not need to create additional indexes on these columns. This is known as a partial key search. You would not want to use this index to search on columns b and c or column c.

If several columns of one table join with several columns in another table, you should create a composite index on the columns of the table with many duplicate values. Adding a unique (or more unique) column to a column that has many duplicate values will increase the uniqueness. The query will be able to perform a partial key search using the first (highly duplicate) field, which will be faster than searching the duplicate lists.

When a table is commonly sorted on several columns, a composite index corresponding to those columns can sometimes be used to implement the ordering.

One of the primary performance objectives in database management is to reduce the number of disk accesses. OnLine uses a unit of I/O, that is, the page. Having as many rows as possible physically on the same block (or page) and in the same order as an index increases the efficiency of an indexed retrieval. By placing rows that are frequently used together in close physical proximity, you can substantially reduce disk access time. Clustering information in a data file in index order puts logically related rows in the same disk block (or page). Clustering is most useful for relatively static tables.

Clustering and reclustering takes a lot of space and time. You can avoid some clustering by loading data into a table in the desired order in the first place. The physical order of rows is their insertion order, so if the table is initially loaded with ordered data, no clustering will be needed.

In some applications, the majority of table updates can be confined to a single time period. Perhaps all updates are applied overnight or on specified dates (the end of the month, for example). When this is the case, consider dropping all nonunique indexes while the updates are being performed, then creating new indexes afterward. This can have two positive effects:

- First, since there are fewer indexes to update, the updating program is likely to run faster. Often it takes less time to drop indexes, update without them, and recreate them afterward than it does to update with the indexes in place.

- Second, newly made indexes are the most efficient ones. Frequent updates tend to dilute the index structure, causing it to contain many partly filled index nodes. This reduces the effectiveness of an index and wastes disk space.

Another time-saving measure is making sure a batch-updating program calls for rows in the sequence defined by the primary key index. That causes the pages of the primary key index to be read in order and only once.

10.5 Creating Views

A view is an alternative way of looking at the data in one or more tables. Views are virtual tables (see Figure 10.13) made up of columns from one or more tables, usually joined by some key or keys they share in common. Views facilitate access to data. They can also provide security, e.g., you can restrict the selection of employee column data such as salary.

Syntax

```
create view [owner.]view_name
       [(column_name [, column_name]...)]
       AS select [distinct] select_statement
       [with check option]
```

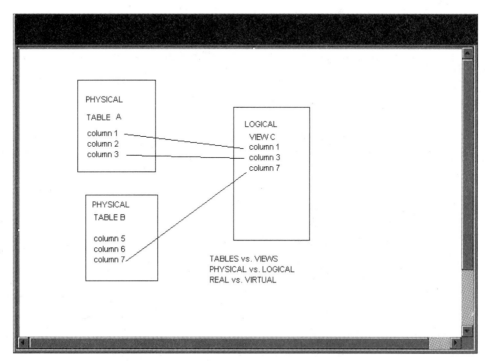

Figure 10.13 Views are not real.

Keywords and options

view_name. The name of the view. The name cannot include the database name. If you have set quoted_identifier on, you can use a delimited identifier. Otherwise, the view name must conform to the rules for identifiers.

column_name. Specifies names to be used as headings for the columns in the view. If you have set quoted_identifier on, you can use a delimited identifier. Otherwise, the column name must conform to the rules for identifiers. It is always legal to supply column names, but it is required only when a column is derived from an arithmetic expression, function, string concatenation, or constant; when two or more columns have the same name (usually because of a join); or when you want to give a column in a view a different name. Column names can also be assigned in the select statement. If no column names are specified, the view columns will acquire the same names as the columns in the select statement.

select. Begins the select statement that defines the view.

distinct. Specifies that the view cannot contain duplicate rows (optional).

select_statement. Completes the select statement that defines the view. It can use more than one table and other views.

with check option. Indicates that all data modification statements are validated against the view selection criteria. All rows inserted or updated through the view must remain visible through the view.

You can modify data through views. Just follow these rules:

- Delete statements are not allowed on multitable views.

- You cannot insert a row through a view that includes a computed column.

- Insert statements are not allowed on join views created with distinct or with check option.

- Update statements are allowed on join views with check option. The update will fail if any of the affected columns appears in the where clause, in an expression that includes columns from more than one table.

- If you insert or update a row through a join view, all affected columns must belong to the same base table.

10.6 Maintaining the Database after Creation

Creating the database and its tables is an iterative process in the development stage of any project. Your administrator will need to back up the database or selected objects, e.g., tables, and then amend the object and restore. Informix provides a fair amount of help in facilitating these amendments.

10.6.1 Modifying DDL statements

You can alter a table in most cases without having to unload and reload the data. If the ALTER TABLE statement causes columns to be physically changed, a complete copy of the table will be made with the specified changes. When the statement has completed, the old copy is deleted and the new copy of the table is used. This means that you must have enough space in your dbspace to hold two copies of the table being altered. Here are some actions the ALTER TABLE statement can perform:

Use the ADD CLAUSE to add a column to the table. The contents of the column will be NULL for rows already existing before the ALTER TABLE statement is run. You can specify where to put the column by adding the BEFORE clause. The following example puts the order_sequence_number column before the order_date column:

```
ALTER TABLE orders ADD order_sequence_num INTEGER BEFORE
order_date
```

Modify a column. You can use the MODIFY clause to change the data type or length, or allow/disallow nulls in a column. You must specify all existing attributes of a column (e.g., the UNIQUE and NOT NULL attributes) or they will be dropped. You can alter a table to change the data type if the data type is compatible with the data already in the column.

Drop a column. You can drop a column using the DROP clause. Dropping a column means that all data in that column is lost.

You can use ALTER TABLE to change the next extent size or lock mode for a table. This will not alter current extents that have been allocated, only the future ones. You can also change the locking mode of the row to either PAGE or ROW.

10.6.2 Data space reclamation

Once an extent has been allocated to a table, that extent will never be freed up for reuse by other tables. If an extent should become empty (due to massive deletes from the table), the extent will remain part of the tblspace. The space will be reused, however, when additional rows are inserted into the same table in the future.

If you want to reclaim the space in empty extents and make it available to the dbspace to use for other tables, you can use the ALTER TABLE command to achieve such a compression. Be aware, however, that ALTER TABLE will only physically restructure the table, if necessary. Thus, running an ALTER TABLE statement that does not actually change the table (e.g., altering a column to be the same as it already is) will not restructure the table. The best way to force a restructuring of the table is to alter one of the table's indexes to CLUSTER; this will always physically restructure the table, even if the index is currently clustered. For example:

```
ALTER INDEX x1_order TO CLUSTER;1
```

This statement will physically restructure the table on which the index x1_order is created. This restructuring will pack the table, freeing up space used by the empty extents. For more information about a clustered index, refer to section 10.4.1, *The CREATE INDEX statement*.

10.6.3 Dropping tables and databases

The DROP TABLE command will free up space allocated for the table to be used for other purposes. The data will no longer be accessible. The DROP DATABASE command frees up space that was allocated for all the tables in the database. The system catalog tables are dropped.

10.7 Utilities for Populating an Informix Database

When developing applications, changes occur frequently and the picture and content of the database as it is forming must be redefined and repopulated to allow development to proceed. Informix provides utilities to facilitate these requirements.

10.7.1 Generating a database schema

The DBSCHEMA utility produces a SQL command file that contains the CREATE TABLE, CREATE INDEX, GRANT, CREATE SYNONYM, and CREATE VIEW statements required to replicate an entire database or a selected table. You must specify the database with the –d option. The following additional options can also be included:

–ttabname. Only the table or view is included. Specify all in place of tabname for all tables.

–ssynname. SYNONYM statements for the specified user (synname) are included. Specify all in place of synname for all synonyms.

–p pname. Print only GRANT statements for the listed user. Specify all in place of pname for all users.

–fstproc. Print the stored procedure that is listed. Specify all in place of stproc for all stored procedures.

–hd tabname. Displays distribution information. Specify all in place of tabname for all tables.

–ss. Generates server-specific information for the specified table, including the lock mode, extent sizes, and dbspace name.

10.7.2 Populating a database

One of the most frequent requirements is loading tables from flat-file extracts from other systems, for example downloads from a mainframe MVS or AS400 legacy or heritage system. Informix provides various options for loading a table, but first a few notes about the target table definition:

The presence of indexes slows down the population of tables. Drop the indexes and then load the table. Create the indexes after the table load is complete. Loading a table that has no indexes at all is a very quick process (little more than a disk-to-disk sequential copy), but updating indexes adds a great deal of overhead.

10.7.3 Utilities to load and unload database data

There are utilities to either unload data from a database or load data into a database. To UNLOAD data you can use dbexport or onunload. To LOAD you can use dbimport, onload, or dbload.

Dbexport utility

Use dbexport to:

- Unload data for an entire database into ASCII files.
- Unload database data and schema to disk or tape.
- Unload database data to tape and schema to disk.

Dbexport unloads data from an entire database into ASCII files. The ASCII files and schema can be retained on disk or on tape. Error messages and warnings are written to a file named dbexport.out.

Dbexport will take a database and create a special directory containing files of ASCII dumps for each of the tables in the specified database, as well as a SQL file containing DDK commands and some additional information. These files will be used by the companion dbimport utility to recreate the database.

```
DBEXPORT -c -d -q destination-option database -ss -V
```

The –c option instructs the program to continue even if errors occur, until a fatal error occurs. The fatal errors are:

- Unable to open the specified tape device.
- Bad writes to the tape or disk.
- Invalid command parameters.
- Cannot open database or no system permission.

The –d option exports blob descriptors only and not blob data. The –q option suppresses the echoing of SQL statements, error messages, and warnings.

The destination options are:

–o directory path. Specifies the directory where the ASCII files are to be stored. The specified directory must already exist. A subdirectory within the specified directory, named database.exp, will be created for you and will hold the data files. The default is the current working directory.

–t device. Directs the output to a tape device.

–b blksize. Specifies the tape block size in kilobytes.

–s tapesize. Specifies the number of kilobytes to be written to each tape.

–f file-path. Directs the SQL command file to disk in the file indicated by the full path name.

The name of the database to be exported, e.g., warehous, is database. The –ss option generates server-specific information for all tables in the specified database. When the database is unloaded, the schemas contain the following information:

- Logging mode of the database.
- Initial extent size of the table.
- Lock mode of the table.
- Dbspace the table is located in.

The –V option displays product version information.

The following command exports the warehous database to tape. The block size is 16 kilobytes, and 24,000 kilobytes are written to each tape. If errors occur, the program will continue:

```
dbexport -c -t /dev/rnt0 -b 16 -s 24000 warehous
```

The following command exports the warehous database to tape and puts the warehous.sql schema file on disk in the /usr/whdirectory:

```
dbexport -c -t /dev/rmo -b 16 -s 2400 -f /usr/wh/warehous.sql warehous -ss
```

The dbimport utility
Use dbimport to :

- Execute the schema and have the database created for you.
- Import ASCII data into the specified database.
- Load the data and schema disk or tape.

Dbimport will create a database and load it with the ASCII input files generated by dbexport.

```
DBIMPORT -c -d -q input-file -i -t -s -f create-option database
```

The option –c instructs the program to continue even if errors occur, until a fatal error occurs. The fatal errors are:

- Unable to open the tape device specified.
- Bad reads from the tape or disk.
- Invalid command parameters.
- Cannot create database or no system permission.

The input file location options are:

−l directory-path. Specifies the directory where the data files are located.

−t device. Directs the input from a tape device.

−b blocksize. Specifies the tape block size in kilobytes.

−s tapesize. Specifies the number of kilobytes to be read from each tape.

−f pathname. Specifies the input path for the SQL command file.

The −q option suppresses the echoing of SQL statements. The name of the database is database. The create options are:

−d dbspace. The destination dbspace for an OnLine database.

−l. Specifies that the imported database is to use transaction logging.

buffered. Specifies that logging is to be buffered. The default is unbuffered logging.

−ANSI. Tells a program to create the new database as MODE ANSI.
Users who runs dbimport are granted DBA permission on the database. Dbimport performs an implicit lock table and unlock table when the database is loaded. If you use tape and the −b and −s options, you must use the same block size and tape size you used to export the database. If you also used the −f option in dbexport, you must use the same block size and tape size you used to export the database, and you must specify the same command file that you specified when you imported the database. A message file, dbimport.out, is always created. It contains error messages and warnings relating to running the program. If you specify the input directory name with the −I option, you can use either a full directory pathname from the root directory (/) or the directory path from your current directory (./).

The file starting with your database name and the .sql extension contains the commands to load your database. If you use the tape option (−t), the commands will be located on the tape. If you use the −t and −f options, you must specify the path and the name of the file to be used as the command file. Typically, it will be the same as that specified for dbexport. Otherwise, the command file is found in the EXP directory of either your current directory or the directory you specified with the −l option. Online databases are created in the dbspace that you specify with the −d option. If you do not specify this option, the database will be created in the root dbspace.

Do not run the program in the background when you use the tape option (−t). Press the Interrupt key to cancel the program. You will be asked to confirm your choice.

The imported database is, by default, created without logging. If you want to have logging turned on for the database, use the −l option. If you use a tape device, you must specify the block size and the amount of data on each tape.

The block size and the tape size are in kilobytes (K). The maximum tape size is 2,097,151 kilobytes.

The following command loads the warehous database from tape into the dbspace dbspace2, and suppresses the echo of SQL statements. The program continues even if errors are found.

```
dbimport -cq -d dbspace2 -t/dev/rmt0 -b 16 -s 24000 warehous
```

The following command imports the warehous database from the directory /usr/warehous.exp using data definition statements and commands from the files warehous.sql in that directory. The new database is put in the root dbspace. The new database is MODE ANSI, with implied unbuffered logging.

```
dbimport -c -i /usr/warehous -ANSI warehous
```

Dbimport and dbexport were originally designed to allow migration from large Informix-SE databases to large Informix-OnLine Dynamic Server databases, but you can also use them to move from one SE database to another, from one OnLine database to another, or from OnLine to SE.

The dbload utility

Dbload is a utility that can load data from one or more ASCII files on disk into one or more existing tables. The ASCII file can be created with the UNLOAD utility or by another means (a program, text editor, or any other unload utility that unloads data to ASCII). Dbload offers more flexibility than LOAD, and can load data into database tables from ASCII files on disk.

Also, dbload differs from dbimport in that the data in the ASCII files can be added to data that already exists in a table. You must create the table before dbload can add data to it. The load file is an ASCII file with each column separated by a specific delimiter. You can alter the delimiter from the default (¦) by setting the DBDELIMITER environment variable.

Dbload has several features that offer more flexibility than using the LOAD statement:

- You can specify a starting point in the load file.
- You can add transaction logic (commit after every x rows).
- You can limit the number of bad rows read, at which time dbload terminates.
- You can use dbload to load fixed-length files into a database.

```
DBLOAD -d database -c commandfile -l errorfile -r -I -n -e -p
```

Here are some possible options to the dbload command:

–c commandfile. Specifies the file name of a dbload command file.

–d database. Specifies the name of the database to receive the data.

–l errorfile. Specifies the filename or pathname of an error log file.

–r. Instructs dbload not to lock the table(s) during loading, enabling users to update data in the table during the load.

–inum-rows ignored. Instructs dbload to ignore the specified number of NEW-LINE characters in the input file.

–n num-rows. Instructs dbload to execute a COMMIT after the specified number of new rows are inserted. This option works only if your database has logging. If this option is not set, a COMMIT will occur every 100 rows.

–e num-errors. Specifies the number of bad rows that dbload will read before terminating.

–p. Prompts for instructions if the number of bad rows exceeds the limit.
You must first create a command file before you can run dbload. There are two types of command files. One uses delimiters and the other uses character positions. The previous example uses the delimiter form. There are two types of statements in a command file:

The FILE statement specifies the location and description of the data files. The fields in the data file are separated by a delimiter that you specify in your FILE statement within quotes. You must also specify how many fields each data row has. When dbload executes, the columns will be assigned the internal names f01, f02, f03, etc.

The INSERT statement specifies what table to insert the loaded rows into. It also specifies the order. In the previous example, the fields are loaded into the stock columns in the order the columns appear in the syscolumns system catalog.

The dbload command file

The character position file statement assumes that the load file has a fixed length, and each field starts at a specific character position within each line. The previous example describes three values: city, state, and zip. Each value is given a start position and a stop position.

The zip value has an optional NULL clause. If dbload encounters the value specified in the NULL clause in the zip position, it will substitute a NULL for the zip value in the INSERT statement.

It is possible to specify more than one INSERT statement for each FILE statement. You might, for example, want to insert a row in the valid addr table and a row into the zip table for each line in the load file.

The onload and onunload utilities

Onunload and onload are very efficient ways to transfer data because the data is read and written in binary pages. The key to these utilities is their performance. The utilities are available only with OnLine databases and cannot be run for databases across a network.

The onunload utility writes an entire database or table in binary disk-page units to tape. It cannot be used to write to a file. You can read the tape using only the onload utility.

You can specify a table or entire database to be created when onload is run. You must have resource privileges on the database to run onload. The owner defaults to the user running onload unless otherwise specified.

Page size varies from machine to machine (check your OnLine configuration file, onconfig, for the page size for your OnLine system). You cannot use the utilities to transfer data from one OnLine system to another with a different page size. Most OnLine systems have either 4K or 2K pages.

You can unload either the entire contents of a database or the entire contents of a table with onunload. The syntax for onunload is:

```
ONUNLOAD tape-options database¦table
```

and the tape options are:

–1. Directs onunload to read the values for tape, device, block size, and tape size from the logical-log backup device parameters in the OnLine configuration file, onconfig.

–t device. Specifies the path name of the tape device. You specify a remote tape device using the following syntax:

```
host machine name:tape device pathname
```

–b blksize. Specifies the block size of the tape device, in kilobytes.

–s tapesize. Specifies the number of kilobytes to be stored on each tape.

- The name of the database is specified by database, and the owner and name of the table is specified by table.

- The logging mode and ANSI compliance are not preserved when a database is unloaded. You must change these options after the database is loaded to the destination.

- You must have DBA privileges to unload a database and either DBA privileges or ownership of the table to unload a single table.

- If you do not specify any tape parameter options, onunload will use the archive tape parameters by default.

Onload creates an entire database or table in a specified dbspace and loads the ASCII data from a tape created by the onunload utility. Onload's syntax is:

```
ONLOAD tape-options create-options database¦table
```

and the tape parameter options are:

–l. Directs onload to read the values for tape device from the OnLine configuration file parameters.

–t device. Specifies the pathname of the tape device. You can specify a remote tape device using the following syntax:

```
host machine name:tape device pathname
```

–b blksize. Specifies the block size in kilobytes of the tape device.

–s tapesize. Specifies the number of kilobytes to be stored on each tape.
The create options are:

–d dbspace. Specifies the name of the dbspace the table or database will reside in. You do not specify the dbspace the table or database will reside in. The table or database being loaded will be placed in the root dbspace.

–I or ind n-ind. Can be used to rename indexes during the load to avoid conflict with existing index names. You must specify a table name on the command line for the –I option to take effect.

- Data loaded as a result of onload will be logged if the database is created with logging. It is recommended that you turn off logging before loading a large amount of data, and then perform an archive after your data is successfully loaded.

- When a new database is loaded, the user who runs onload becomes the owner. Ownership within the database (tables, views, and indexes) remains the same as when the database was unloaded to tape with onunload.

- Synonyms or access privileges are not carried over if you are loading an individual table.

Building the Data
Manipulation Language (DML)

A sometimes gray area in the application design is the database transaction, which is comprised of data manipulation (DML). Where does it start, and where does it end? After you use DML for a while, you will begin to ask questions like ". . . should we use stored procedures or do we use embedded SQL to access and update the database?" Stored procedures allow you to be independant of the front-end GUI, but they neutralize some of the benefits developers can derive from developing native SQL. When developing the application with native SQL, the prudent developer must consider how to manage database transactions and database access during application execution. There are a number of considerations:

- The options available for connecting to the database(s).

- How to manage database-specific logical units of work.

- How to control and avoid potentially expensive database operations.

- How and when to use techniques for dynamically modifying the database interaction.

- How to control and provide viable and concurrent access for multiple users.

11.1 Connecting to the Database

In most contemporary GUI front-end programs, e.g., PowerBuilder, all database connections are managed with a transaction object typically known as SQLCA for relational database systems. Informix uses SQLCA as well. When using a tool like PowerBuilder, the contents of pertinent Informix SQLCA

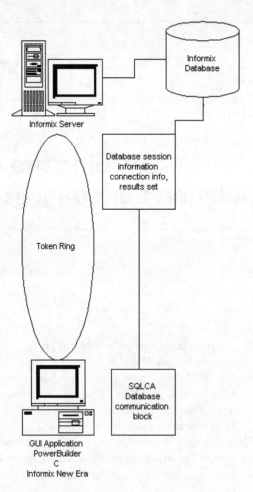

Figure 11.1   SQLCA and the database.

fields, e.g., SQLCODE, are transferred to the PowerBuilder SQLCA so the application can examine the content and determine what to do next. Figure 11.1 depicts the PowerBuilder transaction object SQLCA, which contains all fields used to manage the database access, e.g., user login and database return codes. The default transaction object SQLCA is created when the application is invoked and destroyed when the application terminates.

You can prime SQLCA, i.e., set up the connect to a database (see the following section), using one or more of the following techniques:

- Load values from an application .INI file (static server name, database name, and specifics).

- Prompt the user for values using a logon screen (userid and password).

- Code the values in a script (varying between servers based on availability).

A database CONNECT is generally an expensive operation and should be managed carefully. Try to optimize their invocation. Sometimes they are unavoidable. In Sybase, for example, if you are using a cursor to traverse one table and you want to do INSERTs on another table while continuing to FETCH, Sybase requires a second database thread or connection. You would have to manage the second transaction within a script containing embedded SQL.

11.1.1 The transaction object

In a GUI front-end program like PowerBuilder, all database connections are managed with a transaction object. The default transaction object, SQLCA, is created when the application is invoked and destroyed when the application terminates.

.SQLCA attributes

DBMS.
Specifies which relational database engine will be used (Sybase, Oracle, MDIDB2)

Database.
The name of the database where SYSPB catalog tables will be built

UserID.
Database user ID

DBPass.
Database passwords

Lock.
Type of locking

LogID.
User ID

LogPass.
User password

ServerName.
Name of server (usually a symbolic assignment to a remote connection)

DBParm.
Database parameters specific to the DBMS

> **SQLCode.**
> Return code from the last SQL access (*always* check this after each access)

11.1.2 Priming transaction objects

Before connecting to a database, an application must prime the transaction object (SQLCA or user-defined) with the attribute values required by the target database. Review the particular attribute settings for each DBMS to ensure the proper connection.

These are the basic SQLCA parameters. The ideal technique is to read most of these values from an application .INI file and prompt the user for login ID and password. You can use one, two, or combination of all three methods, depending on the requirements of your site.

11.1.3 Managing database connections

At various times within the course of embedded SQL development, when you invoke the database from within an application execution, a GUI front end like PowerBuilder connects to the database. The connection takes place when either the CONNECT verb is executed or a DML statement coded by the programmer is executed.

11.1.4 Logical units of work

Once connected, you will need to manage the database transactions (logical units of work). A logical unit of work is a set of database operations that must be completed or rejected together, e.g., debiting one account and crediting another. For example, the SQL might look like this:

```
UPDATE tb_acct   SET balance_qty = balance_qty + :arg1_qty
     WHERE acct_no = :arg2_acct;
   IF Sql_code  0 .quit transaction ; return to caller
UPDATE tb_acct    SET balance_qty = balance_qty - :arg1_qty
     WHERE acct_no = :arg3_acct;
   IF Sql_code  0
     ROLLBACK
   ELSE
     COMMIT;
```

Developers need to recognize what constitutes a logical unit of work within the context of the application to guarantee the integrity of the data. For example, if you are deleting a TV series, you must delete all its episodes first before you can delete the series, or you will have orphan episodes.

When several users can access the same data at the same time, you must take precautions to prevent any collisions. Concurrency is a database issue rather than a GUI front-end issue, but that does not relieve developers from understanding the implications of the SQL. Prudent developers must be aware of the various types of concurrent transactions: retrieve only, single-row retrieval with single-row update, multiple-row retrieval with single-row (or limited) update, and multiple-row retrieval with multiple-row update. Each of these will affect how you will manage the logical unit of work. A well-placed stored procedure or a well-constructed user object with an embedded SQL script can overcome shortcomings or semantic GUI front-end snafus.

11.2 Basic Data Manipulation Language

Structured Query Language, or SQL as it is commonly known, is an English-like language that allows you to create, manage, and use databases. The SQL provided with Informix products is an enhanced version of the industry-standard query language that was originally developed by IBM. Data manipulation is a special subset of SQL that includes:

- Data definition (DDL)
- Data manipulation (DML)
- Cursor manipulation
- Dynamic management
- Data access (DCL)
- Data integrity
- Stored procedures (SPL)

Informix's variety of SQL includes just about 50 statements, which can be divided into the following categories:

Data definition statements. Used to create a database and define its structure

Data manipulation statements. Used to select, insert, update, or delete data in a database

Cursor manipulation statements. Used to work with cursors (open, fetch, or close a cursor)

Dynamic management statements. Used to dynamically manage resources at runtime.

Data access statements. Used to determine how data can be accessed (often referred to as data control (DCL) statements)

Data integrity statements. Used to preserve data integrity

Query optimization information statements. Used to obtain information regarding the execution of a query

Stored procedure statements. Used to execute and debug stored procedures

Auxiliary statements. Additional statements that do not fit into the previous categories, yet are part of the SQL provided with Informix products (e.g., WHENEVER, INFO, and OUTPUT)

In this chapter, we will concentrate on data manipulation statements, which in the Informix relational model include:

- Selecting a set of data (one or more rows) from the database.
- Inserting a set of data (one or more rows) into the database.
- Updating a set of data (one or more rows) already in the database.
- Deleting a set of data (one or more rows) already in the database.
- Loading a flat ASCII file containing data (one or more rows) into the database.
- Unloading data (one or more rows) from the database into a flat ASCII file.

In addition, there are the following statements used to control transaction processing:

- BEGIN WORK
- COMMIT WORK
- ROLLBACK WORK

11.2.1 The SELECT statement

The most popular DML statement is SELECT. The SELECT statement is used to retrieve a resulting set of data from the tables in a database. The SELECT statement's WHERE clause describes the contents of the set or set intersection using logical connectors such as AND. SELECT is made up of the following clauses:

```
SELECT select-list
FROM table-name
[WHERE condition]
[GROUP BY column-list]
[HAVING condition]
[ORDER BY column-name]
[INTO TEMP table-name]
```

Only the SELECT and FROM clauses are required. These clauses specify the tables and columns to be retrieved. The remaining clauses are optional. When writing a SELECT statement, keywords, database names, column names, and table names are not case-sensitive. Column values used in the WHERE clause, however, *are* case-sensitive, so NY does not equal ny, which does not equal Ny. This is because the column in the row (physical database content) is case-sensitive. If you use the optional clauses, they must appear in the order shown in the example.

You can use the SELECT statement to look at one, several, or all rows in a table. Unless you specify otherwise by including the WHERE clause, all rows will be retrieved. The select-list, which immediately follows the word SELECT, determines which columns the SELECT statement retrieves. An asterisk (*) is shorthand for saying that you want to retrieve all columns in the table. You can use the asterisk whenever you want all the columns in a table in their defined order. The FROM keyword, which is required, is followed by the name of the table that contains the data you want. In the following example DML, all rows and columns are retrieved from the orders table:

```
SELECT * from orders
```

You can specify which columns you want the SELECT statement to find by including them in the select-list immediately after the keyword SELECT. You can specify any number of columns, and only those columns will appear in the output. The order of the columns in the select-list determines the order of the columns in the output. The previous example selects only a subset of the columns for all rows in the sku_master table.

```
SELECT sku, description, retail_price from sku_master
```

You can suppress duplicate rows of data from being retrieved by including the keyword DISTINCT or its synonym UNIQUE in your SELECT statement at the start of the select-list.

```
SELECT DISTINCT sku, quantity from ship_history
```

You can select part of the value of a column that is of the data type character by including a substring in your select-list. For example, if you wanted to find the geographical distribution of your customers based on their zip codes, you could use the following SELECT statement to retrieve only the first three characters of each customer's zip code:

```
SELECT zip_cde(1,3) from customers
```

11.2.2 The WHERE clause

Probably the most important clause in the SELECT statement, from an impact point of view, is the WHERE clause. This is where the game is won or lost in terms of performance and accuracy of data retrieval.

```
SELECT select-list
FROM table-name
[WHERE condition]
```

The WHERE clause is used for two distinct purposes:

- To specify search criteria for selecting specific rows.
- To create join conditions among multiple tables.

The WHERE clause specifies comparison conditions that define the search criteria for the rows you want to retrieve. You are literally saying "find me the set of rows where . . . (see Figure 11.2). The following keywords can be used in comparison conditions:

SQL SELECT statement

WHERE clause

SELECT columns FROM table1 WHERE property a AND property b

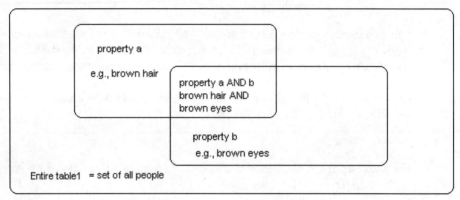

Figure 11.2   The WHERE clause.

BETWEEN. Finds a range of values between x and y

IN. Finds a subset of values in x where x is one or more values

LIKE. Performs variable text searches

IS NULL. Identifies NULL values

NOT. Can be used with any of the previous keywords to specify the opposite condition

AND. Finds the intersection of two WHERE conditions

OR. Finds the union of two WHERE conditions

You can also use the following relational operators in place of a keyword to test for equality:

=. Equals

!= or . Does not equal

>. Is greater than

>=. Is greater than or equal to

<=. Is less than or equal to

<. Is less than

So how do you include or exclude rows? The examples demonstrate how to use the WHERE clause to include or exclude values when selecting rows from a database table.

The first example uses the equal operator (=) to find all rows in which the column equals one particular case. The second example uses the not equal operator (!= or <>) to find all rows except those in which the column equals the target case. As a practical matter, columns used frequently in the WHERE clause of your SELECT statements should be indexed if and only if they have a range of uniformly distributed values whose number exceeds 20 or more.

You can use the keywords BETWEEN and AND to find rows with values in a specified range. The following example finds all rows with a unit price between $20 and $30. You can obtain the same results by using the greater than or equal to (>=) and less than or equal to (<=) relational operators:

```
select  stock num, manu code, description, unit price
   from stock
   where unit price = 20.00

select  stock num, manu code, description, unit price
   from stock
   where unit price <> 20.00

select  stock num, manu code, description, unit price
   from stock
   where unit price BETWEEN 20.00 and 30.00

select  stock num, manu code, description, unit price
   from stock
   where unit price >= 20.00 and unit price <= 30.00
```

The following example finds all customers who live in the states of New Jersey, New York, or Oregon:

```
select * from  customer  where state IN ('NJ', 'NY', 'OR')
```

You can also use the IN keyword of a WHERE clause as shorthand for the OR keyword. The previous example could also have been written as:

```
select *

   from customer
   where state = 'NJ' or
      state = 'NY' or
      state = 'OR'
```

Both statements return the same information, but when you use OR, the customer num column name must be repeated for every value you want to check. You could modify the previous SELECT statement to retrieve all rows except those where the state is equal to NJ, NY, or OR by inserting the NOT keyword prior to the IN keyword.

```
select * from  customer  where state NOT IN ('NJ', 'NY', 'OR')
```

The ORDER BY clause

The ORDER BY clause allows you to sort query results by the values contained in one or more columns. Including the keyword ASC following a column name in the ORDER BY clause specifies that the results should be sorted in ascending order, which is the default. DESC specifies that the results should be sorted in descending order. You might need both if scrolling is required. NULL values are evaluated as less than non-null values when ordering result rows. The OR-DER BY column must be in the select-list. The column listed first in the OR-DER BY clause takes precedence over the second column, which takes precedence over the third column, etc.

```
SELECT select-list
    FROM table-name
    [WHERE condition]
    [GROUP BY column-list]
    [HAVING condition]
    [ORDER BY column-name]
    [INTO TEMP table-name]
```

Make sure that, if the expected result set is large, the ORDER BY column is an index. This will avoid sorting the data and thereby improve performance.

Aggregate functions

In addition to column names and operators, an expression can include one or more functions. There are five aggregate functions you can use:

COUNT (*). Counts the number of rows that satisfy the conditions of the SELECT statement

SUM (column/expression). Sums the values in the given numeric column or expression

AVG (column/expression). Finds the arithmetic mean of the values in the given numeric column or expression

MAX (column/expression). Finds the maximum value in the given column or expression

MIN(column/expression). Finds the minimum value in the given column or expression

You can also use some of these functions with the DISTINCT or UNIQUE keyword:

COUNT (DISTINCT column-name). Counts the distinct value in a particular column

SUM(DISTINCT column-name). Sums the distinct values in a particular numeric column

AVG (DISTINCT column-name). Finds the arithmetic mean of the distinct values in a particular numeric column

You can use display labels to specify the headers to be used when these functions are included in a SELECT statement.

The COUNT (*) function counts the total number of rows in the hypothetical subset of the stock table shown. When the DISTINCT keyword is included with a column name, as shown in the second example, the COUNT (DISTINCT description) function counts only the distinct values in the description column.

The SUM (total price) function sums all the values in the total price column of this subset of the items table and presents the total. When the DISTINCT keyword is included with a column name, as shown in the second example, the SUM (DISTINCT total price) function adds up the distinct values in the total price column.

Algebraic and trigonometric functions

There are many algebraic and trigonometric functions you can use. This section lists some of the more commonly used functions. Refer to the *Informix Guide to SQL: Syntax* for a complete listing.

Hex(column/expression). Returns the hexadecimal encoding of an expression

ROUND (column/expression). Returns the rounded value of a column or an expression

TRUNC(column/expression). Returns the truncated value of a column or an expression

TAN(column/expression). Returns the tangent of a radicand column or an expression

ABS(column/expression). Returns the absolute value of a column or an expression

MOD(dividend, divisor). Returns the modulus or remainder value for two numeric expressions

Statistical functions

The following statistical functions are new starting in the 7.10 release:

Standard deviation. The stdev() function returns the standard deviation of the selected rows, which is computed using the formula for the standard deviation of a sample of the population. The standard deviation is the square root of the variance (see the following).

Variance. The variance() function returns the sample variance of the selected rows. This function uses the following formula:

```
(sum(X**2) - sum(X)**2/N)/(N-1)
```

The value X is each value in the selected column, and the value N is the total number of values in the column.

Range. The range() function returns the difference between the maximum and minimum value of the selected rows.

Time functions

You can use time functions in either the SELECT clause or the WHERE clause of a query. These functions return a value that corresponds to the expression(s) or argument(s) you use to call the function. The time functions are as follows:

DAY (date/datetime expression). Returns an integer that represents the day

MONTH (date/datetime expression). Returns an integer that represents the month

WEEKDAY (date/datetime expression). Returns an integer that represents the day of the week (0 through 6, where Sunday is 0)

YEAR (date/datetime expression). Returns a four-digit integer that represents the year

DATE (nondate expression). Returns a date value corresponding to the character expression you use to call it

EXTEND (date/datetime expression, [first TO last]). Adjusts the precision of a date or datetime value

MDY (month, day, year). Returns the date in MM/dd/yyyy format for a given month, day, and year

CURRENT. Returns a datetime value with the date and time of day of the current instant

Note: A date/datetime expression evaluates to a date or datetime value.

The YEAR function is as follows:

```
select customer_num from orders
   where year (1st_order_date) = 1995
```

This example returns the customer num where the year of the last order date values for all of the rows in the orders table is 1995. The TODAY function returns the system date as a DATE type. The CURRENT function returns a value with the date and time of day, showing the current instant.

The GROUP BY clause

The GROUP BY clause produces a single row of results for each group of rows, which have the same value in a given column. It sorts the data into groups, and then compresses all the rows in each group with like values into a single row. The number of groups depends on the number of distinct values within the column in the table.

```
select customer_number, SUM(order_quantity) from orders
   GROUP BY customer_number
```

In the previous example, the SELECT statement with the GROUP BY clause returns only one row for each distinct customer number in the orders table. You cannot group by a BYTE or TEXT column.

GROUP BY and aggregates

The GROUP BY clause is used with aggregate calculation functions to provide summary information for a group. The previous SELECT statement groups all rows in the orders table with the same customer number together. After the groups are formed, the sum function is applied within each group. The result is a list of customer numbers and the sum total quantity for each customer.

Note: You will get an error if all nonaggregate columns in the SELECT clause are not listed in the GROUP BY clause. For example, the following SELECT statement:

```
select city, state, count (*)
   from customer
   group by city
```

will generate the following error message:

```
294: The column (state) must be in the GROUP BY list
```

You can use an aggregate function to avoid this. The solution is to put the MAX function around the state column as follows:

```
select city, MAX(state), count (*)
   from customer
   group by city
```

Ordering grouped data

The GROUP BY clause does not order data. Make sure to include an ORDER BY clause after your GROUP BY clause if you want to sort the rows returned into a particular order. You can use an integer in an ORDER BY clause or GROUP BY clause to indicate the position of column names or display labels in the group list. Note: Null values are grouped together and will appear first in an ascending sort.

```
select city, state, count (*)
   from customer
   group by 1, state
   order by city, 2
```

You can use the HAVING clause in conjunction with the GROUP BY clause to apply one or more qualifying conditions to groups after they are formed. The HAVING clause provides a filter for grouped results, in the same way a WHERE clause filters individual row results.

```
select customer_num, sum(order_price)
   from orders
   group by 1
   having count(*) > 10
```

Note: The HAVING clause does not require a GROUP BY clause, although it is almost always used with one. If the HAVING clause is used without GROUP BY, the HAVING condition applies to all rows that satisfy the search condition. In other words, all rows that satisfy the search condition make up a single group.

The INTO TEMP clause

By adding an INTO TEMP clause to your SELECT statement, you can temporarily save the results of a query in a separate table that you can query or modify without changing the database. This is not an ANSI standard. Other RDBMSs have temporary tables but are handled differently. For example,

Sybase temp tables are defined and begin with # (a pound sign). The Informix temporary tables that are created by this clause are dropped automatically when:

- You exit dbaccess (the all-purpose database access tool).
- At the end of a SQL session (DISCONNECT).
- When you issue a drop table statement.
- When you exit a program or report.

The INTO TEMP clause is the last clause in a SELECT statement.

Joining together with the FROM clause

Before too long you will want information from more than one table. For example, you might want to see a customer and all of his or her orders. The customer and order tables have a relationship. For every entry in the customer table, there could be one or more entries in the orders table.

To view a customer and all of his or her orders, you would need to find the customer number in the customer table, and then find all occurrences of that customer number in the orders table. In order to access data from two tables, you must enter some additional information into the SELECT, FROM, and WHERE clauses of your SELECT statement:

```
select customer_name, Order_num
  from customer, order
  where customer.Customer_num = order.Customer_num
```

Within the FROM clause, you must list the tables from which you are selecting the columns entered in the SELECT statement. Within the WHERE clause, you must list the columns to be matched in order to join the two tables together, for example customer.customer_num and orders.customer_num columns.

Note: Because both tables being selected from include the column customer_num, you must specify which customer_num you want to see by using the table_name.column syntax. In this, multiple rows are returned for customers with more than one order. And no rows are returned for customers who have not placed orders. Since NULL values represent unknowns, they will not join. Note: When you join large tables, performance will be better when the columns in the join condition are indexed.

If you get an ambiguous column error, look at the column in parentheses and find it in your SELECT statement. This column must have a table prefix everywhere it occurs in the SELECT statement. Because both tables include the column customer_num, you must state which customer_num you want to see. In the case of a join column, it does not matter which one you choose.

When you perform a multiple table query without specifying a join condition, the result is the dreaded "Cartesian product." A Cartesian product consists of every possible combination of rows from the tables you are querying—usually a very large result that contains inaccurate data. Beware of this. Desk-check your SQL to avoid this, or you will have to contact operations to cancel your session before the machine explodes.

Equi-joins and natural joins
An equi-join is a join based on matching values in the WHERE clause of a SELECT statement using the equals(=) operation. In an equi-join, the select-list contains all columns from both tables, as shown in the example in the previous section, so the column(s) in common appears twice in the result.

Natural joins are simply equi-joins with the duplicate column eliminated from the output by means of a more explicit select-list. This is the most common type of join. Note: All joins are associative. The order of the joining terms in the WHERE clause does not affect the meaning of the join. The optimizer will resolve this and choose the best path to the data.

The simple outer join
In an outer join, the tables are treated asymmetrically. One of the tables is dominant (also called preserved); the other is subservient. All the rows of the dominant table are retrieved whether or not there are corresponding rows in the subservient table. The subservient table follows the keyword OUTER. If the subservient table has no rows satisfying the condition, the columns from the subservient table will have NULL values. If an OUTER join is specified, a join condition must exist in the WHERE clause.

There are four logically distinct types of outer joins we will discuss. In the example in the previous section, the orders table is subservient to the customer table because it follows the keyword OUTER. As you can see from the results of the two queries, the simple join query fetches only customers who have placed order. The outer join query, on the other hand, fetches all customers, whether they have placed an order or not. This is because the customer table is the dominant table, and therefore the rows of the customer table that would have been discarded in a simple join are preserved. This outer join example queries only two tables. You can, in fact, use outer joins to query any number of tables. The following example describes the ways you can query three tables using outer joins.

```
select customer_name, Order_num
    from customer, outer order
    where customer.Customer_num = order.Customer_num
```

This outer join query is an example of a nested simple join. It produces a list of all customers with supplemental information (order number). The outer join then combines the customer table with the order information.

Self joins
A join does not always have to involve more than one table. You can join a table to itself, creating a self join. A self join is useful when you want to compare values in a column to other values in the same column. Think of a self join as a join between two tables that are in fact the same table. To resolve column-name am-

biguities in the select-list and WHERE clause, both references to the table must be given an alias in the FROM clause. Note: When you want to join one or more columns in the same table, using a self join is more efficient than creating a temporary table. A self join can result in faster execution and less disk usage.

Self joins are also useful for recursive relationships. A recursive relationship is one in which a row of one table is related to one or more rows of the same table. The complete syntax of the SELECT statement is as follows:

```
select [all ¦ distinct] select_list
 [into [[database.]owner.]table_name]
— used to send data into host variables
[from [[database.]owner.]{table_name ¦view_name}
[,[[database.]owner.]{table_name ¦view_name}
 [where search_conditions]
   [group by [all] aggregate_free_expression
   [, aggregate_free_expression]... ]
   [having search_conditions]
   [order by
      {[[[database.]owner.]{table_name.¦view_name.}]
   column_name ¦ select_list_number ¦ expression}
   [asc ¦ desc]
[,{[[[database.]owner.]{table_name¦view_name.}]
   column_name ¦ select_list_number ¦ expression}
      [asc ¦ desc]]...]
[compute row_aggregate(column_name)
      [, row_aggregate(column_name)]...
   [by column_name [, column_name]...]]
[into TEMP table_name }
```

11.2.3 The UPDATE statement

The UPDATE DML statement changes data in existing rows, either by adding data to previously NULL columns or by modifying existing data presently stored in a column. So you would use the UPDATE statement to change the content of one or more columns in one or more existing rows of the table. The WHERE clause of the UPDATE statement is used to specify precisely which rows are to be updated. Without the WHERE clause, all rows in the table will be updated! Note: If you want to ensure that you will update only one row, specify the primary key columns(s) in the WHERE clause.

Syntax
```
UPDATE [[database.]owner.]{table_name ¦ view_name}
SET [[[database.]owner.]{table_name.¦view_name.}]
   column_name1 ={expression1¦NULL¦(select_statement)}
   [, column_name2 =
{expression2¦NULL¦(select_statement)}]...
   [FROM [[database.]owner.]{table_name ¦ view_name}
   [,[[database.]owner.]{table_name¦view_name}]...]
[WHERE search_conditions] [where current of cursor_name]
```

Keywords and options

SET. Specifies the column name and assigns the new value. The value can be an expression or a NULL. When listing more than one column name and value pair, you must separate them with commas.

FROM. Uses data from other tables or views to modify rows in the table or view you are updating.

WHERE. A standard WHERE clause.

WHERE CURRENT OF. Causes Informix to update the row of the table or view indicated by the current cursor position for cursor_name.

Use UPDATE to change values in rows that have already been inserted, and use INSERT to add new rows. Informix will not prevent you from issuing an UPDATE statement that updates a single row more than once in a given transaction. However, because of the way the UPDATE is processed, updates from a single statement will not accumulate. So if an UPDATE statement modifies the same row twice, the second update will not be based on the new values from the first update, but on the original values. The results are unpredictable since they depend on the order of processing.

Updating variable-length character data or text columns with the empty string ("") inserts a single space. Fixed-length character columns are padded to the defined length. All trailing spaces are removed from variable-length column data, except in the case of a string that contains only spaces. Strings that contain only spaces are truncated to a single space. Updating to a text column initializes the text column, assigns it a valid text pointer, and allocates at least one 2K data page.

Updates and cursors

To update a row using a cursor, first define the cursor with DECLARE CURSOR, then open it. Any update to the cursor result set will also affect the base table row that the cursor row is derived from. The table_name or view_name specified with UPDATE...WHERE CURRENT OF must be the table or view specified in the first FROM clause of the SELECT statement that defines the cursor. If the FROM clause references more than one table or view (using a join), you can specify only the table or view actually being updated. After the update, the cursor position will remain unchanged. You can continue to update the row at that cursor position as long as another SQL statement does not move the position of that cursor. Informix allows you to update columns that are not specified in the list of columns of the cursor's select_statement, but are part of the tables specified in the select_statement. However, when you specify a column_name_list with UPDATE when declaring the cursor, you can update only those specific columns.

Updating SERIAL columns

A column with the SERIAL property cannot be updated, either through its base table or through a view. To determine whether a column was defined with the SERIAL property, use DB-Access to review the base table. A SERIAL column selected into a result table observes the following rules with regard to inheritance of the SERIAL property:

- If a SERIAL column is selected more than once, it will be defined as NOT NULL in the new table. It will not inherit the SERIAL property.

- If a SERIAL column is selected as part of an expression, the resulting column will not inherit the SERIAL property. It will be created as NULL if any column in the expression allows nulls, and NOT NULL otherwise.

- If the select statement contains a GROUP BY clause or aggregate function, the resulting column will not inherit the SERIAL property. Columns that include an aggregate of the SERIAL column are created NULL; others are NOT NULL.

A SERIAL column that is selected into a table with a union or join does not retain the SERIAL property. If the table contains the union of the SERIAL column and a NULL column, the new column will be defined as NULL. Otherwise, it will be defined as NOT NULL.

11.2.4 The INSERT statement

The INSERT DML statement adds a new row or group of rows to a table. You can use it to create a single new row using column values you supply. The values listed in the VALUES clause have one-to-one correspondence with the columns in the stock table. Notice also that the order of the values is exactly the order of the columns in the stock table. These are key requirements when writing an INSERT statement.

Another key requirement is that the values supplied in the VALUES clause of an INSERT statement must be constants, not expressions. If you attempt to insert a value that is not allowed into a column (e.g., putting a NULL value into a column that does not allows nulls), your INSERT statement will fail. Because data is case-sensitive, be careful to enter data in the format you want.

If you are entering every column in a table, the column-list can be omitted. There is one value in the value-list for each column of the table. If you do not have values in your value-list for all the columns in the table, you must specify which columns you want the data inserted into by including a column-list. You must list the data in the value-list in the same order as you list the columns in the column-list. Columns not included in the column-list will receive null or default values. Therefore, they must be defined to allow null values or the INSERT statement will fail. As a practical matter, you should always insert values for the primary key column(s) of the table.

If the table contains a column with the SERIAL data type, use a zero as a placeholder for the serial column customer_num, and a NULL as a placeholder for the nullable columns you do not have data for. These placeholders are necessary for a one-to-one correspondence between the values in the value-list and the columns in the table. Using a zero as a placeholder for a serial column will cause the server to generate the next actual value in sequence before inserting the new row in to the database.

Syntax

```
INSERT [into][database.[owner.]]{table_name|view_name} (column_list)]
{VALUES (expression [, expression]...)  |select_statement }
```

Keywords and options

INTO. Is optional.

column_list. A list of one or more columns to which data is to be added. Enclose the list in parentheses. The columns can be listed in any order, but the incoming data (whether in a VALUES clause or a SELECT clause) must be in the same order. The column list is necessary when some, but not all, of the columns in the table are to receive data. If no column list is given, the insert is assumed to affect all the columns in the receiving table (in create table order).

VALUES. A keyword that introduces a list of expressions.

expression. Specifies constant expressions, variables, parameters, or null values for the indicated columns. The value list must be enclosed in parentheses and must match the explicit or implicit column list. Enclose character and datetime constants in single or double quotes.

select_statement. A standard SELECT statement used to retrieve the values to be inserted.

The Insert column list

- The column list determines the order in which values are entered.
- You can leave out items in the column list and value list as long as the omitted columns allow null values.

Validating column values

- INSERT interacts with the options that are set with the CREATE INDEX command.
- A rule or check constraint can restrict the domain of legal values you can enter into a column.
- A default can supply a value if the user does not explicitly enter one.
- If an INSERT statement violates domain or integrity rules or if it is the wrong data type, the statement will fail and Informix will display an error message.

Treatment of blanks

Inserting an empty string ("") into a variable character type or text column inserts a single space. Char columns are padded to the defined length. All trailing spaces are removed from data inserted into varchar columns, except in the case of a string that contains only spaces. Strings that contain only spaces are truncated to a single space. Strings longer than the specified length of a char, nchar, varchar, or nvarchar column are silently truncated. You can define a trigger that takes a specified action when an INSERT command is issued on a specified table. You can select rows from a table and insert them into the same table in a single statement. To insert data with SELECT from a table that has null values in some fields into a table that does not allow null values, you must provide a substitute value for any NULL entries in the original table. Two tables might be identically structured, but differ in whether null values are permitted in some fields.

Inserting values into SERIAL columns

When inserting a row into a table, do not include the name of the SERIAL column in the column list, or its value in the value list. If the table consists of only one column, a SERIAL column, omit the column list and leave the value list empty, as follows:

```
insert id_table values()
```

The first time you insert a row into a table, Informix assigns the SERIAL column a value of 1. Each new row gets a column value one higher than the last. Server failures can create gaps in SERIAL column values. The maximum size of the gap depends on the setting of the SERIAL burning set configuration variable. Gaps can also result from manual insertion of data into the SERIAL column, deletion of rows, and transaction rollbacks.

11.2.5 The DELETE statement

The DELETE DML statement removes rows from a table. The DELETE statement specifies a table and usually contains a WHERE clause that designates the row or rows to be removed from the table. If the WHERE clause is not included, all rows in the table will be deleted. Without the WHERE clause, all the data in a table would be deleted.

Syntax

```
DELETE [from] [[database.]owner.]{table_name¦view_name}
[WHERE search_conditions]
```

Keywords and options

FROM (after delete).

An optional keyword used for compatibility with other versions of SQL. Follow it with the name of the table or view from which you want to remove rows.

WHERE. A standard WHERE clause.

WHERE CURRENT OF CURSOR_NAME. Causes Informix to delete the row of the table or view indicated by the current cursor position for cursor_name.

Restrictions

You cannot use delete with a multitable view (one whose FROM clause names more than one table), even though you might be able to use UPDATE or IN-

SERT on that same view. When you delete a row through a view you change multiple tables, which is not permitted. INSERT and UPDATE statements that affect only one base table of the view are permitted.

Deleting all rows from a table

If you don't use a WHERE clause, all rows in the table named after DELETE [FROM] will be removed. The table, though empty of data, will continue to exist until you issue a DROP TABLE command.

DELETE transactions

You can define a trigger that takes a specified action when a DELETE command is issued on a specified table. Use the clause WHERE CURRENT OF with cursors. Before deleting rows using the clause WHERE CURRENT OF, you must first define the cursor with DECLARE CURSOR and open it using the OPEN statement. Position the cursor on the row you want to delete using one or more FETCH statements. The cursor name cannot be a SPL parameter or local variable. The cursor must be an updatable cursor or Informix will return an error. Any deletion to the cursor result set will also affect the base table row from which the cursor row is derived. You can delete only one row at a time using the cursor.

You cannot delete rows in a cursor result set if the cursor's SELECT statement contains a join clause, even though the cursor is considered updatable. The table_name or view_name specified with a DELETE . . . WHERE CURRENT OF must be the table or view specified in the first FROM clause of the SELECT statement that defines the cursor. After the deletion of a row from the cursor's result set, the position of the cursor points before the next row in the cursor's result set. You must still use FETCH to access the next row. If the deleted row is the last row of the cursor result set, the cursor will point after the last row of the result set.

The following describes the position and behavior of open cursors affected by a delete. If a client deletes a row (using another cursor or a regular delete) and that row represents the current cursor position of other opened cursors owned by the same client, the position of each affected cursor is implicitly set to before the next available row. However, it is not possible for one client to delete a row representing the current cursor position of another client's cursor. If a client deletes a row that represents the current cursor position of another cursor defined by a join operation and owned by the same client, Informix will still accept the DELETE statement. However, it will implicitly close the cursor defined by the join.

11.2.6 Validating that the user entered data

A GUI front end like PowerBuilder validates the data as it moves it from the edit control into the underlying item(s) in the buffer. Validation begins when the user modifies data in the edit control and one of these conditions occurs:

- The Enter key or its equivalent has been activated.
- The user moves (change focus) to a different item (field) in the DataWindow control.
- A script executes the AcceptText function.

During the validation procedure, the values in the item buffer and the edit control might be different. The edit control receives user-entered data and holds it until the data is validated. The information in the item comes from the database and is updated only after the new data in the edit field has passed all levels of validation. As each column passes a data validation test, it continues to the next test until it passes all levels. When the contents of the edit control pass all validation levels, the item and its status are updated, but the database does not change because no SQL has been submitted for execution.

Did the item change?

In the first validation test, examine the content of the edit control to determine if they have changed from the item in the buffer. When the contents of the edit control are different, this condition is satisfied and additional edit checks and validation are performed, depending on the data type. When you use the Tab key or the mouse to move away from a field, the control determines that there has been no change and the validation stops. If the value has changed, the validation continues to the next level.

Is the entered data of the correct data type?

In the second validation test, a GUI front end like PowerBuilder checks to see if the data type of the entry in the edit control matches the data type of the item. For example, if a numeric column of type integer contains 123 and the user attempts to enter non-numeric characters into the edit control, this action will pass the first-level validation (something changed), but not the second-level validation because ABC is not a valid integer.

If data-type validation fails then what happens?

When the data-type validation fails, an ItemError event occurs. You can let a GUI front end like PowerBuilder handle the error, or you can develop a script to handle the error and perform additional processing. When you let a GUI front end like PowerBuilder handle the validation error, the user receives a standard message that the entry did not pass the validation rules. The cursor returns to the edit control. To discard the entry and start over, the user can press the Escape key, which restores the current item value to the edit control.

11.2.7 Validation rules: beyond just data type

The third validation test checks for any validation rules you defined for a column in the DataWindow object. You can set these validation rules for the database column using extended attributes, i.e., the system catalog tables for a

GUI front end like PowerBuilder. You can populate them in a number of ways, including using CASE design tools such as ERwin and LBMS—both of which contain a GUI front-end interface. You can also use DataWindow object validation rules for anything appropriate.

Range validation. Column1 > 10000 and column1 < 100000

Cross-column validation. If column1 is 1, then column2 must be greater than 1

Specific value checks. Column1 must be A or B or C

When a column fails a DataWindow control validation rule, an ItemError event occurs.

Validation rules

Reference tables provide a good technique for validating data in a DataWindow. Reference tables compare what the user enters in a column against a list of valid values for that column. When entered, if the data does not pass validation, an error status message box will be displayed or the ItemError event will be triggered (if a script is coded).

Validation rules vs. reference tables

Sometimes verifying data values with a reference table is impractical, for example, if a coded number needs to fall in some range but the range is very large (1 to 3000). While it is possible to prime the reference table with valid values, it is impractical for performance reasons. In such situations, you can often use DataWindow validation rules to achieve the same result.

Validation rules are simple expressions that result in a Boolean (TRUE or FALSE) value. When you build a rule, form the expression so it will validate the data while resulting in a Boolean value. Think of a validation rule as an IF statement:

```
if validation rule     (returns TRUE)
   then let the data pass
   else issue an error message
or ItemError event occurs
```

Validation rules are triggered automatically for a modified column when:

- The Enter key interrupt is invoked.
- Focus leaves the column when the Tab or an arrow key is pressed.
- Focus leaves when the mouse is clicked in anotherDataWindow column.

11.3 What Is a Transaction?

A transaction is a set of actions executed as a group. If any of the actions cannot be completed, all other actions must be undone. A transaction always has a beginning and an end. The database server guarantees that operations done within the bounds of a transaction will be completely and perfectly committed to disk; if that is not possible, the database will be restored to the state it was in before the transaction started. Let's take an example transaction that everyone knows: a bank transaction. Transferring money from your savings account to your checking account is a good example of a transaction. The actions involved with this transaction are:

- Updating savings to show a withdrawal.
- Updating checking to show a deposit.

These actions must both be completed successfully before the transfer is complete. If anything goes wrong with either of the actions, the transaction will fail. For example, if you tried to transfer more money into your checking account than you had in your savings account, the transfer would not occur and your account balances would remain as they were before you attempted the transfer.

11.3.1 The transaction log

Many things, such as a hardware or software failure, can make a transaction fail. Because of this, the database server must have a way to track all the changes made during a transaction. This is done in the transaction log. The server uses the transaction log to record each change it makes to the database during a transaction. If for any reason the transaction cannot be completed, the server will automatically use the data in the transaction log to reverse the changes.

Note: Databases do not have automatic transaction logging. The database administrator must decide whether to make a database with transaction logging. If a database does not have logging, transactions are not available.

11.3.2 Specifying transactions

You use SQL statements to specify the boundaries of a transaction. You use the BEGIN WORK statement to specify the start of a multiple-statement transaction, and the COMMIT WORK statement to specify the end of a transaction. When the database server reaches a COMMIT WORK statement, it makes sure that all modifications have been completed properly and committed to disk. If any external failure prevents the transaction from being completed, the partial transaction will be rolled back when the system is restarted. In ANSI databases, you do not need to mark the beginning of a transaction with the BEGIN WORK statement. A transaction is always in effect, and you need to indicate only the end of each transaction with the COMMIT WORK statement.

11.3.3 Rollback work

In some cases, you will want to have your program cancel a transaction deliberately if certain circumstances occur. Use the ROLLBACK WORK statement to do this. ROLLBACK WORK causes the database server to cancel the current transaction and undo any changes that have been made.

11.3.4 Read concurrency

In a fashion similar to other relational DBMSs, Informix provides levels of isolation:

- DIRTY READ
- COMMITTED READ
- CURSOR STABILITY
- REPEATABLE READ

Informix-OnLine provides these four levels of isolation for reading by implementing a "locking" mechanism. It is important to note that Informix-SE databases can use only DIRTY READ. To supply these levels, Informix-OnLine uses shared locks. Shared locks let other processes read rows but not update them.

11.3.5 DIRTY READ

At the isolation level of DIRTY READ, your process is not isolated at all. You get no locks whatsoever, and the process does not check for the existence of any locks before reading a row. During retrieval you can look at any row, even those containing uncommitted changes. Such rows are referred to as "dirty data." Rows containing dirty data might be phantom. A phantom row is inserted with a transaction that is later rolled back before the transaction completes. Although the phantom row never exists in a permanent sense, it could be visible to a process using an isolation level of DIRTY READ. DIRTY READs can be useful when:

- The table is static.
- 100% accuracy is not as important as speed and freedom from contention.
- You cannot wait for locks to be released.

11.3.6 COMMITTED READ

A COMMITTED READ attempts to acquire a shared lock on a row before trying to read it. It does not actually try to place the lock; rather, it sees if it could acquire the lock. If it can, it is guaranteed that the row exists and is not being updated by another process while it is being read. Remember that a shared lock cannot be acquired on a row that is locked exclusively, which is always the case when a row is being updated. A COMMITTED READ provides low-level isolation. During retrieval, you will not see any phantoms or dirty data. You know that the current row was committed (at lease when your process read it). After your process has read the row, though, other processes can change it. COMMITTED READs can be useful for:

- Lookups
- Queries
- Reports yielding general information

For example, COMMITTED READs are useful for summary-type reports such as month-ending sales analyses.

11.3.7 CURSOR STABILITY

With CURSOR STABILITY, a shared lock is acquired on each row as it is read via a cursor. This shared lock is held until the next row is retrieved. If data is retrieved using a cursor, the shared lock will be held until the next fetch is executed. At this level, not only can you look at committed rows, but you are assured the row will continue to exit while you are looking at it. No other process can change (UPDATE or DELECT) that row while you are looking at it. SELECT statements using an isolation level of CURSOR STABILITY can be used for:

- Lookups
- Queries
- Reports yielding operational data

SELECT statements using CURSOR STABILITY are useful for detail-type reports like price quotation or job-tracking systems. If the isolation level of CURSOR STABILITY is set and a cursor is not used, CURSOR STABILITY will behave in the same manner as COMMITTED READ (the shared lock is never actually placed).

11.3.8 REPEATABLE READ

The REPEATABLE READ isolation level places a shared lock on all the rows examined by the database server; all these locks are held until the transaction is committed.

A REPEATABLE READ provides high-level isolation. In explicit transactions, you are assured that the row will continue to exist not only while you are looking at it, but also when you reread it later. No other process can change (UDATE or DELETE) that row until you COMMIT your transaction. REPEATABLE READs are useful when you must treat all row reads as a unit or to guarantee that a value will not change. For example:

- Critical, aggregate arithmetic (e.g., account balancing).
- Coordinated lookups from several tables (e.g., reservation systems).

Warning! It is important to note that with REPEATABLE READs all the rows examined are locked; this includes rows that do not meet the select criteria, but had to be read in order to determine their ineligibility. For example, if you use REPEATABLE READ isolation on a query that requires a table to be read sequentially (if no indexes are available, for example), then all the rows in the table will be locked and those locks will be held for the duration of the transaction.

Additionally, in order to ensure the integrity of the data set (i.e., to ensure that new rows matching the criteria are not added), the corresponding index keys are also locked.

Tip: Use the REPEATABLE READ isolation level on queries that can do indexed reads.

11.3.9 Setting the level of isolation

To make use of process isolation, your database must use logging. To pick an isolation level, use the SET ISOLATION statements. If logging is not turned on, all reads are DIRTY READs and the isolation level cannot be set. Informix-SE databases can use only DIRTY READ.

Each database server process can set its own isolation level. The following is an example SET ISOLATION statement:

```
SET ISOLATION to cursor stability;
```

11.3.10 SET TRANSACTION

The SET TRANSACTION statement complies with ANSI SQL-92. This statement is similar to the Informix SET ISOLATION statement; however, the SET ISOLATION statement is not ANSI-complaint and does not provide access modes.

The isolation levels you can set with the SET TRANSACTION statement are almost parallel to the isolation levels you can set with the SET ISOLATION statement.

Another difference between the SET TRANSACTION and SET ISOLATION statements is the behavior of the isolation levels within transactions. SET TRANSACTION can be issued only once for a transaction. With the SET ISOLATION statement, after a transaction is started, you can change the isolation level more than once within a transaction. The following is an example SET TRANSACTION statement:

```
SET TRANSACTION to Repeatable Read;
```

The default isolation level for a particular database is established when the database is created (see Table 11.1). Table 11.2 relates isolation levels to degrees of tolerable interference.

11.4 Controlling the Cost of the Transaction

The basic language of the relational database management system (RDBMS) is SQL, which is an acronym for structured query language. SQL uses only four

TABLE 11.1

Informix	ANSI	Description
Dirty read	Read uncommitted	Without logging
Committed read	Read committed	With logging that is not ANSI-compliant
Repeatable read	Serializable	ANSI-compliant database

TABLE 11.2

Isolation level	Description
Dirty read or read uncommitted	Let this process look at dirty data
Committed read or read committed	Do not let this process look at dirty data
Cursor stability	Do not let other processes change the current row
(ANSI) repeatable reads or serialize	Do not let other processes change any of the rows I have looked at until I am done

verbs—SELECT, INSERT, DELETE, and UPDATE—to perform data manipulation DML. SQL is a set-oriented language rather than a record-oriented language. In record-oriented systems, such as IBM's VSAM or QSAM, the programmer control file access gets the first record, gets the next record, and so on. In most cases, the programmer also knows how many records can be traversed in a transaction and, therefore, can identify potentially expensive operations. These operations can then be stopped before they start, or the user can be warned that a particular operation might take a while to complete. When the program issues a SQL data manipulation statement (SELECT, INSERT, DELETE, or UPDATE), the programmer usually doesn't know how many rows will be returned and how long the statement will take to complete. In addition, RDBMS databases don't usually provide a way to estimate the cost of execution or determine how many rows will be affected. Some RDBMSs such as DB2/MVS do work with EXPLAIN utilities, which provide this information based on the current state of the database objects to be accessed.

11.4.1 Use unique keys

You can control the nonretrieval SQL verbs (e.g., UPDATE) by including a unique primary key in the WHERE clause for the target table.

```
UPDATE series
   WHERE series_cde  ='BEAVER'
```

For example, deleting SERIES rows based on a single SERIES_CDE guarantees that, at most, only one row will be accessed to complete the statement. Retrieving a SERIES row with SERIES_CDE will have the same limiting effect as in the nonretrieval case, e.g.:

```
SELECT * FROM EPISODE WHERE SERIES_CDE = "LUCY" AND EPISODE_CDE= "225"
```

However, most retrieval situations don't fit into this category. Frequently, the search criteria are supplied entirely by the user in an ad-hoc fashion. It is the programmer's responsibility to provide governing mechanisms to prevent a user from executing a potentially expensive retrieval. For example, the query SELECT * FROM episode will retrieve all rows in the episode table. If the table is large, this query could degrade system performance significantly.

11.4.2 Limit the user to a specific WHERE clause

Limiting the user to a specific WHERE clause requires that the programmer prevent the user from executing any query that might result in retrieving a large number of rows. You need to include some form of WHERE criteria in SELECT, regardless of what options the user is able to specify. Since the programmer is in control during development, the programmer can make a reasonable estimate of the data to be returned.

For example, instead of allowing a user to retrieve information for all episodes in all series, the application would allow the user to retrieve only episodes that reside in a particular television series. This option has a disadvantage. It limits the user's flexibility. In many situations, it is difficult for the programmer to anticipate how the user will want to use the application. For example, some users might be happy viewing episodes one series at a time, but others might want to view them based on a holiday or associated genre. In an addition, this option doesn't consider growth. It is possible that even limiting the user to accessing episodes by series would eventually return a large amount of data.

11.4.3 Perform a COUNT(*) calculation

To provide flexibility for the user while limiting the number of rows retrieved, you can query the database server to determine how many rows will be retrieved. This provides an accurate count of the rows that will be sent to the client requester once the completed query is processed.

For example, if you provide users with the capability of retrieving episode rows completely ad hoc, they might end up executing a wide range of queries:

```
SELECT episode_name, series_name, episode_holiday
    FROM episode
    WHERE series_cde LIKE "L%";
```

It would be difficult to estimate the number of rows that might be retrieved for any of these queries. If, however, the query is executed with a COUNT(*) and no other columns, the single value returned will determine the total number of rows that meet the criteria and should provide you with an accurate estimate of the expense of the query:

```
SELECT count(*) FROM series WHERE series_CDE="LUCY"
```

Since there are no columns in the column list, the database can process the request without sending a lot of data to the client. Once the count is known, you or the educated consumer can decide that any query resulting in more than a certain number of rows will be disallowed. This technique is not always the answer; depending on the volume of data and configuration of the database, the COUNT(*) request can be costly in terms of server time and, therefore, might not be feasible. For example, the WHERE predicate column, especially in the querymode example, might not be an index and a table scan might be needed to determine the COUNT. In addition, if the retrieval is subsequently issued, the server must obtain the rows that meet the WHERE criteria again.

11.4.4 Use a cursor

To have complete control over the retrieval and be able to resume the retrieval after determining that the user wants more rows, you can access the data directly from a SQL cursor. By defining a cursor and issuing each fetch explicitly, you can count the number or rows and determine when to prompt the user. For example, if you want to prompt the user after the first 100 rows, suspend fetches from the server by presenting a MessageBox to the user: Continue? Yes or No. If the user responds Yes, then the FETCH loop will continue until the next point where you want to ask if the retrieval should continue. If the user responds No, the cursor will be closed and no more rows will be sent to the requesting transaction window. You are not only in complete control of the number of rows retrieved, but you can also periodically prompt the user to determine whether to continue. For example (done using PowerBuilder's script language):

```
DECLARE C1 CURSOR FOR
SELECT epsseg.series_cde,
       epsseg.episode_cde,
       epsseg.eps_seg_num,
       epsseg.eps_seg_len
    FROM  epsseg
    WHERE episode_cde = :ls_episode_cde AND
          series_cde = :ls_series_cde ;
//
// check the return code to verify whether the cursor was successfully
created.
// If not successful display error message
    IF sqlca.sqlcode <>  0 THEN &
       f_db_error( sqlca," in epsseg CURSOR build ")
       SetPointer(HourGlass!)
       li_counter = 0
       OPEN C1;
       IF sqlca.sqlcode <   0 THEN &
          f_db_error( sqlca," epsseg CURSOR OPEN ")
// Set the values in the data entry window with the values retrieved
// from the database. Pass through the loop while the FETCH
// is successful
// FETCH result ends with sqlcode = 100
       li_sqlcode = 0
       DO WHILE li_sqlcode = 0
          FETCH C1 INTO :ls_series_cde,
                        :ls_episode_cde,
                        :li_seg_num,
                        :li_seg_len ;
          IF sqlca.sqlcode <> 0  and sqlca.sqlcode <> 100 THEN &
             f_db_error( sqlca," epsseg FETCH error ")
          IF sqlca.sqlcode = 100 THEN li_sqlcode = sqlca.sqlcode
          IF sqlca.sqlcode <> 100 THEN li_counter = li_counter + 1
          IF sqlca.sqlcode <>   100 AND li_counter > 64 THEN &
          MessageBox ( this.title, "This select will caused " + & String(
           li_counter ) + " rows to be returned.~r~nDo you want to continue?"
           & ,question! , okcancel!, 2 ) = 2 then li_counter = 0
       LOOP
CLOSE  C1;
```

Using a cursor in a conversational mode can be very expensive due to the additional overhead for the client (processing queries through a cursor, retrieving the values into local variables, and then setting them into a window). Also, the cursor remains open while you prompt the user whether to continue. This not only ties up resources on the server, but might cause locks on the retrieved records. This can interfere with other users' database access.

11.4.5 Explain SQL

After you get the desired result, then use the Explain SQL option tool to examine the SQL. Explain SQL displays information about the path that Informix will use to access the data. Sometimes there is more than one way to code a SQL statement to obtain the desired result. Explain SQL can help you select the more efficient method. This is most useful when you are retrieving or updating data in an indexed column or using multiple tables.

In many cases, the majority of the work done in an application, in terms of processing time, is that done by the SQL queries used by that application. The most difficult SQL should be identified at an early stage and monitored. In fact, the application should be "tuned" regularly, especially in the early stages of production. In tuning applications, the first area you should examine for optimization possibilities is the SQL queries themselves. Some obvious ways to make SQL faster are to change the SQL query so it:

- Accesses specific data, i.e., reads fewer rows.

- Limits the need to sort results, i.e., avoids a sort, sorts few errors, or sorts on a simpler key.

The way to achieve these ends, however, is not always obvious. The specific methods depend very strongly on the details of the application and the database design. The ideas in this module suggest a general approach, and include some techniques that apply in limited circumstances. Some necessary SQL queries might just be inherently slower than others, and not much can be done to improve their performance.

11.4.6 UPDATE STATISITICS

Before you begin working to optimize your queries, be sure to run the UPDATE STATISTICS statement to ensure that the data in the system catalog tables is current. The optimizer uses this data to determine the fastest way to retrieve the requested data. The database server does not automatically update this data. This should be done regularly, in any event, as it improves overall system performance.

11.4.7 Test the problem SQL

First, select a single query you think is running slow. Then set up an environment in which you can take predictable, repeatable timings of that query.

Without this, you will not be able to tell whether a change helped or not.

- Choose a slow query.
- Set up a consistent system load.
- Simplify the program being tested.
- Use a scaled-down database.

Consistent system load

If you have a multiuser system or network where the system load varies widely from hour to hour, you might need to perform your experiments at the same time each day in order to get repeatable results. You might even need to work at off-peak hours. Some tools can create varying loads of simulated data traffic. Performix uses a neat transaction generator that can simulate users by sending traffic from, let's say, UNIX1 (transaction generator) to UNIX2 (system under test), which contains the database.

A simple program

If the query is presently embedded in a complicated program, consider extracting the statement and executing it interactively, or embedding it in a simpler program.

A scaled-down database

If the real query takes many minutes or hours to complete, it might be a good idea to prepare a scaled-down database in order to run tests more quickly. This can be helpful, but you must be aware of two potential problems:

- The optimizer might make different choices in a small database than in a large one, even when the relative sizes of the tables are the same.
- Execution time is rarely a linear function of table size.
- Sorting time, for example, increases faster than table size, as does the cost of indexed access when an index goes from two to three levels.

What appears to be a big improvement in the scaled-down environment might be less significant with the full database. Any conclusion you reach as a result of tests in the model database must be considered tentative until they are verified in the large database.

11.4.8 Refine the DML select

Look for ways to achieve the same result with less effort. Here are some general recommendations on how to reduce the effort required by a query:

- Avoid or simplify sorts.
- Avoid correlated subqueries.
- Avoid difficult regular expressions.

- Avoid noninitial substrings.
- Avoid joining onto long character strings.

Avoid or simplify sorts

- Avoid sorting by placing your data in a temporary table.
- Simplify sorts by sorting on fewer or narrower columns.

A sort is not necessarily a bad thing. The sort algorithm of the database server is highly tuned and extremely efficient. It is certainly as fast or faster than any external sort program you might apply to the same data. As long as the sort is being done only occasionally or to a relatively small number of output rows, there is no need to avoid it.

However, you should try to avoid or simplify repeated sorts of large tables. Using a temporary table is one way to avoid sorts that is discussed later in this module.

If a sort is necessary, look for ways to simplify it. The sort will generally be quicker if you can sort on fewer or narrower columns.

Avoid correlated subqueries

A correlated subquery is one where a column label appears in both the SELECT list of the main query and the WHERE clause of the subquery. Since the result of the subquery might be different for each row that the database server examines, the subquery is executed anew for every row. This can be extremely time-consuming. Unfortunately, there are some queries that cannot be stated in SQL without a correlated subquery.

When you see a subquery in a time-consuming SELECT statement, look to see if it is correlated. If this is the case, try to rewrite the query to avoid the correlation. If the correlation cannot be avoided, look for ways to reduce the number of rows that are examined. For instance, you might be able to reduce the number of rows by adding other filter expressions to the WHERE clause, or by selecting a subset of records into a temporary table and searching only these records.

Avoid difficult regular expressions

The MATCHES and LIKE keywords support wildcard matches, also referred to as regular expressions. Some regular expressions are more difficult than others for the server to process. A wildcard in the initial position, for example, will force the database server to examine every value in the column because the index cannot be used.

Regular expression tests on an indexed column with wildcards only in the middle or at the end do not force every value to be examined. However, the query can still be slow to execute. Depending on the data in the column, some expressions can be rewritten more simply.

If a difficult regular expression test is essential, avoid combining it with a join. First process the single table, applying the regular expression condition to select the desired rows. Then save the result in a temporary table and join that table to the others.

Avoid noninitial substrings

A filter based on a noninitial substring of a column also requires every value in the column to be tested. Even if an index exists, it will not be used to evaluate this type of filter. If possible, you should rewrite your query to avoid noninitial substrings. However, in some cases, a noninitial substring might be the only way to find the data you need.

Avoid joining onto long character strings

Operations that are applied to character strings are relatively slow. This is because character strings are compared only two bytes at a time. When long strings are used as join columns, the situation is even worse because of the number that have to be compared. Whenever possible, join two tables on a numeric column such as INTEGER, SMALLINT, or SERIAL.

Use a temporary table to speed queries

In some cases, using temporary tables can result in more efficient processing of queries, even when the overhead of the temporary table is taken into account. Temporary tables can be useful for conducting multiple queries on the same subset of data. Select the desired subset of data into a temporary table and then direct your queries against the temporary table.

Note: Any changes made to the primary table after the temporary table has been created will not be reflected in the output.

11.5 Stored Procedures vs. Embedded SQL

Embedded SQL requires that you create your own SQL statements. You use embedded SQL whenever you want something you cannot easily do with a GUI toll, e.g., the PowerBuilder DataWindow. If you add rows to another table in the database not associated with this DataWindow, and you will be explicitly specifying CREATE, DROP, GRANT, REVOKE, and SQL statements.

In general, you use embedded SQL when the data is brought in to be manipulated rather than displayed. When using embedded SQL, you must always check the SQLCode from the transaction object to determine whether the SQL statement executed successfully or not. Embedded SQL can take several forms:

- Static SQL, including cursors
- Stored procedures
- Dynamic SQL

11.5.1 Embedded static SQL

Use embedded static SQL when the components of the SQL statement do not change; only the values passed as arguments to the WHERE clause change.

Remember to use the USING clause to associate the SQL statement with a particular transaction object. For example:

```
SELECT series_cde, series_name
FROM dbo.series  WHERE series_cde = :ls_series_cde
USING Connect1;
```

Host variables are prefixed with a colon and must be declared before being referenced in SQL statements. It is not necessary to use the & character to continue the line when the SQL statement wraps across multiple lines. Always check the SQLCode attribute of your transaction object after executing the SQL statement to verify success or failure. If you do not prefix a table with the owner name, a GUI front end like PowerBuilder will assume that the owner of the table is whatever was specified in your logon ID or user ID. It is a good idea to always use the USING clause, even when the transaction object is SQLCA.

11.5.2 Stored procedures

Stored procedures are named, precompiled sets of modal SQL, e.g., PL/SQL for Informix. Stored procedures hit the ground running, unlike dynamic SQL, which must be parsed, validated, optimized, and compiled before the request can be executed. Database-stored procedures allow you to define procedural SQL statements in the database for use by all applications. Using stored procedures to perform database updates allows you to enhance database security, integrity, and performance. Since stored procedures provide for conditional execution, you can also use them to enforce additional business rules.

11.6 Locking Granularity

Locking granularity refers to the size of the object being locked. Granularity ranges through five levels, from coarse to fine. This range allows you to make trade-offs between currency and locking overhead. Informix-OnLine provides five different levels of locking granularity. The coarsest level is database-level locking; the finest level is row-level locking. Key-level locking is performed on index entries.

11.6.1 Database-level locking

It is occasionally necessary or advantageous to prevent other users from accessing any part of a database for some period of time. This might be the case if you are:

- Executing a large number of updates involving many tables.
- Archiving database files for backups.
- Altering the structure of the database.

To facilitate these DBA-type requirements, you want to eliminate contention from other users who have database permissions. You can lock the entire database by using the DATABASE statement with the EXCLUSIVE option. The EXCLUSIVE option opens the database in an exclusive mode and allows only the current user access to the database.

To allow other users access to the database, you must execute the CLOSE DATABASE statement and then reopen the database. Users with any level of database permission can open the database in exclusive mode. Doing so will not give them any greater level of access than what they normally have.

11.6.2 Table-level locking

Sometimes you want exclusive control over a table to perform some special updates. You want to eliminate contention from other batch or OLTP users who have access, and update permissions on the subject table(s). Informix, as other RDBMS implementations like IBM's DB2, provides table-level locking, which can be used to prevent other users from modifying the database. Use table-level locking to:

- Avoid conflict with other users during batch operations that affect most or all of the rows of a table.

- Avoid running out of locks when running an operation as a transaction (this is covered in detail later).

- Prevent users from updating a table for a period of time.

- Prevent access to a table while altering its structure or creating indexes.

Use table-level locking only when making major changes to a table in a multi-user environment, and when simultaneous interaction by another user would interfere.

Only one lock can apply to a table at any given time. So if a user locks a table, no other user can lock that table until the first user has unlocked it. You cannot lock the system catalog tables.

If your database has transactions, tables can be locked only within transactions. Therefore, be sure that you have executed BEGIN WORK (unless you are using a MODE ANSI database) before attempting to lock a table. The table will be unlocked when the transaction is completed. If you want to give other users read access to the table, but prevent them from modifying any of the data it contains, then use the LOCK TABLE statement with the SHARE MODE OPTION.

When a table is locked in SHARE mode, other users will be able to select data from the table, but they can't insert, delete, or update rows in the table or alter the table.

Important! Note that locking a table in share mode does not prevent row locks from being placed for updates by your process. If you want to avoid exclusive row locks in addition to the share lock on the table, you must lock the table in exclusive mode.

If you want to prevent other users from having any access to the table, then lock it in exclusive mode. In exclusive mode, other users will be unable to use select (unless dirty read isolation is used), insert, delete, or update rows in the table until you unlock the table. Only one lock is used to lock the table, regardless of the number of rows updated within a transaction. In the case of a table that contains BLOBs located in a blobspace, if the table is locked in exclusive mode and changes are made to the associated BLOB values, then each accessed BLOB obtains its own exclusive locks. These locks are placed and released automatically. Two locks are used per blobpage. Tables containing BLOBs located in the table do not obtain additional locks.

Unlocking a table
The UNLOCK TABLE statement restores access to a previously locked database table. Use this statement when you no longer need to prevent other users from accessing and modifying the table. If the table was locked in a transaction, UNLOCK TABLE is disallowed and will generate an error. Finishing the transaction (via COMMIT OR ROLLBACK) will unlock the table.

Setting the lock mode
Use the SET LOCK MODE statement to determine whether calls that alter or delete a locked row must wait for the row to become unlocked. The TO NOT WAIT option causes an error to be returned if a statement attempts to alter or delete a row (or select a row for updating) that another process has locked. This is the default mode.

The TO WAIT option causes a statement to wait on an attempt to alter or delete a row that has been locked by another process until the locked row becomes unlocked. You can optionally specify the number of seconds to wait.

11.6.3 Page- and row-level locking
When you create a table, you choose the lock mode used when any rows from that table are accessed. Page-level locking causes an entire data page to be locked whenever a single row located on that page needs to be locked. Row-level locking causes only the row in question to be locked. The default lock mode when creating a table is page level. The lock level is determined at table creation time. Page locking locks an entire data page, and row locking locks only the row. There are also concurrency/resource trade-offs.

Page locks are useful when, in a transaction, you process rows in the same order as the table's cluster index, or process rows in physically sequential order. Row locks are useful when, in a transaction, you process rows in an arbitrary order. When the number of locked rows becomes large, you run the following risks:

- The number of available locks will become exhausted.
- The overhead for lock management will become significant.

There is a trade-off between these two levels of locking. Page-level locking requires fewer resources than row-level locking, but it also reduces concurrency. If a page lock is placed on a page containing many rows, other processes that need data from that same page could be denied access to the data.

12

Building C Programs with ESQL

When using Informix-ESQL/C, you can embed SQL statements directly into your C programs. Within Informix ESQL/C you will find libraries, header files, and a preprocessor. The extensive library of routines will help you work with all SQL data types, interpret status messages, and work with Informix child processes.

12.1 What Is Informix-ESQL/C?

Informix-ESQL/C is an application development tool that allows C programmers to create customized applications that can interface with an Informix database. Developers can use the libraries, header files, and preprocessor to embed SQL statements directly in their C programs. Informix-ESQL/C has an extensive library of routines that help you work with all SQL data types, interpret status messages, and communicate with Informix child processes. For simplification, in this chapter we will refer to Informix-ESQL/C as ESQL/C.

12.1.1 Setting environment variables in UNIX

Before using ESQL/C, you must define your environment variables; two key variables are the INFORMIXDIR and PATH variables. The INFORMIXDIR variable points to the directory where Informix-ESQL resides, and the PATH variable lists the directories the system will search for programs you want to execute. Depending on which UNIX login shell you are using, you can accomplish this in either of the following ways:

Bourne or Korn shell. Either through your .profile or manually with:

```
INFORMIXDIR=/usr/informix
PATH=$INFORMIXDIR/bin:$PATH
export INFORMIXDIR PATH
```

C Shell. Either through your .login or manually with:

```
setenv INFORMIXDIR /usr/informix
setenv PATH ${INFORMIXDIR}/bin:${PATH}
```

You can set these environment variables at the system prompt or in your .profile (Bourne or Korn shell) or .login (C shell) file. If they are set at the system prompt, you will have to reassign them each time you log on, which will be a manual procedure. If they are set in the .profile or .login file, they will be reassigned automatically each time you log onto your system.

When using Informix-OnLine, you should also set SQLEXEC to point to $INFORMIXDIR/lib/sqlturbo. Depending on your environment, you might also consider setting your TBCONFIG environment variable for compatibility with earlier releases of Informix. TBCONFIG basically defines your Informix system configuration. In addition, you might need to set other environment variables when using Informix-NET, Informix-Star, or Informix-OnLine. Check with your system administrator if this is the case.

12.1.2 What is the benefit of ESQL/C?

ESQL/C is used in conjunction with C code or Informix-SQL's Ace or Perform. It allows the C programmer a means to communicate with the Informix database.

12.1.3 The ESQL/C preprocessor: ESQL

A major component of ESQL/C is its preprocessor. The preprocessor converts ESQL/C code to C code before the C source code is sent to the C compiler. The preprocessor is invoked from the command line and can be run with a variety of arguments to identify source files, desired output file, etc. The ESQL/C preprocessor is what makes it possible to communicate with your Informix database via C programs. When using the preprocessor you invoke what is called esql.

12.2 Incorporating SQL Statements in an Informix-ESQL/C Program

Theoretically any SQL statement that you can type interactively, for example through DB-Access, you can also use in your C program. There may be some slight differences in format, and some SQL statements are simply programming statements, and cannot be used interactively. In order to insert a SQL call within your C program you should prefix the command with either a "$" or "EXEC SQL" so that it will be recognized by the preprocessor.

12.2.1 Rules to remember

■ Signal the preprocessor by prefixing SQL statements with a dollar sign ($) or the ANSI standard keywords EXEC SQL. Though you can mix these two styles in your C code, for maintenance reasons it is not recommended. Also, do not forget to terminate your SQL statement with a semicolon (;).

- SQL statements can include variables. Variables can appear wherever a constant can appear in interactive SQL. Such variables in executable SQL statements are called host variables, which we will describe later in this chapter.

- You can put an executable SQL statement anywhere an executable C statement can appear.

- Portability is perhaps the most important rule. Because the ESQL/C preprocessor allows two different methods to signify an embedded SQL statement, consider choosing a coding standard prior to starting any major development plan. The dollar sign ($) syntax is an Informix-specific construct, while the EXEC SQL notation is an ANSI standard. We recommended that you use the EXEC SQL syntax to enhance the portability of your applications. Since both methods achieve the same results, there is no reason to use the Informix-specific syntax. All of our remaining examples use the EXEC SQL syntax. Although the keywords EXEC SQL can appear in either lower- or uppercase in your code. Our examples will show EXEC SQL in uppercase to make the embedded SQL statements more visible in the code.

12.3 Host Variables in Embedded SQL

Host variables are normal C variables, and can appear in embedded SQL wherever a constant can appear in interactive SQL. When you refer to host variables within a SQL statement, you must distinguish them from SQL names. Doing so cues the preprocessor as to which is the host variable.

```
Using the Dollar Sign ($)
#include <stdio.h>
main( arg1, arg2 )
int arg1;
char **arg2;
{
    $ database warehouse;
    $ update options;
        set max_order_qty = "100"
        where store_num = 323;
    . . .
}
```

```
Using EXEC SQL (ANSI Standard)
#include <stdio.h>
main( arg1, arg2 )
int arg1;
char **arg2;
{
    EXEC SQL database warehouse;
    EXEC SQL update options;
        set max_order_qty = "100"
        where store_num = 323;
    . . .
}
```

Figure 12.1

12.3.1 Communicating with the preprocessor

To distinguish references to host variables in embedded SQL statements, prefix the host variable with a dollar sign ($). However, for portability we recommend that you use the ANSI standard colon (:). Here are some examples:

- A SET clause in an UPDATE statement:

```
EXEC SQL update sku_master set retail_price = :rprice;
```

- A VALUES clause in an INSERT statement:

```
EXEC SQL insert into sku_master sku (:sku);
```

- A WHERE clause in an UPDATE, DELETE, or SELECT statement:

```
EXEC SQL update sku_master ...
   where sku  =  :sku ;
EXEC SQL delete from orders
   where sku  =  :sku;
```

12.3.2 Defining host variables

Host variables are normal C variables and, since they are normal variables, you must define them and declare them to be of some type, like any other C variable. You can define any of these types for a host variable:

- Structure
- Array
- Simple, like integer or double

The following is an example of how to define your data types to the system:

```
EXEC SQL begin declare section;
long  sku  =  0;
int      onfile;
char  desc[30 + 1];   Note:  the +1 allowing for the SQL null char.
int      inpack;
EXEC SQL end declare section;
```

Like other C variables, you can initialize host variables when you declare them. However, since the ESQL/C preprocessor needs to know of their existence and type before it translates the SQL statement, you need to signal the preprocessor as to the definition of host variables. Identify host variables to the preprocessor through a host variable declaration by prefixing the declaration with a dollar sign ($), or enclosing the declaration with the following pair of statements:

```
EXEC SQL begin declare section
EXEC SQL end declare section
```

as was shown in our previous example. The begin/end declare section is the ANSI standard and is the notation we will use in our future examples.

12.3.3 Referencing host variables

There are some considerations you must take into account when you reference host variables, such as naming conventions, case distinction, and C references.

Name independence

Host variables and SQL database objects (databases, tables, columns, constraints, procedures, etc.) can have the same name, even in the same SQL statement. For example, the following statement is fine:

```
EXEC SQL update sku_master
set description = :description
where sku = :sku ;
```

Case sensitivity

The ESQL preprocessor treats uppercase and lowercase letters as unique variables, so it is case-sensitive. For example, the following two host variables are unique and refer to different parts of memory:

```
EXEC SQL begin declare section ;
char description [30+1] ;
char  Description [30+1] ;
EXEC SQL end declare section ;
```

C references

Finally, any host variable can always be used as a normal C variable. When the variable is not used in a SQL statement, it should not be prefixed with a colon (:), but used just as you would for any other C variable.

12.4 SQL and Host Data Compatibility

When data is brought from the database into an ESQL/C application, it should be placed into a data type that is compatible with its SQL data type. Likewise, when data is moved from the application to the database, the data types should be compatible.

12.4.1 Data conversion errors and warnings

If you do not declare a compatible host variable data type, automatic conversion might occur in some cases. If a conversion cannot occur, an error will be returned. For example, when the receiving area is too small, the server will return an error if significant digits would be lost and a warning if significant characters would be lost. Throughout this chapter, we will try to make you aware of some of these cases.

12.4.2 Types of host variables

The chart in Figure 12.2 lists the SQL data types and their corresponding C host variables. The CHAR, SMALLINT, INTEGER, SMALLFLOAT, FLOAT, SERIAL, and DATE SQL types all have corresponding C data types. It is im-

Types of Host Variables			
Simple data Types		**Sophisticated data Types**	
SQL	**C-Host**	**SQL**	**C-Host**
CHAR(n) CHARACTER	char[n+1] char*	DECIMAL DEC NUMERIC	dec_t or struct decimal
SMALLINT	short int	MONEY	dec_t or struct decimal
INTEGER INT	long int	DATETIME	dtime_t or struct dtime
SMALLFLOAT REAL	float		
FLOAT DOUBLE PRECISION	double	INTERVAL	intrvl_t or struct intrvl
SERIAL	long int	VARCHAR	varchar or string
DATE	long int		

Figure 12.2

portant to note that, when using type CHAR within your C program, you must add +1 to account for the SQL null terminator (\0). DECIMAL, MONEY, DATETIME, INTERVAL, and VARCHAR, however, must have special ESQL/C data types defined as the corresponding host variables.

12.4.3 User-defined types: typedef

ESQL/C also supports C-like typedef expressions in host variable declarations. You can accomplish this in the following manner:

```
EXEC SQL begin declare section;

    typedef short      smallint;
    typedef long       date;
    smallint           sku;
    date               week_ending_date;

EXEC SQL end declare section;
```

It is important to note that this must be done within a declare section block. In our example, typedef creates a SMALLINT type as a short integer. We then declare sku as a variable with a SMALLINT type. Using the same method with the SQL type DATE and its equivalent, a long integer, we do the same for the variable week_ending_date. You cannot use typedef to name a multidimensional array or a union as a host variable.

12.5 Structures as Host Objects

You can declare a structure as an Informix-ESQL/C host object. Here is another sample of how you might go about doing this within your program:

```
EXEC SQL begin declare section;

struct orders_t{
    short           sku;
    short           quantity;
}orderrec1 ;
struct orders_t  orderrec1 ;

EXEC SQL end declare section;
```

In our example we declare orders_t as a structure template. Using this template, we then define two structures, orderrec1 and orderrec2. You can also nest structures. In executable SQL statements, you can name the structure variable as a whole or refer to any of its parts. When you name the variable as a whole, the Informix-ESQL/C preprocessor expands it into a list of its parts. For example:

```
EXEC SQL insert into stock ( sku, quantity )
    values( :orderrec1);
```

is equivalent to:

```
EXEC SQL insert into stock ( sku, quantity )
    values( :orderrec1.sku,
            :orderrec1.quantity );
```

12.6 Arrays as Host Objects

To declare an array as an Informix-ESQL/C host object, simply continue using the previous format. Start with the EXEC SQL begin declare section and end with the EXEC SQL end declare section, as with previous constructs. Here is an example of how you might represent it within your program:

```
EXEC SQL begin declare section;

char       *buf[6];      /*   defining buf as an array of
                               pointers to a character      */
static long  unit[6] = {0,0,0,0,0,0};   /*   unit is an array of six
                                             long integers, initialized
                                             to all zeros */
EXEC SQL end declare section;
```

When you declare an array, you must remember to supply an integer value defining the size of the array. In executable SQL statements, you can refer to any element of the array. For arrays of CHAR types, refer to the name alone. For arrays of other types, you cannot refer to the name alone.

12.7 Host Variable Initialization

When you declare host variables, you can use normal C initialization expressions. An exception to this rule, however, is the content of what character-type expressions might contain. Character strings must not contain semicolons (;) or Informix-ESQL/C keywords. The reason for this is that the preprocessor does not check for valid C syntax; it simply passes initialization variables to your C compiler, and the C compiler checks for any such errors.

For portability, avoid initializing host variables when they are declared; instead, assign them values at run time. The manner in which different embedded SQL products handle initializations is not standard.

12.7.1 The scope of host variables

The scope of host variables follow the same rules currently honored within the C programming language. Host variables are automatically considered local, unless you explicitly declare them as external or static, and those variables declared within a function are considered local to that function. Local host variables mask any declaration of the same name that might be external to that function, and you cannot declare a host variable more than once in the same block of code.

12.7.2 Blocks

To ensure that the scope of a local host variable remains local to the block in which it is defined, you should use the combined symbol pair ${ and $} to begin and end the block. It is important to note that the ANSI-standard syntax does not support the ${ and $} pair. By using this construct, you can nest blocks up to 16 levels. For portability, however, we recommend that you avoid nesting host variables with the same name because the manner in which different embedded SQL products handle the nesting might not be consistent. To show you how this works, here is an example:

```
$extern short sku;    /*  here we declare sku to be short external     */

funcA()               /*  within the same program we have function A   */
$double sku;          /*  we re-define sku locally within the function */
${                    /*  here we will use the defined symbol pair      */
        $long sku;    /*  re-defining sku yet another way               */
$}                    /*  closing the defined symbol pair               */
```

If you decide to use the initial definition of sku within a function without redefining it, it would take on its initial form. For example, using the previous code, you could add an additional function definition to the bottom:

```
funcB()
{
$  insert into orders(sku)
     values ($sku);    /*  here sku would be type short as in the external
                           definition that was used initially  */
```

12.7.3 Host variables as function parameters

At times you might feel the need to use host variables as parameters to functions. In order to accomplish this, you should precede the host variable with the parameter keyword when you declare the host variables as function arguments. Following is a sample declaration:

```
EXEC SQL begin declare section; /* in keeping with the ANSI standard
                                   we are using the EXEC SQL form */
char  *col;
EXEC SQL end declare section;
int
foo(col)

EXEC SQL begin declare section; /* Notice that we used the parameter
                                   declaration separately from the
                                   block of C code.    */
parameter char  *col;
EXEC SQL end declare section;
{
}
```

In this example, the col argument to function foo() has already been declared as a host variable, so the parameter keyword is required. If the parameter keyword was not used, the following warning would be generated when compiling:

```
esqlc: "file.ec",line ##: Warning -33011:
```

Current declaration of 'col' hides previous declaration.
If the col argument did not clash with the name of a previously declared host variable, the parameter keyword would not be required.

12.8 Informix-ESQL/C Header Files

Informix-ESQL/C provides a number of header files. Header files contain the definitions of many program objects you might want to access. They can be found in the incl/esql subdirectory of the $INFORMIXDIR directory. The Informix-ESQL/C header files, along with a brief description, are shown in Figure 12.3.

Informix ESQL/C Header Files	
Header File Name	**Description**
sqlca.h	Used to evaluate return codes and other meaningful information, after executing an SQL statement.
decimal.h	Used when working with DECIMAL data.
datetime.h	Used when working with DATETIME and INTERVAL data.
varchar.h	Used when working with VARCHAR data.
locator.h	Used when working with BYTE and TEXT data.
sqlda.h	Used when working with dynamically defined data.
sqlstype.h	Used when working with Dynamic SQL.
sqltypes.h	Used when working with C and SQL data types; used mostly when working with Dynamic SQL.
sqlxtype.h	Used to work with C and SQL data types when in X/OPEN mode.

Figure 12.3

You can include one or more of these header files to simplify your coding. To include, for example, the sqlca header file, use the following syntax:

```
EXEC SQL include sqlca;
```

Including sqlca allows you to determine whether the database server executed your SQL statement successfully. When the preprocessor sees the EXEC SQL include statement, it reads the sqlca.h file and places it into your code at the current position of the include statement. The EXEC SQL include statement is necessary if you need to declare host variables of a type defined in the header file. You can also include the header files in ordinary .c source files with the #include syntax if the files need to access declarations.

12.9 Opening and Closing the Database

Opening the database

Before you can access a table and add rows to it, you need to activate the database in which the table exists. To activate a database and make it current, use the DATABASE statement:

DATABASE. Required keyword

DatabaseName. Name of the database you want to select
DatabaseName can be an identifier naming the database, a quoted string containing the name of the database, or a pointer to such a character string.

Informix-SE only

When specifying a database with Informix-SE that resides neither in your current directory nor in the directory specified by the DBPATH environment variable, you must follow the DATABASE keyword with a string constant or a host variable that evaluates to the full pathname of the database (excluding the .dbs extension). We recommend that you use the DBPATH environment variable to locate databases rather than embedding full paths in your program code. This allows you to use the same program on different databases without having to modify and recompile your code.

Closing the database

Use the CLOSE DATABASE statement to close the current database. CLOSE and DATABASE are both required keywords.

12.9.1 Opening the database examples

Example 1:

```
EXEC SQL database stores;
```

Example 2:

```
EXEC SQL begin declare section;
char dbname[80];
EXEC SQL end declare section;
strcpy("warehous@system1",dbname);
EXEC SQL database :dbname ;
```

In the first example, `stores` is the database name. If Informix-OnLine is used, this database exists in the current instance of OnLine identified by the environment variable TBCONFIG. This database is typically shipped with the product; ask your database administrator if it is available. If Informix-SE is used, this database is either in the current directory or in the directory whose pathname is contained in the DBPATH environmental variable.

In the second example, `warehous` is the database name. This database is neither in the current directory nor accessible through the DBPATH environmental variable. Host variable `dbname` contains the location for the desired database as a result of the `strcpy` function call. Even though this capability exists, it is never a good idea to hard-code a location into a production program. A better coding practice is to get the database name from an environment variable or command-line option, and use the DBPATH environment variable to specify the location of the database.

12.10 Compiling Your Informix-ESQL/C Program

To create an Informix-ESQL/C program, there are three basic steps you must perform: first, you must be able to incorporate Informix specific files into your source code; second, your code must pass successfully through the preprocessor before it can go through the normal C program compile process, which is the third step. In addition to these steps, the UNIX-supplied `make` utility is handy when you are trying to manage large applications.

12.10.1 The Informix-ESQL/C preprocessor

When you preprocess your source files using Informix-ESQL/C, the preprocessor converts SQL statements into C code. You signal the preprocessor either by prefixing your SQL statements with a dollar sign ($) or by enclosing them with EXEC SQL keywords.

Informix-ESQL/C reads in source files that have a .ec suffix, which is a requirement. Then Informix-ESQL/C stores the translated output into a separate file having the same name as your original file but with a .c suffix. For example, preprocessing program1.ec creates program1.c, and the original program1.ec stays intact. Depending on the options specified, you might even pass your code to the C compiler and have it go through the normal compilation process. Once the code is generated, do not attempt future development by directly calling functions generated by the ESQL/C preprocessor. The reasoning behind this is that, with different releases of Informix, the functions and their arguments might change.

12.10.2 Comments

Your code can include standard C comment identifiers /* and */ anywhere in the program. Additionally, on those lines containing SQL statements, you can use ANSI-standard SQL comment identifiers, the double dash (--). The Informix- ESQL/C preprocessor ignores all text to the right of the double dash. In this example:

```
EXEC SQL delete -- has no orders
 from customer;
```

the DELETE statement is incomplete and will cause compile errors because the FROM clause is considered to be part of the comment. However, in this example:

```
EXEC SQL delete -- has no order
from customer;
```

the DELETE statement is complete and will compile fine. Otherwise, you can still code as follows:

```
/*    If customer has no orders  */
EXEC SQL delete from customer ;
```

12.10.3 Using the preprocessor to include other files

At times you might want to include other source files in your program. For example, you might want to store all global variable declarations in a single source file and, through a preprocessor instruction, have them automatically included. When a source file contains no SQL, you can use the standard C preprocessor statement #include. The Informix-ESQL/C preprocessor ignores all #include statements. If the included file contains SQL code, however, you must use one of the following Informix-ESQL/C preprocessor statements, replacing *filename* with the name of the file you want to include:

```
$include filename;
EXEC SQL include filename;
```

In this example, the Informix-ESQL/C preprocessor looks into the current directory and reads the global_var include file. You can include files this way up to a maximum of eight levels. As we mentioned earlier, Informix-ESQL/C comes with nine header files located in $INFORMIXDIR/incl/esql, and you can use them in your Informix-ESQL/C source files. The preprocessor searches multiple directories for the files named in the EXEC SQL include, and the order of the search is as follows:

1. the current directory
2. $INFORMIXDIR/incl/esql
3. /usr/include

```
                    ESQL/C Sample Include statements:

programl.ec                               Sample included file: (global_var)

#include <stdio.h>  /* standard C include */   EXEC SQL include sqlca;  /* sqlca header file */
EXEC SQL include global_var;
main()                                    EXEC SQL begin declare section;
{                                         int    sku;
    ...                                   int    quantity;
}                                         EXEC SQL end declare section;
```

Figure 12.4

If the named file is found, the contents will be placed in the current file at the position of the include statement. The exception to this is if the filename is a pathname, which must be enclosed in double quotes. For example, if you have a file that is not in any of the previously mentioned directories, then you must code as follows:

```
EXEC SQL include "/home/devlp/inclesql/freq_defs";
```

12.10.4 Conditional compilation with preprocessor support

The following is a list of conditional compilation statements you can embed in your Informix-ESQL/C code:

define. Assigns a compile-time value to a name.

undef. Removes a defined name.

ifdef. Tests a name and processes subsequent statements if it has been defined.

ifndef. Tests a name and processes subsequent statements if it has not been defined.

elseif. Begins an alternate section to an ifdef or ifndef condition and checks for the presence of another ifdef.

else. Begins an alternate section to an ifdef or ifndef condition.

endif. Closes an ifdef or ifndef condition.

The define statement is limited to defining only symbols or integer constants. It does not support the definition of string constants or parameterized macros.

12.10.5 Compiling

When your C program contains SQL statements, before using the C compiler, esql must preprocess each file to translate the SQL statements into normal C code. To preprocess and compile such a file, add .ec to the end of the name, and then use the esql command file. Esql preprocesses files that have a .ec suffix, translates them into .c files, and then passes control to the resident C compiler. Once the C compiler creates object files, it links in standard and Informix-ESQL/C libraries as needed. For example:

```
esql pgm1.ec -o pgm1.ece
```

Pgm1 passes through the preprocessor and creates pgm1.c. Then the C compiler (cc) reads in pgm1.c and creates pgm1.o. Then the linker pulls in any required standard system and/or required ESQL/C library routines and creates the executable known as pgm1.ece.

In the example, the final executable pgm1.ece was created because the -o option was specified. If this option had not been specified, then the standard executable name of a.out would have been given to the executable, this being the C default. A word of caution: if you create an ESQL/C source file with the same name as a preexisting C source file, then the C source file will be destroyed when you compile your ESQL/C source file. For instance, given the previous example, if you already had a program named pgm1.c prior to compiling pgm1.ec, then the old pgm1.c would have been overwritten.

The esql command accepts names of files with not only .ec suffixes, but also .c and .o. The preprocessor ignores the .c files, passing them straight to the C compiler. Object files (.o) are passed straight to the linker. Besides preprocessing SQL statements, esql also forces the linking of Informix-ESQL/C libraries at link time. The –l option allows you to link both system libraries and your own libraries.

12.11 ESQL Command Syntax

The following sections will describe the different arguments recognized by ESQL.

12.11.1 General options

Here is the general argument syntax for running the esql command file:

e–. Preprocess only, no compiling or linking.

PreprocessorOptions. Preprocessor options such as routing error and warning messages to a file instead of to standard output. (These options are described later in this section.)

CcArgs. Special arguments passed to the cc (or other C) compiler.

–o Executable File Name. Name of the executable file to be made. If omitted, the name is a.out.

Source.ec. Name of source file(s) containing SQL statements embedded in C code. The filename suffix must be .ec.

CompileLinkOptions. Other files, such as those containing straight C code or object code and other libraries. (These options are described later in this section.)

12.11.2 Preprocessor options

Options you can specify to the esql preprocessor itself are:

–g. Passes the –g flag to the C compiler and also numbers the generated .c files. The numbering of .c files is the default behavior, but the –g flag is not passed to the C compiler.

–{G ¦ nln}. Passes the –g flag to the C compiler but does not number the generated .c files.

–ansi. Gives warnings when Informix extensions to the ANSI standard SQL are encountered.

–t Type. Uses the C compiler named by type instead of cc.

–icheck. Adds error-checking code to generate runtime errors when a SQL NULL is returned and no indicator variable has been used.

–ocal. Keeps cursor names and statement IDs local to the current source file.

–log ErrorFile. Sends compile-time errors and warnings to a specific file, instead of standard out.

–EDSymbolName[=Value]. Defines a preprocessor symbol.

–EUSymbolName. Undefines a preprocessor symbol.

12.12 Compiling and Linking Options

Besides giving arguments to the Informix-ESQL/C preprocessor for compiling your embedded SQL, you can specify other files to compile and link when creating your executable program:

OtherCsource. C source file(s) having a .c suffix you want to recompile and link with your source.ec.

OtherCobject. C object file(s) having a .o suffix you want to link with your source.ec.

–lYourLibrary. Links your library into the executable program.

–lSystemLibrary. Links a system library into the executable program.

12.13 Debugging and Line Numbering

When using a source-level debugger such as dbs or sdb, you need to use one of the –g, –G, or –nln options when compiling .ec files. All three options cause a –g flag to be passed to the C compiler in order to compile the .c files generated by the ESQL preprocessor. This causes the C compiler to include extra information in the resulting object files.

The –G and –nln options both perform the same function, so only –G will be used for the remainder of this discussion.

The difference between –g and –G is whether or not you want the ESQL preprocessor to include #line references to the original .ec file in the generated .c file. The –g option includes these references, while the –G option does not. These references are used by your debugger to display the source code for the application being debugged. If #line references are found in the .c file, the debugger will actually display the lines from the .ec file. If no #line references are found, the source code from the .c file will be displayed.

Whether you want your debugger to display source code from the .ec file or the .c file is a personal preference, probably influenced most by the nature of the bug you are attempting to locate.

Note: It is a common practice to have makefiles automatically remove the .c files generated by the ESQL preprocessor. For source-level debugging, you do not want this behavior since the debugger needs to access the .c files as well as the .o files.

12.14 Using Make: Managing Large ESQL/C Applications

Software projects commonly use a UNIX utility called make. It helps automate the process of compiling and linking a program. To use make, you simply put a series of commands into a file and have make run them. These commands most commonly have to do with building the final, executable program, often from a large number of source files, and with purging junk files. The next few sections provide a brief discussion of how you can use the UNIX make command. Also, you can type in man make on your UNIX system, which will provide you with the UNIX manual pages for this command. Our discussion will show you how to use .ec files and the esql command in the context of make.

You specify these dependencies and the commands to generate each target to make in a description file, often called a makefile.

12.14.1 Make: the description file

The sample makefile in Figure 12.5 contains the instructions necessary to compile a program named pname from two source files, src1.ec and src2.ec. These lines should be placed in a file named makefile. Entering make at the command line causes make to read and carry out the instructions in the file.

Here is a short explanation of the instructions:

```
.SUFFIXES:
```

These lines make a list of file suffixes to use. The first line removes the default list of suffixes.

```
.ec.o:
    esql -c $*.ec
```

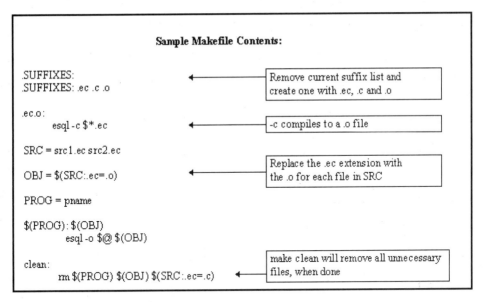

Figure 12.5

This is a suffix rule that indicates how to create a file with a suffix of .o from a file with a suffix of .ec. In this case, esql is executed. The characters $* represent the file with the suffix removed.

Object files needed to create pname are contained in the OBJ macro, which is built from the macro SRC. SRC contains a list of all the .ec files that need to be compiled and linked into the executable.

```
$(PROG):$(OBJ)
esql-o $@$(OBJ)
```

The first line indicates that the macro PROG depends on OBJ. The second line is executed if any of the files in OBJ is newer than PROG or if PROG does not exist. In this case, the esql command is executed with an output file named $@, a built-in macro that represents the target, in this case $(PROG).

12.15 Using Simple Variables in Informix-ESQL/C

Earlier in this chapter, we discussed the different types of host variables that are functional equivalents between SQL and the C language. See Figure 12.6 to refresh your memory.

Now we will show you how you can decide which C data type you should choose to be a host variable. You must understand how storage will be used depending on the SQL and C data types you choose, and which library functions to use when converting both character and numeric data. Here we will begin by working with simple SQL data types. Later we will discuss VARCHAR, which is a complex SQL data type used with variable-length data.

Types of Host Variables			
Simple data Types		**Sophisticated data Types**	
SQL	**C-Host**	**SQL**	**C-Host**
CHAR(n) CHARACTER	char[n+1] char*	DECIMAL DEC NUMERIC	dec_t or struct decimal
SMALLINT	short int	MONEY	dec_t or struct decimal
INTEGER INT	long int	DATETIME	dtime_t or struct dtime
SMALLFLOAT REAL	float		
FLOAT DOUBLE PRECISION	double	INTERVAL	intrvl_t or struct intrvl
SERIAL	long int	VARCHAR	varchar or string
DATE	long int		

Figure 12.6

12.15.1 Types of host variables

Since host variables will contain your SQL data, you must define a compatible type within your C program to store the data value in memory.

Implicit conversion

When you migrate data from memory into your database, the database server converts that data from a C type to a SQL type. When migrating SQL data from the database to your program's memory, Informix converts it from a SQL type to a C type. It is up to you as the programmer to declare the host variable to be a proper type. Figure 12.6 shows the implied relationships between SQL types and C types. If you do not declare your host variables as shown in the figure, the database server will try to convert the data value (if meaningful).

Explicit conversion

Here are two situations where the database server attempts to convert data of one type to another type. In a WHERE clause, you compare a character column to an integer, as in:

```
where prod_num > 99999
```

In an arithmetic expression, you provide values of different types to be operated on, as in:

```
set retail_price = retail_price * pcnt_com (a type DOUBLE)
```

In such expressions, all values are converted to type DECIMAL before operation.

12.15.2 Data conversion in arithmetic expressions

When using Informix-ESQL/C, all arithmetic in an arithmetic expression is done with type DECIMAL. The type of the resulting variable determines the format of the stored or printed result. All the values within an expression, if not already DECIMAL, are converted to DECIMAL, and the resulting number is DECIMAL. This being the case, the following conversions would take place: FLOAT would become DECIMAL(16), SMALLFLOAT would become DECI-MAL(8), INTEGER would become DECIMAL(10,0), and SMALLINT would become DECIMAL(5,0).

If any of these values are a floating-point decimal, then the result would be represented as a floating-point decimal. If the type results in a loss of precision, then ESQL/C would return an error.

12.15.3 Conversion problems

At times, you might want to convert data from one type to another, which might cause the database server to experience problems. These problems could result in either a warning or an error.

Warnings

When converting data to character type, the only problem you might encounter is that the receiving area is too small, which will generate a warning. Here are two examples that will generate such a warning:

- A column is defined as char(5), and you try to insert the string Ear_Cleaners. In this example, the string will be truncated and the column will contain the string Ear_C.
- A column is defined as char(5), and you try to insert the six-digit integer 123456. Here, the number will be ignored and the column will contain a string of five asterisks (*).

Errors

When converting data to some numeric type, the only problem you mighty encounter is that significant digits could be lost, which will generate an error. Here are two examples that will generate such an error:

- A column is defined as a date, and you try to fetch a date value into a host variable of type short.
- A column containing product ID numbers is defined as a char(5), and you try to fetch the value 99999 in a host variable of type SHORT.

In both of these cases, an error is generated because the receiving area is too small. If conversion took place, significant digits would be lost and both host variables would contain undefined values.

12.15.4 Storage of character data type CHAR

On disk, when a SQL character value is shorter than the allotted space, the value is padded with trailing spaces. Host variables of type CHAR accept SQL

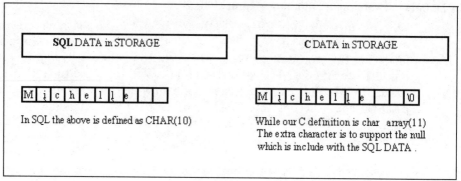

Figure 12.7

data complete with trailing blanks and add a null terminator to the end of the array. To avoid truncation, define the length of this type one greater than the length of the SQL data.

In the example in Figure 12.7, the database column was defined as type char(10), but the host variable array needs to be declared as array[11] to include an extra byte for the terminating null character.

12.15.5 Storage of character data type *CHAR

A host variable of type *CHAR can hold SQL data as long as enough memory has been allocated for the pointer. The amount of memory needed is the length of the CHAR data type plus one byte for the terminating null character. It is imperative that sufficient memory is allocated for the host variable before it is used in any SQL statements. This code fragment shows the use of a host variable of type *CHAR:

```
EXEC SQL begin declare section;
char     *buf;
EXEC SQL end declare section;

buf=(char*)malloc(11);       /* allocate additional memory */
strcpy(buf,"Michelle");      /* copies the string Michelle into buf  */
EXEC SQL update tbl set col = :buf where _;
```

12.15.6 Storage of character data types STRING and FIXCHAR

Besides CHAR and *CHAR, Informix-ESQL/C provides two additional host data types: STRING and FIXCHAR. Another character type, called VARCHAR, is available, but due to its complexity and because it is Informix-On-Line-specific, we have placed it in a separate section within this chapter.

Character strings

STRING types truncate trailing blanks before adding a null terminator. In order to avoid truncation, you should define the length of this type so it is one greater than the length of the SQL data to allow for the null byte.

Fixed-length character data

FIXCHAR is the same as CHAR, except it does not add the trailing null byte to terminate the string. When using this type, you should define the length to be equal to the size of the SQL data.

Typical usage for one of the preceding character types would be to hold SQL character data. SQL character data is stored in a fixed-length format in a database. Sometimes, though, you might need to work with SQL character data of variable length, defined as VARCHARS. For more information on VARCHAR, see the following section.

For portability, it is recommended that you always use host variables of type CHAR instead of the types FIXCHAR and STRING. Although these types provide some coding advantages, they are Informix-specific and might not work with other embedded SQL products.

12.16 Using Data Type VARCHAR in an ESQL/C Program

In this section we will discuss VARCHAR. VARCHAR is utilized when working with variable length data fields. It is important to note that VARCHAR data types are specific to the Informix-Online product, and that usage of its functionality will make your code less portable.

12.16.1 Declaring VARCHAR type variables

The syntax which is used to declare a host variable as type VARCHAR is as follows:

```
varchar HostvarName[n];
```

or

```
string HostvarName[n];
```

A type VARCHAR variable is represented within your program as an array of characters. When you define a variable of type VARCHAR, you must specify the size of the array by providing a value for n, just as you would for any other array. In addition, you must include an extra byte for the null terminator, which is part of the VARCHAR variable, as with any other character type. The size of the array should account for the maximum size of the variable, similar to the way you would use type VARCHAR within your columns. Also note that, even if you use a STRING definition, it will still be treated as an array of characters.

12.16.2 Comparing VARCHAR and STRING

A key issue to consider when deciding whether to use VARCHAR or STRING is the treatment of trailing spaces within the column. When you insert values into a VARCHAR column, the trailing spaces are retained but not added to. When you retrieve data from a VARCHAR column into memory, the database retains all user-entered trailing spaces. When you place the VARCHAR data into a STRING host variable, the server strips off all trailing spaces, leaving only the leading significant characters.

12.16.3 Determining the size of your VARCHAR variables

To aid you in determining the size of your VARCHAR variables, Informix-On-Line provides you with four sizing macros. These macros are useful when you want to know just how big a buffer is required to hold your VARCHAR variable. The macros obtain the size information from the syscolumns catalog under the column collength. Since these values are encoded, the macros enable you to obtain the maximum and minimum lengths defined for a given VARCHAR column. These macros are located in the varchar.h header file. Following is a brief description of each macro:

VCLENGTH(size). Returns the required size of the host array for a VARCHAR (adds 1 for a null terminator).

VCMIN(size). Returns the minimum length of a VARCHAR.

VCMAX(size). Returns the maximum length of a VARCHAR.

VCSIZ(max,min). Returns an encoded value based on maximum and minimum sizes.

The macro parameter size is the encoded integer value in syscolumns.

12.16.4 Using the VARCHAR macros

If you wanted to find the maximum size of the VARCHAR column called prod_descr, you could use the code in Figure 12.8. This example accesses the syscolumns system catalog and retrieves the collength value for the column. VCLENGTH is then used to extract the number of bytes needed to store a VARCHAR value from prod_descr into memory. This return value contains an additional null byte to terminate the character array. In this case, the data is placed into a VARCHAR

```
EXEC SQL begin declare section;
varchar          *vcstr;
 int             collength;
EXEC SQL end declare section;

EXEC SQL select collength into :collength
         from syscolumns where colname=
         "prod_descr";

vcstr = malloc( VCLENGTH( collength ));
```

Figure 12.8

host variable. If it were placed in a host variable of type FIXCHAR, you could have used the VCMAX macro to obtain the maximum length of the column.

12.16.5 Transferring VARCHAR to CHAR

When you transfer data from a VARCHAR column to a host variable of type CHAR, you must check to see if your data has been truncated. Truncation will occur if your VARCHAR variable is longer than your CHAR host variable. You can check the data with an indicator variable and the sqlcaw_s structure within the sqlca. The field sqlwarn1 will show a value of "w" if truncation has occurred. If your data is smaller than the size of the CHAR host variable, then the remaining spaces will be padded with blanks. In both cases, each string will be null-terminated ("\0").

For example, Table 12.1 shows an 8-byte value within a column defined as VARCHAR(255), and a CHAR field with two different definitions.

12.16.6 Transferring VARCHAR to FIXCHAR

When you transfer data from a VARCHAR column to a host variable of type FIXCHAR, you must check to see if your data has been truncated in much the same way as you did with CHAR. Once again, use an indicator variable and the sqlcaw_s structure within the sqlca. The field sqlwarn1 will show a value of "w" if truncation has occurred. Truncation will occur if your VARCHAR variable is longer than your FIXCHAR host variable. If your data is smaller than the size of the FIXCHAR host variable, then the remaining spaces will be padded with blanks. The key difference to using FIXCHAR is that your host variables will not be null-terminated.

Table 12.2 provides the values of an eight-byte value within a column defined as VARCHAR(255), and a FIXCHAR field with two different definitions.

TABLE 12.1

VARCHAR column	I/P data	Host variable	O/P data
8-byte value			
VARCHAR(255)	abcdefg	CHAR(10)	abcdefg_/0
VARCHAR(255)	abcdefg	CHAR(5)	abcd/0

NOTE: Underscores represent blanks

TABLE 12.2

VARCHAR column	I/P data	Host variable	O/P data
8-byte value			
VARCHAR(255)	abcdefg	FIXCHAR(10)	abcdefg_
VARCHAR(255)	abcdefg	FIXCHAR(5)	abcde

NOTE: Underscores represent blanks

12.16.7 Transferring VARCHAR to STRING

When you transfer data from a VARCHAR column to a host variable of type STRING, you must check to see if your data has been truncated just as you did for CHAR and FIXCHAR. Use an indicator variable and the sqlcaw_s structure within the sqlca. The field sqlwarn1 will show a value of "w" if truncation has occurred. Truncation will occur if your VARCHAR variable is longer than your STRING host variable. In the event that your data is smaller than the size of the STRING host variable, no padding will be done. The STRING, however, will be null-terminated ("\0").

Table 12.3 shows an eight-byte value within a column defined as VAR-CHAR(255), and a STRING field with two different definitions.

12.16.8 Transferring CHAR to VARCHAR

When you transfer data from a CHAR column to a host variable of type VAR-CHAR, if the data from the CHAR column data requires more space than the size of the VARCHAR field, truncation will occur once more. You can test to see if this occurs in the same manner as described in the previous three sections. If your VARCHAR field length exceeds the length of the CHAR data string, then the VARCHAR field will take on the length of the CHAR data field and be null-terminated ("\0").

Take, for example, an eight-byte value within a column defined as CHAR(8), and a VARCHAR field with two different definitions (see Table 12.4).

Notice in Table 12.4 that the CHAR column is SQL CHAR(8), which contains the seven characters a through g followed by a blank, and that the host variable is defined as SQL VARCHAR (max = 10). In the first example, abcedfg is transferred and then followed by the null terminator ("\0"), which is the end of the field (eight bytes). In the second case, the truncation is more noticeable.

12.16.9 Portability and VARCHAR

To maintain portability within your code, it is recommended that you define all host variables that will contain VARCHAR columns as type CHAR. You can ac-

TABLE 12.3

VARCHAR column	I/P data	Host variable	O/P data
8-byte value			
VARCHAR(255)	abcdefg	STRING(10)	abcdefg\0
VARCHAR(255)	abcdefg	STRING(5)	abcd\0

TABLE 12.4

CHAR column	Data	Host variable	Data
CHAR(8)	abcdefg	VARCHAR(10)	abcdefg\0
CHAR(8)	abcdefg	VARCHAR(5)	abcd\0

complish this by declaring host variable character arrays as the maximum size of a VARCHAR column, plus one for the null terminator to eliminate possible problems with data truncation. In addition, avoid using VCLENGTH, VCMIN, VC-MAX, and VCSIZ since they are Informix-only macros. The way to avoid these macros is by using host variables of type CHAR for your VARCHAR columns.

12.17 Using Data Type Library Functions

Informix provides a number of library functions, allowing you to work with all data types. You can use these functions in your C programs to manipulate strings of bytes and characters, and to convert from one data type to another. When you compile your program using ESQL, the shell script will automatically link in this library.

12.17.1 Return codes

ESQL/C library routines pass back return codes. Unless otherwise noted, a return code with a value of zero shows success and a return code with a negative value shows failure. Here is an example of how you can determine the return code from a specific function:

```
int sku;                /* define the data types which we will use */
char line[80];
int ret;

printf("SKU NUMBER is ");

fgets(line,7,stdin);  /* get input for length of 7 and store in line */
ret = rstoi(line,&sku);
if(ret)
printf("Error code is %d\n", ret);
```

In this sample code, the function rstoi() converts the character string contained in "line" to an integer and stores the result in sku.

12.17.2 Character functions for null-terminated strings

There are six functions in the ESQL/C library that work on character strings terminated by a null byte.

rdownshift(s). Changes all characters in a string to lowercase. Char *s; is a pointer to the target string.

rupshift(s). Changes all characters in a string to uppercase. Char *s; is a pointer to the target string.

stcat(s,dest). Concatenates one string to another. Char *s; is a pointer to the target string, and char *dest; is a pointer to the destination string.

stcmpr(s1,s2). Compares two strings. Char *s1; is a pointer to the first string, and char *s2; is a pointer to the second string.

stcopy(from,to). Copies one string to another. Char *from; is a pointer to the target string, and char *to; is a pointer to the destination buffer.

stleng(string). Counts the number of bytes in a string. `Char *string:` is a pointer to the target string.

Once again, for portability, you should use equivalent routines in the standard C library instead of the previous routines. You could, for example, use strcpy() instead of stcopy(). All these routines are Informix-specific and will not exist in the embedded products of other vendors.

12.17.3 Character functions for fixed-length strings

There are four functions in the ESQL/C library that work on fixed-length strings that are not null-terminated.

bycmpr(byte1,byte2,len). Compares two groups of contiguous bytes. `Char *byte1;` is a pointer to the first group of bytes, `char *byte2;` is a pointer to the second group of bytes, and `int len;` is the number of bytes to compare.

bycopy(from,to,len). Copies bytes from one area to another. `Char *from;` is a pointer to the target group of bytes, `char *to;` is a pointer to the destination area, and `int len;` is the number of bytes to copy.

byfill(to,len,ch). Fills the specified area with a character. `Char *to;` is a pointer to the area to be filled, `int len;` is the number of bytes to fill, and `char ch;` is the character with which to fill.

byleng(from,count). Counts the number of significant characters. (Significant characters are those in the string minus any trailing spaces.) `Char *from;` is a pointer to the fixed-length string, and `int count;` is the number of bytes in the string.

As with the character functions for null-terminated strings, you should avoid using these routines if equivalent C functions are available. This allows you to keep your code more portable.

12.17.4 Character functions for data manipulation

The following functions perform other operations on character data:

ldchar(from,num,to). Copies (ignoring trailing spaces) a fixed-length string to a null-terminated string. `Char *from;` is a pointer to the fixed-length source string, and `int num;` is the number of bytes in the fixed-length source string.

stchar(from,to,num). Copies a null-terminated string to a fixed-length string. `Char *from;` is a pointer to the null-terminated source string, `char *to;` is a pointer to the fixed-length destination string, and `int num;` is the number of bytes in the fixed-length destination string.

rstod(str,dblval). Converts a null-terminated string to a C double. `Char *str;` is a pointer to the source string, and `double *dblval;` is a pointer to the destination double.

rstoi (str,intval). Converts a null-terminated string to a C integer. `Char *str;` is a pointer to the source string, and `int *intval;` is a pointer to the destination integer.

rstol (str,lngval). Converts a null-terminated string to a C long integer. `Char *str;` is a pointer to the source string, `char *str;` is a pointer to the source string, and `long*lngval;` is a pointer to the destination long integer.

12.18 Storing Simple Numeric Data Types

SQL data of type SMALLINT requires two bytes of storage on disk and is compatible with machine data type of short integers. On all machines, short integers take at least two bytes of memory and are completely compatible with SQL SMALLINT. C integers might alternatively be used as host variables for SMALLINT. Integers take at least the same amount of memory as short integers, and are also compatible with SMALLINT.

SQL data of type INTEGER (or INT) requires four bytes of storage on disk and is compatible with machine data type of long integer. On all machines, long integers take at least four bytes of memory, and are completely compatible with SQL's INTEGER. You should always use a long int to store SQL integer data.

SQL data of type SMALLFLOAT (or real) requires four bytes of storage on disk and is compatible with machine data of type FLOAT. On all machines, data of type FLOAT occupies four bytes of memory and is completely compatible with SQL SMALLFLOAT. C doubles might alternatively be used as host variables for SMALLFLOAT. Smallfloats can track up to eight significant digits.

SQL data of type FLOAT (or double precision) requires eight bytes of storage on disk and is compatible with machine double. On all machines, doubles take eight bytes of memory and are completely compatible with SQL floats. Floats can track up to 16 significant digits.

SQL data of type SERIAL and DATE both correspond to C long integers, since they are internally stored as SQL integers.

12.18.1 Formatting functions for simple numeric values

rfmtdouble(dblval,fmt,str). Formats a double. `Double dblval;` is the target double value, `char *fmt;` is a pointer to the formatting mask, and `char *str;` is a pointer to the destination string.

rfmtlong(longval,fmt,str). Formats a long integer. `Double longval;` is the target long integer value, `char *fmt;` is a pointer to the formatting mask, and `char *str;` is a pointer to the destination string.

In the following section we will show you what characters are considered acceptable when creating a format string. This is an example of how to use rfmtdouble:

```
int     err;
double  val = -354.46;
```

```
char    *fmt = "(<<<,<<<.&&)";
char    str[18];
if( err = rfmtdouble( val, fmt, str ))
printf("Error %d in formatting %g using '%s'\n"
        err val, fmt, str );
```

12.18.2 Numeric formatting characters

Format strings for numeric expressions consist of combinations of the following characters: * & # < , . − + ( ) $. These characters will float: − + ( ) $.

*. Replaces a space with an asterisk.

&. Replaces a space with a zero.

#. Represents a position for a digit or space.

<. Left-justifies.

,. A literal to show a comma. Displays only when there is a digit to its left.

.. A literal to show a decimal point. Only one per format string.

-. A literal to show a minus sign. Displays when the number is negative.

+. A literal to show a plus sign. Displays when the number is not negative.

(. A literal to show a minus sign. Used with) to show a negative value in accounting.

). A literal to show a minus sign. Used with (to show a negative value in accounting.

$. A literal to show a dollar sign.
Table 12.5 shows some examples.

12.19 Date Functions

Informix provides the developer with two distinct sets of date functions: one set for when you want to store a date in the date column of your database, and the other for extracting dates from the database.

12.19.1 Creating internal dates

There are four functions in the ESQ/C library that create date values that can be stored in a date column:

rdefmtdate(jdate,fmt,str). Creates an integer that can be stored in a date column from a formatted string. `Long *jdate;` is a pointer to the destination date value, `char *fmt;` is a pointer to the formatting mask for str, and `char *str;` is a pointer to the source date string.

rmdyjul(mdy,jdate). Creates an internal date from an array of three strings consisting of the month, day, and year. `Short mdy[3];` is an array of integers

TABLE 12.5

Format string	Numeric value	Formatted result
"#####"	0	
"$$,$$$"	–1234	01,234
"$$,$$$"	12345	****** *overflow*
"$$,$$$"	123	$123
"**,***"	123	***123
"###,###.##"	0.01	.01
"<<,<<<.##"	0.01	.01
""–##,###.##"	–12.34	–12.34
"–##,###.##"	–12.34	–12.34
"$***,***.&&"	123.45	$****123.45
"($$$,$$$.&&)"	–1234.5	($1,234.50)
"(($$,$$$.&&)"	–1234.5	($1,234.50)

giving the month, day, and year, and `long *jdate;` is a pointer to the destination date value.

rstrdate(str,jdate). Creates internal date from the default string (mmddyy). `Char *str;` is a pointer to the source date string, and `long *jdate;` is a pointer to the destination date value.

rtoday(jdate). Creates an internal date from the system date. `Long *jdate;` is a pointer to the destination date value.

12.19.2 Extracting date strings

There are four functions in the ESQL/C library that extract date strings from dates in internal format:

rfmtdate(jdate,fmt,str). Creates formatted string from the internal date. `Long jdate;` is the source internal date value, `char *fmt;` is a pointer to the formatting mask for jdate, and `char *str;` is a pointer to the destination date string.

rjulmdy(jdate,mdy). Extracts the month, day, and year from the internal date. `Long jdate;` is the source internal date value, and `short mdy[3];` is an array of integers giving the month, day, and year.

rdatestr(jdate,str). Creates a default date string from the internal date. `Long jdate;` is the source internal date value, and `char *str;` is a pointer to the destination date string.

rdayofweek(jdate). Returns the numeric day of the week (0 to 6). `Long jdate;` is the source internal date value.

There is also a function that determines whether a given year is a leap year:

rleapyear(year). Returns TRUE or FALSE. `Int year;` is the source four-digit year value.

12.20 Data Type As Constants

Some Informix-ESQL/C library routines require that the C or SQL data type be passed as an integer argument. To help you pass the correct integer, you can include the sqltypes.h header file located in $INFORMIXDIR/incl/esql. This file defines constants for all C and SQL data types. The following sections show some of the entries in that header file. These are some of the entries for the C data types:

```
#define CCHARTYPE      100
#define CSHORTTYPE     101
#define CINTTYPE       102
#define CLINGTYPE      103
#define CFLOATTYPE     104
#define CDOUBLETYPE    105
```

These are some of the entries for the SQL data types:

```
#define SQLCHAR        0
#define SQLSMINT       1
#define SQLINT         2
#define SQLFLOAT       3
#define SQLSMFLOAT     4
#define SQLDECIMAL     5
#define SQLSERIAL      6
```

Although you can use either the C or SQL macros as arguments to functions, it is recommended that you use the C macros CINTTYPE, CLONGTYPE, etc., as this states exactly what arguments you are passing. If you were to use SQLINT, someone reading the code might expect an int to be passed as an argument when in fact a long is needed. Using CLONGTYPE makes this point clear.

12.21 Data Type Functions: Working with SQL Nulls

In addition to the aforementioned functions, the ESQL/C library has two additional functions that work with SQL null values:

risnull(type,cvar). Checks whether a C variable is null. `Int type;` is a data type of variable, and `char *cvar;` is a pointer to the variable.

rsetnull(type,cvar). Sets C variable to a SQL null value. `Int type;` is a data type of variable, and `char *cvar;` is a pointer to the variable.

When examining a C variable that contains a SQL null value, risnull returns 1; otherwise, it returns 0. The function rsetnull() assigns the indicated C variable a SQL null value corresponding to the specified type.

The functions risnull() and rsetnull() expect a pointer to a character as the second argument. When you are working with a variable of a different type, you need to cast the second argument as a pointer to a character using the casting operator (char*). The following examples show you how to use these two functions:

```
EXEC SQL include sqltypes;
short prod_num;

if( risnull( CSHORTTYPE, (char*)&prod_num ) != 1 )
    (void) rsetnull(CSHORTTYPE, (char*)&prod_num );
```

12.22 Inserting Rows Using Informix-ESQL/C

In this section we will introduce you to the INSERT statement, which is used within your C programs to add new rows to a table.

12.22.1 The INSERT statement

Use the INSERT statement to insert one or more new rows into an existing table. Here is a sample of the syntax used to execute this statement:

```
INSERT INTO TableName
            [(ColumnList)]
            VALUES(ValueList)
```

And here are descriptions of the verbs and data fields used in this statement:

INSERT INTO. Required keywords.

table-name. Name of the table to which you want to add rows.

column-list. Names of the columns into which you want to insert data. You can enter one column name or a series of comma-separated column names.

VALUES. Required keyword.

value-list. Values that you want to insert into the columns you specified. You can enter one or more comma-separated host variables or constants.

Additionally, note that all constants of type CHAR, DATE, DATETIME, and INTERVAL must be enclosed within quotation marks. You should also enter a zero (0) for a SERIAL column in the INSERT statement if you want the database server to automatically insert the next SERIAL value for the table. If columns are not included within the column list, then they will take on default values, such as SQL nulls, unless the schema has a DEFAULT option specifying some other value for that column. When values violate a CONSTRAINT option (check, foreign key, primary key, or unique) they will cause a SQLERROR condition.

```
EXEC SQL insert into order_history(
                        sku
                        week ending_date,
                        quantity
)
values(
        0,
        :week_ending_date,
        :quantity
);
```

Figure 12.9

12.22.2 INSERT examples

In the first statement of the sample in Figure 12.9, the parenthesized list of column names following the table name indicates which columns in the order_history table will have information inserted into them. Since sku is a SERIAL column, a zero is placed in the VALUES list as a place holder. The content of the two host variables, week_ending_date and quantity, provide values for the second and third columns listed.

In the second sample, Figure 12.10, the table name stands alone. So you must provide one value (host variable or literal) in the VALUES list for each column in the orders table. You need to provide these values in the same order in which the columns were defined in the orders table. In other words, the fields making up the orderrec structure must be in the proper order, and there must be one field for each column.

It is recommended that you follow the first example since it has a number of advantages. First, it is extremely clear when looking at the code what values are being inserted into what columns. Secondly, it is independent of the order in which the columns are actually defined in the database. Finally, the code will always work if new columns are added to the table, as long as they allow null values.

The second example is dependent upon the database columns matching, in both order and number, the definition of the elements in the orderrec structure. Changes to the orders table will cause this code to fail.

Although the first example involves more typing, at least it will not turn out to be a maintenance nightmare in the long term. We recommend that you use this style of code to enhance the long-term maintenance of your applications.

12.22.3 INSERT using prepare/execute

An alternate means of performing the INSERT is to use the prepare and execute commands. The prepare command sends a SQL statement to the engine, where it is parsed and a query plan is created. The execute statement causes the engine to execute the statement that was prepared earlier.

The question mark character (?) is used in SQL statements as place-holders for values that must be passed to the engine when the statement is executed. For example, in the following code:

```
EXEC SQL prepare orderhist_p from
  "insert into order_history
  (sku, week_ending_date, quantity)
  values(?,?,?)";

EXEC SQL execute orderhist_p using
   :sku, :week_ending_date, :quantity;
```

The values for the sku, week_ending_date, and quantity host variables are passed to the engine to be inserted into the corresponding columns in the order_history table.

The advantage of using prepare in this manner is that the SQL statement can be executed any number of times with different values being supplied, but it is parsed by the engine only once. This will have a dramatic effect on your application by increasing the performance of any SQL statement that must be executed a number of times. A common application technique is to prepare the most frequently used SQL statements in an initialization routine at the beginning of the program and actually execute the statements later.

12.22.4 Prepare syntax

The format of the prepare statement is as follows:

```
PREPARE stmnt_id from "string between quotes"
```

or:

```
PREPARE stmnt_id using :our_host_variable
```

```
EXEC SQL insert into orders
       values(:orderrec);
```

Figure 12.10

These examples show that a prepare statement can use either the quoted string or a character array host variable that contains the text of a SQL statement. These examples basically describe what was already done in the previous examples, in which a host variable was used to perform a prepare. The main advantage to using a host variable in your prepare is that you can construct a SQL statement at run time instead of compile time. This allows for greater flexibility in using your program.

12.23 The SQL Communication Area and ESQL/C

The SQL communication area, or SQLCA as it is more commonly referred, is a header file. It is located in the directory known as $INFORMIXDIR/incl/esql, and is in file sqlca.h. The function of this file is to allow you to determine the success or failure of your SQL statements.

After the execution of a SQL statement, the database server returns status data to your program in the SQLCA. You can use the data that is provided to determine whether or not an error has occurred. You can also use this data to monitor performance. The SQLCA is an area within your program that is automatically included when you compile your source file using ESQL. It is defined in the sqlca.h header file.

12.23.1 SQLCA structure

The SQLCA is a globally defined structure that contains data about SQL statements as they execute. When you compile your source code with ESQL, it is automatically included. The SQLCA structure is as follows:

```
struct sqlca_s{
    long      sqlcode;
    char      sqlerm[72];
    char      sqlerrp[8];
    long      sqlerrd[6];
    struct sqlcaw_s
        {
    char sqlwarn0;
    char sqlwarn1;
    char sqlwarn2;
    char sqlwarn3;
    char sqlwarn4;
    char sqlwarn5;
    char sqlwarn6;
    char sqlwarn7;
        } sqlwarn;
    };
extern struct sqlca_s sqlca;
extern long SQLCODE;
```

The five key fields within the structure are listed in Table 12.6.

TABLE 12.6

Field name	Description
long sqlcode	Status indicator
char sqlerrm[72]	Error message parameters (tables, columns or any other objects) specific to the *error* message
char sqlerrp [8]	*Not used at present*
long sqlerrd [6]	Data attributes and performance information
struct sqlwarn	Data exceptions and other warnings

12.23.2 SQLCODE (status indicator)

The sqlcode field in the sqlca structure is the status of the most recently executed SQL statement. After each SQL statement is executed, examine this variable and take whatever action is required if it is not what you expect. The return code can be any of the ones shown in Table 12.7.

12.23.3 SQLNOTFOUND

The database server returns a value of SQLNOTFOUND, which you can determine by performing the following test:

```
if(SQLCODE == SQLNOTFOUND)
```

Its occurrence is caused when a singleton select (which selects only one row) finds no data, if a fetch attempts to go beyond the beginning or end of a set of rows, or when you are in a mode-ANSI database and no rows satisfy the WHERE clause during a delete, insert_select, select_into temp, or update request.

12.23.4 Using SQLCODE

When you compile your source file with ESQL, there is a global variable called SQLCODE. For portability, use the SQLCODE variable instead of testing sqlca.sqlcode.

TABLE 12.7

Return code	Status description
<0	Error occurred
=0	Successful execution, no errors
=1:99	Value of a SQL statement after a DESCRIBE statement. This value can be used by also including sqlstype.h, an additional header file to determine what type of SQL statement was executed (SELECT, INSERT, etc.).
=100	The SQL statement was executed but no rows found the defined field SQLNOTFOUND in the header.
	File has a value of 100.

TABLE 12.8

Array field	Field description
sqlerrd[0]	Estimated number of rows returned, set after a statement is prepared.
sqlerrd[1]	Serial value after an insert or ISAM error code. The ISAM error code is a more specific explanation of the exact error that occurred.
sqlerrd[2]	Number of rows processed.
sqlerrd[3]	Estimated cost, set after a statement is prepared.
sqlerrd[4]	Offset of error into the SQL statement.
sqlerrd[5]	Row ID after an insert.

12.23.5 sqlerrd: data and performance information

The sqlerrd field in the sqlca structure is an array of six long integers. This array contains various information describing certain attributes of the data being manipulated and expected performance. Table 12.8 gives descriptions of each element of the array.

12.23.6 sqlwarn: data exceptions and other warnings

The sqlwarn structure in sqlca has eight character fields to signal various warnings associated with the most recently executed SQL statement. When one of these fields is set, it has a value of W; otherwise, it is blank. Table 12.9 provides descriptions of the different sqlwarn fields.

TABLE 12.9

Field name	Field description
sqlwarn0	One or more of the other fields has been set. If sqlwarn0 is blank, you do not have to check the others.
sqlwarn1	One or more values were truncated to fit into a character host variable, or a database having transactions was opened.
sqlwarn2	An aggregate function (SUM, AVG, MAX, MIN) has encountered a null value, or a mode-ANSI database (with transactions) was opened.
sqlwarn3	Number of items in the select-list is not the same as the number of host variables in the INTO clause, or an OnLine database was opened.
sqlwarn4	An UPDATE or DELETE statement was prepared without a WHERE clause, or float-to-decimal conversion was used.
sqlwarn5	Your program executed an Informix extension to standard ANSI SQL (DBANSIWARN environment variable must be defined).

13

Debugging Your Code

In this chapter, we will discuss the fundamentals of debugging, including problem determination and resolution, locating the problem, and debugging tools.

Debugging is the way to identify and resolve a problem within your program. It is a major factor in the testing process, for this is where you should detect as many of the errors as possible. Debugging occasionally requires as much as 50% of the time it takes to develop an application, and is often considered to be the toughest part of programming.

Debugging can be viewed in multiple fashions. First are the syntax errors, which can most often be found visually. Then there are the execution errors, typically caused by trying to place the wrong data type within a field without the proper description. Finally, there is what we like to call "user anticipation," which is basically having someone unfamiliar with the application use it and provide feedback when errors or perceived errors occur. This will aid in improving the overall application.

13.1 Overview of Debugging Issues

In general, debugging is the means by which the programmer determines what is or is not a problem. Many believe that debugging received its name when some programmers traced a circuit malfunction to the presence of a large moth that had found its way into a computer, therefore calling the problem a "bug." This is not the typical cause, however, for most problems you will experience. The truth of the matter is that there are errors within almost all code as originally written, and sooner or later the programmer will be called upon to resolve the problem.

13.1.1 Quality control through debugging

Although debugging should not be the only path to creating a high-quality application, it is your major tool in determining and ensuring the continued reliability of your application. You need to consider quality in the early design phase, and debugging is your tool to ensure that it is error-free. Good coding practices, careful analysis, and superior design are all part of ensuring a quality application. Debugging is only a tool to assist you on your way.

13.1.2 Variations in debugging performance

Why talk about debugging? Doesn't everyone know how to debug? Studies have found that there is roughly a 20-to-1 difference in the time it takes experienced programmers to find the same set of errors. Moreover, some programmers find more errors and make corrections more accurately. Table 13.1 shows the results of one study that examined how effectively professional programmers with at least four years of experience debugged a program with 12 errors.

The three programmers who were best at debugging were able to find the defects in about one-third the time and made only about two-fifths as many errors as the three who were the worst. The best programmer found all the defects and didn't make any errors in correcting them. The worst missed 4 of the 12 defects and made 11 errors in correcting the 8 defects he found. This wide variation has been confirmed by other studies (Gilb 1977, Curtis 1981).

In addition to providing insight into debugging, the evidence supports the general principle of software quality, that improving quality reduces development costs. The best programmers found the most errors, found them more quickly, and made correct modifications most often. You don't have to choose between quality, cost, and time; they all go hand in hand.

13.1.3 Errors as opportunities

What does having an error mean? Assuming you don't want the program to have errors, it means that you don't fully understand what the program does. The idea of not understanding what the program does is unsettling. After all, if you created the program, it should do your bidding. If you don't know exactly what you're telling the computer to do, then you're merely trying different things until something seems to work. In this type of trial-and-error program-

TABLE 13.1

	Fastest three programmers	Slowest three programmers
Average debug time (minutes)	5.0	14.1
Average number of errors not found	0.7	1.7
Average number of errors made correcting errors	3.0	7.7

SOURCE: "Some psychological evidence on how people debug computer programs" (Gould 1975).

ming, errors are guaranteed. You don't need to learn how to fix errors; you need to learn how to avoid them in the first place.

Most people are somewhat fallible, however, and you might be an excellent programmer who has simply made a modest oversight. If this is the case, an error in your program represents a powerful opportunity. You can:

Learn about the program you're working on. You have something to learn about the program because if you already knew it perfectly, it wouldn't have an error. You would have corrected it already.

Learn about the kind of mistakes you make. If you wrote the program, you inserted the error. It's not every day that a spotlight exposes a weakness with glaring clarity, but this particular day you have an opportunity to learn about your mistakes. Once you find the mistake, you can ask yourself the following questions:

- Why did you make it?
- How could you have found it more quickly?
- How could you have prevented it?
- Does the code have other mistakes just like it?
- Can you correct them before they cause problems of their own?

Learn about the quality of your code from the point of view of someone who has to read it. You have to read your code to find the error. This is an opportunity to look critically at the quality of your code. Is it easy to read? Can it be improved? Use what you have learned to make your future programs even better.

Learn how to solve problems. Do you have confidence in your approach when attempting to debug you code? Does your approach work? Do you find errors quickly? Or are your debugging skills weak? Do you feel anguish and frustration? Do you guess randomly? Do you need to improve? Considering the amount of time many projects spend on debugging, you definitely won't waste time if you observe how you debug. Taking some time to analyze and change the way you debug might be the quickest way to decrease the total amount of time it takes you to develop a program.

Learn to correct your errors. In addition to learning how to locate your errors, you can learn how to correct them. Do you make the simplest correction by inserting a go-to, band-aid, or some cosmetic resolution that doesn't truly eliminate the problem? Or do you systematically, review, diagnose, and correct the problem?

All things considered, debugging is a valuable skill that should be fully developed, providing you with the capability to always improve your application. Debugging truly begins with the application creation process, for it is the readability, design, code quality, etc., that allows you to build in the reliability, availability, and serviceability your applications require. If the code is good, then you will have less debugging to perform.

13.1.4 An ineffective approach

Unfortunately, programming classes in colleges and universities hardly ever offer instruction in debugging. If you studied programming in college, you might have had a lecture devoted to debugging. The extent of the debugging advice given to many, however, was to "put print statements in the program to find the error." This is not adequate. If other programmers' educational experiences were like ours, a great many of them are being forced to reinvent debugging concepts on their own. What a waste!

13.2 A Guide to Debugging

Create a trail.   To locate an error, add print statements in many of the obvious areas throughout your program. Examine the output to determine where the error is. If you can't locate the error with print statements, try changing things in the program until something seems to work. Always keep a backup copy of the original program. Use a secondary copy for modifications so you are free to make whatever changes you deem necessary. Keep a record of the changes you make; build a trail. Stock up on coffee and cake because you're in for a long night in front of your computer.

Don't waste time trying to understand the problem.   It's likely that the problem is trivial, and you don't need to understand it completely to fix it. Simply finding it might be enough.

Correct the error with the most obvious fix.   It's usually best just to fix the specific problem you see, rather than wasting a lot of time making some big, ambitious correction that's going to affect the whole program. This is a perfect example:

```
x = Compute( y )
if ( y = 23 )
x = $22.10 /* Compute()doesn't work for y = 23,so fix it */
```

You don't need to dig all the way into the Compute() function to correct an obscure problem with the value of 23 when you can just write a special case for it in the obvious place. How many times have you taken this approach?

Leave your ego at home.   If you have a problem with a program you've written, it's your fault. It's not the computer's fault, and it's not the compiler's fault. The program doesn't do something different every time. It didn't write itself; you wrote it, so take responsibility for it. Even if an error appears not to be your fault, it's strongly in your interest to assume that it is. This assumption helps you to debug. It's hard enough to locate an error in your code when you're looking for it; the task becomes even more formidable when you assume that your code is error-free. It also improves your credibility because when you do claim that an error arose in someone else's code; other programmers will believe that you have examined the problem carefully. Assuming that an error is your fault also saves you the embarrassment of claiming that an error is someone else's fault and then having to recant publicly when you find out that it was your error after all.

13.3 Locating an Error

Debugging consists of locating an error and correcting it. Locating an error (and understanding it) is typically 90% of the work. Fortunately, there is an ap-

proach to debugging that's better than random guessing. Debugging by thinking about the problem is much more effective and interesting than debugging
via guesswork.

Think of yourself as a detective trying to solve a crime. Which approach
would be more effective: going door to door throughout the country, or examining the scene, searching for clues, and determining the criminal's identity? An
effective programmer who debugs in one-twentieth the time of an ineffective
programmer isn't randomly guessing about how to correct the program. He or
she is using the scientific method.

13.3.1 Adding science to the art of debugging

Here are the steps you go through when using the scientific method:

1. Gather data through repeatable experiments.
2. Form a hypothesis that accounts for as much of the relevant data as possible.
3. Design an experiment to prove or disprove the hypothesis.
4. Carry out the experiment to prove or disprove the hypothesis.
5. Repeat as needed.

This process has many parallels in debugging. Here's an effective approach for
locating an error:

1. Stabilize the error.
2. Locate the source of the error.
3. Correct the error.
4. Test your program.
5. Look for similar errors.

The first step is similar to the scientific method's first step in that it relies on
repeatability. The defect is easier to diagnose if you can make it occur reliably.
The second step uses all the steps of the scientific method. You gather the test
data that divulged the error, analyze the data that has been produced, and
form a hypothesis about the source of the error. You design a test case or an inspection to evaluate the hypothesis and then either declare success or renew
your efforts, as appropriate.

Let's look at each of the steps in conjunction with an example. Assume that
you have a product database program that has an intermittent error. The program is supposed to print a list of products, in alphabetical order, with pricing
information. Here is part of the output:

```
Ear_Cleaners         $5.29
Napkins              $1.66
Nail_Polish_Remover  $3.29
Toothpaste           $2.59
Staples              $2.20
Window_Cleaner       $2.79
```

The error is that Nail_Polish_Remover and Napkins are out of order.

13.3.2 Stabilize the error

If a defect doesn't occur reliably, it's almost impossible to diagnose. Making an intermittent defect occur predictably is one of the most challenging tasks in debugging.

An error that doesn't occur predictably is usually an initialization error or a dangling-pointer problem. If the calculation of a sum is correct sometimes and wrong sometimes, a variable involved in the calculation probably isn't being initialized properly; most of the time it just happens to start at 0. If the problem is a strange and unpredictable phenomenon and you're using pointers, you almost certainly have a pointer that was not initialized or are using a pointer after the memory that it points to has been freed.

Stabilizing an error usually requires more than finding a test case that produces the error. It includes narrowing the test case down to its simplest form that still produces the error. If you work in an organization that has an independent test team, sometimes it's the team's job to make the test cases simple. Most of the time, however, it's your job.

To simplify the test case, you'll use the scientific method. Suppose you have 10 factors that, if used in combination, produce the error. Form a hypothesis about which factors, when used in combination, produce the error. Also form a hypothesis about which factors are irrelevant to producing the error. Change the supposedly irrelevant factors and rerun the test case. If you still get the error, you can eliminate those factors and you've simplified the test. Then you can try to simplify the test further. If you don't get the error, you've disproved that specific hypothesis and you know more than you did before. It might be that some subtle change will still produce the error, but you know at least one specific change that does not.

In the product example, when the program is run initially, Nail_Polish_Remover is listed after Napkins. When the program is run a second time, however, the list is fine:

```
Ear_Cleaners          $5.29
Nail_Polish_Remover   $3.29
Napkins               $1.66
Toothpaste            $2.59
Staples               $2.20
Window_Cleaner        $2.79
```

It isn't until Potato_Chips is entered and shows up in an incorrect position that you remember that Nail_Polish_Remover was entered just before it showed up in the wrong spot, too. What's odd about both cases is that they were entered singly. Products are usually entered in groups. You hypothesize that the problem has something to do with entering a single new product. If this is true, then running the program again should place Potato_Chips in the right position. Here are the results of a second run:

```
Ear_Cleaners          $5.29
Nail_Polish_Remover   $3.29
Napkins               $1.66
Potato_Chips          $1.89
```

```
Toothpaste          $2.59
Staples             $2.20
Window_Cleaner      $2.79
```

This successful run supports the hypothesis. To confirm it, you want to try adding a few new products, one at a time, to see whether they show up in the wrong order and whether the order changes after a second run.

13.3.3 Locate the source of the error

The goal of simplifying a test case is to make it so simple that changing any aspect of it changes the behavior of the error. Then, by changing the test case carefully and watching the program's behavior under controlled conditions, you can diagnose the problem.

Locating the source of an error also calls for using the scientific method. You might suspect that the defect is the result of a specific problem, say an off-by-one error. You could then vary the parameter you suspect is causing the problem (one below the boundary, one on the boundary, and one above the boundary) to determine whether your hypothesis is correct.

In the product example, the source of the problem could be an off-by-one error that occurs when you add one new product but not when you add two or more. Examining the code, you don't find an obvious off-by-one error. Resorting to plan B, you run a test case with a single new product to see whether or not this is truly the problem. You add Hangers as a single product and hypothesize that this record will be out of order. Here's what you find:

```
Ear_Cleaners        $5.29
Hangers             $3.79
Nail_Polish_Remover $3.29
Napkins             $1.66
Potato_Chips        $1.89
Toothpaste          $2.59
Staples             $2.20
Window_Cleaner      $2.79
```

The line for Hangers is exactly where it should be, which means that your first hypothesis is false. The problem isn't caused simply by adding one product at a time. It's either a more complicated problem or something completely different.

Examining the test-run output again, you notice that Nail_Polish_Remover, Window_Cleaner, Potato_Chips, and Ear_Cleaners are the only names containing underscores. Nail_Polish_Remover was out of order when it was first entered, but Ear_Cleaners and Window_Washer weren't—or were they? Although you don't have a printout from the original entry, in the original error Napkins appeared to be out of order, but it was next to Nail_Polish_Remover. Maybe Nail_Polish_Remover was out of order and Napkins was all right.

You hypothesize that the problem arises from product names with underscores, not products that are entered singly. But how does that account for the fact that the problem shows up only the first time a product is entered? You look at the code and find that two different sorting routines are used. One is used when a product is entered, and the other is used when the data is saved.

A closer look at the routine used when a new product is entered shows that it isn't supposed to sort the data completely. It puts the data only in approximate order to speed up the save routine's sorting process. Thus, the problem is that the data is printed before it's sorted. The problem with underscores in product names arises because the rough-sort routine doesn't handle niceties such as underscore characters. Now you can refine the hypothesis even further.

You hypothesize that the names with underscores aren't sorted correctly until they're saved. You later confirm this hypothesis with additional test cases.

13.4 Tips for Tracking Down Errors

Once you have stabilized an error and refined the test case that produces it, finding its source can be either trivial or challenging, depending on how well you have written your code. If you are having a hard time finding an error, it's probably because the code wasn't well written. You might not want to hear that, but it's true. If you're having trouble, consider these tips:

Use all available data in your analysis.   When analyzing the source, try to locate your error by accounting for as much of the data as you can in your analysis. In the example, you might have noticed that Nail_Polish_Remover was out of order and created a hypothesis that names beginning with an N are sorted incorrectly. That's a poor hypothesis because it doesn't account for the fact that Potato_Chips was out of order or that product names are sorted correctly the second time around. If the data doesn't fit the hypothesis, don't discard the data; ask why it doesn't fit and create a new hypothesis. The second hypothesis in the example, that the problem arises from product names with underscores, not product names that are entered singly, didn't initially seem to account for the fact that product names were sorted correctly the second time around. In this case, however, the second hypothesis doesn't account for all of the data at first, but you kept refining the hypothesis so it eventually did.

Modify the test cases that cause the error.   If you can't find the source of an error, try modifying the test cases further than you already have. You might be able to vary one parameter more than you had assumed, and focusing on one of the parameters might provide the crucial breakthrough.

Recreate the error several different ways.   Sometimes trying cases that are similar to the error-producing case, but not exactly the same, is instructive. Think of this approach as triangulating the error. If you can get a fix on it from one point and a fix on it from another, you can determine exactly where it is. Reproducing the error several different ways helps you to diagnose the error. Once you think you've identified the error, run a case that's close to the cases that produced the error, but that should not produce the error itself. If it does produce an error, you don't completely understand the problem yet. Errors often arise from combinations of factors, and trying to diagnose the problem with only one test case sometimes doesn't diagnose the root problem.

Introduce more data to generate more hypotheses.   Choose test cases that are different from the test cases you already know to be erroneous or correct. Run them to create more data, and use the new data to add to your list of possible hypotheses.

Use the results of negative tests.   Suppose you create a hypothesis and run a test case to prove it. Then suppose the test case disproves the hypothesis, so you still don't know the source of the error. You still know something you didn't before, however, such as the error is not in the area where you thought it was. This should narrow your search field and the set of possible hypotheses.

Brainstorm for possible hypotheses.   Rather than limiting yourself to the first hypothesis you think of, try to come up with several. Don't analyze them at first; just come up with as many as you can in a few minutes. Then look at each hypothesis and think about test cases that would prove or disprove it. This mental exercise is helpful in breaking the debugging log-jam that results from concentrating too hard on a single line of reasoning.

Narrow the suspicious region of the code.   If you've been testing the whole program, module, or routine, test a smaller part instead. Systematically remove parts of the program and see whether the error still occurs. If it doesn't, you know it's in the part you took away. If it does, you know it's in the part you've kept.

Rather than removing regions haphazardly, divide and conquer. Use a binary search algorithm to focus your search. Try to remove about half the code the first time. Determine the half the error is in, and then divide that section. Again, determine which half contains the error, and again chop that section in half. Continue until you find the error. If you use many small routines, you'll be able to chop out sections of code simply by commenting out calls to the routines. Otherwise, you can use comments or preprocessor commands to remove code.

If you are using a debugger, you don't necessarily have to remove pieces of code. You can set breakpoints part of the way through the program and check for the error that way instead. If your debugger allows you to skip call routines, eliminate suspicious code by skipping the execution of certain routines and seeing whether the error still occurs. The process with a debugger is otherwise similar to the one in which pieces of a program are physically removed.

Be suspicious of routines that have had errors before.   Routines that have had errors before are likely to continue to have errors. A routine that has been troublesome in the past is more likely to contain a new error than a routine that has been error-free. Reexamine error-prone routines.

Examine code that has recently changed.   If you have a new error that's hard to diagnose, it's usually related to code that has recently changed. It could be in completely new code or in changes to old code. If you can't locate an error, run an old version of the program to see whether the error occurs. If it doesn't, you know the error is in the new version or is caused by an interaction with the new version. Scrutinize the differences between the old and new versions.

Expand the suspicious region of the code.   It's easy to focus on a small section of code if you are relatively sure that the error is in that section. Expand the area of code you suspect, and then focus on pieces of it using the binary search technique described in a previous section.

Integrate incrementally.   Debugging is easy if you add pieces to a system one at a time. If you add a piece to a system and encounter a new error, remove the piece and test it separately. Strap on a test harness and exercise the routine by itself to determine what's wrong.

Force the issue.   If you've used incremental integration and a new error raises its ugly head, you'll have only a small section of code to check for the error. It is sometimes tempting to run the integrated code to locate the error rather than taking the code and checking the new routine by itself. Running a test case through the integrated system, however, might require a few minutes whereas running one through the specific code you're integrating will take only a few seconds. If you don't find the error the first or second time you run the whole system, bite the bullet, isolate the code, and debug the new code separately.

Set a time limit for quick-and-dirty debugging.   It's always tempting to try for a quick fix rather than systematically testing the code and giving the error no place to hide. The risk-taker in each of us would rather try an approach that might find the error in five minutes than the surefire approach that will find the error in half an hour. The risk is that if the five-minute approach doesn't work, you get stubborn. Finding the error the "easy" way becomes a matter of principle, and hours pass unproductively. When you decide to go for the quick victory, set a maximum time limit. If you go past the time limit, resign yourself to the idea that the error is going to be harder to diagnose than you originally thought, and flush it out the hard way. This approach allows you to get the easy errors right away, and not waste time trying to find an easy fix for harder errors.

Check for common errors.   Use code-quality checklists to stimulate your thinking about possible errors. Focus on elements that are part of the error, the data types involved, the specific area of code where the error occurs, other modules or functions entered or exited at the time of error. If you keep a history of past problems that might have occurred in your environment, review them. Create a checklist and follow it through.

Review the problem with someone else.   Sometimes you just have to bite the bullet and tell someone else about your problem. You'll often discover your own error in the act of explaining it to another person. For example, if you were explaining the problem in the product name-sort example, the conversation might sound like this:

"Excuse me, Maria, but have you got a minute? I have this problem. I have a list of product names that are supposed to be sorted, but some of the product names are out of order. They were sorted correctly the second time I printed them out but not the first. I checked to see if it was new product names, but I tried some that worked. I know they should be sorted the first time I print them because the program sorts all the names as they're entered and again when they're saved. Wait a minute; no, it doesn't sort them when they're entered. That's right. It only orders them roughly. Thanks, Maria. You've been a great help." Maria didn't say a word, and you solved your problem. This result is typical, and this approach is perhaps your most potent tool for solving difficult errors.

Give the problem a rest.   Sometimes you concentrate so hard you can't think. How many times have you paused for a cup of coffee and figured out the problem on your way to the coffee machine? Or in the middle of lunch? Or on the way home? If you're debugging and making no progress, once you've tried all the options, let it rest. Go for a walk. Work on something else. Let your subconscious mind tease a solution out of the problem. An auxiliary benefit of giving up temporarily is that it reduces the anxiety associated with debugging. The onset of anxiety is a clear sign that it's time to take a break.

13.5 Syntax Errors

Syntax errors are becoming less and less frequent. As compilers improve, they provide better diagnostic messages; the days when you had to spend two hours finding a misplaced semicolon in a C listing are almost gone. Here is a list of guidelines you can use to speed your way to eliminating syntax errors:

Don't trust line numbers in compiler messages.   When your compiler reports a mysterious syntax error, look immediately before and immediately after the error; the compiler could have misunderstood the problem or simply have poor diagnostic capabilities. Once you find the real error, try to determine the reason the compiler put the message on the wrong statement. Understanding your compiler better can help you find future errors.

Don't trust compiler messages.   Compilers try to tell you exactly what's wrong, but they aren't always clear; often have to read between the lines to know what one really means. For example, in UNIX C, you might get the message "floating exception" for an integer divide-by-0. You can probably come up with many examples of your own.

Resolve your errors in the order of occurrence.   Some compilers are better than others at detecting multiple errors. Some compilers get so excited after detecting the first error that they continue to roll out dozens of error messages that don't mean anything. Other compilers are more level-headed and, although they must feel a sense of accomplishment when they detect an error, they refrain from spewing out inaccurate messages. If you can't quickly find the source of a second or third error message, don't worry about it. Fix the first one and recompile.

Divide and conquer.   The idea of dividing the program into sections to help detect errors works especially well for syntax errors. If you have a troublesome syntax error, remove part of the code and compile again. You'll either get no error (because the errors were in the part you removed), get the same error (meaning you need to remove a different part), or get a different error (because you have tricked the compiler into producing a message that makes more sense).

Find extra comments and quotation marks.   If your code is tripping up the compiler because it contains an extra quotation mark or beginning comment somewhere, insert the following sequence systematically into your code to help locate the error:

```
c language      /*"/**/
```

13.6 Correcting an Error

Once you have found the error, correcting it is normally the easy part. As with many easy tasks, however, the fact that it's easy makes it especially error-prone. Attempting to apply a quick fix after locating the error might be a defective correction. In fact, a quick fix is known to be defective 50% of the time. Here are a few guidelines for reducing the chance of error:

Understand the problem before you fix it.   The best way to make your life difficult and corrode the quality of your program is to fix problems without really understanding them. Before you fix a problem, make sure you understand it to the core. Triangulate the error both with cases that should reproduce the error and with cases that shouldn't reproduce the error. Keep at it until you understand the problem well enough to predict its occurrence correctly every time.

Understand the program, not just the problem.   If you understand the context in which a problem occurs, you're more likely to solve the problem completely rather than only one aspect of it. A study done with short programs found that programmers who achieve a global understanding of program behavior have a better chance of modifying it successfully than programmers who focus on local behavior, learning about the program only as they need to (Littman et al. 1986). Because the program in this study was small (280 lines), it doesn't prove that you should try to understand a 50,000-line program completely before you fix a defect. It does, however, suggest that you understand at least the code in the vicinity of the error correction—the "vicinity" being not a few lines but a few hundred.

Confirm the error diagnosis.   Before you rush to fix an error, make sure that you have diagnosed the problem correctly. Take the time to run test cases that prove your hypothesis and disprove competing hypotheses. If you've proven only that the error could be the result of one of several causes, you don't yet have enough evidence to work on one cause; rule out the others first.

Relax.   A particular programmer was ready to go on vacation. His product was ready to ship, he was already late, and he had only one more error to correct. He changed the source file and checked it into version control. He didn't recompile the program and didn't verify that the change was correct. In fact, the change was not correct and his manager was outraged. How could he change code in a product that was ready to ship without checking it? What could be worse? Isn't this the pinnacle of professional recklessness?

If it isn't the height of recklessness, it's close, and it's common. Hurrying to solve a problem is one of the most time-ineffective things you can do. It leads to rushed judgments, incomplete error diagnosis, and incomplete corrections. Wishful thinking can lead you to see solutions where there are none. Pressure, often self-imposed, encourages haphazard trial-and-error solutions, sometimes assuming that a solution works without verifying that it does.

Relax long enough to make sure your solution is the right one. Don't be tempted to take short cuts. It might take more time, but it will probably take less in the long run. If nothing else, you'll fix the problem correctly and your manager won't call you back from your vacation.

Save the original source code.   Before you begin fixing an error, be sure to make a backup copy of the code that you can return to later. It's easy to forget which change in a group of changes is the significant one. If you have the original source code, at least you can compare the old and the new files and see where the changes are.

Correct the problem, not the symptom.   You should resolve the symptom too, but your focus should be on correcting the underlying problem rather than performing some cosmetic fix that is good for only a specific case. If you don't thoroughly understand the problem, you're not fixing the code. You're fixing the symptom and making the code worse. Suppose you have this code:

```
    int sku;
    int prodnum;
    double total, price;
for (sku = 1; sku <= prodnum; prodnum++)
    total += price;
    printf("%10.2f %10.2f \n", total, price);
return 0;
```

When prodnum equals 25, the total turns out to be wrong by $9.99. Here's the wrong way to fix the problem:

```
int sku;
    int prodnum;
    double total, price;
for (sku = 1; sku <= prodnum; prodnum++)
    total += price;
if (prodnum = 25)                 /*  HERE IS MY FIX  */
    total += 9.99               /*  I solved this problem  */
    printf("%10.2f %10.2f \n", total, price);
return 0;
```

Now when prodnum equals 49, the total turns out to be off by $3.27.

```
    int sku;
    int prodnum;
    double total, price;
for (sku = 1; sku <= prodnum; prodnum++)    total += price;
if (prodnum = 25)                 /*  HERE IS MY FIX  */
    total += 9.99               /*  I solved this problem  */
```

```
    if (prodnum = 49)              /*  HERE IS MY SECOND FIX  */
        total += 3.27              /*  I solved another problem  */
        printf("%10.2f %10.2f \n", total, price);
    return 0;
```

This is by no means a fix, more likely the birth of a monster. It would be impossible to list all the problems that could be created by this type of coding. What you need to do, instead, is to review what might be the root cause of a majority of problems. Correcting just the symptom of a problem has the following drawbacks:

- These type of fixes won't work most of the time, especially when the problem is the result of an initialization error. Initialization errors are, by definition, unpredictable, so the fact that the total for prodnum 25 is off by $9.99 today doesn't tell you anything about tomorrow. It could be off by $1,000,000.00 or it could be correct. That's the nature of initialization errors.

- It's a nightmare to maintain. When code is special-cased to work around errors, the special cases become the code's most prominent feature. The $9.99 won't always be $9.99; the price will change and another error will show up later. The code will be modified again to handle the new special case, and the special case for $9.99 won't be removed. The code will become increasingly entangled with special cases. Eventually the code will be unsupportable, and will come back to haunt you when you least expect it.

- These types of corrections should be done with a calculator and not with a computer. Computers are good at predictable, systematic calculations, but humans are better at fudging data creatively. You'd be wiser to treat the output with white-out and a typewriter than to monkey with the code.

Change your code when you have a good reason to.   As you analyze the symptoms of a problem, you might be tempted to change your code at random until it appears to work. A typical line of reasoning would be: "There appears to be an error in this loop. Perhaps it's an off-by-one error, so let's insert a −1 here and try it. Done. That didn't work, so let's try a +1 instead. Done. It's working. It must be fixed."

Although this practice is popular, it isn't the most effective. Changing code randomly without truly understanding the problem is most often considered the "band-aid approach," where you don't really know if the problem is resolved. This method teaches you nothing and, if your problem is not corrected, then you've just wasted your time. When you change your program randomly, you're actually admitting that you don't understand what the problem is and just hoping that it works. Don't change code randomly. The more modifications you make to it without understanding it, the less chance it has to work correctly.

Control your changes.   Making changes is not a trivial task; you should make them one at a time so you can be confident about your modifications. When you perform two or more changes at a time, they can introduce subtle errors that look like the original errors. This places you in the position of not knowing whether you didn't correct the error, corrected the error but introduced a new one that looks similar, or didn't correct the error and introduced a similar new error. Keep it simple; make just one change at a time.

Test your fix.   Test the program yourself, have someone else test it for you, or walk through it with someone else. Run the same test cases you used to diagnose the problem in order to ensure that all aspects of the problem are resolved. If you've solved only part of the problem, you still have work to do. Rerun the whole program and look for side effects of your changes. The easiest and most effective way to test for side effects is to run the program through an automated suite of regression tests.

Look for similar errors.   When you find one error, look for others that are similar. Errors tend to occur in groups, and one of the values of paying attention to the kinds of errors you make is that you can correct all the errors of that kind. Looking for similar errors requires you to have a thorough understanding of the problem. Watch for the warning sign: If you can't figure out how to look for similar errors, that's a sign that you don't completely understand the problem.

13.7 The Psychology of Debugging

Debugging is as intellectually demanding as any other software-development activity. Your ego tells you that your code is good and doesn't have an error, even when you have a problem in front of you. You have to be methodical, form hypotheses, collect data, analyze the hypotheses, and methodically reject them with a formality that's unnatural to many people. If you're both building code and debugging it, you have to switch quickly between the processes of creative thinking, which goes with design, and the rigidly critical thinking, which goes with debugging. As you read your code, you must fight with the code's familiarity and guard against seeing what you expect to see.

13.7.1 How your "frame of mind" contributes to debugging blindness

When you see a token in a program that says INT, what do you see? Do you see a misspelling of the word *integrate*, or do you see the abbreviation for INTEGER? Most likely, you see the abbreviation for INTEGER. This is an integral part of your mindset. Are you seeing what is expected? Bear in mind the following considerations:

- All programs do not operate in the same fashion; each programmer usually has a different style. Some use top-down programming techniques and go-tos, while others refuse to use go-tos and will use only functions or program calls. Examine programs from point to point; rather than expecting to see the type of techniques you would use, understand how the program itself works.

- Some people expect WHILE loops to be continuously evaluated until they arrive at a false condition and then end there, rather than being evaluated only at the top or bottom.

- Perhaps the most difficult errors to resolve are data-movement errors, when you try to convert data from one type to another, or just move data from one variable to another. You end up being unable to determine what the data looked like before the error occurred or how it even got into your program in the first place. Often programmers look for off-by-one errors and side effects, but overlook problems in simple statements, or perhaps erroneous data.

- Sometimes the problem can be very simple. Let's say that two variables defined as VAR01 and VAR1 are being used within the same program. You might think that both are actually the same and never take notice until unexpected results are produced from the program.

Why is your mindset so important when debugging code? To begin with, if you think about debugging hard enough, you reinforce good programming practices. You begin to appreciate formatting style and insertion of meaningful comments. You realize the significance of naming conventions for variables and functions within your programs. Finally, you end up designing your programs so they have a straightforward flow, which allows you to pinpoint an area at fault in a timely fashion. Once you can focus on a specific area you believe to be at fault, you will feel a sense of accomplishment that allows you to delve further. All of these practices will make you a better, more efficient programmer.

At times, you might find that you have mistakenly chosen the wrong piece of code to be suspect. If you find yourself taking an inordinate amount of time within a small section of code, you might decide that you have chosen the wrong section. If this is the case, review your analysis in locating the offending code. Maybe you didn't choose the correct area to debug.

13.7.2 Relax and step back

Sometimes the problem will be staring right at you, but you have been searching so hard that you feel it must be some super-sophisticated algorithm embedded in there somewhere.

It's times like this when you should step away for a moment and come back with a fresh perspective. After taking a second look, you might determine that there were two variables you mistakenly thought of as one (for instance, VAR01 and VARO1). Other times you might convince yourself that the suspect code is within, let's say, three lines, and never look back to see how the variables used within those lines are populated. If this happens to you, don't become discouraged; just think of it as part of the learning process. It will make you a better programmer for the long term.

13.8 The Debugging Toolkit

As you work on your debugging skills, you will begin to find that you are not out there alone. Although far from perfect, there are some available debugging tools.

13.8.1 Source-code control

On most if not all UNIX systems, you will find SCCS (source-code control system), which allows for controlled modification of your programs, scripts, and files in general. Implementing this facility will provide you with synchronized control of your production applications. By typing `man sccs` from your UNIX terminal, you should be able to find out more details on this topic. In general, the key features are a controlled backup of your original code and a synchronized update process that ensures that only one copy of the file, be it a program, script, or file, is modified at any given time.

13.8.2 Comparing your source

After you have made multiple changes to your source code, you might find that you no longer know what is original and what has been modified. If you are using SCCS, then you can retrieve a copy of the source before you made any modifications to it; if not, hopefully you have made a backup prior to making any changes. In UNIX, you can use the diff command to compare two files. Once again, you can type `man diff` to retrieve the online manual page for different variations of this command.

13.8.3 Compiler messages

One of the best debugging tools you have is your compiler. Compiler messages can be very helpful in creating quality code. Three rules to aid in your development efforts are:

Make the compiler's message level its most sensitive.   When you do this, don't ignore any warning messages if at all possible. Worse yet, don't turn them off as a means of fixing them. If you think this will do any good, you are mistaken. After receiving warning messages, don't ignore them. Try to understand what the compiler is telling you and correct as many errors as possible.

Consider that each warning is a potential error.   Various compilers allow you to treat warnings as errors. Consider this feature, since it will heighten the importance of a warning. This will actually improve the quality of your code over time, as well as ease the transition between different versions of compilers (C 1.0 to C 2.0), when what was once a warning becomes an error.

Compiler option standards for application development.   This is an often overlooked, but key item that must be considered when developing new applications. If everyone is not working with the same standards, you might find that when it comes time to integrate the various modules to create a system, a brand-new set of error messages will appear.

13.8.4 Performance monitoring

Although you might not think of a performance monitor as a debugging tool, consider that your new and improved application might take twice as much memory as its predecessor, or take twice as long to execute as it did before. These are hidden costs that are just as important if not more important than the original problem you set out to resolve. Since these types of problems could affect not only this application, but all other applications on the system as well the system itself, be sure to incorporate them into your overall development plan.

13.8.5 The debugger

Debuggers are typically a more efficient means of analyzing your program than using print statements, scattered randomly throughout your program. Standard UNIX debuggers are usually part of your UNIX system. DBX is probably the most common and can be invoked by typing `dbx runtime_module_name`, provided that you have compiled your program with cc and the –G option, which preserves your object code.

Another tool available to the ESQL/C programmer is the GET DIAGNOSTICS statement, which allows you to pinpoint the area where a problem has occurred. You can execute GET DIAGNOSTICS in two forms: with the statements clause, which tells you how many exceptions exist for an error warning, and with the EXCEPTION clause, which provides error or warning message text associated with a particular SQLSTATE, SQLSTATE standards compliance information, and server connection information.

When it comes to debugging, use both the system debugger and GET DIAGNOSTICS statements whenever necessary. You should also contact your system administrator to determine if any other commercially available debuggers have been installed at your site.

A good debugger will allow you to set breakpoints that break when execution reaches a specific line, at the nth iteration of a specific line, when a global variable changes, or when a variable is assigned a specific value. Good debuggers allow you to step through code line by line, and return to the point where an error originated. They also allow you to log the execution of specific statements, similar to spreading print statements throughout your program.

A debugger should allow you to examine your data, monitoring it as it is read as well as after you modify it. You should be able to monitor dynamically allocated data fields and perform ad-hoc queries of your data. Your debugger must allow you to modify your data and restart your program.

To be perfectly honest, we have yet to find a debugger that provides all of these capabilities within the UNIX platform. The best way we know of today for debugging ESQL/C programs is through the combination of DBX, GET DIAGNOSTICS statements, and the print statement.

In summation, we would have to say that perhaps the best debugging tool is your own train of thought. If you experience a problem within your code, then play computer, understand what your program is supposed to do, read your code, and play computer again. If all else fails, use your debugger to focus on the offending area within your program.

The following is a checklist of items to assist you in your debugging:

Determine the cause of the error

- Examine all the available data before you form a hypothesis.
- Modify test cases that produce the error.
- Recreate your error in multiple ways.
- Create more data and see if it affects your hypotheses.
- Examine cases that negate your hypothesis.
- Don't allow your ego to hold you back; review your problem with others.
- Isolate the area of code that appears to be the problem.
- Review recent changes to your program.
- Modify the offending code incrementally.
- Be wary of routines that have caused problems in the past.
- Don't spend too much time on quick-and-dirty debugging.
- Look for common errors.
- Walk away and come back later with fresh thoughts.

Correct the error

- Understand the cause and effect of the problem.
- Get to know the program as well as the problem.
- Find a means to confirm your diagnosis.
- Don't panic.
- Make backups of your original code.
- Correct the problem, not just the symptom.
- Understand the changes and why you are making them.
- Limit the number of changes you make with each new test.
- After making changes, perform multiple tests.
- Test for other possible errors.

Have the right mindset

- View debugging as an opportunity to learn more about your program, allowing you to reduce your mistakes and improve the overall quality of your code. View it also as a means to enhance your problem-solving capabilities.
- Do not spend too much time with the trial-and-error approach, as this might prove to be a waste of time.
- Always assume that the problem is yours until you have had a chance to diagnose further.

- Take a methodical approach to each problem, which will make you a better programmer as well as a better debugger.
- Use all available tools to locate your errors.
- For your initial diagnosis, keep an open mind and examine all possible causes of the problem.
- Thoroughly test your fix to ensure that it is correct.
- Review all messages; they might provide some hidden clues.
- Check your system logs at the time of execution.

14

Tuning Your Environment

This chapter will guide you through the various areas that could affect the performance of an Informix client/server environment, hopefully allowing you to resolve any issues as soon as possible. We will focus on tuning an application with respect to performance. The performance of an application can be affected by a large number of items, too numerous to cover in a single chapter. However, we will attempt to cover as much of the topic as possible and hopefully uncover some of the gems that we, as developers, have found on our travels.

Although the primary focus of this chapter will be the performance and tuning aspects of the Informix-OnLine Dynamic Scalable Architecture (DSA), we will also provide some coverage of hardware and operating-system issues. If you are looking for very detailed information regarding specific hardware and operating-system software, consult the respective vendors. Some of the details and specific information on tuning are usually provided in the courses offered by these vendors. For more information on application and database design, see chapters 5, 7, and 10.

The source of a performance problem usually stems from one or more of the following areas:

- Application code
- Database system software
- Hardware
- Operating system
- User expectations

We mention user expectations because users might be looking for subsecond response to a "what-if" type of query that requires the database to search, sift through, and join a massive amount of data. This is unrealistic, and it is important to try and soften the user's expectation back down to a more realistic view.

Here's a scenario you might already be familiar with: You've developed the application and you're ready to implement, you've already distributed your application to a pilot group performing a User Acceptance Test (UAT), or, better still, you've rolled out the shiny new application to the complete user environment. How proud you are. So full of pride that you either a) make plans for a well-deserved vacation or b) start a new project to make use of the current development momentum. Then the difficulties begin, slowly at first, with just a trickle of complaints about how long it takes to open a window, save a transaction, or run a report. The complaints escalate until finally the system crashes or the administrator is forced to shut it down and restart it because it is no longer responding. Then you have to deal with angry users who cannot understand how this has happened.

You must now start an investigation. Because of the number of interconnected products, layers, and possibilities involved in a client/server application, however, this task is similar to finding a needle in a haystack. You need to spend a considerable amount of time and effort in trying to diagnose the symptoms and establish where the issues are, and then come up with solutions to the problems. Welcome to the world of performance and tuning, a nightmare if ever there was one. But it need not be with the right amount of planning and execution. As you've probably guessed already, we are into the "planning and execution" solution to all the development issues.

14.1 Performance and Tuning

Performance tuning usually begins with an issue that needs to be solved. The issue can be raised from a complaint from users or a decision about application or database design, hardware and software acquisitions, or some other capacity-planning issue. Before your project starts down the road to potential trouble, you must take the steps necessary to help quickly solve these issues and problems: You must lay down the foundations of a support structure so you can capture and track incidents and problems and any additional data to help you to tune the performance of an application.

14.1.1 Preparing for performance tuning

Before you get down to the task of using tools to measure the performance of any application, you need to gather some basic information about your environments and then establish a way to keep track of problems or incidents as they arise.

14.1.1.1 Documenting your environment

It is important to standardize and document the hardware and software environments that the application is being tested on. This includes the developer workstations, testing workstations, and ultimately end-user workstations that the application will run on. In the case of a commercial product, even if you cannot represent the myriad of hardware and software combinations that are potentially available, it still makes sense to try the product out on a multitude of configurations, ranging from low-end to high-end. If the product is being developed for in-house use, you will probably be able to control the environment issues a little more easily. Many companies standardize on a small number of hardware vendors and very specific configurations of hard disk, memory, and processor. This standard is usually fixed for between one and three years, within which you should be able to research, define, and publish the configuration settings that work with your application.

14.1.1.2 Tracking incidents and problems

An essential tool for supporting an application and its performance is some sort of central log (preferably a database table or spreadsheet) that can track any incidents of unexpected behavior or problems with the application. This database should contain general information describing the incident, as well as any other information that might be useful when analyzing the success of the application. Table 14.1 lists some ideas for the type of information you should consider tracking.

You should also set up a supplement to this log to track any changes to the status of an existing problem or incident. The kinds of things that need to be logged are shown in Table 14.2.

These logs should help you analyze and determine when, where, and under what conditions the system is failing or its performance is less than adequate. These incidents must record as much information as possible about the environment, the time of day of the incident, and any parameters used that might have lead to the error or unacceptable response.

14.1.1.3 Measuring performance

In order to see if what you tuning is having an effect, positive or negative, you need to be able to take measurements so you can compare and contrast the effects. When the area of performance is discussed, the terms in Table 14.3 are used in reference to analysis and measurement.

These definitions are only a guideline. One individual will consider the work performed by the database server as the measure of response time, and another will be more concerned with the I/O portion of response time. End users will probably be more interested in total system response. The crucial point is to define the measure of responsiveness, and clearly document it for all to understand and use.

14.1.1.4 Using monitoring tools

Some database performance issues might require help from the vendor. This help is often provided through the use of monitoring tools that can examine the internals of the database server, and Informix is no different. There are several utilities to monitor activity on an Informix database:

TABLE 14.1

Attribute	Description
Number	Incremental number allocated to new problem or incident
Description	Details of the problem or incident to be investigated
Priority	e.g., 1=high, 5=low
Severity	e.g., 1=high, 5=low
Status	Current status (OPEN, CLOSED)
Occurrence	Number of times the problem or incident has been reported
Symptom	Predefined characteristics attached to the problem
Keyword	Predefined attributes that you attach to the problem or incident
Environment	Predefined code representing hardware/software definition
Notes	Additional notes

TABLE 14.2

Attribute	Description
Date	Date of action
Time	Time of action
Build	Build version number
Cycle	Cycle in which the action took place
By	Person taking the action
Action	Action taken (opened, closed, pending)
To	Person affected by the action
Status	Status after action

TABLE 14.3

Measurement	Description
CPU usage	CPU processing seconds per actual clock second
I/O rate	Device I/O operations per actual clock second
I/O access time	Device busy per I/O second
Paging rate	Paging I/O operations per actual clock second
Response time	Actual clock seconds per unit of work
Transaction rate	Transactions completed per actual clock second

OnCheck. The check utility repairs index and data-page corruption on disk. You can also use it to examine other data structures on disk in the system. Because of its intrusive behavior, however, be aware that during the repair process it creates a shared lock on the table it is repairing, preventing users from updating the table.

OnPerf. This graphical performance utility displays the value of many server metrics, such as disk I/O, buffer cache rates, network information, memory usage, and Parallel Database Query (PDQ) statistics, in graphical display formats. You can display the output in real time or save it to a file for analysis.

OnStat. This status utility shows the contents of the shared memory structures, various internal tables (or data structures) maintained in shared memory. These internal tables track all activity in the system, and give a good picture of what the database server is doing. It is nonintrusive in that it does no disk I/O and only reads from shared memory.

SMI. The System Monitoring Interface is a read-only access of shared memory structures. With a SQL interface to the shared memory data, it allows an administrator to automate the monitoring process.

Refer to Chapter 8 for more detailed information on these utilities and tools.

Type of Performance Data

Performance data typically comes in two flavors: short-term and long-term. Short-term, or snapshot, data is returned by monitoring tools that show information while the activity is still in progress, a quick picture if you like. Short-term data is useful when you are evaluating and reacting to a current performance issue. Long-term data is useful for proactive planning or strategy. Monitoring tools usually allow you to log performance data to disk. You can then use this logged data to produce reports that can be compared to previous instances. This will help identify where significant changes have occurred in the system's usage over a longer period of time. These changes can help you predict future system usage and plan accordingly.

14.1.2 Guide to a diagnosis and cure

What follows is a step-by-step approach to problem solving or diagnosing the problem and some examples of what you can use to speed up your system if it is already exhibiting performance problems.

14.1.2.1 Problem-solving methodology

When you encounter a performance problem, the first and most important step is to ensure that the correct issue is resolved. You can spend many hours and countless amounts of money solving the wrong problem. An example of this mistake might be to upgrade to a faster CPU and then find out that the real problem was an insufficient amount of or badly configured memory resources. Here are the steps to take to help you correctly diagnosis a performance problem:

1. Investigate. The first step is to adequately define the problem. This begins with capturing as much of the pertinent information as possible, including a measurement of the components being used. Use as many of the Informix tools necessary to gather performance data at the lowest component levels.

2. Assess. Compare the component performance data to established standards, or an estimate of what seems reasonable. Highlight the exceptions and consider them first for tuning.

3. Tune. Focus on making changes to one resource at a time. This is so you can determine exactly how successful or unsuccessful the change is.

4. Reevaluate. Compare the new results to the previously problematic one. Even if the issue appears to be resolved, it makes sense to regression-test the remaining parts of your system to ensure that you haven't transferred the issue elsewhere.

14.1.2.2 General query diagnosis and fix
To determine if a query is running inefficiently, follow these steps:

1. Time the query, preferably on a system with little or no activity.

2. Run the query with SET EXPLAIN ON and check the output to determine what query plan the optimizer is choosing.

3. If, in your opinion, the optimizer is not choosing the most efficient query path, you will need to help it do so. You cannot directly specify the required path, but you can greatly influence the optimizer by performing one or more of the following actions:

   - Adding or dropping one or more indexes.
   - Creating data distributions.
   - Using SET OPTIMIZATION LOW to decrease the optimization time.
   - Rewriting the query, e.g., changing a subquery to a join.

4. Rerun the query to see if the response has improved.

14.1.2.3 Improving OLTP query times
The following is a guide for improving the query times of OLTP queries:

- Avoid sort operation due to an ORDER BY clause. By creating an index on the column(s) specified in the ORDER BY, the optimizer will generally use the index and avoid a sort.

- Avoid hash and merge joins. These joins carry significant overhead due to the sort and hash tables that must be created. Creating indexes for the joined columns will help to avoid this overhead.

- Avoid sequential scans. For most OLTP queries, a sequential scan is detrimental. To avoid it, make sure the optimizer uses an index by creating one if necessary.

- The optimizer usually places tables that reduce the highest number the of rows first in the query path. Its premise is that, by eliminating rows early on, less rows need to be joined to the tables later on. You can often influence the optimizer's choice of query path by creating data distributions and/or indexes on the query columns.

14.1.2.4 Improving DSS query times

Decision support queries will most likely benefit the most from OnLine's Parallel Database Query (PDQ) features. This is because PDQ balances the workload by splitting some operations across the CPU, producing faster results. Here are some suggestions for improving the query times of DSS queries:

- Avoid indexes. If a query is using data from most of a large table, it is faster to scan the table without reading it via the index. Removing indexes might speed things up.
- Set OPTCOMPIND to 2. This will let the optimizer consider more query paths.
- Use Parallel Database Query and fragment large tables so it can create parallel scan threads.

14.1.2.5 Other possibilities

You might also consider the following techniques for speeding up queries:

- Run `UPDATE STATISTICS tablename`.
- Drop and recreate the index to improve index contiguity.
- Create a clustered index to recreate the table and reorder the rows by this index. It forces logical and improves physical contiguity.

14.2 Server Considerations

The areas that affect the database server performance are obviously limited to the hardware being used and, less obviously, to the configuration of the operating system and database management system software. The various software configurations are often affected by parameters that can be changed, or "tuned." This section deals with the server's various hardware components and software settings that affect performance.

14.2.1 What affects database performance?

To improve performance, you must first understand what server resources are used and how they collectively affect server performance. In measuring the response time for a database access within an application, focus on the time it takes for a message to be sent from the client workstation to the database server, execute the necessary request, and return the result to the client workstation. Ignore or discount the time it takes for the message to be formatted, sent, and carried over the network and focus on the time being consumed with processing on the database server. You can then summarize the major resources that affect server performance into the following list:

- Central processing unit (CPU)
- Volatile storage (memory)
- Persistent storage (disk)

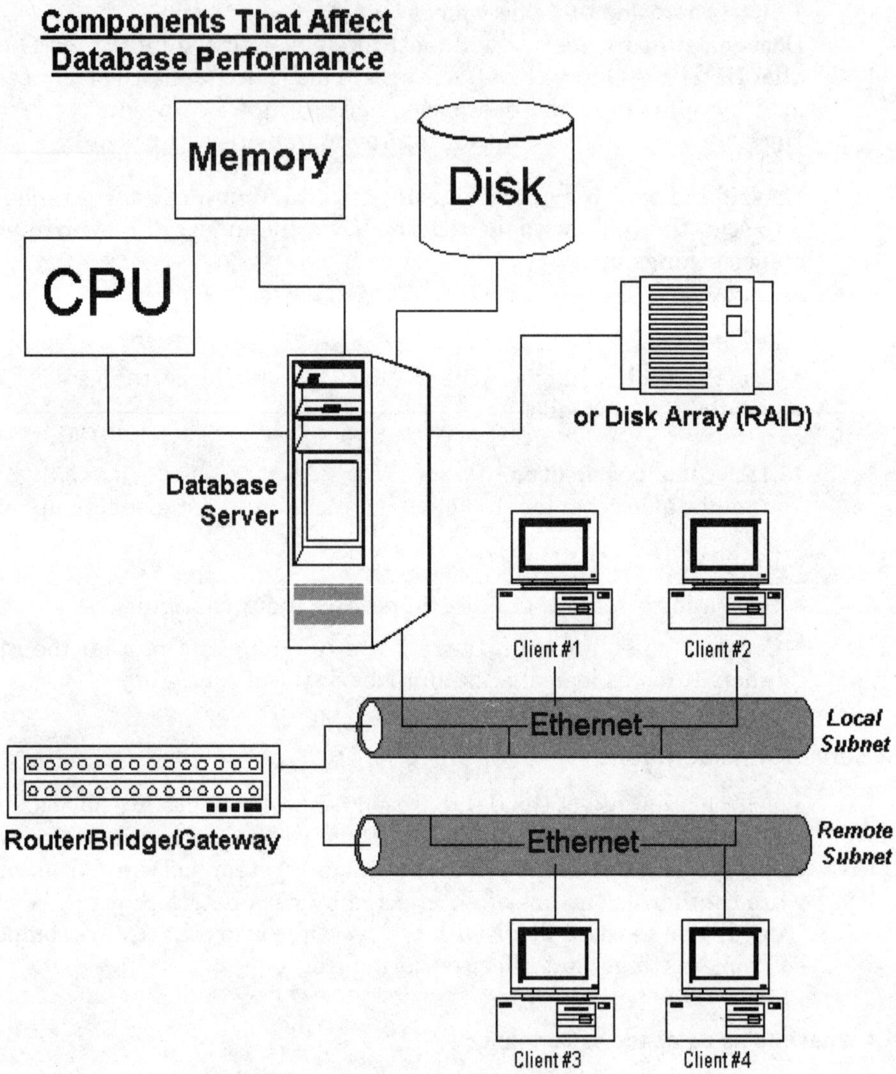

Components That Affect
Database Performance

Figure 14.1   Resources that affect performance.

14.2.2 Central processing unit (CPU)

The CPU component controls the entire application process. The CPU processing speed greatly affects all performance. There are many standard techniques
to measure the relative speed of one CPU against another. The two most common measurements for CPU speed are millions of instructions per second
(MIPS) and millions of floating operations per second (MFLOPS). These measurements are quite narrow in focus and might be of little use when determining the type and amount of CPU resources your product will require. There are
other characteristics of the CPU's time that you should take into account during performance tuning:

User state time. This is the amount of time the CPU spends running under application control. It is a direct reflection of the program's effectiveness and efficiency.

System state time. This is the amount of time the CPU spends executing system calls and administrative functions on behalf of an application.

Dispatching priority. This is the priority of each process running on the system. When CPU time becomes available, the operating system decides which process must run next. The first task with the highest priority that is ready to run will be given the CPU time.

Scheduling algorithm. This is the method used by the operating system to provide each process with access to the CPU. Some possible scheduling algorithms are:

- Round robin, where each process gets the CPU in turn.

- Time slice, where each process is given a fixed amount of CPU time before being interrupted when another process is allowed to run.

- Preemptive, where processes are executed by priority. The highest-priority task is given the CPU until it relinquishes control by either waiting for an I/O operation to complete or intentionally waiting at specific points of operation. The next process with equal or lower priority is started and runs until the higher-priority task is ready to run again. Then the lower priority task is made inactive and CPU time is passed back to the higher-priority task.

Many operating systems use each of these methods to a varying degree, trying to split the CPU time equitably among the available processes. Nonetheless, a higher-priority process will always get more CPU time than a low-priority process, and the CPU time is split in a round-robin fashion for processes of equal priority.

CPU usage. CPU usage is the proportion of time the CPU is busy compared to elapsed real time. Usually, the CPU will be idle only if there is no task to be performed or all processes are waiting for I/O to complete. So if the CPU were busy 54 seconds over a 60-second interval, the usage would be 90%. Prolonged high CPU usage, above 80%, might indicate a lack of CPU capacity for the server.

> It is important to monitor the CPU usage of any database server system. You can use operating-system utilities to monitor CPU usage. Some operating systems have graphical utilities to monitor processor usage.

14.2.2.1 Single- and multiple-CPU machines

Informix can run on single- or multiple-CPU systems. On multiple-CPU or symmetric multiprocessing (SMP) systems, the processors share the system resources, i.e., the disk, memory, and bus. The operating system is responsible for spreading the workload among the CPU's processors, so as processors are added, the performance is typically improved. This ability is also known as scalability. The advantage of a SMP system is that it can execute tasks simultaneously, one task for each processor. This scalability differs among the various hardware and operating system vendors. Most, if not all, systems have a limit of the number of CPUs they can use, after which no performance advantage is perceived.

Nonetheless, a single task will still not run any faster on a SMP system than it will on a single-CPU system, assuming that both systems have the same model CPU and other resources are similarly matched. This is because a single task can run on only one processor, while all other processors execute other tasks or remain idle.

However, many vendors have come up with a way of using the extra CPUs and completing the task in a shorter amount of time by dividing a single task into smaller subtasks, or threads. Each subtask is able to execute, in parallel, on its own CPU. Informix has engineered the OnLine product for this type of parallel processing. OnLine can execute the following subtasks in parallel:

- Aggregation
- Grouping
- Index building
- Recovery
- Scanning
- Sorting

For a fuller discussion on Informix's parallel processing, see section 14.3 later in this chapter.

14.2.2.2 Virtual processors (VPs)
Informix's Dynamic Scalable Architecture (DSA) supports parallel processing by using what Informix calls virtual processors. A virtual processor (VP) functions similar to the way the CPU functions in a computer. A CPU can run multiple processes for multiple users, and a virtual processor can run multiple threads that service multiple SQL requests.

14.2.2.3 Tuning for single-CPU systems
For single-CPU systems:

- Set SINGLE_CPU_VP to 1.
- Set MULTIPROCESSOR to 0.
- Configure only one CPU virtual processor (VP).

With the SINGLE_CPU_VP configuration parameter set to 1, OnLine will bypass many of the internal locking calls that are necessary to protect data structures being used by more than one virtual processor.

> Two-processor systems might also get better performance if they are run in the single-processor mode to avoid internal locking.

14.2.2.4 Tuning for multiple-CPU systems

In multiple-CPU systems, typically those with more than two CPUs, tuning the virtual processors will significantly affect performance. When tuning the CPU virtual processors (VPs), do the following:

- Do not add more virtual processors than actual physical CPUs.
- Add only one virtual processor at a time.
- Monitor the performance to determine if another one needs to be added.

> Adding virtual processors to a system where the actual physical CPUs are already in the 80% to 100% usage range might actually degrade the system performance.

14.2.2.5 Monitoring virtual processor usage

To monitor the virtual processor usage in an OnLine system, use the following utilities:

```
OnStat -g glo
```

and:

```
OnStat -g rea
```

The –g glo option displays information on the virtual processors currently running in the OnLine system. This information is also available from the sysvpprof SMI table. To determine how much of the processor the CPU VP is using, perform the following steps during a period of normal activity:

1. Run `OnStat -g glo`, piping the output to a file.
2. Wait for 60 seconds.
3. Run `OnStat -g glo` again, piping the output to a second file.
4. Subtract the total CPU time for each virtual processor in the second run from the total CPU time for each virtual processor in the first run.

If any of the results are close to 60 seconds, then one of the virtual processors is very busy and the performance might benefit from adding another one. The `-g rea` option displays information on the threads waiting in the ready queue. Table 14.4 shows ready thread information displayed for a command.

If the system continually has threads waiting, you might be able to achieve better performance by adding another virtual processor to increase the throughput of the waiting threads. Although the goal is to reduce the ready queue to 0, at some point adding more virtual processors will not help perfor-

TABLE 14.4

Item	Description
tid	The thread identifier
tcb	Thread control block address for the thread
rstcb	RSAM thread control block address for the thread
prty	Priority of the thread
status	Status of the thread
vp class	The number and class the thread last ran on (see `onstat -g glo` to relate the number to the process ID of the virtual processor).

TABLE 14.5

Parameter	Description
AFF_NPROCS	Number of CPUs eligible for affinity. If this value is zero, the virtual processor will be assigned to a specific CPU.
AFF_SPROC	The CPU number, starting at zero, that OnLine will start with in assigning virtual processors to CPUs. `AFF_NPROCS` + `AFF_SPROC` cannot be greater than the number of actual CPUs.

mance as the physical CPUs might be completely busy. In this case, adding more CPUs could be the best option to improve performance.

14.2.2.6 Affinity parameters

Some multiple CPU machines support processor affinity. On these machines you can assign virtual processors so they exclusively execute on a specific physical CPU. The ONCONFIG parameters in Table 14.5 will work only on systems that support processor affinity if OnLine supports it for that platform.

Leave at least one CPU free for other virtual processors and system processes to run on. If your server runs other nondatabase activity, consider leaving more than one CPU free. Ideally, you want to assign only one virtual processor to one CPU to be eligible for affinity (e.g., if you have three virtual processors, set AFF_NPROCS to 3).

14.2.3 Volatile storage (memory)

Memory is a factor only if your system does not have enough of it or if it is dedicated to an unused type of processing. In both cases, if you limit the amount of memory that a process within a system has, performance will be directly affected. With the relatively low cost to benefit ratio of memory, making that extra investment in more memory up front will pay great dividends in the future. Here's why . . .

> If a process requires more memory than is available, memory occupied by idle processes will be paged out to disk and replaced with the information that is needed immediately. When pages that are needed by active

processes must be paged back in, performance is negatively affected. The rate at which such pages are required is called the paging rate. This process of exchanging pages, or swapping, could escalate to the point where the operating system starts to swap entire processes to disk. When a large amount of paging occurs, the associated disk I/O and transfer rate significantly degrades overall performance.

The amount of memory available on your system and the allocation and usage of this resource is a crucial factor in the overall performance of your system. When determining the optimal memory configuration for your server, consider the following:

- What's the maximum amount of memory that your system supports?
- What is the maximum shared memory that the operating system allows?
- How much memory does your system currently have?
- What shared memory is required by the operating system?
- How much shared memory left for OnLine?

The answers to these questions will help you configure your system appropriately.

14.2.3.1 What consumes memory?

One of the largest consumers of memory is the buffer pool, an area that remains resident in shared memory and is configured by the BUFFERS parameter. Its value depends on the total amount of memory, the size of the database, the number of users, and the type of activities being performed. OLTP applications are large consumers of the buffer pool. Another large consumer of memory is the cache for stored procedures, although this is a factor only for applications that make extensive use of large stored procedures.

Every connection to the database, known as a session pool, consumes memory. The size of a session pool increases depending on the activity. The largest session pools are created when any sort occurs with CREATE TABLE, ORDER BY, GROUP BY, or sort merge join, or when the query uses a hash join. Also, any PDQ activity uses memory for intermediate files and scan buffers.

14.2.3.2 OnLine shared memory

Once you have determined the amount of shared memory available for the server, you must decide how it will be used. Shared memory is divided into three portions, each with a specific use in OnLine (see Table 14.6). When configuring the database kernel, pay particular attention to parameters that affect shared memory usage (see Table 14.7).

14.2.3.3 Monitoring shared memory usage

Use the information in Table 14.8 to examine and monitor the usage of shared memory on your system.

TABLE 14.6

Memory portion	Use
Resident	Contains the buffer cache and other system information. OLTP: Increase buffers to cache pages for performance DSS: Increasing will not help performance
Virtual	Contains session, thread, and sort pools. OLTP: Uses insignificant amount of virtual DSS: Increase for performance
Message	Contains message buffers. This portion is not configurable. It is approximately 12 KB per user connecting via shared memory. Message buffers are used to communicate between clients and the server when using shared memory connections.

TABLE 14.7

Parameter	Description
SHMMAX	Maximum size of the initial shared memory segment. When a shared memory segment is allocated by the OnLine system, only one physical segment is allocated by the operating system instead of several smaller ones, which is less efficient.
SHMSEG	Shared memory segments per process. This memory is allocated in the virtual portion of its shared memory. As memory requirements increase, OnLine dynamically allocates additional virtual shared memory segments.

TABLE 14.8

Command	Description
OnStat –g seg	Displays how much memory is allocated and used by the server. Also displays the usage of shared memory segments. Shared memory segments can also be displayed at the system level by running the appropriate operating system commands.
OnMode –F	Frees unused shared memory segments in your system.

> Performance can degrade when you execute OnMode -F, because the Memory Grant Manager (MGM) examines all the memory pools and memory segments in order to free any unused memory.

14.2.3.4 Balancing memory between DSS and OLTP

If your server is required for a Decision Support System (DSS), then your queries will usually perform better when you allocate all the virtual portion of shared memory to your decision support queries. Conversely, if your server is required for an Online Transaction Processing (OLTP) system, then your queries will usually perform better when you can allocate as much of the shared memory as possible to the resident portion, in the form of BUFFERS. The OnStat -p command allows you to monitor the percent cached; adjust BUFFERS upward until the this figure remains a consistent value.

If your system is being used for a combination of OLTP and DSS, then you need to balance the amount of shared memory between the virtual and resident portions. The way to balance the memory resources between DSS and OLTP is to limit the portion used for DSS. The DS_TOTAL_MEMORY configuration parameter limits the virtual shared memory available for decision support queries, or PDQ. Monitor the usage of the virtual portion of shared memory with the OLTP queries. If you determine that the OLTP queries do not fully use the reserved virtual portion, then consider allocating any unused portion to your DSS queries. The maximum amount of memory you can allocate using the DS_TOTAL_MEMORY configuration parameter is half the total amount of shared memory configured in the OnLine system:

$$DS\_TOTAL\_MEMORY = \frac{SHMTOTAL}{2}$$

You can dynamically override the maximum amount of decision support memory configurable by DS_TOTAL_MEMORY by using the following command:

```
OnMode -M KBAmount
```

14.2.4 Persistent storage (disk)

Disk storage is ultimately where all database information, or data, resides and usually consists of one or more magnetic plates, or platters. These platters are accessed by one or more read/write heads. In the case of multiple head and platter devices, the data is stored across the magnetic surfaces in what is commonly known as a cylinder (see Figure 14.2).

When required, the disk read/write head traverses back and forth across the magnetic surface, in a motion known as seeking. The time it takes to move to the required cylinder is known as the seek time. The disk rotates at a very high

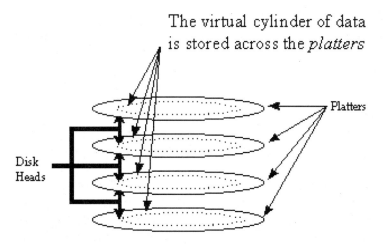

Figure 14.2 Typical disk with platters.

speed and the device waits until the required area is in position under the head before reading or writing; this waiting time is known as the latency time. The transfer rate is the speed by which a specified amount of data can be transferred to or from the disk. A typical disk measurement is access time, which is usually calculated as follows:

access time = seek time + latency time + transfer rate

These disk statistics, or measurements, are normally provided by disk manufacturers for side-by-side comparison. When building the physical location of your most commonly used information, you can minimize the seek time by creating your raw devices toward the middle cylinders. Do this by specifying the cylinder numbers to be used.

14.2.4.1 Determining disk layout

The database administrator's goal is to balance input and output requests across all available disk devices, because excessive usage of any single disk is a bottleneck that can potentially slow the whole system. This balancing of input and output requires the DBA to examine the total disk usage for the system.

For OLTP queries, the placement of logical and physical log files is very important because of their extensive use by the great deal of INSERT, UPDATE, and DELETE activity. In DSS systems, the sort work area is important because most of the complex SELECT queries require sorting (because of ORDER BY or GROUP BY clauses). The sort work area is determined by the DBSPACETEMP configuration and environment variable. There are a few other tips to consider when planning disk usage:

- Always use "raw" instead of "cooked" devices for chunks. Raw devices bypass the operating system's buffering mechanism, accessing the data directly and contiguously.

- Use appropriate extent sizes for tables. This is an important factor when defining very large tables. If the extent size is too large, many unused pages will be created; if the extent size is too small, the data will be fragmented across the disk or disks. There is a limit of approximately 200 extents for a table, which you can monitor with the OnCheck -pe command.

- When planning, remember to take into account other nondatabase activity occurring on the system, such as operating system swapping.

Here are some ideas for determining the actual disk layout for your OnLine system:

Find "hot" tables. Determine the most frequently used or "hot" tables in each database. Examine all SQL and determine the I/O rates. Find the most often used SQL and note which tables are accessed.

Choose disks. Determine which disks are available for OnLine.

Spread I/O. Decide how best to spread online I/O across the available disks. There are several techniques for controlling how the I/O is spread across your disks:

- Single-disk dbspace
- Multiple-disk dbspace
- Round-robin chunk ordering
- Table fragmentation
- Temporary dbspace

14.2.4.2 Single-disk dbspace

A simple technique for ensuring that a table or a group of tables are placed on a specific disk is to create a single dbspace on the disk required and then create the tables in this dbspace. Small or seldom used tables can be placed into a single dbspace. Consider placing tables that are frequently used in the same SELECT statement in separate dbspaces (and disks). Large or frequently used tables should be placed in their own dbspace.

14.2.4.3 Multiple-disk dbspace

Prior to OnLine version 7.0, a common method for spreading I/O was to spread a table, particularly a very large one, across several disks. To do this, you created a dbspace with several chunks, one chunk for each disk. If you are using OnLine version 7.0 or later, however, this method is not advocated. Try using table fragmentation instead, which is explained later in this chapter.

14.2.4.4 Round-robin chunk ordering

Chunks can be added to an OnLine system at any time, but the order in which chunks are added to the system is significant and can affect the time it takes a checkpoint to complete, and therefore the performance in certain situations. This is because when a checkpoint is issued, page cleaners are assigned to the chunks in the order in which the chunks were added to the system.

See the example in Figure 14.3, which has three disks with two chunks per disk. Chunks 1 and 2 were finally added to drive X, then chunks 3 and 4 were added for drive Y, and finally chunks 5 and 6 were added for drive Z. If this system were configured with three page cleaners, then, during a checkpoint, the first page cleaner would start cleaning chunk 1, the second chunk 2, and the third chunk 3. This means you would have disk activity on the X and Y drives, but none on drive Z. If the first page cleaner finished first, it would be assigned to chunk 4 on drive Y with still no disk I/O on drive C.

Ideally, the page cleaning should occur across all three drives in parallel at the start of a checkpoint. In order to do this, you could add the chunks in a round-robin fashion, with chunk 1 on drive X, chunk 2 on drive Y, chunk 3 on

Chunks Added In Sequence

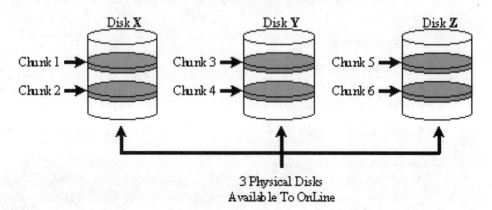

Figure 14.3   Sequential chunks.

Chunks Added In Parallel

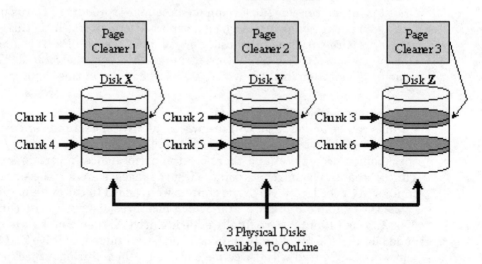

Figure 14.4   Parallel chunks.

drive Z, chunk 4 on drive X, chunk 5 on drive Y, and chunk 6 on drive Z (see Figure 14.4). So at the start of the checkpoint, the three page cleaners would be assigned to chunks 1, 2, and 3. This would ensure that I/O activity commenced on all drives in parallel, potentially decreasing the time it takes the checkpoint to finish.

14.2.4.5 Table fragmentation

Table fragmentation, available since release 7.0, is grouping a set of rows from one table to a specific dbspace. This is similar to the multiple-disk dbspace technique described earlier, but with absolute control over which fragment a given row is placed in. Informix implements this feature by placing each fragment in a dbspace, with each dbspace having one or more chunks on separate disk devices. All these fragments are controlled by a single Informix OnLine system on a single machine.

14.2.4.6 Temporary tables

The most frequently accessed dbspaces are usually the temporary ones. Use the SET EXPLAIN statement prior to the execution of a query and examine the output produced (the default name is sqexplain.out). The output file will list the temporary file requirements. Here is an example:

```
QUERY:
------
SELECT     b.company
           ,a.region
           ,a.type_cd
           ,a.product_cd
           ,count(distinct a.store_cd)
           ,sum(a.quantity)
           ,sum(a.value)
FROM       store a,
           sku_master b
WHERE      m.type_cd in ('f','n')
           and
           b.product_cd = a.product_cd
GROUP BY   b.company,a.region,a.type_cd,a.product_cd
ORDER BY   b.company,a.region,a.type_cd,a.product_cd,a.qty,a.rvn,a.code

Estimate cost: 1077601
Estimate # of Rows Returned: 12
Temporary Files Required For: Order By  Group By

1) warehous.store: SEQUENTIAL SCAN (Parallel, fragments: All)
2) warehous.sku_master: SEQUENTIAL SCAN
   Filters: warehous.sku_master.type_cd IN ('f','n')

DYNAMIC HASH JOIN
   Dynamic Hash Filters:
      warehous.store.product_cd = warehous.sku_master.product_cd
# of Secondary Threads = 14
```

If your queries frequently create and use temporary tables and sort files, consider spreading the temporary tables across one or more dbspaces that are exclusively reserved for temporary tables. For example:

```
DBSPACETEMP dbstemp1, dbstemp2, dbstemp3
```

With this configuration, OnLine will place the first output in the dbstemp1, the second in dbstemp2, and so on in a round-robin fashion. This feature is extremely effective for parallel sorting because the sort threads use separate disks to store temporary tables.

If you do find that temporary dbspace is the most frequently accessed db-space, then consider placing each temporary dbspace on a separate disk to optimize the I/O. A separate dbspace or dbspaces for temporary objects has several advantages:

- You can easily reconfigure temporary space by dropping dbspace or adding new chunks.
- It will not fragment the free space of other dbspaces.
- Temporary tables can be located with `OnStat -t`. Look for a tblnum column with the value of A00xxx, the number of the dbspace used to hold temporary tables.

> Whenever possible, put temporary tables in temporary dbspaces. These dbspaces are not logged (or archived) and can hold only temporary tables. To create a temporary dbspace, use `OnSpaces -t` or specify `Temp[Y]` in the OnMonitor screen option.

14.2.4.7 Monitoring disk activity
To list the contents, including the extents, of a dbspace, run:

```
OnCheck -pe
```

To monitor the disk activity, run:

```
Onstat -g iof
```

If you want to see the chunk numbers, use:

```
Onstat -d
```

The chunks are listed in the same order as the output. If one chunk is receiving more I/O activity than the other, consider either moving a table to another dbspace or splitting a table across disks to even out the I/O activity.

14.2.4.8 RAID
Redundant array of inexpensive disks (RAID) is a method of using disk drives in parallel to achieve higher data availability and performance. Informix can use these disk subsystems because they look the same as any other disk device.

RAID can be configured in several different ways, or levels. Each level has a different impact on performance. Also, hardware vendors might implement the RAID levels differently, so beware. RAID is defined and implemented in the levels listed in Table 14.9.

Some of the RAID levels in Table 14.9 offer forms of disk striping and, as of OnLine version 7, Informix internally offers a form of disk striping called table fragmentation. Mixing hardware disk striping and Informix's own table fragmentation, however, is not recommended.

14.2.5 Table fragmentation

As mentioned earlier, table fragmentation is creating the definition of a set (or fragment) of rows from a table and ensuring that the rows are placed in a specified dbspace. With this technique, Informix can control exactly which fragment a given row is placed in, ensuring the distribution of data across multiple dbspaces. Informix can then evaluate and therefore eliminate table fragments from the search path, allowing the engine to gather the result set in a shorter time period. This splitting, or partitioning, of the data requires careful consideration and ongoing administration. When the data distribution in tables substantially changes, the fragmentation technique that was chosen might no longer be appropriate, so it is important to monitor this periodically. To apply this technique, you must first examine the content of the tables and decide how the data is going to be accessed by the application SQL. This will help detemine how to distribute the data so as to maximize the potential of fragmentation. Here is a list of considerations when analyzing the data:

- Identify the tables used by queries requiring optimal performance.

- Identify tables that are frequently joined together.

- Determine the percentage of table rows being examined by the query.

- Determine what portion of the table is examined most of the time.

Table fragmentation can be carried out in various ways, depending on the results of the analysis. The strategies you apply are related to the data distribu-

TABLE 14.9

Level	Description
0	Disk striping, no redundancy
1	Disk mirroring
2	Error correcting parity information on separate drives
3	Error correcting parity information stored on a single separate drive
4	Disk striping and parity information stored on a single separate drive
5	Data and parity information striped
10 or 1.2	Disk striping and parallel mirroring at the controller level.

tion. If your data is unevenly distributed,, then the best choice is typically to fragment by expression. If your data access is evenly distributed, then the best choice is to fragment with the round-robin approach.

Fragmenting by expression

Expression fragmentation is a technique where you define one or more expressions for a table. Evaluating the expression will determine the dbspace where rows in the table will be physically located. This technique is best if the analysis of your queries reveals that you can easily define expressions that will eliminate fragments to be scanned. The optimal distribution scheme for eliminating fragments is if:

- You can create nonoverlapping fragments on a single column.
- Your queries access tables with a high degree of selectivity.
- Your data is not evenly accessed.

The types of expression that easily eliminate fragments are shown in Table 14.10.

You can fragment by expression to create uneven distributions of data in your fragments. The rows that are read frequently (95%) on an essential table can be distributed across many fragments, while the remaining rows can be placed in a single fragment. Here is an example of fragmentation by expression:

```
FRAGMENT BY EXPRESSION
   type_cd < 'D'                          in dbspace1
   type_cd < 'G' and type_cd > 'C'  in dbspace2
   type_cd < 'L' and type_cd > 'F'  in dbspace3
   type_cd < 'R' and type_cd > 'K'  in dbspace4
   type_cd < 'X' and type_cd > 'Q'  in dbspace5
   type_cd > 'W'                          in dbspace6
```

When performing bulk data loads, there is significant overhead for tables fragmented with expressions. This is because the expression is evaluated each time a row is inserted. Also, when using this technique if the required table fragment for a table is not available, the INSERT statement will fail.

Fragmenting by round robin

If you have a low degree of selectivity where generally all or the majority of the rows in the table are examined, you might benefit fragmenting the table with a round-robin strategy.

Round-robin fragmentation creates an even distribution of data. When performing bulk data loads, there is a significant advantage for tables fragmented by round robin, because no expression must be evaluated each time a row is inserted. Fragmenting by round robin provides the highest level of data avail-

TABLE 14.10

Expression type	If query contains these operators	Example
Range	relational (>, <, <=, >=)	WHERE dept_id>=1000
Equality	equality (=,IN)	WHERE type_cd IN ('A', 'B', 'C')

able, because the engine bypasses any unavailable fragments and continues to insert a row in the next available fragment.

The round-robin distribution is created by the UPDATE STATISTICS command. Here are some suggestions for creating round-robin distributions: Run UPDATE STATISTICS MEDIUM with the default resolution and confidence for all columns that do not have indexes. The sample size for each column with the default resolution and confidence is 2962 rows. For a database with many columns, you might want to run UPDATE STATISTICS MEDIUM on the entire database. Then run UPDATE STATISTICS HIGH for each column that heads an index. The next time to run UPDATE STATISTICS should be relatively short since the index is used to read the data and no sort is executed.

In most cases, this strategy should provide a large enough sample size for the optimizer to pick the correct path for most queries. If there is a problem query, take the following steps:

1. First, run the query with SET EXPLAIN ON to record the query plan.
2. Then run UPDATE STATISTICS HIGH for the columns listed in the WHERE clause.
3. Run the query with SET EXPLAIN ON. Did it run faster?
4. Compare the query plans. If UPDATE STATISTICS HIGH produced a different query plan and the query ran faster, then the optimizer made a better choice and SELECT benefited from having more data available to the optimizer.

You might have received better results with UPDATE STATISTICS HIGH, but the extra time it takes each day to run HIGH mode on these columns often makes it unfeasible. Try using UPDATE STATISTICS MEDIUM for the columns involved in the query, but setting the confidence to .99 and adjusting the resolution value slightly higher so the sample size is higher. Then try rerunning the query and check the query plan to see if it returned the same results as HIGH mode. Repeat this adjustment-and-test process until your query plan matches the query plan of HIGH mode.

The following paragraphs provide recommendations on using UPDATE STATISTICS. Starting with version 7.1, the DISTRIBUTIONS ONLY clause updates only distributions. Index statistics are not updated. Using DISTRIBUTIONS ONLY means that index statistics are generated once using the strategy in the following procedure. This strategy for running UPDATE STATISTICS should decrease the total amount of time needed to update the distribution, table, and index statistics.

1. Run UPDATE STATISTICS MEDIUM DISTRIBUTIONS ONLY for each table or for the entire database. The distributions for columns that head indexes will later be overwritten in step 2 by HIGH-mode distributions; the time wasted creating distributions twice on a few columns might, however, be outweighed by the difficulty of running statistics on individual columns. The default parameters are sufficient unless the table is very large, in which case you should use a resolution of 1.0 and a confidence level of .99.

2. Run UPDATE STATISTICS HIGH DISTRIBUTIONS ONLY for all columns that head an index. For the best performance, execute this command once for each column.

3. Run UPDATE STATISTICS LOW for the database. This command populates index for every table.

To examine the round-robin data distribution, execute the following command:

```
DbSchema -d DatabaseName -hd TableName
```

Monitoring fragmentation

To monitor the success of your fragmentation strategy, you need to determine if the I/O is balanced across fragments. The `onstat -g ppf` command displays the number of reads and writes for each fragment. Note that this just indicates information because the calls do not show how many disk reads and writes have actually occurred.

The system stores a row for each fragment in sysfragments, a system catalog table. You can determine the table for the fragment by joining the partnum column in the output of `OnStat -g ppf` to the partn column in this table. The sysfragments table will display the associated table ID in the tabid column. If you then join this column to the table ID column in systables, you can determine the table name in column tabname for the fragment. The sysfragments table contains the useful information listed in Table 14.11.

To determine the accurate fragment information, you need to run UPDATE STATISTICS after loading data in the fragments.

14.2.6 Tuning I/O

Informix has several parameters that influence input and output of data. Tuning the I/O parameters affects when pages are read or written to disk, and how fast can they can be read or written to disk. The factors that influence Informix's I/O capabilities are in the following areas:

- Asynchronous IO (AIO)
- Buffer cache sizes
- Checkpoint intervals
- Least recently used queues
- Page-cleaner threads
- Read-ahead buffers

14.2.6.1 Asynchronous I/O

OnLine can use the following methods to perform asynchronous I/O:

AIO virtual processors. AIO virtual processors (VPs) can perform read and write operations if the kernel AIO is not used. AIO VPs performs I/O on cooked files as opposed to raw devices.

Kernel AIO. Kernel asynchronous I/O (also referred to as kernel AIO or kaio) is a method of performing nonblocking disk reads and writes via the operating system. Kernel AIO can be used only with raw devices.

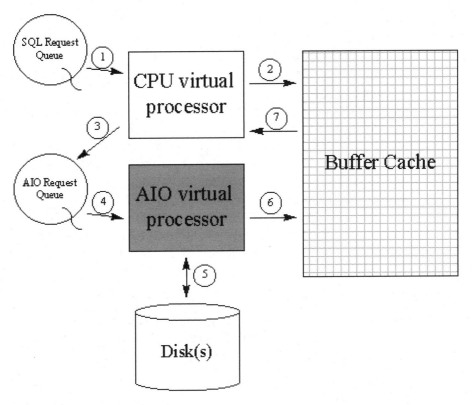

Figure 14.5 I/O with AIO virtual processors.

TABLE 14.11

Column	Description
fragtype	Table or index (T or I)
tabid	Table identifier in systables
partn	Unique number for each fragment
strategy	Expression or round robin (E or R)
evalpos	Fragment number (beginning at 0)
exprtext	Expression text
dbspace	Dbspace name where the fragment is located
npused	Number of pages used
nrows	Number of rows in the fragment

Some configurations can use a combination of the two methods, which is typically the case if your system has a mixture of raw devices and cooked files. To determine if your system uses kernel AIO, run the `onstat-g ath` command to list all the currently executing threads. One or more kaio threads will be seen running on systems that use kernel AIO.

Figure 14.5 shows how a SQL request is satisfied by a database server using asynchronous I/O with virtual processors. The procedure is as follows:

1. The SQL statement is parsed and optimized.
2. The system reads the buffer cache for the pages needed to satisfy the query.
3. If a page does not exist in the buffer cache, then a request for the appropriate chunk is sent to the AIO request queue.
4. The CPU VP thread yields to another thread on the ready queue and puts itself in the sleep queue until the AIO VP processes the request.
5. The AIO VP reads the data from disk.
6. The AIO VP places the disk data in the buffer cache.
7. This causes the CPU VP thread in the wait queue to put itself in the ready queue so it can read the page(s) from the buffer cache and continue processing the SQL statement.

AIO VPs are also used to write to control files, such as the message log. Figure 14.6 shows how a SQL request is satisfied by the database server using kernel asynchronous I/O. Kernel asynchronous I/O is coordinated by the operating system kernel and handled by a kaio thread. This thread is started when the first raw device is opened. Here is the procedure shown in Figure 14.6:

1. The SQL statement is parsed and optimized.
2. The system reads the buffer cache for the pages needed to satisfy the query.
3. If a page does not exist in the buffer cache, then a request for the appropriate chunk is sent to the AIO request queue. At this point the CPU VP thread yields to another thread on the ready queue and puts itself in the sleep queue until the IO request is processed.
4. The AIO manager reads the request.
5. The AIO manager sends the request to the kaio thread queue.
6. The kaio thread reads the request.
7. The kaio thread sends the request to the operating system kernel.
8/9. The kaio thread polls the operating system kernel to determine if the operation is complete.
10. When the operation is complete, the kaio thread places the data in the buffer cache.
11. This causes the CPU VP thread in the wait queue to put itself in the ready queue so it can read the page(s) from the buffer cache and continue processing the SQL statement.

The optimum number of AIO virtual processors to allocate depends on the system's use of kernel AIO. Refer to Table 14.12 for recommended NUMAIOVPS settings.

The OnStat -g ioq command displays information about I/O queue lengths. There is a queue for every chunk and for every CPU VP. The len col-

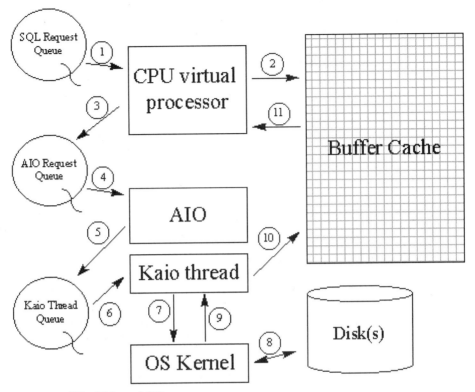

Figure 14.6 I/O with kernel AIO.

TABLE 14.12

AIO type	NUMAIOVPS setting
No kernel AIO	Equal to the number of disks that have database tables
Kernel AIO with mixture of raw devices and cooked files	Equal to the number of disks that use cooked files for chunks holding database tables
Kernel AIO with just raw devices	2 (or 1 for smaller systems) needed for control files, e.g., message log

umn shows the current length of the queue. The maxlen column shows the largest the queue length has been since the time the database was started or since the last time the following command ran.

```
OnStat -z
```

If the queue length is large for many or all of the AIO queues, adding another AIO VP could increase performance. When you add another AIO VP, reset the queue information and then monitor the maxlen column again to see if the maximum queue lengths decrease.

14.2.6.2 Buffer cache size

The performance of OLTP applications is affected by the amount of work that can be satisfied in memory buffers, as opposed to requiring a read or write to disk. If more of the required data is in memory, the performance will improve.

You can obtain the amount of memory-cached read and write information by running the `OnStat -p` command. The cache amounts displayed are calculated with the following formulas:

$$\% \text{ read} = \frac{100 * (\text{bufreads} - \text{diskreads})}{\text{bufreads}}$$

$$\% \text{ written} = \frac{100 * (\text{bufwrites} - \text{diskwrits})}{\text{bufwrits}}$$

Informix minimizes actual write I/O by deferring the writes back to disk for as long as possible, retaining the most recently used buffers in memory. You can increase the number of shared memory buffers by changing the BUFFERS configuration parameter. However, adding buffers beyond the requirements of your applications will not increase performance, so do it incrementally and monitor the cached percentages carefully.

Also note that, for every buffer that is added, an extra page of shared memory is required. The page size is determined by the value of BUFFSIZE in the OnConfig file.

> For Decision Support Systems (DSS) that use parallel database query, note that the PDQ feature bypasses these memory buffer caches and uses an alternate form of cache in the virtual portion of shared memory.

14.2.6.3 Checkpoints

A checkpoint can be thought of as synchronizing the data on disk with the data in the buffer cache. The time it takes for this synchronization process to occur is called the checkpoint duration. Since OnLine suspends most other activity when a checkpoint is occurring, it is important to keep checkpoint duration to a minimum. The factors that effect checkpoint duration are described in the following sections.

How many dirty pages from the buffer pool must be written to disk

The bulk of the work during a checkpoint is writing modified buffers from memory to disk. Some of the things that affect how many pages must be written during a checkpoint are:

The size of the buffer pool. As you increase the number of buffers in the OnLine system, there can be more dirty pages to write during a checkpoint. You influence the size of the buffer pool with the BUFFERS configuration parameter.

The LRU parameters. The LRU_MAX_DIRTY and LRU_MIN_DIRTY parameters influence how many pages are written between checkpoints. As more pages are written between checkpoints, there might be less pages to write during a checkpoint.

The random nature of writes. If many of the writes are localized in a small number of pages, the number of dirty pages might be less than the size of the buffer pool.

The amount of write activity. If very little accrues during a period of time, the number of dirty pages will be minimal.

How fast dirty pages can be written to disk

Some of the factors that influence how quickly dirty pages can be written are:

Number and speed of disks. As you increase the number and speed of disks, checkpoint duration should decrease as well.

Disk layout. As discussed earlier, it is important to spread I/O between disks so no disk becomes a bottleneck. This is particularly important during checkpoints.

Number of AIO VPs. Having more AIO VPs than necessary should not be a problem. However, having less AIO VPs than necessary will not keep the disks as busy as possible and will increase checkpoint duration.

Number of page cleaners. As with AIO VPs, having too few page cleaners will increase checkpoint duration because they will not be able to keep the AIO VPs busy, and hence the disks will not be fully used.

The time between the end of one checkpoint and the start of another is known as the checkpoint interval or checkpoint frequency. OnLine suspends most other activity when a checkpoint is occurring. If the checkpoint intervals are too short, performance will be hampered because OnLine must keep suspending threads until the checkpoint completes.

You can use the OnStat -m command to monitor the checkpoint duration and interval, and edit the message log to sample a longer period of time. You can derive the checkpoint interval by subtracting the time stamps between two checkpoint entries in the log. The checkpoint duration is listed after every checkpoint entry. The checkpoint interval is affected by the following:

- The CKPTINTVL configuration parameter, whose default is 300 seconds, specifies the number of seconds between the checkpoints.
- When the physical log is 75% full, an automatic checkpoint is issued.

The more data created or modified (through INSERT, UPDATE, and DELETE) in a system increases the amount of write and therefore checkpoint activity. It also fills the physical log, causing the automatic triggering of a checkpoint.

During a checkpoint, page-cleaner threads are each assigned to a particular chunk in the database. Each page-cleaner thread then searches through the buffers, gathering pages associated with its chunks. The page cleaner then sorts the gathered pages into disk sequence, and sends a request to the AIO subsystem to write these pages back to disk.

You can measure the page-cleaning efficiency by analyzing the types of buffer writes performed by the page-cleaner threads. The types of buffer writes that occur are listed in Table 14.13. These writes decrease performance, but you can avoid them by tuning the LRU parameters. The OnStat -F command displays detailed information about the activity of the page-cleaner threads. In general, you want to maximize LRU writes, minimize chunks writes, and eliminate foreground writes. Optimal performance seems to occur when you have a page-cleaner thread continuously do a moderate amount of work, thereby reducing the amount of work and wait times during a checkpoint.

Systems that are oriented toward batch processing with fewer OLTP requirements might perform better by keeping LRU percentages higher and performing most page cleaning during checkpoints, thereby increasing the number of chunk writes. Chunk writes are sorted writes and help performance in batch-related applications.

14.2.6.4 Least recently used (LRU) queues

The shared memory buffer pool is managed through the use of several linked lists of pointers to the buffer table. The LRUS configuration parameter establishes the number of paired queues for the system, with a maximum of 32 pairs. They are considered pairs because there is one queue for free pages (FLRU) and another for modified pages (MLRU). As mentioned earlier, page-cleaner threads scan these LRU queues during their cleaning activity, and the sqlexec threads use the queues when searching for a page. When configuring these type of queues, it is important to try to reduce any contention. For a large multiple-CPU system, you can achieve this by allocating as many LRU queues as there are CPU virtual processors. For a small, multiple-CPU or single-CPU system, set the minimum number of queues to four.

To monitor and display information about these LRU queues, use OnStat -R. For each queue pair, there is a line displaying the percentage of the queue pair that is free and the percentage of the queue that is modified.

14.2.6.5 Page cleaning

The number of page-cleaner threads is configured with the CLEANERS configuration parameter. As a general guideline, it is recommended that you allocate page-cleaner threads equal to the number of active disks. In a complete

TABLE 14.13

Write	Description
Chunk	Very efficient stored writes that occur during a checkpoint.
LRU	Initiated by a page cleaner thread when the number of dirty buffers relative to the total number of buffers exceeds the LRU_MAX_DIRTY threshold.
Foreground	When a thread cannot find the page in shared memory and needs to read the page from disk to a clean buffer in the FLRU queue. If a clean buffer cannot be located in the FLRU queue, a dirty buffer must be written to disk before it can be used.

decision support system where few disk writes occur, you can use fewer page-cleaner threads. Generally, you should not have to tune the value. However, you can monitor the activity of the page-cleaner threads using the OnStat -F command.

Two more parameters also control the page-cleaning activity: LRU _MAX_DIRTY and LRU_MIN_DIRTY. The LRU_MAX_DIRTY parameter defines the maximum percent of LRU queue pairs that can remain dirty before page-cleaning activity takes place. If the percentage of dirty buffers on the modified LRU (MLRU) queue exceeds the value in LRU_MAX_DIRTY, then the page-cleaner threads will start to flush dirty buffers to disk. The page cleaners will continue their cleaning activity until the percent of modified LRU (MLRU) queues equals the value in LRU_MIN_DIRTY. The default setting for LRU_MAX_DIRTY is 60%, and the default setting for LRU_MIN_DIRTY is 50%. Decreasing the LRU percentages will cause more page cleaning to occur between checkpoints. Setting the LRU percentages very high will allow the queues to become very dirty, potentially increasing the number of foreground writes that have to take place, decreasing performance.

Page cleaning between checkpoints is different than cleaning during a checkpoint in the following ways:

- The order of dirty pages in LRU queues is completely random, based on system activity. When a page-cleaner thread writes dirty pages to disk, it can write pages in several different areas of the chunks, causing substantial disk-head movement, as opposed to the sorted chunk writes that occur at checkpoint time.

- Page cleaning between checkpoints is asynchronous and does not slow down any user processes. Page cleaning during a checkpoint stops all user attempts to change a page until the checkpoint is finished.

14.2.6.6 Read-ahead pages

The read-ahead parameter affects users performing sequential reads of data. For example, an index build or sequential scan via a SELECT statement will cause a read ahead to occur. The RA_PAGES configuration parameter specifies how many pages will be read ahead if OnLine detects a sequential read. The RA_THRESHOLD parameter specifies how many pages are left to be read in shared memory by the requester before more pages are read ahead from disk. You can set read-ahead parameters higher (30 to 40) if users are reading the same data or if there are very few users connected on the OnLine system. Keep read-ahead parameters lower (5 to 10) if multiple users are performing reads on separate data.

Key or index searches

Read-aheads with key-only searches and sequential scans that use an index work differently than read-aheads with sequential scans. Read-aheads begin when the database server starts at the level-1 page (the page above the level-0 or leaf page) and reads all the leaf pages the level-1 page points to. The read-ahead is complete when one of the following items occur:

- The database server reaches the end of the key range for the query.
- The database server reads ahead all the leaf pages pointed to by the level-1 page.
- The limit of the number of pages to be read-ahead is reached. This limit is defined as the maximum of one of the following calculations:

(#buffers / #sessions)

75% of the total number of buffers

If both calculations yield a number less than what RA_PAGES is set to, then RA_PAGES will be used as the number of pages to read-ahead.

Sequential scans

Read-aheads with sequential scans that use an index have to read-ahead index pages and data pages. Read-ahead begins when the database server starts at the leaf page and reads all the data pages the leaf page points to. The read-ahead is complete when one of the following occurs:

- The database server reaches the end of the key range for the query.
- The database server has read all the data pages points to by the current leaf page.
- The limit of the number of pages to be read-ahead is reached. This limit is defined as the maximum of one of the following calculations:

(#buffer / #sessions)

75# of the total number of buffers.

If both calculations yield a number less than what RA_PAGES is set to, then RA_PAGES will be used as the number of pages to read-ahead. To turn off read-ahead, set RA_PAGES to 0. There are several ways to monitor the effectiveness of the read-ahead configuration parameters:

- If the read-ahead parameters are set too high, you might see a decrease in the read cache rate. Too many pages read from disk for one user could cause pages needed by other users to be flushed.
- If the read-ahead operation is still being performed by the AIO subsystem when the user needs a specific page, the bufwaits field in OnStat -p will be incremented. If you see this field unusually high, the RA_PAGES parameter might be too high or the RA_THRESHOLD parameter might be too low.
- Totally effective read-aheads means that all pages read from disk are used by the session. If this is true, then RA-pgsused (pages used by sessions) would be equal to the sum of the ixda-RA, idx-RA, and da-RA fields.

14.2.7 Logging

There are two types of database logging: buffered and unbuffered. In buffered logging, transactions are written to a memory buffer first and, when the buffer becomes full, it is flushed (applied) to disk. In an unbuffered database, transactions are still written to a memory buffer, but the buffer is flushed immediately after any transaction is committed.

Unbuffered logging is less efficient than buffered logging because valuable time is spent writing the buffer contents to disk after every transaction instead of when it is full. Also, more disk space is used because the entire buffer is written to disk even though much of it could be empty. On the other hand, there is a potential for data loss using buffered logging if the database or system crashes before the log buffer is flushed to disk.

Because all databases share the same logical log buffer, if you mix databases with both types, the logical log buffer will be flushed after every transaction committed to the database with unbuffered logging.

For optimal performance, you want the physical and logical log buffers to be large enough to minimize the amount of physical I/O required for writing to the physical log or logical logs, while at the same time being only as large as necessary because they occupy shared memory space. (The more shared memory needed, the less memory there is for other processes.)

You can use the `OnStat -1` utility to verify if the log buffer sizes chosen are optimal. Examine the following output fields from the Physical Logging and Logical Logging sections of the output:

bufsize. The current buffer size, measured in pages.

pages/io. The average number of pages written for all physical I/O to the log.

The buffers are being used efficiently if the value of pages/io is greater than or equal to 75% of the bufsize value. Increasing the buffer size even further will reduce the amount of physical I/O carried out when writing to the logs, and consequently improve the performance.

The buffers are not being used efficiently if the value of pages/io is less than 75% of the bufsize value. As such, you should decrease the buffer size until you reach the more optimum 75% value. This buffer size reduction will use less of the shared memory and possibly aid the performance of other parts of the system.

14.2.8 Indexes

All database vendor indexing methods are typically implemented through what is known as a balanced B+ tree, which is a set of nodes, or pages, that contain index keys and pointers arranged in a hierarchy (see Figure 14.7).

It is balanced because there are an equal number of levels in all parts of the tree. When the database server attempts to access a row via an index, it reads the tree starting from the root page, and traverses the branch pages until it reaches a leaf page.

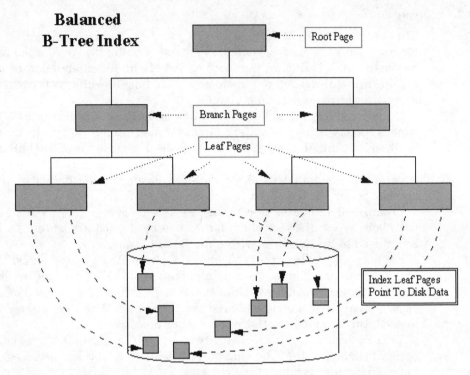

Figure 14.7   Index B+ tree.

As rows are inserted into an indexed table, the pages fill up. When you attempt to add a key to a full page, the page splits into two pages and the middle key value is promoted into a page at the higher level. So a full page becomes two pages that are half full, leaving room. These splits do, however, come at a cost. The split operation itself requires extra processing. While the keys are split across two pages, the pages are locked. Half-full index pages are generally less efficient because they increase the size of the tree, use more disk space, and require more memory cache pages.

When an index is initially built via the CREATE INDEX statement, you can determine the percentage of each index page that will be filled by specifying a FILLFACTOR (the default is 90%). It makes sense to choose a higher FILL-FACTOR for tables that will not receive many new inserts, and a lower FILL-FACTOR for tables that will.

With that in mind, it is also very important to consider the number of indexes on tables that will receive many SQL INSERT, UPDATE, and DELETE statements, because these statements also check and maintain the index entries. Table 14.14 lists these SQL statements and the associated index action and requirements.

To monitor the indexes on a table, use the `OnCheck -pT TableName` command. This will produce an index usage report showing the average number of keys and average free bytes for each index for the specified table.

14.2.9 Query optimizer

The Informix engines use cost-based optimization to determine the best way to satisfy SQL statements. Most of the top RDBMS vendors use this or similar optimization techniques. Another approach is rule-based optimization. In rule-based optimization, the sequence of tables and columns specified in several parts of the SQL statement (e.g., FROM, WHERE, and ORDER BY in a SELECT statement) determine the plan for the engine. This type of optimization is therefore very sensitive and much less forgiving to SQL, which was constructed without taking into account the design of the database and the current data distribution.

The cost-based optimizer used in Informix examines the inbound SQL request and analyzes internal statistics that correspond to the tables being referenced by the SQL in order to determine what is commonly termed the execution or query plan. The plan specifies to the engine which indexes to use, what work tables to create, and the sequence in which to access the tables.

The internal statistics referred to in the previous paragraph are stored in the database catalog tables as systables, syscolumns, sysindexes, and sysdistrib. The optimizer examines the following information in these catalog tables:

- Number of rows in the table
- Whether a column is unique
- Type, availability, and efficiency of indexes
- Number of data pages
- Number of index pages

These statistics are not maintained on a continual basis, but when updated they reflect the data in the tables at a specific point in time. It is important to make sure that the information in the catalog is as accurate as possible in order for the optimizer to produce the most efficient plans for accessing the data. A specific SQL command, UPDATE STATISTICS, makes the engine take a fresh snapshot and update these statistics.

The UPDATE STATISTICS command has several options: You can use it to update statistics for all the tables, stored procedures, or both in the current database. You can also use the command to update statistics for a specific table

TABLE 14.14

SQL statement	Index action	Requirement
INSERT	Reads every index	Locates the correct index page to place the new key value
DELETE	Reads every index	Locates the key value to mark it for deletion
key value update	Reads every index (possibly twice)	Locates and deletes old key value, and then locates the page to place the new key value

or stored procedure. Here are some examples of the UPDATE STATISTICS command:

```
//All tables and procedures in current database
   UPDATE STATISTICS
//All procedures in current database
   UPDATE STATISTICS FOR PROCEDURE
//Specific procedure
   UPDATE STATISTICS FOR PROCEDURE pr_customer
//All tables in current database
   UPDATE STATISTICS FOR TABLE
//Specific table, gathering minimum amount of information for column
   UPDATE STATISTICS LOW FOR TABLE tb_customer (cust_id)
//Specific table, sampling the data stored in table for column specified
   UPDATE STATISTICS MEDIUM FOR TABLE tb_customer (cust_id)
//Specific table, scanning all data stored in table for column specified
   UPDATE STATISTICS HIGH FOR TABLE tb_customer (cust_id)
```

You should update the statistics when you make a significant number of modifications to the data in a table (i.e., a batch bulk load) or perform extensive modifications to a table, or when changes are made to tables that are used by one or more procedures and you do not want the engine to reoptimize the procedure at execution time. You should also update statistics when you upgrade to a new database engine. This ensures that the indexes, the form of which is typically changed in the next release, are converted to the newer form.

Based on the statistical information in the catalogs, the optimizer tries to create several alternative plans. Then it computes the cost of executing each plan. It does this by estimating the number of disk accesses, the amount of CPU required, and—in the case where the query is on a distributed database—the basic cost of interaction to another engine over the network. This is a sophisticated strategy that allows the optimizer to select the best overall alternative. For large complex queries involving several joins, however, it can incur more overhead than desired, and in some extreme cases, the engine can run very low on or out of memory. For this reason, programmers can force the optimizer to be less adventurous by issuing the SET OPTIMIZATION LOW statement prior to executing this type of query. By using this statement, you invoke an alternative algorithm, one that eliminates unlikely join strategies during the early stages of optimization. This reduces the amount of time and memory resources spent trying to come up with alternative plans. But be aware that, if you choose to use this command, the "optimal" plan might be eliminated from consideration during the early stages of plan creation. Note that this optimization level stays in effect until you issue the SET OPTIMIZA-TION HIGH command. Also note that the HIGH setting is the default optimization level when you first start your connection to the engine.

> Sometimes the number of tables in the query increases the time required for optimization of the query, since all possible query paths must be examined. To determine if SET OPTIMIZATION LOW will help this type of query:

1. Execute and time the query.
2. SET EXPLAIN ON, reexecute the query, and note the query path used.
3. SET OPTIMIZATION LOW, SET EXPLAIN OFF, reexecute, and time the query.
4. If the query runs faster, SET OPTIMIZATION LOW, SET EXPLAIN ON, and reexecute the query.

   If the optimizer chooses the same query path in steps 2 and 4 and executes the query faster, then it makes sense to issue SET OPTIMIZATION LOW before you execute this query in the future. Be aware that, after executing this query, you should issue the SET OPTIMIZATION HIGH statement in order to return to the normal optimization methods for subsequent queries.

There are times you may want to see what plan the optimizer chooses for a given query, especially in the situation where you find that the performance of a particular query is slower than expected or is unacceptable. In order to see this plan, use the SET EXPLAIN ON statement. With this option set on, when the optimizer selects the plan, it creates a file (sqexplain.out) in the user's current directory. The file includes a copy of the query and plan the optimizer has chosen. Table 14.15 lists the items that might appear in the output file. The methods that OnLine uses when joining two tables in a query are described in Table 14.16.

If you have not run UPDATE STATISTICS, the optimizer will have no way to make a decision on the query path. Queries that should take seconds to run might take minutes or even hours to run if UPDATE STATISTICS has not been run. Consider running UPDATE STATISTICS daily or weekly, or after

TABLE 14.15

SET EXPLAIN ON output file	Description
AUTOINDEX PATH	Creates a temporary index
DYNAMIC HASH JOIN	Uses a hash join
Estimated Cost:	A numerical evaluation of the overall cost
Estimated # of Rows Returned:	Estimated number of rows returned
INDEX PATH	Scanning one or more indexes
MERGE JOIN	Using sort/merge join instead of a nested loop join
REMOTE PATH	Access to another distributed database
SEQUENTIAL SCAN	Reading table in sequence (a.k.a., a table scan)
SORT SCAN	Sorting result of preceding join or table scan
Temporary Files Required For:	Reason for temporary tables, e.g., Order By
QUERY:	A copy of the SQL evaluated by the optimizer

TABLE 14.16

Type of join	Description
Nested loop	The most efficient join method when the filter on both tables are indexed. The first table is scanned in any order, and the join column is matched with corresponding columns in the second table.
Sort merge	This requires that both tables, after filtering, are sorted in the order of the join column. A sort can be avoided if an index exists on the join column.
Hash (since v7.0)	This is where the second table is read and put into a hash table. The first table is scanned and matched against the hash table.

specific application activity occurs on your system. For example, if an application inserts a significant number of rows to a table, it would probably be worth running UPDATE STATISTICS to help subsequent queries. It might get to a point where you need to run UPDATE STATISTICS once a day in order to keep the optimizer supplied with decent data statistics. You could run it at night or at a period during the day when there is little activity or no demand on the system. Another way to affect the optimizer's choice for a query path is through the OPTCOMPIND environment (or configuration) parameter.

> For versions 7.0 to 7.10.UD1, the default value is 0. For subsequent versions starting at 7.10.UD1, the default is 2.

The OPTCOMPIND parameter determines when the optimizer is free to compare a dynamic join method with an existing index join method for a specific join pair only. For example, if you have two tables, header and detail, with an index on detail.orderid and you execute the following query:

```
SELECT D.*
FROM header, detail
WHERE header.orderid = detail.orderid
```

The optimizer will consider the two possible join orders: (header, detail) and then (detail, header). When it considers the (header, detail) join order, it checks the value of OPTCOMPIND to determine the join strategy. See Table 14.17 to see what the optimizer does with the various OPTCOMPIND settings.

When the optimizer considers the (detail, header) join order, there are no useful indexes on header, so it costs out a query path for a dynamically constructed index, hash, or sort merge join. In the final step, the optimizer chooses the lowest cost of the query path for either (header, detail) or (detail, header). If the cost of path (detail, header), which in this case is a dynamic method, is less than the cost of (header, detail), an index path, then the dynamic join path will be chosen.

TABLE 14.17

OPTOCOMPIND setting	Optimizer action
0	Either use an index join, or scan, using the index on detail.orderid
1 (and repeatable read transaction mode)	Same as OPTCOMPIND = 0
1 (not repeatable read transaction mode)	Same as OPTCOMPIND = 2
2	Choose the lowest cost between the index, hash, and sort merge joins

14.3 Parallel Database Query (PDQ)

Parallel Database Query distributes the execution of a SQL query across several processors. The goal of PDQ is to facilitate performance improvements of complex data queries that form the basis of many decision support systems. Before deciding how to set the PDQ parameters, consider some of the following factors:

- How many users will be running decision support queries at one time? By estimating how many users are running DSS queries at any one time, you can make better decisions on how to set the PDQ parameters.

- Do some queries have higher priority than others? Less important queries (e.g., queries that run in the background) can be run with a lower PDQPRIORITY.

- Should all DSS queries run at once, or should some wait? By increasing the PDQPRIORITY of some queries, you might cause other queries to wait. Because running queries have more resources they might run quicker, but the performance of waiting queries might suffer. To determine the best mix of running queries to wait queries, consider running a benchmark test and varying the PDQ parameters to determine the best settings.

- Is OLTP SQL running at the same time as DSS queries? If so, does OLTP SQL have a higher priority? DSS queries can use a large amount of system resources, which can decrease the performance of OLTP SQL. If OLTP SQL is important, decrease DS_TOTAL_MEMORY and DS_MAX_SCANS.

Before applying the answers to these questions, let's take a look at some of the history relating to parallel computing.

14.3.1 What is a parallel query?

The '80s were the decade of the relational database (RDBMS) and the '90s has quickly become known as the decade of the parallel relational database (P-RDBMS), with Informix currently leading the way.

The early parallel database market was captured by DBC 1012 (from Teradata Corporation) and NonStop SQL (from Tandem Computers). Soon the parallel database was dominating discussions surrounding decision support systems, and more recently data warehousing. Let's dig a little deeper into the science of parallel databases, specifically how these DBMSs achieve high performance by processing queries in a parallel fashion. It is still worth mentioning that the performance of any system is still determined by a successful mix of hardware, software, and the application code.

> Shared disk: Oracle, IBM's DB2 for MVS, and Red Brick Systems' Red Brick
> Shared nothing: Informix, Sybase, Teradata, and DB2 Parallel Edition

Early parallel-query processing systems implemented a technique known as interquery parallelism, where the system allocated one physical processor to each query. This approach is easy to implement, but the obvious downside is that it does not provide faster results for an individual query. The processor assigned to the query is fully used, while the other processors either stand idle or service other users' queries. The focus of parallel queries soon changed to intraquery parallelism, where the engine parallelizes parts of a query. Intraquery parallelization typically uses the following two types of parallelism to achieve faster results:

Pipelining. The output of one query process is input to the next part of the query before the first process is finished (e.g., a sort process passes rows to a merge process before the sort process completes).

Partitioning. Data is organized by some form of expression and spread across multiple disk volumes (e.g., table fragmentation).
Database vendors differ significantly in their use of pipeline parallelism. Oracle7, Sybase Navigation Server, and Teradata do not make much, if any, use of it. Informix and IBM's DB2 Parallel Edition, however, use significant amounts of pipelining.

> The crucial problems in parallel database implementation focus on resource management. In this area, the query optimizer is a key player, particularly in its relationship to the runtime resource management system.

What SQL can be parallelized? Typically, parallel queries require a large percentage of system resources, especially memory and CPU, in order to process complex queries involving large volumes of data. Managing these resources becomes an essential and crucial part in the administration of an Informix server.

Informix, through its configurable parameters, provides the flexibility to manage resources allocated to PDQ at a generic or high level, as well as at a specific level, providing the ability to balance server resources between queries of an OLTP and DSS nature. Informix's PDQ can parallelize the following parts of a query:

- Aggregation
- Grouping
- Joining
- Scanning
- Sorting

PDQ has software components that concentrate on each part of a query. It does this by starting a thread for each parallel software component, allowing each component to perform its unit of work. These threads can be configured to execute on different virtual processors, which in turn can execute on different physical processors. Informix can also make use of PDQ software components during inserts of the following form:

```
INSERT INTO ... SELECT FROM
SELECT ... INTO TEMP
```

Parallelization does not take place if the query:

- Contains a call to a stored procedure, such as:
  ```
  SELECT name FROM customer
  WHERE state = pr_get_state_by_area (212)
  ```
- Has no parallel PDQ operations.
- Is a parent query of a correlated subquery.
- Is optimized with CURSOR STABILITY isolation mode.
- Uses a cursor declared FOR UPDATE or WITH HOLD.

14.3.2 The parallel database query parameters

Several parameters control the allocation of resources to PDQ. They are shown in Table 14.18.

The DS_MAX_QUERIES parameter (the default is 3) determines the maximum number of parallel database queries requiring PDQ memory that can run concurrently.

The DS_MAX_SCANS parameter is the maximum number of scan threads the server can start. A scan thread is likely to be started for every table fragment to be examined. Obviously, if the table is comprised of many fragments, then the number of scan threads required can quickly exceed this value, affecting performance.

The DS_TOTAL_MEMORY parameter (the default is SHMVIRTSIZE/4) is the total amount of shared memory, measured in kilobytes, available for parallel database queries. The maximum is 1,048,576.

TABLE 14.18

Parameter	Description
DS_MAX_QUERIES	Maximum concurrent parallel database queries
DS_MAX_SCANS	Maximum number of PDQ scan threads
DS_TOTAL_MEMORY	Total memory (KB) that PDQ can use
MAX_PDQPRIORITY	Maximum PDQPRIORITY% allowed
PDQPRIORITY	Degree of parallelism that PDQ attempts
RA_PAGES	Number of read-ahead pages

The MAX_PDQPRIORITY parameter limits the maximum percentage of the PDQPRIORITY that any query will execute with.

The PDQPRIORITY parameter determines the amount of parallization to apply. The possible parameter values are one of the following:

OFF or 0. All queries run without any parallel assistance.

LOW or 2. Only scan portion of queries execute in parallel.

2 through 99. Run with a percentage of available parallel resources.

HIGH or 100. Use all available parallel resources for parallel queries.

You can determine the degree of parallelization by using the following equations:

#_secondary_ PDQ threads = (PDQPRIORITY / 100) * #_virtual_processors
#_scan_threads = #_fragments_scanned_for_all_tables

Because the PDQPRIORITY can be set in one of three ways—a configuration parameter, an environment variable, or explicitly via SQL statements—it is important to know the order of precedence:

1. SQL statement (SET PDQPRIORITY . . .)

2. Environment variable

3. Configuration parameter

In order to be certain that the desired amount of parallel resources are used, you might find it necessary to explicitly set the amount prior to each query, as opposed to relying on any current setting.

14.3.3 Changing PDQ parameters dynamically

You can change the server's configuration parameters dynamically while the server is running. Table 14.19 shows how to do this.

As mentioned earlier, you can change the PDQPRIORITY parameter prior to executing any query by issuing one of the following SQL statements before issuing the query:

```
SET PDQPRIORITY DEFAULT
SET PDQPRIORITY LOW
SET PDQPRIORITY OFF
SET PDQPRIORITY HIGH
SET PDQPRIORITY percent-of-resource
```

14.3.4 Memory Grant Manager (MGM)

All system resources for PDQ are allocated and managed by the Memory Grant Manager (MGM). The MGM accomplishes this by controlling:

- The number of threads started for each parallel query.
- The number of scan threads started for the OnLine system.
- The number of simultaneous parallel queries.
- The percentage of available memory and CPU resources for each parallel query.

The MGM allocates memory for parallel query activities such as sorting, joining, and grouping data. The total amount of memory allocated to all parallel queries cannot exceed the value specified by the DS_TOTAL_MEMORY parameter. The MGM grants memory to parallel queries in multiples of a parallel memory quota (PMQ). The quota is calculated in the following way:

$$PMQ = \frac{\text{Total memory available for PDQ}}{\text{Maximum PDQ queries allowed}} \text{ or } \frac{\text{DS\_TOTAL\_MEMORY}}{\text{DS\_MAX\_QUERIES}}$$

So when a parallel query enrolls with the MGM, the MGM calculates the memory to be allocated to the parallel query using the following formula:

Amount of memory to be allocated = INTEGER (PDQPRIORITY x (PMQ / DS_MAX_QUERIES))

For example, if a parallel query with a PDQPRIORITY of 26 enrolls with the MGM of an OnLine system that is configured with a DS_MAX_QUERIES of 10

TABLE 14.19

Configuration parameter	Command
DS_MAX_QUERIES (*)	OnMode –Q NewValue
DS_MAX_SCANS	OnMode –S NewValue
DS_TOTAL_MEMORY (*)	OnMode –M NewValue
MAX_PDQPRIORITY	OnMode –D NewValue

(*) The NewValue's for DS_MAX_QUERIES and DS_TOTAL_MEMORY will not take effect until all parallel database queries that are currently in progress have completed. New database queries that register with the MGM will not execute until the new setting takes effect.

and a DS_TOTAL_MEMORY of 1024, then the amount of memory to be reserved for the query would be 265, the result of:

INTEGER (26 × (1024 / 10))

A parallel query can use less than what was actually allocated by the MGM.

14.3.5 Monitoring parallel database query activity

It is essential for the administrator of an OnLine system to periodically check
the activity of PDQ and MGM. There are utilities provided by Informix that allow an administrator to monitor the PDQ and MGM activity inside an OnLine
server: OnMonitor and OnStat.

OnMonitor. The OnMonitor utility provides the current configuration parameters to the OnLine system, and resembles the following:

```
PDQ Priority                        [100]
Max PDQ Priority                    [100]
Decision Support Queries            [3]
Decision Support Memory (Kbytes)    [20000]
Maximum Decision Support Scans      [100]
Dataskip                            [off]
Optimizer Hint                      [0]
```

OnStat. The OnStat utility provides information about the status of the On-
Line system, and the OnStat -g mgm form of the command gives information
specifically about the status of PDQ and MGM. The output from this command
is broken down into sections with detailed information on the configuration parameters, memory and thread usage, and active (and pending) parallel queries
currently in the system.

14.4 Additional Considerations

Having tuned the database server, including the Parallel Database Query feature, the only other areas to take a look at are network issues and some of the
ways you can load information into and remove data from the server.

14.4.1 Network capacity

On systems with a large number of clients who access a database server, the
administrator is duty-bound to examine and monitor the network closely, making adjustments to the database server where necessary. When a network is
overloaded, systems will most likely try to send packets over the network at
the same time, causing collisions. If the network software detects a collision, it
will resend the packet. This duplication of work delays messages passed back
and forth between the application and the database. A certain amount of collisions within a network is normal. If your network is experiencing collisions for
a prolonged period of time, however, it probably means that the network
should be either upgraded or reconfigured.

TABLE 14.20

Section	Description
Configuration parameters	Displays current setting of the PDQ parameters
Queries	Displays current parallel database queries: *Active* = # of active parallel database queries *Ready* = # of parallel database queries waiting for MGM to allow them to run *Maximum* = # of concurrent parallel database queries allowed
Memory	The usage of memory for parallel database queries: *Total* = Amount of PDQ memory available *Free* = Amount of PDQ memory not currently in use *Quantum* = Smallest amount of memory that can be allocated
Scans	The usage of scan threads for parallel queries: *Total* = # of scan threads that can be started *Free* = # of scan threads not currently in use *Quantum* = Smallest unit of scan threads that will be started when required
Load control	Queries requiring resources pass through a series of gates to test if enough resources are available. The length of the queue for each gate is displayed under this section: *Memory* = # of queries waiting for memory to be allocated *Scans* = # of queries waiting for scan thread to be allocated *Priority* = # of queries waiting for higher priority queries to complete *Max Queries* = # of queries waiting for other queries to complete *Reinit* = # of queries waiting for the re-initialization of the DS_MAX_QUERIES or DS_TOTAL_MEMORY parameters
Active queries	This section shows the parallel database queries that are either active or waiting for resources: *Session* = session identifier (OnStat –g ses for session details) *Query* = address of internal control block for query *Priority* = PDQPRIORITY of query *Thread* = MGM's thread address *Memory* = # of memory gets requests *Scan* = # of scan threads allocated / # of scan threads used *Gate* = Gate number at which the query is waiting (see Load control)
Free resource and queries	Displays information about the average free resources and queries since the time the system started, or since the last execution of OnMode –Q, OnMode –M, or OnMode –S. The section also lists average and minimum amounts of memory for parallel database queries in units of 8K bytes. It displays the average number of scan threads used at any one time: *Average #* = Average of memory / scans, and standard deviation from average *Minimum #* = Minimum available memory / scans at any one time *Average #* = Average active and ready queue length *Maximum #* = Maximum size of the active and ready queue *Total #* = number of queries that are active and ready

Some obvious network-configurable parameters you might consider altering are:

Window size. The number of messages sent before an acknowledgment. This is typically a 1:1 ratio, but you might see better usage by increasing the size to 5.

Packet size. The number of bytes per message. A large number is better suited to DSS, and a smaller size is potentially (depending on the size of message) better suited to OLTP.

14.4.2 Reducing network traffic

An obvious way to avoid congestion on a network is to reduce the amount of traffic or move some of it elsewhere. Most corporate networks are a collection of subnetworks interconnected by one or more routers. If client workstations are on a different subnetwork than the database server, then any traffic needs to hop from one subnetwork to the other. If the subnetworks are configured with multiple routers between them, then this hopping, or hop count, will possibly delay the messaging, and you might want to consider connecting the database server to the same subnetwork as the clients, or at least a closer one, by installing an additional network card in the database server. This allows the database to simultaneously connect to multiple subnetworks, rather than letting the traffic flow through and be delayed by a combination of routers.

14.4.2.1 Configuring multiple-network cards

Informix OnLine can communicate with multiple-network interface cards by having entries in several relevant system files that define TCP/IP connections. In order to use the multiple-network cards, follow these steps:

1. Add one entry per network card in the /etc/services file:

```
ol1    4096/tcp
ol2    4097/tcp
```

2. Add one entry per network card in /etc/hosts, with a separate IP address:

```
199.177.177.21 tribeca1
104.124.177.22 tribeca2
```

3. Add one entry per network card to Informix's sqlhosts file:

```
trib_ol1 onsoctcp tribeca1 ol1
trib_ol2 onsoctcp tribeca2 ol2
```

4. In the ONCONFIG file, add the DBSERVERNAME for one of the network card sqlhosts entries, and DBSERVERALIASES for the other sqlhosts entry:

```
DBSERVERNAME trib_ol1
DBSERVERALIASES trib_ol2
```

Once configured, applications can choose a particular route to the database server by specifying the sqlhosts entry name or defaulting to the dbservername given by the INFORMIXSERVER environment variable.

14.4.2.2 Programming techniques

Here are some programming techniques that can reduce the amount of network traffic:

- Use stored procedures for tasks that have groups of SQL statements, because they reduce the number and size of messages. Ensuring database referential integrity, instead of coding it in the application, will also reduce unnecessary traffic.

- Return only data that's necessary in the application. Filter out all rows and columns not needed by the application.

- Use the fetch buffer when sending and receiving client data. Increasing the FET_BUF_SIZE environment variable might decrease network traffic when transferring a large number of rows, particularly wide rows.

14.4.3 Using stored procedures

A large number of sites have a policy of using stored procedures for database interaction, typically because of security and potential speed benefits. More specifically:

- They prefer stored procedures because it is easier for them to see exactly what SQL has been executed, and it is easier to tackle performance problems.

- You can use any front end to your system, which also makes it easy to test procedures in isolation from your front end.

- Database administrators can control access to objects, right down to an individual user in the database, regardless of the front end being used.

- Stored procedures are considered more efficient during execution. When a procedure is created, the SQL is parsed, the indexes are selected, and the query plan is built and optimized based on the current database statistics. If you pass dynamic SQL to a database engine, it has to perform these steps for every database access, making the stored procedure approach scale better when the number of users increases.

- If you are using stored procedures, you can change the database without affecting the front end. This allows you to easily add performance enhancements, debug code, check for errors, etc., without affecting the front end.

This should give you an idea why many sites advocate or demand the use of stored procedures. Most sites we have worked in have used stored procedures, and we recommend that you consider using stored procedures too.

Using stored procedure arguments in joins

When joining tables and supplying the parameters to one table, supply them to the other one as well, if it is part of the join to the other table instead of the column.

14.4.4 Using binary large objects (BLOBs)

If you are using BLOB data types, you can place them in a blobspace. A blobspace can hold BLOBs from multiple tables. Storing large BLOBs in blobspaces will be more efficient if the blobspace is created with a large page size.

Blobspaces are not seen through the buffer pool and the logical log. When a BLOB in a blobspace is updated, the original BLOB value remains on disk until the associated logical log file is backed up to tape. So it is necessary to have enough space available to all copies of the BLOB.

Set the blobspace's page size to the average BLOB for that blobspace. This will help prevent BLOB fragmentation.

14.4.5 Mass migration

When you are loading or removing large amounts of data into or from one or more tables, consider the situation carefully in order to maximize the throughput and minimize the time it takes for the operation to complete.

Loading data

In addition to using the bulk load programs already mentioned in Chapters 10 and 16, there are some additional techniques you can use to reduce the time it takes to load a large volume of data into a table:

- Turn off database logging while the data loads.

- Drop any indexes and re-create than after the data is loaded. This is so obvious that it is often forgotten or ignored. Once you drop any indexes and load the tables, you can quickly and efficiently rebuild them using Informix's parallel index build feature. You can also help the parallel indexing process out by increasing the PSORT_NPROCS environment variable. The value in this variable sets the number of sort threads the parallel sort routines can use during index rebuilds.

- Use a cursor to insert the data. When using a cursor, several rows are inserted into a memory buffer before they are sent to the database server. If you are using INET version 7.10 or greater, this memory buffer is determined by the FET_BUF_SIZE environment variable (the default is 4096 bytes). Increasing the buffer decreases the frequency of network traffic between the client application and database server. It is worth noting that, in the event of a SQL error, coding is required to determine which row caused the error. Because of this, a cursor is not a practical solution to inserting data into several tables during the same transaction.

Removing data

The following are some techniques and suggestions you can employ when deleting large amounts of data from one or more tables:

- Drop any indexes.

- Monitor the tablespace for empty extents after DELETE operation. Extents that are allocated to a tablespace are not returned to the dbspace's free space until after the table is dropped. The DELETE operation might have left the tablespace with empty or near-empty extents, so if you do not plan to repopulate the table soon, it is a good idea to reclaim the free space.

- Reclaim space from extents that are allocated but empty or nearly empty by dropping and rebuilding the table. The easiest way to do this is to alter the index to cluster, which creates a new table in the same dbspace as the existing table, inserts the rows in index order, and then drops the old table:

```
ALTER INDEX x1usage TO CLUSTER
```

  Note: You need enough free pages in the dbspace to contain two copies of the table while the ALTER command is executing. If the first extent of the table contains a large number of free pages, you cannot reorganize it with this technique because the new table it creates will have the same first extent size. In order to rebuild the table with a new first extent size, you must unload it, drop it, and re-create it with the new first extent size. Then you have to reload the table.

- Watch for long transactions. If a DELETE statement removes a large number of rows, make sure you have enough free space in the logical log to hold the log entries for the statement. There is one log entry for each row and index key deleted. If the transaction starts in the first log, it must be completed after a certain percentage of the log fills. That percentage is given by the LTXHWM configuration parameter. If the transaction does not complete by then, it will be rolled back, which is a very lengthy operation.

Chapter

15

Building Common Database Procedures

15.1 Using Stored Procedures

You can group SQL statements and control-of-flow stored procedure language (SPL) in a stored procedure to improve the performance of Informix. Stored procedures are collections of SQL statements and SPL. They are stored in the database and the SQL is parsed and optimized. An execution plan is prepared and cached when a procedure is run, so the subsequent execution is very fast. The SQL is reoptimized only at execution if necessary. Stored procedures can:

- Receive parameters passed by the calling object (e.g., PowerBuilder GUI front end).
- Call other procedures.
- Return a status value to a calling procedure or GUI front end to indicate success or failure, and the reason for failure.
- Return values of parameters to a calling procedure or GUI front end.
- Be executed on remote Informix, i.e., remote procedures calls (RPC).

The ability to write stored procedures greatly enhances the power, efficiency, and flexibility of SQL. Compiled procedures dramatically improve the performance of SQL statements and batches. In addition, stored procedures on other Informix servers can be executed if your server and the remote server are both set up to allow remote logins. You can write triggers on your local Informix that execute procedures on a remote server whenever certain events, such as deletions, updates, or inserts, take place locally. Stored procedures differ from ordinary SQL statements and from batches of SQL statements in that they are precompiled. When you create a procedure, Informix's query processor analyzes it and prepares an execution plan that is ultimately stored in the system

427

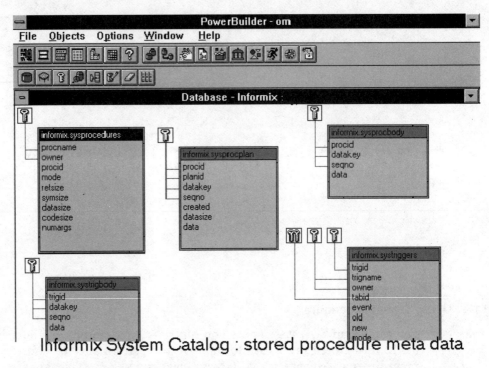

Figure 15.1   Informix system catalog, stored procedure meta data.

tables SYSPROCEDURES, SYSPROCBODY, and SYSPROCPLAN (see Figure 15-1).

Subsequently, the procedure is executed according to the stored plan. Since most of the query processing work has already been performed, stored procedures execute almost instantaneously. The following example stored procedures work with the warehouse sample database. We will use examples here to fast-track all of you through most of the important SPL statements. They are documented to give an integrated flavor to stored procedures construction. The stored procedure comments begin with --.

```
------------------
-- CREATE a Stored procedure upd_ship_hist
--      the procedure passes two arguments, integer and smalllint
--      they are passed as sku and qty
--      the procedure returns one arguments integer
--      they are passed as nrows (the number of rows updated)
create procedure upd_ship_hist(sku integer, qty smallint)
returning int;
-- define variables of type date, smallint, and integer
   define w_e_date date;
   define old_qty smallint;
   define nrows integer;
-- uncomment the following to begin debugging
   -- set debug file to "/tmp/sqltrace" with append;
   -- trace on;
-- SQL select a date from the options table and
-- assign it to w_e_date
```

```
      let w_e_date = (select week_ending_date from options);
-- use SQL update ship_history table rows that :
--                  have sku = the passed parm sku
--                  and week-ending date = option table value
--    >>>  increase  the quantity by the passed argument qty
   update ship_history
         set quantity = quantity + qty
         where ship_history.sku = sku and
                ship_history.week_ending_date = w_e_date;
   -- CHECK the sqlcode returned from the SQL invocation
if sqlca.sqlcode < 0 then
      error " Error code = ", sqlca.sqlcode "has occurred"
      ..................

-- assign the SQLCA variable containing the number of rows
--                   affected by the UPDATE
   let nrows = dbinfo("sqlca.sqlerrd2");
-- use the IF/THEN/ELSE construct
--   if the number or rows updated = 0, then INSERT a row
--      if there is no history, then create some
   if nrows = 0, then
-- SQL inserts a row into ship_history using the
--            passed arguments and the option table value
   insert into ship_history (sku, week_ending_date, quantity)
                 values (sku, w_e_date, qty);
-- CHECK the sqlcode returned from the SQL invocation
-- if the sqlcode is less than zero, then something might be wrong
--      it is prudent to log such occurrences for de-facto review
if sqlca.sqlcode < 0 then
      error " Error code = ", sqlca.sqlcode "has occurred"
      ..................
-- end the IF block
   end if
-- return # of rows affected
   return nrows;
-- end the procedure definition
end procedure;
-------------------
-- DROP Procedure  (used in construction/development cycle)
drop procedure item_lookup;
-- CREATE Procedure to lookup receiving one value, return 7 values
create procedure item_lookup(sku integer)
      returning int, char(30), int, char(1), int, int, float, int, int;
-- DEFINE variables
  define desc char(30);
  define inpack int;
  define taxflag char(1);
  define retail int;
  define promo int;
  define histavg float;
  define backstock int;
  define ordqty int;
  define nrows int;
  define w_e_date date;
  define osflag char(1);
-- uncomment for use of DEBUG IF NECESSARY
  -- set debug file to "/tmp/sqltrace" with append;
  -- trace on;
-- SQL Select into the host variables from product or sku_master
--           where the sku = the passed value
select description, inner_pack, tax_flag, retail_price, promo_price
      into desc, inpack, taxflag, retail, promo
      from sku_master
      where sku_master.sku = sku;
-- CHECK the sqlcode returned from the SQL invocation
if sqlca.sqlcode < 0 then
```

```
                       error " Error code = ", sqlca.sqlcode "has occurred"
                       ..................
-- Return 7 (zero or blank) values if desc null
   if desc is null then
     return 0, " ", 0, " ", 0, 0, 0, 0, 0;
   end if
--select columns for the options table ( 1 row table)
   select week_ending_date, order_ship_flag
     into w_e_date, osflag
     from options;
-- CHECK the sqlcode returned from the SQL invocation
if sqlca.sqlcode < 0 then
       error " Error code = ", sqlca.sqlcode "has occurred"
       .................:.
-- if the options flag is "O" then calculate
--    the average quantity for all orders in the last 14 weeks
--      based upon ORDER history, ELSE use SHIPMENT history
  if osflag = "O" then
     select avg(quantity) into histavg from order_history
       where order_history.sku = sku and
             week_ending_date between (w_e_date - (14 * 7))
and                                   (w_e_date - 7);
   else
     select avg(quantity) into histavg from ship_history
       where ship_history.sku = sku and
             week_ending_date between (w_e_date - (14 * 7))
and                                   (w_e_date - 7);
   end if
   if histavg is null then
     let histavg = 0;
   end if
   select quantity into backstock
     from back_stock
     where back_stock.sku = sku;
-- CHECK the sqlcode returned from the SQL invocation
if sqlca.sqlcode < 0 then
       error " Error code = ", sqlca.sqlcode "has occurred"
       .................

   if backstock is null then
     let backstock = 0;
   end if
     select quantity into ordqty
        from orders
        where orders.sku = sku;
-- CHECK the sqlcode returned from the SQL invocation
if sqlca.sqlcode < 0 then
       error " Error code = ", sqlca.sqlcode "has occurred"
       .................
   if ordqty is null then
     let ordqty = 0;
   end if
-- RETURN 7 values
   return 1, desc, inpack, taxflag, retail, promo, histavg,
   backstock, ordqty;
--   END Procedure
end procedure;
--------------------
-- DROP Procedure  (used in construction/development cycle)
drop procedure drop_sku_master;
-- CREATE Procedure to drop a table if it exits
create procedure drop_sku_master()
  on exception in (-206)
-- table doesn't exist
  end exception;
-- execute DDL to DROP a table
```

```
    drop table sku_master;
end procedure;
--------------------
-- DROP Procedure  (used in construction/development cycle)
drop procedure make_sku_tr;
create procedure make_sku_tr()
-- execute procedure to CREATE TRIGGER (special stored procedure)
    create trigger sku_ins_tr
-- the TRIGGER is based on INSERTS to table sku_master
        insert on sku_master
-- new rows in sku_master are referenced with qualifier post_ins
        referencing new as post_ins
-- for each row execute the procedure passing the new values
        for each row (execute procedure upd_ship_hist
        (post_ins.sku,post_ins.ship_qty));
end procedure;
------------------
-- DROP Procedure  (used in construction/development cycle)
drop procedure make_sku_master;
-- This stored procedure creates the sku_master table
create procedure make_sku_master()
  create table sku_master
   (sku integer,
    description char(30),
    retail_price integer,
    promo_price integer,
    inner_pack integer,
    tax_flag char(1),
    ship_qty smallint);
-- CHECK the sqlcode returned from the SQL invocation
if sqlca.sqlcode < 0 then
     error " Error code = ", sqlca.sqlcode "has occurred"
        .................
-- execute the stored procedure make_sku_tr
   execute procedure make_sku_tr();
-- CHECK the sqlcode returned from the SQL invocation
if sqlca.sqlcode < 0 then
     error " Error code = ", sqlca.sqlcode "has occurred"
        .................
end procedure;
------------------
-- DROP Procedure  (used in construction/development cycle)
drop procedure make_sku_idx;
-- create a procedure to CREATE a UNIQUE INDEX
create procedure make_sku_idx()
   create unique index sku_master_idx on sku_master (sku);
end procedure;
------------------
-- DROP Procedure (used in construction/development cycle)
drop procedure backup_sku;
-- procedure to backup table by renaming it & creating a new one
create procedure backup_sku()
-- test the situation -206 no table -319 no index -634 no object
  on exception in (-206, -319, -634)
   end exception with resume;
-- if objects exist, drop them
   drop index sku_master_idx;
   drop trigger sku_ins_tr;
   drop table sku_master_old;
   rename table sku_master to sku_master_old;
   execute procedure make_sku_master();
      insert into sku_master
         select * from sku_master_old;
end procedure;
------------------
drop procedure restore_sku;
```

```
create procedure restore_sku()
  -- -206 no table -319 no index -634 no object
  on exception in (-206, -319, -634)
  end exception with resume;

  execute procedure drop_sku_master();
  rename table sku_master_old to sku_master;
  execute procedure make_sku_tr();
  execute procedure make_sku_idx();

  drop table ship_history;
  execute procedure make_ship_hist();
  insert into ship_history
    select * from ship_hist_old;
  execute procedure make_ship_hist_idx();
end procedure;
-------------------
End of Example procedures
-------------------
```

15.1.1 Setting up stored procedures

You create stored procedures with the CREATE PROCEDURE command. You can run this command from DB-Access or any database administration tool, e.g., PowerBuilder (see Figure 15-2). The syntax for creating a stored procedure named pr_table1 is as follows:

```
create procedure pr_table1
..-- SPL & SQL statements
end procedure
```

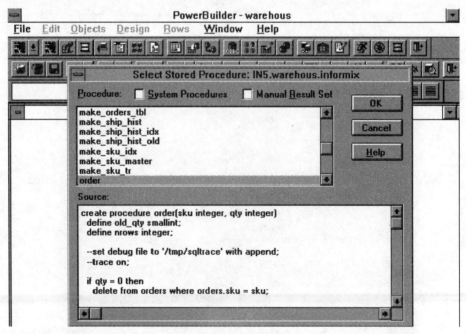

Figure 15.2 Displaying stored procedures with PowerBuilder.

To execute the stored procedure pr_table1, use the EXECUTE PROCEDURE or CALL command, invoked within an E/SQL C program or a GUI front end (PowerBuilder):

```
execute procedure pr_table1
```

The syntax for creating a simple stored procedure without special features such as parameters is:

```
create procedure procedure_name
    SQL_statements & SPL statements
end procedure
```

Stored procedures are database objects, and their names must follow the rules for identifiers. You can include any number and kind of SQL statements, with the exception of CREATE PROCEDURE and CREATE DATABASE statements. A procedure can be as simple as a single statement that lists the names of all the users in a database:

```
create procedure pr_proclist
    select procname from sysprocedures
end procedure
```

To execute a stored procedure, use the keyword `execute` and the name of the stored procedure. You can execute pr_proclist in this way:

```
execute pr_proclist
```

To execute a stored procedure on a remote Informix, you must give the machine name. The full syntax for a remote procedure call is:

```
execute db@server_name:procedure_name
```

A procedure can include more than one statement:
```
create procedure pr_showall

    select count(*) from sysusers
    select count(*) from sysobjects
    select count(*) from syscolumns
end procedure
```

When the procedure is executed, the results of each command occur and are displayed (DB-Access) in the order that the statement appears in the procedure. Control-of-flow statements such as IF THEN ELSE determine the path or sequence of the command execution. When a CREATE PROCEDURE command is successfully executed, the procedure's name is stored in sysprocedures, and its text in a sysprocbody table.

Stored procedures can serve as security mechanisms, since users can be granted permission to execute a stored procedure even if they do not have permission for tables or views referenced in it, or permission to execute specific commands. The stored procedure must be owned by the same person who owns the table or view. As a database changes, you must reoptimize the original query plans used to access its tables by recompiling them. Informix saves you

the work of having to find, drop, and recreate every stored procedure and trigger by recompiling at each procedure invocation (more on this later). The complete syntax for the CREATE PROCEDURE command is:

```
create procedure [owner.]procedure_name[;number] [[
(]@parameter_name datatype
   [= default] [output] [, @parameter_name datatype [=
default] [output]]...[)]]
   sql_statements
end procedure
```

You can create a procedure in the current database only. Here is the complete
syntax statement for the EXECUTE command:

```
execute : [execute] [@return_status = ] [[[ server .]
database .] owner .] procedure_name
      [[@ parameter_name  =] value ¦ [@ parameter_name
      =] @ variable [output]
   [,[@ parameter_name =] value ¦ [@ parameter_name =]
   @ variable [output]...]]
```

For example:

```
create procedure raise prices (per cent int) parameters
update stock     /* statement block*/
   set unit price=unit price +(unit price * (percent/100));
end procedure
```

15.1.2 CREATE PROCEDURE

To reiterate, a stored procedure is created with a SQL statement called CRE-
ATE PROCEDURE. When this statement is executed, the procedure is parsed,
optimized, and stored in the database, ready for execution. The procedure
name can be any unique name up to 18 characters used to reference the stored
procedure. The statement block is the group of Informix SPL (stored procedure
language) statements and Informix SQL statements that are executed when
the procedure is executed. All the statements in the statement block must be
delimited by semicolons (;). The parameters are composed of data passed to the
procedure from the process that executes the stored procedure.

WITH LISTING IN

The WITH LISTING IN option allows you to put compile-time warnings in a
file. This option stores the compile-time warnings in a file. Without this option,
the compiler will not generate a list of warnings.

A procedure must not exceed 64K in size. This includes all SQL, SPL, blanks,
and tabs. (Blanks, tabs, and new lines are allowed anywhere in the stored procedure text).

Stored procedure comments

```
create procedure sp_raise_prices (per_cent int)
update sku_master −increase by percentage procedure comments
set retail_price = retail_price+(retail_price * (per_cent / 100))
```

```
end procedure
 document
     "USAGE: EXECUTE PROCEDURE "p_raise_price" (xxx)",
        "xxx = Percentage from 1 - 100"
with listing in "warn file";
```

This stored procedure raises the price of all sku_master items in a specified percentage (whatever is passed in when the procedure is executed). The statement block begins with the first statement after the CREATE PROCEDURE statement and ends with an END PROCEDURE statement.

Document clause

The document clause lets you put any comments in your procedure that can be selected by a program at run-time, if needed. The example document clause in the previous section contains a usage statement that shows a user or programmer how to run the stored procedure. You can extract executing the following SQL statement:

```
select data, seqno
from sysprocbody b, sysprocedures p
where b.procid = p.procid
     and p.procname = "sp_raise_prices"
     and b.datakey = "D"
order by b.seqno;
```

This option is helpful for users or programmers who want to understand the purpose of a stored procedure without having to extract and read the code.

15.1.3 Executing a stored procedure

```
Procedure name
execute procedure sp_raise_prices (5)
execute procedure db@servername:sp_raise_prices(5)
```

The EXECUTE PROCEDURE command is a SQL statement and can be run from DB-Access or most Informix and third-party application tools, e.g., PowerBuilder. You must either own the procedure or have permission to execute the procedure (given via the GRANT statement).

You can execute a remote procedure by specifying the server name and database. This feature is useful because you have to store code in only one database, and that code can be shared by users connected from remote systems. This feature is available only with OnLine and not the SE version of Informix. The tables that are in SQL statements in the remote procedure belong to the database where the procedure resides unless they are qualified by a database name. You cannot call a remote procedure from another remote procedure, as this constitutes a multihop connection. Calling a remote procedure from another remote procedure will cause the following error:

```
-556 Cannot create, drop, or modify a remote object
```

Note that your OnLine database server must be configured properly to access a remote database. For more information, consult the Informix-Online Dynamic Server Administrator's Guide.

As mentioned, a stored procedure is recompiled at each invocation. This can be expensive if the procedure is used many times in a process. You can avoid this recompilation by using the PREPARE command. Preparing the EXECUTE PROCEDURE statement improves performance if the statement is executed many times within a program.

```
let p_percent = 5
prepare proc_stmt from "execute procedure sp_raise_prices (?)"
execute proc_stmt using p_percent
```

15.1.4 Preparing an EXECUTE PROCEDURE

Preparing the EXECUTE PROCEDURE statement improves performance if the statement is executed many times within a program. The PREPARE statement eliminates the need to parse and optimize the EXECUTE PROCEDURE statement every time it is executed. Preparing the EXECUTE PROCEDURE statement is also necessary if the application tool does not support the EXECUTE PROCEDURE syntax. For example, you must prepare the EXECUTE PROCEDURE statement if you are compiling with Informix-4GL version 4.*x* or version 6.0. Failure to do so will result in a syntax error during the compile. It is not necessary to prepare the statement if you are using Informix-NewEra.

The example in the previous section shows the Informix-4GL syntax to prepare the EXECUTE PROCEDURE statement.

15.1.5 Passing variables into a stored procedure

```
create procedure sp_delete_order (p_sku_num int default null)
   delete from order
      where order.sku = p_sku_num;
   end procedure;
execute procedure sp_delete_order (1001)
```

You can pass variables into a stored procedure at runtime. In this example, the value of the item also known as the sku number p_sku_num (1001) to be deleted is passed via the EXECUTE PROCEDURE statement. Note that the CREATE PROCEDURE statement must declare every value being passed in. The variables must be declared inside of the parentheses. You can give default values to variables that are passed into procedures. The number of parameters in the EXECUTE statement should be less than or equal to the number of parameters in the CREATE PROCEDURE statement. Any parameters not passed in are given their default value or else are undefined. The assignment of values is from left to right.

You can also execute the procedure by tagging each value with its respective variable name (as defined in the stored procedure). For example:

```
execute procedure sp_delete_order (p_sku_num=1001)
```

15.1.6 Returning values from a stored procedure

You can return one or more values from a stored procedure. Typically in an update you are sending a row image (the key or a set of columns), and receiving back a return code and perhaps a row count. To set up a procedure to accomplish this, you need to make two additions to your procedure:

A RETURNING clause in the CREATE PROCEDURE statement. This clause describes the type of data that will be returned from the procedure. In this example, you know that the procedure will return two integers.

A RETURN SPL statement. This statement, when executed, returns execution back to the calling routine along with any variables to be returned.

The values in the RETURNING clause must match, in number and type, the values in the RETURN statement. You can, however, return no values back to the calling routine (so your choices are all or none). Any variables returned should either be assigned a value through a LET statement, passed into the procedure with a value, or assigned a default value.

You can return values up to 32K in length. You use the DEFINE statement to define variables used in a stored procedure. Depending on which front end you use, you will need to determine and set up a command set for executing Informix-stored procedures, i.e., initiating, sending data to, and receiving data from the procedure. There are a host of tools: PowerBuilder, Forte, Delphi, and Visual Basic, as well as the Informix tools we will discuss in this section. The application tool receives returned values from a stored procedure similar to the way it receives returned values from a SELECT statement. Review the following procedure and note the RETURNING and RETURN syntax:

```
create procedure sp_delete_order (p_sku_num int)
   returning int, int;           Two integers will be returned
   define item_count   int;
   select count (*) into item_count from items
      where item.sku = p_sku_num;
   delete from items
      where item.sku = p_sku_num;
   delete from  orders
      where item.sku = p_sku_num;
   return p_sku_num, item_count;   here count is returned
end procedure
executive procedure sp_delete_order (1001)
```

The following examples illustrate how some Informix application interfaces execute stored procedures. Notes on the front-end procedure interfaces follow the code. It is prudent to check with each vendor to ensure that your GUI-to-Informix interface is set up properly and is optimized for integrity and performance.

Informix-4GL

```
prepare prep statement from "execute procedure
                         sp_delete_order(?)"
declare del_curs cursor for prep stmt
open del_curs using p_sku_num
   fetch del_curs into p_sku_num,   p_item_count
close del_curs
```

You must prepare the EXECUTE PROCEDURE statement because Informix-4GL version 4.*x* does not recognize EXECUTE PROCEDURE syntax. You must use a cursor even if only one set of values is being returned. (The EXECUTE statement cannot store returned data.)

Informix-ESQL/C

```
exec sql execute procedure
   sp_delete_order (:p_sku_num) into
   :p_sku_num, :p_item_count ;
```

You can use the EXECUTE PROCEDURE statement in ESQL/C (version 5.0 or later). In ESQL/C, host variables are used for values passed into the stored procedure and values returned from the stored procedure.

DB-Access

```
execute procedure sp_delete_order (1001)
```

DB-Access displays the returned values on the screen for you. Using the INTO clause for the EXECUTE PROCEDURE statement is not necessary (and not allowed).

PowerBuilder

```
DECLARE logical_procedure_name PROCEDURE FOR
   INFORMIX_procedure_name
   ({:arg1,:arg2, ...})
   {USING transaction_object};
create procedure "p_delete_order (:p_sku_num) into
   :p_sku_num, :p_item_count as _..
end procedure

declare del_order_proc procedure for
"p_delete_order(:p_sku_num)
into :p_sku_num, :p_item_count using sqlca;

execute del_order_proc (1001);
```

PowerBuilder requires a declarative statement to identify the database-stored procedure that is being used and specify a logical name. The logical name is used to reference the procedure in subsequent SQL statements. The general syntax for declaring a procedure is:

```
DECLARE logical_procedure_name PROCEDURE FOR
   INFORMIX_procedure_name
   ({:arg1,:arg2, ...})
   {USING transaction_object};
```

where logical_procedure_name can be any valid PowerBuilder identifier and INFORMIX_procedure_name is the name of the stored procedure in the Informix database. The parentheses after INFORMIX_procedure_name are required even if the procedure has no parameters. You can create a stored procedure within PowerBuilder by changing the TerminatorCharacter value in database preferences to something other than a semicolon (;), for example, the ¦ character, which is available on some keyboards by pressing Shift–\ (holding down Shift and pressing the backslash key). You must do this because Informix uses semicolons in its internal syntax. You can then create stored procedures in the Database Administration painter. The parameter references can take the form of any valid parameter string that Informix accepts. PowerBuilder does not inspect the parameter list format except for purposes of variable substitution. The USING clause is required only if you use a transaction object other than the default transaction object (SQLCA).

You specify the EXECUTE statement the same way regardless of whether a stored procedure takes arguments. The arguments used in the DECLARE statement get passed automatically, without your having to state them in the EXECUTE statement.

15.1.6.1 The RETURN statement

There are two ways to use the RETURN statement. When a RETURN is executed, control is returned to the calling routine (either another stored procedure or the application), and all variables are reset to undefined. The next time the procedure is called, it is started over. When a RETURN WITH RESUME is executed, control is returned back to the calling routine. But the next time the stored procedure is called (via a fetch or the next iteration of a FOREACH) by the calling routine, all variables keep the same values and execution continues at the statement immediately following the RETURN WITH RESUME statement.

You can return variables, the result of another stored procedure call, or an expression back to the calling routine. Returned values can include variables, expressions, or procedures.

```
return p_sku_ num;
return p_sku_num with resume;
```

WITH RESUME will resume execution of the stored procedure. All variables keep their same value. The next fetch will cause the control to go to a statement after RETURN.

15.1.6.2 Returning multiple sets of values

You can return more than one set of values to an application from a stored procedure. This happens most frequently when more than one row has been selected in the stored procedure and needs to be returned. It is necessary to open a cursor and call a procedure in a loop using FETCH or FOREACH when using ESQL, Informix-NewEra, Informix-4GL, or perhaps PowerBuilder to call a stored procedure returning more than one row. The DB-Access query language option handles the looping for you. In ESQL, every time the fetch executes, the procedure that has RETURN WITH RESUME continues and a new row is returned. Once the procedure ends, the END PROCEDURE statement is executed and no values are returned, and the next FETCH statement executed for the cursor returns a SQLCODE of 100 or NOTFOUND. A RETURN without values or END PROCEDURE signals the NOTFOUND condition. You can use a scroll cursor in the application to move through the returned rows in different ways (previous, last, first, etc.).

DB-Access

```
execute procedure get items ( )
```

Informix-4GL

```
prepare prep stmt from "execute procedure get items ( ) *
declare geti cursor for prep stmt
foreach geti into p stock num, p mfg code, p quality
end foreach
```

PowerBuilder

```
FETCH sp_procedure_example
     INTO :part_var1,:part_var2,:part_var3;;
IF (sqlca.sqlcode =100 ) _. You are through
```

The example at the end of this section shows how to select and return more than one row in a stored procedure. The FOREACH statement opens a cursor for the SELECT statement immediately following the FOREACH keyword. The FOREACH statement does the following:

- Declares a cursor.
- Opens the cursor.
- Fetches a row.
- Executes any statements within the FOREACH loop.
- Repeats the fetch and executes until no more rows are found.

The RETURN . . . WITH RESUME statement returns three variables back to the calling routine (either another stored procedure or the application program). The statement that will be executed the next time the stored procedure is called by the calling routine (via a fetch or the next iteration of a FOREACH) is the END FOREACH statement. Rows will continue to be returned until no more rows are found. At that time, control automatically breaks from the FOREACH statement and the procedure ends. Here is an example of returning multiple sets of values:

```
create procedure sp_get_items ( )
   returning integer, char (3), integer;
      define p_stock_no integer;
      define p_mfg code char (3)/
      define p_quantity integer;
      foreach
         select stock_num, mfg_code, quantity
         into p_stock_no p_mfg_code, p_quantity
         from items
         return p_stock_no p_mfg_code, p_quantity
                   with resume;
      end foreach; <-Control will continue from this point after the resume
end procedure
```

15.1.7 Remote procedure calls

Remote procedure calls are not treated as part of a transaction, i.e., there is no two-phase COMMIT. If you execute a remote procedure call after beginning the transaction, and then roll back the transaction, data modification remote procedure calls and any changes the remote procedure call made on remote data will not be rolled back. You must make sure to check all conditions that might trigger a rollback before issuing a remote procedure call that will alter remote data.

You can execute procedures on another Informix from your local Informix. Once both servers are properly configured, you can execute any procedure on the remote Informix simply by using the server name as part of the identifier. You can pass one or more values as parameters to a remote procedure from the batch or procedure that contains the EXECUTE statement for the remote procedure. Therefore, if you execute a remote procedure call as part of a transaction and then roll back the transaction, any changes that the remote procedure call made on a remote Informix will not be rolled back.

15.2 What Are Batches and Control-of-Flow Language?

Up to this point, each example in the chapter has consisted pretty much of an individual statement. You submit individual statements to Informix one at a time, entering statements and receiving results interactively. Informix can also process multiple statements submitted as a batch, either interactively or from a file. A batch of SQL statements is terminated by an end-of-batch signal that instructs Informix to go ahead and execute the statements. Technically speaking, a single SQL statement can constitute a batch, but it is more common to think of a batch as containing multiple statements. Frequently, a batch of statements is written to an operating system file before being submitted to ESQL or DB-Access. Stored Procedure Language provides special keywords called control-of-flow language that allow users to control statements' flow of execution. You can use control-of-flow language in single statements, batches, stored procedures, and triggers. Without control-of-flow language, separate SQL statements would be performed sequentially, as they occurred. Control-of-flow language permits statements to connect and to relate to each other via programming-like constructs.

Control-of-flow language constructs such as if . . . elif (for conditional performance of commands) and for, foreach, and while (for repetitive execution) let you refine and control the operation of SQL statements. Stored Procedure Language's control-of-flow language transforms standard SQL into a very high-level programming language.

if. Defines conditional execution.

elif. Defines alternate execution when the if condition is false.

begin. Beginning of a statement block.

end. End of a statement block.

while. Repeat performance of statements while condition is true.

end while. Exit from the end of the next outermost while loop.

continue. Transfer execution to next loop iteration.

define. Declare local variables.

return. Exit unconditionally.

raisexception. Print a user-defined message or local variable on the user's screen and set a system flag in the global variable.

if . . . elif . . . else construct

The keyword if, with or without its companion else, introduces a condition that determines whether or not the next statement is executed. The SQL statement executes if the condition is satisfied, that is, if it returns TRUE. The else keyword introduces an alternate SQL statement that executes when the if condition returns FALSE. The syntax for if, elif, and else is:

```
if boolean_expression
    statement
elif boolean_expression
    statement
else statement
end if;
```

A Boolean expression is an expression that returns TRUE or FALSE. It can include a column name, a constant, any combination of column names and constants connected by arithmetic or bitwise operators, or a subquery, as long as the subquery returns a single value. If the Boolean expression contains a SELECT statement, it must be enclosed in parentheses and it must return a single value.

If . . . else constructs are frequently used in stored procedures where they test for the existence of some parameter. You can nest if . . . else condition if tests either within another if test or following an else. The expression in the if test can return only one value. Also, for each if . . . else construct, there can be only one SELECT statement for the if and one for the else. To include more than one SELECT statement, use the begin . . . end keywords as described in the following section.

begin . . . end construct

The begin and end keywords enclose a series of statements and specify that they be treated as a unit by control-of-flow constructs like if...else. A series of statements enclosed by begin and end is called a statement block. The syntax of begin . . . end is:

```
begin
    statement block
end
```

Without begin and end, the if condition would apply only to the first SQL statement. The second statement would execute independently of the first.

With control of flow, you also need some variables to save and restore data while the procedure is executing. A variable is an entity assigned a value that can change during the batch or stored procedure in which the variable is used. Informix has two kinds of variables: local and global. Local variables are user-defined; global variables are supplied by the system and are predefined.

Local variables are declared, named, and typed with the Define keyword, and assigned an initial value with a SELECT command variable assignment and LET statement. They must be declared, assigned a value, and used all within the same batch or procedure. Local variables are often used in a batch or stored procedure as counters for FOREACH loops or if . . . else blocks. When they are used in stored procedures, they are declared for automatic, noninteractive use by the procedure when it executes. You can use local variables as arguments to print or raisexception. Local variables are assigned the value NULL when they are declared, and can be assigned the null value by a LET statement. The special meaning of NULL requires that comparison between null-valued variables and other null values follows special rules.

15.2.1 Defining variables

All variables used in a stored procedure must be defined in the stored procedure with the DEFINE statement. DEFINE is not an executable statement and must appear before any other statements in a statement block.

```
create procedure sp_todays_orders(p_sku_num int)
   define p_order_date date;
   define p_customer_num like orders.customer_num;
...
end procedure
```

You can use any SQL data type except SERIAL to define a variable. If you define a variable for TEXT or BYTE data, the variable is only a pointer to the data. Variables passed into a program must be defined in the CREATE PROCEDURE statement. Variables can have the same name as columns. If there is a variable with the same name as a column used in a SQL statement, the procedure will assume that the variable name is being referenced, not the column name. To reference the column, qualify the column name with the table name. For example:

```
SELECT * from orders where orders.sku_num =
```

15.2.1.2 Types of variables

A variable can be defined as local (the default) or global. A local variable is defined for the duration of the execution of the stored procedure or statement block. A global variable is defined in a stored procedure for the duration of the session. It can be used in any stored procedure, although it must be defined in each stored procedure where it is used (even though space is allocated only once). A global variable carries its value from procedure to procedure until the session process ends. You must supply a default value for every global variable that is defined. The default is used only the first time a procedure references the global variables. The default is ignored on all subsequent calls.

```
create procedure sp_proc1( )
    returning int;           A default value is required
    define global gi_variable int default 1;
    let gi_variable = gi_variable + 1;
    return gi_variable;
end procedure;
create procedure sp_proc2( )
    returning int;
    define global gi_variable int default 4;
    let gi_variable = gi_variable + 1;
    return global var;
end procedure;
```

In the previous example, the variable gi_variable is defined with a default value in both procedures, but it is effectively the same variable. The first procedure executed with the global variable supplies the default value. If the procedures were executed in the following order:

```
execute procedure sp_proc1( );
execute procedure sp_proc2( );
```

the value of gi_variable would be 3. If the procedures were executed in this order:

```
execute procedure sp_proc2 ( );
execute procedure sp_proc1 ( );
```

the value of gi_variable would be 6.

15.2.1.2 Assigning values to variables

If variables are not assigned a value, they have an undefined value. The undefined value is treated very differently than a NULL value. Any attempts to use those variables will result in an error. It is best to assign a value to a variable before it is used, by using a LET statement.

The LET keyword is required. The right-hand side of the LET statement can contain any SQL expression that can be used in a WHERE clause except an aggregate expression. For example:

```
let c = 10; let d = 5;
let p_order_date = today;
let a,b = 10, c+d;
let a,b = (select columna, columnb from table1 where columna=10);
let a = proc_name ( );
let a = c||d
```

You can assign values to more than one variable at a time, as shown in the previous example. When a value is assigned to a variable in a stored procedure, the procedure attempts to convert the value to the data type supplied. The LET statement will fail if it cannot convert the value.

15.2.2 Statement blocks

Every stored procedure has at least one statement block, which is a group of SPL and SQL statements. There is an implicit statement block that begins after the CREATE PROCEDURE statement and continues to the end of the procedure. You can define explicit statement blocks by using the BEGIN and END statements. Explicit statements blocks allow you to:

- Define variables to be used only within the statement block.
- Handle exceptions differently within the statement block.

A variable is valid within a statement block and any statement block nested within that statement block, unless it is redefined.

```
create procedure sp_show_var ( )
    returning integer;
    define variable_1 integer;
    let variable_1 = 1
    begin
        define variable_1  integer;
        let variable_1  = 2;
    end
    return variable_1 ;
end procedure
```

In this example, variable_1 is defined in the outer statement block and in the nested statement block. This means there are two different, independent variables called variable_1, and variable_1 takes on a value of 2 only within the nested statement block. The value that gets returned for the other variable_1 is 1. Don't try this at home.

15.2.2.1 FOREACH loop

A FOREACH loop declares and opens a cursor, fetches rows, and then closes the cursor. A cursor is a pointer to the results of either a SELECT statement or a stored procedure. A FOREACH loop is required if a SELECT statement or an EXECUTE PROCEDURE might return more than one row.

```
foreach select ship charge into p ship charge
Select statement returning>1 row
                    from orders
...
end foreach;
foreach execute procedure delete order ( ) into p item num
...
end foreach;
```

The statements inside this loop will be executed as many times as there are rows returned from the SELECT or EXECUTE PROCEDURE statements. When the FOREACH statement contains an EXECUTE PROCEDURE statement, the loop continues until:

- The RETURN statement in the called procedure is executed without any parameters.
- The END PROCECURE statement in the called procedure is executed.

If no rows are returned, the statements in the loop will not be executed at all. Scroll cursors are not allowed in a stored procedure. (A scroll cursor allows you to move backward within a selected list.)

15.2.2.2 Using an update cursor

An update cursor puts an update lock on a row so no other process can update the row until either the next row is fetched (if it was only read) or an update or delete has occurred and the transaction has ended. An update cursor is useful if you do not want other users to change the row between the moment it is fetched into your procedure and the moment it is changed.

A stored procedure will use an update cursor automatically if there is a WHERE CURRENT OF clause in any UPDATE or DELETE statement in the statement block within the FOREACH loop. You must explicitly name the cursor (as in the previous example) if you are using the WHERE CURRENT OF clause.

```
create procedure sp_delect_order ( )
   define p_ship_date date;
   begin work;
   foreach cursorl for
      select ship date into p_ship_date from orders
         where order_date < today - 100
      if p_ship_date is not null then
         delete from orders where current of cursorl;
      end if;
   each foreach;
   commit work;  Locks are released for updated rows.
end procedure;
```

15.2.2.3 IF-THEN-ELSE

The IF-THEN-ELSE structure in a stored procedure consists of three clauses and their corresponding statements:

IF condition. If the condition following the IF statement is evaluated to true, then the statements following are executed.

ELIF condition. The ELIF condition is evaluated only if the IF condition is evaluated to false. If the condition following the ELIF keyword is evaluated to true, then the statements following are executed.

ELSE condition. The statements following the ELSE are executed if neither the IF condition nor any of the ELIF conditions are true. An IF statement can include 0 or more ELIF conditions are 0 or 1 ELSE clauses.

```
create procedure sp_check_order (p_order_num int)
...
   if p_ship_date is null then
      execute procedure sp_notify_shipping (p_order_num);
      let exception code = 1;
   elif p_paid_date is null then
      execute procedure sp_notify_acctrecv (p_order_num);
      let exception code = 2;
   else
      let exception code =3
   end if;
...
end procedure;
```

15.2.2.4 WHILE loop

A WHILE statement evaluates any statement that can evaluate to true or false, and executes until the condition is false. The condition is evaluated at the beginning of each iteration. If the condition is evaluated to null, it will be translated to false and the loop will terminate.

```
create procedure sp_test_rows (nbr_rows int)
   define i integer;
   let i =1;
   while I < nbr rows
      insert into table1 values (I);
      let i=i+1;
   end while;
end procedure;
```

15.2.2.5 FOR loop

You can execute and control the FOR loop in a number of times. The loop can be executed in two ways:

Using a range (e.g., 1 to 20). You can include the increment if you want. The default increment is 1 (or –1, as in the case of FROM 20 TO 1).

Including expressions (e.g., IN(I,5,10)). You can include any expression (the result of a singleton SELECT statement if okay) within the parentheses, as long as it matches the variable type after the FOR keyword.

Since a FOR loop is guaranteed to terminate, there are two controls in place to assure that termination occurs:

- You cannot change the value immediately following the FOR keywork (I in the previous example) within the FOR loop.

- When the FOR statement is executed, the expressions are evaluated before the loop begins execution.

```
for I=1 to 10 step 2                    Loop executed 5 times
...
end for;
for i in (1, 5, 10, 15, 20, 25)   Loop executed 6 times
...
end for;
```

You can exit a FOR, FOREACH, or WHILE loop with an EXIT statement in a stored procedure. The EXIT statement exits the innermost loop and resumes execution at the statement following the loop. You can skip the rest of the statements in the loop with the CONTINUE statement. Execution continues at the top of the loop with the next iteration.

```
for i=1 to 10
   if  i=5 then
      continue for;
   elif  i=8 then
      exit for;
   end if;
end for;
```

15.2.2.6 Operating system commands

```
system "backup -i tables >backup.1st"
system "echo" "Backup Operation Started""¦ mail dba";
```

You can execute operating system commands with the SYSTEM command. You enclose the command in quotes, as shown in the example. You can also use the double pipe symbol (¦¦) to concatenate expressions together for the SYSTEM statement. The database server will wait until the command is complete before continuing. You cannot use values returned from the command in your stored procedure. If the system call fails (a nonzero status is returned), that value will be placed in the ISAM error code with an appropriate value in the SQL error code.

Semicolons (;) should be placed after every statement in a stored procedure: the FOR, FOREACH, and WHILE statements and the END FOR, END FOREACH, and END WHILE statements. The rules are similar with the IF and ON EXCEPTION statements. If you have a RETURNING clause in the CREATE PROCEDURE statement, use a semicolon after the RETURNING clause.

15.3 What Is a Trigger?

A trigger is a special kind of stored procedure that goes into effect when you insert, delete, or update data in a specified table. Triggers can help maintain the referential integrity of your data by maintaining consistency among logically related data in different tables. Referential integrity means that primary key values and corresponding foreign key values must match exactly.

The main advantage of triggers is that they are automatic. They work no matter what caused the data modification: a clerk's data entry or an application action. A trigger is specific to one or more of the data modification operations (update, insert, or delete). The trigger is executed once per SQL statement; it fires immediately after the data modification statements are completed. The trigger and the statement that "fires" it are treated as a single transaction that can be rolled back from within the trigger. If a severe error is detected, the entire transaction will roll back.

15.3.1 In what situations are triggers most useful?

Triggers can "cascade" changes through related tables in the database. Triggers can disallow, or "roll back," changes that would violate referential integrity, canceling the attempted data-modification transaction. Such a trigger might go into effect when you try to insert a foreign key that does not match its primary key. Triggers can enforce restrictions much more complex than those defined with rules. Unlike rules, triggers can reference columns or database objects. Triggers can also perform simple "what if" analyses. For example, a trigger can compare the state of a table before and after a data modification, and take actions based on that comparison.

As an alternative to using triggers, you can use the referential integrity constraint of the CREATE TABLE statement to enforce referential integrity across tables in the database. However, referential integrity constraints differ

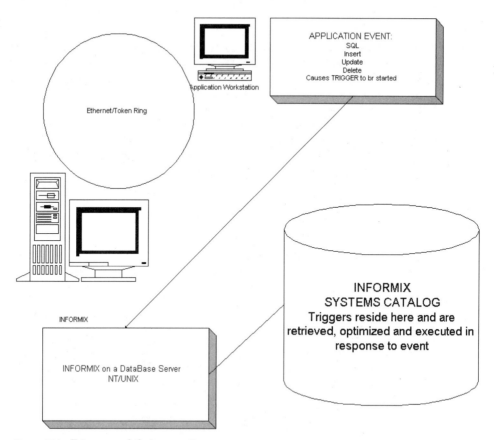

Figure 15.3 Triggers and their execution.

from triggers in that they cannot perform the following tasks (as previously described):

- "Cascading" changes through related tables in the database.
- Enforcing complex restrictions by referencing other columns or database objects.
- Performing "what if" analyses.

In addition, referential integrity constraints do not roll back the current transaction as a result of enforcing data integrity. With triggers, you can roll back or continue a transaction depending on how you handle referential integrity. If your application requires one of the tasks that can be performed only by triggers, obviously you need to use triggers. Otherwise, referential integrity constraints offer a simpler way to enforce data integrity. Note that Informix checks referential integrity constraints before any triggers, so a data-modification statement that violates the constraint does not also fire the trigger.

15.3.2 Creating triggers

A trigger is a database mechanism that executes a SQL statement automatically when a certain event occurs. It is available starting in the 5.01 release of Informix-SE and Informix-OnLine. The event that can trigger an action can be an INSERT, UPDATE, or DELETE statement on a specific table. The UPDATE statement that triggers an action can specify either a table or one or more columns within the table. The table that the trigger event operates on is called the triggering table. When the trigger event occurs, the trigger action is executed. The action can be any combination of one or more INSERT, UPDATE, DELETE, or EXECUTE PROCEDURE statements.

Triggers are a feature of the database server, so the type of application tool used to access the database is irrelevant in the execution of a trigger. By invoking triggers from the database, a DBA can ensure that data is treated consistently across application tools and programs.

A trigger is a database object. When you create a trigger, you specify the table and the data modification commands that should "fire" or activate the trigger. Then you specify the action or actions the trigger is to take. Since triggers execute as part of a transaction, the following are not allowed in a trigger: All CREATE commands, including CREATE DATABASE, CREATE TABLE, CREATE INDEX, CREATE PROCEDURE, CREATE DEFAULT, CREATE RULE, CREATE TRIGGER, and CREATE VIEW. Triggers are used to maintain referential integrity, which assures that vital data in your database—such as the unique identifier for a given piece of data—remains accurate and can be used as the database changes.

You coordinate referential integrity by using primary and foreign keys. The primary key is the column or combination of columns that uniquely identifies a row. It cannot be null and it must have a unique index. A table with a primary key is eligible for joins with foreign keys in other tables. Think of the primary key table as the master table in a master-detail relationship. The foreign key is a column or combination of columns whose values match the primary key. A foreign key doesn't have to be unique. They are often in a many-to-one relationship to a primary key. Foreign key values should be copies of the primary key values: no value in the foreign key should ever exist unless the same value exists in the primary key. A foreign key can be null; if any part of a composite foreign key is null, the entire foreign key must be null.

Tables with foreign keys are often called detail or dependent tables to the master table. Referential integrity triggers keep the values of foreign keys in line with those in the primary keys. When a data modification affects a key column, triggers compare the new column values to related keys by using temporary work tables containing the table column deltas or changes. When you write your triggers, you base your comparisons on data that is temporarily stored in the trigger test tables. When you insert a new foreign key row, you want to make sure the foreign key matches a primary key. The trigger should check for joins between the inserted row or rows and the rows in the primary key table, and then roll back any inserts of foreign keys that do not match a key in the primary key table.

When you delete a primary key row, you should delete corresponding foreign key rows in dependent tables. This preserves referential integrity by ensuring that detail rows are removed when their master row is deleted. If this were not done, you could end up with a database that had detail rows that could not be retrieved or identified. A trigger that performs a cascading delete is required.

In actual practice, you might want to keep some of the detail rows, either for historical purposes (to check how many sales were made on discontinued titles while they were active) or because transactions on the detail rows are not yet complete. A well-written trigger should take these factors into consideration. Since a primary key is the unique identifier for its row and for foreign key rows in other tables, you want to be very careful when updating a primary key. In this case, you want to protect referential integrity by rolling back the update unless specified conditions are met.

Generally speaking, it's best to prohibit any editing changes to a primary key, for example by revoking all permissions on that column. But if you do want to prohibit updates only under certain circumstances, use a trigger.

A change or update to a foreign key by itself is probably an error. A foreign key is just a copy of the primary key; the two should never be independent. If for some reason you want to allow updates of a foreign key, you might want to protect integrity by creating a trigger that checks updates against the master table and rolls them back if they don't match the primary key.

Multirow considerations are particularly important when the function of a trigger is to automatically recalculate summary values, that is, ongoing tallies. Triggers used to maintain summary values should contain GROUP BY clause triggers that use GROUP BY clauses, or subqueries that perform implicit grouping, to create summary values when more than one row is being inserted, updated, or deleted.

The trigger is stored in two system catalog tables, systriggers and systribody, and other dictionary tables are put in the database server memory. Before an INSERT, UPDATE, or DELETE statement is executed by the database server, the dictionary in the database server memory is scanned for a trigger that exists for the table and type of SQL statement being executed. If a trigger exists, it is retrieved, optimized, and executed by the database server at the appropriate time.

15.3.3 Why use triggers?

Triggers can restrict how data is manipulated in a database. Without some enforcement of these restrictions, the programmer or SQL user is free to manipulate data in any way (assuming that he/she has permission to do so). Some examples of how triggers can be used are:

Business rules. This term refers to the way a business uses data. Triggers can be used to enforce business rules for data within a database. An example of a business rule might be: If inventory for an item reaches a certain level, automatically place an order to restock the item.

Derived values. In some cases, it might be necessary to store a derived value, such as an account balance, in a database. Using triggers to do this forces the derived value to be synchronized with the values from which it is derived.

Table replication. You can use triggers to replicate changes to a table automatically. Three triggers would be needed: one for inserted rows, one for updated rows, and one for deleted rows. The duplicate table could reside in the same database, or in a different database on another machine.

Audit trials. An organization might need to record certain transactions in an audit table. Triggers will assure that all the specified transactions are recorded. For example, if an employee's salary gets changed, you can add an audit record to the audit table, specifying the change made and the login of the person who made the change.

Cascading deletes. By using triggers, you can specify if a row in a table is deleted, that corresponding information in another table is automatically deleted at the same time. For example, if an order is deleted, the corresponding items for an order is also deleted. Although cascading deletes are part of referential integrity starting with version 6.0 database servers, earlier versions of the database server can use triggers to perform the same function.

Security authorization. You can use triggers to augment database security that already exists. For example, triggers can check for a date before authorizing a change, or allow only certain people to create orders greater than $1000.
You use the CREATE TRIGGER statement to store the trigger event and trigger action in the database server. It is an SQL statement that can be executed by applications compiled with tools that support the statement. You must be either the owner of the table or the database administrator to create a trigger on a table. Each trigger must be given a trigger name, which is unique within the database for which it is created. Each trigger also has a trigger event and trigger action. You can use the correlation names to reference values of the row before and after it is changed.

15.3.4 Trigger events

Multiple UPDATE triggers are allowed for a table, but column lists must be mutually exclusive. If columns are not listed, all columns are assumed, and only one UPDATE trigger is allowed.

A trigger event is the SQL statement that triggers the specified action. The trigger event can be an INSERT, UPDATE, or DELETE SQL statement. The table that the trigger event operates on is sometimes referred to as the triggering table. Only one trigger is allowed for the operation and table combination, except for the UPDATE statement. This means that there can by only one INSERT trigger event for a table and only one DELETE trigger event for a table.

The UPDATE trigger event can include one or more columns within a table, but columns in UPDATE triggers for a table must be mutually exclusive. This means that, if there are five columns in a table, there can be at most five UP-DATE triggers for the table (one for each column). If you have an UPDATE trigger for the entire table (not specifying columns), only one UPDATE trigger is allowed. The table specified by the trigger event must be a table in the current database. You cannot specify a remote table. The following is an example of a trigger:

```
drop procedure make_sku_tr;
create procedure make_sku_tr()
   create trigger sku_ins_tr
         insert on sku_master
         referencing new as post_ins
         for each row(execute procedure
                          upd_ship_hist(post_ins.sku,
post_ins.ship_qty));
end procedure;
```

15.3.5 Trigger action

Every trigger has a trigger action, the action that occurs when the trigger event occurs. The trigger action consists of one or more INSERT, UPDATE, DELETE, or EXECUTER PROCEDURE statements that can be executed at one of the following times:

Before the trigger event occurs. The BEFORE trigger action executes once before the trigger event executes. Even if no rows are processed by the trigger event, the BEFORE trigger actions will still be executed.

After each row is processed by the trigger event. The FOR EACH ROW trigger action occurs once after each row is processed by the trigger event.

After the trigger event completes. The AFTER trigger action executes once after the trigger event executes. If no rows are processed by the trigger statement, the AFTER trigger action will still be executed.

You cannot reference the trigger table in any of the trigger action SQL statements, with the exception of an UPDATE statement that updates columns not listed in the trigger table and SELECT statements in a subquery or stored procedure.

16

Preparing the Operational Database

In this chapter we discuss some of the planning you must do prior to installing Informix-OnLine on a UNIX system. We examine special considerations you should take into account, based on dependencies you might have and system resources. We also discuss various disk considerations, with respect to performance and recovery, as well as which system files must be updated. In addition, we describe some UNIX security commands and show you how to designate ownership and permissions for access to designated file systems.

16.1 Planning for the Informix-OnLine Dynamic Server

When planning for OnLine, you need to consider certain priorities, such as what type of performance you expect and what resources will be available for its implementation.

16.1.1 Getting started

As you prepare to install Informix OnLine software on your UNIX system, you should examine the system to see what resources are available. The specific items you must take into account are:

- How much memory is available on the system?
- How many tape drives are available?
- How much disk space do I require?
- Is there enough disk space available?
- How many CPUs are on the system?
- What other applications are running on the system?
- What type of availability is required?

```
SunOS Release 5.4 Version Generic_Patch [UNIX(R) System V Release 4.0]
Copyright (c) 1983-1994, Sun Microsystems, Inc.
mem = 65536K (0x4000000)                    ← How much memory is installed on this system?
avail mem = 63528960                        ← How much memory is available to the users?
Ethernet address = 8:0:20:11:xx:xx
root nexus = SUNW,Sun 4_75
sbus0 at root: obio 0xf8000000
dma0 at sbus0: SBus slot 0 0x400000
esp0 at sbus0: SBus slot 0 0x800000 SBus level 3 sparc ipl 3
sd3 at esp0: target 3 lun 0                 ← What disk or disks are attached to this system?
sd3 is /sbus@1,f8000000/esp@0,800000/sd@3,0
    <SUN0424 cyl 1151 alt 2 hd 9 sec 80>
Unable to install/attach driver 'isp'
root on /sbus@1,f8000000/esp@0,800000/sd@3,0:a fstype ufs
zs0 at root: obio 0xf1000000 sparc ipl 12
zs0 is /zs@1,f1000000
zs1 at root: obio 0xf0000000 sparc ipl 12
zs1 is /zs@1,f0000000
cgsix0 at sbus0: SBus slot 2 0x0 SBus level 5 sparc ipl 7
cgsix0 is /sbus@1,f8000000/cgsix@2,0
cgsix0: screen 1152x900, single buffered, 1M mappable, rev 6
Unable to install/attach driver 'stc'
le0 at sbus0: SBus slot 0 0xc00000 SBus level 4 sparc ipl 5
le0 is /sbus@1,f8000000/le@0,c00000         ← How many hardware communications
                                               interfaces do I have?
stl2: <Exabyte EXB-8500 8 mm Helical Scan>  ← This segment was taken from another system to
                                               show how a tape drive is displayed.
stl2 at esp1:
target 5 lun 0
stl2 is /io-unit@f,e1200000/sbi@0,0/dma@0,81000/esp@0,80000/st@5,0
```

Figure 16.1

16.1.2 Gathering the information

The instructions in this chapter will allow you to answer all these questions (the commands have been executed on both a SunOs 4.1.3 system as well as on a Solaris 2.4 system). To determine the system's hardware resources, perform a dmesg command. The output will resemble Figure 16.1.

To see which file systems are currently mounted on your system, issue the df (SunOs) or df -k (Solaris or SVR4) command. Refer to Table 16.1, which is a sample output from a df -k command from a Solaris 2.4 system.

TABLE 16.1

File system	Kilobytes	Used	Avail.	Capacity	Mounted on
/dev/sd0a	47863	18397	24686	43%	/
/dev/sd0b	225383	200601	2252	99%	/usr
/proc	0	0	0	0%	/proc
fd	0	0	0	0%	/dev/fd
/dev/sd0e	47863	21027	22056	49%	/var
swap	826520	1020	816200	1%	/tmp
/dev/sd1a	71943	64426	327	99%	/opt

Additionally, the directory /var/adm contains multiple message files. You can browse these files, which contain output from the UNIX syslog facility, with the more command. There you will see messages similar to the messages displayed with the dmesg command. Another location where you can browse for disk assignment information is /etc/fstab on a SunOs system, or /etc/vfstab on Solaris 2.4 and other SVR4-based systems. You can use the UNIX cat utility to browse these files.

16.1.3 Examining the disk

In order to determine the layout of disks installed on your system, you have to use the UNIX format command. Here is a brief session of invoking the format command. To execute this command, you must become the super-user, root.

1. Upon initial invocation of the format command, the system will return the screen shown in Figure 16.2.

2. Once you have selected your disk, you receive the format primary menu, shown in Figure 16.3.

3. Format returns the following prompt:

   ```
   format> p (option "p" has been selected for partition)
   ```

   and you receive the partition menu, shown in Figure 16.4.

4. After selecting `print`, the format utility returns the display shown in Figure 16.5.

5. You can now see the actual size of each partition on the disk. In addition, the response to the partition prompt of help will return the screen in Figure 16.6.

6. At this point, respond with `quit` and you will exit the format program.

In this example, done on a Solaris 2.4 system, there is only a single disk attached to the system: an internal disk divided into eight partitions, numbered 0 through 7. Partition 2 is a reserved partition and should never be modified. It defines the total size of the disk, the disk in the example being 404.65MB in size. This disk is the system disk, and there are currently three partitions. Partition 0 is the root directory (50.27MB), partition 1 is used for swap space, and partition 6 is the /usr file system (and directory).

You can use this utility to see how the disk space installed at your sight is partitioned. You can also use this utility to modify the partitions on your disks. For a complete description of all the features provided, use the manual pages on your system.

16.2 Disk Performance Considerations

What type of disk space should you use: a raw or a cooked (UFS) partition? The UNIX operating system provides you with two types of disk spaces, raw and cooked, or, as it is more commonly called, a UFS file system. A raw file system

```
        # format                        ← Enter the format command
        Searching for disks...done      ← The system responds


        AVAILABLE DISK SELECTIONS:
           0. c0t3d0 <SUN0424 cyl 1151 alt 2 hd 9 sec 80>   ← This system has only one disk
              /sbus@1,f8000000/esp@0,800000/sd@3,0
        Specify disk (enter its number): 0                   ← The disk has been selected
        selecting c0t3d0
        [disk formatted]
        Warning: Current Disk has mounted partitions.        ← This disk is currently in use
```

Figure 16.2

```
        FORMAT MENU:
            disk      - select a disk
            type      - select (define) a disk type
            partition - select (define) a partition table
            current   - describe the current disk
            format    - format and analyze the disk
            repair    - repair a defective sector
            label     - write label to the disk
            analyze   - surface analysis
            defect    - defect list management
            backup    - search for backup labels
            verify    - read and display labels
            save      - save new disk/partition definitions
            inquiry   - show vendor, product and revision
            volname   - set 8-character volume name
            quit
```

Figure 16.3

is a partition or slice of disk that, if used in this form by an application, leaves the I/O responsibility in the hands of the application. To access the disk in this manner, you must prefix the device name with the letter *r*. Figure 16.7 is a short session of commands, performed on a SunOs 4.1.3 system, that shows you how to locate your raw file systems. The output from these commands might vary slightly on other UNIX systems, depending on the device-naming standards of the vendor.

For file systems not considered to be raw, the rsd0a is sd0a. Even though rsd0a and sd0a are the same physical device, access to the device from a performance standpoint can be very different depending on how the device is referenced. A disk is considered to be a block device in UNIX terminology. It can be configured with an interface that provides buffering, or it can be treated as

```
         PARTITION MENU:
             0    - change `0' partition
             1    - change `1' partition
             2    - change `2' partition
             3    - change `3' partition
             4    - change `4' partition
             5    - change `5' partition
             6    - change `6' partition
             7    - change `7' partition
             select - select a predefined table
             modify - modify a predefined partition table
             name   - name the current table
             print  - display the current table
             label  - write partition map and label to the disk
             quit
         partition> print          ← "print" has been selected to view the disk layout
```

Figure 16.4

```
      Current partition table (original):
      Total disk cylinders available: 1151 + 2 (reserved cylinders)

      Part    Tag    Flag   Cylinders     Size       Blocks
       0     root     wm     0 - 142      50.27MB    (143/0/0)
       1     swap     wu    143 - 370     80.16MB    (228/0/0)
       2     backup   wm     0 - 1150    404.65MB    (1151/0/0)  ← shows total disk capacity
       3 unassigned   wm      0            0         (0/0/0)        Do not modify partition 2
       4 unassigned   wm      0            0         (0/0/0)
       5 unassigned   wm      0            0         (0/0/0)
       6      usr     wm    371 - 1150    274.22MB   (780/0/0)
       7 unassigned   wm      0            0         (0/0/0)

      partition> help                        ← "Help" can be entered at any time
```

Figure 16.5

a character special device (or raw device), which uses a special interface that informs UNIX that the buffering mechanism for the device is provided by the application.

16.2.1 Cooked vs. raw file systems

When the UNIX kernel reads data from a cooked file system, it places the data into a kernel buffer pool. Later, a second copy operation copies the data from the buffer and places it in the location that the application has designated for it. This means that, although the data has been read from the disk once, if multiple users want to read the data, then it will be copied from the buffer multi-

```
Expecting one of the following: (abbreviations ok):
    0    - change `0' partition
    1    - change `1' partition
    2    - change `2' partition
    3    - change `3' partition
    4    - change `4' partition
    5    - change `5' partition
    6    - change `6' partition
    7    - change `7' partition
    select - select a predefined table
    modify - modify a predefined partition table
    name   - name the current table
    print  - display the current table
    label  - write partition map and label to the disk
    quit
```

Figure 16.6

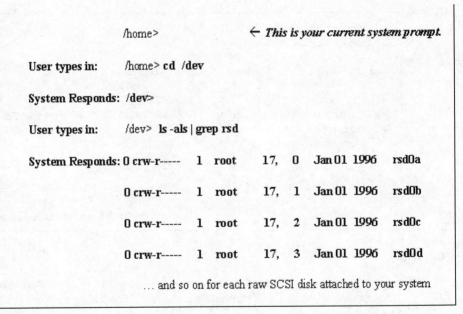

Figure 16.7

ple times. Had this been a raw disk device, given the proper application the kernel buffer would have been bypassed and the data copied directly to the location requested by the application.

Informix-OnLine places the data into shared memory, where it immediately becomes available to all OnLine virtual processors and running threads without any further copying. Although it might be easier to define a cooked file system, you could sacrifice performance by not using a raw file system. If you decide to use a raw file system, you will have to change the ownership and permissions for the raw device.

16.2.2 Changing the ownership of a raw file system

In order to change the ownership of a raw file system, you need the root ID. File systems are typically assigned by the system administrator. Prior to issuing any of these commands, check with your system administrator to ensure that the partition you are using is the proper size and is not being used by any other application running on your system. The following commands describe how to change the ownership of a raw file system.

First, the user must check to see which directory he or she is in by typing:

```
/home> pwd
```

The system responds with:

```
/home
```

The user types in:

```
/home> cd /dev
```

The system responds with:

```
/dev>
```

The user types in:

```
/dev> ls -als | grep rsd
```

The system responds with:

```
0 crw-r-----   1   root   17,   0   Jan 01  1996   rsd0a
0 crw-r-----   1   root   17,   1   Jan 01  1996   rsd0b
0 crw-r-----   1   root   17,   2   Jan 01  1996   rsd0c
0 crw-r-----   1   root   17,   3   Jan 01  1996   rsd0d
```

The user types in:

```
/dev> chmod 660 rsd0a
```

and:

```
/dev> ls -als | grep rsd0a
```

The system responds with:

```
0 crw-rw----  1   root   17,   0   Jan 01 1996   rsd0a
```

The user types in:

```
/dev> chown informix rsd0a
```

and:

```
/dev> chgrp informix rsd0a
```

and:

```
/dev> ls -als ¦ grep rsd0a
```

The system responds with:

```
0 crw-rw----  1   informix   informix 17,  0   Jan 01 1996 rsd0a
```

Note: Managing file systems is an important function and should always be performed with caution. The system will not prevent you from modifying the permissions of an active file system, so you should document the usage of raw file systems within /etc/fstab or /etc/vfstab (depending on the release of UNIX you are using). Do this by using a comment, since raw file systems are not mounted via the UNIX mount command. You can also see which UFS file systems are currently mounted on your system by issuing the df command.

Warning: If you decide to use a raw partition and decide to use partition A (SunOs) or partition 0 (Solaris or most SVR4-based systems), be certain that you skip cylinder 0. This is where the disk's internal information is kept, and it will be destroyed if you make this a raw partition and load your database onto it. You can use the format utility to redefine this partition, starting at cylinder 1.

16.3 Modifying the Appropriate System Files

If this is the first time you have installed Informix on your system, then you must perform some initial tasks before you can get started. The four main files that need to be updated are /etc/group, /etc/passwd, /etc/services, and /etc/hosts.

16.3.1 The /etc/group file

The /etc/group file is part of the UNIX security scheme. Each login ID must be a member of a group, so you must define a group that the Informix login ID belongs to. To do this on a single system, you have to edit the /etc/group file. Here is a sample of what the /etc/group file entries look like on a SunOs system:

```
informix:*:101:
```

(The basic structure of an entry within the group file would be as follows: groupname:password:group-id-#:user-list. In addition, the group ID must be greater than 100, and the numbers from 0 through 100 are reserved for system functions. The user list should always be left blank, which will prevent any other users from becoming a member of this group.) The entries continue:

```
daemon:*:1:
kmem:*:2:
bin:*:3:
tty:*:4:
operator:*:5:
news:*:6:
uucp:*:8:
audit:*:9:
staff:*:10:
other:*:20:
+:
```

(If the file has a last entry with a plus sign, this means that you are using NIS, which is Sun's Network Information System. If this is the case, you might want to consider having your system administrator define your informix group to NIS so it is global to all UNIX systems within the same domain.)

On Sun's Solaris systems, you will not see the plus sign because the implementation is somewhat different. Instead, there is a file known as /etc/nss-witch.nis. It is here that you will find commonly used system filenames and the search order. The group ID number must be unique for each group entry. The order of search in this group file definition would be: first the one on the local system, then the NIS map (or group file) if NIS is active. On a Solaris system, you should review the nsswitch.nis file to see what the order of search is. If you are using NIS, then be sure to run the system's make utility on the NIS server to ensure that the file has been updated for all systems within the network. If this is the case, then there should be no Informix entry in the local system's /etc/group file. Instead, you can do a ypcat group ¦ grep informix to see your entry in the NIS map.

16.3.2 The passwd file

Next, your system administrator will have to create an entry for your informix ID in the /etc/passwd file, which will belong to group 101 given the previous example. The entry in the password file should look something like this:

```
informix:Xyz/FgpySZo1:123:101:Informix id 010196:/home/informix:/bin/ksh
```

The breakdown for this entry is as follows:

```
username:pwd:unique user id #:group id #:comment field:
    home directory:login shell
```

Where username is the name you are known to the system by, pwd is your encrypted password, unique user id # a numerical ID by which the system knows the user, group id # must be the same number for the informix group file entry (a general comment field), home directory is the default directory available to the user at login, and login shell is the default shell you are placed in at login time.

Note: If you are using NIS, then be consistent with your entries; if you made the group entry into the NIS map, then you should update the NIS password in the same manner. If you are running on a Solaris or other SVR4-based system, an additional file known as /etc/shadow will contain your actual password.

The key benefit of using the NIS password file is that you have to remember only one password to access Informix on each system within your network.

16.3.3 The /etc/services file

When you configure OnLine to use the TCP/IP network protocol, you use information from this file to prepare your sqlhosts file. This file is maintained by your network administrator. The file contains an entry for each service available through TCP/IP. Table 16.2 lists some sample entries. This file can also be NIS controlled, as discussed for the passwd and group files.

16.3.4 The /etc/hosts file

This file contains an entry for each host you want to be known to TCP/IP. Each entry within the file defines a single host. Table 16.3 describes the format, along with some sample entries.

Each host that uses the Informix client/server product requires an entry in the hosts file. Each entry must be unique in order to prevent errors on your network. This file can also be controlled by NIS. If you don't find your entries in the local /etc/hosts file, then you can view the NIS map by typing `ypcat hosts`.

TABLE 16.2

Service name	Port/protocol	Aliases	Comments
online1	1526/tcp		# Informix Online
nfsd	2049/udp	nfs	# NFS server daemon

Entry online1 will be known as the service for TCP port 1526. The Online database server will be able to use this port to service client-application requests.

TABLE 16.3

Internet address	Official host name	Alias or alternate name
123.45.678.12	hoster	
123.45.678.13	rickster	
123.45.4.13	informix1	
123.45.7.14	micky3	

TABLE 16.4

# File system	Directory	File system type	Options	Freq	Pass
/dev/sd0a	/	4.2	rw	1	1
/dev/sd0g	/usr	4.2	rw	1	2
/dev/sd1g	/usr/informix	4.2	rw	1	2
/dev/fd0	/pcfs	pcfs	rw,noauto,usermount_access	0	0
#					
#	The following raw partitions have been saved for the Informix Databases				
#					
#/dev/rsd2a	this raw disk partition is reserved for the Informix database *DBname*				
#					

16.4 Creating a Directory to Install the Informix Product

Once you have the proper amount of disk space on your system, you must make a few decisions. Although Informix recommends that you call your file system /usr/informix, you can actually call it whatever you want, as long as it is local to the system. To relieve you from reproducing the installation documentation just because you decided on a different name, you can use a soft link to point to an alternate file system name. If you are using a unique partition on one of your local disks, you can create a subdirectory under the /usr directory by using mkdir and adding an entry to your /etc/fstab or /etc/vfstab file with a separate mount point for /usr/informix.

Table 16.4 is a sample of what fstab looks like on a SunOs system. In this example, we have created a directory under /usr and called it informix. When the system is booted, it will automatically be mounted. Prior to using any UFS or cooked file system, you have to run the newfs command against the particular slice or partition you want to use. If you have just created this file system with the newfs command, you can issue the UNIX mount command to make it available without rebooting your system. In addition, you should use the chown command to prevent others from writing to this directory. Since all Informix users will need access to the file system, however, you can give the group and world permissions of read and execute, using the root ID.

Following is an example of using chown and chmod for such a purpose. The user begins by typing in:

```
/> pwd
```

The system responds with:

```
/
```

The user types in:

```
/> cd /usr
```

The system responds with:

```
/usr>
```

The user types in:

```
/usr> ls -als | grep informix
```

The system responds with:

```
1 drw-r---    2    root       512 Jan    1 1996    informix
```

The user types in:

```
/usr> chmod 755 informix
```

and:

```
/usr> chown informix informix
```

and:

```
/usr> ls -als | grep informix
```

The system responds with:

```
1 drw-r-xr-x    2    informix       512 Jan    1 1996    informix
```

Optionally, you can have a file system called oemprds, as we do in sample fstab, shown in Table 16.5.

If there is sufficient space, you can create a directory under the oemprds directory and call it informix. You can still access it by using the name /usr/informix if you create what is referred to as a link. Links are a way to refer to a particular object using an alternate name. By using a link, you can refer to the

TABLE 16.5

# File system	Directory	File system type	Options	Freq	Pass
/dev/sd0a	/	4.2	rw	1	1
/dev/sd0g	/usr	4.2	rw	1	2
/dev/sd1g	/oemprds	4.2	rw	1	2
/dev/fd0	/pcfs	pcfs	rw,noauto,usermount_access	0	0

```
#
#      The following raw partitions have been saved for the Informix Databases
#
#/dev/rsd2a   this raw disk partition is reserved for the Informix database DBname
#
```

directory /oemprds/informix by the name /usr/informix. The user begins this process by typing in:

```
/> cd /oemprds
```

The system responds with:

```
/oemprds>
```

The user types in:

```
/oemprds> mkdir informix
```

and:

```
/oemprds> ls -als ¦ grep informix
```

The system responds with:

```
1 drw-r---    2    root        512 Jan    1 1996      informix
```

The user types in:

```
/oemprds> chmod 755 informix
```

and:

```
/oemprds> chown informix informix
```

and:

```
/oemprds> ls -als ¦ grep informix
```

The system responds with:

```
1 drw-r-xr-x    2    informix     512 Jan    1 1996     informix
```

The user types in:

```
/oemprds> cd /usr
```

The system responds with:

```
/usr>
```

The user types in:

```
/usr> ln -s /oemprds/informix informix
```

and:

```
/usr> ls -als ¦ grep informix
```

The system responds with:

```
1 lrwxrwxrwx  2  root  512 Jan  1 1996    informix -> /oemprds/informix
```

Note: Two items need to be clarified in this example. First, even though the permissions on the link show that everyone can read, write, and execute, this is not the case. The permissions of the informix directory under the /oemprds directory takes precedence. Second, when you refer to directory /usr/informix, you are really accessing the files under /oemprds/informix.

To ensure that you have done everything properly, provided you have taken this approach, then change to directory /usr/informix and enter the command df. The directory /oemprds/informix should appear as a result of this command.

16.5 Preparing the User Environment

Before users can begin to use Informix, the UNIX system must know where to locate files required by the product, depending on which shell you have set for your users: the Bourne, Korn, or C shell. The following environment variables are essential to all Informix users. In addition, I have included a small code segment you can insert into your .profile or .login files that will permit you to make these environment variable modifications for Informix users only, without affecting any other users of the system. The manner in which it is implemented depends on how you have defined the current users of UNIX within your company. If everyone shares a common .profile or .login file (possible via a UNIX link), then you have to make this change in only a single place. However, if everyone has his or her own individual .profile or .login file, then perhaps you can mail the code segment to your Informix users and have them make the change themselves.

The minimum required environment variables are INFORMIXDIR, which points to the directory or file system where you have installed the INFORMIX product, and the user's PATH variable, which defines the location of the binaries (or INFORMIX executables). For each INFORMIX user, create the following file in his or her HOME directory. The filename is:

```
.profile.informix
```

The file content for a Bourne or Korn shell is:

```
INFORMIXDIR=/usr/informix
export INFORMIXDIR
PATH=$PATH:$INFORMIXDIR/bin
export PATH
```

The file content for C shell users is:

```
setenv INFORMIXDIR /usr/informix
setenv PATH ${PATH}:${INFORMIXDIR}/bin
```

Add the following lines into your .profile or .login if INFORMIX is available only on specific hosts:

```
#
# (This is for INFORMIX USERS on HOST1 or HOST2)
```

```
#
if [[ `uname -n` = host1 !! `uname -n` =  host2 ]]
then
#
# (This will execute the setup for INFORMIX users)
#
if [[ -r ${HOME}/.profile.informix ]]
then
    . ${HOME}/.profile.informix
fi
#
```

This will provide you with a means of control for your Informix user community. After users log into the UNIX system, have them do a `cd $IN-FORMIXDIR`, which should put them into the /usr/informix directory. You can expand these files to provide additional INFORMIX variables, depending on which INFORMIX products and features you want to use.

For administrative purposes, consider creating links to these files so, if you decide to make changes, you will have to make the change in only a single place rather than having to customize multiple files for each individual user.

16.6 Gathering System Performance Information

Prior to installing Informix on your system, collect as much data as possible. The following system performance utility descriptions will aid you in collecting performance data. The items you must consider are the amount of memory, the amount of disk space you initially require, connectivity to the network, the number of disk controllers, and the number of tape drives. In addition to these items, you need to know the answers to the following questions:

- How many users are logged onto this system, and at what times?

- What is the peak number of users?

- What time of day is the system busiest?

16.6.1 UNIX performance utilities

Depending on which release of the UNIX operating system you are running, you might have all or none of the following performance tools on your system. The utilities covered in this section include mpstat, vmstat, iostat, swap, and sar. I have seen only mpstat, swap, and sar on SVR4 systems, such as Sun's Solaris and Pyramid systems DCOSX. The vmstat and iostat utilities are available on both architectures, as well as on SunOs.

16.6.2 MPSTAT

The mpstat utility allows you to determine cpu usage on a per-processor basis within a predetermined time interval. The output produced by mpstat shows averages for each cpu in the system. If no time interval is specified, then the output will consist of a one-line summary from the time the system was booted.

```
158 /home> mpstat 5 5

    CPU minf mjf xcal  intr ithr  csw icsw migr smtx  srw syscl  usr sys  wt idl

      0   0   0    0   104    4   33    5    0    0    0    60    2   2    0  96

      0   2   0    0   132   32   34    7    0    0    0    56    2   3    1  94

      0   0   0    0   105    5   30    5    0    0    0    46    1   1    0  97

      0   0   0    0   102    2   30    5    0    0    0    48    1   2    0  97

      0   0   0    0   105    5   31    5    0    0    0    72    1   2    0  97
```

Figure 16.8

Figure 16.8 shows an example of mpstat output on a single-cpu system. The format of the mpstat command is:

```
mpstat [time_interval_in_seconds] [number_of_times_to_run_command]
```

The definitions for the headings on the display are as follows:

CPU. Processor ID

minf. Minor faults

mjf. Major faults

xcal. Interprocessor cross-calls

intr. Interrupts

ithr. Interrupts as threads (not counting clock interrupt)

csw. Context switches

icsw. Involuntary context switches

migr. Thread migrations (to another processor)

smtx. Spins on mutexes (lock not acquired on first try)

srw. Spins on readers/writer locks (lock not acquired on first try)

syscl. System calls

usr. Percent user time

sys. Percent system time

wt. Percent wait time

idl. Percent idle time

Figure 16.9 is an example of mpstat output on a multiprocessor. In this diagram, we executed mpstat to take three snapshots at five-second intervals. This execution of mpstat was run on a multi-CPU system.

16.6.3 VMSTAT

The vmstat utility reports virtual memory statistics on a UNIX system. Like the mpstat utility, you can monitor CPU usage and determine what percentages are used by the system and the user, and how much of the CPU is idle. In addition, you can collect virtual memory, and disk and trap activity statistics. The vmstat utility is typically available on both Berkley and SVR4 systems. Figure 16.10 is an example of vmstat output.

In the following, we executed vmstat using the same parameters as input, which were previously used to execute mpstat:

```
vmstat [time_interval_in_seconds] [number_of_times_to_run_command]
```

```
172 /home> mpstat 5 3

CPU minf mjf xcal  intr ithr  csw icsw migr smtx  srw syscl  usr sys  wt idl

  0   16   5    0   455   73 1742  447   57 1633    0  6363   25  59   4  12

  1   14   4    0   625  354 1470  384   58 1431    0  6220   25  59   4  12

  2   15   4    0   618  357 1491  361   61 1473    0  6323   25  58   4  13

  3   16   4    0   386   53 1843  458   65 1534    0  6394   27  54   5  14

CPU minf mjf xcal  intr ithr  csw icsw migr smtx  srw syscl  usr sys  wt idl

  0   26  27    0   711   69 1663  805   34 1469    0  7765   33  67   0   0

  1   36  11    0  1303 1147  490  237   29 1058    0  6877   20  80   0   0

  2  110  24    0   923  571 1732  813   28 1116    0  5183   39  61   0   0

  3   54  43    0   740  279 1164  534   39 1323    0  7280   32  68   0   0

CPU minf mjf xcal  intr ithr  csw icsw migr smtx  srw syscl  usr sys  wt idl

  0   79  36    0   459   65  939  366   37 1297    0  5065   37  54  10   0

  1   21   7    0  1461 1258  761  338   22 1030    0  4825   12  85   3   0

  2   93  32    0   959  466 1400  573   42 1393    0  7106   29  61  10   0

  3   43  38    0   668  309 1411  603   42 1256    0  7048   28  64   9   0
```

Figure 16.9

```
163 /home> vmstat 5 5
 procs     memory            page            disk          faults      cpu
 r b w   avm   fre  re at  pi  po  fr  de  sr s0 dl d2 d3  in   sy  cs us sy id
 1 0 0     0   516   0  1   0   0   0   0   0  0  0  0  0  11   94  50 10  2 88
 0 0 0     0   356   0  4  12   0  12  16   8  2  0  0  0  22  155  89 27  2 71
 0 0 0     0   408   0  1   0   0   0   0   1  0  0  0  0   8  149  90 27  0 73
 2 0 0     0   456   0  0   0   0   0   0   0  0  0  0  0   3  151  91 27  2 72
 0 0 0     0   472   0  0   0   0   0   0   0  0  0  0  0   0  148  92 27  0 73
```

Figure 16.10

Once again we chose to take five snapshots in five-second intervals. The heading descriptions for the vmstat report are as follows:

procs

This is the number of processes in each of the three following states:

r. In run queue

b. Blocked for resources (i/o, paging, etc.)

w. Runable, but swapped

memory

This reports the usage of virtual and real memory. Virtual memory is considered active if it belongs to processes that either are running or have run in the last 20 seconds.

avm. Number of active virtual kilobytes

fre. Size of the free list in kilobytes (K)

page

This is information about page faults and paging activity. The information for each activity is averaged every five seconds, and given in units per second.

re. Page reclaims

at. Number of attaches

pi. Page in, kilobytes per second

po. Page out, kilobytes per second

fr. Freed, kilobytes per second

de. Anticipated short-term memory shortfall in kilobytes

sr. Pages scanned by clock algorithm per second

disk

This reports the number of disk operations per second (the field is system-dependent). In the example in Figure 16.10, s0 is for SCSI disks and the entries indicate that three additional disks are being monitored. Depending on the system type and disk device type, these headings might vary.

faults

This reports trap/interrupt rate averages per second over the last five seconds.

in. (Nonclock) device interrupts per second

sy. Number of system calls per second

cs. CPU context switch rate (switches/sec)

cpu
This gives the CPU time usage, in percentages.

us. Percentage of time performing user processes

sy. Percentage of time used by the operating system

id. Percentage of time the CPU is idle

Another format for executing the vmstat command is with a –S option. When executed this way, the vmstat command displays swapping information rather than paging information.

Figure 16.11 is an example of the vmstat command using the –S option. Note: The difference between this display and the previous example is that, under the page heading, the first two columns are si for swap in and so for swap out. Previously, they were displayed as re for page reclaims and at for number of attaches.

There are other variations of vmstat you can explore. Since vmstat is a reporting tool, you can do no harm by experimenting with it. Refer to your systems manual pages (MAN command) to see what other information you can obtain.

16.6.4 IOSTAT

The iostat utility reports I/O statistics, and can be particularly useful when you are trying to determine which disk to install the Informix product on. In addition to disk I/O activity, iostat provides reports for terminal I/O and CPU usage. Iostat obtains its information through a number of counters maintained by the system kernel. For each disk attached to your system, the kernel counts reads, writes, bytes read, and bytes written. In addition, the kernel takes time stamps at queue entry and exit points, which allows it to track residence time and the cumulative residence length for each queue. When iostat processes this information, it can measure throughput, CPU usage, transaction rates, queue lengths, and service time. For terminal devices, iostat reports the number of input and output characters.

Figure 16.12 is a sample iostat report. By default, iostat reports information on terminals, disks, and CPUs. By using various execution parameters, you can modify the reports to display only information about the particular device types you are interested in. In the example in Figure 16.12, we chose the options x, t, and c, which told iostat we wanted to report on extended disk statistics, terminal I/O counts, and CPU user, system, waiting, and idle percentage

```
165 /home> vmstat -S
 procs     memory              page                    disk        faults      cpu
 r b w    avm    fre    si so  pi  po  fr  de  sr s0 d1 d2 d3  in   sy  cs us sy id
 1 0 0      0    452 1025009  2   0   0   0   0   0  0  0  0  0  11   94  50 10  2 88
```

Figure 16.11

```
iostat -xtc 5 5
                              extended disk statistics       tty        cpu
disk    r/s  w/s   Kr/s   Kw/s wait actv  svc_t  %w  %b  tin tout us sy wt id
fd0     0.0  0.0    0.0    0.0  0.0  0.0 2251.5   0   0    0    1  2  2  0 96
sd3     0.0  0.1    0.0    0.3  0.0  0.0   39.2   0   0
                              extended disk statistics       tty        cpu
disk    r/s  w/s   Kr/s   Kw/s wait actv  svc_t  %w  %b  tin tout us sy wt id
fd0     0.0  0.0    0.0    0.0  0.0  0.0    0.0   0   0    0   61  3  2  0 96
sd3     0.0  0.0    0.0    0.0  0.0  0.0    0.0   0   0
                              extended disk statistics       tty        cpu
disk    r/s  w/s   Kr/s   Kw/s wait actv  svc_t  %w  %b  tin tout us sy wt id
fd0     0.0  0.0    0.0    0.0  0.0  0.0    0.0   0   0    0   61  3  2  0 95
sd3     0.0  0.0    0.0    0.0  0.0  0.0    0.0   0   0
                              extended disk statistics       tty        cpu
disk    r/s  w/s   Kr/s   Kw/s wait actv  svc_t  %w  %b  tin tout us sy wt id
fd0     0.0  0.0    0.0    0.0  0.0  0.0    0.0   0   0    0   61  2  3  0 94
sd3     0.0  1.4    0.0    8.8  0.0  0.1   56.1   1   3
                              extended disk statistics       tty        cpu
disk    r/s  w/s   Kr/s   Kw/s wait actv  svc_t  %w  %b  tin tout us sy wt id
fd0     0.0  0.0    0.0    0.0  0.0  0.0    0.0   0   0    0   61  3  2  0 95
sd3     0.0  0.0    0.0    0.0  0.0  0.0    0.0   0   0
```

Figure 16.12

information. Additionally, we told iostat that we wanted to take five snapshots in five-second intervals.

The following list of options are available to the iostat utility:

–c. Percentage of time the system spent in user mode, system mode, waiting for I/O, and idling.

–d. The number of kilobytes transferred per second, number of transfers per second, and average service time in milliseconds for each disk.

–D. The number of reads and writes per second, as well as the percentage of disk usage.

–l. The counts in each interval, rather than rates (where applicable).

–t. The number of characters read and written to terminals per second.

–x. Extended disk statistics.

For additional information on the execution parameters, review your manual pages. Following is a description of the headings in the report in Figure 16.12:

disk. Name of the disk

r/s. Reads per second

w/s. Writes per second

Kr/s. Kilobytes read per second

Kw/s. Kilobytes written per second

wait. Average number of transactions waiting for service, the length of the queue

actv. Average number of transactions actively being serviced

svc_t. Average service time, in milliseconds

%w. Percent of time transactions are waiting on the queue for service

%b. Percent of time the disk is busy

16.6.5 SWAP

The swap utility provides the system administrator with the capability to add, delete, and monitor swap space. Using this utility to add and delete swap space requires the super-user root ID. However, root privilege is not required for monitoring. For the purposes of this discussion, we will discuss only the monitoring capability. Figure 16.13 shows two samples that do not require the root privilege.

The following describes the O/P that was created as a result of our execution:

–l

This option lists the status of all the swap areas. The output has five columns:

swapfile. The path name for the swap area (or disk partition)

dev. The major/minor device number in decimal if it is a block special device; zeros otherwise

swaplo. The swap low value for the area in 512-byte blocks

blocks. The swaplen value for the area in 512-byte blocks

free. The number of 512-byte blocks in this area that are not currently allocated

Note: The list does not include swap space in the form of physical memory because the space is not associated with a particular swap area. For a more accurate representation of swap area usage, we prefer the –s option:

```
174 /home> swap -s
total: 468592k bytes allocated + 182172k reserved = 650764k used, 827720
175 /home> swap -l
swapfile             dev   swaplo blocks    free
/dev/dsk/c0t0d0s1    32,1       8 201592  85256
/dev/dsk/c0t1d0s1    32,9       8 610392 466160
/dev/dsk/c0t3d0s1    32,25      8 201592  94688
```

Figure 16.13

–s

This options prints summary information about total swap space usage and availability:

allocated. The total amount of swap space (in 1024-byte blocks) currently allocated for use as backing store

reserved. The total amount of swap space (in 1024-bytes blocks) not currently allocated, but claimed by memory mappings for possible future use

used. The total amount of swap space (in 1024-byte blocks) either allocated or reserved

available. The total swap space (in 1024-byte blocks) currently available for future reservation and allocation

Note: These numbers include swap space from all configured swap areas as listed by the –l option, as well as swap space in the form of physical memory.

16.6.6 SAR

Up to this point we have discussed only performance utilities that are especially useful for immediate diagnosis. Using the sar utility requires that you first enable the UNIX system accounting facility. The sar utility samples cumulative activity counters in the operating system at n intervals of t seconds, where t should be 5 or greater. If t is specified with more than one option, all headers are printed together, making the output difficult to read. If the sampling interval is less than 5, the activity of sar itself might distort the sample.

If the –o option is specified, it saves the samples in an output file in binary format. The default value of n is 1. An alternate means of execution is to specify no interval. In this case, sar will extract data from a previously recorded file, either the one specified by the –f option or, by default, the standard system activity file, known by its full pathname of /var/adm/sa/sadd, where dd represents the current day.

You can set a start and end time within your report by using the –s and –e arguments, where time is specified in the form hh:mm:ss. Optionally, you can use the –i parameter to select records at second intervals. Otherwise, all intervals found in the file are reported.

You can use the sar utility to generate many different reports, but rather than trying to produce every report, we will display just a few sample reports in the areas of disk management and CPU usage.

A sample disk usage report is shown in Figure 16.14. In this sample run, we asked sar to report all block device activity between the hours of 6 P.M. and 7 P.M. (see Figure 16.14). This report is truncated; had I displayed the full report, the bottom of the listing would have included averages for each device in the display.

The headings on the report have the following meanings:

%busy. Percentage of time that the device was busy servicing a transfer request

```
238 /var/adm/sa> sar -d -s 18:00:00 -e 19:00:00

SunOS system1 5.4 Generic sun4d      01/01/96

18:19:01   device      %busy   avque   r+w/s   blks/s   avwait   avserv

18:39:01   sd0           1      0.0       1       9       0.0     25.2
           sd1           1      0.0       0       1       0.0     13.1
           sd15          1      0.0       1       3       0.0     12.0
           sd16          1      0.0       1       6       0.0     18.9
           sd17          0      0.0       0       1       0.0     11.5
           sd19         10      0.1       7     689       0.0     14.4
           sd2           0      0.0       0       1       0.0     13.2
           sd21          1      0.0       1       5       0.0     12.2
           sd3           2      0.0       1      11       0.0     25.7
           sd30          0      0.0       0       0       0.0      0.0
           sd31          0      0.0       0       0       0.0      0.0
           sd32          0      0.0       0       0       0.0      0.0
           sd33          0      0.0       0       5       0.0     14.7
           sd34          0      0.0       0       0       0.0      0.0
           sd35          0      0.0       0       2       0.0     10.5
           sd6           0      0.0       0       0       0.0      0.0
           ssd0          1      0.0       1       3       0.0     12.2
           ssd1          0      0.0       0       1       0.0      9.6
           ssd10         0      0.0       0       1       0.0     13.8
```

Figure 16.14

avque. Average number of requests outstanding during the time in question

r+w/s. Number of reads and writes or device I/O

blk/s. Number of bytes transferred in 512-byte units

avwait. Percentage of I/O time waiting on the device

avserv. Percentage of I/O time for seek and fetch operations

For the example in Figure 16.15, we chose to monitor the CPU for a one-hour time period. You can see that, between the hour of 6 P.M. and 7 P.M., the system from a CPU standpoint is mostly waiting on I/O.
The definitions for the headings are as follows:

%usr. Percentage of time running in user mode

%sys. Percentage of time running in system mode

%wio. Percentage of time the CPU is idle with some process waiting for block I/O

idle. Percentage of CPU that is just idle

These reports are just a small portion of the information that can be reported on when you use the sar command. Additionally, if you run sar and eliminate the header on the various reports, you can then use the sar O/P as input to a spreadsheet program in order to produce charts and graphs for a better picture

```
239 /var/adm/sa> sar -u -s 18:00:00 -e 19:00:00

SunOS system1 5.4 Generic sun4d     01/01/96

18:19:01    %usr    %sys    %wio    %idle
18:39:01      7      11      82       1
18:59:01      5       8      86       0

Average        6      10      84       0
```

Figure 16.15

of what is occurring over extended periods of time. As a reminder, the manual pages can provide a world of information on this topic.

16.7 Configuration Overview

Up until now we have reviewed the system so you can see what resources are available. Much of the data we have collected will help you tailor the configuration files required by Informix OnLine. At this point, you should have decided which directory will contain the Informix product. Once you have used the UNIX tar utility to load the software onto your system, you have to decide whether you want to use a cooked file system or a raw file system for your database. Additionally, you must update key several configuration files prior to starting the Informix OnLine product. Some questions you have to answer are:

- How much data will the database hold?
- How many tables will there be in the database?
- What types of data will be processed?
- Which hardware will we be using?
- How many users will this database support?
- Are there any security concerns that need to be addressed?

16.7.1 The onconfig.std configuration file

The $INFORMIXDIR/etc/onconfig.std file is the configuration file template that comes with the Informix OnLine product. It is loaded into the $INFORMIXDIR/etc directory during the OnLine installation procedure. The onconfig.std file contains default values for the configuration parameters and serves as the template for all other configuration files that you create. Prior to building your Informix database, you should copy the onconfig.std file into an alternate file with a meaningful name, one that represents the specific use of the configuration. For example, if your database contains a company product inventory, then use the filename onconfig.prodinv. Here is a list of entries you must address:

ROOTNAME. Specifies the name of the root dbspace for this configuration. If this is the first time you are using Informix OnLine, you should probably call it rootdbs.

ROOTPATH. This is the full pathname, including the device or filename of the initial chunk of the root dbspace. If you have chosen raw disk space, Informix recommends that you create a link to the raw device name instead of the actual name.

SERVERNUM. Specifies a relative location in shared memory. Pick a number from 0 through 255. It must be unique for each online database server on your system.

DBSERVERNAME. Although the default is the hostname for the system you have installed your database on, you should pick a more descriptive name, possibly including the name of the host. If you are using multiple communications protocols, such as IPX/SPX and TCP, then you also need to assign a name to the DBSERVERALIAS variable.

TAPEDEV. Specifies the device the ontape utility uses to archive your data. Additionally, it specifies the default device to which data is loaded or unloaded when you use the –l option of the onload or onunload utilities.

LTAPEDEV. Specifies the device where the logical logs are backed up to when you use the ontape utility. Additionally, it specifies to which device data is loaded or unloaded when you use the –l option of the onload or onunload utilities.

16.7.2 The sqlhosts configuration file

The $INFORMIXDIR/etc/sqlhosts file is the connectivity file. It contains information that enables an Informix client application to connect to any Informix database server on the network. It specifies the database server name, type of connection, name of the host computer, and service name. You must prepare the sqlhosts file even if both the client application and the OnLine database server are on the same computer.

The sqlhosts file has the following format: The DBSERVERNAME is myhost_prodinv; the NETTYPE is ontlitcp; the HOSTNAME is myhost, and the SERVICENAME is online1, where DBSERVERNAME is the value you provided in the onconfig.prdinv name.

The nettype is broken down in the following manner: The first two characters are either on or ol for the Informix OnLine product, se for Informix-SE, or dr for Informix-Gateway with DRDA. The middle three characters are ipc for interprocess communications, soc for a socket connection, or tli for transport-level interface. The final three characters are shm for shared memory, tcp for the TCP/IP network protocol, or spx for the IPX/SPX network protocol.

16.7.3 Environment variables used by OnLine

We have mentioned Informix variables in various areas throughout this book, even earlier in this chapter when describing the .profile file. We therefore thought it would be appropriate to list the following variables, since they are required to initialize the Informix OnLine product:

INFORMIXDIR. The directory or full pathname where you installed the product.

PATH. The directory or directories that UNIX will search to locate your executables.

ONCONFIG. The full pathname, including the onconfig filename, you have chosen.

INFORMIXSERVER. The same value you assigned to the DBSERVERNAME variable in your onconfig file.

Depending on which shell you are using, you will use either the setenv commands for the C shell or export to set the variables.

Note: If the ONCONFIG environment variable is not present, OnLine will use configuration values from the file $INFORMIXDIR/etc/onconfig. If INFORMIXSERVER is not set, OnLine will not build the sysmaster tables. Also, INFORMIXSERVER is required for the ON-Monitor and DB-Access utilities.

The following environment variables are not required for initialization, but they must be set before you can use OnLine with an application:

- TERM

- TERMCAP or TERMINFO (optional)

- INFORMIXTERM (optional)

The TERM, TERMCAP, TERMINFO, and INFORMIXTERM environment variables specify the type of terminal interface. You might need assistance from the UNIX system administrator to set these variables because they are highly system-dependent.

16.8 Configuring an OnLine Test Environment

If you have never configured an OnLine environment, the following step-by-step approach is a good starting point. You might want to follow this test to become more familiar with the product. The test environment allows you to prepare a working OnLine database server with a minimum of time and effort. It is also a quick way to check that the new OnLine system is working correctly, i.e., that the installation was successful.

The instructions in this section allow you to build an OnLine database server that is suitable for a few users and moderate-sized databases. This environment is not expected to serve as a final configuration; it just allows you to see a working OnLine database server. After you have some practice using OnLine, you can reconfigure the database server for a production environment.

The following is the sequence for creating a test environment, and each step is then described in detail in the following sections:

1. Log in as user informix.
2. Choose names for your configuration file and your database server.
3. Set environment variables.
4. Allocate disk space for data storage.
5. Prepare an ONCONFIG configuration file.
6. Prepare the connectivity file (sqlhosts).
7. Start OnLine.
8. Experiment with OnLine.

16.8.1 Log in as user informix

Most administrative tasks require that you log in as user informix or user root. For this example, you should log in as user informix.

16.8.2 Choose configuration names

Choose a name for your ONCONFIG configuration file that indicates how the file is used. The examples in this section use the name onconfig.test for the ONCONFIG file. Choose a name for your OnLine database server. This name is called the dbservername. You will use the dbservername when you set environment variables in the ONCONFIG configuration file and in the sqlhosts file. The examples in this section use the name test_online. The dbservername must be 18 or fewer characters and can include lowercase characters, numbers, and underscores. It should begin with a letter. The database sever name must be unique within your network, so we recommend choosing a descriptive name, such as online_hostname or testsrv_online1.

16.8.3 Set environment variables

Before you start the configuration process, set the following environment variables:

INFORMIXDIR. Environment variable to the full pathname of the directory in which OnLine is installed.

PATH. Environment variable to include the $INFORMIXDIR/bin directory. You should place this in front of your existing PATH.

ONCONFIG. Environment variable to the configuration file you just chose: onconfig.test.

INFORMIXSERVER. Environment variable to the database server name you just chose: test_online.

If you have forgotten how to set your environment variables, then just refer back to our description of the .profile file earlier in the chapter. The following example illustrates setting the ONCONFIG environment variable in the C shell and the Bourne (or Korn) shell. For the C shell:

```
setenv ONCONFIG onconfig.test
```

For the Bourne or Korn shell:

```
ONCONFIG=onconfig.test
export ONCONFIG
```

16.8.4 Allocate disk space for data storage

The UNIX operating system allows you to use two different types of disk space: raw and cooked. Cooked disk space or UFS file system refers to ordinary UNIX files. It is space that has already been organized and that UNIX administers for you. Raw disk space is unformatted space that OnLine administers. OnLine allows you to use either type of disk space (or a mixture of both types).

To gain the full benefits of OnLine, you must use raw space. However, cooked space is easier to use and is acceptable for many environments. The instructions for the test environment assume that you are using cooked space. To understand the benefits of raw vs. cooked file systems, see the discussion earlier in this chapter. Informix refers to its biggest unit of physical disk storage as a chunk. For your test environment, you will create an ordinary UNIX file (a cooked file). The file you create becomes one chunk.

The cooked file for your test environment should be in a directory that you control and that has sufficient allocated space. The default values given in the configuration file require 20 megabytes of disk space. Do not put your cooked file space in the home directory of user informix, nor in the directory where the executable code for the OnLine database server is installed ($INFORMIXDIR).

Hint: The default values in the configuration file assume that you are starting an active, medium-sized production system. If your test environment is short of space, you can reduce the default value of ROOTSIZE from 20 megabytes to 7 megabytes, without changing other parameters in your ONCONFIG file.

16.8.5 Preparing the cooked file space

The details for setting up a cooked file space vary slightly from one UNIX installation to another. Table 16.6 shows a typical example of the commands you need to prepare the cooked disk space. This example assumes that you plan to store the cooked space in the file /test/data/root_chunk.

16.8.6 Prepare the ONCONFIG configuration file

The ONCONFIG configuration file contains values for parameters that describe the OnLine environment. You can have several different ONCONFIG

TABLE 16.6

Step	Command	Comments
1	% cd /test/data	Change directories to the directory where the cooked space will reside.
2	% cat /dev/null > root_chunk	Create your root chunk by writing nulls to a file. We recommend that you name this file something descriptive, such as root_chunk, to simplify keeping track of your space.
3	% chmod 660 root_chunk	Set the permissions of the file to 660 (rw-rw--).
4	% ls – lg root_chunk	Verify that both group and owner of the file are Informix.
	–rw-rw----1 informix informix 0 Apr 13 08:12	You should see something similar to this line (which is wrapped around in this example).

configuration files to describe different environments, such as test, development, and production.

All OnLine configuration files reside in the $INFORMIXDIR/etc directory. One of the files loaded during the installation of OnLine is onconfig.std (OnLine configuration standard). It contains default values for the ONCONFIG parameters and serves as the template for any other ONCONFIG configuration files that you create. Do not modify onconfig.std since others might want to use it as a template for their own personalized copy of this file.

To prepare a configuration file for the test environment, copy onconfig.std into your own configuration file and then modify the parameters. Informix provides a menu-based utility called ON-Monitor, which you can use to modify the configuration file. Since you need to modify only a few values for the test environment, however, it will probably be simpler to use a text editor, such as vi or emacs.

16.8.7 Prepare the ONCONFIG file for a test environment

To prepare the ONCONFIG file for a test environment, follow the steps outlined in this section. First, change directories to $INFORMIXDIR/etc and copy the onconfig.std file into a new file in that directory, using the name that you chose for your ONCONFIG file. For example:

```
cd $INFORMIXDIR/etc
cp onconfig.std onconfig.test
```

You can use $INFORMIXDIR as a variable to relieve you from excessive typing. The second step is to edit onconfig.test to modify the following parameters:

ROOTPATH /test/data/root_chunk. ROOTHPATH is the full directory pathname of the cooked file space that you created in the previous section. In this example, the pathname of the cooked space is /test/data/root_chunk.

TAPEDEV /dev/null and LTAPEDEV /dev/null. Setting these parameters to /dev/null allows OnLine to behave as if tape drives were present and log files were being backed up, but in fact the output to tape is discarded. With these settings, you cannot restore data. Also, ON-Archive does not work if LTAPEDEV is set to /dev/null. For a production environment or to gain experience working with archive-and-backup tools, set TAPEDEV and LTAPEDEV to actual devices.

DBSERVERNAME test_online. Change the DBSERVERNAME parameter to the dbservername you chose for your database server. This example uses test_online. You already used the dbservername when you set the INFORMIX SERVER environment variable. You will also use the dbservername in the next section when you prepare the sqlhosts file. INFORMIXSERVER tells an application which database server to use, and sqlhosts tells the application how to connect to the database server.

SERVERNUM some_number. Change the SERVERNUM parameter to some integer between 0 and 255. Each different OnLine instance must have a distinct value. You could leave SERVERNUM set to its default value 0 for your first OnLine instance, but that could cause problems in ON-Monitor when you start to initialize a second OnLine instance. It is safer to set SERVERNUM to a unique, nonzero value each time you make a new ONCONFIG file.

MSGPATH a_pathname. If you installed the OnLine executables in the /usr/informix directory, then set this parameter to /usr/informix or whatever directory you want your message log to be stored in.

16.8.8 Prepare the connectivity file

The sqlhosts file contains information that allows a client application to connect to a database server. For the test environment, you can use the simplest possible connection using shared memory.

16.8.9 Prepare the sqlhosts file for the test environment

The sqlhosts file should already be present. If it is not, create it. Edit the sqlhosts file using a text editor, as shown in the following example:

```
vi $INFORMIXDIR/etc/sqlhosts
```

You need to add one line (one entry) to the sqlhosts file. The entry has the following four fields:

- The dbservername. You already used the dbservername to set the INFORMIX SERVER environment variable and as the value of the DBSERVERNAME parameter. This example uses test_online.
- The type of connection. For a shared-memory connection, the necessary value is onipcshm.
- The name of your host computer (UNIX command: uname –n).
- The service name.

For a shared-memory connection, the following statements are true:

- The service name can be any short group of letters and numbers. This example uses the value ontest.

- The service name for a shared-memory connection does not need to appear in a network connectivity file (/etc/services).

You can separate the fields in the sqlhosts file with spaces or tabs. If the host name of your computer is myhost, the sqlhosts entry will look like this:

```
test_online onipcshm myhost ontest
```

16.8.10 Start OnLine running

To start OnLine running for the first time, you must initialize both the disk space and the shared memory used by the OnLine database server. To do this, execute the following command (Warning: When you execute this command, all existing data in the OnLine disk space is destroyed. Use the –i flag *only* when you are starting a brand-new OnLine system):

```
% oninit -i
```

If you want to stop OnLine, execute the following command:

```
% onmode -k
```

This command asks if you really want to take OnLine offline. It then tells you how many users are currently using OnLine and asks if you want to proceed. If you answer Y to both questions, OnLine will go to offline mode (stop running). If you stop OnLine and want to restart it without destroying the information on disk, use this command:

```
% oninit
```

You can also start or stop OnLine using the ON-Monitor Mode menu.

16.8.11 Experiment with OnLine

The OnLine product includes DB-Access, an application that allows you to create and query databases and tables. DB-Access is installed as part of the installation process for OnLine. DB-Access includes scripts to create a practice database that you can use to try out various OnLine features.

16.9 Informix OnLine Startup and Shutdown

To automate your Informix OnLine startup and shutdown, we have included a sample script you can use in a UNIX SVR4 environment (see Figure 16.16). We recommend that you place this script into your /etc/init.d directory, and create links to it in either your /etc/rc2.d or /etc/rc3.d directories. This decision is based on which run state your system normally operates in. To find out your

```
#!/sbin/sh
#
# /etc/rc3.d/S85informix - start/stop Informix server process
#
# Created by: Rich Bambara          DATE: January 1, 1996
#
##################################################################################
#
INFORMIXDIR=/usr/informix
export INFORMIXDIR
PATH=$INFORMIXDIR/bin:/home/informix

case $1 in
'start')

    if [ -f /usr/informix/bin/oninit ]; then
         /home/informix/.profile .informix
    su - informix -c /usr/informix/bin/oninit
    fi
    ;;

'stop')

    if [ -f /usr/informix/bin/oninit ]; then
         /home/informix/.profile .informix
    su - informix -c /usr/informix/bin/onmode -k
    fi
    ;;
*)
    echo "usage: /etc/rc3.d/S85informix {start|stop}"
    ;;
esac
```

Figure 16.16

system's run state, issue the UNIX command who -r. If you are using a UNIX
BSD system, add the start section to your rc.local file and the stop section to
your shutdown script.

To use this script as both a start and stop script for Informix OnLine, perform the following steps:

1. Place this script into your /etc/init.d directory under the name informixol.scr.

2. Set your directory with cd /etc/rc3.d.

3. Use the link command: ln -s /etc/init.d/informixol.scr S85in
formix (The S indicates start).

4. Use the link command: ln -s /etc/init.d/informixol.scr K85in
formix (The K indicates stop).

Note: The first time you start Informix OnLine, you have to do it manually by issuing the command `oninit -i` to initialize the database; all subsequent execution can then be done via the script.

16.10 Summary

This chapter covers the following topics:

- Disk file systems (raw and cooked or UFS)
- UNIX system files (/etc/group, /etc/passwd, /etc/services, and /etc/hosts)
- Defining environment variables for your UNIX users
- UNIX performance utilities (mpstat, vmstat, iostat, swap, and sar)
- Informix OnLine configuration files
- Creating a test environment for your Informix product

17

Distributing the Application

After developing the application and creating an executable, you need to consider the distribution of the application. In order to do this, you need to know how the application is configured so you can determine what files are to be distributed. You also need to understand the end-user production environment so you can determine where the components of the application are going to reside. This chapter recaps the various components that can be configured to create an application. With the configuration of the application defined, we'll discuss the what, where, and how of distribution: what needs to be delivered, where it is to be delivered, and how to get it there.

Once you have determined the delivery mechanism and procedures, it is still very important to carry out extensive testing on a subset of the production environment prior to the complete rollout. This will not only tell you whether or not the process works, but also allow you to make the necessary adjustments and document them accordingly.

17.1 What Do You Need To Distribute?

Having decided the configuration of the application, you need to consider exactly what is to be distributed. This can be broken down into two categories. The first category is: "What does the client need in order to run an executable that was developed with the development tool, in the production environment? The second is: "What parts of the application are needed in the production environment?"

17.1.1 Application runtime requirements

The files needed to deploy an application developed with most Windows development tools typically have one of the following file extensions:

*.DLL. Runtime and any other third-party DLLs

*.EXE. The application executable file

*.BMP. Bitmaps

*.CUR. Cursor(s)

*.ICO. Icons

*.INI. The application INI file(s)

*.RLE. Run-length encoded bitmaps (compressed)

*.WMF. Windows meta files

17.1.2 Development tool runtime requirements

Each development tool has very specific runtime requirements. The requirements vary from a small amount of additional code that is compiled into your application to a whole list of accompanying files, commonly referred to as the "runtime kit." These individual tool requirements are most often listed in the documentation that accompanies the product, or other third-party books.

17.2 Where Is It Going?

The environment in which you run the application is called the production environment. The design of the environment is a major factor in determining how you shape the application and consequently how you distribute it.

We are now going to review the major elements of a production environment, which can range from a stand-alone workstation to a more complicated local area network (LAN) to a collection of LANs spread over a wide area (WAN).

What follows is a more detailed description of the workstation environments you might encounter when deploying an application.

17.2.1 Stand-alone client workstation

The stand-alone client workstation (see Figure 17.1) is the most straightforward hardware configuration you will deal with when considering software distribution. It is either an IBM-compatible personal computer, Apple Macintosh, or a UNIX workstation with its own hard disk for storing programs and data.

By definition, a stand-alone workstation is not continuously connected to any other workstations or servers (i.e., a LAN), so the methods available for distribution are typically restricted to what media devices are installed on the workstation. You can distribute the software using:

- Floppy disk
- CD-ROM
- Magnetic tape

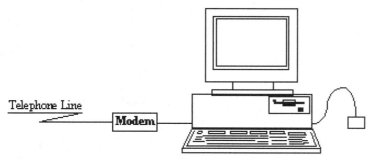

Figure 17.1 Stand-alone workstations.

This is provided that the client workstation has the media device for the same size and format media you choose. The most common media are 3.5-inch floppy disks and CD-ROM, which is appropriate for larger products. If the workstation has a modem installed with access to a telephone line, however, you need not be restricted to using one of these three types of devices. With the appropriate communications software, a modem and telephone line provides you with many more options for distributing the application software:

- You can dial into your client using a remote communications package (e.g., Norton pcAnywhere) to transfer applications.

- Bulletin boards and services can provide clients with the ability to dial-in and download the latest version of software you have previously uploaded. This is very popular today with services like Compuserve, Prodigy, and America Online.

- If you and your client workstation have access to the Internet, the client can FTP (file transfer protocol) the latest copy from a directory on your distribution machine.

Even with all these techniques for getting software to the workstation, it must still be installed and configured correctly. You can ensure this by doing something as simple as enclosing a text file of written instructions for the client user to carry out. This is somewhat susceptible to human error, however, and likely to dissatisfy the client. Or you could make a simple script that creates the appropriate directories and then copies the files to these directories. Or you could use one of the many third-party tools to allow you to completely script an installation of your product. See Chapter 20 for more information on distribution tools.

17.2.2 Local area network (LAN)

The local area network (LAN), shown in Figure 17.2, is a collection of client workstations and file and database servers that are all connected together.

The distribution methods for a client workstation on a local area network include all the methods available for a stand-alone workstation. But if you have a LAN, it makes sense to use it. If you do, however, there is another considera-

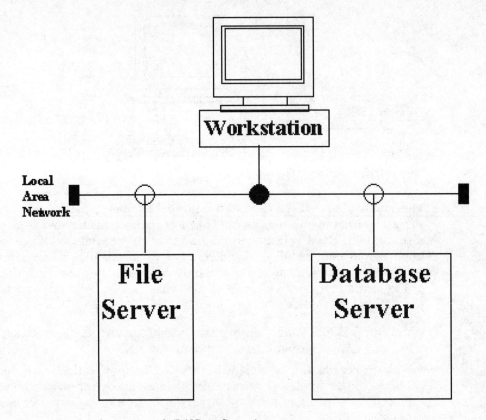

Figure 17.2 Local area network (LAN) configuration.

tion. Does every client workstation run the application from a shared storage device on a file server? This is a definite if the client is a diskless workstation. Does every client workstation run the application from its local storage device? Or does the user community need a mixture of both? Let's examine the various scenarios . . .

Running from the server
The pros if you choose to run the application from the server are that:

- You can distribute any application updates more quickly.
- There is no need for an additional distribution process for each client work-station (reduced administration).
- There is a single copy of the application held on the server (reduced dupli-cation).
- It is a solution for diskless or space-restricted workstations.

The one con is when it comes to network traffic. The application and support-ing files have to be loaded from the network to the workstation for every client.

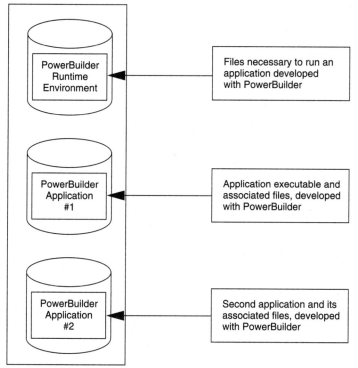

Figure 17.3 Running from a server.

If everyone chooses to load the application at the same time, it might temporarily affect the response on the network.

Running from the client

Here are the pros if you choose to run the applications from the client workstation:

- There is reduced traffic on the network.
- If the file server goes down, the application will still be available.
- Loading the application will not be affected by network traffic.

The cons for running an application from the client are:

- There is an additional distribution process for each client workstation.
- It requires widespread duplication.
- Client machines need disks and therefore disk space for applications.

17.2.3 Wide area network (WAN)

A wide area network (WAN), shown in Figure 17.5, is practically the same as a local area network (LAN), but routers, bridges, and gateways that connect the

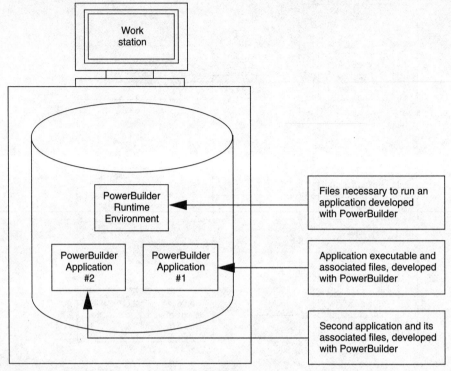

Figure 17.4   Running from each client workstation.

various LANs control the type of messaging or traffic that is allowed to pass through. You must verify that it allows traffic to flow from the distribution server to the client workstations, and take this feature into account during the planning stages.

The distribution methods for a client workstation on a wide area network include all the methods available for a local area network's stand-alone workstation. The only additional process is coping the distribution package from the distribution server to each LAN's file server.

17.3 How Do You Get It There?

Having decided on the destinations for the distribution package, there are a few questions you should pose:

- How are you going to deploy the software files to the client workstation?
- How will it be done the first time?
- How can you make it easier for any subsequent times?

See Chapter 18 for more information on commercial software distribution products. If you do not use a commercial product, then you must develop your own methods for getting files to the client environments. Depending on the network size, product size, and general accessibility of the clients, you have to consider what one method or combination of delivery methods are best suited for this assignment. These methods are typically:

- WAN server-to-server copy
- LAN server-to-client copy
- Dial-up networking
- Removable media

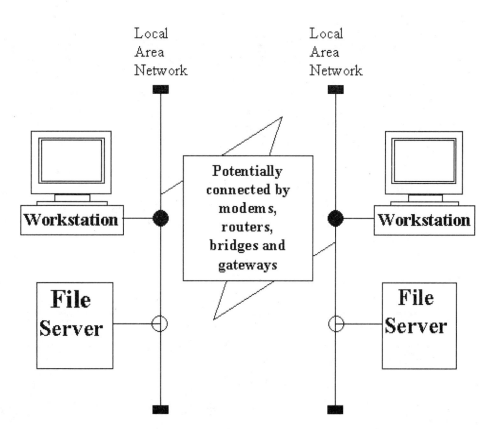

Figure 17.5   Wide area network (WAN) configuration.

17.3.1 Server-to-server copy (WAN)

Copying server to server is useful in a situation involving clients on a wide area network (WAN). The software is copied, or pushed, from the development file server, or distribution server, to the production file servers, or staging servers. You can do this by using the following types of commands and utilities:

- DOS XCOPY
- Windows LZCopy
- UNIX FTP

17.3.2 Server-to-client copy (LAN)

Once the software is on the file server that serves a local area network (LAN), you can copy server to client if the software is to reside on each workstation. The software is copied, or pulled, from the local file server, or staging server, to the client workstations.

17.3.3 Dial-up networking

With more workstations gaining access to external services, such as Compuserve, another method has become available for delivering software to remote clients. The modem connection introduces multiple possibilities, ranging from dial-up remote control to third-party service providers.

Remote-control products, like Norton pcAnywhere for DOS, allow you to take control of a remote client workstation and its resources, including file services, from your workstation. You can then copy and install the software remotely.

Service providers, like Compuserve, allow you to send information to subscribing clients via an upload or simple mail attachments. Upon receipt, the client can download and install the files accordingly.

17.3.4 Removable media

If you have limited access to client machines or if you are distributing a commercial product, then the good old floppy disk might be what you need to use. If you do use this method, however, make a note of the following:

- You must install from one or more floppy disks for each client.
- Floppy disks must be installed on each workstation, typically carried out during off-peak hours.
- What about emergency fixes?
- Using floppies is very human-resource-intensive, and subsequently prone to error.
- Be aware of floppy disk management and version control.
- Floppy disks wear out!

17.4 Distribution Tools

Now that you know that you need some kind of tool, you have to decide whether to use the setup disk builder that might have been included with the development tool (such as Install Disk Builder for PowerBuilder or Setup Builder for Visual Basic), purchase a third-party software distribution tool, construct your own software distribution utility, or use a combination of all these methods.

If you want to distribute a commercial package or one that is targeted for stand-alone workstations, then it probably makes sense to either use the Install Disk Builder or buy a third-party tool. If the target audience is predominantly on a LAN or WAN, then you will probably need to purchase a tool and possibly supplement its features with your own routines.

17.4.1 Product tools

Many development tools (e.g., Delphi, Visual Basic, and PowerBuilder) come with an executable packaging tools, providing an inexpensive way to deploy an application. They typically create install disks for your application that contain the standard Windows installation program, SETUP.EXE, just like the ones used to install professional products. Some of them also allow you to configure initialization files, registry entries, and runtime libraries.

17.4.2 Buying third-party deployment tools

See Chapter 18 for more information on commercial software deployment and distribution tools.

17.4.3 Building a distribution tool

This applies to client configurations linked by a network and running the application from a local disk. It does not apply to the client configurations that run software from a shared network device. This type of distribution method requires only the server-to-server or file-distribution technique.

If you plan on building your own distribution tool, the following areas might apply to your product:

- Auditing: create/maintain, print/display, purge/clean
- Scheduling/connection/transmission
- Packaging: development issues/roles
- Configuration management: file distribution only

And here is a list of the types of tools you might consider creating:

- A client workstation agent
- A software load program
- Application functions

Client workstation agent

This type of distribution tool is started on the client workstation and waits for the notification of change to the managed software. You can implement it using one or more of the Windows notification messages, which prompts the tool to copy the latest software from a shared network device to the client workstation. This would probably require the workstation to be left powered on during the period of time the update will most likely occur in order to receive the latest software.

Software load program

This type of distribution tool is started when the user on the client machine selects to execute an application. It is typically installed in the application icon's start-up command line. For example, if you had an application that had the following properties:

Command line: `c:\app\crva\crva.exe allenpa`
Working directory: `s:\data\crva`

It could be replaced with an icon with the following properties:

Command line: `c:\sl\sloader.exe c:\app\crva\crva.exe allenpa s:\data\crva`
Working directory: `c:\sl`

The software load program, sloader.exe, would parse the command line and extract the program pathname (c:\app\crva\crva.exe), optional parameters (allenpa), and working directory. Using the program name, the software loader could check that the software on the C: drive was the same (date, time, and file size checks) as the network copy and download accordingly. When the download was complete or if no download was necessary, the software loader would start the application.

Application functions

This could be several application functions responsible for checking that the software on the C: drive was the same (date, time, and file size checks) as the network copy, and download accordingly. Here is the list of possible functions and some pseudocode for them:

of_distribution()

```
IF of_upgrade_required (THIS) = TRUE THEN
   IF of_perform_upgrade(THIS) = TRUE THEN
      MessageBox("Distribution Control","Upgrade Successful.")
   ELSE
      MessageBox("Distribution Control","Upgrade Failed.")
   END IF
END IF
```

of_upgrade_required()

- Check dates of all the executable and supporting files with entries in the current application's DC table (or .INI file).

- Call f_get_current_build for each library and compare with entries in the DC table (or .INI file).

- RETURN TRUE if version numbers are different or the dates are different.

of_perform_upgrade()

- Run the homegrown installation routine to install the latest version of the application.

- Run the third-party installation routine to install the latest version of the application.

- Wait for this utility to complete before continuing with the application.

17.4.4 Installation/setup routines

Once the software is delivered to the client, it must still be correctly set up or installed. This might be as simple as copying all the files from the floppy disk to a standard directory and using an icon in Windows that starts the executable. There are also more advanced and therefore more complicated installation routines, which must be carefully constructed by the development team, taking into account the various combinations of hardware configurations of the client workstations. You can create these install scripts using countless third-party tools. Some of the more popular ones are mentioned later in this book.

Chapter

18

Related Tools and Publications

This chapter contains information on a number of products that can combine with PowerBuilder to provide a feature-rich application development environment, with connectivity to enterprise-wide server systems. Your demand for these products in a development project depend on a number of factors: the size and functionality of the application, time constraints, and budget constraints. The last section in the chapter lists publications that are either dedicated to or contain regular columns on development techniques for Informix specifically or client/server in general.

18.1 Case Tools

18.1.1 Acu4GL

Acucobol, Inc.
7950 Silverton Ave., Suite 201
San Diego, CA 92126-6344
Tel: 800.262.6585 or 619.689.7220
Fax: 619.566.3071

Allows software written in ACUCOBOL-85 to interface with Informix (and Sybase or Oracle) RDBMSs by generating SQL queries. Allows developers to use 4GL tools such as report writers and query tools while retaining the use of COBOL for the database maintenance application.

18.1.2 Bachman

Bachman Information Systems, Inc.
8 New England Executive Park
Burlington, MA 01803

Tel: 800.BACHMAN or 617.273.9003
Fax: 617.229.9904

Uses Bachman data models to create PowerBuilder DataWindows, validation rules, PowerBuilder system table information, and PowerBuilder functions necessary to develop PowerBuilder applications.

18.1.3 EasyCASE System Designer

Evergreen CASE Tools, Inc.
8522 154th Ave. North East
Redmond, WA 98052
Tel: 206.881.5149
Fax: 206.883.7676

Supports a wide range of methods for process events and data modeling. It can be used for logical and physical data modeling, which generates SQL DDL scripts and supports forward and reverse engineering of *x*BASE databases. The professional edition also supports Watcom, SQL Base, SQL Server, XDB, Access, and Paradox.

18.1.4 ERwin/ERX

Logic Works, Inc.
1060 Route 206
Princeton, NJ 08540
Tel: 800.78ERWIN or 609.252.1177
Fax: 609.252.1175

Entity-relationship logical data modeling tool. Facilitates the design of client/server database applications with a bidirectional link of the Power-Builder user interface development environment to the database logical model in ERwin. You can define the PowerBuilder catalog of extended attributes for each database column from within ERwin, or capture and synchronize the existing definitions, enabling both client- and server-side information to be defined and managed in one place: the model. These models can then be stored in and retrieved from the DBMS. Provides DBMS support for forward and reverse engineering, as well as support for table-level and schema-level prescripts and postscripts, direct system catalog synchronization, multiple subject areas and stored displays, physical storage parameters, and stored procedures.

18.1.5 Excellerator II

Intersolv, Inc.
3200 Tower Oaks Boulevard
Rockville, MD 20852
Tel: 800.547.4000 or 301.230.3200
Fax: 301.231.7813

Analysis and design tool that supports multiple approaches for distributed design of data, process, events and user interfaces, and RAD and object-oriented methods. Includes multiuser LAN repository that enables teams to share information and reuse design elements under multiple methodologies.

18.1.6 IE:Advantage

Information Engineering Systems Corporation
201 North Union Street, 5th Floor
Alexandria, VA 22314
Tel: 703.739.2242
Fax: 703.739.0074

CASE product with central repository that supports an information system's development life cycle. Develops logical data models, process models, and system designs in implementation priority sequence. Includes goal and objectives of organization, which can be linked to logical data/process models. Generates databases and application systems in various formats and languages. Includes an IEW/ADW conversion utility, cross-reference reports, and IDEF1X data modeling capabilities. Implementation includes user-customizable SQL schema generation with interface to PowerBuilder for application/code generation.

18.1.7 InfoModeler

Asymetrix Corporation
110 110th Avenue North East, Suite 700
Bellvue, WA 98004

InfoModeler uses conceptual modeling tools based in ORM (object role modeling) that help to communicate and automate the process of building sound RDBMSs. Designers and end users use English-language business rules and sample data to build the information model. InfoModeler then automatically generates a correctly normalized database and builds the PowerBuilder data dictionary.

18.1.8 LexiBridge Transformer

LexiBridge Corporation
605 Main Street
Monroe, CT 06468
Tel: 203.459.8228
Fax: 203.459.8220

LexiBridge provides a rule-driven interface that allows users to specify migration objectives at three levels: the data model, the process model, and the user model. LexiBridge parses the COBOL/CICS source-code modules, performs restructuring and code clean-up, and then generates the appropriate PowerBuilder and SQL constructs.

18.1.9 MidPoint for IEF

MidCore Software, Inc.
49 Leavenworth Street, Suite 200
Waterbury, CT 06702
Tel: 203.759.0906
Fax: 203.759.2131

Provides a level of open access, while allowing IEF applications to maintain complete integrity and security of business data and business rules. Provides access to data in IEF applications to the following: GUI tools (such as Power-Builder, Visual Basic, and SQL Windows), report writers (including Report-Smith and Crystal Reports), and analytical tools (such as Microsoft Excel).

18.1.10 S-Designor

SDP Technologies, Inc. (subsidiary of Powersoft Corp.)
One Westbrook Corporate Center, Suite 805
Westchester, IL 60154
Tel: 708.947.4250
Fax: 708.947.4251

Database design tool that allows users to construct entity-relationship data models and describe entities and their attributes in the dictionary. Produces analysis documentation, generates database-creation scripts, and offers reverse-engineering functionalities.

18.1.11 Silverrun Relational Data Modeler, Silverrun Informix Bridge

Computer Systems Advisers, Inc. (division of CSA Group)
300 Tice Boulevard
Woodcliff Lake, NJ 07675
Tel: 800.537.4262 or 201.391.6500
Fax: 201.391.2210

Relational data modeler: GUI object-oriented modeling tool that supports the creation of multiple physical models from a single logical model for client/server applications. Models contain necessary specifications to generate DDL to many target environments. Bidirectional interfaces exist for major databases, client/server development environments, and object-oriented 4GLs.

Informix bridge: Bridge between Informix and Silverrun, allowing developers to transform specifications from validated Silverrun relational models into Informix SQL script files ready for execution. Generates Informix database schema from Silverrun relational models, and can also performs reverse transformation.

18.1.12 System Architect

Popkin Software & Systems, Inc.
11 Park Place
New York NY 10007-2801
Tel: 800.REAL.CASE or 212.571.3434
Fax: 212.571.3436

SQL smart, Windows rich, object easy, MIS friendly. Two-way connection between System Architect's analysis and design capabilities and PowerBuilder's development environment. Uses logical and physical model information in the SA repository to generate database tables for target RDBMSs. Creates extended attribute tables. Uses screen and menu layouts created in System Architect to generate menus and response windows in PowerBuilder. Provides support for Sybase SQL server, MS SQL server, Oracle 6 and 7, and Informix.

18.1.13 Systems Engineer/Open

LBMS, Inc.
1800 West Loop South, Suite 1800
Houston TX 77027-3210
Tel: 800.231.7515 or 713.623.0414
Fax: 713.623.4955

Transfers CASE-based design data from Systems Engineer to PowerBuilder for developing applications. Systems Engineer is a multiuser, concurrent-access CASE tool and integrated life-cycle development tool. Provides data-driven, process-driven, rapid application development (RAD), and joint application development (JAD) capabilities.

18.2 Connectivity Tools

18.2.1 Data Pump for Windows

Borland International, Inc.
100 Borland Way
Scotts Valley, CA 95066-3249
800.233.2444 or 408.431.1000
Fax: 408.431.4122

Allows developers to move data and schema between different database sources. Allows users to create, populate, and move databases from one source to another, leveraging Borland native connections to Informix, InterBase, Microsoft, Oracle, and Sybase database servers.

18.2.2 DataLink for Lotus Notes (version 2.0)

Brainstorm Technologies, Inc.
64 Sidney St.
Cambridge, MA 02139
Tel: 617.621.0800
Fax: 617.621.8519

The MS-Windows GUI interface for migrating and synchronizing data between Lotus Notes and relational databases via ODBC. Supports Borland (dBase and Paradox), Informix, Microsoft (Access, FoxPro and SQL server), Oracle, and Sybase.

18.2.3 DBtools.h++

Rogue Wave Software, Inc.
260 S.W. Madison Ave., P.O. Box 2328
Corvallis, OR 97339
Tel: 800.487.3217 or 503-754-3010
Fax: 503.757.6650

Provides portable C++ interface to APIs from DB2/2, Informix, Ingres, Microsoft, Oracle, SQLBase, and Sybase database engines. Allows developers to exploit features specific to each supported database. Contains classes for incorporating complex data types stored as BLOBs in the database. Supports Borland, Microsoft, and CFront compilers.

18.2.4 HyperSTAR

VMARK Software, Inc.
50 Washington St.
Westboro, MA 01581-1021
Tel: 800.966.9875 or 508.366.3888
Fax: 508.366.3669

Object-messaging middleware that enables integration of client/server applications by providing connectivity to disparate databases across the enterprise. Allows transparent, read/write access to corporate database on more than 30 different platforms, including most popular DBMSs (Oracle, Informix, Sybase, Ingres, and others) and open systems hardware.

18.2.5 Intelligent Warehouse

Hewlett-Packard Co.
3000 Hanover St.
Palo Alto, CA 94304
Tel: 800.752.0900 or 415.857.1501

Warehousing tool for loading data from a variety of sources (Informix, Ingres, Oracle, Red Brick, and Sybase), enabling users to summarize and analyze business information. Consists of software that manages data, a warehouse database that stores the data, and client software that allows end users to access the data. Suitable for sites with 20 to 35 users and 15 to 25 gigabytes of data.

18.2.6 Tun SQL

Esker, Inc.
350 Sansome St., Suite 210
San Francisco, CA 94104
Tel: 800.88.ESKER or 415.675.7777
Fax: 415.675.7775

A single multidatabase MS Windows ODBC driver for accessing relational databases. Supports Informix, Oracle, and Sybase.

18.2.7 UniSQL C++ Interface

UniSQL, Inc.
8911 N. Capital of Texas Hwy., Suite 2300
Austin, TX 78759-7200
Tel: 800.451.DBMS or 512.343.7297
Fax: 512.343.7383

Consists of C++ class libraries and class-generation facilities that developers can use to work with either UniSQL/X DBMSs or with relational database systems including Informix, Ingres, Oracle, and Sybase.

18.3 Database Administration Tools

18.3.1 DB-Toolkit-1 and DB-Toolkit-2

Breakaway Technologies
P.O. Box 681092
Schaumburg, IL 60168
Tel: 708.582.3512
Fax: 708.582.3515

Provide toolkits that allow the DBA to get into shared memory and the disk structures.

18.3.2 DB Privileges

Advanced DataTools Corporation
4510 Maxfield Drive
Annandale, VA 22003
Tel: 703.256.0267

Allows DBA to quickly modify permissions to the database, tables, and columns.

18.3.3 Desktop DBA

Platinum Technology, Inc.
1815 S. Meyers Rd.
Oakbrook Terrace, IL 60181-5241
Tel: 800.378.7528 or 708.620.5000
Fax: 708.691.0710

DBA utility for SQL database servers. Allows simultaneous management of multiple databases/servers. Permits users to drag-and-drop copy databases from server to server or database objects from database to database.

18.3.4 Intelligencia

DCC/4GL
1256 Cabrillo Avenue, Suite 250
Torrance, CA 90501
Tel: 310.320.4300
Fax: 310.320.3579

Enhanced backup and restore tool for Informix OnLine database systems. Allows very flexible backup criteria, to the table or row level.

18.3.5 ISQLPERL

This program is in the public domain.

18.4 Database Multimedia Extensions

18.4.1 DocuData

LaserData
300 Vesper Park
Tyngsboro, MA 01879
Tel: 508.649.4600
Fax: 508.649.4436

Offers three development approaches: a built-in viewer and browser that enables document management capabilities with little or no programming, document- or image-enabling applications via a dynamic data exchange (DDE) interface, or creation of new applications with an extensive application programming interface (API).

18.4.2 Illustra DataBlade

Illustra Information Technologies, Inc.
(division of Informix Software, Inc.)
1111 Broadway, Suite 2000
Oakland, CA 94607
Tel: 510.652.8000
Fax: 510.869.6388

A RDBMS that enables users to store, manage, and analyze complex data types (audio, video, and image) in a single database along with simple data types (text and numbers) using SQL. The products are Illustra Server database engine, Illustra Object Schema Knowledge tool for visualizing complex data queries, and Illustra DataBlade modules that allow you to extend the capabilities of the server with new user-defined data types and related methods.

18.4.3 MediaDB

MediaWay, Inc.
3080 Olcott Street, Suite 220C
Santa Clara, CA 95054
Tel: 708.748.7407
Fax: 408.748.7402

MediaDB is a DBMS optimized for the storage and retrieval of multimedia information. The Application Development Kit is a class library that provides custom controls necessary to develop multimedia applications.

18.4.4 Verity

18.4.5 Watermark Discovery Edition

Watermark Software
129 Middlesex Turnpike
Burlington, MA 01803
Tel: 617.229.2600
Fax: 617.229.2989

Uses object linking and embedding (OLE) technology to enable images of incoming faxes and scanned documents to be stored, manipulated, copied, and distributed by applications.

18.4.6 WorkFLO

FileNet Corporation
3565 Harbor Boulevard
Costa Mesa, CA 92626
Tel: 714.966.3197
Fax: 714.966.3490

WorkFlo Application Libraries (WAL) enable applications to manage images and documents stored on the FileNet system. WAL is available for the following platforms: Windows 3.1, OS/2, Macintosh, SunOS, HP-UX, and IBM-AIX.

18.5 Distributed Computing Tools

18.5.1 Connection/DCE

Open Horizon, Inc.
1301 Shoreway Road, Suite 116
Belmont, CA 94002
Tel: 415.593.1509
Fax: 415.593.1669

Database connectivity product that offers full integration with DCE services, such as security, encryption, directory/name services, and transport-independent RPCs. The connection DLL has the same name and is binary-compatible with the database vendor's software products.

18.5.2 Distributed Computing Integrator (DCI)

Tangent International, Inc.
30 Broad Street
New York, NY 10004
Tel: 212.809.8200
Fax: 212.968.1398

Allows a PowerBuilder application to act as a client in a transaction processing environment. The integrator is composed of two parts: the transaction processing interface (TPI) and the transaction monitor connector (TMC). The TPI is a set of APIs that unite the different processing paradigms of PowerBuilder with the transaction processing systems. The TMC takes advantage of the connectivity and features of specific transaction monitors (currently Novell's Tuxedo and AT&T's TopEnd).

18.5.3 EncinaBuilder for Windows

Transarc Corporation (an IBM subsidiary)
707 Grant Street, Gulf Tower, 20th Floor
Pittsburgh, PA 15219
Tel: 412.338.4400
Fax: 412.338.4404

Interface between PowerBuilder and the Encina transaction monitor, based on OSF's distributed computing environment (DCE). Allows developers to create applications using the OLTP concept of transaction processing software that will interface with Encina servers running on UNIX systems.

18.5.4 Encompass

Open Environment Corporation
25 Travis Street
Boston, MA 02134
Tel: 617.562.0900
Fax: 617.562.0038

Suite of tools that enables client/server developers to build enterprise-wide distributed applications based on a three-tiered architecture. Includes a RPC code generator, application management, security, distributed naming services, and application testing and debugging facilities. Can be used in conjunction with RPCPainter, from Greenbrier & Russel, for connecting to existing legacy systems.

18.5.5 EZ-RPC

NobleNet
337 Turnpike Road
Southboro, MA 01772-1708
Tel: 508.460.8222
Fax: 508.460.3456

Suite of multiplatform tools that facilitate the distribution of applications across TCP/IP and SPX/IPX networks. EZ-RPC generates C-language executables for UNIX, WinRPC generates RPC DLLs, RPCWare generates RPC NLMs, and MacRPC generates C-language executables for Macintosh.

18.5.6 Magna X

Magna Software Corporation
275 Seventh Avenue
New York, NY 10001-6708
Tel: 800.431.9006 or 212.727.6719
Fax: 212.691.1968

Application generator for COBOL OLTP applications. Operates across distributed UNIX platforms and incorporates enterprise data on mainframes via generated COBOL programs. Includes a GUI development environment and shared workgroup dictionary, and produces applications for Novell Tuxedo and Transarc Encina.

18.5.7 RPCpainter

Greenbrier & Russel
1450 East American Lane, Suite 1640
Schaumburg IL 60173
Tel: 800.453.0347 or 708.706.4000
Fax: 708.706.4020

Allows developers to build enterprise-wide, client/server applications in distributed computing environments using the three-tiered architecture of Encompass from Open Environment Corporation. Includes graphical tools for preparing and editing remote procedure interface definitions (IDL), the automatic generation of remote procedure call (RPC) stubs for the server, the automatic population of DataWindows with RPC results, and the automatic upload of DataWindow changes through RPCs.

18.6 Help and Web Authoring Tools

18.6.1 Doc-To-Help

WexTech Systems, Inc.
310 Madison Avenue, Suite 905
New York, NY 10017
Tel: 800.939.8324 or 212.949.9595
Fax: 212.949.4007

Add-on to Microsoft Word that lets users create tailored online help systems in the Windows environment by converting documents (.DOC) to help files (.HLP).

18.6.2 Hot Dog Pro

18.6.3 HyperHelp

Bristol Technology, Inc.
241 Ethan Allen Highway
Ridgefield, CT 06877
Tel: 203.438.6969
Fax: 203.438.5013

Provides the same capability as the Help Compiler (HC.EXE) for Microsoft Windows. It uses the same rich text format (.RTF), project (.HPJ) and bitmap (.BMP) files, and compiles an online help file for use on UNIX platforms that run PowerBuilder for Motif applications. Enables you to maintain a single source for your help system across Windows and UNIX platforms.

18.6.4 Internet Assistant for Word and Internet Studio

Microsoft Corporation
One Microsoft Way
Redmond, WA 98052
Tel: 206.936.3468

18.6.5 RoboHELP

Blue Sky Software Corp.
7486 La Jolla Boulevard, Suite 3
La Jolla, CA 92037-9583
Tel: 800.677.4946 or 619.459.6365
Fax: 619.459.6366

Help-authoring tool that offers bidirectional conversion from Microsoft Word documents (.DOC) to help files (.HLP). Designs, tests, and generates context-sensitive help systems.

18.6.6 Web Developer's Kit (WDK)

VMARK Software, Inc.
50 Washington St.
Westboro, MA 01581-1021
Tel: 800.966.9875 or 508.366.3888
Fax: 508.366.3669

Allows user to create client/server applications that enable any HTML browser to dynamically interact with a variety of relational and legacy databases. Contains a visual query builder, C-language-compatible API, database-specific access server, and documentation. There are versions available for Informix, Ingres, Oracle, Sybase, and uniVerse. Supports Windows, Windows NT, and Macintosh clients.

18.7 Software Distribution Tools

18.7.1 BrightWork Utilities

McAfee Associates, Inc.
2710 Walsh Avenue, Suite 200
Santa Clara, CA 95051-0963
Tel: 800.866.6585 or 408.988.3832
Fax: 408.970.9727

Suite of applications for small and medium-sized LANs. Tracks network software and hardware. Allows users to support and troubleshoot Windows or DOS workstations on a LAN. Monitors system performance, security, capacity, and configuration. Provides LAN users with access to printers attached to any PC on the network.

18.7.2 Courier

Tivoli Systems, Inc.
9442 Capital of Texas Highway North, Arboretum Plaza One, Suite 500
Austin, TX 78759
Tel: 800.2TIVOLI or 512.794.9070
Fax: 512.794.0623

Allows system managers to automatically distribute software updates. Identifies any application package or collection of files, indicates machines that subscribe to the software, and automatically distributes new modules to these computers.

18.7.3 Doughboy Professional Install for Windows (V.2.0)

NeoPoint Technologies
P.O. Box 2281

Winnipeg, Manitoba R3C 4A6
Canada
Tel: 800.665.9668 or 204.668.8180
Fax: 204.661.6904

Installation program generator, allowing developers to specify where directory applications are located, modify customization options, and build master disks. Includes high-speed data compression, CRC-32 data integrity checking, automatic splitting of large files across multiple disks, and creation of program manager groups and items.

18.7.4 Enterprise Desktop Manager (EDM)

Novadigm
One International Boulevard
Mahwah, NJ 07495
Tel: 708.527.0490
Fax: 708.527.0492

Manages the deployment of applications, including configuration management, distribution management, desktop installation, and version control of the PB execution environment. Direct links to the version control system enable applications to automatically be distributed to clients when a new version is promoted.

18.7.5 LAN Management System for Netware

Saber Software Corporation
5944 Luther Lane, Suite 1007
Dallas, TX 75225
Tel: 800.338.8754 or 214.361.8086
Fax: 214.361.1882

Combination of several Saber products featuring menuing, centralized file and software distribution, scripting languages, automatic software/hardware inventorying, remote control, disk/print management, real-time information viewing, and management of tracking, prioritizing, and queuing predefined activities.

18.7.6 NetWare Navigator

Novell, Inc.
122 East 1700 South
Provo, UT 84606
Tel: 800.NETWARE

Management tool that enables managers to distribute files from a single workstation. The administration console allows managers to create distribution lists, create packages that contain files for distribution, schedule jobs, and receive network feedback. A distribution server holds utilities used by the administration console and stages servers' route files from the distribution server to their intended client destination in the distribution list.

18.7.7 Norton Administrator For Networks

Symantec Corporation
10201 Torre Avenue
Cupertino, CA 95014-2132
Tel: 800.441.7234 or 408.253.9600
Fax: 408.253.3968

Allows network managers to control software and hardware inventory, distribute software, manage licensing system security, and protect against anti-viruses from the central console. Automatically builds a database of information each time a user logs onto the machine, capturing information on system resources and configuration.

18.7.8 Q

Voyager Systems, Inc.
Pine Tree Place, 360 Route 101, Suite 1501
Bedford, NH 03110-5030
Tel: 603.472.5172
Fax: 603.472.8897

Q, developed with PowerBuilder 3.0a, is a batch scheduler and remote execution system for networks. It uses a reference database on the network to control scheduling and agent programs executing on client PCs. A client agent "registers" with the database to see if there is work to be done; if so, it executes the instructions accordingly.

18.7.9 Software Update and Distribution System (SUDS)

Frye Computer Systems, Inc.
19 Temple Place
Boston, MA 02111-9779
Tel: 800.234.3793 or 617.451.5400
Fax: 617.451.6711

SUDS/LAN: Software update and distribution system designed for remote distribution of shrink-wrapped packages as well as network drivers, tools, and utilities. Works across bridges and routers. Includes distribution lists and user menu procedures, alarm options, master procedures, procedure retry, and a per-user log summary. A Macintosh version is also available.

SUDS/WAN: Extends the range of software update and distribution system by letting network manager create a set of procedures at one server to be automatically copied to any or all installations of SUDS on a WAN. Includes a package inspection security feature, ability to define and save target lists, and report writing.

18.7.10 WinInstall

Aleph Takoma Systems
Distributed by: On Demand Software, Inc.
1100 Fifth Avenue South, Suite 208

Naples, FL 33940
Tel: 800.368.5207 or 813.261.6678
Fax: 813.261.6549

Automates installation, uninstallation, and upgrades of Windows and DOS applications on any network. Modifies all initialization files, copies necessary files including OLE registration database, and installs icons and program groups. Supports environment application and global variables. Displays custom messages, calls other programs, and keeps logs. Also allows you to record an installation, discover what has changed, and build the necessary installation scripts for automated use.

18.8 Testing Tools

18.8.1 ANSWER: Testpro for Windows

Sterling Software, Inc.
9340 Owensmouth Avenue, Box 2210
Chatsworth, CA 91311
Tel: 818.716.1616
Fax: 818.716.5705

Designed to build a repeatable test script library for Windows and host-based applications. Features a capture/playback mechanism, script language, flexible image and text capture capabilities, and the ability to synchronize with host-based applications as well as the Windows environment.

18.8.2 Automated Test Facility (ATF)

Softbridge, Inc.
125 Cambridge Park Drive
Cambridge, MA 02140
Tel: 617.576.2257
Fax: 617.864.7747

Tests client/server or stand-alone OS/2, Windows, and NT applications. From a central point, it can perform simultaneous, unattended tests on up to 50 machines. Handles GUIs, distributed applications, and legacy system testing.

18.8.3 Automator QA

Direct Technology Ltd.
551 London Road
Isleworth TW7 4DS
England
Tel: 44.181.847.1666
Fax: 44.181.847.0003
U.S. Tel: 212.475.2747

Consists of four integrated modules: QA Plan, QA Run, QA Track, and QA Stress. Supports all aspects and stages of the software testing process.

18.8.4 AutoTester

AutoTester, Inc. (Software Recording Corporation subsidiary)
8150 N. Central Expressway, Suite 1300
Dallas, TX 75206
Tel: 800.326.1196 or 214.368.1196
Fax: 214.750.9668

Handles organization and execution of regression tests, including test synchronization, dynamic window placement and positioning, advanced control querying and manipulation, and actual text retrieval. Creates audit trails and conducts review and comparison of expected results to actual results.

18.8.5 EMPOWER/CS

Performix, Inc.
8200 Greensboro Drive, Suite 1475
McLean, VA 22102
Tel: 703.448.6606
Fax: 703.893.1939

Permits multiuser load testing without requiring a PC for each emulated user. Uses C language for flexible scripts, a global variable and synchronization capability to emulate complex workloads, and an interactive monitoring feature that allows for control and debugging of scripts during testing.

18.8.6 Microsoft Test

Microsoft Corporation
One Microsoft Way
Redmond, WA 98052
Tel: 206.936.3468

Microsoft Test is a tool for automating software testing of Windows-based applications.

18.8.7 ODBC Sniffer and SQL Sniffer

Blue Lagoon Software
6659 Hesperia Avenue
Reseda, CA 91335
Tel: 818.345.2200
Fax: 818.345.8905

ODBC (ODBC Sniffer) and DBLIB (SQL Sniffer) are trace and performance analysis tools for GUI programmers and database administrators. Allows users to see the amount of time in seconds or milliseconds spent on a call, which application made the call, parameters passed to the call, and return values from the call. Traces can be logged into a text file in ASCII format.

18.8.8 PowerRunner

Mercury Interactive Corporation
470 Potrero Avenue

Sunnyvale, CA 94086
Tel: 800.TEST.911 or 408.523.9900
Fax: 408.523.9911

Object-oriented testing tool that allows unattended testing. Results are analyzed with DataWindows verification and execution reports. Test scripts can be ported to run on Windows NT, OS/2, Open Look, and Motif platforms. LoadRunner/PC tests system functionality and response under stress-load conditions; it replicates heavy use of a system by distributing applications across the network. Allows you to find critical failures and unacceptable performance issues before going to production.

18.8.9 QA Partner

Segue Software, Inc.
1320 Centre Street
Newton Centre, MA 02159
Tel: 800.922.3771 or 617.969.3771
Fax: 617.969.4326

Creates superclasses of objects based on functions that allows developers to create generic regression suites of tests using a scripting language. Translates scripts using appropriate GUI drivers for each environment.

18.8.10 Rhobot/Client-Server

Promark, Inc.
8 Campus Drive
Parsippany, NJ 07054
Tel: 201.540.1980
Fax: 201.540.8377

Automates stress-testing of client-server architectures by emulating their online and batch functions via scripts representing transactions. Supports multiple scripts, executed simultaneously. You can review the results or export them for further analysis by spreadsheet, statistical, and graphics packages.

18.8.11 SQA TeamTest

Software Quality Automation (SQA), Inc.
10 State Street
Woburn, MA 01801
Tel: 800.228.9922 or 617.932.0110
Fax: 617.932.3280

Automated GUI testing solution implemented on team/work group model. Based on network test repository, which is updated during all stages of the testing process: test planning, test development, unattended test execution, test results analysis, and extensive incident/problem tracking and reporting.

18.9 Version Control Tools

Version control tools are crucial to managing the source.

18.9.1 CCC/Manager

Softool Corporation
340 S. Kellogg Avenue
Goleta, CA 93117
Tel: 800.723.0696 or 805.683.5777
Fax: 805.683.4105

Using GUI and command-line interfaces, provides change and version management for any type of software component, application management, change packaging, access control, and user hierarchy maintenance centralized or distributed database.

18.9.2 Endeavor Workstation (NDVR)

Legent Corporation
575 Herndon Parkway
Herndon VA 22080-5226
Tel: 800.676.LGNT or 703.708.3000

Endeavor Workstation is a software management system that controls and manages changes to both workstation applications and to mainframe applications developed on the workstation.

18.9.3 LBMS Systems Engineer

See section 18.1.13, Systems Engineer, earlier in this chapter.

18.9.4 MKS Revision Control System (RCS)

Mortice Kern Systems, Inc.
185 Columbia Street West
Waterloo, Ontario N2L 5Z5
Canada
Tel: 800.265.2797 or 519.884.2251
Fax: 519.884.8861

Customizable revision control system that tracks changes to source code as it is created, tested, and revised by programmers. Includes configuration and document management, encryption, visual difference locking, branching, merging, locking, a menu-driven interface, and support for binary and text files.

18.9.5 ObjectCycle

18.9.6 PVCS Version Manager

PVCS (Polytron Version Control System) Version Manager keeps track of revision, version, and release information of all development objects, including source code, ASCII files, graphics, documentation, and binary files. Another of its services is the Configuration Builder. Its job is to record relationships between components and re-create the specific sequence of steps to construct a software system reliably, completely, and accurately at any time.

18.9.7 SCCS

Standard UNIX source-code control system, free with most varieties of the UNIX operating system.

18.10 Magazines and Journals

Unfortunately, this is very short list.

18.10.1 Informix Times

Informix Times
4100 Bohannon Drive
Menlo Park, CA 94025

Informix quarterly customer newsletter. To subscribe, send a message to Michael Pooley, Editor, at pooley@informix.com or the above address.

18.10.2 Informix CS Times

CS Times
4100 Bohannon Drive
Menlo Park, CA 94025

Informix's customer service newsletter. Published every quarter, *CS Times* is designed to deliver up-to-the-minute news about Informix services and support. To subscribe, send a message to Angela Sanchez, Editor, at angelas@informix.com or the above address.

18.10.3 Informix Tech Notes

Informix Tech Notes are available for customers subscribing to Informix-OpenLine. If you are interested in Tech Notes and OpenLine support, please call Informix Service Sales at (800) 274-9464 ext. 43, or send an e-mail message to moreinfo@informix.com.

Figure 18.1 *Informix CS Times* logo.

18.10.4 Informix Systems Journal

Informix Systems Journal
400087 Mission Boulevard, Suite 167
Freemont, CA 94539-9930
Tel: 800.943.9300

An independent publication focusing exclusively on the Informix product line. The rate is $84 (U.S.) a year, for six issues.

Figure 18.2   *Informix Systems Journal* logo.

19

Getting Familiar with the Development O/S

Unix is a multiplatform operating system. In other words, it can be used to run on a machine as small as a desktop PC as well as on machines as large as mainframes. The means by which we communicate with UNIX is through what is commonly called a shell. To date, there are three primary shells: the C shell or csh, the Bourne shell or sh, and the Korn shell or ksh. I have chosen the Korn shell for this book because it is the newest, and combines the features of both the C shell and the Bourne shell. After reading this chapter, you should have a good understanding of UNIX and how to communicate with the UNIX operating system.

19.1 The UNIX Operating System

UNIX is the name of a computer operating system and its family of related utility programs. Over the past few years, the UNIX operating system has matured and gained unprecedented popularity. This chapter starts by defining an operating system and discussing some of the features of the System V, Release 4 version of UNIX. It continues with a brief history and overview of the UNIX system and explains why it has become so popular.

19.1.1 What is an operating system?

An operating system is a control program for a computer. It allocates computer resources and schedules tasks. Computer resources include all the hardware, the central processing unit, system memory, disk and tape storage, printers, terminals, modems, and anything else connected to or inside the computer.

An operating system performs many varied functions almost simultaneously, it keeps track of filenames and where each file is located on the disk, and it monitors every keystroke on each of the terminals. Memory must be allocated so only one task uses a given area of memory at a time. Other operating system functions include fulfilling requests made by users, running accounting programs that keep track of resource use, and executing backups and other maintenance utilities. An operating system schedules tasks so the central processor is working on only one task at a given moment, although the computer might appear to be running many programs at the same time.

19.1.2 UNIX System V features

The UNIX operating system was developed at Bell Laboratories in Murray Hill, New Jersey, one of the largest research facilities in the world. Since the original design and implementation of the UNIX operating system by Ken Thompson in 1969, many people have contributed to it. The most recent releases are based on UNIX System V, Release 4. For the remainder of this chapter, we will refer to System V, Release 4 as UNIX SVR4 or just SVR4.

UNIX SVR4 is the culmination of the efforts of many people over many years and the consolidation of many different strains of UNIX, most notably AT&T Bell Labs UNIX and the Berkeley Software Distribution (BSD) UNIX. The following sections discuss the most commonly used features of SVR4. This discussion only touches the surface of what is UNIX SVR4. Many features, such as shared memory and named pipes, are beyond the scope of this book. Many others are significant only if you are familiar with previous versions of the UNIX system. This chapter is meant to give you a basic understanding of UNIX. If UNIX is new to you, you will want to read this chapter to learn some of the features that UNIX has to offer.

19.1.3 Shell functions

One of the most important features of the shell (the UNIX command interpreter) is that you can use it as a programming language. Because the shell is an interpreter, it does not compile the programs you write for it, but interprets them each time you load them in from the disk. Interpreting and loading programs can be time-consuming.

You can write shell functions that the shell holds in main memory so it does not have to read them from the disk each time you want to execute them. The shell also keeps functions in an internal format so it does not have to spend as much time interpreting them.

19.1.4 Job control

Job control allows you to work on several jobs at once, switching back and forth between them as you need to. Normally, when you start a job it is in the foreground, so it is connected to your terminal. This is especially important when you are not working in an X-Window system environment. Using job control, you can move the job you are working with into the background so you can work on another job while the first is running. If a background job needs your attention, you can move it into the foreground so it is once again attached to your terminal. The concept of job control was borrowed from Berkeley UNIX, although the SVR4 implementation differs from that of Berkeley. Under SVR4, job control is coordinated by the shell layer manager (ksh). The name is derived from the concept of shell layers, each layer running a different job.

19.1.5 Screen-oriented editor

Although the vi (visual) editor from Berkeley has been widely available for many years, it became an official part of UNIX only with AT&T's release of System V. The vi editor is an advance over its predecessor, ed, because it displays a context for your editing; where ed displayed a line at a time, vi displays a full screen of text.

19.1.6 Delayed execution of jobs

The at utility lets you schedule a job to run at a certain time. You can tell at you want to run the job in a few hours, next week, or even on a specific date in the future. This utility allows you to schedule jobs that slow the machine down or tie up the printer so they run when your machine is not normally used (e.g., at night or on weekends).

19.1.7 Scrolling through a file

The more utility displays a file on your terminal, one full screen at a time. When you finish reading what is on the screen, you can ask for another full screen by pressing the spacebar and, for single line, the Enter key. It also allows you to scroll backward through a file.

19.2 History of the UNIX Operating System

Since its inception 27 years ago, the UNIX operating system has gone through a maturing process, bringing it to its current state, SVR4. When the UNIX operating system was developed, many computers still ran single jobs in a batch mode. Because these systems served only one user at a time, they did not take full advantage of the power and speed of the computer. Furthermore, this work environment isolated programmers from each other and did not make it easy to share data and programs.

The UNIX time-sharing system provided two major improvements over single-user batch systems. It allowed more than one person to use the computer at the same time (the UNIX operating system is a multiuser operating system), and it allowed a person to communicate directly with the computer via a terminal, making it interactive.

UNIX was not the first interactive, multiuser operating system. An operating system named Multics was in use briefly at Bell Labs before the UNIX operating system was created. The Cambridge Multiple Access System had been developed in Europe, and the Compatible Time-Sharing System (CTSS) had also been used for several years. The designers of the UNIX operating system took advantage of the work that had gone into these and other operating systems by combining the most desirable features of each of them.

The UNIX system was developed by researchers who needed a set of modern computing tools to help them with their projects. It allowed a group of people working together on a project to share selected data and programs, while keeping other information private.

Universities and colleges have played a major role in furthering the popularity of the UNIX operating system through the "four year effect." When the UNIX operating system became widely available in 1975, Bell Labs offered it to educational institutions at minimal cost. The schools, in turn, used it in their computer science programs, ensuring that all computer science students became familiar with it. Because the UNIX system is such an advanced development system, the students became acclimated to an optimum programming environment. As these students graduated and went into industry, they expected to work in a similarly advanced environment. As more of these students worked their way up in the commercial world, the UNIX operating system found its way into industry.

In addition to introducing its students to the UNIX operating system, the Computer Science Department of the University of California at Berkeley made significant additions and changes to it. They made so many popular changes that one version is called the Berkeley Software Distribution (BSD) of the UNIX system. SunOS from Sun Corporation was primarily based on the BSD version of UNIX. System V from AT&T adopted many of the features appearing in UNIX systems produced by software companies that specialized in adapting the UNIX system to different computers.

It is this heritage of development and research that has made the UNIX operating system such a powerful software development tool.

19.2.1 The UNIX system on microcomputers

In the mid-1970s, minicomputers began challenging the large mainframe computers. Minicomputer manufacturers demonstrated that in many applications their products could perform the same functions as mainframe machines for much less money. Today, microcomputers are challenging the minis in much the same way. Powerful 16- and 32-bit processor chips, inexpensive memory, and lower-priced disk storage have allowed manufacturers to install multiuser operating systems on microcomputers. The cost and performance of these systems are rivaling those of the minis.

19.2.2 Why is the UNIX system popular with manufacturers?

Advances in hardware technology and the need for greater processing power required an operating system that would take advantage of available hardware power. Among other reasons, there was a need to share information throughout large diverse networks of systems.

With the cost of hardware dropping, hardware manufacturers could no longer afford to develop and support proprietary operating systems. In a similar manner, application software developers could not afford to convert their products to run under many different proprietary operating systems. Software developers had to keep the price of their products down in line with the price of the hardware.

Hardware manufacturers needed a generic operating system that they could easily adapt to their machines. They wanted to provide a multiplatform environment for third-party software. Software manufacturers needed a generic operating system as a common environment for their products.

The UNIX operating system satisfied both needs. Because it was initially designed for minicomputers, the UNIX operating system file structure took full advantage of large, fast hard disks. Equally important, the UNIX operating system was intended to be a multiuser operating system and it was not modified to serve several users as an afterthought. Finally, because the UNIX system was originally designed as a development system, it provided an ideal working environment for a software company.

The advent of a standard operating system legitimized the birth of the software industry. Now software manufacturers can afford to make one version of one product available on many different machines. No longer does one speak of "the company that makes the ABC package for the IBM machine," but rather "the company that makes the ABC package for the UNIX operating system." The hardware manufacturer who offers a UNIX-based system can count on third-party software being available to run on the new machine.

19.2.3 UNIX has arrived!

The UNIX operating system has gained widespread commercial acceptance. UNIX system user groups are very common today, and UNIX system magazines are appearing daily. Even non-UNIX operating systems, such as MS-DOS, have adopted some of the traits of the UNIX system. In addition, many companies have created operating systems that are variations of the UNIX system. SUN corporation has created both SunOS and Solaris, and IBM has created AIX and Pyramid systems (DCOSX) to name a few.

19.2.4 How can it run on so many machines?

UNIX is an operating system that can run on many different machines. About 95% of the UNIX operating system is written in a high-level language (C), which is a machine-independent language. Today, UNIX is distributed by many different vendors and runs on machines as small as PCs, as well as on large mainframe systems.

19.2.5 Overview of the UNIX system

The UNIX operating system has many unique features. Like other operating systems, UNIX is a control program for computers. But it is also a well-thought-out family of utility programs with a built-in set of tools that allow you to connect and use these utilities to build systems and applications. This section discusses both the common and unique features of the UNIX operating system.

Utilities

The UNIX system includes a family of several hundred utility programs that perform functions universally required by users. An example is sort. The sort utility puts lists (or groups of lists) in order. It can put lists in alphabetical or numerical order, or it can order by part number, author, last name, city, zip code, telephone number, age, size, costs. The sort utility is an important programming tool and is part of the standard UNIX system. Other utilities allow you to display, print, copy, search, and delete files. There are also text editing, formatting, and typesetting utilities. The man (manual) utility provides online documentation of the UNIX system itself. Because UNIX provides these frequently used utilities, you don't have to write them. You can incorporate them in your work, allowing you to spend more of your time working on the unique aspects of your project and less time on the aspects common to many other projects.

UNIX can support many users

The UNIX operating system is a multiuser operating system. Depending on the components that make up the machine being used, a UNIX system can support from one to over one hundred users, each concurrently running a different set of programs or what is more commonly called processes in UNIX jargon. The cost of a computer that can be used by many people at the same time is less per user than that of a computer that can be used by only a single person at a time. The cost is less because one person cannot generally use all the resources a computer has to offer. No one can keep a printer going 24 hours a day, all the system's memory in use, the disk busy reading and writing, the tape drives spinning, and the terminals busy. A multiuser operating system allows many people to use the system resources almost simultaneously. Thus, resource usage can approach 100%, and the cost per user can approach zero. These are the theoretical goals of a multiuser system.

The UNIX operating system allows you to run more than one job at a time. You can run several jobs in the background while giving all your attention to the job being displayed on your terminal. In addition, with X-Window software installed, users can access more than one system at a time and display each concurrently. When using the system's job control features, you can even switch back and forth between jobs, with or without an X-Window. This multitasking capability allows you to be more productive.

The shell

As discussed earlier in this chapter, The shell is the utility that processes your request. When you enter a command at a terminal, the shell interprets the command and calls the program you want. There are three popular shells in use today: the Bourne shell (standard System V UNIX), the C shell (BSD UNIX system), and the Korn shell. More shells are available, including menu shells that provide easy-to-use interfaces for computer-naïve users. Because separate users can use different shells at the same time on one system, a system can appear different to its various users. The choice of shells demonstrates one of the powers of the UNIX operating system: the ability to provide a customized user interface.

The shell can also be considered to be a high-level programming language. You can use this language to combine standard utility programs to build entire applications in minutes instead of weeks. Using the tools described in this book, you can even construct many useful applications right on the command line. A shell program can, for example, allow an inexperienced user to easily perform a complex task. The shell is one of the UNIX system tools that makes your job easier.

File structure

A file is a set of data, such as a memo, report, or group of sales figures, that is stored under a name, frequently on a disk. The UNIX system file structure is designed to assist you in keeping track of a large numbers of files. It uses a hierarchical or tree-like data structure that allows each user to have one primary directory with as many subdirectories as required.

Directories are useful for collecting files pertaining to a particular project. In addition, the UNIX system allows users to share files by means of links, which can make the same file appear to be in more than one user's directory.

Security: private and shared files

Like most multiuser operating systems, the UNIX system allows you to protect your data from access by other users. The UNIX system also allows you to share selected data and programs with certain users by means of a simple but effective protection scheme.

Filename generation

Using special characters that the shell command processor recognizes, you can construct patterns. These patterns generate filenames that you can use to refer to one or more files whose names share a common characteristic. You can include a pattern in a command when you do not know the exact filename you want to reference or when it is too tedious to specify it. You can also use a single pattern to reference many filenames.

Device-independent input and output

Devices (such as a printer or terminal) and disk files all appear as files to UNIX programs. When you give the UNIX operating system a command, you can instruct it to send the output to any one of several devices or files. This diversion is called output redirection.

In a similar manner, you can redirect a program's input that normally comes from a terminal so it comes from a disk file instead. Under the UNIX operating system, input and output are device-independent. You can redirect them to or from any appropriate device.

As an example, the cat utility normally displays the contents of a file on the terminal screen. When you enter a cat command, you can cause its output to go to a disk file, a printer, or even into another program instead of the terminal.

Interprocess communication

The UNIX system allows you to establish both pipes and filters on the command line. A pipe redirects the output of a program so it becomes input to another program. A filter is a program designed to process a stream of input data and yield a stream of output data. Filters are often used between two pipes. A filter processes another program's output, altering it in some manner. The filter's output then becomes input to another program. Pipes and filters are frequently used to join utilities to perform a specific task.

What are UNIX's limitations?

The most commonly heard complaints about the UNIX operating system are that it has an unfriendly, terse, treacherous, unforgiving, and non-mnemonic user interface. These complaints are well founded, but many of the problems have been rectified by newer versions of the operating system and by some application programs. The implementation of the GUI (graphical user interface) has helped provide UNIX with a more user-friendly interface. You can usually solve those problems that haven't been addressed directly by UNIX by writing a simple shell program.

The UNIX system is called unfriendly and terse because it seems to follow the philosophy that "no news is good news." The ed (editor) does not prompt you for input or commands, the cp (copy) utility does not confirm that it has copied a file successfully, and the who utility does not display a banner before its list of users.

This terseness is useful, however, because it facilitates redirection, allowing the output from one program to be fed into another program as its input. Thus, you can find out how many people are using the system by feeding the output of who into the utility wc (word count), which counts the numbers of lines and characters in a file. If who displayed a banner before it displayed the list of users, you could not make this connection. (The latest version of who has an option that displays a banner and another that tells you how many people are using the system.)

In a similar manner, although it would be nice if ed prompted you when you are using it as an interactive editor, it would not be as useful when you wanted to feed it input from another program and have it automatically edit a group of files.

The UNIX system was initially designed for slow hard-copy terminals. The less a program printed out, the sooner it was done. With today's high-speed terminals, this is no longer true. Editors that display more information (e.g., vi) now run on the UNIX system with these newer high-speed terminals.

The shell user interface can be treacherous, however. A typing mistake on the command line can easily destroy important files, and it is possible to inadvertently log off the system. You must be cautious when working with a powerful operating system. If you want a foolproof system, you can use the tools that the UNIX system provides to modify the shell. Many manufacturers have produced menu-driven user interfaces that make it very difficult to make mistakes with such far-reaching consequences. The Korn shell has optional built-in safeguards against many of these problems.

Due to its simplicity, the UNIX operating system still has some limitations. In versions prior to System V, mechanisms to synchronize separate jobs were poorly implemented and there was no way to lock files—an important feature in a multiuser operating system. System V has rectified these problems.

Although the UNIX operating system has some shortcomings, you can rectify most of them by using the tools that UNIX itself provides. The unique approach that the UNIX operating system takes to the problems of standardization and portability, its strong foothold in the professional community, its power as a development tool, and its chameleon-like user interface are causing it to emerge as the standard choice of users, hardware manufacturers, and software manufacturers.

Getting started

This section is intended to make you more familiar on how you as a user appear to the UNIX system. It discusses several important names and keyboard keys that are specific to you, your terminal, and your installation. After showing you how to log on and off, it explains what is actually happening while you are connecting to the system. Finally, it guides you through a short session with the vi editor and introduces other important utilities that manipulate files. With these utilities, you can obtain lists of filenames, display the contents of files, and delete files.

The best way to learn is by doing. Prior to accessing the system, you must contact your system administrator and get a user ID on the system. In the following pages, we will give you a brief outline of what actually happens when you log on to your system. Once you obtain a feel for your environment, you will better understand how to navigate through your system. Feel free to experiment with different commands and utilities. Create test files with test data and maneuver the files. The worst thing you could do is delete a test file.

Before you log on to a UNIX system for the first time, take a couple of minutes to answer the following questions. Ask your system administrator or someone else who is familiar with your installation.

- What is my user ID? This is the name or owner that the system assigns to the processes that are being executed by you, the user.

- What is my password? On multiuser systems, this is the means by which the system provides the user a layer of security. Your system administrator should assign you a password. Upon receipt, you should change it immediately. The system typically has a passwd command that allows you to do it. On systems that use Sun's NIS or NIS+, the command will be yppasswd or nispasswd, respectively.

- What is my location on the network? In other words, by what name or IP address is my system known? Do I have access to the proper applications? What applications are running on my local system and which are running on machines across the network? If you are a beginner, you should first become familiar with your local system and the applications running on it. You will soon be able to determine what the system components are and which resources are required to run your application.

- What key or key combinations will be helpful in using the system? What key or key combination can I use to interrupt an application? On most systems, Ctrl–C or Ctrl–D will typically interrupt an application.

- What type of terminal am I using? You can issue the set or env commands and look for the TERM value. You need to know this name if you use vi (the visual editor). Some applications require this information, typically for display purposes.

- Which shell will I be using? The shell tells UNIX how to interpret your commands. Your system administrator sets the default in the password file. At login time, various actions will take place depending on the type of shell you are running under. The three most common (Bourne, C, and Korn) are similar in many respects, but the Korn shell is the latest and combines many of the features of the Bourne and C shells. The examples in this book use the Korn shell.

19.2.6 Using the UNIX system

Now it is time to become acquainted with the system and what happens when you log in. This section will lead you through a brief session, explaining how to log on, change your password, and log off.

Logging on

Since many people can use the UNIX operating system at the same time, it must be able to differentiate between you and other users. You must identify yourself before the UNIX system will process your requests.

Figure 19.1 shows how a login procedure appears on a SunOS terminal screen. Your login procedure might look different. If your terminal does not have *login:* on it, check to see that the terminal is turned on, then press the Enter key a few times. If *login:* still does not appear, try pressing Ctrl–Q, Ctrl–C, or Ctrl–D. If these procedures don't work, check with your system administrator.

You must end every message or command to the UNIX system by pressing the Enter key. Pressing Enter signals that you have completed giving an instruction and are ready for the operating system to execute the command or respond to the message.

The first line of Figure 19.1 shows the UNIX system login: prompt followed by the user's response. The user entered *maria*, her login name, followed by an Enter. Try logging on, making sure that you enter your login name and pass-

```
SunOS UNIX (system_name)
login: maria
password:
SunOS Release 4.1.2 (GENERIC) : Wed Oct 23 10:52:58 PDT 1991
>
```

Figure 19.1 Logging on

word appropriately. UNIX is case-sensitive; it differentiates between upper-case and lowercase letters.

The second line of Figure 19.1 shows the password: prompt. If your account does not require a password, you will not see this prompt. This, however, could be a security weakness, and you should probably assign yourself a password. In our example, the user responded to the prompt with a password followed by an Enter. For security, the UNIX operating system never displays a password. Enter your password in response to the password: prompt, then press Enter. The characters you enter will not appear on the terminal screen.

You will see a message and a prompt when you successfully log on. This "message of the day" is generally something like "SunOS Release *n.n.*" If you are using the Korn shell, the prompt is usually a greater-than sign (>) or a number followed by the greater-than sign. The C shell generally prompts you with a percent sign (%) or a number followed by a percent sign, and the Bourne shell prompts you with a dollar sign ($). Any one of these prompts indicates that the system is waiting for you to give it a command.

Most systems expect your commands in lowercase, so be sure to type in low-ercase. The exception to this rule is your environment variables, which we will discuss later in the chapter.

At login time

Once you log on, you are communicating with the command interpreter known as the shell. The shell plays an important role in all of your communications with the UNIX operating system. When you enter a command at the terminal (in response to the shell prompt), the shell interprets the command and initi-ates the appropriate action. This action might be executing your program, call-ing a standard program such as a compiler or a UNIX utility program, or giving you an error message telling you that you have entered a command incorrectly.

Changing your password

When you first log on to a UNIX system, you will either not have a password or have a password that the system administrator assigned. In either case, it is a good idea to give yourself a new password. An optimal password is seven or eight characters long and contains a combination of numbers, uppercase let-ters, and lowercase letters. Don't use names or other familiar words that some-one can easily guess.

Figure 19.2 shows the process for changing a password using the passwd utility. For security reasons, none of the passwords you enter are ever dis-played by this or any other utility.

```
$ passwd
Changing password for maria
Old password:
New Password:
Re-enter new password:
>
```

Figure 19.2   The passwd utility.

Give the command `passwd` (followed by an Enter) in response to the shell prompt. This command causes the shell to execute the passwd utility. The first item the passwd utility asks you for is your old password (it skips this question if you do not yet have a password). The passwd utility verifies this password to ensure that an unauthorized user is not trying to alter your password. Next, passwd requests the new password. Your new password must meet the following criteria:

- It must be at least six characters long.
- It must contain at least two letters and one number.
- It cannot be your login name, the reverse of your login name, or your login name shifted by one or more characters.
- If you are changing your password, the new password must differ from the old one by at least three characters. Changing the case of a character doesn't make it count as a different character.

After you enter your new password, passwd asks you to retype it to ensure that you did not make a mistake when you entered it. If the new password is the same both times you enter it, your password is changed. If the passwords differ, it means that you made an error in one of them; the passwd utility will display the following message:

```
They don't match; try again.
New Password:
```

After you enter the new password again, passwd will ask you to reenter it. If your password does not meet the proper criteria, passwd will display the following message:

```
Password is too short - must be at least 6 digits.
New password:
```

Enter a password that meets the criteria in response to the New password: prompt.

When you successfully change your password, you change the way you log on. You must always enter your password exactly the way you created it. If you forget your password, you will have to contact your system administrator to reset it. Since your password is encrypted, no one else knows it; only your system administrator can change it.

Logging off

Once you have changed your password, log off and try logging on again using your new password. To log off, enter the command `exit`. This will terminate your shell and end your session.

19.2.7 Correcting mistakes

This section explains how to correct typing and other errors you make while you are logged on. (The techniques covered here do not work to correct errors you make while entering your name and password.) Log on to your system and try making and correcting mistakes as you read this section.

Because the shell and most other utilities do not interpret the command line (or other text) until after you press the Enter key, you can correct typing mistakes before you press Enter. There are two ways to correct typing mistakes. You can erase one character at a time, you can back up to the beginning of the command line, or you can press Ctrl–C (this will abort the command line). After you press the Enter key, it is too late to correct a mistake; you must either wait for the command to run to completion or abort execution of the command.

19.3 What Actually Happens When You Log In

At login time, a sequence of events takes place as a result of your logging in. Following is a description of what happens when you log in.

First, the system places you in your default directory, usually known as your home directory, which is determined by your entry in the passwd file. Your .profile is then executed (this sets up your default environment). Other commands or scripts might also be executed, depending on the content of your .profile.

Other files that might be used to modify the environment in which you are running are commonly called dot (.) files, called by this name because they are prefixed by a dot, or period. Some examples are .login (executed when you login with the C shell), .cshrc (executed each time you spawn a new C shell), .kshrc (executed when you spawn a new Korn shell) and many more to enhance your usage of the UNIX system.

To see which dot files have been defined for your user ID, do the following:

1. Type `cd` and press Enter. (This will place you in your home directory.)

2. Type `ls -als` ¦ more (The first files in the list should be your dot files).

For most dot files, there is usually a man page that will provide a reasonable explanation of the individual file's function; if not, contact your system administrator, who should be able to provide you with some information about the file. The man pages are a part of a facility that is basically an online manual, which you should use whenever trying a command with which you are unfamiliar.

This is probably a good time to become more familiar with your environment. Try the following commands to obtain a better understanding of what has been provided to you. The env or set commands will display your environment variables. Some common examples are:

```
MANPATH=/usr/man:/export/vol/man (the search path for your manual pages)
INFORMIXDIR=/usr/local/informix (the home directory for your INFORMIX install)
PATH=.:/usr/bin:$INFORMIXDIR/bin (the search path for your executables or pro-
grams)
ONCONFIG=$INFORMIXDIR/config.dbname (the Informix configuration file)
INFORMIXSERVER=value_of_dbservername (the dbservername in
$INFORMIXDIR/etc/sqlhosts)
EDITOR=vi (determines your default editor)
TERM=vt100 (determines what terminal type you are using)
```

19.4 Creating and Editing a File Using vi

A file is a collection of information stored on a disk you can refer to with a filename. Text files typically contain reports or manuscripts. An editor is a utility program that allows you to create a new text file or change a text file that already exists. There are many editors in use on UNIX systems. This section shows you how to create a file using vi (visual), a powerful (although sometimes cryptic), interactive, visually oriented text editor. It also covers elementary vi editing commands. The vi editor is not a text formatting program. It does not justify margins, center titles, or provide the features of a word processing system. You can use nroff, a UNIX utility, to format the text you edit with vi.

19.4.1 Specifying a terminal

Because vi takes advantage of features that are specific to various kinds of terminals, you must tell it what type of terminal you are using. The TERM environment variable describes the type of terminal you are using. If you are using the Korn shell, follow the command formats in this section to identify the type of terminal. You can also place these commands in your .profile file so the UNIX system automatically executes them each time you log on. Replace *name* with the Terminfo name for your terminal.

```
TERM=name
export TERM
```

Following are the actual commands you would enter if you were using a vt100 terminal:

```
$ TERM=vt100
$ export TERM
```

You can place such a command in your .login file for automatic execution.

19.4.2 An editing session

This section describes how to start vi, enter text, move the cursor, correct text, and exit from vi. Most vi commands take effect immediately. Except as noted, you do not need to press Enter to end a vi command. When giving vi a command, it is important that you distinguish between uppercase and lowercase letters. The vi editor interprets the same letter as two different characters, depending on whether it is uppercase or lowercase.

Start vi with the following command line (the first line only) to create a file named sqlhosts. Terminate the command line with Enter.

```
$ vi sqlhosts
```

The tilde character will run down the left side of your screen or window, depending upon what type of system is on your desktop.

The terminal screen will look similar to the one described. If it does not, your terminal type is probably not set correctly. If you need to reset your terminal type, press Escape and then give the following command to get the shell prompt back:

```
:q!
```

When you enter the colon, vi will move the cursor to the bottom line of the screen. You must press Enter after you give this command.

Once you get the shell prompt back, type env ¦ grep TERM, which will tell you what type of terminal is defined in your environment.

If the sqlhosts file is new, there is no text in it yet. The vi editor will display the following message on the status (bottom) line of the terminal to show that you are creating and editing a new file (your system might display a different message):

```
"sqlhosts" (New File)
```

When you edit an existing file, vi displays the first few lines of the file and gives status information about the file on the status line.

19.4.3 Command and input modes

The vi editor has two modes of operation: command mode and input mode. While vi is in command mode, you can give vi commands. For example, in command mode you can delete text or exit from vi. You can also instruct vi to enter threw input mode. While in the input mode, vi accepts anything you enter as text and displays it on the terminal screen. You can press Escape to return vi to command mode.

The vi editor does not normally keep you informed about which mode it is in. If you give the following command, vi will display INPUT MODE at the lower right of the screen if it is in input mode:

```
:set showmode
```

When you enter the colon, vi will move the cursor to the status line. Type the command and press Enter.

19.4.4 Entering text

Once you have called up vi, you have to put it in input mode before you can enter text. Put vi in input mode by pressing the I key. If you have not set showmode, vi will not let you know that it is in input mode.

If you are not sure if vi is in input mode, press the Escape key; vi will return to command mode if it was in input mode or beep (some terminals flash) if it was already in command mode. You can put vi back in input mode by pressing the I key again.

While vi is in input mode, you can enter text by typing and using the Enter key to end each line. As you are entering text, prevent lines of text from wrapping around from the right side of the screen to the left by pressing the Enter key before the cursor reaches the far right side of the screen. Also, make sure that you do not end a line with a space. Some vi commands will not behave properly when they encounter a line that ends with a space.

While you are using vi, you can always correct any typing mistakes you make. If you notice a mistake on the line you are entering, you can correct it before you continue (refer to the next section). You can correct other mistakes later. When you finish entering text, press the Escape key to return vi to command mode.

19.4.5 Correcting text as you insert it

The keys that allow you to back up and correct a shell command line (the erase and line kill keys mentioned earlier) are usually # and @, and serve the same functions when vi is in input mode. Although vi might not remove deleted text from the screen as you back up over it, it will remove it when you type over it or press Escape.

There are two restrictions to using these correction keys. They allow you to back up over only text on the line you are entering, and they back up over only text that was just entered. For example, assume that vi is in input mode, you are entering text, and you press the Escape key to return vi to command mode. Then you give the I command to put vi back in input mode. Now you cannot back up over text you entered the first time you were in the input mode, even if the text is part of the line you are working on.

The following represents a screen in vi after you enter the command on the first line:

```
vi sqlhosts
~

~
```

The tildes are repeated depending on the number of rows supported by your terminal. At the bottom you will see:

```
"sqlhosts" (New File)
```

After entering I, you are in insert mode and can begin typing:

```
This a test
~
~

~
```

Once again, the tildes are repeated depending on the number of rows supported by your terminal. At the bottom you will see:

```
"sqlhosts" (New File) 1 lines, 11 characters
```

After typing the file content, you can save the file by pressing Escape and then entering a colon (:), followed by wq to write the file and quit vi, which will bring you back to your UNIX prompt.

Moving the cursor
When you are using vi, you need to move the cursor on the screen so you can delete text, insert new text, and correct text. While vi is in command mode, you can use the Enter key, the spacebar, and the arrow keys to move the cursor.

Deleting text
You can delete a single character by moving the cursor until it is over the character you want to delete and then giving the command x. You can delete a word by positioning the cursor on the first letter of the word and giving the command dw (delete word). You can delete a line of text by moving the cursor until it is anywhere on the line you want to delete and then giving the command dd.

The undo command
If you delete a character, line, or word by mistake, give the command u (undo) immediately after you give the delete command, and vi will restore the deleted text.

Inserting additional text
When you want to insert new text within text you have already entered, move the cursor so it is on the character that will follow the new text you enter. Then type I to put vi in input mode, enter the new text, and press Escape. When you are finished entering text, press Escape to return vi to command mode.

To enter one or more lines, position the cursor on the line above where you want the new text to go. Give the command o (open). The vi editor will open a blank line, put the cursor on it, and be in input mode. Enter the new text, ending each line with an Enter. When you are finished entering text, press Escape to return vi to command mode.

Correcting text
To correct text, use dd, dw, or x to remove the incorrect text. Then use i or o to insert the correct text. For example, one way to change a word is by positioning the cursor at the beginning of the line and using your arrow keys to move the cursor until it is at the beginning of the word you want to change. Give the command dw to delete the word, then hit Escape, type I for insert, and type in the new word.

Saving your file
When you have completed typing the data into your file, you can save the file by first hitting the Escape key. Then type :wq to write the file and quit from the vi editor.

19.5 Summary

Obviously, there is much more to the UNIX operating system than we have presented here, but hopefully this will help you along the way. The following checklist is meant as an aid to help you better understand your environment.

- When in doubt, use the man pages to find out more about the commands you are executing.
- Examine your dot files to see how they affect your environment.
- To understand your INFORMIX environment, use the env command.

Other helpful commands to help get you started are:

at. A UNIX scheduling command.

cat. Displays the contents of a file.

cd. Changes your current directory.

cp. Copies a file.

cron. Built-in UNIX scheduler.

fg and bg. Used for job control (foreground and background).

find. Searches directories.

grep. Finds data strings within files.

history. Shows you a list of recently executed commands.

kill. Cancels a job or process.

ln. Creates a link to a file (creates a pointer to a file).

lp and lpr. Prints files.

ls. Lists directories.

man. Gives you more information about the different parameters of each command.

mkdir. Creates directories.

more. Displays a file a page at a time.

mv. Removes a file.

ping. Tells you if you can communicate with another system on the network.

rm. Removes a file.

rmdir. Removes a directory.

set. Defines environment variables.

sort. Sorts a file.

uname. Tells you what operating system you are using, and the name of the host you are currently logged on to.

vi. The built-in UNIX editor.

who. Tells you who is logged onto the system.

This list is merely a small subset of the available UNIX commands, but it should help you to get a reasonable start in using your UNIX system.

20

Standards and Guidelines

The purpose of this chapter is to provide model standards and guidelines for development of client/server applications for the Windows environment, using Informix as the development tool. This chapter assumes the developer has at least a base-level familiarity with the Windows environment, i.e., personal or professional use of Windows software, at a minimum. This chapter also assumes at least a working knowledge of the Informix tool, i.e., that you have read the first chapters of this book.

The kinds of standards and guidelines that should be in place at the start of the development include:

- User-interface guidelines
- Naming standards
- Programming guidelines
- Documentation standards
- Standard error and status routines

If you're working on a project team, it's common to have one or more team members who are responsible for maintaining and enforcing particular sets of standards and guidelines. For example, a database administrator (DBA) might handle standards related to database implementation, while someone in the role of object manager might oversee most of the application development standards. If you're working solo, there are still plenty of reasons for coming up with standards and guidelines to follow. They promote consistency and order, especially on projects that involve many components and whose development life cycle extends over long periods of time. Enforced standards and guidelines are especially valuable later in the cycle because they make it easier for you to maintain or enhance an application in which the original development team is not available.

20.1 General Design Guidelines

The development team should assume that at least some users have no Windows expertise, and design the interface to be as foolproof as possible. A good design allows for varying operating preferences and levels, i.e., provides menus with both keyboard and mouse access capabilities. A good design provides for visual and functional consistency within the application and, to the extent possible, is consistent with other commercially available Windows-based applications. Consistency, as we have mentioned, provides several advantages, including but not limited to the following development environment objectives. It will:

- Help in migrating from one application to another with ease and speed.
- Facilitate the learning process, i.e., what is expected of each developer.
- Minimize training requirements for additional applications that the team will develop.
- Increase overall productivity and harmony, i.e., give the workplace a good rhythm.
- Minimize user confusion and the time it takes a new user to become confident.
- Provide users with a sense of stability, thereby increasing their confidence in the reliability of the provided application(s).

Remember to design the application as a tool for those who want to use it. Try to make it self-explanatory and, if possible, intuitive. Prototype the product through consultation with representatives of the user community early in the development process. This is sometimes referred to as JAD, or joint application development. Try keep any user messages polite and friendly and avoid computer jargon. Get to know the users' business and use labels for data that are familiar to the users. This will allow users to be in control of the application, not the reverse. A good open design provides the ability to get from any point in the application to any other appropriate point in the application directly, i.e., without having to return through levels of windows in a modal fashion. If the users must wait for processing to complete, it should be visually obvious, e.g., the pointer should change to an hourglass. The users should receive timely and tangible feedback for their actions. For example, if a user selects an object, visual feedback that the object has been selected should be provided; this can be in the form of graphical, textual, or even auditory feedback. Accommodate user mistakes without pain or penalty. A good design minimizes opportunities for error and, when the inevitable occurs, it should handle errors consistently in a soft-fail fashion. The application should provide error messages that state the problem objectively and, where possible, offer viable solutions.

Provide the appropriate tools or utilities within the application to aid the user. The application should provide functions, rather than expect the user to remember or calculate information offline (e.g., the day of the week corresponding to a certain date). The application should present choices explicitly rather than expecting users to recall an involved set of options or commands.

Build iterations of design review with the users into the early phases of the development process and, if required, a rework of the interface design. In designing and testing an interface, make sure to consider the larger context within which the application will initially be used, to the extent it is known or predictable. For example:

- Will the distributed software be used on a stand-alone machine or on a network?
- Will the application be used alone or with other applications?
- Is this a custom application with different components for each user?
- Will the application be used with other commercially available applications or software?

Reflect and facilitate any required integration with other applications by providing data exchange techniques that are consistent across the applications. It is recommended that you identify and name any common functions during the design phase, thus allowing function development to be assigned as a separate project task. And other developers can avoid having to develop these function calls during script development. They need only mark a place in the application where the function call and arguments are inserted later.

GUI development tools provide a wide variety of components and options that you can use to construct the user interface of your application. While this gives you a great deal of flexibility, it also requires you to make choices about what is appropriate for your project. By making these choices early on and establishing them as conventions, you can make the application more consistent, attractive, and usable while saving yourself from a lot of cleanup work later.

To gather intelligent user-interface conventions, you must either learn something about good graphical design or draw on the expertise of someone who does. You can find a lot of good ideas for your user-interface conventions by looking at existing graphical applications, especially some of the more popular commercial products (for instance, Microsoft Word, Excel, and Lotus 1-2-3). You probably already use several of these applications and know which aspects of their user interfaces you like and which you don't. If the intended users of your application work frequently with a particular product, e.g., Microsoft Word, you might even consider adopting a similar user interface in order to take advantage of their experience and lower the learning curve.

Earlier you learned that an application can employ different styles of user interface: SDI (single-document interface), MDI (multiple-document interface), or a combination of the two. MDI is the most popular choice because of the flexibility it gives the user and all the built-in services it provides. You should probably think about using it by default.

SDI might be appropriate if your application is very simple, especially if it deals with only one kind of data and the user needs to perform only one operation at a time. A combination interface might be useful in an application that performs very diverse operations, but you must design it with great care to avoid confusing the user.

TABLE 20.1

Window area	Possible convention
Kinds of controls	To keep the interface intuitive, use an appropriate kind of control for each feature you want to implement in a window. For instance, don't use a RadioButton to initiate a command; use a CommandButton or PictureButton instead.
Number of controls	Limit the number of controls you place in a window to avoid overwhelming the user. Use multiple windows instead of trying to cram too many controls into one.
Spacing of controls	Leave enough white space in a window. Don't crowd controls together.
Borders of controls	To make them stand out, display other controls (such as Static Text) without any borders.
Availability of controls	Gray out (disable) a control when it is not available to the user.
Length of list controls	Limit the number of items in a ListBox or DropDownListBox control to prevent it from becoming too long to scroll through. You'll usually want to keep the number of items well under 50.
MDI sheets and buttons	Avoid placing CommandButton or PictureButton controls in MIDI sheets. Use menu items instead.
Keyboard support	Provide keyboard access to every control in a window
Colors	Use color judiciously. It is most effective for bringing out those portions of a window that you want the user to see most readily. Where possible, use color defaults so that the user's settings (from the windowing system) can take effect
Fonts	Limit the number of fonts to one or two (and make sure that users will have those fonts installed on their computers). Keep font size large enough to be easily legible and use a very limited number of different font sizes.
Modality	Try to use nonmodal windows whenever possible to give the user maximum control over the interface. Use modal (response) windows only when the application must focus the user's attention.

Table 20.1 lists window conventions you can apply to the windows in your application. Table 20.2 lists menu conventions you might want to apply to the menus in your application.

If users might have small, low-resolution monitors, make sure you design your windows for them and not just for larger, high-resolution monitors, such as those that many developers have.

The choice of some user-interface conventions depend on the particular platform on which your application is to be deployed. For example, certain conventions that might be appropriate for Microsoft Windows users might not make sense for Apple Macintosh users. Make sure you are familiar enough with your target platform to choose conventions that suit it. If you're planning to deploy an application on multiple platforms, your user-interface conventions should take any platform differences into account and specify how to handle them.

20.1.1 Development environment

A good development environment is a prerequisite to successful application development. New developers should be able to hit the ground running when they receive their user ID. Standards, guidelines, and the like should be available and up to date. Global functions, etc., should be placed in a specific PBL file (such as FUNCLIB.PBL) that exists in all library lists. Virtual objects to be used throughout the application should be placed in a specific PBL file (such as *xxx*VIRTS.PBL, where *xxx* is an identifier of the application) that exists in all library lists in the application. A development environment should be established consisting of Informix libraries in directories for various levels of development/support activities, including:

- A development directory for work in progress shared among developers.

- Personal libraries for each developer working on a new or existing version of an application component; existing versions should be checked out.

TABLE 20.2

Menu area	Possible convention
Number of menu items	Limit the number of menu items you place in a menu to avoid overwhelming the user with choices.
Depth of menu items	If you use a cascading menu, go down only one level. Deeper menus confuse users.
Availablity of menu items	Gray out (disable) a menu item when it is not available to the user.
Length of menu items	Try to make menu items just one or two words long (and never more than four).
Wording of menu items	Make sure the name you use is descriptive of what the menu item does. To indicate a menu item that displays a dialog box, include ellipses at the end of its name (for example, Find . . .). Be consistent in your use of either nouns or verbs for menu items.
Standard menu item names	Where possible, use standard names and positions for menu items (for instance, a typical menu bar should begin with File Edit).
Toggles	If a menu item serves as a toggle between one state and another (such as on or off), indicate the current state to the use either by displaying a checkmark (for example, √ On) or by switching the menu item name (such as from On to Off).
Help	Make sure that every menu bar provides menu items that display your application's help system and information about the application.
Keyboard support	Provide keyboard access to every menu item.
MDI frame and sheet	In a MDI application, provide a menu for the frame menus (which displays when no sheets are open) and a separate menu for each kind of sheet (which displays when a sheet of that kind is active).
MDI toolbars	In a MDI application, display toolbar buttons for a few of the most common menu items.
MDI MicroHelp	In a MDI application, provide MicroHelp text (which displays in the frame's status area) for every menu item.

- A staging directory for production-ready code and rollout support.
- A production directory for released code (fully rolled out).
- Backup libraries that are copies of production libraries (optional).

20.1.2 Using directories/libraries

The development libraries should be used for developing the application and any or all major enhancements made to the application. It should also be used as the starting point for preparing releases of the application, frozen at a point in time. It should be frozen only temporarily, however, long enough to capture and migrate to the staging directory of libraries. It will probably always be active until the entire application is complete, i.e., it will last forever. It should be fully accessible to all developers.

The staging libraries are used for rollout preparation. They should be used for support during rollout, i.e., they will contain the source code corresponding to the application executable being rolled out. They will be emptied (by the administrator) after rollout is complete, i.e., at the conclusion of migrating to the production libraries. They should be accessible to all developers, but should be used only on rare occasions. Note: Take care that any changes made in these libraries are also reflected in the development libraries for future releases of the application.

The production libraries should be used for reference. They contain the source code corresponding to the application executable that has been fully released. They should be used as the starting point of source code for fixes after rollout is complete and new development has begun. They should be accessible to all developers on a read-only basis. They are fully accessible only to the administrator for capturing the source code corresponding to the application executable that has been fully rolled out by migrating from the staging directory of libraries.

20.2 Naming Standards

While developing your application, you'll create a lot of different components and have to specify names for them, too. These components include database objects such as tables and indexes, Informix objects such as windows and menus, controls that go into your windows, and variables for your event and function scripts. To keep those names straight, you should devise a set of naming conventions and follow them faithfully throughout your project. This is crucial when you're working on a team (to enforce consistency and enable others to understand your code), but it's important even if you work on your own (so you can easily read your own code).

In general, all component names in Informix can be up to 40 characters long. Developers typically use the first few characters to specify a prefix that identifies the kind of component it is. Then they use an underscore character (_), followed by a string of characters that uniquely describes the particular component.

20.2.1 Relational database object-naming convention

Future releases of relational databases could cause modifications or additions to the information in this section. All names for relational database objects are in lowercase. The standards suggested here provide various naming standard formats. One format should be chosen by the application and followed for all objects. Any text marked in italics represents a variable and the application can substitute an appropriate value. The data definition language for database objects named throughout this section should be stored in the DDL subdirectory in the application file structure. Today, it is not uncommon to be migrating from mainframe DB2 to a server-based DBMS. If this is the case, then there are several reasons to use the DB2 naming standards for relational database objects:

- For a database that might be ported to DB2 from Sybase or Oracle, follow the DB2 naming standards so names do not have to be changed for DB2.

- For a database that will be used in conjunction with a DB2 database, the DB2 standards are recommended for the relational database. This will provide a consistent standard for the cross-platform databases.

- For a database ported from DB2 where the DB2 database will not be retained, the DB2 standards are optional. However, using these standards may ease the transition for developers familiar with the DB2 database.

If you are using the DB2 standard, then limit database and table names to eight characters and columns to 18 characters.

Database Name

This object name describes an application database.

Format	db_*aaa_database name*	
Max Length	21 characters	
Where	db	Two-character constant (required)
	_	Underscore (optional)
	aaa	Three-character application ID (optional)
	_	Underscore (optional)
	database name	This name describes the objects contained within the database. The maximum length of this name can range from 14 to 18 characters, depending on the optional parts chosen. (required)
Example	db_abc_pgmtrk dbpgmtrk	

Figure 20.1

Table Name

This object name describes a table contained within a database.

Format	tb_*aaa*_table name	
Max Length	27 characters (limited length because of view, index and trigger names)	
Where	tb	Two-character constant (required)
	_	Underscore (optional)
	aaa	Three-character application ID (optional)
	_	Underscore (optional)
	table name	This name describes the contents of a table. The maximum length of this name can range from 20 to 24 characters, depending on the optional parts chosen. (required)
Example	tb_abc_series tbseries	

Figure 20.2

Table column names

This object name describes a column associated with a table. It is strongly recommended that you use the business names with some abbreviation list to construct the column names.

Create the column name from an appropriate business name by applying an abbreviation list to each component word in the business name. Abbreviations for words and phrases should be maintained in the organization's central dictionary. If you cannot find a word used in the business name in the abbreviation list, you need to add it to the list or search for suggestions for an alternative from among available words or phrases. A maximum of 18 characters is permitted for each standard abbreviated name, including separators. This is to ensure compatibility with SQL requirements.

Refer to Table 20.3 for a summary of relational object name formats.

20.2.2 Naming standards for other objects

Naming these objects is important both for recognition and for logically grouping the objects together. In order for these objects to be grouped together in the application's libraries, the names must all begin with the same prefix. This grouping of objects will be helpful in migration and library management activities.

The object name can begin with a one- or two-letter abbreviation indicating the object type, followed by an underscore and a descriptive name (the descriptive name can start with a one- to three-letter abbreviation designating a portion of the application, such as a subsystem or conversation group). Short descriptive abbreviations are recommended. All letters should be lowercase.

Views

There are usually two types of views:

- Views
- Base views

View Name

This object name describes any view on a table. A view can be comprised of columns from one or more tables.

Format	vw_*aaa_view name*	
Max Length	30 characters	
Where	vw	Two-character constant (required)
	_	Underscore (optional)
	aaa	Three-character application ID (optional)
	_	Underscore (optional)
	view name	This name describes the contents of the view. The maximum length of this name can range from 24 to 28 characters, depending on the optional parts chosen. (required)
Example	vw_abc_series vwseries	

Figure 20.3

Base View Name

This object name describes a view based on a single table. In addition, this view will always contain the same number, order, and name of the columns in the table from which the view is based.

Format	vb_*aaa_view name*	
Max Length	30 characters	
Where	vb	Two-character constant (required)
	_	Underscore (optional)
	aaa	Three-character application ID (optional)
	_	Underscore (optional)
	view name	This name should be the same as the table on which it is defined, excluding the table prefix (tb) and application ID if used. (required)
Example	vb_abc_series vbseries	

Figure 20.4

Index Name

This object name describes an index defined on a table.

Format	*xn_table name*	
Max Length	30 characters	
Where	x	One-character constant (required)
	n	A one-digit number from 0–9 will be used to sequence multiple indexes defined on a table. (required)
		The number 0 should be used for the clustering index and the numbers 1–9 should be used for nonclustering indexes.
	aaa	Three-character application ID (optional)
	_	Underscore (optional)
	table name	This name should be the same as the table on which it is defined excluding the table prefix (tb) and application ID if used. (required)
Example	**Clustering**	
	x0_abc_series x0series	
Example	**Nonclustering**	
	x1_abc_series x1series	

Figure 20.5

Stored procedure name (application)

This object name describes of a collection of SQL and program control language statements bound into an executable plan.

Format	pr_*aaa_procedure name*	
Max Length	30 characters	
Where	pr	Two-character constant (required)
	_	Underscore (optional)
	aaa	Three-character application ID (optional)
	_	Underscore (optional)
	procedure name	This name describes the purpose of the stored procedure. The maximum length of this name can range from 23 to 27 characters, depending on the optional parts chosen. (required)
Example	pr_abc_series prseries	

Figure 20.6

Trigger name

This object name describes a stored procedure that is executed when an insert, update, or delete is performed on a specified table.

Format	t *type_table name*	
Max Length	30 characters	
Where	t	One-character constant (required)
	type	One-character constant indicating the SQL operation that causes the trigger. The allowable values are **i**, **u**, and **d** (Insert, Update, and Delete). (required)
	_	Underscore (optional)
	table name	This name should be the same as the table on which it is defined, excluding the table prefix (tb) and application ID if used. (required)
Example	tu_abc_series tuseries	

Figure 20.7

TABLE 20.3

Object type	Format
Database	db_*aaa_database name*
Table	tb_*aaa_table name*
View	vw_*aaa_view name*
Base view	vb_*aaa_view name*
Index	xn_*table name*
Stored procedure (application)	pr_*aaa_procedure name*
Stored procedure (system)	sp_*procedure name*
Trigger	t *type_table name*

TABLE 20.4

Type	Abbreviation	Example
Menu	m_	m_main_menu
Window	w_	w_customer
Data object	d_	d_series

20.2.3 Naming variables

When working with or using variables in programs, please refer to this section for guidelines and standards for naming, declaration, and use. The concepts regarding scope of access can be loosely applied to structure and function declarations and use. Please keep this in mind while reading this section. Development languages typically support variables with varying scope, e.g., PowerBuilder supports global, shared, instance, and local variables. Each type of variable has a different life expectancy, a different scope of access, and a different overhead.

In the case of PowerBuilder, global, shared, and instance variables are all considered to be static because they are declared at design time, are loaded into memory once, and remain in memory even while no code is being executed. Local variables, on the other hand, are loaded into memory when their script is executed and disappear when the script completes. Choosing the right scope of declaration for a variable is extremely important in good Informix development. The following sections describe the behavior of each variable type. As a general rule, when choosing the scope (type) of a variable, consider what code is going to have to access this variable. The whole application? A particular window? A specific script? The answer to this question will steer you toward the right choice for the type of variable required.

> Use the following naming convention when declaring variables:
>
> st_b
>
> Where s is the scope abbreviation (e.g., g for global), t_ is the data type abbreviation (e.g., s for string), and b is the business or application relevant name.

The scope information is crucial because it gives developers an instant understanding of where the variable has been declared and therefore what its life expectancy is and what objects have access to it. The data type is also a very important part of the variable name because it indicates, without having to refer to the declaration of the variable, what the data type is.

The business or application name tells the developer what the significance of the variable is, thus giving it meaning outside of a particular code context.

Table 20.5 lists example scope abbreviations for PowerBuilder, and Table 20.6 lists example data type abbreviations for PowerBuilder.

The business or application portion of the name should indicate the type of information that is contained in the variable and should comply with the application-specific abbreviation standards of your project. If the name is a conglomerate of a multiword description, the various words should have their first letters capitalized. If the name contains an abbreviation or word commonly displayed as all uppercase, it should be named consistently.

Table 20.7 lists example variable names for PowerBuilder.

TABLE 20.5

Abbreviation	Scope
g_	global
s_	shared
i_	instance
l_	local (script-defined)

TABLE 20.6

Abbreviation	Data type	Abbreviation	Data type
a	Any	l	Long
bl	Blob	o	Object
bo	Boolean	po	PowerObject
dt	Date	r	Real
dtm	DateTime	s	String
de	Decimal	t	Time
db	Double	ui	UnsignedInteger
do	DraggedObject	ul	UnsignedLong
i	Integer	w	Window

TABLE 20.7

Variable	Description
gs_version	Global string containing the application version number
si_acctnum	Shared integer representing an account number
ib_winmod	Instance Boolean to keep track of whether a window has been modified
li_counter	Local integer used for counting in a loop

20.2.4 Naming functions

Functions are like variables in that they have a certain scope. They are typically either global or they are methods in specific objects. Many developers choose to name global function names with a prefix of gf_. It should have the first letter capitalized, the remainder should be in lowercase, and there should be no underscores separating words. If the name is a conglomerate of a multiword description, the various words should have their first letters capitalized. If the name contains an abbreviation or word commonly displayed as all uppercase, it should be named consistently. Use the firm's abbreviation list. Object-level functions are typically named with a prefix of of_. Some examples are:

gf_ExcelPromptSave. A global function to prompt for the name and save the data to an Excel spreadsheet as that name.

of_SetBase. Where a window function to set the base portion of the WHERE clause of a SQL SELECT statement to be executed to retrieve the data for this window.

20.2.5 Naming constants

A constant should be in all uppercase, with words separated by underscores. Some examples are:

```
END_OF_FILE
OK
NOT_FOUND
```

20.2.6 Internal naming standards

Use the following naming convention when developing objects:

`t_s_b`

> Where t_ is the object type (see Table 20.8), s_ is the application or function to which the object is related, and b is the business or application relevant name.

The last portion of the name should be specific to the functionality of the window you are developing. Table 20.9 lists window name examples.

20.2.7 Functions

A function can be global or object-specific in scope. It should have the first letter capitalized, the remainder should be in lowercase, and there should be no underscores separating words. If the name is a conglomerate of a multiword description, the various words should have their first letters capitalized. If the name contains an abbreviation or word commonly displayed as all uppercase, it should be named consistently. Some function abbreviations are shown in Table 20.10, and some examples are shown in Table 20.11.

TABLE 20.8

Object type (t)	Abbreviation
Window	w_
Virtual window	wcls_
Standard visual user object	u_controlprefix
Custom visual	u_cv
External visual	u_ex
VBX visual	u_vbx
Standard class	u_sc
Custom class	u_cc
C++ class	u_cpp

TABLE 20.9

Window	Description
w_series_sheet	The window for the series planning tool
w_ctrk_login	The login window for the tracking application
wcls_mdi_sheet	A class MDI window sheet to be inherited, e.g., by w_series_sheet

TABLE 20.10

Type	Truth
Global function object	gf_
Object function	of_

TABLE 20.11

Function name	Description
f_ExcelPromptSave( )	A global function to prompt for the name and save the data to an Excel spreadsheet of that name
wf_SetBaseWhere( )	A window function to set the base portion of the WHERE clause of the SELECT statement to be executed to retrieve the data for this window
mf_GetFrame( )	A menu function that returns the MDI frame window.

20.3 Headers and Comments

Commenting code acts as inline documentation for the benefit of other developers. The application specifications are essential in order to understand where the localized logic has probably been placed in an event-driven application component. There are two forms of comments that are a common to most, if not all, development languages: comment headers and inline comments.

20.3.1 Comment headers

Figure 20.8 is an example of a comment header block that should be placed at the beginning of all scripts.

20.3.2 Inline comments

You use inline comments to explain particular lines or sections of code. A comment should consist of a description of change and reason for change, followed by developer name and date:

```
//Description of change. Made by JSMITH 10/09/96
```

This is especially important if you comment something out:

```
//The following line was commented out. ALLENPA 10/25/96
```

Put a comment before any major addition to a piece of code or to explain why code has been commented out:

```
//Check to see if the file exists
IF NOT FileExists(L_sINIFile) THEN
    MessageBox("Error",L_sINIFile + "does not exist.")
    Return -1
END IF
```

Use the block comment (/* . . . */) for large multiline comments. Comments are placed at the beginning of scripts that are complex or difficult to follow. Com-

```
/*****************************************************************************

[FUNCTION]
      Put function name here in mixed case.
      (EXAMPLE)
      f_GetConnectInfo( )

[DESCRIPTION]
      Write a description of the function which says only what the function does
      not how it does it or in what order. This function description should be
      used for verification.

[ACCESS]
      Public, Private, Protected.

[INPUTS]
      Put a description of all inputs to the functions. This includes PARAMETERS,
      TABLES, EXTERNAL FUNCTIONS (DLLs), FILES, GLOBAL VARIABLES, etc.

      (EXAMPLE)
      PARAMETERS:
            AV_sINIFile - A string variable containing the name of an INI file.
      EXTERNAL LIBRARY:
            XXXX.DLL - A custom written DLL that this function makes calls to.

[ASSUMPTIONS]
      List here any assumptions that the program makes or dependencies that exist.
      For example, the function may require the existence of certain global variables
      or files. List these assumptions below.

[RETURNS]
      Describe all possible return values of the function in the following format.

      (EXAMPLE)
      POSSIBLE VALUES:
      0    =     Function completed successfully
      -1   =     INI file not found
      -2   =     INI section not defined
      -3   =     etc. . .

[CHANGE LOG]
      NAME    DATE          CHANGE DESCRIPTION
      PRA     9/20/94       original function
      JJB     10/25/94      added error checking code

*****************************************************************************/

// VARIABLE DECLARATIONS
int   L_iRetVal

//************************** BEGIN SCRIPT ***************************
//
//    !!!!!! FUNCTION BODY GOES HERE !!!!!!
//
Return L_iRetVal
//************************** END SCRIPT ***************************
```

Figure 20.8

ments at the beginning of functions should describe the valid values for parameters and what the possible return codes are.

20.3.3 Spacing

Single spaces should be placed:

- Before and after all operators and the assignment operator (=).
- After the comma of each argument in function parameter lists.
- Before a close parenthesis, if there are nested parentheses.
- Before the THEN clause of an IF . . . THEN . . . END statement.

Do not put spaces before the open parenthesis, (, of a function call.

20.3.4 Capitalization

Mixed case:

- Development tool function names (TriggerEvent, SetFocus)
- User-defined function names (gf_dbConnect, of_CheckSQL)

Lowercase:

- Windows and window controls (w_main, cb_ok)
- Object attributes (text, title, x, y, enabled, visible)

Uppercase:

- Script control words (IF, THEN, ELSE, WHILE, NEXT)
- Reserved words (THIS, TRUE, FALSE)

20.3.5 Tabs and indenting

Use tabs to align assignment statements for greater readability. The following is incorrect:

```
I_sFName = "Rosanne"
I_sLastName = "Silinonte"
I_sTelephoneNumber = "(718) 347-4703"
```

This is correct:

```
I_sFName            = "Rosanne"
I_sLastName         = "Silinonte"
I_sTelephoneNumber  = "(718) 347-4703"
```

Use tabs to indent. Statement blocks used with the following statements are indented one tab stop from the corresponding statement: CASE, DO UNTIL, DO WHILE, DO..LOOP, FOR..NEXT, and multiline IF..THEN.

20.3.6 Variable declaration

For static variables declared using the declaration dialog boxes (global, shared, instance variables), put the following comment header in the dialog box to indicate the object for which the variables are being defined. These, for example, are globals:

```
/* GLOBAL VARIABLES for Application "SAMPLE"
data type      variable name                */
string         G_sUserName
boolean        G_bLoggedOn
```

These are shared:

```
/* SHARED VARIABLES for Window "w_main"
data type      variable name                */
string         I_sUserName
boolean        I_
```

These are instance:

```
/* INSTANCE VARIABLES for Window "w_main"
data type      variable name                */
integer        I_iAcctNum
boolean        I_bWinModified
```

and these are local:

```
// VARIABLE DECLARATIONS
data type      variable name                */
integer        I_iAcctNum
boolean        I_bWinModified
```

20.4 Potpourri

20.4.1 Tips and good coding practices

Do not use an evaluated expression in the <end> portion of a FOR or WHILE loop. For example:

```
FOR L_iCounter = 1 TO Len(this.text)
   <statement block>
NEXT
```

In this code segment, the statement Len(this.text) will be evaluated (the Len( ) function will be invoked) during each iteration of the loop. A preferred coding method would be:

```
L_iStrLen = Len(this.text)

FOR L_iCounter = 1 TO L_iStrLen
   <statement block>
NEXT
```

20.4.2 Object referencing

Make implicit references to objects using indirect reserved words whenever possible instead of explicit references using object names. Using these generic references insulate code from particular object names and therefore make it more flexible and reusable. A PowerBuilder example might be:

```
THIS.Title = "Details for Account" + String(L_iAcctNum)
```

instead of:

```
RemoteWin.Title = "Details for Account" + String(L_iAcctNum)
```

To accomplish this, you might need to send a message to the window to invoke the local code.

20.4.3 User documentation and error handling

In addition to comments and online help, you might also want to address printed documentation in your standards. For instance, you might consider requiring one or more of the following:

Developer reports. You can use the library painter of PowerBuilder to print reports about the application components you've developed. You should determine which reports you need to print and how often.

Developer manuals. Would it be useful to have someone write one or more internal documents that developers could then reference for information on application components? If so, you need to specify what is to be described as well as how it is to be organized and formatted.

End-user manuals. Do users need training or reference documents to assist them as they run your application? If so, indicate what these documents are to cover as well as how they are to be organized and formatted.

Standard error and status routines. Housekeeping chores such as error and status checking are often good candidates for standardization. That's because you'll usually want to handle them the same way across many applications and because you'll want to minimize the chance of accidentally omitting a particular test.

For example, you might consider standardizing the way you check for:

- Network connection errors
- Database access errors
- Data entry errors

Fortunately, the object-oriented features of many development languages make it easy to standardize and implement common chores like these. For example, in PowerBuilder, you will want the DataWindow controls in your windows to check for various data entry and database access errors. The hard way to accomplish this is to write the appropriate event scripts in each individual DataWindow control. The easy, object-oriented way is to:

- Create your own version of a generic DataWindow control by defining a user object for it.

- Write your error-processing event scripts in this user-object DataWindow control.

- Inherit the DataWindow controls you want to place in windows from your user-object DataWindow control. These inherited controls can automatically perform your error processing.

20.5 What's On the CD?

The accompanying CD provides various presentations, worksheets, and documents, including the Warehouse data model that is referred to throughout this book. Figure 20.9 illustrates the CD directory structure.

What's On The CD?

Root

— Document

About.doc	*About the authors*
Ifmx.ppt	*Informix presentation*
Ifmxinst.doc	*Installation tips*
Ifmxsize.xlw	*Database sizing guide*
Pb5.ppt	*PowerBuilder presentation*

— Warehous

Warehous.cdm	*S-Designor conceptual*
Warehous.er1	*ERwin model*
Warehous.erx	*ERwin export*
Warehous.pcx	*Picture of database*
Warehous.pdm	*S-Designor physical model*
Warehous.sql	*SQL statements*

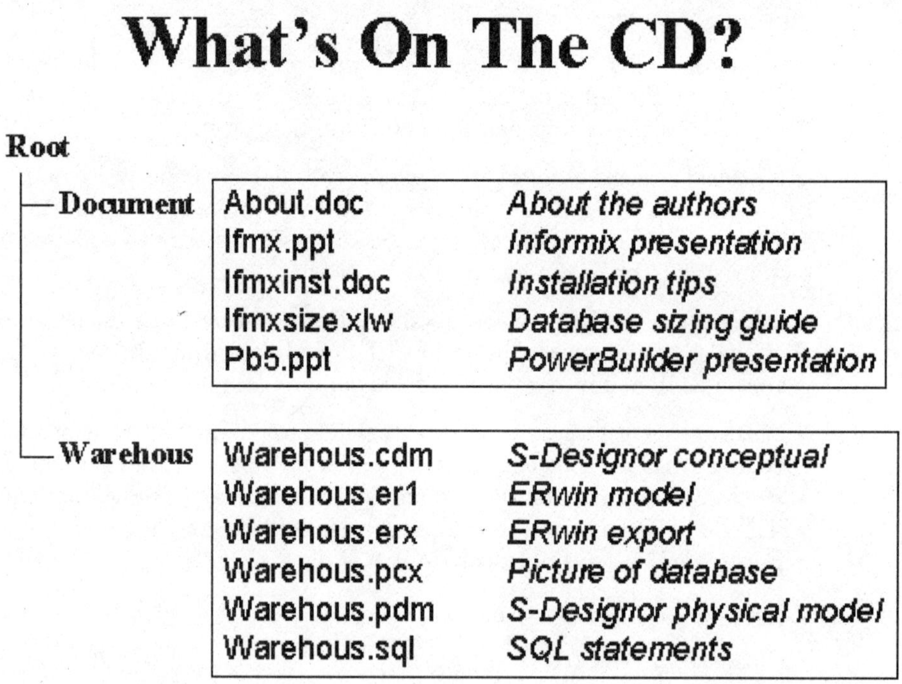

Figure 20.9 CD directory structure.

Index

A

ABS function, 293
abstraction, 131-132
accelerator keys, 231
access tools (*see* information access)
Ace development tool, 29
Acu4GL, 501
administration (*see* database creation and management)
administration utilities, 167-213
ADW, 39, 40, 64
agents, client workstation agents, 498
Agents, MetaCube, 13
aggregate functions, 292-293, 294-295
algebraic functions, 293
ALLBASE/SQL, 98
ALLOCATE DESCRIPTOR, 31
AlphaServer, 4, 5
ALTER TABLE, 28
analysis stage of application development, 154
ANSI, 30, 31
ANSI-compliant databases, 240-241
ANSWER: Testpro for Windows, 515
application development and programming (*see* also database creation and management; ERwin; ESQL), 9, 25, 103-128
    4GL, 26, 27, 28, 33
    4GL Rapid Development System, 26, 27
    Ace development tool, 29
    ADW, 39, 40
    analysis stage of application development, 154
    ANSI, 30
    application programming interface (API), 28
    architectures, 133-136, 151-152

attributes, 38, 41, **44**, 106-108, 109
backups, 113
batch interface/batch utilities, 111-113, 164-165, 441-448
BEGIN statement, 441
BEGIN . . . END statement, 442-443
breakpoints, 125
"build and test" routines, 61-62
building an application, 32
business rules, 104, 145-146
C language, 26, 27, 30, 33
case sensitivity, 557
CASE tools, 36, 38, 39-40, 107, 501-505
checkpoints, 205
class libraries, 114-115
classes, 149, 163-164
client/server architecture, 31-32, 51-52, 104, 129-131, **130**
COBOL, 26, 27, 30, 33
code review, 52
columns, 107
commands, 30-31
comments, 555-557
compatibility, 148
compiler, 26, 28, 124
connection management, 31
consistency in system, 143-144
construction stage of application development, 155
CONTINUE statement, 442
control-of-flow language, 441-448
CREATE PROCEDURE statement, 434-435
creating a database (*see also* database creation and management), 32, 239-241
data access objects, 32, 120-123, **122**
data and system management (DASM), 164

Illustrations are in **boldface**.

About The Authors

Paul R. Allen of UCNY, Inc. specializes in helping companies improve their operations by using object technology. He has more than a decade of experience in developing application systems for the financial, brokerage, and manufacturing industries. He has extensive experience with a multitude of development platforms, has lectured at several industry-related conferences, and teaches courses in computing at Columbia University in New York. He is also the coauthor of *PowerBuilder: A Guide to Developing Client/Server Applications*, published in 1995 by McGraw-Hill (ISBN 0-07-05413-4).

Joseph J. Bambara of UCNY, Inc. has been developing application systems for over 20 years, and relational databases for the last 10 years. He has extensive experience with PowerBuilder-based application development using Informix and Sybase. His has experience in the financial, brokerage, manufacturing, medical, and entertainment industries. He has a Bachelors and Masters degree in Computer Science, and has taught various computer courses for CCNY's School of Engineering. He also holds a Juris Doctorate in Law and is admitted to the New York Bar. He has taught numerous courses in computing, including several client/server development tools. He is the coauthor, with Paul Allen, of *PowerBuilder: A Guide to Developing Client/Server Applications*. Paul and Joe have presented seminars on client-server and multitiered development in the United States, Europe, and Scandanavia.

Richard J. Bambara is a senior systems software engineer with an investment banking firm. For the past 19 years, he has been installing software, creating documentation, and training users and support personnel on using multiple software products. He is an operating systems support expert on various platforms, including Sun Corporation's SunOS, Solaris, Pyramid DCOSX, and IBM's MVS operating system. He attended the College of Staten Island, where he attained an A.A.S. in Computer Science. He continued his education at Brooklyn College and PACE University. He has programmed in Assembler, PL/1, COBOL, and C. He is presently working in a diverse environment, which includes the deployment and support of software on systems ranging from workstations to mainframes. He is the author of the book *UNIX/MVS Programming Guide* (McGraw-Hill, 1997).

For more information, you can contact us at:

UCNY, Inc.
6th Floor
143 Madison Avenue
New York, NY 10016

+1.212.576.2030   (voice/fax)
e-mail: pwrtouch@tribeca.ios.com
www: http://tribeca.ios.com/~pwrtouch/index.html

SOFTWARE AND INFORMATION LICENSE

The software and information on this diskette (collectively referred to as the "Product") are the property of The McGraw-Hill Companies, Inc. ("McGraw-Hill") and are protected by both United States copyright law and international copyright treaty provision. You must treat this Product just like a book, except that you may copy it into a computer to be used and you may make archival copies of the Products for the sole purpose of backing up our software and protecting your investment from loss.

By saying "just like a book," McGraw-Hill means, for example, that the Product may be used by any number of people and may be freely moved from one computer location to another, so long as there is no possibility of the Product (or any part of the Product) being used at one location or on one computer while it is being used at another. Just as a book cannot be read by two different people in two different places at the same time, neither can the Product be used by two different people in two different places at the same time (unless, of course, McGraw-Hill's rights are being violated).

McGraw-Hill reserves the right to alter or modify the contents of the Product at any time.

This agreement is effective until terminated. The Agreement will terminate automatically without notice if you fail to comply with any provisions of this Agreement. In the event of termination by reason of your breach, you will destroy or erase all copies of the Product installed on any computer system or made for backup purposes and shall expunge the Product from your data storage facilities.

LIMITED WARRANTY

McGraw-Hill warrants the physical diskette(s) enclosed herein to be free of defects in materials and workmanship for a period of sixty days from the purchase date. If McGraw-Hill receives written notification within the warranty period of defects in materials or workmanship, and such notification is determined by McGraw-Hill to be correct, McGraw-Hill will replace the defective diskette(s). Send request to:

Customer Service
McGraw-Hill
Gahanna Industrial Park
860 Taylor Station Road
Blacklick, OH 43004-9615

The entire and exclusive liability and remedy for breach of this Limited Warranty shall be limited to replacement of defective diskette(s) and shall not include or extend to any claim for or right to cover any other damages, including but not limited to, loss of profit, data, or use of the software, or special, incidental, or consequential damages or other similar claims, even if McGraw-Hill has been specifically advised as to the possibility of such damages. In no event will McGraw-Hill's liability for any damages to you or any other person ever exceed the lower of suggested list price or actual price paid for the license to use the Product, regardless of any form of the claim.

THE McGRAW-HILL COMPANIES, INC. SPECIFICALLY DISCLAIMS ALL OTHER WARRANTIES, EXPRESS OR IMPLIED, INCLUDING BUT NOT LIMITED TO, ANY IMPLIED WARRANTY OF MERCHANTABILITY OR FITNESS FOR A PARTICULAR PURPOSE. Specifically, McGraw-Hill makes no representation or warranty that the Product is fit for any particular purpose and any implied warranty of merchantability is limited to the sixty day duration of the Limited Warranty covering the physical diskette(s) only (and not the software or in-formation) and is otherwise expressly and specifically disclaimed.

This Limited Warranty gives you specific legal rights; you may have others which may vary from state to state. Some states do not allow the exclusion of incidental or consequential damages, or the limitation on how long an implied warranty lasts, so some of the above may not apply to you.

This Agreement constitutes the entire agreement between the parties relating to use of the Product. The terms of any purchase order shall have no effect on the terms of this Agreement. Failure of McGraw-Hill to insist at any time on strict compliance with this Agreement shall not constitute a waiver of any rights under this Agreement. This Agreement shall be construed and governed in accordance with the laws of New York. If any provision of this Agreement is held to be contrary to law, that provision will be enforced to the maximum extent permissible and the remaining provisions will remain in force and effect.